THE HISTORY OF THE FRANKS

ADVISORY EDITOR: BETTY RADICE

GREGORY OF TOURS was Metropolitan Bishop of that city from 573 until his death in 594. He was a Gallo-Roman who spoke and wrote sixth-century Latin as his native language. On both his mother's and his father's side he came of distinguished senatorial families. During his episcopate the civil rule in Tours passed from Sigibert to Chilperic and then again to Childebert II, during whose minority Guntram exercised control. Gregory wrote many books. The most famous of them, *The History of the Franks*, begins with the Creation; but much of it is an eye-witness account of the bloodthirsty behaviour of these four Merovingian Kings and their savage consorts. Gregory was later canonized.

LEWIS THORPE, BA, L-ès-L, PhD, D de l'U, LLD, FIAL, FRSA, FR HistS, was Professor of French at Nottingham University from 1958 to 1977. He joined the staff of that university in 1946 after distinguished war service. He was President of the British Branch of the International Arthurian Society, and editor of the Society's *Bulletin Bibliographique*. He was also editor of *Nottingham Mediaeval Studies* and *Nottingham French Studies*. He published many articles, and his books include *La France Guerrière* (1945), *Le roman de Laurin, fils de Marques le Sénéchal* (1950), *Le roman de Laurin, text of MS. B.N.f.fr. 22548* (1960), *Guido Farina, Painter of Verona, 1896–1957* (1967) with Barbara Reynolds, *Einhard the Frank: The Life of Charlemagne* (1970), *Le roman de Silence, by Heldris de Cornuälle* (1972) and *The Bayeux Tapestry and the Norman Invasion* (1973). He also translated *Geoffrey of Monmouth: The History of the Kings of Britain*, *Two Lives of Charlemagne* and *Gerald of Wales: The Journey through Wales and The Description of Wales* for the Penguin Classics. Lewis Thorpe was a member of the MCC. He died on 10 October 1977.

GREGORY OF TOURS

THE HISTORY OF THE FRANKS

Translated with an Introduction by
Lewis Thorpe

PENGUIN BOOKS

PENGUIN BOOKS

Published by the Penguin Group
Penguin Books Ltd, 27 Wrights Lane, London W8 5TZ, England
Penguin Books USA Inc., 375 Hudson Street, New York, New York 10014, USA
Penguin Books Australia Ltd, Ringwood, Victoria, Australia
Penguin Books Canada Ltd, 10 Alcorn Avenue, Toronto, Ontario, Canada M4V 3B2
Penguin Books (NZ) Ltd, 182–190 Wairau Road, Auckland 10, New Zealand

Penguin Books Ltd, Registered Offices: Harmondsworth, Middlesex, England

This translation first published 1974
17 19 20 18 16

Copyright © the Estate of Lewis Thorpe, 1974
All rights reserved

Printed in England by Clays Ltd, St Ives plc
Set in Intertype Times

CONTENTS

INTRODUCTION   7

I   *Gregory of Tours*   7
    Genealogical table: the family of Gregory of
    Tours   11

II   *The Times in which Gregory lived*   16
    Genealogical table: the Merovingians, down to
    Dagobert   18

III   *Gregory's Writings*   22

IV   *The History of the Franks*   23
    1. Intention and shape   23
    2. Historical and literary debts   27
    3. Personal knowledge   31
    4. Credibility   33
    5. Other historians of the period   36
    6. Language   38
    7. Style   41
    8. Humour and irony   46
    9. Nature notes   50
    10. The manuscripts   53
    11. Earlier translations   54
    12. This translation   54

V   *Gregory down the Centuries*   54

VI   *Short Bibliography*   56

    ABBREVIATIONS USED FOR THE BOOKS
    WRITTEN BY GREGORY OF TOURS   59

    MAP OF GAUL   60

    PREFACE   63

BOOK I	65
BOOK II	101
BOOK III	159
BOOK IV	195
BOOK V	251
BOOK VI	325
BOOK VII	383
BOOK VIII	431
BOOK IX	479
BOOK X	541
INDEX	605

INTRODUCTION

I. GREGORY OF TOURS

The historian who was to become known to the world as Gregory, nineteenth Bishop of Tours, was born on 30 November *c*. 539,[1] in what is now Clermont-Ferrand, Puy-de-Dôme, and what was then *Arvernus* or *Arvernorum civitas*, the chief city of *Arvernia* or Auvergne. He was baptized Georgius Florentius. On both his father's and his mother's side he came of distinguished senatorial families with a long tradition of service to the Catholic Church, that is to say of wealthy Gallo-Roman landed gentry whose ancestors had enjoyed the rank of Senators under the Empire and were still extremely proud of the fact. His father was the Senator Florentius and his paternal grandfather was the Senator Georgius, both of Clermont.[2] His mother was Armentaria,[3] grand-daughter of Saint Tetricus, Bishop of Langres, 539–72, and great-grand-daughter of Saint Gregory, also Bishop of Langres, 507–39. Gregory's immediate predecessor as Bishop of Tours, Saint Eufronius, 556–73, was his first cousin once removed. Duke Gundulf and his brother Saint Nicetius, Bishop of Lyons, 552–73, were two of Armentaria's uncles.[4] When Bishop Eufronius was introduced to

1. See *MBA*, 38, where Gregory tells us that he was born on Saint Andrew's day. See *VSM*, III, 10, where he tells us that his mother came to Tours after his consecration and was cured by Saint Martin of muscular pains which had troubled her ever since his own birth thirty-four years before.

2. See *VP*, XIV, 3, where Gregory's father, as a boy, was taken to be cured by Saint Martius of a tertian fever: 'Famulus tuus est puer Florentius, Georgi quondam filius senatoris.'

3. She is mentioned in *VP*, VII, 4, when she was taken to Saint Gregory of Langres to be cured of a quartan fever: 'Armentaria autem, neptis eius ...'

4. 'I received him kindly, the more so as I realized that he was my mother's uncle,' writes Gregory of Gundulf, *HF*, VI, 11.

7

King Lothar I as a descendant of Saint Gregory of Langres, the King replied: 'That is one of the noblest and most distinguished families in the land.'[5] Gregory had many other famous forbears; and, indeed, he himself said that of the eighteen Bishops who preceded him in Tours all but five were his blood-relations.[6] There was even an early Christian martyr in the family, Vettius Epagatus, who was killed in Lyons in 177.[7]

These rather indigestible details are made the more strange for us by the fact that so many of Gregory's relations were canonized by the Catholic Church, as he was to be himself. What I have given is, however, more than sufficient to prove that in his family there was a long and constant tradition of service to the state and to the Church, even more marked perhaps on his mother's side than on his father's, and directed more often towards ecclesiastical than lay office, but rewarded by high place in both spheres.[8]

Gregory does not mention his father or mother by name in the *History of the Franks*. He describes in some detail and with much feeling the murder in 574 of his brother Peter, who was a deacon in Langres.[9] He had a sister, who married a man called Justinus, neither of whom is mentioned, but their daughter, Gregory's niece, plays a valiant part in the story as Justina, Prioress of Saint Radegund's nunnery in Poitiers.[10] There is also a reference to the husband of another niece, Eustenia, who was presumably Justina's sister,[11] although Eustenia herself is not named.

It is inferred that Gregory's father died while he was still a boy. His mother went to live in Burgundy, where she had property, especially near Cavaillon, Vaucluse, and there Gregory visited her.[12] When he was about eight he was sent to Clermont-Ferrand to be brought up in the household of his uncle,

5. *HF*, IV, 15.   6. *HF*, V, 49.   7. *HF*, I, 29, 31.
8. See the family tree on p. 11.
9. *HF*, V, 5.   10. *HF*, X, 15.   11. *HF*, V, 14.
12. *VSM*, III, 60. 'Oportunitatis causa nuper exteterat, ut ad visitandam genetricem meam in terretorium Cavellonensis urbis adirem.'

Saint Gallus, Bishop of that city, 525–51;[13] and, when Gallus died, the boy, still in his early teens, stayed on with the Archdeacon Avitus, who was to succeed Cautinus as Bishop *c*.572.[14] From Clermont he paid long and frequent visits to his grand-uncle, Saint Nicetius, Bishop of Lyons,[15] and to his first cousin once removed, Saint Eufronius, Bishop of Tours.[16] It can have been no surprise to anyone when he was ordained a deacon in 563, at the age of twenty-five.[17] In 573, when Eufronius died, Gregory, who was by then well-known in the city, was elected to replace him as nineteenth Bishop, and King Sigibert approved the election. Gregory held the bishopric of Tours for twenty-one years, from his consecration on 20 August 573 until his death at the age of fifty-five on 17 November 594.

To become a bishop in Merovingian Gaul in the sixth century was to shoulder great responsibility and to wield great power. Once elected, bishops had security of tenure, and most of them occupied their episcopal thrones until the day of their death. It is true that Praetextatus of Rouen was murdered in his own cathedral,[18] that the politically-minded Egidius of Rheims was sent into exile for treason and narrowly escaped a worse fate,[19] and that Gunthar of Tours drank himself to death;[20] but they were exceptions. In contrast with this, quite apart from the likelihood of their being killed on the battlefield or mortally wounded in some affray, those in positions of secular authority were liable to be deposed at any moment, to have their lands and property sequestered, to be tortured to death in the most inhuman and bestial way, irrespective of whether they were innocent or guilty of whatever charge had been levelled against them, or indeed of whether or not there was any such charge. The bishops were the upholders of the tenets of the

13. *VP*, II, 2. 'Tempore, quo Gallus episcopus Arvernam regebat ecclesiam, horum scriptor in adolescentia degens graviter aegrotabat, et ab eo plerumque dilectione visitabatur, eo quod patruus eius esset.'

14. *HF*, IV, 35, where Gregory writes with great feeling about the kind hospitality of Avitus: 'To this day, when a stranger comes to him, he is so warmly welcomed that he finds in Avitus at once a father and a fatherland.'

15. *VP*, VIII, 3.   16. *VSM*, I, 32–3.   17. *VSM*, I, 32.
18. *HF*, VIII, 31.   19. *HF*, X, 19.   20. *HF*, X, 31.

Catholic faith and of the canons of the numerous Gallican Councils, in the face of Jews, of unbelievers, of Arians and of any other sectarians with whom they might come into contact, including the Kings of their own country[21] and impostors who maintained that they were the returned Christ.[22] At the beginning of his *History* Gregory felt the need to state explicitly and at some length his own Catholic credo;[23] and he is constantly in debate and argument and disputation on points of theology.[24] The bishops were the defenders and exemplars of public morality; and they were virtually the only individuals in a position of authority who had any sense whatsoever of human compassion, and who practised Christian charity and loving kindness. They were responsible for church plate,[25] for the tombs and relics of the Saints and martyrs,[26] for the repair and maintenance of existing churches and for the erection of new places of worship.[27] They acted as Visitors to the monasteries and nunneries in their diocese; and just how onerous a task this could be is shown by the revolt in Saint Radegund's nunnery in Poitiers which Gregory described at such length.[28] They supervised the refectories attached to their cathedrals.[29] They had many properties to administer, numerous servants to govern

21. *HF*, V, 44.   22. *HF*, X, 25.

23. *HF*, preface to Book I.

24. E.g., *HF*, V, 43, where he disputes with an Arian; *HF*, VI, 5, where he argues with a Jew; and *HF*, X, 13, where he is in debate with one of his own priests who denies the resurrection of the body.

25. Maroveus, Bishop of Poitiers, had to melt down one of his gold chalices and make it into coins, in order to buy off King Guntram's troops, who were sacking his city and molesting his person, *HF*, VII, 24.

26. Gregory gives a fascinating account of himself and his verger examining with a lighted taper the reliquaries in Saint Martin's church, *HF*, X, 31.

27. Among Gregory's predecessors in Tours, Eufronius built four churches, Baudin two churches and two whole villages, Injuriosus two churches and two whole villages, Perpetuus seven churches, *HF*, X, 31. To turn to another period, it has been estimated that, between 1050 and 1350, eighty cathedrals, five hundred large churches and tens of thousands of village churches were built in France alone (Jean Gimpel, *Les bâtisseurs de cathédrales*, 1969, p. 3).

28. *HF*, IX, 39, X, 15–17.

29. Bishop Baudinus started a *mensa* for his canons in Tours, *HF*, X, 31.

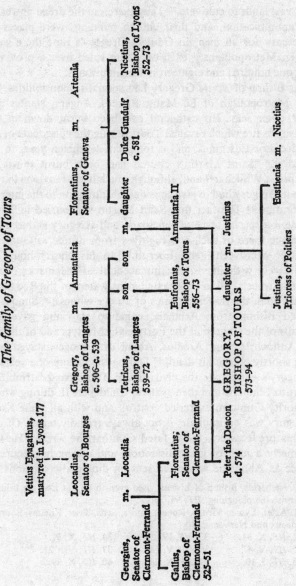

The family of Gregory of Tours

Vettius Epagathus,
martyred in Lyons 177

Leocadius,
Senator of Bourges

Georgius, **m.** Leocadia
Senator of
Clermont-Ferrand

Florentius,
Senator of Clermont-Ferrand

Gallus,
Bishop of
Clermont-Ferrand
525–51

Peter the Deacon
d. 574

GREGORY,
BISHOP OF TOURS
573–94

Gregory, **m.** Armentaria
Bishop of Langres
c. 506–c. 539

Tetricus,
Bishop of Langres
539–72

son   son   son

Eufronius,
Bishop of Tours
556–73

Armentaria II

Florentinus, **m.** daughter
Senator of Geneva

Duke Gundulf
c. 581

Nicetius,
Bishop of Lyons
552–73

Artemia

daughter **m.** Justinus

Justina,
Prioress of Poitiers

Eusthenia **m.** Nicetius

and vast lands to cultivate.[30] They exercised the dread power of
excommunication; and their church buildings were places of
sanctuary for all men. In Gaul in Gregory's time there were
eleven Metropolitans,[31] each of whom ruled over a province,
and one hundred and eighteen suffragan bishops.

As Bishop of Tours Gregory had special responsibilities. He
was Metropolitan of Le Mans, Rennes, Angers, Nantes and
four other sees. His cathedral had been burnt down in the
disastrous fire which ravaged Tours during the episcopate of his
predecessor Eufronius, and it took him seventeen years to rebuild it.[32] Saint Martin's church had been burnt down by
the priest Willichar[33] and, although much had been done to restore it, Gregory had to give considerable attention to the interior
decoration.[34] The fact that Saint Martin was buried in Tours
made it a special place of sanctuary, and Gregory endured the
presence there of such evil fugitives from justice as Guntram
Boso,[35] Merovech[36] and Eberulf.[37] In his church-house he
was rarely without visitors: his account of the marks of the
chariot-wheels still to be seen under the waters of the Red Sea is
based upon the traveller's tales of an eye-witness;[38] Simon, an
exiled Bishop from Armenia, came to stay and gave him
details of the Church of the Forty-eight Martyrs and of the fall
of Antioch;[39] Saint Aredius, Abbot of Limoges, stayed with
him shortly before his death.[40] During the twenty-one years of
Gregory's episcopate the civil rule of Tours passed from Sigibert to Chilperic and then again to Childebert II, during whose
minority Guntram exercised control: and with all these Kings
Gregory was on intimate, if not always friendly terms. Of one
of his predecessors, the ill-fated Gunthar, he wrote: 'He was
formerly a man of great discretion, and during his tenure of
office as Abbot he was often sent on diplomatic missions be-

30. Aetherius, Bishop of Lisieux, used even to go out into the fields to
supervise the ploughing, *HF*, VI, 36.
31. Arles, Lyons, Vienne, Rouen, Tours, Sens, Trier, Rheims, Bourges,
Bordeaux and Narbonne.

32. *HF*, X, 31.	33. *HF*, IV, 20.	34. *HF*, X, 31.
35. *HF*, V, 4.	36. *HF*, V, 14.	37. *HF*, VII, 21.
38. *HF*, I, 10.	39. *HF*, X, 24.	40. *HF*, X, 29.

tween the Frankish Kings.'[41] The second part of this sentence was equally true of himself: he was with King Chilperic at Nogent-sur-Marne in 581;[42] he was in Chalon-sur-Saône in 587 as the envoy of Childebert II sent to ease away any doubts which King Guntram might be entertaining about the terms of the Treaty of Andelot;[43] and he was one of the judges of Clotild and Basina after the revolt in Saint Radegund's nunnery in Poitiers.[44]

Within the limits of a certain area in Gaul Gregory travelled very widely. We find him in Autun,[45] Berny-Rivière,[46] Blaye,[47] Bordeaux,[48] Carignan,[49] Cavaillon,[50] Chalon-sur-Saône,[51] Clermont-Ferrand,[52] Coblenz,[53] Dijon (?),[54] Lyons,[55] Metz,[56] Nogent-sur-Marne,[57] Orleans,[58] Paris,[59] Poitiers,[60] near Rheims,[61] Riez,[62] Saintes,[63] Soissons[64] and Vienne.[65] He never had occasion to leave Gaul, and the journey to Coblenz seems to have been the longest which he undertook.

Gregory is supposed to have been a very small man. There is an apocryphal story that he once visited Gregory the Great in Rome, knelt in obeisance before him and, as he rose, saw the Pope eyeing him quizzically, whereupon he is supposed to have said: 'It is God that hath made us, and not we ourselves.'[66] He is also said to have been ill frequently, but this is largely based upon his habit of mixing for himself odd and noisome potions made from infusions of the dust and relics of the Saints.[67] In

41. *HF*, X, 31. 42. *HF*, VI, 2. 43. *HF*, IX, 20.
44. *HF*, X, 15. 45. *GC*, 74. 46. *HF*, V, 49.
47. *GC*, 45. 48. *GC*, 46–7. 49. *HF*, VIII, 15–17.
50. *VSM*, III, 60. 51. *HF*, IX, 20. 52. *HF*, X, 15.
53. *HF*, VIII, 13–14. 54. *HF*, III, 19. 55. *VSJ*, 2, etc.
56. *HF*, IX, 13, 20, X, 19.
57. *HF*, VI, 2–5. 58. *HF*, VIII, 1–7. 59. *HF*, V, 18, IX, 6.
60. *HF*, IX, 2, X, 15. 61. *HF*, IX, 13. 62. *GC*, 82.
63. *VSM*, III, 51, IV, 31. 64. *HF*, IV, 19. 65. *VSJ*, 2.
66. Psalm 100, 3, the Jubilate Deo. This story was first put about by Odo de Cluny, in his tenth-century *Vita Sancti Gregorii*, 24.
67. In 573, for example, only two months before his consecration, he fell seriously ill with dysentery and despaired of his life. He had recourse to his favourite remedy, the *potio de pulvere sepulchri*, made an infusion of dust from Saint Martin's tomb and recovered almost immediately, *VSM*, II, 1.

any case the fact that he felt ill occasionally can have caused no surprise to anyone in those days of bubonic plague and raging dysentery. Small and sometimes ailing in body he may have been, but he was big in heart: he refused point-blank to surrender Guntram Boso to Chilperic's insolent emissary Roccolen;[68] in similar circumstances he refused to surrender Merovech;[69] he alone spoke up for Bishop Praetextatus at the Council of Paris;[70] he argued firmly with King Chilperic about the distinction of Persons;[71] instead of fleeing the country, as he was urged to do, he defended himself valiantly at the Council of Berny-Rivière against the charge of having slandered Queen Fredegund;[72] and he resisted strenuously the attempts of Childebert's collectors to levy tax on the townsfolk of Tours.[73]

As one reads the *History of the Franks*, certain pleasing peculiarities of Gregory's character and personality strike one forcibly. He was proud of his distinguished relatives, but it was for their sake, not his, for he himself was really the most modest of men. As we have seen, he played a big part in the history of his own times, but he rarely refers to himself; and when he does it is in passing and in deprecating terms. In fact, as he unravels for us the bewildering events of these two decades, he seems to go out of his way to understate his own role. His summing up of his manifold activities in Tours between 573 and 591 is typical. He rebuilt the cathedral and re-decorated Saint Martin's church, and that he could hardly omit, for it was common knowledge and the very stones cried out for witness. He discovered, identified, blew the dust off and placed in suitable vantage-points various jars full of putrefying relics. Having related at great length the architectural achievements of his predecessors, he then concludes: 'In many other places in Tours and its immediate neighbourhood I dedicated churches and oratories, and these I enriched with relics of the Saints. It would be too long to give you a complete list.'[74] Gregory was not a

68. *HF*, V, 4. 69. *HF*, V, 14. 70. *HF*, V, 18.
71. *HF*, V, 44. 72. *HF*, V, 49. 73. *HF*, IX, 30.
74. *HF*, X, 31.

garrulous man; but his education had been sketchy,[75] and that perhaps accounts for the relish with which he sets out for us in such detail his disputations and his skill in matching quotation by quotation, Biblical text by Biblical text.[76] He had a very keen sense of justice: and, as his innumerable characters cross the stage, most of them reprehensible in this way or that, he gives from the wings a succinct and honest judgement of each, not always that of history, for like any man he had his prejudices. The *History of the Franks* is spattered with the blood and festering pus, it re-echoes with the animal screams of men and women being tortured unto death: yet Gregory never once questions this effective method of exacting confession, implicating confederates, or simply satisfying the blood-lust of Queens and Kings. For all that, he was a man of deep compassion. One passage is often quoted. In 580 dysentery once again decimated the inhabitants of Gaul. He wrote: 'The epidemic began in the month of August. It attacked young children first of all and to them it was fatal: and so we lost our little ones, who were so dear to us and sweet, whom we had cherished in our bosoms and dandled in our arms, whom we had fed and nurtured with such loving care. As I write I wipe away my tears and I repeat once more the words of Job the blessed: "The Lord gave, and the Lord hath taken away; as it hath pleased the Lord, so is it come to pass. Blessed be the name of the Lord, world without end." '[77] Finally, he had a wry and pawkish sense of humour, which to my knowledge has never been noticed before.[78] Time and time again, usually at the conclusion of some most serious passage, of some stomach-turning description, he adds an amusing comment, often a sly quip at himself. One example will suffice here. At the end of his account of the activities of an impostor, a false healer, a self-announced Christ, he writes: 'Just about this time I had occasion to come to Paris myself and I was put up in the church-house of Saint Julian the martyr. The very next night this poor wretch broke out of his prison and, with his chains wrapped round him, made

75. See p. 30.   76. *HF*, II, 10, V, 43, VI, 5, VI, 40, X, 13.
77. *HF*, V, 34.   78. See pp. 46–9 for fuller treatment.

his way to Saint Julian's church, where he collapsed on the stone floor on the exact spot where I was due to stand. Exhausted and sodden with wine, he fell asleep where he lay. In the middle of the night I got up to say my prayers to God, quite unaware of what had happened. There I found him sleeping. He smelt so foul that compared with the stench which rose from him the noisome fetor of lavatories and sewers quite pales into insignificance. I was quite unable to step into the church for this odour. One of the junior clergy ventured forward holding his nose and tried to rouse the man. He was unable to do so, for the poor wretch was completely drunk. Four other priests went up to him, lifted him up in their hands and threw him into a corner of the church. Water was brought, the stone floor was washed clean and then strewn with sweet-smelling herbs, and so eventually I came in to perform the office. Even my singing failed to wake him.'[79] In case you have missed the point, or been too overawed to smile, in the next sentence he re-writes for you a line of Virgil: 'When daylight returned to the world and the sun's bright lamp climbed up the sky,[80] I handed the man back to Bishop Ragnemod and asked that he might be pardoned.' Pardoned, you note, not punished. However hateful may have been his times, this was a lovable man.

II. THE TIMES IN WHICH GREGORY LIVED

The *History of the Franks* is largely a parade of Kings and Queens. As will be explained on p. 24, Gregory's personal narrative probably begins with the assassination of King Sigibert in 575, soon after his own consecration, and it fills Books V–X. Until then Gregory had been looking backwards; and if we are to understand the history of his times we shall have at first to do the same.

79. *HF*, IX, 6.
80. *Aeneid*, VII, 148–9:
        Postera cum prima lustrabat lampade terras
        Orta dies . . .

The Kings of the Merovingian dynasty ruled over Gaul from the early fifth century until 751, although the last hundred years or more of this period was for them a time of ever-increasing decadence and subjection to the Mayors of the Palace, who, as the Carolingians, were eventually to replace them. Chlogio or Clodio, the half-legendary founder of the line, is mentioned briefly by Gregory, as is also Merovech, d. 456, his successor and putative son, after whom the dynasty is named.[81] Two chapters only are devoted to the events of the reign of Childeric, d. 481, the third Merovingian King.[82] As is to be expected, Gregory gives much fuller treatment to Clovis, who, by his victories over the last representatives of Roman power, and then over the leaders of the Alamanni, the Burgundes and the Arian Visigoths, united most of Gaul under the rule of the Salian Franks. He defeated the Roman general Syagrius near Soissons in 486 and executed him;[83] he married the Burgundian Princess, Clotild, and in 496 she persuaded him to accept baptism as a Christian and a Catholic;[84] he defeated and killed Alaric, King of the Visigoths, at Vouillé in 507.[85] In 511, the thirtieth year of his reign, he died in Paris and was buried in the church of the Holy Apostles, afterwards Sainte Geneviève, which he had founded.[86]

Clovis left four sons: Theuderic, the child of a concubine, and Chlodomer, Childebert I and Lothar I, the three surviving sons of Clotild. Their interminable quarrels, their wars in Burgundy, Septimania and Spain, how, with the connivance of Childebert, Lothar murdered the children of Chlodomer, and then destroyed his own rebellious son Chramn, all this is described spasmodically but graphically in Books III–IV.

Lothar I died in 561. All his brothers had predeceased him. He left four sons, three of them, Charibert, Guntram and Sigibert, the children of Ingund, his second wife, and Chilperic, the only child of his third wife, Aregund. Frankish Gaul, which Lothar, like Clovis, had united under his rule, was now once

81. *HF*, II, 9. See the family tree on p. 18 of the Introduction.
82. *HF*, II, 12 & 18.   83. *HF*, II, 27.   84. *HF*, II, 28–9.
85. *HF*, II, 37.   86. *HF*, II, 43.

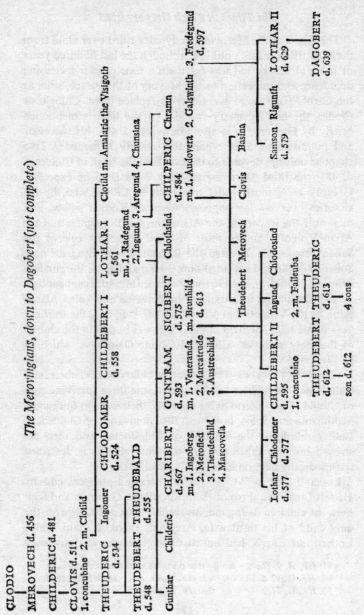

The Merovingians, down to Dagobert (not complete)

CLODIO

MEROVECH d. 456

CHILDERIC d. 481

CLOVIS d. 511
1. concubine   2. m. Clotild

THEUDERIC
d. 534

Ingomer   CHLODOMER
d. 524

CHILDEBERT I
d. 558

LOTHAR I
d. 561
m. 1. Radegund
2. Ingund 3. Aregund 4. Chunsina

Clotild m. Amalaric the Visigoth

THEUDEBERT
d. 548

THEUDEBALD
d. 555

Gunthar   Childeric

CHARIBERT
d. 567
m. 1. Ingoberg
2. Merofled
3. Theudechild
4. Marcovefa

GUNTRAM
d. 593
m. 1. Veneranda
2. Marcatrude
3. Austrechild

SIGIBERT
d. 575
m. Brunhild
d. 613

Chlotsind   CHILPERIC
d. 584
m. 1. Audovera 2. Galswinth 3. Fredegund
d. 597

Chramn

Lothar   Chlodomer
d. 577   d. 577

CHILDEBERT II
d. 595
1. concubine

Ingund   Chlodosind

Theudebert   Merovech   Clovis   Basina

Samson   Rigunth   LOTHAR II
d. 579   d. 629

THEUDEBERT
d. 612

THEUDERIC
d. 613
2. m. Faileuba

DAGOBERT
d. 639

son d. 612

4 sons

more divided between four brothers, with Paris, Orleans, Rheims and Soissons as their capitals.[87] The events of their reigns down to the death of Charibert in 567 are described in a rough-and-ready fashion in Book IV, 21–45. With the death of the oldest brother a fresh partition was necessary. The activities of Guntram, Sigibert and Chilperic down to 575 are set out in Book IV, 46–51. In 575 Sigibert was assassinated on the royal estate of Vitry, between Douai and Arras. 'Two young men who had been suborned by Queen Fredegund then came up to Sigibert, carrying the strong knives which are commonly called scramasaxes and which they had smeared with poison. They pretended that they had something to discuss with him, and they struck him on both sides. He gave a loud cry and fell to the ground. He died soon afterwards.'[88] Gregory was in his thirty-sixth year when Sigibert was murdered. He had lived through many of the events set out in the last two paragraphs, but he had played no part in them. From 575, or a little before, he began to write with authority and personal knowledge, from his vantage-point as Metropolitan Bishop of Tours.

Chilperic lived for nine more years after the murder of Sigibert. The events of this period are given in considerable detail in Books V and VI. Chilperic had three wives: Audovera, who was confined in a nunnery and later murdered by Fredegund;[89] Galswinth, sister of Brunhild, Sigibert's Queen, whom Chilperic had garrotted;[90] and the redoubtable Fredegund herself, who was to die peacefully in her bed many years later in 597. Theudebert, Chilperic's eldest son, died on the battlefield;[91] Chilperic forced the rebellious Merovech to kill himself;[92] Clovis, Audovera's third son, was murdered by Fredegund;[93] and Chilperic's daughter Clotild became the ringleader of the revolt in Saint Radegund's nunnery in Poitiers.[94] Rigunth, Chilperic's daughter by Fredegund, set out on her ill-fated journey to marry Recared, the son of Leuvigild, King of the Visigoths; she had travelled as far as Toulouse

87. *HF*, IV, 22.   88. *HF*, IV, 51.   89. *HF*, V, 39.
90. *HF*, IV, 28.   91. *HF*, IV, 50.   92. *HF*, V, 18.
93. *HF*, V, 39.   94. *HF*, IX, 39–43, X, 15–17, 20.

when her father's death was announced, and then, after many vicissitudes, she returned home to her widowed mother, with whom she lived in extreme enmity.[95] In 584 Chilperic was assassinated in the royal villa at Chelles. 'One day when he returned from the chase just as twilight was falling, he was alighting from his horse with one hand on the shoulder of a servant, when a man stepped forward, struck him with a knife under the armpit and then stabbed him a second time in the stomach. Blood immediately streamed both from his mouth and through the gaping wound, and that was the end of this wicked man.'[96]

The death of Chilperic left Guntram as the sole remaining son of Lothar I. Sigibert had been succeeded by his son Childebert II, who was a boy of five, in 575; Chilperic was succeeded by Lothar II, Fredegund's only son, who was four months old when his father was assassinated in 584. Guntram had long before lost all his four sons: his second wife, Marcatrude, murdered Gundobad, his only son by Veneranda, and then lost her own son; and the two children of Austrechild, Lothar and Chlodomer, died of dysentery in 577. From 584 onwards Guntram acted as a more or less benevolent uncle to Childebert II, whom he called his adopted son.

Books VII–X of the *History* are much more full in their treatment. They cover the years 584–91. Forty of the hundred and sixty-eight chapters in these four Books are devoted to Church affairs. Through the other chapters runs a constant spirit of revolt: the challenge to the authority of the Kings made by the great nobles of the state, Gundovald, Eberulf, Mummolus, Guntram Boso, Rauching, Ursio, Berthefried; the constant enmity of the Bretons; the rebellion against Leubovera, second Abbess of Saint Radegund's nunnery in Poitiers, led by Clotild and Basina, both of them princesses of the blood royal. One after another these uprisings were crushed, always with terrible bloodshed and loss of life. Lothar II was still a child. Childebert II gradually grew to manhood, and his relationship with King Guntram centred round the Treaty of Andelot of

95. *HF*, IX, 34.   96. *HF*, VI, 46.

587. Behind Childebert II stood his mother, Queen Brunhild, the hated enemy of Queen Fredegund, Chilperic's widow.

The *History of the Franks* is also a procession of bishops, abbots and other great dignitaries of the Church. Gregory first recorded their activities in a desultory fashion, as he came to hear of them, or as he inquired into them for his other books. He then went back in a systematic way and added sixty-eight chapters, most of which deal with churchmen, to Books I, II, IV, V and VI.[97] Finally, in Book X, he passes in review the eighteen Bishops of Tours who had preceded him.

Beneath the Kings and Queens, the great noblemen, some of them upstarts, and the princes of the Church, are the common people. Armies march up and down, their aim being to ravage and to loot rather than to engage the enemy. Great conflagrations blaze: at Mareuil outside Blois,[98] in Poitiers,[99] in Paris,[100] in Tours itself.[101] There are frequent floods, famines and epidemics, all of which show respect to no man. Assassins lurk and pounce, most of them, if Gregory is to be believed, the emissaries of Queen Fredegund. Feuds arise between whole townships: the men of Orleans and Blois unite to ravage Châteaudun and Chartres.[102] Inside the towns there are savage quarrels between the comparatively well-to-do: in Tours Sichar attacks Austregesil and kills Auno;[103] Chramnesind, the son of Auno, tries to take vengeance on Sichar;[104] these two then become friends, but in the end Chramnesind feels the call of his blood, murders Sichar with his dagger and hangs his naked body on his garden-fence.[105] We see little of the really poor: among their greatest anxieties is the payment of taxes;[106] and their most gruesome fate is to be thrown into gaol, where they are chained to logs and left to moulder away.[107]

97. See note 120.　　98. *HF*, VII, 12.　　99. *HF*, VII, 13.
100. *HF*, VIII, 33.　　101. *HF*, X, 31.　　102. *HF*, VII, 2.
103. *HF*, VII, 47.　　104. *HF*, VII, 47.　　105. *HF*, IX, 19.
106. *HF*, IX, 30, X, 7.　　107. *HF*, X, 6.

For a man who lived to be fifty-five only and who for the last twenty-one years of his life must have been extremely busy, Gregory was much given to putting pen to parchment. As he says good-bye to us at the end of the *History of the Franks,* he gives a list of his literary compositions: 'I, Gregory, have written the ten books of this *History,* seven books of *Miracles,* and one of the *Lives of the Fathers.* I have composed a book of *Commentaries on the Psalms*; I also wrote a book on the *Offices of the Church.*'[108] The complete list, as we have it, seems to be:

1. The *Historiae Francorum* [=*HF*], Books I–X, the subject of this translation. Book I has the title *Historiae Aeclestiasticae Liber Primus,* and again *Liber Historiarum Primus*; and in the explicit Book X is called *Liber Historiarum Decimus.* These are no doubt scribal additions. Gregory's exact words in the passage quoted above are 'decem libros Historiarum', so that for him the book was the *Historiae.* His final summing-up in Book X, 30 concerns the year 591. At the very end he refers to 'the twenty-first [year] after my own consecration',[109] which was 593–4.

2. The *Liber in Gloria Martyrum Beatorum* [=*GM*], one Book in 106 chapters. The latest reference is to the return from Rome of Gregory's deacon Agiulf in 590.[110]

3. The *Liber de passione et virtutibus Sancti Juliani martyris* [=*VSJ*], one Book, in fifty chapters. The latest reference is to Gregory's consecration on 20 August and his arrival in Tours as Bishop on 28 August 573. [111]

4. The *De virtutibus beati Martini episcopi* [=*VSM*], Books I–IV. The latest entry is to the feast of Saint Martin, 4 July 593.[112]

5. The *Liber vitae Patruum* [=*VP*], one Book, in twenty chapters. The latest reference once again is to the return from Rome of Gregory's deacon Agiulf in 590.[113]

108. *HF*, X, 31.   109. *HF*, X, 31.   110. *GM*, 82; cp. *HF*, X, 1.
111. *VSJ*, 34.   112. *VSM*, IV, 45.   113. *VP*, VIII, 6.

6. The *Liber in gloria Confessorum* [=*GC*], one Book, in 110 chapters. For the third time, the latest reference is to the return home of Agiulf, 'mihi vir fidelis', in 590.[114] Items 2, 3, 4 and 6 together make up the 'seven books of *Miracles*' referred to by Gregory in the passage quoted above.

7. The *Liber de miraculis beati Andreae apostoli* [=*MBA*], one Book in thirty-eight short chapters.

8. The *Passio sanctorum Martyrum Septem Dormientium apud Ephesum* [=*PMSD*], one Book in twelve very short chapters, translated into Latin by Gregory.

9. The *De Cursu Stellarum ratio* [=*CS*], one Book in forty-seven very short chapters. This contains a reference to a comet seen in Gaul just before the assassination of King Sigibert in 575.[115] In the passage by Gregory quoted above it is the *Offices of the Church*.

10. The *In Psalterii tractatum commentarius*, which is lost except for the incipit and the chapter-headings.

11. A book on the Masses of Sidonius Apollinaris, which is lost.[116]

It is impossible to put these books into any firm order of composition. Items 3, 7, 8, 9, 10 and 11 are all comparatively short works, each of which could have been written as a complete whole. The evidence seems to suggest that the book on Saint Julian was an early work, written for the most part before Gregory's consecration. This may well be true of some of the others. On the contrary, items 1, 2, 4, 5 and 6 consist, so to speak, of running-account entries, to which Gregory could continue to add as long as his health permitted, and this is probably what he did. All five of them bring us down to the 590s.

IV. THE HISTORY OF THE FRANKS

1. *Intention and shape*

In his preface Gregory laments the fact that in the Gaul of his time 'there is not one man to be found who can write a book

114. *GC*, 60.   115. *CS*, 34; cp. *HF*, IV, 51.   116. *HF*, II, 22.

23

about what is happening today . . .'[117] At some moment after his consecration in August 573, having weighed carefully the demands upon his time and strength of all his new responsibilities, and having, one can well imagine, begun already to feel a pressing need for relaxation from them, he took upon himself the task of writing such a contemporary history. He continued to work at this book until the year of his death, although the last year treated in detail is 591. He would naturally think in terms of a chronicle, for in the sixth century a historian of contemporary events meant a historiographer, and a historiographer meant a chronicler, a recorder who listed happenings in quasi-diary form more or less as they occurred, choosing and sifting his material no doubt, but setting it down in chronological order. Gregory's *History* is, of course, much more than a chronicle, for there is a strong sense of narrative about it, the more important events are built up into dramatic sequences, and Gregory is no mean raconteur; but the smaller self-contained incidents are entered in chronicle fashion. The alternative of collecting material over a period of years and then, at some propitious moment, of sitting down to write a reasoned philosophical history, seen in perspective, with cause linked to effect, with due proportion and proper balance, can hardly have occurred to Gregory. From his vantage-point in Tours, he wanted to describe what was happening at the moment. Life was much more uncertain then than now, and, had he adopted this modern method, or even conceived of it, the probability was great that he would have died with all his notes around him and no book written. There remains the problem of deciding at which point in the *History* as we have it this contemporary narrative begins. We can assume, if we wish, that Gregory was writing smoothly and consecutively from the beginning of Book V, with its passionate prologue and its opening reference to the murder of Sigibert in 575, in short that Books V–X form the *History* proper. This does not prevent us from accepting the possibility that during the first three years of his episcopate he had already made rough drafts of certain parts of

117. Preface, p. 63.

Book IV, or even of earlier Books, and that, as he forged ahead with his story, he was at the same time casting an occasional glance backwards at his wake.[118]

Inspired by his reading of the chronicles of Eusebius, Saint Jerome and Orosius, and by his knowledge of the Bible, Gregory took upon himself the task of prefixing to the narrative of his own times the Old Testament story from the days of the Creation onwards, then the Nativity of Christ and then the later events of the New Testament. This became Book I; but Book I does not stop there. It moves on to the death of Saint Martin of Tours in 397, and, according to Gregory's ingenious reckoning, by the time that he had finished it he had covered in one Book of thirty-five chapters no fewer than 5596 years of world history. It is possible, of course, that Book I, or much of Book I, was written before Books V–X.

The third stage was to close the gap between the death of Saint Martin in 397 and the murder of Sigibert in 575, in a word to compose Books II, III and IV. It is perhaps too ingenuous to suggest that Gregory acted in a simple logical way: that at one end of a table he had a heap of manuscript sheets which contained the text of Book I, 1–26, his paraphrase of the Biblical story, prefaced by his personal confession of faith; that at the other end lay the gradually increasing pile of folios in which were being recorded contemporary events from Book V onwards; and that, in between, in moments of leisure, he methodically accumulated the remainder of Book I and the whole of Books II, III and IV, running from Trajan to the early years of his own episcopate, and slightly overlapping in time with the beginning of Book V. Something of this sort may well have happened. With Eusebius to help him, with Saint Jerome down to 378 and then Orosius to the early years of the fifth

118. There are indications of this. Book V has a particularly ornate prologue; but the opening sentence of Book IV, 50 seems to foreshadow it. There is the oddity that all the manuscripts of Class B, including Bibl. Nat.f.lat.17655, have VII, 7–8 inserted in error at the end of Book IV. Book IV ends with a detailed computation of the years which elapsed between the Creation and the assassination of Sigibert.

century, he could have worked in an orderly fashion if he had
wished. Again, it is not impossible that Books I–IV were written, or at least drafted, before Books V–X.

What appeared at first to be a consecutive narrative of more
or less contemporary events has now become an affair of some
complexity and a cause of no little bewilderment to the modern
reader, who finds it odd that what we call the *History of the
Franks*, but what was for Gregory his 'decem libros Historiarum',[119] should begin with the Creation and the first man
Adam before he committed sin. There is still a fourth stage of
composition to be considered. At some moment, probably in
584, Gregory turned back and began to interpolate chapters.
None of these is found in Books VII–X, which begin with the
death of Saint Salvius in 584. As he continued with his task,
Gregory saw more and more clearly that, once the Bible story
was completed, his *History* was at once an account of the major
secular events in Gaul and a record of the Saints, martyrs and
bishops of the Church. He came to the opinion that he had
perhaps treated this second aspect too sparingly in his earlier
books. The fact that in all probability he was at the same time
compiling the *Liber in gloria Martyrum Beatorum*, the *Liber
vitae Patruum* and the *Liber in gloria Confessorum* would re-
inforce this opinion. There are sixty-eight of these interpolated
chapters.[120] They all, or nearly all, deal with churchmen and
Church affairs.

In Book X, 30, Gregory, in his engaging way, sums up the
weather for 591, the last year described in his *History*. Unlike

119. *HF*, X, 31.
120. Book I, 28, 29, 31, 33, 34, 35, 36, 37, 38, 44, 45, 46, 47; Book II, 14,
15, 16, 17, 21, 22, 23, 26, 36, 39; Book IV, 5, 6, 7, 11, 12, 15, 19, 32, 33,
34, 35, 36, 37, 43, 48; Book V, 5, 6, 7, 9, 10, 12, 20, 32, 36, 37, 40, 42, 45,
46, 47, 48, 49; Book VI, 7, 8, 9, 10, 11, 13, 15, 22, 29, 36, 37, 38, 39. There is
none in Book III. They are marked with an asterisk in this translation.
Book I, 47 is the improving tale of the chaste spouses. Book V, 47–9 is the
grim story of Count Leudast and, most interestingly, the account of
Gregory's own trial for alleged calumny at Berny-Rivière. Book VI, 13
relates a scandal-column imbroglio at Tours and it could well have been
omitted.

the genial sundial, he records only the tempestuous hours: 'The
hay was destroyed by incessant rain and by the rivers which
overflowed, there was a poor grain harvest, but the vines
yielded abundantly. Acorns grew, but they never ripened.'[121]
With the acorns still unripe on the oak-trees, he lay down his
pen. He could not have known that he was not to die for three
more years; but perhaps he felt old and dispirited, and had had
enough. In a last renewal of strength he picked his pen up again.
He had mentioned all eighteen of the previous Bishops of Tours
in passing: in a sort of Appendix he decided to list them all in
proper order from Gatianus to Eufronius and to write a paragraph about each, adding a modest one about himself. Then he
hands his 'decem libros Historiarum' to us, begs us, in a passage
which is at once self-deprecating and yet written from the heart,
not to do it violence,[122] and tots up his figures for the last
time: 'quorum omnis summa est anni MMMMMDCCXCII.'

2. *Historical and literary debts*

Much of Book I of the *History* is a re-writing of the Old and
New Testaments. In this Book, and again in Book II, Gregory
several times mentions the three chroniclers Eusebius, Jerome
and Orosius.[123] The Greek text of the *Chronicles* of Eusebius
is for the most part lost, and in any case Gregory could not have
read it, but a number of passages in Book I are adapted from
Jerome's Latin translation and continuation. These run as far as
I, 41, where Gregory notes: 'So far Jerome; from this point
onwards the priest Orosius took on the task of writing.'[124] The
borrowings from the *Historiae adversum Pagano*s of Orosius
are, in effect, few.[125] In Book I Gregory also refers to the

121. *HF*, X, 30.   122. *HF*, X, 31. See pp. 602–3.
123. Eusebius, Bishop of Caesarea, *c.* 260–*c.* 340: *HF*, preface to Book
I, p. 69; preface to Book II, p. 103; see also *HF*, IX, 15. Saint Jerome, *c.* 347–
c. 420: *HF*, preface to Book I, p. 69; I, 41. Paulus Orosius, *fl. c.* 415: *HF* preface
to Book I, p. 69; *HF*, I, 6, I, 41, II, 9; see also preface to Book V, p. 254.
124. The main borrowings from Jerome are in *HF*, I, 17, 24, 26–8, 32,
37–41.
125. *HF*, I, 10, II, 9, preface to Book V, p. 254.

apocryphal book known as the *Gesta Pilati*,[126] to Sulpicius
Severus, *c.* 353–*c.* 410, author of the *Historiae Sacrae*,[127] and
to Victorius of Aquitaine, fl. *c.* 457, author of the *Cursus Paschalis*.[128] There is a one-sentence quotation from the *Passio
Sancti Saturnini*,[129] d. *c.* 257, and three chapters are based
partly on Jerome's *De viris illustribus*.[130] One chapter is
largely taken from the *Passio Sancti Irenaei*,[131] d. 202, and
another is based on the *Vita Sancti Hilarii Pictavensis episcopi*,[132] d. 366. Further debts have been traced to the *Itin-
erarium Theodosii de situ terrae sanctae*[133] and to the
Inventio Sanctae Crucis.[134]

In Book II, 8–9, Gregory sets out to discover the very first
mentions of Frankish kings, and for his material he goes to two
sources which are now lost to us, the *Historia* of Renatus Profuturus Frigeridus and the *Historia* of Sulpicius Alexander, fl.
late fourth century, from both of which he quotes long passages. He takes more material from Orosius.[135] He refers to
the *Vita Sancti Aniani*,[136] d. 453, to two letters by Sidonius
Apollinaris,[137] *c.* 430–*c.* 488, and to the *Letters* and *Homilies*
of Saint Avitus,[138] d. *c.* 518. He also gives a brief quotation
from a letter by Saint Eugenius,[139] d. 505. Other details have
been culled from the *Passiones martyrum in Africa*,[140] the
Vita Sancti Remigii episcopi Remensis,[141] 437–533, and the
Vita Sancti Maxentii,[142] c. 447–515.

In the last eight Books things are very different. Gregory
mentions Eusebius once, in order to quote the story of how
Arius lost his entrails in the lavatory.[143] He gives one sentence
from Orosius[144] and one from Sidonius Apollinaris, calling
him 'Sollius noster'.[145] The poetry written by King Chilperic
is said to have been imitated from that of Sedulius, fl.

126. *HF*, I, 21, 24.   127. *HF*, I, 7.
128. *HF*, preface to Book I, p. 69; see also X, 23.   129. *HF*, I, 30.
130. *HF*, I, 22, 26, 28.   131. *HF*, I, 29.   132. *HF*, I, 39.
133. *HF*, I, 7.   134. *HF*, I, 36.   135. *HF*, II, 9.
136. *HF*, II, 6.   137. *HF*, II, 24–5.   138. *HF*, II, 34.
139. *HF*, II, 3.   140. *HF*, II, 3.   141. *HF*, II, 31.
142. *HF*, II, 37.   143. *HF*, IX, 15.
144. *HF*, preface to Book V, p. 254.   145. *HF*, IV, 12.

425–50.[146] In the farewell address there is a long passage devoted to Martianus Capella, the fifth-century outhor of the *Satiricon*.[147] The lost letters of Ferreolus, d. 581, Bishop of Uzès, are compared with those of Sidonius Apollinaris.[148] Sulpicius Severus, Bishop of Bourges, d. 591, is mentioned as a poet.[149] There is one passing reference to Venantius Fortunatus, *c.* 530–600, who was to become Bishop of Poitiers.[150] Three of these men were Gregory's contemporaries, Ferreolus, Sulpicius Severus and Venantius Fortunatus; but the all-over impression of written sources remains thin. Gregory strengthened it in two ways. He had already quoted the *Aeneid* in Book II.[151] In these last eight Books he included three more quotations from Virgil,[152] with a fourth passing reference.[153] He also quoted Sallust twice.[154] His second device, which is much more important, was to insert the original text of a number of supporting documents. There are seven of these and they are all to be found in Books IX and X:

1. The letter of foundation sent to all neighbouring bishops by Saint Radegund when she was busy establishing her nunnery in Poitiers.[155]

2. The answer sent to Saint Radegund by seven Bishops, Eufronius of Tours, Praetextatus of Rouen, Germanus of Paris, Felix of Nantes, Domitianus of Angers, Victorius of Rennes and Domnolus of Le Mans.[156]

3. The text of the Treaty of Andelot signed between King Guntram and King Childebert II in 587.[157]

4. The address which Pope Gregory delivered to the plague-stricken inhabitants of Rome just before his consecration in 590.[158]

5. The letter of commiseration and support sent in 590 by ten of

---

146. *HF*, V, 44, VI, 46.
147. *HF*, X, 31. See p. 49 for a discussion.
148. *HF*, VI, 7.   149. *HF*, VI, 39.
150. *HF*, V, 8.   151. *HF*, II, 29, *Aeneid* I, 47.
152. *HF*, IV, 30, *Aeneid* I, 104–5, 118; *HF*, IV, 46, *Aeneid* III, 56–7; *HF*, VIII, 22, *Aeneid* III, 56.
153. *HF*, IX, 6.   154. *HF*, IV, 13; VII, 1.   155. *HF*, IX, 42.
156. *HF*, IX, 39.   157. *HF*, IX, 20.   158. *HF*, X, 1.

his fellow-prelates to Gundegisil, Bishop of Bordeaux, the Metropolitan concerned, on the occasion of his failure to quell the rebellion in Saint Radegund's nunnery in Poitiers.[159] The Bishops who signed the letter were Aetherius of Lyons, Syagrius of Autun, Aunacharius of Auxerre, Hesychius of Grenoble, Agricola of Nevers, Urbicus of Riez, Felix of Belley, Veranus of Cavaillon, Felix of Châlons-sur-Marne and Bertram of Le Mans.

6. The judgement given in 590 on the Abbess Leubovera and the two rebellious nuns Clotild and Basina by Gregory himself, Metropolitan of Tours, Ebregisel, Bishop of Cologne, Maroveus, Bishop of Poitiers, Gundegisil, Metropolitan of Bordeaux and other Bishops of the Bordeaux province.[160]

7. The Lists of Fasts and Vigils observed in the cathedral and the other churches of Tours.[161]

This is an impressive list. It is seen in its true light only when we remember that these seven documents have been preserved nowhere else but in the *History of the Franks*. With items 3, 6 and 7 Gregory had close personal connections. Presumably item 4 was brought back from Rome in 590 by the deacon Agiulf in his head or on parchment. The three letters concerning Saint Radegund's nunnery in Poitiers Gregory may have copied from his own chapter archives in Tours.

Gregory's education had been an ecclesiastical rather than a secular one. As we have seen, from the age of twelve onwards he was taught by the kindly Archdeacon Avitus in Clermont-Ferrand. The Latin texts which he studied as a boy were the Psalms, the Gospels, the Acts and the Epistles,[162] rather than such of the works of the great classical writers of ancient Rome as were available. He seems to have done little in later life to remedy this, apart from reading parts of the *Aeneid*, although here, too, the few quotations which he gives may be memories of the teaching of Avitus. For all that, the historical and literary documentation behind the *History* is far from negligible.

159. *HF*, IX, 41.　　160. *HF*, X, 15.　　161. *HF*, X, 31.

162. *VP*, II, introduction: 'Non enim me artis grammaticae studium imbuit, neque autorum secularium polita lectio erudivit . . .'

3. *Personal knowledge*

For information about events which occurred before Theudebert's invasion of Italy in 539[163] Gregory could rely only
upon bookish sources and hearsay. His own observation of
national events, and still less his participation in them, can
hardly have begun before 563, when, at the age of twenty-five,
he was ordained a deacon. On the other hand, as we have seen,
he had many friends and relations in high place, and no doubt he
often had serious talks about recent happenings with Avitus
of Clermont-Ferrand, with his grand-uncle Bishop Nicetius and
his cousin Bishop Eufronius. For the period 538–*c.* 563 and for
the ten years which ensued before his consecration in 573, he
certainly had means of gaining reliable information, even if he
himself can have played little or no part in the events which he
described. This takes us from Book III, 32 to about Book IV,
57. It is clearly in Books V–X that we must look for his personal
contribution. A close analysis of the happenings recorded in
these Books in which Gregory himself played a part would
become almost a résumé of the *History* itself. He appears in
sixty-seven of the 265 chapters of the last six Books and in many
of them his role was a central one.

The first time that Gregory had occasion to mention himself
was when Roccolen marched on Tours and sent hostile messages to him: 'Next Roccolen marched on Tours, having received orders to do so from Chilperic. He was full of
braggadocio as to what he proposed to do there. He pitched his
camp on the further bank of the River Loire and sent messengers to me to say that I must expel Guntram from my church,
for he was accused of having killed Theudebert. If I did not
carry out his commands, he would order the city and all its
suburbs to be burnt to the ground.'[164] From that moment
onwards Gregory was as often as not present at the happenings
which he described. Many of them were major events of
national importance: the arrival of Merovech in Tours to seek
sanctuary;[165] the Council of Paris at which Praetextatus,

163. *HF*, III, 32.   164. *HF*, V, 4.   165. *HF*, V, 14.

31

Bishop of Rouen, was tried;[166] the visit which Gregory paid to King Chilperic at Nogent-sur-Marne;[167] the period which he spent in Orleans with King Guntram;[168] the visit to Coblenz with King Childebert II;[169] the stay in Metz with Child-ebert;[170] the embassy to King Guntram in Chalon-sur-Saône;[171] the trial of Clotild and Basina, at which Gregory was one of the judges;[172] and the trial of Egidius, Bishop of Rheims, in Metz.[173] There is then the long series of local affairs in Tours: the robbery in Saint Martin's church;[174] the devastation of the whole neighbourhood by Duke Berulf;[175] the quarrels with Leudast;[176] Gregory's relationships with the infamous Count Eberulf;[177] the murder of the Jew Armentarius;[178] the affrays between Sichar, Austregesil and Chramnesind;[179] and the upsets in Ingitrude's convent.[180] Finally there is a host of minor happenings, extremely interesting in themselves, but sometimes treated at excessive length in view of their comparative unimportance: the personal quarrel with Felix, Bishop of Nantes;[181] the argument with King Chilperic about the distinction of Persons;[182] Gregory's attendance at the funeral of Saint Radegund;[183] and poor Wistrimund, surnamed Tatto, who had toothache.[184] Perhaps the most curious of all these personal reminiscences is the account of Gregory's own trial at Berny-Rivière for having slandered Queen Fredegund, not because of the details which he gives, but because this is one of the interpolated chapters, for in the original text he had chosen to make no mention of it.[185]

These lists could be lengthened at will. They are more than sufficient to prove the personal nature of Gregory's narrative in Books V–X of the *History*.

166. *HF*, V, 18.
167. *HF*, VI, 2,
168. *HF*, VIII, 1–7.
169. *HF*, VIII, 13–14.
170. *HF*, IX, 20.
171. *HF*, IX, 20.
172. *HF*, X, 15.
173. *HF*, X, 19.
174. *HF*, VI, 10.
175. *HF*, VI, 12.
176. *HF*, VI, 32.
177. *HF*, VII, 22.
178. *HF*, VII, 23.
179. *HF*, VII, 47, IX, 19.
180. *HF*, X, 12.
181. *HF*, V, 5.
182. *HF*, V, 44.
183. *HF*, IX, 2.
184. *HF*, X, 29.
185. *HF*, V, 49.

4. *Credibility*

Within the limits set by his circumstances Gregory of Tours was a painstaking and accurate recorder of events. He has been recognized as such down the centuries. In the sixteenth century Claude Fauchet called him 'le pere de nostre Histoire Françoise' and 'le plus ancien et fidele Autheur qui ait parlé des Roys et du Gouvernement François'; and for J. J. Ampère in the nineteenth century he was 'l'Hérodote de la barbarie'.[186] Much of what he described he had seen with his own eyes. From time to time he copied out original documents in full to support his arguments. The *History* contains references to a great number of books which Gregory had consulted with care. Where he had gathered oral information, he added the words *fertur, ferunt*, so it is said, so they say, to make it clear that he was reporting the opinions of others. Whenever he was not sure of something, he admitted it.[187] Although his findings are a little muddled, in that they are given en route and not summed up properly at the end of the journey, Gregory's attempt to discover the first occasion on which a Frankish leader had actually been given the title of King is a first-rate piece of historical research, with the authorities set out in an orderly fashion and the relevant passages quoted *in extenso*, the whole investigation being made the more fascinating by the fact that Gregory was copying his evidence from books which we do not possess written by fourth-century authors of whom we have never heard.[188] Gregory was one of the first to question the naïve statement still so frequently heard today: it must be true, for I read it in such and such a book.[189] Finally, while he

186. *Histoire littéraire de la France avant Charlemagne*, 3rd edn, Paris, 1870, Vol. I, p. 8.

187. *HF*, III, 8, where, when Hermanfrid fell to his death from the walls of Zülpich, Gregory writes: 'He died, but who pushed him we shall never know.' He had a shrewd idea.

188. *HF*, II, 9.

189. *VP*, XVII, introduction: '. . . non omnia quae in scripturis leguntur obtutibus propriis cerni potuerunt; sed quaedam ipsius scripturae relatione firmata, quaedam aliorum autorum testimonio conprobata, quaedam vero proprii intuitus autoritate creduntur.'

wrote with great verve and strength, and would have agreed enthusiastically with Professor R. W. Southern's recent dictum 'that a historian should aim at satisfying the same emotional and intellectual needs as a novelist and poet',[190] on the other hand Gregory rarely indulged in fine purple-passage writing as a literary exercise, and when he did we can be sure that he was being ironic or simply droll, rather than wilfully obscuring the truth by fanciful diction.[191]

All this is on the credit side of the ledger; but adverse comments have been made. Gregory was a Gallo-Roman writing a history of the Franks: he has been accused by patriotic Teutons of being unfair to the Merovingians in that he exaggerated their brutality.[192] Gregory was a zealous churchman: naturally enough, he always saw situations from the viewpoint of the Church; and a king who was regular in his attendance at the offices of the Church or a count who made a strenuous effort to protect church buildings and church property might hope to find his vices more readily condoned in the *History*. As has been said already, Gregory recorded many spirited conversations which he himself invented to fit the circumstances of the moment; but this is a dramatic device still used with great effect by English historians of the late nineteenth century. The personal documentation for which I have praised Gregory has been turned against him: he has been accused of expatiating at undue length on minor events in which he himself was involved, to the detriment of larger issues of great moment to which scant attention was given. He is said to have looked out at the round world from the windows of the church-house in Tours and to have indulged occasionally in local tittle-tattle. This cannot be denied: it is to impugn his sense of judgement and his choice of material; but in these days when the common man takes his

190. 'The classical tradition from Einhard to Geoffrey of Monmouth', *Proceedings of the Royal Historical Society*, 5th series, 1970, p. 175.

191. One thinks of the florid verse of Gregory's contemporary, Venantius Fortunatus, or, at the other extreme, of the terse classical style of Einhard.

192. K. G. Kries, *De Gregorii Turonensis episcopi vita et scriptis*, Breslau, 1859, *passim*.

stand in the history books beside the most puissant princes, such deft and delicate brushwork, trivial as it may sometimes seem, has much to teach us that we wish to know of the society of the time. There is also to be considered the painter's concept of the balance of blocks of colour: after some massive panoramic canvas, say of Pope Gregory addressing the plague-stricken citizens of Rome,[193] we turn with a sense of relief to the petty marital problems of Eulalius and Tetradia.[194] There are factual errors in the *History*, and nineteenth-century collectors of historical minutiae have made great play with them:[195] Gregory said that Alboin ravaged Italy for seven years whereas he should have said four;[196] as successor to Aptachar or Authari, King of the Longobards, he named a certain Paul of whom no one else seems ever to have heard;[197] he made the Emperor Justin rule for eighteen years, whereas in reality he reigned from 565 to 578 only.[198] However much they may err in their judgement, historians should not be wrong in their facts; but, given the difficulties under which a sixth-century chronicler laboured, these occasional lapses, few in number and so easily corrected, are surely to be expected, if not to be excused.

The farther one moves in time and space from the city of Tours in the years 573 to 591 the more likely it is that Gregory may unwittingly mislead us in some statement which he makes. Even for the central events in which he himself played a leading part we often have no other contemporary source by which to control him. It remains true that the *History of the Franks,* in the sober words of Gabriel Monod, is 'un livre exceptionnel où l'auteur lui-même n'est pas le moins intéressant des grands personnages qu'il met en scène'.[199] O. M. Dalton is more explicit in his judgement: '[Gregory] sometimes states things which are not true, but this is either because he did not know

---

193. *HF*, X, 1.   194. *HF*, X, 8.

195. For example, R. A. Lecoy de la Marche, *De l'autorité de Grégoire de Tours*, Paris, 1861.

196. *HF*, IV, 41.   197. *HF*, X, 3.   198. *HF*, V, 30.

199. *Etudes critiques sur les sources de l'histoire mérovingienne*, Paris, 1872, p. 146.

the truth, or because he was misled by his sources. He is never found guilty of calumny or falsehood.'[200]

5. *Other historians of the period*

Venantius Fortunatus, *c.* 530–600, whom, as we have seen, Gregory mentions in passing as 'the priest Fortunatus',[201] and who, after Gregory's death, was to become Bishop of Poitiers, was the only other contemporary historian of any importance in Gaul. Most of his works are in verse. He was born near Treviso, studied in Ravenna and came to Gaul in 564 or 565 to visit the tomb of Saint Martin in Tours. He settled in Poitiers, where he became the close friend of Saint Radegund and of Agnes, the first Abbess of her nunnery. He was the author of a number of Lives of Saints in prose and of a verse *Vita Sancti Martini* in four Books. His main claim to fame is his *Carmina*, a series of *poèmes de circonstance* divided into eleven Books.[202] In Book V, 3, Fortunatus writes to the citizens of Tours in 573 to congratulate them on the election of Gregory as their Bishop. Twelve of the poems in Book V and eleven of the poems in Book VIII are addressed to Gregory; and there is one poem to him in Book IX.[203] In many of these Fortunatus simply sends greetings to Gregory or thanks him for gifts which he has received. In others he deals with more important matters: the conversion of the Jews in Clermont-Ferrand by Bishop Avitus;[204] and the riots in the nunnery in Poitiers.[205] The

200. *The History of the Franks by Gregory of Tours*, Oxford, 1927, 2 vols., of which see Vol. I, p. 36. Dalton is translating from the introduction to *Monumenta Germaniae Historica, Scriptores rerum Merovingicarum* by W. Arndt, p. 21: '... falsa interdum protulit, aut inscius recti, aut fontibus suis delusus, sed nunquam calumniator, aut homo mendas exstitit.'
201. *HF*, V, 8.
202. There are many editions of the poems of Fortunatus. The standard one is the *Opera Poetica* in the *Monumenta Germaniae Historica* series, *Auctorum Antiquissimorum Tomi IV Pars Prior*, ed. by Friedrich Leo, Berlin, 1881, reprint 1961.
203. *Carmina*, V, 4–5, 8–17; VIII, 11–21; IX, 6.
204. *Carmina*, V, 5.
205. *Carmina*, VIII, 12–13.

poems are delightful to read, but they really add little to our knowledge of the major events of the period.

Marius, Bishop of Avenches, a few kilometres to the north-west of Fribourg in Switzerland, lived *c.* 530–94. Like Fortunatus, he was thus almost an exact contemporary of Gregory. He was the author of a *Chronicle*[206] which added to Jerome's translation and continuation of Eusebius, listing names and events from 455 to 581. The *Chronicle* of Marius contains a number of personal reminiscences of the happenings of his own lifetime, but much of it consists of names only. It is succinct and arid, and it can in no way be compared with Gregory's *History*, for it fills only eight pages of modern print. An essential difference is that it was written from a Burgundian viewpoint. It is thought that Marius composed his *Chronicle* towards the end of his life. Like Gregory he knew King Guntram well and it has been suggested that the two men may have met at the Council of Chalon-sur-Saône in 579.[207] What is sure is that Marius used part of Gregory's *History* when he was composing his own *Chronicle*.[208]

John, Abbot of Biclar, near Barcelona, d. 621, an orthodox Catholic, wrote a short *Chronicle*[209] which covers the period 567–90. It fills only ten pages of modern print and, like the *Chronicle* of Marius, it is in no way comparable with Gregory's *History*. Its interest is that it is Catholic and not Arian, and that it describes happenings from a Visigothic viewpoint. John of Biclar gives a short account of the reign of Leuvigild, King of the Visigoths in Spain, and of the first years of the reign of his son Recared.

206. There are many editions. The standard one is in the *Monumenta Germaniae Historica* series, *Chronica Minora saeculorum IV, V, VI, VII*, ed. by Theodor Mommsen, Berlin, 1894, reprinted 1961, Vol. II, pp. 232–9.

207. *HF*, V, 27. Gregory does not actually say that he was present. He nowhere mentions Marius.

208. Marius tells the stories of the revolt of Chramn (*HF*, IV, 20), the collapse of Mount Tauredunum (*HF*, IV, 31) and the disgrace of Bishops Salonius and Sagittarius (*HF*, V, 27). What is more remarkable is a series of textual borrowings made by Marius from *HF*, II, 33, III, 11 and IV, 10.

209. For an edition, see the volume listed in note 206, pp. 211–20.

The so-called *Chronicle of Fredegar*,[210] put together by three anonymous writers, in 613, 642 and *c.* 658, paraphrases parts of Gregory's *History* and carries it forward for another seventy years. It is thought to have been composed in Avenches and it describes events from a Burgundian standpoint. It contains four Books. Much of the material of Book III is taken from Gregory.

Of these four texts only the *Chronicle of Fredegar* can be set beside the *History of the Franks*. The most cursory examination of the works of Gregory's three contemporaries makes it clear that as an historian he stood alone in his own century.

6. *Language*

Gregory wrote as he spoke. His language is the everyday spoken Latin of Gaul in the sixth century, as used by a man who had been brought up in a cultured family of considerable distinction and who was conscious of his own standing as a Metropolitan Bishop. There is no evidence that he dictated the *History of the Franks*.[211] As far as the earlier Books are concerned, he consulted his sources and prepared his own account of the circumstances which he wished to describe. In the later and more interesting part of the *History*, events occurred, Gregory took part in them himself or gathered information about them, and then, at a suitable moment, added a new page or more to his growing heap of manuscript. No doubt he had amanuenses to make fair copies. He was a busy man and his recording may sometimes have lagged well behind the actual events; his very first sentence is written with some feeling: 'A great many things keep happening, some of them good, some of them bad . . .'[212] There is no particular point in comparing his Latin with the

210. For an edition, see *Monumenta Germaniae Historica, Scriptores rerum Merovingicarum*, vol. II, ed. by Bruno Krusch, Hanover, 1888, reprinted 1961, pp. 18–168.

211. Contrast, for example, the garrulousness of a dictated text such as Joinville's *Le livre des saintes paroles et des bonnes actions de Saint Louis*.

212. *HF*, preface, p. 63.

classical tongue of Caesar or Cicero; it is unfair to compare it with the Latin of Einhard or the other writers of the Carolingian Renaissance. It is a vernacular language, moving on fast from the day-to-day speech of the Augustan era towards the first texts in Old French. It is rich in its vocabulary; its syntax is gradually freeing itself from restraint; its morphology is progressing from a synthetic to an analytical structure which will become the two-case system of Old French, where prepositions and articles largely replace the old declensions, just as pronouns bolster up the decaying verbal endings. One may say that it is incorrect, but no linguist would use the word: secondary or tertiary principles are replacing primary ones.[213] It is true that some of the manuscripts which we possess may well be called incorrect, for the copyists did great violence to what Gregory had written.[214]

In an earlier paragraph I have examined his knowledge of the writers who preceded him and of the works of his contemporaries. For the moment it is enough to say that he is most familiar with the Old and New Testaments, and that the Latin of the Bible influenced his language profoundly.

In the *History* Gregory refers only once to his language. 'My Latin may be provincial,' he writes, 'but I could hardly pass over in silence the things which I have seen, or which I have

213. In an excellent article based on two lectures given at the Courtauld Institute of Art in 1968, Roberto Salvini draws a parallel between the way in which the spoken Latin of the men with whom Gregory of Tours, whom he has no reason to mention, must have mixed eventually became Old French and the other early Romance languages, with the Latin of the Carolingian Renaissance as an artificial side-development, and the comparable direct development of pre-Romanesque painting, sculpture and architecture into the Romanesque, with the Carolingian and Ottonian again as a side-development. This is a commonplace for linguists; it seems still to be a point of debate with art historians. See 'Pre-Romanesque, Ottonian and Romanesque', by Roberto Salvini, *Journal of the British Archaeological Association*, 3rd series, XXXIII, 1970, pp. 1–20.

214. This is particularly true of Books VII–X, where MS. Bruxelles 9403 is used. For example, in Book VII, 1, a corrector has thought fit to make eighty-four changes in what the original scribe wrote.

been told by the faithful.'[215] It is provincial in that it is of the
Province of Gaul. In effect, he is the first to complain when
someone else speaks badly. Of the impostor from Bigorra he
writes: 'He spoke the language of the common people, his accent
was poor and the words he used vulgar. It was not easy to
follow what he was trying to say.'[216] On the very few occasions when he departs from his natural language and gives a
false polish to what he has to say one is immediately aware of
the fact.[217] As we shall see, he sometimes draws attention to
his modest jokes by a sentence or two of over-ornate writing.[218]

Gregory was surrounded by Franks, many of whom must
have spoken their own tongue in preference to Latin, or, indeed,
have spoken only Frankish. There is no evidence that he himself
could speak the Frankish dialect.[219] He never mentions Greek.
There is one instructive passage about the tongues being used in
Orleans, when Guntram entered the town on 4 July 585. 'A vast
crowd of citizens came out to meet him, carrying flags and
banners, and singing songs in his praise. The speech of the
Syrians contrasted sharply with that of those using Gallo-
Roman, and again with that of the Jews, as they each sang his
praises in their own tongue.'[220] His only other linguistic comment is on Chilperic's additions to the Latin alphabet. 'He also
added certain letters to our alphabet, the ω of the Greeks, and
the *ae, the* and *wi*, these four to be represented by the characters
ω, Ψ, Z and Δ. He sent instructions to all the cities in his
kingdom, saying that these letters should be taught to boys in
school, and that books using the old characters should have

215. *HF*, V, 6. The exact words are important: 'Et licet sermone
rustico ...' His self-deprecating remarks in *HF*, X, 31 concern his style
rather than his language. There are many other similar references in
Gregory's other writings.

216. *HF*, IX, 6.

217. The preface has been over-polished and so has the first paragraph
of Book I. One could say the same of Book X, 31.

218. See p. 16.

219. See p. 157, note 64, and p. 297, note 66 for the two words *leudes* and
morgengabe.

220. *HF*, VIII, 1.

them erased with pumice-stone and the new ones written in.'[221]

7. *Style*

Gregory's style is plain and unadorned. In the *History of the Franks* there are few figures of speech. One looks almost in vain for exciting comparisons, for arresting metaphors, for any other of the numberless stylistic devices with which he could have enlivened his long account. For Gregory words have a simple narrative function, they tell a story, they record a judgement, on very rare occasions they express an emotion, but there must be no grace notes, no flourishes, no blandishments, no tricks of the writer's trade: these words must never be permitted to stand between the author and us. Gregory marches them this way and that like well-drilled soldiers, but for most of their engagements they are clad in khaki. Part of his own trade as a Bishop was to sway large congregations, in noble and impressive ceremonies to play the central part, to speak up bravely in public assemblies for the cause of justice and Christian loving kindness, to bring a whispered word of comfort at the midnight hour. His language is certainly not lacking in richness and variety, and no doubt it met all these different needs; but it remains true that his literary style has little ornamentation. He is well aware of this. 'My style is not very polished,' he writes in his preface.[222] When the time comes for him to bid farewell to us, he says it again: 'I know very well that my style in these Books is lacking in polish: ... if ... what I have written seems uncouth to you ... do not, I beg you, do violence to my Books.'[223]

Certain positive things strike one immediately about Gregory's style. He will exchange Biblical quotations with us until the evening Angelus rings out and the cows come lumbering home to be milked.[224] When in the mood he will use one of the oldest devices known to Christian apologists and draw broad ethical and spiritual deductions for us from events which hap-

221. *HF*, V, 44.   222. *HF*, preface, p. 63.   223. *HF*, X, 31.
224. *HF*, II, 10, V, 43, VI, 5, VI, 40, X, 13.

41

pened long ago, preferably in the days of the Old and New Testaments.[225] For effect he will readily and constantly move from a past to a present sequence. Above all, and this on nearly every page, he will report to us in spirited direct speech conversations which no one overheard and none had ever recorded. Most of his comparisons are simple. When he comes to the font Clovis is like Constantine;[226] Leudast is as proud as a peacock;[227] Riculf is as proud as Simon Magus;[228] Chilperic is like Nero of old,[229] he is 'the Nero and Herod of our time';[230] a priest goes back to his fornicating 'like some dog which had returned to its vomit'.[231] Occasionally Gregory is more fanciful: '... the bed of the river was piled high with their corpses and ... the Franks crossed over them to the other side as if they were walking on a bridge';[232] men plunge into a river 'like so many bees entering a hive'.[233] His most striking comparison concerns the portent which he saw in the sky at Carignan. 'A cloud gleamed bright in the middle of the heavens, and these rays were all focused on it, as if it were a pavilion the coloured stripes of which were broad at the bottom but became narrower as they rose, meeting in a hood at the top.'[234] All public speakers like a strong contrast, and this reappears when they write: '... their minds ... now strove unjustly to destroy the Just';[235] 'He, the sinless, who had so often set free the sinful ...'[236] '... so that ... the adversaries who prowl about our frontiers may have cause to fear because they see us in agreement, rather than reason to rejoice in our discord.'[237] Gregory is not averse to a good climactic sequence, although this last device must not be used too often: 'Scarcely a day passed without someone being murdered, scarcely an hour without some quarrel or other, scarcely a minute without some person or

225. The Ark is the symbol of the Mother Church, *HF*, I, 4; our earthly existence is like the sea, *HF*, I, 10; the temple of Christ is within us, *HF*, I, 15.

226. *HF*, II, 31.	227. *HF*, V, 48.	228. *HF*, V, 49.
229. *HF*, VI, 46.	230. *HF*, VI, 46.	231. *HF*, VI, 36.
232. *HF*, III, 7.	233. *HF*, IV, 33.	234. *HF*, VIII, 17.
235. *HF*, I, 20.	236. *HF*, VI, 36.	237. *HF*, X, 3.

other having cause for sorrow.'[238] From time to time he gives us a modest aphorism: 'Anyone who does exactly what he wishes is plainly in subjection to none.'[239] Sometimes he quotes a proverb: 'Amico inimicoque bonum semper praebe consilium, quia amicus accepit, inimicus spernet.'[240] Then there are the changes of humour: we have seen Gregory in a tender, loving mood;[241] in the next section we shall watch his face-muscles twitch with irony which must not become sarcasm.[242]

Gregory of Tours is a recorder and a narrator. He can list dull ordinary things, like other people's births and deaths, and who begat whom: this never bores him, because he is a neat man, and putting things in order gives him satisfaction. He can tell us a short tale, describe for us a brief encounter: how the men of Poitiers and the men of Tours vied for Saint Martin's body;[243] how the first-born son of Clotild and Clovis died the moment he was baptized;[244] or how Fredegund had three heads cut off with three axes which swung through the air in unison to end a feud.[245] He can paint a picture, but it must be small, with lots of men and women walking about, none of them quite as large as life, Pieter Brueghel in his thirties, but not a Delacroix: the siege of Chastel-Marlhac;[246] fire raging through the streets of Paris;[247] or deacon Theudulf falling off Angers city-wall when he was tipsy.[248] He can tell an improving story,[249] although, indeed, when he reaches his own era, there are few improving stories to tell. There is one really large canvas, Guntram questioning whether or not Childebert is observing the terms of the Treaty of Andelot, but Gregory fluffs it: we see the roll of parchment and we listen to the clauses of the Treaty, but Guntram, Gregory and Felix are all slightly out of focus,[250] as indeed were Childebert, Brunhild and Faileuba

238. *HF*, X, 15.   239. *HF*, VI, 18.
240. *HF*, VI, 32. Give the same good advice to him who loves you and him who hates you: your friend has accepted it, even if your enemy will scorn it.
241. See p. 15.   242. See pp. 46–9.   243. *HF*, I, 48.
244. *HF*, II, 29.   245. *HF*, X, 27.   246. *HF*, III, 13.
247. *HF*, VIII, 33.   248. *HF*, X, 14.
249. *HF*, I, 47.   250. *HF*, IX, 20.

on the day when the Treaty was negotiated.[251] There is one really long narrative, the *scandalum* in the nunnery in Poitiers, and with the description of this none can quarrel. Gregory first brings us to the convent to witness the pathetic death of Disciola and the vision of the spring of living water seen by the nameless nun.[252] Years pass, Saint Radegund dies and Gregory goes to her funeral.[253] Agnes, the first Abbess, dies in her turn and is replaced by Leubovera. Then the great revolt begins and Gregory is immediately involved. The story continues through Book IX, 39–43, which contain Saint Radegund's letter of foundation, an answer of approval and promised support from seven bishops and a letter of commiseration to Gundegisil from ten bishops. It is taken up again in Book X, 15–17, which include the text of the judgement against Clotild and Basina. Gregory comes back to it a last time in Book X, 20. It is by far the longest and most detailed account in the *History*; it is supported by more documentary evidence than any other event; and the *entrelacement* makes it even more vivid.

Bishop he may be, but when he wishes Gregory can describe a military engagement in full and compelling detail, as when he sets the scene for the siege of Comminges and then goes on to tell how Leudegisel forced Gundovald to surrender.[254] In these military passages he occasionally lapses into a more colloquial style in order to give us the language of the soldiery.[255] Sometimes, on the other hand, he tries a sentence or two of more figurative speech. 'The time came for Leudast to go into service and he was given a job in the royal kitchens. His eyes were weak when he was a young man and the acrid smoke was harmful to him. He was therefore promoted from the kitchen pestle to the baker's basket.'[256] Leudast was Gregory's bitter enemy.

Character studies are built up with infinite patience, not by editorial comment, not by analysis on the couch, not by the old hackneyed devices of monologue, soliloquy, dialogue, dreams, personification of Heredity and Environment, but by reaction to circumstance and by the gradual accumulation of points of

251. *HF*, IX, 11. 252. *HF*, VI, 29. 253. *HF*, IX, 2.
254. *HF*, VII, 34 and 37. 255. *HF*, VII, 36. 256. *HF*, V, 48.

physical detail. A good example is King Guntram, whom we come to know so well that in the end we can predict his reaction to any emergency. In effect, we are introduced formally to no one. If you meet Rigunth, or Brunhild or even Fredegund in the street tomorrow, you will not recognize her until it is too late, for Gregory has told us nothing about her shape, her hair-style or the colour of her eyes.

When we find ourselves in Barcelona or Bellinzona or Carthage there is ample opportunity for local colour on a large scale, but Gregory, who has never been out of Gaul himself, does not take it. 'All the plate which you see here belonged to the traitor Mummolus,' said Guntram to Gregory when they were feasting together in Orleans. 'By the grace of God, it has now passed into my possession. I have had fifteen other dishes out of the set broken up, all as large as the one which you see before you. I have kept only this plate, with a second one which weighs one hundred and seventy pounds.'[257] Guntram was working very hard, but Gregory did not take the hint: there is no description of the King's plate in the *History*. He was surrounded by Franks, yet in the ten Books there are only two words of Frankish, technical terms which I myself have had to explain in a footnote.[258]

Gregory rarely passes judgement: when he does so what he says is clear and unequivocal.[259] In all these ghastly scenes of torture, which will sicken the mind of the gentle reader as much as they have sickened that of the gentle translator, there is no word of comment from the author.[260]

257. *HF*, VIII, 3.
258. They are *leudes*, *HF*, II, 42, III, 33, IX, 20; and *morgengabe*, *HF*, IX, 20.
259. These judgements usually consist of one condemning sentence. Much longer is the scathing chapter on Chilperic, *HF*, VI, 46.
260. 'Some Government sources have argued that the authorities are virtually powerless to stop torture. They claim the torturers are not on the staff lists of the police security forces.' See *The Times*, 26 May 1972, the day on which I wrote this chapter, of a country in South America.

8. *Humour and irony*

I have mentioned Gregory's wry sense of humour. In so sober a narration of events, which are themselves so uniformly grim, we can expect to have no opportunity even to smile. That we laugh occasionally is a pleasant tribute to Gregory's personality.

There are no examples of humour in Books I–IV. Book V starts with the heading: 'Here, I am glad to say, begins Book V. Amen.' Now that Gregory was at last in a position to describe the events of his own period he no doubt found his task much easier. When the savage Count Roccolen marched on Tours to demand the expulsion of Guntram Boso from sanctuary, his men dismantled one of the church-houses and stole the very nails from the woodwork. God and Saint Martin punished Roccolen with jaundice, from which he died: '. . . he fell ill with jaundice, the King's evil,' wrote Gregory, who must have seen him, 'and became bright saffron.'[261] In the next chapter he recorded his exchange of letters with Felix, Bishop of Nantes, whose Metropolitan he was and whom he disliked. 'What a pity it was not Marseilles which elected you as its bishop!' he wrote to Felix. 'Instead of bringing you cargoes of oil and other wares, its ships could have carried only papyrus, which would have given you more opportunity for writing libellous letters to honest folk like me. As it is, only lack of paper cuts short your long-windedness.' Unlike Nantes, Marseilles was not in the province of Tours. 'I will say no more about this,' added Gregory, addressing his readers, 'for fear that you begin to think that I am much the same myself.'[262]

There came a moment when it was reported that Felix was dying of bubonic plague. His last request was that his nephew Burgundio should be elected to replace him as Bishop of Nantes. His perplexed fellow-suffragans sent the callow young man to Gregory, with a letter asking their Metropolitan if he would consider travelling all the way to Nantes in order to make Burgundio a priest or at least a deacon, and then to consecrate

261. *HF*, V, 4.   262. *HF*, V, 5.

46

him. Burgundio was only twenty-five: he was possessed of no
very obvious talents and he was a layman. Gregory gave him
some fatherly advice. 'It is set out here in the canons, my dear
boy,' he said, no doubt speaking very slowly and clearly, 'that
no one can be consecrated as a bishop until he has passed
through the various ranks of the Church in the normal way.
You had better go back to Nantes and ask the person who is
sponsoring you to give you the tonsure. Once you have been
found worthy of admission to the priesthood, apply yourself
seriously to all that the Church asks of you. When God decides that the moment has come to remove your uncle the
Bishop to a better world, it may well be that you yourself will
be given episcopal rank.'[263] Gregory was glad to be about to
see the back of Felix; but if the Bishop of Nantes were to live to
be a hundred instead of only seventy, his Metropolitan clearly
saw little hope of Burgundio's being thought worthy to succeed
him. In the same Book, as part of the conspiracy to defame
Aetherius, Bishop of Lisieux, Gregory told how it was bandied
about that he was in the habit of sleeping with a woman. 'Only
the Devil can have put into their heads the idea of bringing such
a charge against the Bishop,' he added testily, 'for he was nearly
seventy years old!'[264]

When the diocese of Avignon became vacant, Lothar I proposed to appoint Abbot Domnolus. The Abbot asked to be
excused: '... and he begged the King not to submit him, a
simple man, to the boredom of having to listen to sophisticated
arguments by old senatorial families, or to counts who spent
all their time discussing philosophical problems.'[265] Later
Domnolus accepted without demur the episcopate of Le Mans.
There is some personal joke here. Le Mans was in the province
of Tours. Perhaps Domnolus was a noted anti-establishment
man; or perhaps he had made adverse comments on Gregory's
pride in his senatorial ancestors. It is possible that Gregory is
making fun of the Avignonnais: he may have had in mind some
particular families, or some specific count.

In the whole of Gregory's *History*, there is only one play on a

263. *HF*, VI, 15.   264. *HF*, VI, 36.   265. *HF*, VI, 9.

proper name: when Abbot Buccovald put in for the bishopric of Verdun, Gregory, who clearly did not like him, could not prevent himself from adding: '. . . they used to say that he was a proud man, hence his nickname, Buccus Validus.'[266]

Much of Book IX, 20 is devoted to Gregory's efforts, which he shared with a certain Felix, to persuade King Guntram that King Childebert II really was observing the terms of the Treaty of Andelot. They were in Chalon-sur-Saône. When their business was done, they went off to Mass together, and then the King invited Gregory and Felix to have dinner with him. Gregory had had a hard day; but now he could relax. 'The abundance of the dishes on the table was only rivalled by the full contentment which we felt in our hearts,' he wrote, as usual making it clear from his style that he has a joke to offer us. King Guntram was in good form. 'From time to time he laughed out loud, as he coined some witty phrase,' wrote Gregory, and he added drily, 'thereby ensuring that we shared his happiness.' The King turned to Gregory's companion. ' "Tell me, Felix," he said, "is it really true that you have established warm friendly relations between my sister Brunhild and that enemy of God and man, Fredegund?" Felix replied that it was not. I spoke up and said: "The King need not question the fact that the 'friendly relations' which have bound them together for so many years are still being fostered by them both. That is to say, you may be quite sure that the hatred which they have borne each other for many a long year, far from withering away, is still as strong as ever." '[267]

Fredegund is the raging virulent virago of the *History*. There was no love lost between her daughter Rigunth and the widowed Queen. 'She would often insult her mother to her face,' wrote Gregory of the Princess, 'and they frequently exchanged slaps and punches.' The story of how Fredegund tried to murder her daughter by shutting her head in a treasure-chest is unpleasant enough, but Gregory saw the bathos of these undignified goings-on in high places. 'Rigunth was stretching her arm into the chest to take out some more things,

266. *HF*, IX, 23.   267. *HF*, IX, 20.

when her mother suddenly seized the lid and slammed it down on her neck. She leant on it with all her might and the edge of the chest pressed so hard against the girl's throat that her eyes were soon starting out of her head. One of the servant-girls who was in the room screamed out at the top of her voice: "Quick! Quick! Mistress is being choked to death by her mother!" '[268] Gregory concludes his chapter in a tone of ironic disapproval. 'The quarrels between the two were even more frequent after this . . . The main cause was Rigunth's habit of sleeping with all and sundry.'

There remains the farewell address,[269] which is a mixture of heartfelt seriousness and rather heavy humour. Gregory conjures us not to destroy or rewrite his *History*, and certainly not to permit selected extracts from it to be published. Then comes the reference to Martianus Capella and the listing of the Seven Liberal Arts, grammar, dialectic, rhetoric, geometry, astronomy, arithmetic and music, with the implication that none is present in the *History* and the obvious fishing for a hot denial. We are expected to reply: We know that all your training was designed for your subsequent career in the Church, and, indeed, how extraordinarily successful that career has been; but, if any further proof were still needed, the *History of the Franks* confirms us in our admiration of your consummate mastery of the Latin language (= disciplinae grammaticae) and your great skill in analysing and shaping your rather difficult material (= disciplinae dialecticae).[270] Gregory would then dismiss us as incorrigible flatterers, for his modesty was genuine. He concludes by giving us permission, if we are so inclined, to rewrite the whole of the *History* as a narrative poem.[271]

268. *HF*, IX, 34. 'Curritte, quesu, curritte; ecce domina mea graviter a genetricae (sic) sua suggillatur.'

269. *HF*, X, 31.

270. *Disciplinae rhetoricae*, the art of writing poetry, are not relevant; nor are *disciplinae geometricae, arithmeticae* and *armoniae*. One could make a case for *disciplinae astrologicae*. I give Gregory's terms, *HF*, X, 31.

271. This is not meant to be funny. Fortunatus sent his verse *Vita Sancti Martini* to Gregory, with his verse redaction of the *Dialogues* of Sulpicius Severus. He then offered to rewrite Gregory's *De virtutibus beati Martini*

9. *Nature notes*

Gilbert White spent most of his life wondering where swallows, swifts and house-martins went in the winter-time. He should have read the *History of the Franks*.[272] Gregory was a keen observer of nature. In the ten Books he found room for thirty-two nature notes, although most of them record pestilence and storm.

The first six concern the years of his youth: the extremely harsh winter of 548;[273] stars moving round the moon in 555 as a sign that Theudebald was soon to die;[274] a plague of locusts in Auvergne and the Limousin in 559;[275] the flickers of lightning which presaged the death of Lothar I in 561;[276] the great landslide which occurred at Tauredunum, probably Les Evouettes, in 563, and by blocking its course flooded the banks of the River Rhône as far up as Geneva,[277] and a comet which caused an epidemic in Auvergne.[278]

Gregory was no astronomer, but he watched the night sky constantly. In 578, while in Paris, he saw in the heavens rays of light which foretold the death of Merovech;[279] later on in this same year, after he had returned to Tours, there was a circle round the moon, which then went into eclipse, while meteors appeared near the sun.[280] In 582 the comet of 563 was seen again, there was thunder and lightning, a great beacon shone in the sky, it rained blood in Paris and Senlis, and the bubonic plague caused by the comet raged in Narbonne and elsewhere;[281] later in the year the moon was in eclipse and a fiery light traversed the sky.[282] In 583 a ball of fire fell near Tours;[283] lights shone in the northern sky in 584,[284] and later

episcopi in verse. This part of the farewell address may well have been written with Fortunatus in mind, 'sacerdos Dei, quicumque es.' If so, Fortunatus did not accept the challenge!

272. *HF*, IX, 17. 273. *HF*, III, 37. 274. *HF*, IV, 9.
275. *HF*, IV, 20. 276. *HF*, IV, 51. 277. *HF*, IV, 31.
278. *HF*, IV, 31. 279. *HF*, V, 18. 280. *HF*, V, 23.
281. *HF*, VI, 14. 282. *HF*, VI, 21.
283. *HF*, VI, 25. 284. *HF*, VI, 33.

that year there were multi-coloured rings round the sun;[285] in 585 beacon-lights and columns of fire foretold the death of Gundovald,[286] and later in the same year there were again fiery rays in the northern sky.[287] While in Carignan with Vulfolaic in 586 Gregory saw in the north the vivid rays and blood-red clouds which made him think of a military pavilion,[288] and towards the end of the year a light in the shape of a serpent swept across the sky.[289] In 587 there were again bright lights in the north and snakes fell from the clouds;[290] while in 590 fiery globes traversed the heavens and then there was an eclipse of the sun.[291]

These astronomical prodigies were usually followed by extremely inclement weather, which in its turn brought plague or dysentery or both. The tides were high in 578;[292] in 580 there were torrential rains, floods and earthquakes,[293] and later on flood-waters and tempestuous winds.[294] In 582 there was heavy rain;[295] the river-waters rose in 583;[296] in 584 there was frost and hail, followed by prolonged drought;[297] in 585 'the Spring and Summer months were so wet that it seemed more like Winter in Summer.'[298] In 587 it first rained in torrents[299] and then there were unseasonable frosts;[300] at Easter in 589 there were terrible rains and hail-storms;[301] and in 590 it rained torrentially and the rivers rose in flood.[302] All this foul weather destroyed the crops. Wolves prowled about inside the walls of Poitiers[303] and Bordeaux,[304] eating any dogs they chanced to meet, while locusts did immense damage in Toledo.[305] Even more remarkable phenomena were seen: on an island off Vannes a fish-pond was found filled with blood;[306] and in 587 'in the homes of a number of people vessels were discovered inscribed with unknown characters which could not be erased

285. *HF*, VI, 44.   286. *HF*, VII, 11.   287. *HF*, VIII, 8.
288. *HF*, VIII, 17.   289. *HF*, VIII, 42.   290. *HF*, IX, 5.
291. *HF*, X, 23.   292. *HF*, V, 18.   293. *HF*, V, 33.
294. *HF*, V, 41.   295. *HF*, VI, 14.   296. *HF*, VI, 25.
297. *HF*, VI, 44.   298. *HF*, VIII, 23.   299. *HF*, IX, 5.
300. *HF*, IX, 17.   301. *HF*, IX, 44.   302. *HF*, X, 23.
303. *HF*, V, 41.   304. *HF*, VI, 21.
305. *HF*, VI, 33 and 44.   306. *HF*, VIII, 25.

or scraped off however hard they tried.'[307] The rains often made travelling impossible. Nothing could be more dreary than the arrival of Clotild and the rebellious sisters at Gregory's church-house in Tours: 'She and her fellow-nuns had come on foot from Poitiers. They had no horses to ride on. They were quite exhausted and worn-out. No one had offered them a bite to eat on the journey. They reached our city on the first day of March. The rain was falling in torrents and the roads were ankle-deep in water.'[308] The destruction of the crops brought starvation to the peasantry. 'In this year 585 almost the whole of Gaul suffered from famine. Many people made bread out of grape-pips or hazel catkins, while others dried the roots of ferns, ground them to powder and added a little flour. Some cut green corn-stalks and treated them in the same way. Many others, who had no flour at all, gathered grasses and ate them, with the result that they swelled up and died.'[309] Time and time again there were outbreaks of dysentery and bubonic plague.

There are lighter touches. Men cross the frozen rivers as if on dry ground.[310] An elder-tree produces grapes instead of black berries.[311] A crested lark flies into a church in Clermont-Ferrand and extinguishes the lamps.[312] Roses bloom in January.[313] The army of Tiberius captures twenty elephants.[314] Gundovald uses camels as pack animals.[315] One of the servants of Mummolus is a giant, two or three feet taller than a normal man: he is a carpenter by trade, but he dies young.[316] Acorns grow, but they fail to ripen.[317] The vine-harvest is abundant.[318]

307. *HF*, IX, 5. 308. *HF*, IX, 39. 309. *HF*, VII, 45.
310. *HF*, III, 37. 311. *HF*, IV, 9. 312. *HF*, IV, 31.
313. *HF*, VI, 44. 314. *HF*, V, 30. 315. *HF*, VII, 35.
316. *HF*, VII, 41. 317. *HF*, X, 30. 318. *HF*, X, 30.

10. *The manuscripts*

In the introduction to their 1886–93 edition of the Latin text of the *Historia*,[319] Henri Omont and Gaston Collon list twenty-eight manuscripts still in existence which contain the whole or a considerable portion of what Gregory wrote. There is also a great number of fragments. It is not known which manuscript Josse Bade used for his *editio princeps* of 1512.[320] In their own edition Henri Omont and Gaston Collon followed MS. B5 for Books I–VI and MS. B2 for Books VIII–X. The essential details of these two manuscripts are as follows:

B5: Bibliothèque Nationale, Paris, MS. latin 17655. This contains Books I–IV. It was copied in a Merovingian hand, apparently by a single scribe, in the seventh century. It belonged formerly to the Abbaye de Saint Pierre in Corbie and was listed there in two catalogues of the twelfth century. The text runs from f° 2r° to f° 96v°.

B2: Bibliothèque Royale, Bruxelles, MS. 9403, which contains the text from Book II, 3 to the middle of Book X, 29. It was copied at some time in the eighth and ninth centuries by four different scribes, of whom the second was responsible for Books VII–VIII, the third for Book IX and the fourth for Book X. Nothing seems to be known about its early history. The text of Books VII–X runs from f° 181r° to f° 334v°. The remainder of Book X, 29 and the whole of Book X, 30–31 are missing from this manuscript, and Omont and Collon completed their text from the edition published in 1885 by W. Arndt and Bruno Krusch in the *Monumenta Germaniae Historica* series.

319. *Grégoire de Tours. Histoire des Francs. Texte des manuscrits de Corbie et de Bruxelles*, Collection des Textes pour servir à l'Etude et à l'Enseignement de l'Histoire, originally published in Paris, 1886–93, republished by René Poupardin, Paris, 1913.

320. *B. Gregori Turonēsis episcopi Historiarum precipue gallicarū Lib. X*, etc., Paris, 1512.

11. *Earlier translations*

The *Historia* has been translated many times. The first French version was published by Claude Bonet in 1610. Bonet was followed by the Abbé de Marolles in 1668, by François Guizot in 1823, by J. Guadet and N. R. Taranne in 1836–41, by Henri Bordier in 1859–61 and, more recently, by Robert Latouche in 1963–65. The standard German translation was made by W. Giesebrecht in 1851. In 1927 O. M. Dalton published an excellent English translation, with a very full introduction and copious notes. This was reprinted in 1971.

12. *This translation*

This new translation is a faithful rendering into modern English of the Latin text of Henri Omont and Gaston Collon. I have consulted earlier editions, particularly those produced by the *Société de l'Histoire de France* in 1836, by J. P. Migne, and by W. Arndt and Bruno Krusch in the *Monumenta Germaniae Historica* series, mainly for the sake of the variants. It would be idle to pretend that I had not looked at the translations by O. M. Dalton and Robert Latouche.

V. GREGORY DOWN THE CENTURIES

According to the *Vita Sancti Gregorii*,[321] when he died in 594 Gregory was buried beneath one of the flag-stones of his own cathedral in Tours. In the seventh century Saint Ouen, Archbishop of Rouen, 640–83, built a rich tomb for Gregory's bones beside that of Saint Martin. This was overturned by the Northmen in the ninth century, but in the early years of the eleventh century it was restored by Hervé de Buzançais, Treasurer of the cathedral. It was destroyed completely by the Huguenots in 1562.

As we have seen, Marius of Avenches had access to at least Books I–V of the *Historiae* before Gregory's death,[322] and the

321. *Vita Sancti Gregorii*, 26. See note 324.
322. See p. 37.

various authors of the *Chronicle of Fredegar* used it in the seventh century.[323] Two manuscripts which we still possess, a possible third and a fragment date from the seventh century. A tenth-century *Vita Sancti Gregorii* is attributed by some to Odo, Abbot of Cluny, *c.* 879–942.[324] The first printed edition of the *Historiae* is that of Josse Bade of 1512.[325] Ronsard gave a brief account of the Merovingians, from Clodio to Dagobert, in Book IV of *La Franciade*, 1572, but his sources seem to have been secondary ones only, Jean Lemaire de Belges and Jean Bouchet rather than Gregory himself. On the other hand, Claude Fauchet (1530–1601) had the greatest admiration for Gregory, whom he called 'le pere de nostre Histoire', and he quoted from him frequently in *Les Antiquitez Gauloises et Françoises* of 1579, the *Recueil de l'origine de la Langue et Poesie Françoise* of 1581 and *Les Origines des Chevaliers* of 1600. The seventeenth century saw the first French translations of the *Historiae*, by Claude Bonet in 1610 and by the Abbé de Marolles in 1668.

In the eighteenth century Edward Gibbon had obviously read the *Historiae*, but he made little use of it, failing to realize what an important source-book it was for events in Gaul in the period 575–91.[326] In his *Histoire des Français* J. C. L. Simonde de Sismondi took the opposite view, quoting from Gregory on nearly every page of his book which deals with the second half of the sixth century and expressing warm admiration for him.[327] Gregory's name appears frequently in the indexes to the nine books of Thomas Hodgkin's *Italy and her*

323. See p. 38.

324. For an edition, see Martin Bouquet, *Recueil des historiens des Gaules et de la France*, Vol. II, Paris, 1738.

325. See p. 53.

326. See especially ch. XXXVIII, note 117 of the *Decline and Fall of the Roman Empire* (1776–82), where Gibbon is extremely critical of Gregory: '... in a prolix work ... he has omitted almost everything that posterity desires to learn.'

327. See *Histoire des Français* (1821–44), Part I, ch. 2–8. When describing the early Merovingians, Sismondi writes: 'Grégoire de Tours ... a travaillé avec une érudition et une diligence rares pour son siècle ...' (Part I, ch. 4).

Invaders, 1879–99, but Hodgkin was critical of him.[328] Meanwhile a great number of monographs were being written, and the French and the Germans were vying with each other in bringing out editions and translations of the *Historiae*.[329]

Our own century has given great attention to Gregory. The 1886–93 edition of the *Historiae* by H. Omont and G. Collon was reprinted by René Poupardin in 1913. In the same year Volume II of the *Cambridge Medieval History* appeared, with three authoritative chapters on the period by Christian Pfister (IV–V) and Rafael Altamira (VI). In 1927 O. M. Dalton published the first English translation of the *Historiae*, with a long introduction, full notes and a series of indexes. Erich Auerbach discussed Gregory with great sympathy in his two books *Mimesis. The Representation of Reality in Western Literature* and *Literary Language and its Public in Late Latin Antiquity and in the Middle Ages*, first issued in German in 1946 and 1958 respectively. The *Monumenta Germaniae Historica* text of the *Historiae*, with the rest of the series, was reprinted in 1961. Robert Latouche published a new French translation in 1963–5. O. M. Dalton's excellent book was reprinted in 1971.

VI. SHORT BIBLIOGRAPHY

1. *The Latin text of the Historiae*

1885: W. Arndt and Bruno Krusch, *Monumenta Germaniae Historica, Scriptores rerum Merovingicarum*, Vol. I, Hanover. Reprinted 1961.

1886–93: Henri Omont and Gaston Collon, *Grégoire de Tours. Histoire des Francs. Texte des manuscrits de Corbie et de Bruxelles*, Paris, *Collection des textes pour servir à l'étude et à l'enseignement de l'histoire*, Volumes 2 and 13.

328. See for example: 'Gregory of Tours ... supplies some meagre details ...' (Book II, 3); 'Gregory of Tours ... adds some information, of a questionable kind' (Book III, 4).

329. See the Short Bibliography on pp. 56–8 for these books and for all those mentioned in the remainder of this section.

2. *Modern translations of the Historiae*

1927: O. M. Dalton. *The History of the Franks by Gregory of Tours,* translated with an Introduction, Oxford, 2 vols., of which the second, pp. 2–478, is the translation. Reprinted 1971.

1963–5: Robert Latouche, *Grégoire de Tours. Histoire des Francs, traduite du latin,* Paris, *Classiques de l'Histoire de France au Moyen Age,* Volumes 27–28.

3. *Recent critical works*

1872: Gabriel Monod, *Etudes critiques sur les sources de l'histoire Mérovingienne, 1ère partie, Introduction, Grégoire de Tours, Marius d'Avenches,* Paris.

1913: Christian Pfister, 'Gaul under the Merovingian Franks. Narrative of events' and 'Institutions', chs. IV and V in *Cambridge Medieval History,* Vol. II, Cambridge.

1913: Rafael Altamira, 'Spain under the Visigoths', ch. VI in *Cambridge Medieval History,* Vol. II, Cambridge.

1926: Sir Samuel Dill, *Roman Society in Gaul in the Merovingian Age,* London. See especially Book II, ch. 4, 'Gregory of Tours and his circle in Auvergne'.

1927: O. M. Dalton, *The History of the Franks by Gregory of Tours, translated with an Introduction,* Oxford, 2 vols., of which the first, pp. 1–447, is the introduction. Reprinted 1971.

1952: Wilhelm Levison, *Deutschlands Geschichtsquellen im Mittelalter,* Weimar, Vol. I, of which see pp. 99–108.

1953: Erich Auerbach, *Mimesis. The Representation of Reality in Western Literature,* Princeton, translated by Willard R. Trask from *Mimesis. Dargestellte Wirklichkeit in der abendländischen Literatur,* Bern, 1946. See ch. 4, 'Sicharius and Chramnesindus.' Reprinted 1957, 1968, 1971.

1962: J. M. Wallace-Hadrill, *The Long-haired Kings and Other Studies in Frankish History,* London. See especially ch. 3, 'The work of Gregory of Tours in the light of modern research', and ch. 7, iii, 'Gregory's Kings'.

Introduction

1965: Erich Auerbach, *Literary Language and Its Public in Late Latin Antiquity and the Middle Ages*, New York and London, translated by Ralph Manheim from *Literatursprache und Publikum in der lateinischen Spätantike und im Mittelalter*, Bern, 1958. See especially ch. 2, 'Latin Prose in the Early Middle Ages'.

1 June 1972

LEWIS THORPE

ABBREVIATIONS
USED FOR THE BOOKS WRITTEN
BY GREGORY OF TOURS

HF:	*Historiae Francorum*
GM:	*Liber in Gloria Martyrum Beatorum*
VSJ:	*Liber de passione et virtutibus Sancti Juliani martyris*
VSM:	*De virtutibus beati Martini episcopi*
VP:	*Liber vitae Patruum*
GC:	*Liber in Gloria Confessorum*
MBA:	*Liber de miraculis beati Andreae apostoli*
PMSD:	*Passio sanctorum Martyrum Septem Dormientium apud Ephesum*
CS:	*De Cursu Stellarum ratio*
PC:	*In Psalterii tractatum commentarius*

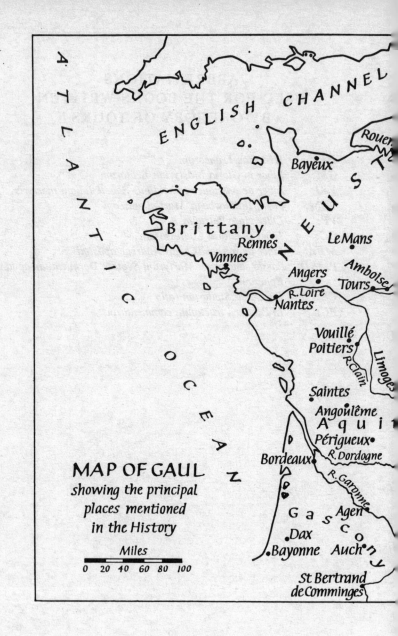

ATLANTIC

ENGLISH CHANNEL

Rouen

Bayeux

B r i t t a n y

Rennes

Vannes

Le Mans

N
E
U
S
T

Angers

Amboise

Tours

R. Loire

Nantes

O

C

Vouillé

Poitiers

R. Clain

Limoges

E

Saintes

Angoûlême

A

Périgueux

A q u i t

A

R. Dordogne

Bordeaux

N

R. Garonne

MAP OF GAUL

*showing the principal
places mentioned
in the History*

G a s

c

o

Agen

Auch

n

Dax

Bayonne

y

Miles

0 20 40 60 80 100

St Bertrand
de Comminges

THE PREFACE OF GREGORY, BISHOP OF THE CHURCH IN TOURS

A great many things keep happening, some of them good, some of them bad. The inhabitants of different countries keep quarrelling fiercely with each other and kings go on losing their temper in the most furious way. Our churches are attacked by the heretics and then protected by the Catholics; the faith of Christ burns bright in many men, but it remains lukewarm in others; no sooner are the church-buildings endowed by the faithful than they are stripped bare again by those who have no faith. However, no writer has come to the fore who has been sufficiently skilled in setting things down in an orderly fashion to be able to describe these events in prose or in verse. In fact in the towns of Gaul the writing of literature has declined to the point where it has virtually disappeared altogether. Many people have complained about this, not once but time and time again. 'What a poor period this is!' they have been heard to say. 'If among all our people there is not one man to be found who can write a book about what is happening today, the pursuit of letters really is dead in us!'

I have often thought about these complaints and others like them. I have written this work to keep alive the memory of those dead and gone, and to bring them to the notice of future generations. My style is not very polished, and I have had to devote much of my space to the quarrels between the wicked and the righteous. All the same I have been greatly encouraged by certain kind remarks which, to my no small surprise, I have often heard made by our folk, to the effect that few people understand a rhetorical speechifier, whereas many can follow a blunt speaker.

So that the sequence of time may be properly understood, I have decided to begin my first book with the foundation of the world. I have set out the chapter-headings in proper order.

BOOK I

IN THE NAME OF CHRIST HERE BEGINS THE FIRST BOOK
OF THE ECCLESIASTICAL HISTORY OF GEORGIUS
FLORENTIUS, KNOWN AS GREGORY, BISHOP OF TOURS

CHAPTER-HEADINGS

1. Adam and Eve.
2. Cain and Abel.
3. Enoch the Righteous.
4. The Flood.
5. Chus, who made the graven image.
6. Babel.
7. Abraham and Ninus.
8. Isaac, Esau, Job and Jacob.
9. Joseph in Egypt.
10. The Crossing of the Red Sea.
11. The people in the Desert and Joshua.
12. The Captivity of the Israelites, and their generations down to David.
13. Solomon and the building of the Temple.
14. The Division of the Kingdom of Israel.
15. The Captivity in Babylon.
16. The Birth of Christ.
17. The different kingdoms of the Gentiles.
18. The time when Lyons was founded.
19. The gifts of the Three Wise Men and the Massacre of the Innocents.
20. The miracles and the Passion of Christ.
21. How Joseph buried Him.
22. James the Apostle.
23. The day of the Resurrection of our Lord.

24. The Ascension of our Lord, and the death of Pilate and Herod.
25. The Passion of the Apostles; Nero.
26. James, and the Evangelists Mark and John.
27. The persecution under Trajan.
28. Hadrian and the inventions of the heretics; the Passion of Saints Polycarp and Justin.
29. Saint Photinus, Saint Irenaeus and the other martyrs of Lyons.
30. The Seven sent to preach among the Gauls.
31. The church at Bourges.
32. Chroc and the shrine in Clermont-Ferrand.
33. The martyrs who died in Clermont-Ferrand.
34. Saint Privatus, martyr.
35. [Quirinus], Bishop and martyr.
36. The birth of Saint Martin, and the Finding of the Cross.
37. James of Nisibis, the Bishop.
38. The passing of the monk Anthony.
39. The coming of Saint Martin.
40. The matron Melania.
41. The death of the Emperor Valens.
42. The Empire of Theodosius.
43. The death of the tyrant Maximus.
44. Urbicus, Bishop of Clermont-Ferrand.
45. Saint Illidius, the Bishop.
46. The Bishops Nepotianus and Arthemius.
47. The chaste lovers.
48. The passing of Saint Martin.

HERE END THE CHAPTER-HEADINGS

IN THE NAME OF CHRIST HERE BEGINS
BOOK I OF THE HISTORY

Proposing as I do to describe the wars waged by kings against hostile peoples, by martyrs against the heathen and by the Churches against the heretics, I wish first of all to explain my own faith, so that whoever reads me may not doubt that I am a Catholic. For the sake of those who are losing hope as they see the end of the world coming nearer and nearer, I also think it desirable that, from material assembled from the chronicles and histories of earlier writers, I should explain clearly how many years have passed since the world began. Before I do that, I apologize to my readers lest by syllable or even letter I offend against grammatical usage, a matter in which I am far from being expert. My one desire is that, without the slightest deviation and with no hesitation whatsoever in my heart, I may hold fast to what is ordained in church that we should believe, for I know that one given to sin may obtain pardon with God through the purity of his faith.

I believe therefore in God the Father Almighty and in Jesus Christ His only Son, our Lord, born of the Father and not made, who was always with the Father, not in the passage of time, but before all time. God could not have been called the Father unless He had the Son, nor would He be the Son had He not had the Father. I renounce with execration those who say: 'There was a time when He was not', and I maintain that they are cut off from the Church. I believe this Christ to be the Word of the Father, by whom all things were made. I believe that this Word was made flesh, and that by His Passion the world was redeemed; and I believe that He suffered Passion in His manhood and not in His Godhead. I believe that He rose again on the third day, that He delivered man which was lost, that He ascended into Heaven and now sitteth on the right hand of the Father, and that He shall come again to deliver the quick and the dead. I believe in the Holy Ghost, who proceeded from the Father and the Son, that He was not after or before them in time, but was equal, the God co-eternal always with the Father and the Son, in nature consubstantial, in omnipotence equal, in essence co-sempiternal with them. He was never without the Father or the Son, nor was He less than the Father or the Son. I believe that this Holy Trinity exists in distinction of the Persons, and that the Person of the Father is one, the Person of the Son one, and the Person of the Holy Ghost one. In this Trinity I confess one Godhead, one power and one essence. I believe in the Blessed Mary, who was virgin before the birth, and was virgin after the birth. I believe in the immortality of the soul, which yet has no part in the Godhead. All things which were established by the three hundred and eighteen Bishops of Nicaea I do faithfully believe.[1] Of the end of the world I truly believe those things which I have learnt from those who have gone before, but that before this the Antichrist shall come. First the Antichrist brings in circumcision, proclaiming himself to be Christ. Then in the Temple of Jerusalem he places his image to be worshipped, for we read that the Lord said: 'Ye shall see the abomination of desolation stand in the holy place';[2] but concerning that day the Lord makes clear to all men when He says: 'But of that day and that hour knoweth no man, no, not the angels which are in heaven, neither the Son, but the Father.'[3] Here we answer the heretics, who attack us and say that the Son

1. The first Council of Nicaea was convened by the Emperor Constantine in A.D. 325. It was attended by some 220 bishops. The Council accepted almost unanimously the Nicene Creed, one essential point of which is that the Son is 'of one substance' with the Father. It thus condemned out of hand the Arian heresy of the subordination of the Son to the Father. Nicaea, in Bithynia, is now Isnik in Turkey.

2. Matthew 24, 15. All English quotations from the Bible given in this translation are taken from the Authorized Version of 1611. Gregory himself was using the Latin translation completed by Saint Jerome *c*. 404 and known as the Vulgate. He often quotes passages from memory, whereas I have had to look most of them up.

3. Mark 13, 32.

is less than the Father, because He does not know this day. They should understand that by this Son is meant the Christian people, of whom God says: 'I will be to them for a Father, and they shall be to Me for Sons.'[4] If God had spoken thus of His only-begotten Son, He would not have placed the angels before Him. He said: 'Not the angels which are in heaven, neither the Son,' showing that He said these things not of His only-begotten Son but of His adopted people. Christ Himself is our end, for in the fullness of His Grace He will give us eternal life, if we have been converted to Him.

The chronicles of Eusebius, Bishop of Caesarea, and of the priest Jerome, explain clearly how the age of this world is computed, and set out in systematic form the entire sequence of the years. Orosius, too, who looked very diligently into these matters, made a list of all the years from the beginning of the world until his own day. Victorius did the same thing, when he was making inquiries about the dating of the Easter festival. If our Lord is willing to give me His help, I will follow the example of these writers whom I have mentioned and in my turn reckon the entire series of years from the very first creation of man down to our own time. I will do this more easily if I begin with Adam himself.

1. In the beginning God made the heaven and the earth in His own Christ, that is in His own Son, who is the origin of all things. When the basic elements of the whole earth had been created, He took a lump of malleable clay and shaped man in the form of His own image and breathed into his face the breath of life, so that he was turned into a living soul. While he was asleep a rib was taken from him and the woman Eve was created. There is no doubt at all that, before he committed sin, this first man Adam was similar to our Lord and Saviour. Christ in His Passion fainted and, when He produced water and blood from His side, He procured for Himself a Church which was pure and immaculate, redeemed by His blood and cleansed

4. Cp. II Samuel 7, 14 and II Corinthians 6, 18.

by the water, having no blemish, and no wrinkle,[5] that is to say
washed clear by the water and stretched on the Cross to remove
any wrinkle. These first human beings lived happily in the pleasant place of Paradise. Then they were enticed by the Serpent's
guile and they transgressed the divine commandments, and so
were expelled from their angelic abode and driven out into the
travails of the world.

2. Once Adam's companion had known intercourse, the
woman conceived and bore two sons. When God graciously
accepted the sacrifice offered by one of these, the other was
inflamed with jealousy and he swelled up with anger. He was
the first man to shed his brother's blood and to murder a
member of his own family, for he seized hold of his brother and
overcame him and slew him.

3. From that moment onwards the entire human race never
ceased to commit one execrable crime after another, except
Enoch the Just, who walked with God. Because of his
righteousness he was taken up by God Himself and delivered
from the midst of a sinful people. 'And Enoch walked with
God: and he was not seen; for God took him.'[6]

4. The Lord was therefore filled with anger by the iniquities of
a people which did not walk in His ways. He sent the Flood, and
the deluge which came down removed every living soul from
the surface of the earth. In the Ark the Lord saved only Noah,
His most faithful servant who was made in His image, with his
own wife, his three sons and their wives, for the sake of pre-
serving the human race for the future. On this point the heretics attack us, asking why the Holy Scripture says that God
lost His temper. They should realize that God did not show
anger as a man would do: He is moved to anger so that He may
fill us with awe, He drives us forth so that He may call us back,
He is enraged so that He may reform us. I have no doubt at all
that the shape of the Ark represented the concept of the mother

5. Cp. Ephesians 5, 27.   6. Genesis 5, 24.

Church, which moves forward through the waves and between the rocks of life here below, protecting us in her maternal bosom from the evils which threaten us, and defending us in her loving embrace and guardianship.

From Adam to Noah there are ten generations: Adam, Seth, Enosh, Kenan, Mahalaleel, Jered, Enoch, Methuselah, (Lamech) and Noah.[7] Two thousand two hundred and forty-two years are included in these ten generations. Adam was buried in the land of the Anakim, which was formerly called Hebron, as is clearly explained in the Book of Joshua.[8]

5. After the Flood Noah had three sons, Shem, Ham and Japheth. Whole races of men were born from Japheth, Ham and Shem. As ancient history tells us, the human race was spread out beneath the whole heaven by these people. Chus was the first child of Ham: by the inspiration of the Devil he was the first inventor of idolatry and of the whole art of magic. He was encouraged by the Devil to be the first to set up an image to be worshipped; and by his false power he revealed to men the stars and fire falling from the sky. He went to live among the Persians, who called him Zoroaster, that is the Living Star.[9] They acquired from him the habit of worshipping fire, and when he was himself consumed by fire from heaven they adored him as a god.

6. As men multiplied and began to spread across the whole earth, they migrated from the East and discovered the grassy plain of Senachar. There they built a city and made great efforts to construct a tower which should reach to the skies. God made them confused in this futile plan and in each man's language, and He spread mankind far and wide across the entire earth. The name of this city was Babel, that is confusion, because God confused their languages on that spot. This is Babylon, built by

7. Cp. I Chronicles 1, 1–3.
8. Joshua 14, 15.
9. Gregory gives a fanciful but ingenious etymology of the Greek name Zoroaster, which really comes from the Persian Zarathustra.

the giant Hebron, who was the son of Chus.[10] As the history of Orosius tells us, it was laid out in a square on a remarkably flat plain. Its wall was built of burned brick with bitumen for mortar. It was fifty cubits thick and two hundred cubits high. The distance round the wall was four hundred stadia and each stadium had about six hundred and twenty-five feet. There were twenty-five gateways built on each side, which makes a hundred in all. The doors of these gateways were made of cast bronze and they were of remarkable size. The same historian tells us many other things about this city, but he finishes with these words: 'Although it was so strongly built, nevertheless it was captured and thrown to the ground.'

7.   The first son of Noah was called Shem, and from him, in the tenth generation, was born Abraham. The line of descent ran as follows: Noah, Shem, Arphaxad, Shelah, Eber, Peleg, Reu, Serug and Terah, who was the father of Abraham.[11] Nine hundred and forty-two years are included in these ten generations. At that time Ninus was King, he who built the city Ninus, which they call Nineveh, the entire administrative area of which, according to the prophet Jonah, took some three days to cross.[12] Abraham was born in the forty-third year of the reign of Ninus. This is the Abraham who was the beginning of our faith. It was he who received the promises: for Christ our Lord revealed to him that He would be born and that He would suffer for us in place of a sacrifice. In the Gospels Christ says: 'Abraham rejoiced to see my day; and he saw it, and was glad.'[13] Sulpicius Severus tells us in his chronicle that this sacrifice of Abraham's was offered on Mount Calvary, where our Lord was crucified, and to this day this is generally accepted in the city of Jerusalem. On this hillside stood the Holy Cross, to which our Redeemer was nailed and from which flowed His blessed blood. This man Abraham accepted the sign of circumcision, indicating that what he bore in his body we should carry in our heart. 'Circumcise yourselves to the Lord,' says the

10. Hebron in error for Nimrod. Cp. Genesis 10, 8–10.
11. Cp. I Chronicles 1, 17–27.   12. Jonah 3, 3.   13. John 8, 56.

prophet, 'and take away the foreskins of your heart.'[14] Later he
says: 'Go not after other gods';[15] and then again: 'No stranger,
uncircumcised in heart, shall enter into my sanctuary.'[16] After
he had added a syllable to his name, God called this Abraham
the father of many peoples.[17]

8. When he was a hundred years old Abraham became the
father of Isaac. In his sixtieth year twin sons were born to Isaac
himself, with Rebecca as the mother. The first-born was Esau,
also known as Edom, that is the 'earthly one', who sold his
birthright because of greediness. He is the ancestor of the Idumaeans and from his line Jobab was born in the fourth generation: that is, Esau, Reuel, Zerah and Jobab, also called Job.[18]
Job lived for two hundred and forty-eight years. In his eighty-
ninth year he recovered from a disease, and after this he lived
another hundred and sixty years with all his wealth restored to
him in double measure, and he was blessed with as many sons as
he had lost.[19]

9. Jacob came next after Esau, Jacob the beloved of God, as
He spoke by the prophet: 'Yet I loved Jacob. And I hated
Esau.'[20] After he had struggled with the angel, Jacob was called
Israel, and the Israelites took their name from him.[21] He was
the father of twelve patriarchs. Their names are: Reuben,
Simeon, Levi, Judah, Issachar, Zebulun, Dan, [Joseph, Ben-
jamin, Naphtali], Gad and Asher.[22] After this, in the ninety-
second year of his life, he became the father of Joseph, with
Rachel as the mother.[23] Jacob loved Joseph more than all his
children.[24] By Rachel he also had Benjamin, the last of them

14. Jeremiah 4, 4.   15. Jeremiah 35, 15.   16. Ezekiel 44, 9.
    17. Cp. I Chronicles 1, 27.
    18. Cp. I Chronicles 1, 35–44.
    19. Cp. Job 42, 16. As we have it, the text of Gregory says 'another
hundred and seventy years'.
    20. Malachi 1, 2–3.   21. Cp. Genesis 32, 24–8.
    22. Cp. I Chronicles 2, 1–2. As we have it, the text of Gregory omits three
of the twelve.
    23. Cp. Genesis 30, 22–4.   24. Cp. Genesis 37, 3.

all.[25] When Joseph was sixteen he had visions, in this being a
forerunner of the Redeemer. He related them to his brothers:
once, when he was binding sheaves of corn, his brothers'
sheaves worshipped him; on another occasion it was as if the
sun and the moon, with eleven stars, fell prostrate before him.
This caused his brothers to hate him very much.[26] As a result
they were filled with burning jealousy, and they sold him for
thirty pieces of silver to some Ishmaelites who were on their
way to Egypt. Later there came a famine and the brothers went
to Egypt in their turn. They were recognized by Joseph, but
they did not know who he was. Only when they had suffered
many exhausting experiences and had been forced to send for
Benjamin, who had been born to Joseph's own mother Rachel,
and when Benjamin had arrived, did Joseph reveal himself to
them. After this all the Israelites travelled to Egypt, where,
thanks to Joseph, they were well treated by Pharaoh. After he
had blessed his sons Jacob died in Egypt. He was buried by
Joseph in Canaan, in the tomb of his father Isaac. Joseph and
Pharaoh died in their turn, and the entire race of Israelites was
thrown into slavery.[27] After the plagues of Egypt they were
freed by Moses, and Pharaoh was drowned in the Red Sea.[28]

10. Since so much has been written by so many authors about
this passage of the Red Sea, I have thought it a good idea to
include in this book some description of the place itself and of
the crossing.[29] As you know very well, the Nile flows through
Egypt and irrigates the land with its flood-water, so that the
Egyptians are called the dwellers on the Nile. Many travellers
who have visited those places tell how the banks of the Nile are
now covered with holy monasteries. Beside the river stands the
city of Babylon,[30] not the Babylon which I have described
already, but the one where Joseph built granaries of wonderful
workmanship made of square stones and cement.[31] They are

25. Cp. Genesis 35, 18.   26. Cp. Genesis 37, 5–8.
27. Cp. Genesis 37–50 *passim*.   28. Cp. Genesis 14.
29. For this chapter, see Exodus 14 *passim*.
30. Babylon, a fortress in Lower Egypt, opposite to the Pyramids.
31. What Gregory takes for granaries are the Pyramids.

constructed in such a way that they are very broad at the base but narrow at the top, so that corn could be poured into them through a small aperture. These granaries are still to be seen to this day. From this city, then, the King set out to pursue the Hebrews with squadrons of chariots and a great force of foot-soldiery. The river about which I have told you flows in from the east and makes its way round towards the western shore of the Red Sea. A lake or arm of water runs from the west away from the Red Sea and then flows eastwards, being about fifty miles long and eighteen miles wide. At the head of this water stands the city Clysma, built there, not because of the fertility of the site, for nothing could be more sterile, but for its harbour.[32] Ships which come from the Indies lie quietly at anchor here because of the fine position of the harbour, and the goods collected here are then distributed all over Egypt. The Hebrews made their way across the desert to this lake, and then came to the sea. As soon as they found fresh water, they pitched their camp. They bivouacked in this narrow space between the desert and the sea itself, as it is written: 'And Pharaoh, hearing that the sea and the desert had shut them in, and that there was no way by which they might go farther, commanded that they should be pursued.'[33] As the Egyptians came nearer, the people appealed to Moses for help. God ordered Moses to stretch out his rod over the sea and it parted and they travelled across on dry land. As the Scripture says, they were protected on both sides by a wall of water.[34] With Moses as their leader they cross-ed over completely unharmed to the shore which is near Mount Sinai, but the Egyptians were drowned. As I have said, many accounts have been given of this crossing. Since I myself have learnt the true story from informed sources and, indeed, from men who have visited the place in question, I have taken care to include it in my book. They say that the ruts which the chariot-wheels made remain to this day and that, as far as the eye can reach, they can be seen at the bottom of the sea. When the motion of the sea begins to cover them up, they are mir-

32. Clysma is now Tell Kolzum, at the head of the Gulf of Suez.
33. Cp. Exodus 14, 3–4.   34. Cp. Exodus 14, 22.

aculously renewed and made just as they were before, as soon as the water becomes calm again. Some say that the Israelites made only a short circuit in the water and then turned back to the same shore from which they had set out. Some maintain that they all entered the water at the same spot; but others think that a separate way was opened for each tribe. These last are misinterpreting the statement in the Psalms: 'which divided the Red Sea into parts'.[35] These parts must be constructed in a metaphorical way, and not according to the letter of the text. In this earthly existence of ours, too, which is figuratively called a sea, there are many parts; but we cannot all pass through it into life in the same way, or along one road. Some pass through in the very first hour: these are they who are reborn by baptism, and are thus able to remain unsullied by any defilement of the flesh until they reach the end of their life here below.[36] Those who are converted in later life pass through at the third hour. Those who control the lust of the flesh pass through at the sixth hour. As the Evangelist says, at one or other of these hours, according to the strength of their faith, they are hired to work in the Lord's vineyard. These are the parts in which we make our way through this sea. Support to the argument that, when they reached the sea, they turned back along the shore of that arm of water, is given by the fact that God says to Moses that 'they turn and encamp before Pi-hahiroth, between Migdol and the sea, over against Baal-zephon'.[37] There is no doubt at all that this crossing of the sea and this pillar of cloud are symbols of our baptism. The blessed Apostle Paul says: 'Moreover, brethren, I would not that ye should be ignorant, how that all our fathers were under the cloud, and were all baptized unto Moses in the cloud and in the sea.'[38] The column of fire is a symbol of the Holy Spirit.

Four hundred and sixty-two years are counted from the birth of Abraham to the departure of the Children of Israel from Egypt and the passage of the Red Sea, which happened in the eightieth year of the life of Moses.

35. Psalms 136, 13.   36. Cp. II Corinthians 7, 1.
37. Exodus 14, 2.   38. I Corinthians 10, 1–2.

11.   For forty years after this the Israelites dwelt in the desert
and familiarized themselves with their laws, and lived on the
food of the angels. Once they had assimilated the Law, they
crossed the Jordan with Joshua and were given permission to
enter the Promised Land.

12.   After the death of Joshua, they ceased to observe God's
commandments and were often forced to submit to the domination of foreign peoples. With great lamentation they repented
of their sins, and the Lord allowed them to be set free by main
force by their strong men. It was then, through Samuel, that
they asked the Lord if they might have a King, as other peoples
have, and they received first Saul and then David.

From Abraham to David there are fourteen generations: Abraham, Isaac, Jacob, Judah, Pharez, Hezron, Ram, Amminadab, Nahshon, Salma, Boaz, Obed, Jesse and David.[39]
David was the father of Solomon, who was borne by Bathsheba.[40] Through the combined efforts of Nathan the prophet,
his own brother and his mother Bathsheba, Solomon was raised
to the throne.[41]

13.   When David was dead and his son Solomon had begun to
reign, the Lord appeared to him and promised to give him
whatever he asked. He scorned earthly riches and asked for
wisdom instead. The Lord granted this, and Solomon heard
Him say: 'Because thou hast asked wisdom and hast not asked
the kingdoms of the world, neither hast thou asked for thyself,
take then this thing; so that there was none wise like thee before
thee, neither after thee shall any arise like unto thee.'[42] The
judgement which Solomon delivered on two women who had
begun a law-suit for a single child was proof of this.[43] It was
Solomon who, in the name of the Lord, built the Temple with
wonderful workmanship, using much gold and silver, and
bronze and iron, so that there were some who said that

39. Cp. I Chronicles 2, 3–15.
40. Cp. I Chronicles 3, 5.   41. Cp. I Kings, 1 *passim*.
42. Cp. I Kings 3, 11–12.   43. Cp. I Kings 3, 16–28.

no comparable building had ever been constructed in the world.[44]

From the departure of the Children of Israel from Egypt until the building of the Temple, which happened in the seventh year of the reign of Solomon, there elapsed two hundred and eighty years, as we learn in the Book of Kings.[45]

14.   After the death of Solomon, the kingdom was divided up into sections, as the result of the harsh rule of Rehoboam. Two tribes remained under Rehoboam and were called Judah. The other ten tribes accepted Jeroboam as King, and what they held was called Israel. These later turned to idolatry. The predictions and the death of their prophets, the destruction of their homeland, the ruin of their kings, nothing served to soften their hearts.[46]

15.   Finally the Lord lost patience with them and stirred up Nebuchadnezzar, who led them captive to Babylon, with all the adornments of the Temple.[47] Daniel, the great prophet, who remained unharmed among the famished lions, and the three servants moistened by dew in the midst of the flames went into captivity with them.[48] During this captivity Ezekiel prophesied and the prophet Ezra was born.

From David to the destruction of the Temple and the Babylonian captivity there are fourteen generations: David, Solomon, Rehoboam, Abijah, Asa, Jehoshaphat, Jehoram, Uzziah, Jotham, Ahaz, Hezekiah, Manasseh, Amon and Josiah.[49] Three hundred and ninety years are included in these

44. Cp. I Kings 6 *passim*.

45. Cp. I Kings 6, 1, which places the building of the Temple in the fourth year of Solomon's reign, 480 years after the passing of the Red Sea.

46. Cp. I Kings 12 *passim*.

47. Cp. II Chronicles 36, 7–10.

48. Cp. Daniel 6, 16–23 and Daniel 3, 12–30. The three servants, *pueri*, are Shadrach, Meschach and Abed-nego.

49. The accounts of the last twelve of these Kings are contained in I Kings 12 to II Kings 25 and in II Chronicles 10 to II Chronicles 35.

fourteen generations.[50] They were freed from this captivity by Zerubbabel, who later restored the Temple and the city.[51] In my opinion this captivity is a symbol of the enslavement into which the soul of a sinner is led, and indeed such a soul will be carried off into fearful exile unless some Zerubbabel, that is Christ Himself, can rescue it. The Lord Himself says in the Gospel: 'If the Son therefore shall make you free, ye shall be free indeed.'[52] May He then build for Himself a temple within us, in which He may deign to dwell, where faith may shine as bright as gold, where the word of the preacher may gleam like silver and where all the ornaments of that other visible temple may be seen clearly in the integrity of our hearts. May He grant a successful outcome to our good intentions, for 'Except the Lord build the house, they labour in vain that build it.'[53] This captivity is said to have lasted seventy-six years.

16. As soon as the Israelites were brought back home by Zerubbabel, as I have already told you, they began to make complaints against God, to rush off to worship idols and to copy the abominations practised by the Gentiles. As long as they continued to scorn God's prophets, they were left in the power of the Gentiles, and enslaved and put to death. In the end our Lord Himself, as was promised in the sayings of the patriarchs and prophets, entered the womb of the Virgin Mary through the Holy Ghost and allowed Himself to be born again for the redemption of the Israelites and of all other races.

From the beginning of the Captivity until the birth of Christ there are fourteen generations: Jechonias, Salathiel, Zerubbabel, Abiud, Eliakim, Azor, Sadoc, Achim, Eliud, Eleazar, Matthan, Jacob and Joseph, Mary's husband, from whom our Lord Jesus was born.[54] Joseph is counted as the fourteenth of these.[55]

50. Gregory omits the last four Kings, Jehoahaz, Jehoiakim, Jehoiachin and Zedekiah. The reign of David and the first seven years of Solomon are included twice, as they were counted already in ch. 13.

51. Cp. Ezra 3.   52. John 8, 36.

53. Psalms 127, 1.   54. Cp. Matthew 1,12–16.

55. Joseph is thirteenth. In his 'fourteen generations' Gregory presumably includes Christ.

17. So that I may not seem to have information only about the Hebrew race, I now tell you about other kingdoms at the time of the Israelites, who they were and what sort of people. At the time of Abraham Ninus reigned over the Assyrians,[56] and Europs over the town of Sicyon.[57] Over the Egyptians ruled the sixteenth race of kings, or dynasty, as they would say in their language.[58] At the time of Moses Trophas reigned over the Argives and Cecrops was the first King in Attica.[59] Cenchris, who was drowned in the Red Sea, was the twelfth King of the Egyptians.

Agatadis was the sixteenth King of the Assyrians, and Maratis governed the Sicyonians. At the time when Solomon reigned over Israel, Silvius was the fifth King of Latium, Festus ruled the Lacedaemonians, Oxion was the second King of the Corinthians and Thephei was the hundred and twentieth King of the Egyptians. Eutropes governed the Assyrians and Agasastus was the second King of the Athenians. At the time when Amon reigned over Judaea[60] and when the captivity in Babylon began, Argaeus was King of the Macedonians, Gyges of the Lydians and Vafres of the Egyptians. Nebuchadnezzar, who led the Israelites away as captives, reigned in Babylon[61] and Servus was the sixth King of the Romans.[62]

18. After these Julius Caesar was the first Emperor to gain jurisdiction over the whole Empire.[63] The Second was Oc-

---

56. Modern archaeological evidence seems to imply that Abraham was a real person and that he lived at some time in the twentieth–nineteenth centuries B.C. Ninus, the legendary founder of Nineveh, is given the approximate date of 800 B.C.

57. Sicyon was a few miles west of Corinth.

58. The word dynasty is Greek, not Egyptian. The sixteenth dynasty was that of the Hyksos or 'Shepherd Kings'.

59. Cecrops, the legendary first King of Attica, is supposed to have founded Athens.

60. Amon, son of Manasseh. Cp. II Kings 21, 19–26.

61. Nebuchadnezzar was King of Babylon from 605–562 B.C.

62. Servius Tullius, sixth King of Rome, reigned traditionally from 578–535 B.C.

63. Julius Caesar was not Emperor.

tavian, the nephew of Julius Caesar, who is known as Augustus and after whom the month of August is named. In the nineteenth year of his reign, Lyons, a city in Gaul, was founded, as we are clearly informed.[64] Later on this city was made famous for the blood shed there by martyrs, and it bears a most noble name.[65]

19. In the forty-fourth year of the reign of Augustus, our Lord Jesus Christ, as I have already said, was born in the flesh of the Virgin Mary, in Bethlehem, a city of David. The Wise Men saw His great star from the East and came with gifts. When they had made their offerings, they worshipped the Child in great humility. Herod feared for his kingdom and massacred all the small children in an attempt to hunt down Christ our God. Later on he himself was punished by the justice of God.[66]

20. Jesus Christ, our Lord and Master, preached repentance, gave us the grace of baptism, promised the heavenly kingdom to all nations and gave portents and performed miracles among the people. He changed water into wine, put an end to fevers, gave sight to the blind, restored life to those who were buried, freed those possessed of unclean spirits and cured lepers who were foul with skin disease. While He was performing these miracles and many others like them, and making it most clear to the people that He was indeed God in person, the Jews became incensed and were roused to hatred against Him: their minds, which had fed on the blood of the prophets, now strove unjustly to destroy the Just. Therefore, in order that the predictions of

64. Lyons was founded in 43 B.C. by Lucius Munatius Plancus, one of the officers of Julius Caesar, as Copia Lugdunum, on a hill above the confluence of the Rivers Rhône and Saône. In 43 B.C. Augustus, then Octavianus, was only twenty.

65. In A.D. 177 the Christian community of Lyons was persecuted by the Emperor Marcus Aurelius and in 197 the city was burnt and largely destroyed by the Emperor Septimus Severus. Gregory returns to the subject in *History of the Franks* (*HF*), I, 29.

66. For this chapter, cp. Matthew 2, 1–16.

the ancient prophets might be fulfilled, He was betrayed by His disciple. He was condemned unjustly by the high priests, mocked by the Jews, crucified along with thieves, and, when His spirit had left His body, watched over by soldiers. Once all these things had been accomplished, darkness fell upon the whole earth, and with great lamentation many were converted and confessed that Jesus was the Son of God.

21.   Joseph, who had embalmed Christ's body with spices and hidden it in his own tomb, was arrested and shut in a prison-cell.[67] He was guarded by the high priests themselves, for, as is related in the accounts sent by Pilate to the Emperor Tiberius, the hatred which they bore him was fiercer than that which they felt for our Lord himself.[68] Christ was guarded by soldiers, but Joseph was watched over by the high priests themselves. Our Lord rose again, and when He could not be found in the tomb, the guards were terrified by the vision of the angel. During the night the walls of the cell where Joseph was incarcerated were raised up in the air and he was freed from imprisonment, for an angel came to release him. Then the walls were put back in their proper place. When the high priests upbraided the guards and ordered them to hand over the sacred body immediately, the soldiers replied: 'You give back Joseph and we will give back Christ; but we know very well that you can no more restore God's benefactor than we can return God's Son.' The priests were confounded by this, but after what they had said the soldiers were allowed to go free.

22.   When he had seen our Lord dead on the Cross, the Apostle James is said to have sworn an oath that he would never eat bread again unless he saw Him risen once more. When our Lord finally came again on the third day, having vanquished and triumphed over Hell, He showed Himself to James and said: 'Arise, James, and eat, for I am now risen from the dead.' This

67. For Joseph of Arimathaea, cp. Matthew 27, 57–60.
68. The accounts sent by Pilate are an apocryphal book, the *Gesta Pilati* or *Acts of Pilate*.

was James the Just, whom they call the brother of our Lord, for he was the son of Joseph, borne to him by another wife.[69]

23.　We maintain that the Sunday of the Resurrection was the first day of the week, and not the seventh, as many believe. This is the day of the Resurrection of our Lord Jesus Christ, which we rightly call Sunday because of His holy rising again. In the beginning this was the first day to see the light, and it deserved to be the first to see our Lord rise from the tomb.

Between the captivity of Jerusalem and the destruction of the Temple and the Passion of our Lord Jesus Christ, which occurred in the seventeenth year of Tiberius, there elapsed six hundred and sixty-eight years.

24.　When our Lord had risen again, He spent forty days discussing the Kingdom of God with His disciples. Then as they watched He was taken up on a cloud and carried to heaven, where He sits in glory on the right hand of the Father. Pilate sent a report of what had happened to Tiberius Caesar, and told him of the miracles of Christ and of His Passion and Resurrection.[70] We still possess this written report today. Tiberius presented it to his senators; but the members of the Senate rejected it angrily because it had not been sent to them in the first place. Thus were sown the first seeds of hatred against the Christians. Pilate did not go unpunished for his wicked crime, that is for having slain our Lord Jesus Christ, for he killed Him with his own hands. Many consider that he was a Manichaean, in accordance with what may be read in the Gospel: 'There were present at that season some that told him of the Galilaeans, whose blood Pilate had mingled with their sacrifices.'[71] King Herod, who persecuted the Lord's Apostles,

69. The substance of this chapter is taken from Saint Jerome, *De viribus illustribus*, ch. 2.

70. This again is from the *Acts of Pilate*.

71. Luke 12, 1. Pontius Pilate is supposed to have committed suicide during the reign of the Emperor Caligula, A.D. 37–41. Manes, the Persian founder of the Manichaean sect, lived much later, in the third century after Christ.

was in the same way punished by God for his many crimes: swollen up and swarming with vermin, he took a knife to cure his disease and so killed himself with his own hand.[72]

25.   Under Claudius, who was the fourth Emperor after Augustus, the blessed Apostle Peter came to Rome to preach and proved clearly, by His manifold virtues, that Christ was indeed the Son of God. From those days onwards there began to be Christians in the city of Rome. As the name of Christ spread more and more among the people, the old Serpent rose up in hatred of what was happening and the heart of the Emperor Nero was filled with loathing for the Christians. This vain and arrogant debauchee, who submitted himself to the blandishments of other men and then lusted after them in his turn, this filthy seducer of his own mother, his sisters and any other women who were closely related to him, was the first to persecute the true believers and to satisfy his boundless hatred for the cult of Christ. To help him in this he had Simon Magus, a man of immense malice and a master of every form of necromancy, who had been rejected by Peter and Paul, the Apostles of our Lord.[73] The Emperor was furious with them for preaching Christ the Son of God and for the scorn with which they refused to worship idols. He ordered Peter to be killed on the cross and Paul by the sword. Nero died by his own hand at the fourth mile-stone outside the city, when trying to escape from a revolt which had been stirred up against him.

26.   At this time James, the brother of our Lord, and Mark the Evangelist received in Christ's name the glorious crown of martyrdom; but the first man to walk the martyr's path was Stephen the Levite.[74] After the death of the Apostle James, a great disaster happened to the Jews: for with the coming to power of Vespasian the Temple was burned down and six hundred thousand of them died in battle, from famine and the sword.[75]

72. Cp. Acts 12, 23.   73. For Simon Magus, cp. Acts 8, 9–24.
74. Cp. Acts 6, 1–15 and 7, 1–60.
75. Vespasian, Roman Emperor A.D. 69–79: in 67 he had been appointed as special commander to suppress the Jewish rebellion.

Domitian was the second Emperor after Nero to vent his rage
upon the Christians, for he sent the Apostle John into exile on
the island of Patmos and was responsible for many cruelties
practised on the people.[76] After Domitian's death the blessed
John, Apostle and Evangelist, returned from exile. When he
was very old and had come to the end of his life, which he had
spent in perfect communion with God, he climbed into the
tomb while still alive. It is said that John will not experience
death until our Lord shall come again at the Judgement Day,
for he himself said in his Gospel: 'I will that he tarry till I
come.'[77]

27.   Trajan was the third Emperor after Nero to persecute the
Christians. Saint Clement, who was the third Bishop of the
church in Rome, suffered death during his reign. Saint Simeon,
Bishop of Jerusalem and son of Cleophas, is said to have been
crucified in Christ's name; and Ignatius, Bishop of Antioch, was
taken to Rome and handed over to the wild beasts. These are
the things which were done in the days of Trajan.

28.*   After Trajan Aelius Hadrianus was made Emperor. It is
from the name of Aelius Hadrianus, this successor to Domitian,
that Jerusalem is called Aelia, because it was he who restored
the city.[78] Even when the saints whom I have mentioned had
suffered martyrdom, the Devil was not satisfied with having
aroused heathen people against the followers of Christ, for he
stirred up schisms among the Christians themselves. He inspired
them to heresies, and the Catholic faith was split and divided in
various ways. When Antoninus was Emperor there began the
absurd heresy of Marcion and Valentinus; and the philosopher
Justin, who wrote a number of works on the Catholic Church,
was crowned as a martyr in the name of Christ. Persecution

76. Domitian, Roman Emperor A.D. 81–96. For the exile of John see
Revelation 1, 9.

77. John 21, 22.

78. Hadrian, Roman Emperor A.D. 117–38. After the building of a shrine
to Jupiter Capitolinus on the site of the Temple, Jerusalem was renamed
Colonia Aelia Capitolina.

started in Asia, and Saint Polycarp, who had been the disciple of
John the Apostle and Evangelist, was consecrated by fire to our
Lord, becoming a pure holocaust in his eightieth year. In Gaul,
too, many were crowned with heavenly gems and received martyrdom in Christ's name. The story of their persecution is still
faithfully preserved among us to this day.

29.*   The first among these was Photinus, Bishop of the church
of Lyons, who was tortured repeatedly when he was a very old
man and suffered death in the name of Christ. Saint Irenaeus,
next in the line after the martyred Photinus, and who had been
sent to the town of Lyons by Saint Polycarp, made a great name
for himself there by his remarkable powers. In a very short
time, particularly by his preaching, he converted the whole city
to Christianity. Then the persecution began again: and by the
hand of a tyrant the Devil made such assaults and so great a
number of Christians was put to death for confessing our
Lord's name that rivers of Christian blood ran through the
streets. We cannot tell how many were killed or what their
names were; but our Lord has written them down in the Book
of Life. After having had him tortured repeatedly in his presence, the executioner dedicated Saint Irenaeus in martyrdom
to Christ our Lord. After Irenaeus forty-eight other martyrs
suffered death, the first of them, so we have read, being called
Vettius Epagatus.[79]

30.   When Decius was Emperor, a long series of wars was
waged against those who bore the name of Christians, and such
slaughter was made among the believers that it is not possible to
list those who died. Babylas, the Bishop of Antioch, with three
boys called Urbanus, Prilidanus and Epolon, Sixtus, Bishop of
the church in Rome, Laurentius the Archdeacon and Hippolytus all died as martyrs through confessing the name of our
Lord. Valentinianus and Novatianus were then the leaders of
the heathen, and the Devil drove them on to vent their rage

79. Vettius Epagatus was a remote ancestor of Gregory himself. See the
Introduction, p. 8, and the family tree on p. 11.

against our faith. At this time seven men who had been consecrated as bishops were sent to preach among the Gauls, as we learn from the story of the holy martyr Saturninus, where we read the following sentence: 'The record has been carefully kept of how, when Decius and Gratus were consuls, the city of Toulouse received Saint Saturninus as its first and greatest priest.' The seven Bishops were sent to their sees: Bishop Gatianus to the men of Tours; Bishop Trophimus to the men of Arles; Bishop Paulus to Narbonne; Bishop Saturninus to Toulouse; Bishop Dionysius to the men of Paris; Bishop Stremonius to the men of Clermont-Ferrand; and Martialis was made Bishop of Limoges. Of these Saint Dionysius, Bishop of Paris, suffered repeated torture in Christ's name and then ended his earthly existence by the sword. When he saw that he was about to be martyred, Saturninus said to two of his priests: 'Now I am about to be sacrificed and the moment of my immolation is at hand. Stand by me, I beg you, until I meet my end.' He was seized and led off to the Capitol, but he was dragged there alone, for the two priests deserted him. When he saw that they had run away, he is said to have prayed in the following words: 'Lord Jesus Christ, hear me from where You are in heaven: may this church never to the end of time have a bishop chosen from its own citizens.' We know that this has never happened in the city down to our own days. Saturninus was tied to the heels of a wild bull and driven out from the Capitol, ending his life in this way. Gatianus, Trophimus, Stremonius, Paulus and Martialis passed their lives in great holiness, winning many people over to the church and spreading the faith of Christ among all whom they met; then they died in joyous confession of their belief. They passed away from earthly existence, some in martyrdom, others in full confession, and now they are reunited in heaven.

31.* One of their disciples went to the city of Bourges and preached to the people that Christ our Lord had come to save mankind.[80] Only a few believed him. These were ordained as

80. Saint Ursinus, first Bishop of Bourges, *fl.* 2nd century A.D.

priests. They were taught how to chant psalms, and they were
given instruction in building churches and in celebrating the
rites due to Almighty God. As yet they had little chance of
building a church, so they asked for the use of the house of one
of the townsfolk, so that they could make a church of it. The
Senators and the other leading men of the place were still committed to their own heathen religion, and those who had come
to believe in God were from the poorer classes, in accordance
with what our Lord said when He rebuked the Jews: 'The pub-
licans and the harlots go into the kingdom of God before
you.'[81] They did not obtain the use of the house for which
they had asked; and they therefore went to see a man called
Leocadius, the leading Senator of Gaul, who was of the same
family as that Vettius Epagatus who, as I have already told
you, suffered martyrdom in Lyons in the name of Christ.[82]
They told him of their Christian faith and explained what they
wanted. 'If my own house,' he replied, 'which I possess in
Bourges, were worthy of being put to such a use, I would be
willing to offer it to you.' When they heard him they fell at his
feet. They said that his house was indeed suitable to be used for
religious ceremonies and they offered him three hundred golden
pieces for it, together with a silver salver. Leocadius accepted
three of the golden coins for luck and refused the rest. Up to
this moment he had believed in heathen gods, but now he
became a Christian and turned his house into a church. This is
now the most important church in the town of Bourges, constructed with great skill and famous for the relics of Stephen,
the first martyr.

32.   Valerianus and Gallienus were the twenty-seventh in succession to rule the Roman Empire and in their days they began
a bitter persecution of the Christians. It was then that Cornelius
made Rome famous by shedding his blood in glory there, and
Cyprian did the same for Carthage. At the same time, Chroc,
King of the Alamanni, assembled an army and invaded Gaul.

81. Matthew 21, 31.
82. One of Gregory's ancestors: see p. 86, note 79.

There is said to have been no limit to this Chroc's overweening pride. He was the perpetrator of a long series of crimes, being under the influence, so they say, of his wicked mother, and now, as I have told you, he mobilized the people of the Alamanni, invaded the whole of Gaul, and destroyed down to its very foundations every single building which had been put up in ancient times. When he reached Clermont-Ferrand, he set fire to the temple which was called in the Gallic language Vasso Galatae, tearing it down and completely destroying it.[83] It had been constructed with great skill and was solidly built, for it had a double wall, the inner one made of small stones and the outer one of great squared masonry. Altogether this wall was thirty feet thick. It was decorated inside with marble and mosaics; the floor of the building was paved with marble and the roof was covered with lead.

33.* The two martyrs Liminius and Antolianus are buried outside this town. It was here, too, that Cassius and Victorinus, united as brothers in their love of Christ, both won their place in the kingdom of heaven by pouring forth their blood. An old tradition maintains that Victorinus was the servant of the priest of the temple about which I have told you. He often used to go into that quarter of the town where the Christians lived, and there he made the acquaintance of Cassius, who was himself a Christian. He was greatly moved by the sermons of Cassius and by the miracles which he performed, and so himself came to believe in Christ. He abandoned his wretched heathen practices, accepted the consecration of baptism, and became famous for the miracles which he himself performed. Not long afterwards these two, who had been friends on earth, suffered martyrdom and so went together to the kingdom of heaven.

34.* During the invasion of Gaul by the Alamanni, Saint Privatus, Bishop of the town of Javols, was found in a moun-

83. The site of the Gallic shrine called Vasso Galatae has been identified with that on the Puy de Dôme of Mercurius Dumias, a Roman god adapted from the Celtic Teutates.

tain cavern near Mende, where he was fasting and praying while his people were shut up in the fortified castle of Grèzes. This good shepherd was not willing to surrender his sheep to the wolves, and so the Alamanni tried to force him to make sacrifices to their devils. Privatus refused to do anything so foul and he made his revulsion clear. They beat him with sticks until he was thought to be dead. Within a few days he died as a result of the beating. Chroc was later captured in the town of Arles in Gaul. He was submitted to various tortures and then died by a blow from a sword, paying the penalty which he deserved for the sufferings which he had inflicted on God's elect.

35.* Under Diocletian, who ruled the Roman Empire as the thirty-third in succession, a savage persecution of the Christians lasted for four years, so that, on one occasion, at the holy feast of Easter, great multitudes of Christians were slaughtered because of their worship of the true God. At that time Quirinus, who was Bishop of the church of Siscia, suffered the glory of martyrdom in Christ's name. A millstone was tied to his neck and the savage pagans threw him into a swift-flowing river. As he fell into the whirlpool, through God's intervention he floated for a long time on the waters, which could not pull him to the bottom because no weight of sin dragged him down. The crowd of people which stood on the banks were astounded at what had happened: they took no notice of the fury of the Gentiles, but rushed forward to free their Bishop. Quirinus saw what they were going to do, but he did not want to be rescued from his martyrdom. He raised his eyes to heaven and said: 'Lord Jesus, You who sit in glory on the right hand of the Father, do not allow me to be taken from my course, but receive my soul and deign to add me to Your martyrs in eternal rest.' As he said these words he died. His body was recovered by the Christians and was buried with great reverence.

36.* Constantine was the thirty-fourth to hold the Roman Empire and he reigned happily for thirty years. In the eleventh year of his rule, when peace had been restored to the churches after the death of Diocletian, in the town of Sabaria in Pannonia[84] the most blessed Bishop Martin was born of parents who were pagans living in fairly easy circumstances. In the twentieth year of his reign Constantine killed his son Crispus with poison and his wife Fausta in a hot bath, because they had planned to remove him from his throne by treason. During Constantine's life-time the revered wood of our Lord's Cross was discovered, thanks to the zeal of the Emperor's mother Helena. It was a Hebrew called Judas who revealed it. He was later baptized and given the name Quiriacus. The historian Eusebius continued to write his chronicle down to this time. From the twenty-first year of Constantine's rule the priest Jerome took it over. It is he who tells us that a priest called Juvencus rewrote the Gospels in verse, at the request of the Emperor Constantine himself.[85]

37.* When Constans was Emperor there lived James of Nisibis. God in His clemency listened to the prayers of this James, and many perils were diverted from his city. Maximinus, the Bishop of Trier, had great influence because of his saintliness.

38.* In the nineteenth year of the reign of Constantine II the monk Anthony died at the age of one hundred and five. Saint Hilary, Bishop of Poitiers, was sent into exile at the request of the heretics. There he wrote books on the Catholic faith. He sent these books to Constantius, who, in the fourth year of his exile, ordered him to be pardoned and permitted him to return home.

39. At that period, too, our new luminary began to shine, and Gaul became bright with new rays coming from its lamps, for this is the moment when Saint Martin began to preach in this country. By his many miracles he overcame the disbelief of the

84. Sabaria is now the town of Szombathely in Hungary.

85. Juvencus is the name given to a Spanish priest Caius Vettius Aquilinus, fl. A.D. 330. His metrical version of the Gospels still exists.

Gentiles and made it clear to the people that Christ, the Son of God, is Himself the true God. He destroyed pagan temples, suppressed heresy, built churches and earned great renown for many miracles, crowning his claim to fame by restoring three dead men to life. In the fourth year of the Emperors Valentinianus and Valens, in the town of Poitiers, Saint Hilary went up to heaven, full of holiness and faith, and famous for his many miracles. He, too, is said to have restored the dead to life.

40.   A married woman of noble birth, called Melania, who lived in Rome, travelled to Jerusalem in her piety, leaving her son Urbanus behind. She seemed so good and saintly to everyone that she was called Thecla by her fellow-citizens.

41.   After the death of Valentinianus, Valens succeeded to the whole Empire. He decreed that all monks should be compelled to do military service and those who refused he ordered to be flogged. Some time later the Romans waged a most bitter war in Thrace. So great was the slaughter that the Roman cavalry lost their horses and fled on foot. They suffered heavy losses at the hands of the Goths. Valens was wounded by an arrow and sought refuge in a poor hovel. The enemy found him there and burned the hut over his head, so that he died without the burial which we all expect. In this way God's vengeance caught up with him in the end for the blood of the saintly men which he had shed.[86]

So far Jerome: from this point onwards the priest Orosius took on the task of writing.

42.   When he saw that the state was left defenceless, the Emperor Gratianus made Theodosius his colleague in the imperial power. This man Theodosius put all his hope and all his trust in the mercy of God. He held many peoples in check, more by vigils and prayer than by the sword, and so he strengthened the Roman state and was able to enter the city of Constantinople as a conqueror.

86. The Emperor Valens died at the battle of Adrianople, A.D. 378.

43.   Maximus was victorious over the Britons, for he crushed them by his tyrannical behaviour. As a result he was made Emperor by his soldiers. He made Trier his capital. He captured the Emperor Gratianus by a stratagem and had him put to death. Saint Martin, who had become a Bishop, visited Maximus. Theodosius, the man I have told you about, who placed all his hope in God, therefore took over the entire Empire in the place of Gratianus. With God's help he later stripped Maximus of the imperial power and had him put to death.

44.*   Urbicus was the first Bishop of Clermont-Ferrand after the prelate and preacher Stremonius. He had been converted from a senatorial family. He was a married man and, according to the custom of the church, his wife lived as a religious, apart from her husband. They both devoted themselves to prayer, charity and good works. As they were pursuing the even tenor of their lives, the woman was filled with the Devil's own malice, which is always hostile to holiness: for he inflamed her with desire for her husband and turned her into a second Eve. The Bishop's wife burned so hot with passion, and was overwhelmed by dark thoughts of such a sinful nature, that she made her way through the pitch-black night to the church-house. When she found that everything was shut up for the night, she started to beat on the doors of the church-house and to shout something like the following: 'Bishop! How long do you intend to remain asleep? How long do you propose to refuse to open these closed doors? Why do you scorn your lawful wife? Why do you shut your ears and refuse to listen to the words of Paul, who wrote: "Come together again, that Satan tempt you not."[87] I am here! I am returning to you, not as to a stranger, but to one who belongs to me.' For a long time she went on shouting these things and others like them. In the end the Bishop forgot his religious scruples and ordered her to be admitted to his bedroom, where he had intercourse with her and then said that it was time for her to go. Later on he recovered his wits, and

87. I Corinthians 7, 5.

grieved for the sin which he had committed. He went off to a monastery in his diocese, with the intention of doing penance. With lamentation and tears he atoned for his misdeeds, and finally came back to his own town. When he reached the end of his life, he departed from this world. His wife had become pregnant and she bore a daughter, who passed her life as a religious. The Bishop was buried in a crypt beside a public thoroughfare at Chantoin, with his wife and daughter at his side. Legonus was elected as Bishop in his place.

45.*   When Legonus died, Saint Illidius replaced him. He was a man of such remarkable holiness and impeccable virtue, and his sanctity was so clear for all to see, that his fame reached lands outside Gaul. As a result he was summoned to Trier by the Emperor, so that he might cure his daughter of an unclean spirit. I have told this story already in the book which I wrote on the life of Illidius.[88] He lived, so the story goes, to be a very old man, full of days and full of good works. When he had completed his life's journey, he died peacefully and went off to join our Lord. He was buried in a crypt in a suburb of his own city of Clermont-Ferrand. He had an Archdeacon who was with good reason called Justus. When this Justus had come to the end of a life filled with good works, he was placed beside his master in the same tomb. After the death of this saintly Bishop Illidius so many miracles were performed at his tomb that it is not possible to record them or even to remember them. The holy Nepotianus succeeded to Illidius.

46.*   Saint Nepotianus counts as the fourth Bishop of Clermont-Ferrand. Envoys were sent to Spain from Trier; and one of them, a man called Arthemius, who was remarkable both for his wisdom and his good looks, fell ill of a high fever, although he was in the prime of life. The other envoys continued their journey, and Arthemius was left behind ill in Clermont. He had recently become engaged in Trier. Nepotianus came to see him and anointed him with holy oil. With our Lord's help Ar-

88. *Liber vitae Patruum (VP)*, 2.

themius was restored to health. When he had been prayed over
by the saintly man, he forgot both his earthly spouse and his
private fortune. He became a member of the holy Church, and
was ordained as a priest and gained such fame for his saintliness
that he succeeded Nepotianus as Bishop and took charge of the
folds of the Lord's flock.

47.* At the same time a certain Injuriosus, who was a wealthy
man sprung from a senatorial family in Clermont-Ferrand,
asked for the hand in marriage of a young woman in similar
circumstances. The dowry had been handed over and he
arranged a day for the wedding. Each of the two was an only
child. The day of the ceremony arrived and the marriage service
was duly performed. According to the custom the two were
placed in the same bed. The young woman was greatly distressed: she turned her face to the wall and wept bitterly. Her
husband said to her: 'Tell me what is the matter. Tell me, I beg
you.' She remained silent and he said again: 'I beg you, in the
name of Jesus Christ, the Son of God, be sensible and tell me
what is making you so sad.' She turned to him and answered: 'If
I were to weep every day of my life there would still not be
enough tears to wash away the great grief which fills my heart.
I had determined to preserve my poor body for Christ, untouched by intercourse with man. Now to my great sorrow I am
deserted by Him and I have not had the strength to achieve
what I wanted so much; for on this day, which I could have
wished never to see, I have lost that which I have preserved
from the beginning of my life. I am forsaken by the sempiternal
Christ, who promised me heaven as my dowry, for now it is my
fate to be the consort of a mortal man. In place of the roses
which shall never wither, the remains of my own faded roses
disfigure rather than adorn me. At the moment when, beside the
river of the Lamb, with its four separate streams,[89] I should
have put on the stole of purity, this wedding-gown brings me
shame instead of honour. What is the use of our talking any

89. Cp. Revelation 14, 1. From Mount Sion flowed the four rivers of
Paradise, symbols of the four Gospels.

longer? How unhappy I am! I should have had heaven as my reward, instead I am plunged into hell. If this was to be my fate, why could not the very first day of my life have also been my last? How I wish that I could have passed through death's dark portal before I had even sucked my mother's milk! If only the kisses of my gentle nurses could have been bestowed upon my dead body! The things of this world are loathsome to me, for my eyes are fixed on the hands of the Redeemer, which were pierced to bring life to the world. I no longer see diadems glittering with precious jewels, but in my mind I gaze upon His crown of thorns. I have nothing but scorn for your vast estates and your lands which spread so far and wide, for it is the joys of Paradise for which I yearn. Your sun-drenched rooms are hateful to me when I gaze at our Lord sitting in majesty above the stars.' As she raved on and the tears ran down her face, her young husband was moved with compassion. 'Our parents are the most nobly-born in Clermont,' he said. 'We are their only children, and they have planned this marriage for us to produce children, so that when they are dead no heir from outside our families may claim the succession.' 'This earthly existence of ours is of no value,' she replied. 'Wealth is of no value, the pomp and circumstance of this world is of no value, the very life which we enjoy is of no value. We should look instead to that other life which is not ended when death finally comes, which is not dissolved by any illness, which is not closed by any accident, but where man lives for ever in eternal bliss, in a radiance which never fades, and, what is more than all this, where he is translated to cohabit with the angels and enjoys a happiness which is eternal, rejoicing in a meditation which lasts for ever, in the presence of our Lord Himself.' 'Your sweet words have brought eternal life to me,' answered her husband, 'and this shines on me like a bright star. If you are determined to abstain from intercourse with me, then I will agree to what you want to do.' 'It is difficult for a man to make such a compact with women,' she answered. 'All the same, if you can agree that we shall remain unsullied in our human existence, then I will share with you the dowry which is promised to me by my

spouse, the Lord Jesus Christ, to whom I have vowed myself as
handmaiden and bride.' Her husband crossed himself and said:
'I will do what you ask.' Hand in hand they went to sleep, and
for many years after this they lay each night in one bed, but
they remained chaste in a way which we can only admire, as
was revealed when the time came for them to die. When her
life's journey was over and the young woman had gone to join
Christ, after he had performed all her funeral rites and had
placed her in the tomb, her husband said: 'I thank you, Lord
Jesus Christ, Master, and eternal God, for granting that I may
hand back to Your loving care this treasure as unsullied as
when I received her from Your hands.' As he spoke, she smiled
up at him. 'Why do you say that,' she said, 'when no one asked
you to?' Not long after she was buried her husband followed
her. Although their two tombs were placed by different walls, a
new miracle occurred which proved their chastity. When morning dawned and the people came to visit the place, they found
the two tombs side by side, although they had left them far
apart. This shows that when heaven unites two people the
monument which covers their buried corpses cannot hold them
apart. Down to our own times the inhabitants of the place have
chosen to call them 'The Two Lovers'. I have told their story in
my *Book of Miracles*.[90]

48.   In the second year of the rule of Arcadius and Honorius,
Saint Martin, Bishop of Tours, who had done so many good
deeds for the sick, who was so holy and had performed so many
miracles, died at Candes, a village in his own diocese, in the
eighty-first year of his age and the twenty-sixth year of his episcopate, and so went happily to meet Christ.[91] He died at midnight on a Sunday, during the consulship of Atticus and
Caesarius. As he passed away, many heard a chanting of psalms
in the sky, which I have described at greater length in the first
book of his Miracles.[92] As soon as this holy man was taken ill

90. *Liber in gloria Confessorum* (*GC*), 31.
91. A.D. 397.
92. *De Virtutibus beati Martini episcopi* (*VSM*), 1.

in the village of Candes, as I have said already, the people of
Poitiers and Tours began to assemble at his death-bed. When he
was dead, a great altercation arose between the two groups. The
men of Poitiers said: 'As a monk he is ours. He became an
abbot in our town. We entrusted him to you, but we demand
him back. It is sufficient for you that, while he was a Bishop on
this earth, you enjoyed his company, you shared his table, you
were strengthened by his blessing and above all you were
cheered by his miracles. Let all these things suffice for you, and
permit us at least to carry away his dead body.' To this the
men of Tours replied: 'If you say that we should be satisfied
with the miracles which he performed for us, then admit that
while he was with you he did more than in our town. If all his
other miracles are left out of the count, he raised two dead men
for you and only one for us; and, as he himself used often to
say, his miraculous power was greater before he was made
Bishop than it was afterwards. It is therefore necessary that
what he did not achieve with us when he was alive he should
complete now that he is dead. God took him away from you,
but only so that He might give him to us. If the custom established by the men of old is observed, then by God's will he shall
be buried in the town where he was consecrated. If you propose
to claim him because you have his monastery, then you must
know this, that his first monastery was in Milan.' They went on
with their argument until the sun went down and night began to
fall. The body was placed in the middle of the room, the doors
were locked and he was watched over by the two groups. The
men of Poitiers planned to carry off the body as soon as morning came, but Almighty God would not allow the town of
Tours to be deprived of its patron. In the end all the men of
Poitiers fell asleep in the middle of the night, and there was not
one who remained on guard. When the men of Tours saw that
all the Poitevins had fallen asleep, they took the mortal clay of
that most holy body and some passed it out through the window
while others stood outside to receive it. They placed it in a boat
and all those present rowed down the River Vienne. As soon as
they reached the River Loire, they set their course for the city

of Tours, praising God and chanting psalms. The men of Poitiers were awakened by their voices and they went back home in great confusion, taking nothing of the treasure which they were supposed to be guarding. If anyone should ask why from the death of Bishop Gatianus down to Saint Martin there was only one Bishop of Tours, to wit Litorius, let him know that for a long time the pagans were so hostile that the city remained without episcopal benediction. In those days those who were Christians celebrated the divine office secretly and in hidden places. If any were discovered by the pagans to be Christians they were either beaten severely or had their heads cut off with a sword.

From the Passion of our Lord until the death of Saint Martin four hundred and twelve years passed.

HERE ENDS THE FIRST BOOK, WHICH COVERS FIVE
THOUSAND, FIVE HUNDRED AND NINETY-SIX YEARS
FROM THE BEGINNING OF THE WORLD DOWN TO THE
DEATH OF SAINT MARTIN

BOOK II

HERE BEGIN THE CHAPTER-HEADINGS
OF THE SECOND BOOK

1. The episcopate of Bricius.
2. The Vandals and how the Christians were persecuted during their rule.
3. Cyrola, bishop of the heretics, and the holy martyrs.
4. The persecution carried out during the reign of Athanaric.
5. Bishop Aravatius and the Huns.
6. The church of Saint Stephen in the town of Metz.
7. The wife of Aetius.
8. What the historians have written about Aetius.
9. What they say about the Franks.
10. What the prophets of the Lord write about the idols of the Gentiles.
11. The Emperor Avitus.
12. King Childeric and Aegidius.
13. The episcopate of Venerandus and that of Rusticus, both of Clermont-Ferrand.
14. The episcopate of Eustochius of Tours and that of Perpetuus. The church of Saint Martin.
15. The church of Saint Symphorian.
16. Bishop Namatius and the church in Clermont-Ferrand.
17. The wife of Namatius and the church of Saint Stephen.
18. How Childeric came to Orleans and Odovacar to Angers.
19. The war between the Saxons and the Romans.
20. Duke Victorius.
21. Bishop Eparchius.
22. Bishop Sidonius.
23. The saintly behaviour of Bishop Sidonius and how the injuries done to him were requited by the vengeance of God.

24. The famine in Burgundy and Ecdicius.
25. Euric the persecutor.
26. The death of Saint Perpetuus. The episcopate of Volusianus and Verus.
27. How Clovis became King.
28. How Clovis married Clotild.
29. When he had been baptized, their first son died in his white robes.
30. The war against the Alamanni.
31. The baptism of Clovis.
32. The war against Gundobad.
33. The death of Godigisel.
34. How Gundobad wished to be converted.
35. The meeting of Clovis and Alaric.
36. Bishop Quintianus.
37. The war with Alaric.
38. The title of Consul is bestowed upon King Clovis.
39. Bishop Licinius.
40. The death of the elder Sigibert and of his son.
41. The death of Chararic and his son.
42. The death of Ragnachar and his brothers.
43. The death of Clovis.

HERE END THE CHAPTER-HEADINGS

As I continue to follow the march of history I recount for you at one and the same time, and in the muddled and confused order in which these events occurred, the holy deeds of the Saints and the way in which whole races of people were butchered. It will not, I am sure, be held unreasonable of me if I describe the blessed lives of the Saints together with the disasters of the unfortunate: for it is the course of events which demands this and not my own fantasy as a writer. Indeed, if the attentive reader looks carefully he will discover that, in the histories of the Kings of Israel, the sacrilegious Phineas met his end during the reign of the just Samuel; and that the Philistine Goliath died when the strong man David was King. Let him remember how many peoples were slaughtered and what famine and drought our miserable earth suffered in the time of the distinguished prophet Elisha, who caused the rains to cease whenever he wished, or at his will made them pour down again on the parched ground, and who by his prayer gave riches to the poor widow-woman. Let him remember, too, what disasters befell Jerusalem in the time of Hezekiah, whose life God prolonged for fifteen years. Even in the days of the prophet Elisha, who restored the dead to life and performed many other miracles among the people, how much carnage and what miseries were suffered by the children of Israel! Just as I have done myself, so Eusebius, Severus and Jerome mingled together in their chronicles the wars waged by kings and the holy deeds of martyrs. I have composed my book in the same way, so that the onward march of the centuries and the succession of the years down to our own times may be studied in their entirety. So far I have been following the chronicles of the authors whom I have named; and now, according to the will of God, I will describe for you what happened next.

1.* After the death of Saint Martin, Bishop of the city of Tours, that most eminent and indeed incomparable man, concerning whose miracles large tomes have been written in our own country, Bricius succeeded to the episcopate. When he was a very young man this Bricius would often set snares for Saint Martin, who was then still living in the flesh, because the Saint used very frequently to rebuke him for spending too much of his time on trivial matters. One day when a sick man came to Saint Martin to be healed, he met Bricius, who was still a deacon, in the square. 'I am hanging about here waiting for the holy man,' said he in his rough way, 'but I don't know where he is or what he's doing.' 'If you are looking for that crazy fellow,' answered Bricius, 'just cast your eyes in that direction. In his usual half-witted way, he is staring at the sky.' The poor man went over to Saint Martin and was given what he wanted. The Saint then turned to his deacon Bricius and said: 'So I seem to you to be half-witted, do I?' Bricius was so confused when he heard this that he denied that he had said any such thing, but Saint Martin went on: 'I was listening to your words, even though you were some distance away. Amen say I to you, for I have just had granted to me by God that you shall succeed to the honour of this bishopric after my death, but you must know this, that during your tenure of the episcopate you will suffer much ill-treatment.' When Bricius heard this he laughed and answered: 'Wasn't it true what I alleged, that much of what you say is sheer lunacy?' Even when he had been ordained as a priest, Bricius continued to cause pain to the Saint by his sarcastic remarks. However, when he was elected to the bishopric, with the full approval of the citizens of Tours, he spent his time in prayer.

Although Bricius was arrogant and vain, he was considered to be chaste in body. In the thirty-third year after his ordination, a lamentable charge was levelled against him. A woman to whom his servants used to give his clothes to wash, and who for religious reasons had herself given up wearing lay garments, became pregnant and bore a child. At this news the entire population of Tours rose in its anger. They laid the whole guilt on their Bishop and as one man wanted to stone him to death. 'Your piety as a holy man has all this time been just a cover for your depraved habits,' they cried. 'God no longer permits us to defile ourselves by kissing your unworthy hands.' Bricius stoutly denied the charge. 'Bring the child to me,' he commanded. The baby was carried in, still only thirty days old. 'In the name of Jesus Christ, the son of God the all-powerful,' said Bricius to the infant, 'if I am really your father, I order you to say so, with all these people listening.' 'You are not my father,' answered the baby. When the people begged Bricius to ask who the father was, he replied: 'That is not for me to do. I was only concerned insofar as the matter affected me. If you have any more interest in what has happened, then ask the question yourselves.' They then alleged that he had done this by his magic arts. They rose up in rebellion against him and dragged him away, shouting: 'You shall no longer rule over us with the false name of pastor.' To justify himself to the people, he placed burning coals in his cassock and pressed them against his body and went in procession with the whole mob to the tomb of Saint Martin. When he reached the tomb he dropped the coals on the ground, but his cassock had no marks of burning on it. Then he went on with what he was saying: 'Just as you see that my clothing is completely unmarked by these burning coals, so is my body undefiled by intercourse with woman.' They still would not believe him, but refused to accept what he had said. He was dragged away and reviled, and they expelled him from their city, so that the saying of Saint Martin might be fulfilled: 'Know this, that during your tenure of the episcopate you will suffer much ill-treatment.'

When they had expelled Bricius, the people of Tours chose Justinian to be their Bishop. Bricius made his way to the Pope of the City of Rome. Weeping and lamenting his fate, he said to the Pope: 'I deserve to suffer all these insults, for I sinned against the holy man of God, calling him a madman and a lunatic on a number of occasions. When I saw the miracles which he performed I did not believe them.' After Bricius had left, the people of Tours said to their new Bishop: 'Go after him and give attention to your own situation, for if you do not follow him you will deserve to be despised by us all.' Justinian thereupon left Tours and came to the city of Vercelli in Italy. There he died on his journey, for he was struck by the judgement of God. When the people of Tours heard of the death of Justinian they persisted in their wrong-doing and appointed Armentius in his place. As soon as Bishop Bricius arrived in Rome he told the Pope all that he had suffered. He took up residence in the Papal see and frequently celebrated Mass there, but he continued to lament his offensive behaviour towards the holy man of God. When seven years had passed he left Rome and with the Pope's permission set out once more for Tours. He came to a village called Mont-Louis, some six miles from the town, and there he took up residence. Armentius fell ill of a fever and died in the middle of the night. This was revealed to Bishop Bricius in a vision and he said to his servants: 'Get up quickly and let us hurry to the funeral of our brother the Bishop of Tours.' As they came to one of the gates of the city and were preparing to pass it, the dead man was being carried out by another gate. After the funeral Bricius returned to his own cathedral and lived there happily for seven years. He died in the forty-seventh year of his episcopate. Saint Eustochius, a man of remarkable sanctity, succeeded him.

2. The next thing which happened was that the Vandals left their homeland and invaded Gaul with Gunderic as their King.[1] When they had ravaged Gaul they attacked Spain.[2] The Suebi, also called the Alamanni, followed the Vandals, and seized Galicia. Not long afterwards a quarrel arose between these two peoples, for their territories were adjacent. They had taken up arms and marched out to war and were on the very point of attacking each other when the King of the Alamanni said: 'How much longer is war going to devastate an entire people? In my opinion the armed forces of both peoples should not be slaughtered, but two champions chosen one from each side should meet fully armed on the field of combat and should

1. A.D. 406.   2. A.D. 409.

fight it out between them. That side whose champion is victorious should take over the territory in dispute without further
contest.' All those present agreed to this, rather than that the
entire multitude should rush upon each other's swords. Some
time later King Gunderic died and Trasamund took over the
kingship of the Vandals in his place.[3] In the single-combat
between the two champions, the man representing the Vandals
was beaten and killed. Once he was dead Trasamund gave his
word that he would carry out his promise to withdraw and that,
as soon as the preparations necessary for the journey back had
been made, he would retire from Spain.

About this time Trasamund began to persecute the Christians
and by tortures and all sorts of executions forced the whole of
Spain to accept the heresy of the Arian rite. It so happened that
a young girl of strong religious convictions was dragged forward for this torment. She was extremely wealthy and according to the class-distinctions of this world she belonged to a noble
senatorial family. What is nobler still than all this, she was
strong in the Catholic faith and served Almighty God in a fault-
less way. When she was brought into the presence of the King
he spoke to her kindly and tried first to persuade her to be re-
baptized. The shield of her faith turned aside the poisonous
barb and the King ordered all her possessions to be confiscated,
but in her mind she already possessed the Kingdom of Heaven.
Then he ordered the instruments to be applied and she was
tortured to the point where her life was despaired of. What
more can I say? She was tortured repeatedly and all her earthly
possessions were removed from her, but her will was not broken
by this and she would not renounce the Holy Trinity. As she
was dragged off to be re-baptized against her will and compelled to suffer immersion in the filthy font, she shouted: 'I
believe the Father with the Son and the Holy Ghost to be of one
substance.' As she said this she stained all the water with her
blood, for her menstrual period began. Then she was submitted
to a legal interrogation, and tortured by the rack, the flames and

3. Gaiseric succeeded Gunderic and then came Huneric. Trasamund
became King of the Vandals in 496 only.

the pincers. Finally she was consecrated to Christ our Lord by having her head cut off.

After this the Vandals crossed the sea and were dispersed throughout the whole of Africa and Mauretania. The Alamanni followed them as far as Tangiers.

3.   The Christians[4] were persecuted even more cruelly in the time of the Vandals, as I have already told you. It is therefore only right and proper that I should recount to you some of the crimes which they committed against the churches of God and then the way in which their rule was brought to an end. Trasamund died and so finished his maltreatment of God's elect. Huneric became King of the Africans,[5] having been chosen by the Vandals to rule over them, and he was even more sadistic than his predecessor. None can tell how many Christian peoples were slaughtered in his time in the most sacred name of our Lord. Africa is their witness, the land which bore them, and so is the right hand of Christ, which crowned them with the sempiternal gems of martyrdom. I have read the accounts of some of their sufferings and these I propose to tell once more in order to fulfil my promise to you.

Cyrola, who is wrongly called bishop, was considered to be the greatest champion of the heretics. When the King of the Vandals sent messages to all his provinces that the Christians should be molested, this persecutor laid hands on Bishop Eugenius, whom he discovered in a suburb of his city. So suddenly did Cyrola seize Eugenius, a man of ineffable holiness who also had a reputation for great wisdom, that he gave him no opportunity of saying a few words of encouragement to his Christian flock.[6] When he realized that he was to be dragged away forcibly, Eugenius managed to convey the following letter[7] to the

4. By the Christians Gregory means the Catholics, as distinct from the Arians.

5. Huneric preceded Trasamund.

6. Eugenius became Bishop of Carthage in 479. He was exiled to Gaul and died in Albi in 505.

7. This is the first example of Gregory's commendable habit of quoting original documents at length. See Introduction, pp. 29–30. The full text of the letter still exists.

local inhabitants to exhort them to be steadfast in their Catholic faith:

Eugenius the Bishop sends this message to the sons and daughters of the church committed by God to his care, to you who are most cherished and most dear to him. The King's edict has gone forth and by this order he commands me to come to Carthage to answer for the fact that I have continued to exercise the Catholic faith. So that by my departure I may not leave the church of God in any doubt or suspense, or abandon Christ's flock without a word and like a false shepherd, I have decided to send this letter to speak to you in my name. In it I beg you with my tears, I exhort you, I warn you and I adjure you, with all the strength at my command, you who are God's elect, by the very majesty of God and by the fearful Day of His Judgement and by the coming again of Christ when all will be seen with a clarity hardly to be borne, that you hold firm to the Catholic faith and that you proclaim that the Son and the Father and the Holy Ghost all three have the same Godhead with the Father and the Son. Preserve the grace of the single baptism and the anointing with the holy unction. None of you who has been born again of the water must return again to that water for re-baptism. By God's will you are made the salt of the earth in that water, but, if that salt is placed back in the water, all its virtue is immediately lost. That is why our Lord rightly says in the Gospel: 'If the salt have lost its savour, wherewith shall it be salted?'[8] This is indeed to lose savour, to be baptized a second time, when once is sufficient. Have you not heard the word of Christ: 'He that is washed needeth not to wash again'?[9] My brothers and sons and daughters in Christ, do not let my departure distress you. If you hold fast to the Catholic doctrine, I shall not forget you. However far away from you I may be, I shall not be separated from you even in death. However far away from you I may be borne in my anguish, remember this, that the palm of victory will be mine. If I am driven into exile, I have Saint John the Evangelist for an example; if I pass through the portals of death, 'to me to live is Christ, and to die is gain.'[10] If I am to return, then, brethren, God will be granting your wish. It is enough for you that I have not left you without a message. I have warned you and I have given you such advice as I could in the circumstances. I am innocent of the blood of all who are killed,

8. Matthew 5, 13.   9. John 13, 10.   10. Philippians 1, 21.

and I know that this letter will be read in their presence before the judgement-seat of Christ, when He comes again to requite each man according to his works. If I am to return, I shall see you in this world; if I am not to return then I shall see you in the next. This is my message to you: Farewell, pray for me, and fast, for charity and fasting have always brought the mercy of God. Remember what is written in the Gospel: 'Fear not them which kill the body, but are not able to kill the soul: but rather fear him which is able to destroy both soul and body in hell.'[11]

Saint Eugenius was then led before the King and there he disputed with this bishop of the Arians in defence of the Catholic faith. He was successful in refuting Cyrola completely on the mystery of the Holy Trinity, and, what is more, Christ wrought many miracles through his agency, with the result that the Arian bishop became more and more incensed. With the holy Eugenius at this time were two wise and saintly men, the Bishops Vindimialis and Longinus, his equals in rank and no way inferior to him in their miraculous power; for the holy Vindimialis was said to have raised the dead at that time and Longinus had restored to health many who were afflicted. For his part Eugenius not only cured the blindness of the seeing eye but also that of the spirit.

When the infamous bishop of the Arians saw this, he summoned to his presence a man who shared the same heresy which marred his own life. 'I cannot bear,' said Cyrola, 'that these Bishops should perform so many miracles among the people and that everyone should follow them but neglect me. Do what I tell you. Here are fifty pieces of gold. Go and sit in the square. As I walk by, shut your eyes and press your hand over them. As I come near with the others, shout out at the top of your voice: "Blessed Cyrola, high-priest of our religion, look at me, I beg you, and give proof of your glory and miraculous power by opening my eyes so that I may be held worthy to see the light which I have lost." ' The man did as he was told and sat down in the square. As the heretic Cyrola passed by with the holy men of God, he who thought to make a mockery of the Almighty

11. Matthew 10, 28.

shouted out as loud as he was able: 'Cyrola the blessed, listen to
me! Hear me, holy priest of God! Behold me in my blindness!
Let me, too, have evidence of your healing power, from which
other blind men have profited, which lepers have experienced
and the effects of which the very dead have felt. I beg you, by
the miraculous power which you have, to restore to me the sight
for which I long, for I am stricken with complete blindness.'
Without realizing it, he was speaking the truth, for avarice had
made him blind, and for the sake of money he thought to make
a mockery of the power of God Almighty. The bishop of the
heretics then turned aside, as if about to cure the man's blindness by his miraculous power. Beside himself with vanity and
pride, he placed his hand on the man's eyes and proclaimed: 'By
virtue of our faith, through whose tenets we so rightly believe in
God, may your eyes be opened.' He had hardly uttered this
blasphemy when joy was changed to grief and the trickery of
the bishop was made plain to all. The eyes of this miserable
creature began to hurt so much that he was forced to press them
in with his fingers to stop them bursting out of their sockets.
Then in his anguish he began to shout: 'A terrible thing has
happened! I have been led astray by an enemy of God's law.
The catastrophe has befallen me because I thought to make a
mockery of God for money. I have been bribed with fifty pieces
of gøld to commit this outrage.' Then he said to the bishop:
'Take your gold! Give me back my sight which I have lost
through your trickery! And you, glorious followers of Christ,
do not despise me in my misery, but help me, for I am on the
point of death. This at least I have learnt, that God is not
mocked.'[12]

The two saintly men were moved with compassion. 'If thou
canst believe,' they said, 'all things are possible to him that
believeth.'[13] The man answered at the top of his voice:
'Anyone who will not believe that Christ the Son of God and
the Holy Ghost are of equal substance and deity with the
Father ought to suffer what I am now enduring. I believe in
God the Father Almighty,' he went on. 'I believe that Jesus

12. Galatians 6, 7.   13. Mark 9, 23.

111

Christ the Son of God is equal to the Father, I believe that the Holy Ghost is consubstantial and coeternal with the Father and the Son.' When they heard this, a pious debate began between them as to which should mark the sign of the Holy Cross upon his eyes, and each in turn was willing to yield the honour to the others. Vindimialis and Longinus begged Eugenius to lay his hands upon the blind man, but he asked them to do it. It was they who laid their hands upon his head and Saint Eugenius who marked the Cross of Christ on the blind man's eyes. 'In the name of the Father and the Son and the Holy Ghost,' said he, 'very Godhead, which we hold to be three Persons, omnipotent and equal, may your eyes be opened.' The pain immediately stopped and the man recovered his former health. By the blinding of this man it was made quite clear how the bishop of the heretics was covering the eyes of men's hearts with the miserable veil of his doctrine, so that none could see the true light with the eyes of faith. Wretched creature, who entered not by the gate, that is, by Christ, the true gate, who became a wolf rather than the shepherd of his flock, who, in the depravity of his own heart, strove to put out the torch of faith which he ought rather to be kindling in the hearts of believers! The holy men of God performed other miracles among the people, who all proclaimed with one voice: 'The Father is true God, the Son is true God, the Holy Ghost is true God, each to be worshipped in one faith, each to be feared with one fear, each to be honoured with a single honour! It is quite clear to us that Cyrola's doctrine is false.'

When King Huneric saw that what he believed was being exposed in this way by the glorious faith of these saintly men, that his heretical sect was being destroyed instead of exalted and that the reputation of his arch-priest had been brought to an end, he ordered God's saints to suffer many tortures, first the rack, then the flames, then the pincers and after all that death itself. Eugenius he ordered to be beheaded, but with the proviso that, if at the moment when the sword was about to descend on his neck, he still refused to turn to the heretical sect, he should not be killed but should be sent into exile, for Huneric did not

want the Christians to venerate him as a martyr. As everyone
knows, that is what happened. As he was about to be executed
he was asked if he was determined to die for the Catholic faith.
'To die for the true cause is life eternal,' he answered. The
sword did not fall. Eugenius was sent into exile to Albi, a town
in Gaul. There he lived out his life and to this day many miracles are frequently wrought at his tomb. The King ordered
the holy Vindimialis to be beheaded with the sword, and this
was done. In this persecution the Archdeacon Octavianus and
many thousands of men and women who confessed our faith
were killed and broken by torture. To suffer torment for the
love of glory seemed nothing to those saintly persons of our
own persuasion, for, if harassed in small matters, they knew
that they would be rewarded in great ones, as the Apostle said:
'The sufferings of this present time are not worthy to be compared with the glory which shall be revealed in the saints.'[14]

At this time many strayed from the faith for the sake of
money and so brought suffering upon themselves, like the unhappy Bishop Revocatus, who abjured the Catholic faith. Three
times the sun was in eclipse, so that only a third part of it was
visible. In my opinion this happened because of all the crimes
which had been committed and all the blood which had been
shed. After all the wrong which he had done Huneric was seized
by the devil. Having glutted himself for so long on the blood of
the saints, he tore himself to pieces with his own teeth and
ended his unworthy life in this torment which was a befitting
death. Childeric succeeded him. When he died, Geilamir
became King.[15] He was broken in battle by the forces of the
Roman Empire and ended his life and his reign at the same
moment. So perished the Kingdom of the Vandals.

4.   At this period the churches of God were assailed with a
long series of heresies, and quite a few of them were visited with
divine vengeance. Athanaric, King of the Goths, began a great

14. Romans 8, 18.
15. Huneric died in A.D. 484. Childeric became King of the Vandals in
523 only. Geilamir deposed Childeric in 530.

persecution. He subjected many Christians to various forms of torture and then he cut off their heads with a sword. As a result of his misdeeds he felt the weight of God's judgement. This man who kept attacking God's churches was expelled from his kingdom and banished from his country for having shed the blood of the righteous. I must now, however, return to what I was writing about before.

5. A rumour spread that the Huns were proposing to invade Gaul. At that time in the fortified township of Tongres there lived an extremely saintly Bishop called Aravatius, who spent his time in vigils and fasting. Constantly bathed in a flood of tears, he prayed that God in his pity should not permit this unworthy and unbelieving race to enter Gaul. Because of the sins of the people, he felt in his heart that his prayer had not been granted to him: he therefore decided to journey to Rome, so that he might add the power of intercession of the Apostle to his own and be considered worthy of being granted what he was asking of God's compassion with such humility. He made his way to the tomb of the Apostle; and there in great abstinence he continued to pray for the support of his loving kindness, wearing himself out with long fasts and indeed often going two or three days without food or drink, in order to avoid having to interrupt his prayer and so that there need be no interval of silence. When he had remained there in such mortification for many days, he is said to have received the following answer from the blessed Apostle: 'Why, holy man, do you keep on praying to me? It is decreed most clearly by God in His wisdom that the Huns will invade Gaul and that they will devastate that country like some great tornado. You must take my advice. Go home quickly and put your domestic affairs in order, prepare your place of burial and have ready a clean shroud. You are about to leave this earthly life, and your eyes will not see the devastation which the Huns will cause in Gaul, for that is the decision announced by our Lord God.'

As soon as the Bishop had received this answer from the holy Apostle, he made ready for his journey in all haste and then he travelled back to Gaul. When he reached the town of Tongres, he quickly made all the preparations necessary for his own burial. He said goodbye to his clergy and all the other citizens of the town, and then with tears and lamentation he told them that they would never see his face again. They wept and groaned as they walked behind him, and they addressed the following humble supplication to him: 'Do not leave us, holy father! Good shepherd, do not forget us!' He gave them his blessing and the kiss of peace, and then they went back home, for with all their tears they could not turn him back. He made his way to the town of Maestricht and there he fell ill of a mild fever. As soon as his soul had left his body he was washed by the faithful and buried beside the public highroad. How, after the lapse of many years, his holy body was moved elsewhere I have described in my *Book of Miracles*.[16]

6.   The Huns migrated from Pannonia and laid waste the countryside as they advanced. They came to the town of Metz, so people say, on Easter Eve. They burned the town to the ground, slaughtered the populace with the sharp edge of their swords and killed the priests of the Lord in front of their holy altars. No building in the town remained unburnt except the oratory of Saint Stephen, Levite and first martyr. I will now tell you the story of this oratory as I heard it from various people. They say that, before these enemies arrived, one of the faithful in a vision saw Saint Stephen the Levite discussing this destruction with the holy Apostles Peter and Paul. 'I beg you, masters,' said he, 'that by your intervention you prevent the town of Metz from being burnt down by the enemy, for there is a spot there in which the relics of my own humble existence are preserved. If you do this you will make the people realize that I have some influence with the Lord. If the wickedness of the inhabitants is too great, and nothing can be done to protect the town from a holocaust, at least stop my oratory from being burnt.' 'Go in peace, beloved brother,' answered the Apostles, 'for your oratory alone will escape the flames. As for the town,

16. *GC*, 71.

we can do nothing, for the judgement of God has already been passed on it. The evil-doing of the inhabitants has reached such a point that the reverberation of their wickedness has already come to God's ears. The town must therefore be burnt to the ground.' There is no possible doubt, then, that, when the town was destroyed, the oratory remained unscathed thanks to their intervention.

7.   Attila the King of the Huns marched forward from Metz and ravaged a great number of other cities in Gaul.[17] He came to Orleans and did all he could to capture it by launching a fierce assault with his battering-rams. At that time the Bishop of Orleans was the saintly Anianus, a man of great wisdom and admirable holiness, the story of whose miracles has been faithfully handed down to us. The besieged inhabitants begged their Bishop to tell them what to do. Putting his trust in God, he advised them to prostrate themselves in prayer and with tears to implore the help of the Lord, which is always present in time of need. As they carried out his orders and prayed to the Almighty the Bishop said: 'Keep a watch from the city wall, to see if God in his pity is sending us help.' His hope was that, through God's compassion, Aetius might be advancing, for Anianus had gone to interview that leader in Arles when he foresaw what was going to happen. They watched out from the wall, but they saw no one. 'Pray in all faith,' said Anianus, 'for this day the Lord will deliver you.' They continued their prayers. 'Look out a second time,' said the Bishop. They peered out, but they saw no one bringing help. The Bishop said a third time: 'If you continue to pray in faith, God will come quickly.' With much weeping and lamentation, they begged for God's succour. When their prayer was finished, they were ordered by the old man to look out a third time. Far away they saw what looked like a cloud of dust rising from the ground. This they reported to the Bishop. 'It is the help sent by God,' said he. The walls were already rocking under the shock of the battering-rams and about to collapse when Aetius arrived, and with him Theodoric,

17. A.D. 451.

the King of the Goths, and his son Thorismund. They hastened
forward to the city with their armies and drove off the enemy
and forced them to retreat. Orleans was thus saved by the
prayers of its saintly Bishop. They put Attila to flight, but he
made his way to the plain of Moirey and there drew up his
forces for battle. When they learned this, they bravely prepared
to attack him.

Soon afterwards the rumour reached Rome that Aetius was
in great danger with the troops of the enemy all round him.
When she heard this his wife was very anxious and distressed.
She went frequently to the churches of the holy Apostles and
prayed that she might have her husband back safe from this
campaign. This she did by day and by night. One night a poor
man, sodden with wine, was asleep in a corner of the church of
Saint Peter. When the great doorways were closed according to
custom, he was not noticed by the porters. In the middle of the
night he got up. He was dazzled by the lamps shining bright in
every part of the building and he looked everywhere for the
exit, so that he could make his escape. He tugged at the bolts of
first one doorway and then another, but, when he found that
they were all closed, he lay down on the floor and anxiously
awaited an opportunity of escaping from the building at the
moment when the people should come together for their morning hymns. Then he noticed two men who saluted each other
with great respect and asked how the other was prospering in his
affairs. The older of the two began as follows: 'I cannot bear
any longer the tears of the wife of Aetius. She keeps on praying
that I should bring her husband back safe from Gaul. God in
His wisdom has decreed otherwise, but nevertheless I have obtained this immense concession that Aetius shall not be killed.
Now I am hurrying off to bring him back alive. I order the man
who has overheard this to keep his counsel and not be so rash as
to reveal my secret, for otherwise he will die immediately.' The
poor man, of course, heard this, but he was not able to keep the
secret. As soon as day dawned in the sky, he recounted what he
had heard to the wife of Aetius. He had no sooner finished
speaking when he became blind.

Meanwhile Aetius and his allies the Goths and the Franks
had joined battle with Attila. When he saw that his army was
being exterminated, Attila fled from the battlefield. Theodoric,
the King of the Goths, was killed in this conflict. No one has
any doubt that the army of the Huns was really routed by the
prayers of the Bishop about whom I have told you; but it was
the patrician Aetius, with the help of Thorismund, who gained
the victory and destroyed the enemy. When the battle was over,
Aetius said to Thorismund: 'Now you must go back home
quickly, for otherwise you will be cheated out of your father's
kingdom by the machinations of your brother.' Thorismund
hurried off as soon as he received this advice, hoping to forestall
his brother and to occupy their father's throne before him. By a
similar stratagem Aetius persuaded the King of the Franks to
leave. As soon as they had both gone, Aetius collected all the
booty lying about on the field of battle and set off with it for
home.

Attila retreated with the few men left to him. Soon after
Aquileia was captured, burnt and destroyed by the Huns, who
roamed all over Italy and laid waste to the country. Thorismund, about whom I have been telling you, conquered the
Alani in battle. Later on, after many disputes and wars, he was
beaten by his brothers, who had him garrotted.

8.   Now that I have explained all this and set out in proper
order certain facts about Aetius, it seems only right that I
should tell you what the *Historia* of Renatus Frigeridus has to
say about him.[18] In Book XII he describes how after the death
of the deified Honorius the five-year-old boy Valentinian was
made Emperor by his cousin Theodosius. In Rome the tyrant
John usurped the imperial power, but the envoys whom he sent
to Valentinian were treated by him with contempt. Renatus
Frigeridus adds:

   While these things were taking place, the envoys came back to the
tyrant and duly reported the insults sent by Valentinian. John was

   18. The *Historia* of Renatus Profuturus Frigeridus has been lost. See
Introduction, p. 28.

incensed and sent Aetius, who was then Governor of the Palace, to the Huns with a great sum in gold, for they were already well-known to him from the days when he was their hostage, and they still accepted him as their friend. Aetius bore the following message: as soon as the enemy troops had entered Italy, the Huns were to attack them from the rear and he himself would come to meet them as they advanced. Since there is so much to be related later on about the man Aetius, I must tell you about his family and his character. His father was Gaudentius, a man of no mean rank in the province of Scythia, who had begun his career in the Praetorian Guard and who rose to the high position of Master of the Horse. His mother was an Italian noblewoman of vast possessions. Their son Aetius, who was admitted to the Praetorian Guard while still a youth, spent three years in the hands of Alaric as a hostage, and then was passed on to the Huns. Later in life he became the son-in-law of Carpilio, one-time Head of the Imperial Household and then Governor of the Palace. Aetius was of medium height, manly in his habits and well-proportioned. He had no bodily infirmity and was spare in physique. His intelligence was keen, he was full of energy, a superb horseman, a fine shot with an arrow and tireless with the lance. He was extremely able as a soldier and he was skilled in the arts of peace. There was no avarice in him and even less cupidity. He was magnanimous in his behaviour and never swayed in his judgement by the advice of unworthy counsellors. He bore adversity with great patience, was ready for any exacting enterprise, he scorned danger and was able to endure hunger, thirst and loss of sleep. From his earliest youth it was clear that he was destined by fate to hold high position and that much would be heard of him when his time came and occasion offered.

That is what Renatus Frigeridus has to say about Aetius. When the Emperor Valentinian became a grown man he was afraid that in his desire for supreme power Aetius might destroy him, and he therefore had him killed, although there was no open charge which he could level against him. Not long afterwards, when Valentinian was seated in the Campus Martius and haranguing the people from his dais, a certain Occila, the trumpeter of Aetius, came up to him and ran him through with his sword. So these two men perished, each in his turn.

9.   Many people do not even know the name of the first King of the Franks. The *Historia* of Sulpicius Alexander[19] gives many details about them, while Valentinus does not name their first King but says that they were ruled by war-leaders. What Sulpicius Alexander says about the Franks seems to be worth quoting. He tells how Maximus gave up all hope of the imperial throne, lost his reason and went to live in Aquileia. Then he adds:

At that time the Franks invaded the Roman province of Germania under their leaders Genobaud, Marcomer and Sunno. As these Franks crossed the frontier, many of the inhabitants were slaughtered and they ravaged the most fertile areas. The townsfolk of Cologne were terrified: and, when this news reached Trier, Nanninus and Quintinus, who commanded the Roman armies and to whom Maximus had entrusted his infant son and the defence of Gaul, collected their troops together and marched to that city. The enemy, who were heavily laden with booty, for they had pillaged the richest parts of the province, crossed back over the Rhine, but left many of their men behind in Roman territory, where they were planning to continue their ravaging. The Romans found it easy to deal with these, and a great number of Franks were cut down in the forest of Charbonnière. After this success, the Roman leaders held a meeting to decide whether or not they should cross into Frankish territory. Nanninus refused to do so, for he knew that the Franks were waiting for them and that on their own soil they would undoubtedly be much the stronger. This did not meet with the approval of Quintinus and the other military leaders, and so Nanninus retreated to Mainz. Quintinus crossed the Rhine somewhere near the fortress of Neuss with his army. After two days' march away from the river, he attacked a number of dwellings abandoned by their inhabitants and a few townships of no mean size, which were, however, deserted. The Franks had pretended to retire in panic and had withdrawn into the remote woodland regions, all round which they had erected barricades of forest trees. The Roman soldiers burned down all the houses, imagining in their cowardly stupidity that by doing so they had gained a conclusive victory: then they spent an anxious night without daring to take off their heavy equipment. At first light they marched out into the woods, with Quintinus

19. The *Historia* of Sulpicius Alexander has been lost.

to lead them in battle. By about mid-day they had lost themselves completely in a maze of pathways and had no idea where they were. They ran up against an endless barricade solidly constructed from huge tree-trunks, and then they tried to break out over the marshy fields which bordered the forests. Here and there enemy troops showed themselves, standing on the boles of trees or climbing about on the barricades as if on the ramparts of turrets. They kept shooting arrows as if from war-catapults, and these they smeared with poisons distilled from plants, so that wounds which did little more than graze the skin and touched no vital organ were followed by death against which there was no protection. Then the Roman army, now surrounded by the main force of the enemy, rushed desperately into the open meadows, which the Franks had left unoccupied. There the cavalry was bogged down in marshland and the bodies of men and animals, all mixed up together, were borne to the ground in one common catastrophe. Such infantry as was not trodden under foot by the heavy horses was caught in thick mud from which the men had difficulty in lifting one foot after the other. With fear in their hearts they rushed back to hide in the very woodlands out of which they had marched only a short time before. As the legions were cut down the ranks were broken. Heraclius, tribune of the Jovinian Legion, and almost all the officers were wiped out. Darkness and the deep recesses of the forests offered safety and refuge to a few survivors.

That is what Sulpicius Alexander had to say in Book III of his *Historia*.

In Book IV, when he is describing the murder of Victor, the son of the tyrant Maximus, he says:

At that time Carietto and Sirus, appointed in the place of Nanninus, were stationed in the province of Germania with an army collected to oppose the Franks.

A little further on, after stating that the Franks had gone home laden with booty from Germania, he goes on:

Arbogast, who would brook no delay, urged the Emperor to inflict due punishment on the Franks unless they immediately restored all the plunder which they had seized the previous year when the legions were slaughtered, and unless they surrendered the warmongers who had been responsible for such a treacherous violation of peace.

He says that these events occurred at a time when the Franks were ruled by war-leaders. Then he continues:

A few days later there was a short parley with Marcomer and Sunno, the royal leaders of the Franks. Hostages were insisted upon, as was the custom, and then Arbogast retired into winter quarters in Trier.

When he says 'regales' or royal leaders, it is not clear if they were kings or if they merely exercised a kingly function. When he is recording the straits to which the Emperor Valentinian was reduced, he says:

When these events were taking place in the East in Thrace, the government was in great difficulty in Gaul. The Emperor Valentinian was shut in the palace in Vienne and reduced almost to the status of a private citizen. The control of the army was handed over to Frankish mercenaries and the civil administration was in the control of Arbogast's accomplices. There was not one among all those who were bound by their military oath of obedience to him who dared to obey the private orders let alone the public commands of the Emperor.

He goes on:

That same year Arbogast, urged on by tribal hatred, went in search of Sunno and Marcomer, the kinglets of the Franks. He came to Cologne in the full blast of winter, for he knew well that all the retreats of Frankland could be penetrated and burnt out now that the leaves were off the trees and that the bare and sapless forests could offer no concealment for an ambushed foe. He therefore collected an army together, crossed the River Rhine, and laid waste the land nearest to the bank, where the Bructeri lived, and the region occupied by the Chamavi. He did this without meeting any opposition, except that a few Amsivarii and Chatti showed themselves on the far-distant ridges of the hills, with Marcomer as their war-leader.

A few pages further on, having given up all talk of 'duces' and 'regales', he states clearly that the Franks had a king, but he forgets to tell us what his name was.

The next thing which happened was that the tyrant Eugenius led a military expedition as far as the frontier marked by the Rhine. He renewed the old traditional treaties with the kings of the Alamanni and the Franks, and he paraded his army, which was immense for that time, before their savage tribesmen.

So much for the information which this chronicler Sulpicius Alexander has to give us about the Franks.

As for Renatus Profuturus Frigeridus, whom I mentioned above, when he comes to tell us how Rome was captured and destroyed by the Goths, he writes:

Meanwhile Goar had gone over to the Romans, and Respendial, the King of the Alani, therefore withdrew his forces from the Rhine. The Vandals were hard-pressed in their war against the Franks, their King Godigisel was killed and about twenty thousand of their front-line troops had been slaughtered, so that, if the army of the Alani had not come to their rescue in time, the entire nation of Vandals would have been wiped out.

It is an extraordinary thing that, although he tells us about the kings of these various peoples, including the Franks, when he describes how Constantine, who had become a tyrant, summoned his son Constans to come from Spain to meet him, he goes on:

The tyrant Constantine summoned his son Constans, who was also a tyrant, from Spain, so that they might confer together about affairs of state. As a result Constans left his wife and the administrative affairs of his court in Saragossa, entrusted all his interests in Spain to Gerontius and hurried to meet his father by forced marches. They duly met. Quite a few days passed, but no news arrived from Italy to disturb Constantine. He therefore returned to his daily round of over-drinking and over-eating, and told his son that he might as well go back to Spain. No sooner had Constans sent his troops on ahead, while he himself lingered a little longer with his father, than messengers arrived from Spain to say that Gerontius had proclaimed Maximus, one of his own dependants, as

Emperor. Maximus was supported by a horde of troops collected from various barbarian tribes and he was ready for any contingency. Constans and the Prefect Decimus Rusticus, one-time Master of the Offices, were very frightened by this news. They sent Edobech to contain the people of Germania and they themselves set out for Gaul, with the Franks, the Alamanni and a whole band of soldiery, intending to return to Constantine as soon as they could.

Later on, when he describes how Constantine was besieged, he adds:

Constantine had been beleaguered for about four months when messengers arrived all of a sudden from northern Gaul to announce that Jovinus had assumed the rank of Emperor and was about to attack the besieging forces with the Burgundes, the Alamanni, the Franks, the Alani and a large army. Things then moved very quickly. The city gates were opened and Constantine came out. He was immediately packed off to Italy, but the Emperor sent a band of assassins to meet him and he was beheaded up on the River Mincio.

After a few more sentences, Frigeridus goes on:

At the same time Decimus Rusticus, the Prefect of the tyrants, Agroetius, one-time Head of Chancery of Jovinus, and many other noblemen were captured by the army commanders of Honorius and cruelly put to death. The city of Trier was sacked and burnt by the Franks in a second attack.

He notes that Asterius was made a patrician by a patent signed by the Emperor and then he continues:

At this time Castinus, Master of the Imperial Household, was sent to Gaul, as a campaign had been begun against the Franks.

That concludes what these two historians have to say about the Franks.

In Book VII of his work the chronicler Orosius adds the following information:

Stilicho took command of an army, crushed the Franks, crossed the Rhine, made his way across Gaul and came finally to the Pyrenees.

The historians whose works we still have give us all this information about the Franks, but they never record the names of their kings. It is commonly said that the Franks came originally from Pannonia and first colonized the banks of the Rhine. Then they crossed the river, marched through Thuringia, and set up in each country district and each city long-haired kings chosen from the foremost and most noble family of their race. As I shall show you later, this is proved by the victories won by Clovis. We read in the consular lists that Theudemer, King of the Franks, son of Richemer, and his mother Ascyla, were executed with the sword. They also say that Clodio, a man of high birth and marked ability among his people, was King of the Franks and that he lived in the castle of Duisburg in Thuringian territory.[20] In those parts, that is towards the south, the Romans occupied the territory as far as the River Loire. Beyond the Loire the Goths were in command. The Burgundes, who believed in the Arian heresy, lived across the Rhône, which flows through the city of Lyons. Clodio sent spies to the town of Cambrai. When they had discovered all that they needed to know, he himself followed and crushed the Romans and captured the town. He lived there only a short time and then occupied the country up to the River Somme. Some say that Merovech, the father of Childeric, was descended from Clodio.

10. This particular race of people seems always to have followed idolatrous practices, for they did not recognize the true God. They fashioned idols for themselves out of the creatures of the woodlands and the waters, out of birds and beasts: these they worshipped in the place of God, and to these they made their sacrifices. If only the inner recesses of their hearts could have been moved by that awe-inspiring Voice which spoke to the people through Moses! 'Thou shalt have no other Gods before me,' it said. 'Thou shalt not make unto thee any graven image, or any likeness of any thing that is in heaven above, or

20. See on p. 18 of the Introduction the line of descent of the Merovingian Kings down to **Dagobert.**

that is in the earth beneath, or that is in the water under the earth. Thou shalt not bow down thyself to them, nor serve them.'[21] 'Thou shalt fear the Lord thy God,' said the Voice, 'and serve him, and shalt swear by his name.'[22] If only they could have known what vengeance pursued and crushed the people of Israel for having worshipped the molten calf, after all the feasting and the songs, after the wantonness and the dancing, when with their lips defiled they said of this graven image: 'These be thy gods, O Israel, which brought thee up out of the land of Egypt.'[23] Twenty-four thousand of the Israelites perished. What of those who were initiated into the worship of Belphegor and who fornicated with the women of Moab and were cut down and slaughtered by their own people? In this massacre, when all the others were destroyed, the priest Phineas appeased the wrath of God, 'and so the plague was stayed'.[24] If only their ears had heard the words which the Lord thundered forth through the mouth of David, saying: 'For all the gods of the nations are idols: but the Lord made the heavens.'[25] 'The idols of the heathen are silver and gold, the work of men's hands,'[26] He said in another passage. 'They that make them are like unto them: so is every one that trusteth in them.'[27] We also read: 'Confounded be all they that serve graven images, that boast themselves of idols.'[28] The prophet Habakkuk gives this testimony: 'What profiteth the graven image that the maker thereof hath graven it; the molten image, and a teacher of lies, that the maker of his work trusteth therein, to make dumb idols? Woe unto him that saith to the wood, Awake; to the dumb stone, Arise, it shall teach! Behold, it is laid over with gold and silver, and there is no breath at all in the midst of it. But the Lord is in his holy temple: let all the earth keep silence before him.'[29] To this another prophet adds: 'The gods that have not made the heavens and the earth, even they shall perish from the earth and from under those

---

21. Exodus 20, 3–5.   22. Deuteronomy 6, 13.   23. Exodus 32, 4.
24. Psalms 106, 30.   25. Psalms 95, 5.   26. Psalms 135, 15.
27. Psalms 135, 18.   28. Psalms 97, 7.   29. Habakkuk 2, 18–20.

heavens.'[30] In one place we read: 'For thus saith the Lord that created the heavens: God himself that formed the earth and made it; he hath established it, he created it not in vain, he formed it to be inhabited ... I am the Lord: that is my name: and my glory will I not give to another, neither my praise to graven images.'[31] Elsewhere we find: 'Are there any among the vanities of the Gentiles that can cause rain?'[32] The following passage is in Isaiah: 'I am the first and I am the last; and beside me there is no God ... Is there a God beside me? – yea, there is no God; I know not any. They that make a graven image are all of them vanity; and their delectable things shall not profit; and they are their own witnesses; they see not, nor know; that they may be ashamed ... Behold, all his fellows shall be ashamed: and the workmen, they are of men ... The smith with the tongs both worketh in the coals and fashioneth it with hammers, and worketh it with the strength of his arms ... The carpenter ... marketh it out with the compasses, and maketh it after the figure of a man, according to the beauty of a man; that it may remain in the house. He heweth him down cedars ... yea, he maketh a god, and worshippeth it ... with nails and hammers hath he constructed it, that it be not broken asunder. They are carried because they cannot walk ... He burneth part thereof in the fire, and they warmeth themselves ... And the residue thereof he maketh a god, even his graven image: he falleth down unto it, and worshippeth it, and prayeth unto it, and saith, Deliver me; for thou art my god ... I have burned part of it in the fire; yea, also I have baked bread upon the coals thereof; I have roasted flesh, and eaten it; and shall I make the residue thereof an abomination? – shall I fall down to the stock of a tree? A part of it is burnt to ashes. A deceived heart hath turned him aside, that he cannot deliver his soul, nor say, Is there not a lie in my right hand?'[33]

At first the Frankish people knew nothing of all this; but they learned it later, as my *Historia* will tell in its later chapters.

30. Jeremiah 10, 11.   31. Isaiah 45, 18.
32. Jeremiah 14, 22.   33. Isaiah 44, 6–20.

11. The Senator Avitus, who, as is well known, came from Clermont-Ferrand, succeeded in becoming Emperor, but his way of life was too libidinous, and he was deposed by the other Senators. Later he was ordained bishop at Piacenza. When he discovered that the Senate was still hostile to him and wished to have him killed, he set out for the church of Saint Julian, the martyr of Clermont, taking with him many gifts. On the journey he died and his body was carried to the village of Brioude, where it was buried at the foot of the above-named martyr. Avitus was succeeded by Maiorianus, and in Gaul the Roman Aegidius was appointed as commander of the armies.

12. Childeric, King of the Franks, whose private life was one long debauch, began to seduce the daughters of his subjects. They were so incensed about this that they forced him to give up his throne. He discovered that they intended to assassinate him and he fled to Thuringia. He left behind a close friend of his who was able to soothe the minds of his angry subjects with his honeyed words. Childeric entrusted to him a token which should indicate when he might return to his homeland. They broke a gold coin into two equal halves. Childeric took one half with him and the friend kept the other half. 'When I send my half to you,' said this friend, 'and the two halves placed together make a complete coin, you will know that you may return home safe and sound.' Childeric then set out for Thuringia and took refuge with King Bisinus and his wife Basina. As soon as Childeric had gone, the Franks unanimously chose as their king that same Aegidius who, as I have already said, had been sent from Rome as commander of the armies. When Aegidius had reigned over the Franks for eight years, Childeric's faithful friend succeeded in pacifying them secretly and he sent messengers to the exile with the half of the broken coin which he had in his possession. By this token Childeric knew for sure that the Franks wanted him back, indeed that they were clamouring for him to return, and he left Thuringia and was restored to his throne. Now that Bisinus and Childeric were both kings, Queen

Basina, about whom I have told you, deserted her husband and joined Childeric. He questioned her closely as to why she had come from far away to be with him, and she is said to have answered: 'I know that you are a strong man and I recognize ability when I see it. I have therefore come to live with you. You can be sure that if I knew anyone else, even far across the sea, who was more capable than you, I should have sought him out and gone to live with him instead.' This pleased Childeric very much and he married her. She became pregnant and bore a son whom she called Clovis. He was a great man and became a famous soldier.

13.   After the death of Saint Arthemius, Venerandus, a man of senatorial rank, was consecrated as Bishop of Clermont-Ferrand. Paulinus gives us information as to what sort of a man this Bishop was:

> Today when you see Bishops as worthy of the Lord as Emperius of Toulouse, Simplicius of Vienne, Amandus of Bordeaux, Diogenianus of Albi, Venerandus of Clermont, Alithius of Cahors and now Pegasus of Périgueux, you will see that we have excellent guardians of all our faith and religion, however great may be the evils of our age.[34]

Venerandus is said to have died on Christmas Eve. The next morning the Christmas procession was also his funeral cortège. After his death the most shameful argument arose among the local inhabitants concerning the election of a bishop to replace him. Different factions were formed some of which wanted this man and others that, and there was great dissension among the people. One Sunday when the electing bishops were sitting in conclave, a woman wearing a veil over her head to mark the fact that she was a true servant of God came boldly in and said: 'Listen to me, priests of the Lord! You must realize that it is true that not one of those whom they have put forward for the bishopric finds favour in the sight of God. This very day the Lord in person will choose Himself a bishop. Do not inflame

34. The source of this quotation has not been traced.

the people or allow any more argument among them, but be patient for a little while, for the Lord will now send to us the man who is to rule over our church.' As they sat wondering at her words, there came in a man called Rusticus, who was himself a priest of the diocese of this city of Clermont-Ferrand. He was the very man who had been pointed out to the woman in a vision. As soon as she set eyes on him she cried: 'That is the man whom the Lord elects! That is the man whom He has chosen to be your bishop! That is the man whom you must consecrate!' As she spoke the entire population forgot all its previous disagreement and shouted that this was the correct and proper choice. To the great joy of the populace Rusticus was set on the episcopial throne and inducted as Bishop. He was the seventh to be made Bishop in Clermont-Ferrand.

14.*   In the city of Tours Bishop Eustochius died in the seventeenth year of his episcopate. Perpetuus was consecrated in his place, being the fifth bishop after Saint Martin. When Perpetuus saw how frequently miracles were being performed at Saint Martin's tomb and when he observed how small was the chapel erected over the Saint's body, he decided that it was unworthy of these wonders. He had the chapel removed and he built in its place the great church which is still there some five hundred and fifty yards outside the city. It is one hundred and sixty feet long by sixty feet broad; and its height up to the beginning of the vaulting is forty-five feet. It has thirty-two windows in the sanctuary and twenty in the nave, with forty-one columns. In the whole building there are fifty-two windows, one hundred and twenty columns and eight doorways, three in the sanctuary and five in the nave. The great festival of the church has a threefold significance: it marks the dedication of the building, the translation of the Saint's body and his ordination as a bishop. You should observe this feast-day on 4 July; and you should remember that Saint Martin died on 11 November. If you celebrate this faithfully you will gain the protection of the saintly Bishop in this world and the next. The vault of the tiny chapel which stood there before was most elegantly designed, and so Bishop Perpetuus thought it wrong to destroy it. He built another church in honour of the blessed Apostles Peter and Paul, and he fitted this vault over it. He built many other churches which still stand firm today in the name of Christ.

15.* At this time the church of the blessed martyr Symphorian of Autun was built by the priest Eufronius, and later on Eufronius was elected as Bishop of that city. It was he who, in great devotion, sent the marble lid which covers the tomb of Saint Martin.

16.* After the death of Bishop Rusticus, Saint Namatius became the eighth Bishop of Clermont-Ferrand. It was he who built by his effort the church which still stands and which is considered to be the oldest within the city walls. It is one hundred and fifty feet long, sixty feet wide inside the nave and fifty feet high as far as the vaulting. It has a rounded apse at the end, and two wings of elegant design on either side.The whole building is constructed in the shape of a cross. It has forty-two windows, seventy columns and eight doorways. In it one is conscious of the fear of God and of a great brightness, and those at prayer are often aware of a most sweet and aromatic odour which is being wafted towards them. Round the sanctuary it has walls which are decorated with mosaic work made of many varieties of marble. When the building had been finished for a dozen years, the saintly Bishop sent priests to Bologna, the city in Italy, to procure for him the relics of Saint Agricola and Saint Vitalis, who, as I have shown, were assuredly crucified in the name of Christ our Lord.[35]

17.* The wife of Namatius built the church of Saint Stephen in the suburb outside the walls of Clermont-Ferrand. She wanted it to be decorated with coloured frescoes. She used to hold in her lap a book from which she would read stories of events which happened long ago, and tell the workmen what she

35. *Liber in Gloria Martyrum Beatorum* (*GM*), 43.

wanted painted on the walls. One day as she was sitting in the church and reading these stories, there came a poor man to pray. He saw her in her black dress, a woman already far advanced in age. He thought that she was one of the needy, so he produced a piece of bread, put it in her lap and went on his way. She did not scorn the gift of this poor man, who had not understood who she was. She took it, and thanked him, and put it on one side. She ate it instead of her other food and each day she received a blessing from it until it was all eaten up.

18.   Childeric fought a battle at Orleans. Odovacar with his Saxons penetrated as far as Angers. A great pestilence caused the death of many people. Aegidius died and left a son called Syagrius. After the death of Aegidius, Odovacar took hostages from Angers and other places. The Bretons were expelled from Bourges by the Goths and many were killed at Bourg-de-Déols. Count Paul, who had Roman and Frankish troops under his command, attacked the Goths and seized booty from them. Odovacar reached Angers, but King Childeric arrived there on the following day: Count Paul was killed and Childeric occupied the city. On that day the church-house was burnt down in a great fire.

19.   While these things were happening a great war was waged between the Saxons and the Romans. The Saxons fled and many of their men were cut down by the Romans who pursued them. Their islands[36] were captured and laid waste by the Franks, and many people were killed. In the ninth month of that year there was an earthquake. Odovacar made a treaty with Childeric and together they subdued the Alamanni, who had invaded a part of Italy.

20.   During the fourteenth year of his reign Euric, King of the Goths, put Duke Victorius in charge of the seven cities. Victorius went straight to Clermont-Ferrand and made certain ad-

36. These were islands in the River Loire between Saumur and Angers which had been occupied by piratical bands of Saxons.

ditions to the city. The underground chapels which he
constructed are still there today. It was he who had erected
in the church of Saint Julian the columns which are still part of
the building. He also built the church of Saint Lawrence and
the church of Saint Germanus in Saint-Germain-Lanbron.
Victorius was nine years in Clermont. He spread a number of
scandalous rumours about the Senator Eucherius. Eucherius
was thrown into prison. In the middle of the night Victorius had
him brought out, he was attached to an old wall and then Victorius had the wall knocked down on top of him. Victorius was
far too much given to irregular affairs with women. He was
afraid of being assassinated by the men of Clermont and he fled
to Rome. There he began to live the same loose life and he was
stoned to death. Euric reigned for another four years after the
death of Victorius. He died in the twenty-seventh year of his
reign. There again occurred a big earthquake.

21.*   When Bishop Namatius died in Clermont-Ferrand, Eparchius succeeded him. He was a most saintly and devout man. At
that time the church had very little property inside the city walls.
The Bishop had his lodging in what is now called the sacristy.
He was in the habit of getting up in the middle of the night to
give thanks to God before the high altar in his cathedral. One
night it happened that as he went into the church he found it
full of devils and Satan himself sitting on his own episcopal
throne made up to look like a painted woman. 'You hideous
prostitute,' said the Bishop, 'is it not enough that you infect
other places with every imaginable sort of foulness, without
your defiling the throne consecrated to the Lord by sitting your
revolting body down on it? Leave the house of God this
instant and stop polluting it with your presence!' 'Since you give
me the title of prostitute,' said Satan, 'I will see that you yourself are constantly harassed with sexual desire.' As he said this he
disappeared into thin air. It is true that the Bishop was tempted
by the lusts of the flesh, but he was protected by the sign of the
Cross and the Devil was unable to harm him.

According to all accounts it was Eparchius who built the

monastery on the top of Mont Chantoin, where the oratory now is, and there he would go into retreat during the holy days of Lent. On the day of the Lord's Supper he would process down to his cathedral, escorted by his clergy and the townsfolk, and accompanied by a great singing of psalms.

When Eparchius died he was succeeded by Sidonius Apollinaris, one-time Prefect of the City, a man of most noble birth as honours are counted in this world, and one of the leading Senators of Gaul, so noble indeed that he married the daughter of the Emperor Avitus. In his time, while Victorius, about whom I have already told you, was still in Clermont, there lived in the monastery of Saint-Cyr in the same city an abbot called Abraham, who, thanks to his predecessor and namesake, was greatly distinguished by his faith and good works, as I have told you in my other book where his life is recorded.[37]

22.* The saintly Sidonius was so eloquent that he would often speak extempore in public without hesitating in the slightest and express whatever he had to say with the greatest clarity. One day it happened that he went to the monastery church of which I have told you, for he had been invited there for a festival. Some malicious person removed the book with which it was his habit to conduct the church service. Sidonius was so well versed in the ritual that he took them through the whole service of the festival without pausing for a moment. This was a source of wonder to everyone present and they had the impression that it must be an angel speaking rather than a man. I have described this in more detail in the preface of the book which I wrote about the Masses composed by Sidonius.[38] He was a very saintly man and, as I have said, a member of one of the foremost senatorial families. Without saying anything to his wife he would remove silver vessels from his home and give them away to the poor. When she found out what he had done, she used to grumble at him; then he would buy the silver vessels back from the poor folk and bring them home again.

37. *VP*, 3.   38. This book has been lost.

23.*   At the time when Sidonius was living a saintly life here
on earth and was completely devoted to the service of the Lord,
two priests rebelled against him. They removed from him all
control over the property of his church, reduced him to a very
straitened way of life and submitted him to every kind of
contumely. God in His clemency did not permit this insult to go
long unpunished. One of these two insidious men, who was
unworthy to be called by the name of priest, had threatened the
night before to drag Sidonius out of his own church. When he
got up the next morning on hearing the bell which called to
matins, this man was full of spite against the holy man of God,
and was busy turning over in his mind how he could best carry
out a plan which he had formed the previous evening. He went
off to the lavatory and while he was occupied in emptying his
bowels he lost his soul instead. A boy was waiting outside with a
candle, expecting his master to emerge at any moment. Day
dawned. His accomplice, the other priest, sent someone to see
what had happened. 'Come quickly,' said the messenger, 'don't
hang about in there any longer, we must do together what we
planned yesterday.' The dead man gave no answer. The boy
lifted up the curtain of the lavatory and found his master dead
on the seat. From this we may deduce that this man was guilty
of a crime no less serious than that of Arius, who in the same
way emptied out his entrails through his back passage in the
lavatory. This, too, smacks of heresy, that one of God's bishops
should not be obeyed in his own church, the man to whom had
been entrusted the task of feeding God's flock, and that someone else to whom nothing at all had been entrusted, either by
God or by man, should have dared to usurp his authority.

After that the saintly Bishop, to whom, mark you, there still
remained one of his two enemies, was restored to his authority.
Some time later Sidonius fell ill with a very high temperature.
He ordered his attendants to carry him into the church. He was
borne inside and a great crowd of men and women, and of little
children, too, gathered round him, weeping and saying: 'Good
shepherd, why are you deserting us? To whom will you abandon us, your orphan children? If you die, what sort of life can

we expect? Will there be anyone left to season our lives with the salt of wisdom and to inspire in us the fear of the Lord's name with the same insight which you have shown?' The citizens of Clermont wept as they said these things and others like them. Finally Bishop Sidonius answered them, for the Holy Spirit moved him to do so. 'Do not be afraid, my people,' said he. 'My brother Aprunculus is still alive and he will be your Bishop.' Those who were present did not understand him, and they thought that he was wandering in his mind.

After the death of Sidonius, the evil priest, the second of the two, the one who was still alive, blinded with greed, immediately laid hands on the property of the church, as if he were already bishop. 'God has at last taken notice of me,' said he, 'for He knows that I am more just than Sidonius and He has granted me this power.' He rode proudly through the whole city. On the Sunday following the death of the holy Bishop, this priest prepared a feast in the church-house and ordered all the townspeople to be invited. He showed no respect for the senior among them, but took his place at table first. The cup-bearer passed him a goblet of wine and said: 'My lord, I have just seen a vision and this I will describe to you, if you permit. I saw it this very Sunday evening. I perceived a great hall, and in this hall there was placed a throne, and on this throne there sat a man, a sort of judge who seemed to have authority over everyone else present. A great throng of priests in white garments stood round him, and there were immense crowds of people of all sorts, so many that I could not count them. While I watched, and trembled as I watched, I saw the blessed Sidonius standing far off as if on a dais, and he was rebuking that dear friend of yours, the priest who died some years ago. The priest was worsted in this argument, and the King had him shut up in the deepest and smallest dungeon. When he had been put away, Sidonius turned on you, saying that you had been implicated in the crime for which the other had just been condemned. Then the judge began to make urgent inquiries to find someone whom he could send to you. I hid myself in the crowd and stood well back, holding my own counsel, for fear that I myself should be sent, for after all I know you very well. While I stood silent and lost in thought everyone else disappeared and I was left all alone in this public place. The judge called me forward and I went up to him. At the sight of him in all his dignity and splendour I lost control of myself and began to sway on my feet from sheer panic. "Do not be afraid, my boy," said he. "Go and tell that priest: 'Be present to answer the charge, for Sidonius has stipulated that you be summoned.'" You must go quickly, for the King commanded me to say what I have said, and he made this dire threat to me: "If you do not speak you will die a frightful death." ' As his servant said this the priest fell down dead on the spot and the goblet slid out of his hand. He was picked up dead from the couch on which he was reclining, and they buried him and so despatched him to join his accomplice in hell. The Lord passed this earthly judgement on those two unruly priests: one suffered the fate of Arius, and the other was dashed headlong from the very summit of his pride, like Simon Magus at the behest of the holy Apostle. No one can doubt that these two who plotted together against their holy Bishop now have their place side by side in nethermost hell.

Meanwhile rumours of the approach of the Franks were being repeated on all sides in these regions and everyone looked forward with great excitement to the moment when they would take over the government. Saint Aprunculus, the Bishop of the city of Langres, had fallen into ill-favour with the Burgundes. The hatred which they bore him became daily more bitter and an order went out that he should be executed in secret. This came to his ears and one night he was lowered down from the walls of Dijon. He escaped to Clermont-Ferrand and in accordance with the word of God, placed in the mouth of Sidonius, he became the eleventh bishop of that city.

24.   In the days of Bishop Sidonius there was a great famine in Burgundy. The inhabitants were widely scattered over the countryside and there was nobody to distribute food to the poor. Then Ecdicius, one of the Senators and a close relative of Sidonius, with the help of God found a wonderful solution. He

sent his servants with horses and carts through the neighbouring cities and brought in those who were suffering from starvation. They went out and collected all the poor and needy they could find and brought them in to where Ecdicius lived. Throughout the long period of famine he provided them with food and so saved them from dying of hunger. There were, so they say, more than four thousand of them, both men and women. When the time of plenty returned, he arranged transport home again for them and took each man and woman back to where he or she lived. After they had gone a voice was heard from Heaven, saying to him: 'Ecdicius, Ecdicius, because you have done this thing you and your descendants shall never lack food; for you have obeyed my word and by feeding the poor you have stayed my hunger, too.' Many witnesses have reported how swift this Ecdicius was to take action. There is a story that he once repelled a strong force of Goths with only ten men to help him. Saint Patiens, Bishop of Lyons, is said to have succoured his people in just the same way during the famine. There is still in existence a letter written by Saint Sidonius in which he praises Patiens very highly for this.

25. At the same time Euric, King of the Goths, crossed the Spanish frontier and began a terrible persecution of the Christians in Gaul. Without more ado he cut off the heads of all who would not subscribe to his heretical opinions, he imprisoned the priests, and the bishops he either drove into exile or had executed. He ordered the doorways of the churches to be blocked with briers so that the very difficulty of finding one's way in might encourage men to forget their Christian faith. It was mainly the district between the River Garonne and the Pyrenees and the towns of the two Aquitaines which suffered from this violent attack.[39] We still possess a letter by the noble Sidonius written to Bishop Basilus about this, in which he gives full

39. The district between the Garonne and the Pyrenees, then known as Novempopulana, is now Gascony. The 'two Aquitaines', Aquitania Prima and Aquitania Secunda, are the district between the River Garonne and the River Loire.

details.[40] Soon afterwards the persecutor died, struck down by the vengeance of God.

26.* Not long afterwards Saint Perpetuus, Bishop of the city of Tours, reached the end of his life, having been bishop for thirty years. Volusianus, a man of senatorial rank, was appointed in his place. He was regarded with suspicion by the Goths. In the seventh year of his episcopate he was dragged off as a captive to Spain and there he soon died. Verus succeeded him and was ordained as the seventh Bishop after Saint Martin.

27. The next thing which happened was that Childeric died. His son Clovis replaced him on the throne. In the fifth year of his reign Syagrius, the King of the Romans[11] and the son of Aegidius, was living in the city of Soissons, where Aegidius himself used to have his residence. Clovis marched against him with his blood-relation Ragnachar, who also had high authority, and challenged him to come out to fight. Syagrius did not hesitate to do so, for he was not afraid of Clovis. They fought each other and the army of Syagrius was annihilated. He fled and made his way as quickly as he could to King Alaric II in Toulouse. Clovis summoned Alaric to surrender the fugitive, informing him that he would attack him in his turn for having given Syagrius refuge. Alaric was afraid to incur the wrath of the Franks for the sake of Syagrius and handed him over bound to the envoys, for the Goths are a timorous race. When Clovis had Syagrius in his power he ordered him to be imprisoned. As soon as he had seized the kingdom of Syagrius he had him killed in secret.

At that time many churches were plundered by the troops of Clovis, for he still held fast to his pagan idolatries. The soldiers had stolen an ewer of great size and wondrous workmanship, together with many other precious objects used in the church service. The bishop of the church in question sent messengers to the King to beg that, even if he would not hand back any of the

40. Sidonius Apollinaris, *Epistolae*, 7, 6.
41. Syagrius was not King; he was probably Master of the Soldiers.

other sacred vessels, this ewer at least might be restored to the church. The King listened to them and replied: 'Follow me to Soissons, where all the objects which we have seized are to be distributed. If this vessel for which your bishop is asking falls to my share, I will meet his wishes.' They came to Soissons and all the booty was placed in a heap before them. King Clovis addressed his men as follows, pointing to the vessel in question: 'I put it to you, my lusty freebooters, that you should agree here and now to grant me that ewer over and above my normal share.' They listened to what he said and the more rational among them answered: 'Everything in front of us is yours, noble King, for our very persons are yours to command. Do exactly as you wish, for there is none among us who has the power to say you nay.' As they spoke one of their number, a feckless fellow, greedy and prompt to anger, raised his battle-axe and struck the ewer. 'You shall have none of this booty,' he shouted, 'except your fair share.' All present were astounded at his words. The King hid his chagrin under a pretence of long-suffering patience. He took the vessel and handed it over to the envoy of the church; but in his heart he resented what had happened. At the end of that year he ordered the entire army to assemble on the parade-ground, so that he could examine the state of their equipment. The King went round inspecting them all and came finally to the man who had struck the ewer. 'No other man has equipment in such a bad state as yours,' said he. 'Your javelin is in a shocking condition, and so are your sword and your axe!' He seized the man's axe and threw it on the ground. As the soldier bent forward to pick up his weapon, King Clovis raised his own battle-axe in the air and split his skull with it. 'That is what you did to my ewer in Soissons,' he shouted. The man fell dead. Clovis ordered the others to dismiss. They were filled with mighty dread at what he had done. Clovis waged many wars and won many victories. In the tenth year of his reign he invaded the Thuringians and subjected them to his rule.

28. The King of the Burgundes was called Gundioc: he was of

the family of that King Athanaric who persecuted the Christians and about whom I have told you. He had four sons: Gundobad, Godigisel, Chilperic and Gundomar. Gundobad killed his brother Chilperic and drowned Chilperic's wife after tying a stone round her neck. He drove Chilperic's two daughters into exile: the elder, whose name was Chroma, became a religious, and the younger was called Clotild. Clovis often sent envoys to Burgundy and they saw the girl Clotild. They observed that she was an elegant young woman and clever for her years, and they discovered that she was of the blood royal. They reported all this to Clovis and he immediately sent more messengers to Gundobad to ask for her hand in marriage. Gundobad was afraid to refuse and he handed Clotild over to them. They took her back with them, and presented her to their King. Clovis already had a son called Theuderic by one of his mistresses, but he was delighted when he saw Clotild and made her his wife.

29. The first child which Clotild bore for Clovis was a son. She wanted to have her baby baptized, and she kept on urging her husband to agree to this. 'The gods whom you worship are no good,' she would say. 'They haven't even been able to help themselves, let alone others. They are carved out of stone or wood or some old piece of metal. The very names which you have given them were the names of men, not of gods. Take your Saturn, for example, who ran away from his own son to avoid being exiled from his kingdom, or so they say; and Jupiter, that obscene perpetrator of all sorts of mucky deeds, who couldn't keep his hands off other men, who had his fun with all his female relatives and couldn't even refrain from intercourse with his own sister,

'. . . Jovisque
Et soror et coniunx,'[42]

to quote her own words. What have Mars and Mercury ever done for anyone? They may have been endowed with magic arts, but they were certainly not worthy of being called divine.

42. *Aeneid*, 1, 46–7: 'at once sister and wife of Jupiter'.

You ought instead to worship Him who created at a word and out of nothing heaven, and earth, the sea and all that therein is,[43] who made the sun to shine, who lit the sky with stars, who peopled the water with fish, the earth with beasts, the sky with flying creatures, at whose nod the fields became fair with fruits, the trees with apples, the vines with grapes, by whose hand the race of man was made, by whose gift all creation is constrained to serve in deference and devotion the man He made.' However often the Queen said this, the King came no nearer to belief. 'All these things have been created and produced at the command of *our* gods,' he would answer. 'It is obvious that *your* God can do nothing, and, what is more, there is no proof that he is a God at all.'

The Queen, who was true to her faith, brought her son to be baptized. She ordered the church to be decorated with hangings and curtains, in the hope that the King, who remained stubborn in the face of argument, might be brought to the faith by ceremony. The child was baptized; he was given the name Ingomer; but no sooner had he received baptism than he died in his white robes. Clovis was extremely angry. He began immediately to reproach his Queen. 'If he had been dedicated in the name of my gods,' he said, 'he would have lived without question; but now that he has been baptized in the name of your God he has not been able to live a single day!' 'I give thanks to Almighty God,' replied Clotild, 'the Creator of all things, who has not found me completely unworthy, for He has deigned to welcome to His kingdom a child conceived in my womb. I am not at all cast down in my mind because of what has happened, for I know that my child, who was called away from this world in his white baptismal robes, will be nurtured in the sight of God.'

Some time later Clotild bore a second son. He was baptized Chlodomer. He began to ail and Clovis said: 'What else do you expect? It will happen to him as it happened to his brother: no sooner is he baptized in the name of your Christ than he will die!' Clotild prayed to the Lord and at His command the baby recovered.

43. Psalms 146, 6.

30.   Queen Clotild continued to pray that her husband might recognize the true God and give up his idol-worship. Nothing could persuade him to accept Christianity. Finally war broke out against the Alamanni and in this conflict he was forced by necessity to accept what he had refused of his own free will. It so turned out that when the two armies met on the battlefield there was great slaughter and the troops of Clovis were rapidly being annihilated. He raised his eyes to heaven when he saw this, felt compunction in his heart and was moved to tears. 'Jesus Christ,' he said, 'you who Clotild maintains to be the Son of the living God, you who deign to give help to those in travail and victory to those who trust in you, in faith I beg the glory of your help. If you will give me victory over my enemies, and if I may have evidence of that miraculous power which the people dedicated to your name say that they have experienced, then I will believe in you and I will be baptized in your name. I have called upon my own gods, but, as I see only too clearly, they have no intention of helping me. I therefore cannot believe that they possess any power, for they do not come to the assistance of those who trust in them. I now call upon you. I want to believe in you, but I must first be saved from my enemies.' Even as he said this the Alamanni turned their backs and began to run away. As soon as they saw that their King was killed, they submitted to Clovis. 'We beg you,' they said, 'to put an end to this slaughter. We are prepared to obey you.' Clovis stopped the war. He made a speech in which he called for peace. Then he went home. He told the Queen how he had won a victory by calling on the name of Christ. This happened in the fifteenth year of his reign.

31.   The Queen then ordered Saint Remigius, Bishop of the town of Rheims, to be summoned in secret. She begged him to impart the word of salvation to the King. The Bishop asked Clovis to meet him in private and began to urge him to believe in the true God, Maker of heaven and earth, and to forsake his idols, which were powerless to help him or anyone else. The King replied: 'I have listened to you willingly, holy father.

There remains one obstacle. The people under my command will not agree to forsake their gods. I will go and put to them what you have just said to me.' He arranged a meeting with his people, but God in his power had preceded him, and before he could say a word all those present shouted in unison: 'We will give up worshipping our mortal gods, pious King, and we are prepared to follow the immortal God about whom Remigius preaches.' This news was reported to the Bishop. He was greatly pleased and he ordered the baptismal pool to be made ready. The public squares were draped with coloured cloths, the churches were adorned with white hangings, the baptistry was prepared, sticks of incense gave off clouds of perfume, sweet-smelling candles gleamed bright and the holy place of baptism was filled with divine fragrance. God filled the hearts of all present with such grace that they imagined themselves to have been transported to some perfumed paradise. King Clovis asked that he might be baptized first by the Bishop.[44] Like some new Constantine he stepped forward to the baptismal pool, ready to wash away the sores of his old leprosy and to be cleansed in flowing water from the sordid stains which he had borne so long. As he advanced for his baptism, the holy man of God addressed him in these pregnant words: 'Bow your head in meekness, Sicamber.[45] Worship what you have burnt, burn what you have been wont to worship.'

Saint Remigius was a bishop of immense learning and a great scholar more than anything else, but he was also famous for his holiness and he was the equal of Saint Silvester for the miracles which he performed. We still have an account of his life, which tells how he raised a man from the dead. King Clovis confessed his belief in God Almighty, three in one. He was baptized in the name of the Father, the Son and the Holy Ghost, and marked in holy chrism with the sign of the Cross of Christ. More than three thousand of his army were baptized at the same time. His sister Albofled was baptized, but she soon after died and was gathered to the Lord. The King grieved over her death, but

44. A.D. 496.
45. The Merovingians claimed to be descended from the Sicambri.

Saint Remigius sent him a consoling letter which began with these words:

I am greatly distressed and I share your grief at the loss of your sister of pious memory. We can take consolation in this, that she has met her death in such a way that we can look up to her instead of mourning for her.[46]

Another sister of Clovis, called Lanthechild, was converted at the same time. She had accepted the Arian heresy, but she confessed the triune majesty of the Father, the Son and the Holy Ghost, and received the holy chrism.

32. At this time the two brothers Gundobad and Godigisel ruled over the territory round the Rhône and the Saône and the province of Marseilles. Like their subjects they belonged to the Arian sect. They were enemies, and when Godigisel heard of the victories won by King Clovis he sent envoys to him in secret. 'If you help me to attack my brother,' he said, 'so that I can kill him in battle or drive him out of his territory, I will pay you any annual tribute which you may care to exact.' Clovis gladly accepted the offer and in his turn promised to help Godigisel wherever occasion should arise. They chose a suitable moment and Clovis marched his army against Gundobad. As soon as he heard of this, Gundobad, who knew nothing of his brother's treachery, sent a message to Godigisel. 'Come to my assistance,' he said, 'for the Franks are marching against us and are invading our territory which they plan to capture. Let us make a common front against this people which hates us, for if we are not united we shall suffer the fate which others have met before us.' Godigisel answered: 'I am coming with my army and I will support you.' The three kings each put his army in the field, Clovis marching against Gundobad and Godigisel. They arrived with all their military equipment at a fortified place called Dijon. When battle was joined on the River Ouche Godigisel went over to Clovis and their united forces crushed the army of Gundobad. Gundobad turned his back and fled when

46. The text of this letter still exists.

he saw the treachery of his brother, about whom he had had no
suspicion. He made his way along the banks of the Rhône and
took refuge in the city of Avignon. As for Godigisel, once the
victory was won, he promised to hand over a part of his kingdom to Clovis and then went home in peace and entered Vienne
in triumph, as if he were still master of his own territory.
Clovis called up more troops and set out in pursuit of Gundobad, planning to extract him from Avignon and kill him.
When Gundobad learned this he was panic-stricken, for he was
afraid of being killed at any moment. He had with him a man
of some distinction called Aridius. Aridius was astute and full
of energy. Gundobad summoned this man to him and said: 'I
am surrounded by pitfalls and what to do I cannot tell. These
barbarians have launched this attack against me. If they kill us
two they will ravage the whole neighbourhood.' 'You must do
all you can to propitiate this savage creature,' answered
Aridius, 'or else you are done for. If you agree, I will run away
from you and pretend to go over to his side. When I have joined
him I will see to it that no harm is done to you or to this region.
If you will only carry out my plan in all its details, the Lord
God in his compassion will assure you a happy outcome.' 'I will
do whatever you say,' replied Gundobad. Having received his
answer, Aridius bade him good-bye and left him. He made his
way to Clovis. 'I am your humble slave, most pious King,' said
he. 'I have deserted the wretched Gundobad and come to join
your forces. If you are prepared to accept me kindly, then you
and your descendants will find in me a faithful and trustworthy
retainer.' Clovis accepted this offer without hesitating for a
moment and kept Aridius by his side. He was a wonderful
raconteur, full of good advice, sound in judgement and apparently trustworthy. Clovis remained encamped with his entire
army round the city walls. 'If you who are a king with absolute
power would deign to accept a little advice from me who am no
one,' said Aridius to him, 'this is the loyal proposition which I
should like to put to you. What I am going to say will be to
your advantage and at the same time to the advantage of the
cities through which you propose to pass. What is the point of

keeping all these troops under arms when your enemy is safe in a stronghold which is too well fortified for you to capture? You are destroying the fields, spoiling the meadows, cutting up the vineyards, ruining the olive-groves and ravaging the whole countryside, which is a very fruitful one. In doing this you are causing no harm whatsoever to Gundobad. Why don't you send an ultimatum to him to say that he must pay whatever annual tribute you care to exact? In that way the region will be saved and he will have to submit to you and pay tribute to you for ever. If he doesn't accept this, you can do whatever you wish.'
Clovis accepted the advice of Aridius and sent his army home. Then he dispatched envoys to Gundobad and ordered him to pay yearly tribute. Gundobad paid up for the year in question and promised that he would do the same from then onwards.

33.   Later on Gundobad recovered his strength and scorned to pay to King Clovis the tribute which he had promised. He marched his army against his brother Godigisel and besieged him inside his city of Vienne. Once provisions began to run short among the common people, Godigisel was afraid that the lack of food might extend to him also, and he ordered them to be driven out of the town. This was done, but along with them was expelled the engineer who was in charge of the aqueduct. He was very indignant at having been ejected with the others. He went in a rage to Gundobad and revealed to him how he might break into the city and take vengeance on his brother. With this engineer to show them the way, Gundobad's army was led along the aqueduct. At their head marched a number of sappers with iron crowbars. There was a water-gate blocked by a great stone. Under the direction of the engineer they heaved this stone on one side with their crowbars, made their way into the city and attacked from the rear the defenders, who were still busy shooting their arrows from the wall. A trumpet-call was sounded from the centre of the city, the besiegers attacked the gateways, burst them open and rushed in. The townsfolk were caught between two fires and cut to pieces by two forces. Godigisel took refuge in one of the heretic churches, but he was

killed there and his Arian bishop with him. The Franks who had
been with Godigisel banded together in one of the towers. Gundobad gave orders that none of them should be maltreated.
When he had disarmed them he sent them in exile to King
Alaric in Toulouse. All the Gallo-Roman senators and the Burgundes who had sided with Godigisel were killed out of hand.
This whole region, which is now called Burgundy, Gundobad
took under his own rule. He instituted milder laws among the
Burgundes, to stop them treating the Romans unjustly.[47]

34.   Gundobad came to realize that the religious tenets of the
heretics were of no avail. He accepted that Christ, the Son of
God, and the Holy Ghost are equal with the Father, and he
asked the saintly Bishop of Vienne to arrange for him to be
anointed with the chrism in secret. 'If you really believe what
the Lord has Himself taught us,' said the Bishop, 'then you
should carry it out. Christ said: "Whosoever therefore shall
confess me before men, him will I confess also before my
Father which is in heaven. But whosoever shall deny me before
men, him will I also deny before my Father which is in
heaven."[48] In the same way He gave advise to the holy and
blessed Apostles, whom He loved so much, saying: "But beware
of men: for they will deliver you up to the councils, and they
will scourge you in their synagogues; and ye shall be brought
before governors and kings for my sake, for a testimony against
them and the Gentiles."[49] You are a king and you need not fear
to be taken in charge by anyone: yet you are afraid of your
subjects and you do not dare to confess in public your belief in
the Creator of all things. Stop being so foolish and confess in
front of them all what you say you believe in your heart. The
blessed Apostle said: "For with the heart man believeth unto
righteousness; and with the mouth confession is made unto salvation."[50] Similarly the prophet said: "I will give thee thanks in
the great congregation: I will praise thee among much
people."[51] And again: "I will praise thee, O Lord, among the

---

47. The *Lex Gundobada.*   48. Matthew 10, 32–3.
49. Matthew 10, 17–18.   50. Romans 10, 10.   51. Psalms 35, 18.

people: I will sing unto thee among the nations."[52] You are afraid of your people. Do you not realize that it is better that the people should accept your belief, rather than that you, a king, should pander to their every whim? You are the leader of your people; your people is not there to lord it over you. When you go to war, you yourself march at the head of the squadrons of your army and they follow where you lead. It is therefore preferable that they should learn the truth under your direction, rather than that at your death they should continue in their errors. For "God is not mocked,"[53] nor can He love the man who for an earthly kingdom refuses to confess Him before all the world.' Gundobad was worsted in this argument, but to his life's end he persisted in his obstinacy, refusing to confess in public that the three persons of the Trinity are equal.

At this time Saint Avitus was at the height of his eloquence. Certain heresies began to be current in the town of Constantinople, first that of Eutyches[54] and then that of Sabellius,[55] who maintained that our Lord Jesus Christ had nothing about Him which was divine. At the request of King Gundobad Avitus wrote polemics against these heresies. We still possess these admirable letters, which at once denounced the heresy and supported the Church of God. He wrote a book of *Homilies*, six books in verse on the creation of the world and other cognate subjects, and nine books of *Letters*, among which are included the ones already mentioned.[56] In the homily which he composed on the Rogations he says that these ceremonies, which we celebrate before the triumph of our Lord's Ascension, were instituted by Mamertus, Bishop of that same town of Vienne of which Avitus held the episcopate when he was writing, at a time when the townsfolk were terrified by a series of portents. Vienne was shaken by frequent earthquakes, and savage packs of wolves and stags came in through the gates and

52. Psalms 57, 9.   53. Galatians 6, 7.
54. Eutyches, *fl. c.* 440, denied the twofold nature of Christ, maintaining that He was not man, but divine. Gregory says the opposite.
55. Sabellius, *fl. c.* 250, had preached the same heresy.
56. The text of these letters still exists, as does also that of the *Homilies*.

ranged through the entire city, fearing nothing and nobody, or so he writes. These portents continued throughout the whole year. As the season of the feast of Easter approached, the common people in their devotion expected God's compassion on them, hoping that this day of great solemnity might see an end of their terror. However, on the very vigil of the holy night, when the rite of Mass was being celebrated, the King's palace inside the city walls was set ablaze by fire sent by God. The congregation was panic-stricken. They rushed out of the church, for they thought that the whole town would be destroyed by this fire, or else that the earth would open and swallow it up. The holy Bishop was prostrate before the altar, imploring God's mercy with tears and lamentations. What more should I say? The prayers of this famous Bishop rose to heaven above and, so to speak, his floods of tears put out the fire in the palace. While this was going on, the feast of the Ascension of our Lord was coming nearer, as I have told you. Mamertus told the people to fast, he instituted a special form of prayer, a religious service and a grant of alms to the poor in thanksgiving. All the horrors came to an end. The story of what had happened spread through all the provinces and led all the bishops to copy what this particular prelate had done in faith. Down to our own times these rites are celebrated with a contrite spirit and a grateful heart in all our churches to the glory of God.

35.   When Alaric II, the King of the Goths, observed that King Clovis was beating one race of people after another, he sent envoys to him. 'If you agree,' said he, 'it seems to me that it would be a good thing, my dear brother, if, with God's approval, we two were to meet.' Clovis did agree. He travelled to meet Alaric and the two of them came together near the village of Amboise, on an island in the Loire, in territory belonging to Tours. They conferred with each other, sat side by side at the meal table, swore eternal friendship and went home again in peace. At that time a great many people in Gaul were very keen on having the Franks as their rulers.

36.* It was as a direct result of this that Quintianus, the Bishop of Rodez, fell into disfavour and was driven out of his city. The townsfolk started saying to him: 'If you had your way, the Franks would take over our territory.' Not long after this an open quarrel started between him and his flock. The Goths who were resident in Rodez suspected him, and the Ruthénois themselves went so far as to accuse him of wishing to accept the rule of the Franks. They plotted together and planned to assassinate him. When Quintianus came to hear of this, he fled one night and left the city with the more trustworthy among his attendants. He reached Clermont-Ferrand and there he was kindly received by Saint Eufrasius, who had succeeded to Aprunculus, himself a native of Dijon. Eufrasius gave him accommodation, with fields around and vineyards, for, as he said: 'The resources of this diocese are sufficient to support us both: that charity which the blessed Apostle preached must continue between God's ministers.' The Bishop of Lyons also made over to Quintianus certain church property which he administered in Clermont. Other details concerning Saint Quintianus, the wrongs which were done to him and the miracles which the Lord deigned to perform through his agency, are described in my *Vitae Patruum*, in the chapter devoted to him.[57]

37.   'I find it hard to go on seeing these Arians occupy a part of Gaul,' said Clovis to his ministers. 'With God's help let us invade them. When we have beaten them, we will take over their territory.' They all agreed to this proposal. An army was assembled and Clovis marched on Poitiers.[58] Some of his troops passed through land belonging to Tours. In respect for Saint Martin Clovis ordered that they should requisition nothing in this neighbourhood except fodder and water. One of the soldiers found some hay belonging to a poor man. 'The King commanded that nothing should be requisitioned except fodder, didn't he?' said this man. 'Well, this is fodder. We shan't be disobeying his orders if we take it.' He laid hands on the poor

57. *VP*, 4.   58. A.D. 507.

man and took his hay by main force. This was reported to
Clovis. He drew his sword and killed the soldier on the spot. 'It
is no good expecting to win this fight if we offend Saint Martin,'
said he. This was enough to ensure that the army took nothing
else from this region. The King sent messengers to the church of
Saint Martin. 'Off with you,' he said, 'and see if you can bring
me some good tidings from God's house.' He loaded them with
gifts which they were to offer to the church. 'Lord God,' said he,
'if You are on my side and if You have decreed that this people
of unbelievers, who have always been hostile to You, are to be
delivered into my hands, deign to show me a propitious sign as
these men enter Saint Martin's church, so that I may know that
You will support your servant Clovis.' The messengers set out
on their journey and came to Tours as Clovis had commanded.
As they entered the church, it happened that the precentor was
just beginning to intone this antiphon: 'For thou hast girded me
with strength unto the battle: thou hast subdued under me those
that rose up against me. Thou hast also given me the necks of
mine enemies: that I might destroy them that hate me.'[59] When
the messengers heard this psalm, they gave thanks to God. They
made their vows to the Saint and went happily back to report to
the King. When Clovis reached the Vienne with his army, he
was at a loss to know where to cross, for the river was swollen
with heavy rains. That night he prayed that God might deign to
indicate a ford by which he might make the crossing. As day
dawned an enormous doe entered the water, as if to lead them
at God's command. The soldiers knew that where the doe had
crossed they could follow. The King marched towards Poitiers,
and while he and his army were encamped there a pillar of fire
rose from the church of Saint Hilary. It seemed to move
towards Clovis as a sign that with the support of the blessed
Saint he might the more easily overcome the heretic host,
against which Hilary himself had so often done battle for the
faith. Clovis forbade his troops to take any booty as they
marched in, or to rob any man of his possessions.

At that time on the outskirts of Poitiers there dwelt a saintly

59. Psalms 18, 39–40.

Abbot called Maxentius, who lived as a God-fearing recluse in his monastery. There is no point in my giving the name of the monastery, as it is now called the Cell of Saint Maxentius. When the monks saw a squadron of troops coming nearer and nearer to their monastery they begged their Abbot to come out of his cell to give his blessing to the soldiers. He was a long time coming, and they were so frightened that they burst the door open and pushed him out of his cell. He showed no fear. He walked towards the troops, as if to ask them not to molest him. One of the soldiers drew his sword to strike Maxentius over the head. His arm went stiff on a level with the Saint's ear and his sword fell to the ground. The soldier in question knelt at the Saint's feet and asked his forgiveness. When his companions saw what had happened, they rushed back to the army in great consternation, for they were afraid that they might all pay for it with their lives. The blessed Saint rubbed the man's arm with holy oil, made the sign of the Cross over him, and he immediately recovered. As a result of what Maxentius had done the monastery remained unharmed. He performed many other miracles, as the diligent reader will discover if he peruses the Abbot's *Vita*.[60] This happened in the fifteenth year of the reign of Clovis.

Meanwhile King Clovis met Alaric II, King of the Goths, on the battlefield of Vouillé, near the tenth milestone outside Poitiers.[61] Some of the soldiers engaged hurled their javelins from a distance, others fought hand to hand. The Goths fled, as they were prone to do, and Clovis was the victor, for God was on his side. As one of his allies he had the son of Sigibert the Lame,[62] called Chloderic. Sigibert had been lame since he was wounded in the knee when fighting against the Alamanni at the fortress of Zülpich. Clovis killed Alaric, but, as the Goths fled, two of them suddenly rushed up in the scrum, one on this side and one on that, and struck at the Frankish King with their spears. It

60. There exist two *Vitae Sancti Maxentii*, but neither seems to date back to the time of Gregory.

61. A.D. 507.

62. Sigibert the Lame, King of the Ripuarian Franks.

was his leather corselet which saved him and the sheer speed of his horse, but he was very near to death. A large force of Auvergnats took part in this battle, for they had come under the command of Apollinaris: their leaders, who were of senatorial rank, were killed. Amalaric, the son of Alaric, escaped from the conflict and fled to Spain, where he later ruled his father's kingdom wisely. Clovis sent his own son Theuderic through Albi and the town of Rodez to Clermont-Ferrand. As he moved forward Theuderic subjected to his father's rule all the towns which lay between the two frontiers of the Goths and the Burgundes. Alaric II had reigned for twelve years. Clovis wintered in the town of Bordeaux. He removed all Alaric's treasure from Toulouse and went to Angoulême. There the Lord showed him such favour that the city walls collapsed of their own weight as he looked at them. Clovis drove the Goths out of Angoulême and took command of the city. With his victory consolidated he then returned to Tours. There he gave many gifts to the church of Saint Martin.

38. Letters reached Clovis from the Emperor Anastasius to confer the consulate on him. In Saint Martin's church he stood clad in a purple tunic and the military mantle, and he crowned himself with a diadem. He then rode out on his horse and with his own hand showered gold and silver coins among the people present all the way from the doorway of Saint Martin's church to Tours cathedral. From that day on he was called Consul or Augustus. He left Tours and travelled to Paris, where he established the seat of his government. Theuderic came to join him in Paris.

39.* When Eustochius, Bishop of Tours, died, Licinius was ordained Bishop in his place. He was the eighth after Saint Martin. The war which I have just described was waged during the episcopate of Licinius, and it was in his time that King Clovis came to Tours. Licinius is said to have been in the East and to have visited the holy places. They even say that he went to Jerusalem and saw on a number of occasions the site of our

Lord's Passion and Resurrection, about which we read in the Gospels.

40.   While Clovis was resident in Paris he sent secretly to the son of Sigibert, saying: 'Your father is old and he is lame in one leg. If he were to die, his kingdom would come to you of right, and my alliance would come with it.' Chloderic was led astray by his lust for power and began to plot his father's death. One day Sigibert went out of the city of Cologne and crossed the Rhine, for he wanted to walk in the forest of Buchau. At midday he took a siesta in his tent, and his son set assassins on him and had him murdered, so that he might gain possession of his kingdom. By the judgement of God Chloderic fell into the pit which he had dug for his own father. He sent messengers to King Clovis to announce his father's death. 'My father is dead,' said he, 'and I have taken over his kingdom and his treasure. Send me your envoys and I will gladly hand over to you any-thing which you may care to select from this treasure.' 'I thank you for your goodwill,' answered Clovis. 'I ask you to show all your treasure to my messengers, but you may keep it.' The envoys came and Chloderic showed his father's treasure to them. They inspected everything. 'It was in this coffer that my father used to keep all his gold coins,' said Chloderic. 'Plunge your hand right to the bottom,' they answered, 'to see how much is there.' As he leant forward to do this, one of the Franks raised his hand and split Chloderic's skull with his double-headed axe. This unworthy son thus shared the fate of his father. When Clovis heard that both Sigibert and his son were dead, he came to Cologne himself and ordered the inhabitants to assemble. 'While I was out sailing on the River Scheldt,' and he, 'Chloderic, the son of your King, my brother, was busy plotting against his father and putting it out that I wanted him killed. As Sigibert fled through the forest of Buchau, Chloderic set assassins on him and had him murdered. While Chloderic was showing his father's treasure, he in his turn was killed by some-body or other. I take no responsibility for what has happened. It is not for me to shed the blood of one of my fellow kings, for

that is a crime; but since things have turned out in this way, I will give you my advice and you must make of it what you will. It is that you should turn to me and put yourself under my protection.' When they heard what he had to say, they clashed their shields and shouted their approval. Then they raised Clovis up on a shield and made him their ruler. In this way he took over both the kingship and the treasure of Sigibert and submitted Sigibert's people to his own rule. Day in day out God submitted the enemies of Clovis to his dominion and increased his power, for he walked before Him with an upright heart and did what was pleasing in His sight.

41. Clovis next marched against Chararic.[63] When Clovis was fighting against Syagrius, this Chararic, who had been summoned to his aid, remained neutral, giving help to neither side and awaiting the issue of the conflict, so that he might offer the hand of friendship to whichever leader was victorious. This was the reason why Clovis now attacked him in his wrath. He hemmed Chararic in by some stratagem and made him prisoner. Chararic and his son were both bound and then Clovis had their hair cut short. He ordered Chararic to be ordained as a priest and he made his son a deacon. Chararic objected to this humiliation and burst into tears. His son is said to have exclaimed: 'These leaves have been cut from wood which is still green and not lacking in sap. They will soon grow again and be larger than ever; and may the man who has done this deed perish equally quickly.' The statement came to the ears of Clovis. As they were threatening to let their hair grow again and then to kill him, he had their heads cut off. When they were dead he took possession of their kingdom, their treasure and their people.

42. There lived in Cambrai at this time a King called Ragnachar who was so sunk in debauchery that he could not even keep his hands off the women of his own family. He had an adviser called Farro who was given to the same filthy habits. It

63. Chararic, King of the Salian Franks.

was said of Farro that when food, or a present, or indeed any
gift was brought to the King, Ragnachar would say that it was
good enough for him and his dear Farro. This situation roused
their Frankish subjects to the utmost fury. Clovis gave a bribe.
of golden arm-bands and sword-belts to the *leudes*[64] of Ragnachar, to encourage them to call him in against their King.
These ornaments looked like gold, but they were really of
bronze very cleverly gilded. Clovis marched his army against
Ragnachar. Ragnachar sent spies to discover the strength of the
invaders. When the spies returned, he asked them just how
strong the enemy was. 'Strong enough for you and your dear
Farro,' they replied. Clovis arrived in person and drew up his line
of battle. Ragnachar witnessed the defeat of his army and prepared to slip away in flight. He was arrested by his own troops
and with his arms tied behind his back he was brought before
Clovis. His brother Ricchar was dragged in with him. 'Why
have you disgraced our Frankish people by allowing yourself to
be bound?' asked Clovis. 'It would have been better for you had
you died in battle.' He raised his axe and split Ragnachar's
skull. Then he turned to Ricchar and said: 'If you had stood by
your brother, he would not have been bound in this way.' He
killed Ricchar with a second blow of his axe. When these two
were dead, those who had betrayed them discovered that the
gold which they had received from Clovis was counterfeit.
When they complained to Clovis, he is said to have answered:
'This is the sort of gold which a man can expect when he deliberately lures his lord to death.' He added that they were lucky to
have escaped with their lives, instead of paying for the betrayal
of their rulers by being tortured to death. When they heard this,
they chose to beg forgiveness, saying that it was enough for
them if they were allowed to live. The two Kings of whom I
have told you, Ragnachar and Ricchar, were relatives of Clovis.
At his command their brother Rignomer was also put to death
in Le Mans. As soon as all three were slain, Clovis took over

64. The *leudes*, cp. MG *Leute*, were the nobles who had sworn a special
oath of loyalty to the king and from whom his personal bodyguard was
formed.

their kingdom and their treasure. In the same way he encompassed the death of many other kings and blood-relations of his whom he suspected of conspiring against his kingdom. By doing this he spread his dominion over the whole of Gaul. One day when he had called a general assembly of his subjects, he is said to have made the following remark about the relatives whom he had destroyed: 'How sad a thing it is that I live among strangers like some solitary pilgrim, and that I have none of my own relations left to help me when disaster threatens!' He said this not because he grieved for their deaths, but because in his cunning way he hoped to find some relative still in the land of the living whom he could kill.

43. At long last Clovis died in Paris. He was buried in the church of the Holy Apostles,[65] which he and his Queen Clotild had built. He expired five years after the battle of Vouillé.[66] He had reigned for thirty years and he was forty-five years old. From the passing of Saint Martin until the death of King Clovis, which happened in the eleventh year of the episcopate of Licinius, Bishop of Tours, there are counted one hundred and twelve years. After the death of her husband Queen Clotild came to live in Tours. She served as a religious in the church of Saint Martin. She lived all the rest of her days in this place, apart from an occasional visit to Paris. She was remarkable for her great modesty and her loving kindness.

HERE ENDS BOOK II

65. Afterwards Sainte Geneviève.
66. A.D. 511.

BOOK III

HERE BEGIN THE CHAPTER-HEADINGS
OF BOOK III

1. The sons of Clovis.
2. The episcopates of Dinifius, Apollinaris and Quintianus.
3. How the Danes attacked Gaul.
4. The kings of the Thuringians.
5. How Sigismund killed his own son.
6. The death of Chlodomer.
7. The war against the Thuringians.
8. The death of Hermanfrid.
9. How Childebert went to Clermont-Ferrand.
10. The death of Amalaric.
11. How Childebert and Lothar went to Burgundy, and Theuderic to Clermont-Ferrand.
12. The destruction wrought in Clermont.
13. Vollore and the fortress of Chastel-Marlhac.
14. The death of Munderic.
15. The enslavement of Attalus.
16. Sigivald.
17. The Bishops of Tours.
18. The murder of Chlodomer's sons.
19. Saint Gregory. The site of the fortress of Dijon.
20. How Theudebert became engaged to Wisigard.
21. How Theudebert went to Provence.
22. How Theudebert later married Deuteria.
23. The death of Sigivald.
24. How Childebert rewarded Theudebert.
25. The goodness of Theudebert.
26. How Deuteria murdered her daughter.
27. How Theudebert married Wisigard.
28. How Childebert joined Theudebert against Lothar.

159

29. How Childebert and Lothar went to Spain.
30. The Kings of Spain.
31. The daughter of Theodoric, King of Italy.
32. How Theudebert went to Italy.
33. Asteriolus and Secundinus.
34. The generosity of Theudebert to the townsfolk of Verdun.
35. The murder of Syrivald.
36. The deaths of Theudebert and Parthenius.
37. A harsh winter.

HERE END THE CHAPTER-HEADINGS

I would like to make a brief comparison between the happy
outcome of the Christians who have believed in the Holy Trinity and the disasters which have befallen those who have
sought to destroy it. I shall leave out how Abraham worshipped
the Trinity at the oak-tree, how Jacob proclaimed it in his blessing, how Moses saw it in the bush and how the children of Israel
followed it in the cloud and trembled before it on the mountain.
I shall not describe how Aaron bore the Trinity on his breastplate and how David prophesied it in a psalm, praying that a
proper spirit might be reborn in him, that the Holy Ghost
should not be removed from him and that he might be strengthened by the free Spirit of the Lord.[1] It is, by the way, a great
mystery to me why the voice of the prophet calls *spiritus prin-
cipalis* what the heretics maintain to be something of minor
importance. However, as I promised, I must leave that and
move on to our own times. Arius, that evil man, the founder of
that evil sect, lost his entrails in the lavatory and so was hurried
off to hell-fire;[2] Saint Hilary, on the other hand, who defended
the undivided Trinity and was sent into exile for having done
so, was restored to his own country and went at last to heaven.[3]
Clovis, who believed in the Trinity, crushed the heretics with
divine help and enlarged his dominion to include all Gaul; but
Alaric, who refused to accept the Trinity, was therefore deprived of his kingship, his subjects and, what is more important,
the life hereafter. As the Devil prowls around the true believers

1. Psalms 51, 11–12.
2. Arius died in A.D. 336. The conversion of Recared, King of the Visigoths in Spain, in 587, cp. *HF*, IX, 15, put an end to the long hostility
between the Arian Visigoths and the Catholics of Merovingian Gaul.
3. Hilary, Bishop of Poitiers, was banished to Phrygia in A.D. 356. He
returned to Poitiers in 360 and died in 368.

may well lose many things, but the Lord restores them a hundredfold; the heretics on the other hand have not much advantage to show, and even that which they have is taken away from them. The deaths of Godigisel, Gundobad and Godomar are a proof of this, for they lost their homeland and their souls at one and the same moment.[4] I myself believe in God the Father, one and invisible, infinite, incomprehensible, glorious, everlasting and eternal, one in three Persons in the Trinity, that is the Father, the Son and the Holy Ghost. I believe Him three in one, with equality of substance, godhead, omnipotence and divine power, one God, almighty and supreme, reigning world without end.

1.   Once Clovis was dead, his four sons, Theuderic, Chlodomer, Childebert and Lothar, inherited his kingdom and divided it equally among themselves.[5] Theuderic already had a son called Theudebert, an elegant and able young man. These four princes had considerable courage and their armies made them a great power in the land. Amalaric, the son of Alaric, who was King of Spain, asked for the hand of their sister in marriage. This they graciously granted and they sent her off to Spain with a great dowry of expensive jewellery.

2.   When Licinius, the Bishop of Tours, died, Dinifius ascended the episcopal throne. In Clermont-Ferrand, after the death of Saint Aprunculus, the holy Eufrasius was inducted as the twelfth Bishop. Eufrasius lived on for four years after the death of Clovis, dying in the twenty-fourth year of his episcopate. The people elected in his place Saint Quintianus, who had been expelled from Rodez. Alchima and Placidana, the wife and sister of Apollinaris, went to Saint Quintianus and said: 'It should be enough for you in your old age, holy prelate, that you have

---

4. Godigisel, Gundobad and Godomar were Arian Kings of Burgundy. Gregory omits Sigismund, who reigned between Gundobad and Godomar. Sigismund was a Catholic, but he was defeated in battle and murdered by Chlodomer in A.D. 523, cp. *HF*, III, 6.
5. See Introduction, p. 17.

already been appointed to one bishopric. Won't you, who are so pious, allow your servant Apollinaris to hold the episcopate here? If he does gain this high honour, he will obey your command in all things. You will give the orders, and he will carry out your wishes. Please listen sympathetically to this humble proposal of ours.' 'What can I do for you,' asked Quintianus, 'I who have no control whatsoever over this election? I certainly ask nothing more than that the Church should give me enough to eat each day, so that I may devote myself to prayer.' When they had heard his reply, the two women sent Apollinaris to King Theuderic.[6] He took plenty of gifts with him and he was given the bishopric. When he had been Bishop for four months only he died. This news was reported to Theuderic and he ordered Saint Quintianus to be inducted and to take over full control of the diocese. 'It was for love of me that he was expelled from his own city,' said the King. Messengers were sent to Clermont. The local bishops and the townsfolk were called together and they elected Quintianus to the bishopric of the city, where he was the fourteenth prelate to rule the diocese. All else which he did, his miracles and the date of his death, are recorded in the book which I wrote of his life.[7]

3.   The next thing which happened was that the Danes sent a fleet under their King Chlochilaich and invaded Gaul from the sea.[8] They came ashore, laid waste one of the regions ruled by Theuderic and captured some of the inhabitants. They loaded their ships with what they had stolen and the men they had seized, and then they set sail for home. Their King remained on the shore, waiting until the boats should have gained the open sea, when he planned to go on board. When Theuderic heard that his land had been invaded by foreigners, he sent his son Theudebert to those parts with a powerful army and all the

6. Apollinaris, the son of Sidonius Apollinaris, Bishop of Clermont-Ferrand 472–88, was present at the battle of Vouillé, *HF*, II, 37.

7. *VP*, 4.

8. This is the Hygelac of *Beowulf*. See G. Storms, 'The Significance of Hygelac's Raid' in *Nottingham Mediaeval Studies*, Volume XIV (1970), pp. 3–26.

necessary equipment. The Danish King was killed, the enemy
fleet was beaten in a naval battle and all the booty was brought
back on shore once more.

4.   At this time three brothers called Baderic, Hermanfrid and
Berthar ruled over the Thuringians. Hermanfrid beat his
brother Berthar in battle and killed him. When Berthar died he
left an orphaned daughter called Radegund;[9] he also left a
number of sons, about whom I shall have a deal to say later on.
Amalaberg, the wife of Hermanfrid, was a wicked and cruel
woman: it was she who sowed the seeds of civil war between the
two remaining brothers. One day when her husband came in to
have a meal, he found only half the table laid. When he asked
Amalaberg what she meant by this, she answered: 'A king who
is deprived of half his kingdom deserves to find half his table
bare.' Hermanfrid was roused by this and by other similar
things which Amalaberg did. He decided to attack his brother
and sent secret messengers to King Theuderic to invite him to
make war on Baderic in his turn. 'If we can only manage to
kill him,' said Hermanfrid, 'we will share his kingdom equally
between us.' Theuderic was delighted when he heard this and he
marched against Baderic with his army. Theuderic and Hermanfrid made contact, gave each other pledges of good faith,
and set out for battle. They encountered Baderic, destroyed his
army and cut off his head. Once this victory was won, Theuderic returned home. Hermanfrid broke his word without
more ado, and made no attempt to carry out the promises

9. The Thuringian Princess Radegund afterwards became the first wife
of King Lothar I, but she preferred the religious life and founded the
famous Nunnery of the Holy Cross in Poitiers. She died in 587 and Gregory
went to her funeral, *HF*, IX, 2. See Index for further references and for the
revolt in the nunnery of Clotild and Basina during the rule of Leubovera,
the second Abbess. Jesus College, Cambridge, was built on the site of a
priory dedicated *c.* 1157–64 to Saint Radegund by Malcolm IV, King of
Scotland and Earl of Huntingdon. Malcolm had fought with Henry II
against the French in the district round Poitiers. Jesus Lane in Cambridge
was formerly called Radegund Lane. See F. Brittain, *Jesus College, Cambridge*, 1940, pp. 13–14.

which he had given to Theuderic. As a result there was a great enmity between the two Kings.

5.   After the death of Gundobad, his son Sigismund inherited his kingdom. With great care and attention to detail Sigismund built the monastery of Saint-Maurice d'Agaune, providing it with chapels and living accommodation. Sigismund lost his first wife, the daughter of Theodoric, the King of Italy, although he had a son by her called Sigeric. He then married a second wife who, as is the habit of step-mothers, proceeded to maltreat and abuse her step-son. It happened as a result that when, on a certain feast-day, the boy noticed that she was wearing clothes which had belonged to his mother, he said to her bitterly: 'Shame on you for covering your back with those garments which, as everyone knows, belonged to your mistress, my own mother!' The Queen was furious at what he had said. She went straight to her husband and stirred him up with her spiteful tongue. 'That wicked son of yours is plotting to seize your throne,' said she. 'Once he has killed you, he intends to extend his power as far as Italy, so that he may take over the kingdom which his grandfather Theodoric held in that country. He knows that he cannot realize his plans as long as you live: he cannot rise unless you fall.' Sigismund was roused by his wife's word and by a lot of similar allegations which she made. He agreed to the suggestion of this evil woman and became the foul murderer of his own son. One day when the boy had drunk wine with his lunch Sigismund sent him to lie down in the afternoon. As he slept a cloth was slipped under his neck and knotted under his chin. Two servants tugged at the ends and so the boy was throttled. The father was grief-stricken at what he had done, but it was too late. Sigismund threw himself on the dead body and wept most bitterly. An old man who was present is said to have remarked: 'Weep for yourself, Sigismund, for, on your wife's evil advice, you have murdered your own son in this barbarous fashion. There is no point in weeping for your boy, who has been strangled in his innocence.' Nevertheless Sigismund went to the monastery of Agaune where he wept and

spent a long time praying for pardon. He then made his way to Lyons, but the vengeance of God followed fast on his heels. King Theuderic married his daughter.

6.   Queen Clotild arranged a meeting with Chlodomer and her other sons. 'My dear children,' said she, 'do not give me cause to regret the fact that I have brought you up with such care. You must surely resent the wrong which has been done to me. You must do all in your power to avenge the death of my mother and father.' When they had listened to her appeal they set out for Burgundy. They marched their troops against Sigismund and his brother Godomar. The Burgundian army was beaten and Godomar fled. Sigismund tried to escape to the monastery of Agaune. He was captured by Chlodomer with his wife and sons, and was held a prisoner somewhere in the neighbourhood of Orleans. When the Frankish kings had departed, Godomar rallied his forces: he mobilized the Burgundes and won back his kingdom. Chlodomer made preparations to attack him a second time. He decided to have Sigismund killed. Saint Avitus, the Abbot of Saint-Mesmin de Micy, a powerful churchman of the period, addressed this plea to Chlodomer: 'If you change your plans and show respect to God by refusing to have these men killed, the Lord will be with you and you will go forth to victory. On the other hand, if you do kill them, you will fall into the hands of your enemies and you will suffer a fate similar to theirs. Whatever you do to Sigismund and his wife and children, the same will be done to your children and your wife and you yourself.' Chlodomer refused to listen to the advice of Avitus. 'It would be foolish to do what you suggest,' he said, 'and leave some of my enemies behind me when I march out to meet the others. They will attack me from the rear while the others meet me face to face, and I shall be destroyed between two enemy armies. I shall win an easier victory and a more complete one if I keep the two of them separate. If I kill Sigismund now, it will be a simpler matter to dispose of the others.' Sigismund and his wife and children were murdered out of hand: Chlodomer ordered them to be thrown down a well at Saint-Péravy-la-

Colombe, a small township in the Orléanais. He summoned
King Theuderic to his assistance and set out for Burgundy.
Theuderic showed no desire to avenge the wrong done to his
father-in-law, but promised to march in support of Chlodomer.
The two armies met at Vézeronce in the Viennois, and joined
battle with Godomar. Godomar and his army turned in flight.
Chlodomer pursued him and soon out-distanced his own troops.
The Burgundians imitated Chlodomer's rallying-cry and
shouted to him: 'This way! This way! We are your own
troops!' Chlodomer believed them, wheeled in their direction
and rushed headlong into the middle of his enemies. They
hacked off his head, stuck it on a stake and raised it in the air.
The Franks saw what had happened and realized that Chlodomer was dead. They rallied their forces and put Godomar to
flight. They conquered the Burgundes and took over their
country. Later Lothar married the widow of his brother
Chlodomer: her name was Guntheuc. When her period of
mourning was over, Queen Clotild took Chlodomer's sons into
her own household and brought them up. The eldest was Theudovald, the second Gunthar and the third Chlodovald. Godomar won back his kingdom a third time.

7.   Theuderic could not forget the wrongs done to him by Hermanfrid, the King of the Thuringians. He summoned his
brother Lothar to his support and prepared to march against
Hermanfrid. He promised Lothar a share in the booty, if victory were once theirs. He called a meeting of the Franks. 'You
have every reason to be furious,' said he, 'both because of the
injury done to me and for the slaughter of your own relations.
Remember that not so long ago these Thuringians made a violent attack upon our people and did them much harm. Hostages
were exchanged and our Franks were ready to make peace with
them. The Thuringians murdered the hostages in all sorts of
different ways. They attacked our fellow-countrymen and stole
their possessions. They hung our young men up to die in the
trees by the muscles of their thighs. They put more than two
hundred of our young women to death in the most barbarous

way: they tied their arms round the necks of their horses, stampeded these animals in all directions by prodding them with goads, and so tore the girls to pieces; or else they stretched them out over the ruts of their roads, attached their arms and legs to the ground with stakes, and then drove heavily-laden carts over them again and again, until their bones were all broken and their bodies could be thrown out for the dogs and birds to feed on. What is more, Hermanfrid has now broken his promise to me and refuses utterly to do what he said he would. There is no doubt that we have right on our side. With God's help we must attack them!' The Franks listened to what he had to say: they were furious at this recital of the crimes committed by their enemy and they all agreed to invade Thuringia. Theuderic summoned his brother Lothar and his son Theudebert to his support and set out at the head of his army. The Thuringians had prepared a few pitfalls for the advancing Franks. They dug a series of ditches in the field where the battle would be fought. Then they covered these holes over with turves and made them level again with the rest of the grass. When the battle began many of the Frankish cavalry rushed headlong into these ditches and there is no doubt that they were greatly impeded by them. Once they had spotted the trick, they advanced with more circumspection. King Hermanfrid was driven from the battlefield and the Thuringians realized that they were being cut to pieces. They turned in flight and made their way to the River Unstrut. Such a massacre of the Thuringians took place here that the bed of the river was piled high with their corpses and that the Franks crossed over them to the other side as if they were walking on a bridge. When their victory was complete the Franks took over the country and subjected it to their own rule.

When the time came to return home Lothar took with him as his share of the booty Radegund, the daughter of King Berthar. Later he married her. This did not stop him afterwards from arranging for her brother to be murdered by assassins. Radegund turned to God, took the habit of a religious and built a nunnery for herself in Poitiers. She was famous for her prayers, her vigils and her charities, and she became so well known that the common people looked upon her as a saint.

While the Frankish Kings were still in Thuringia, Theuderic plotted to kill his brother Lothar. He prepared an ambush of armed assassins and then summoned Lothar to his presence, saying that he had something which he wished to talk over in secret. In a courtyard of his house he stretched a piece of canvas across from one wall to another, and he told the armed men to stand behind it. The canvas was not long enough to reach the ground, and the men's feet were plainly visible beneath it. Lothar observed this and marched into the house still protected by his own bodyguard. In his turn Theuderic realized that Lothar had seen through his plot, so he had to think up a pretext while he chatted on about one thing after another. Not quite knowing how to cover up his treachery, he finally handed Lothar a great silver salver as a present. Lothar thanked Theuderic for the gift, said good-bye and went back to his lodging. Theuderic then complained to his family that he had handed over the silver salver without any valid reason for doing so. 'Run after your uncle,' said he to his son Theudebert, 'and ask him to be so good as to hand back to you the present which I have just given to him.' The young man set off and was given what he asked for. Theuderic was very good at this sort of trick.

8.   When he reached home Theuderic summoned Hermanfrid to his presence, assuring him of safe-conduct. He loaded him with valuable gifts. One day they were seen chatting together on the city walls of Zülpich.[10] Somebody accidentally gave Hermanfrid a push and he fell to the ground from the top of the wall. He died, but who pushed him we shall never know. Certain people have ventured to suggest that Theuderic may have had something to do with it.

9.   While Theuderic was still in Thuringia, the rumour reached Clermont-Ferrand that he had been killed. Arcadius, one of the

10. Zülpich, *civitas Tulbiacensis*, had no bishop and was not a city.

Senators of Clermont,[11] sent a message to Childebert to invite him to take command of the district. Childebert did not lose a moment, but came straight to Clermont. The fog was so thick that day that one could see only a short distance. Childebert was in the habit of saying: 'How I should love to see the plain of Limagne in Auvergne, which is said to be so gay and attractive!' God did not permit him to do so. The city gates were locked and there was no entrance open to him. Arcadius sawed off the lock of one of the gates and invited Childebert in. At that moment the news arrived that Theuderic had returned safe and sound from Thuringia.

10.   As soon as Childebert was sure of this he left Clermont and set off for Spain, for the sake of his sister Clotild. She was being very badly treated by her husband Amalaric on account of her Catholic faith. Several times when she was on her way to church he had dung and other filth thrown over her. Finally he struck her with such violence that she sent to her brother a towel stained with her own blood. He was greatly moved and set off immediately for Spain. When Amalaric heard of this he had boats launched and made ready his escape. Just as Childebert was arriving, Amalaric, who was on the point of going aboard one of the boats, remembered that he had left a fortune in precious stones in his treasury. He rushed back into the city[12] to collect them, but the soldiery blocked his return to the sea-port. Seeing that all escape was cut off, he ran to take refuge in one of the Christian churches. Before he could cross the threshold of the building, a soldier threw a javelin at him and wounded him mortally. He fell to the ground and died on the spot. Childebert planned to take his sister home with him, and at the same time to carry off a vast mass of treasure. By some ill chance Clotild died on the journey. She was carried to Paris and buried beside her father Clovis. Along with the other treasure Childebert removed a most valuable collection of

11. Arcadius was the son of Apollinaris and the grandson of Sidonius Apollinaris.
12. Barcelona.

church plate. He carried off sixty chalices, fifteen patens and
twenty Gospel bindings, all made of pure gold and adorned
with precious gems. He did not have them broken up. He do-
nated them all to various churches and monastery chapels.

11.   After this Lothar and Childebert decided to attack Burgundy. They called upon Theuderic to support them, but he
refused to move. The Franks under his command said: 'If you
refuse to march against Burgundy with your brothers, we shall
assuredly desert you, for we much prefer to follow the others.'
Theuderic knew that the men of Clermont-Ferrand were ready
to betray him. 'Follow me,' said he to his people, 'and I will lead
you to a land where you will be able to lay your hands on so
much gold and silver that even your lust for loot will be
satisfied. If only you will agree not to go off after my brothers,
in this other land you may capture as many cattle and slaves
and seize as much clothing as you wish.' The Franks were persuaded by what Theuderic said and they promised to do as he
wished. As he made ready to march into Clermont, he told his
troops again and again that they had his permission to bring
home with them not only every single thing which they could
steal in the region which they were about to attack but also the
entire population. Meanwhile Lothar and Childebert were
marching against Burgundy. They besieged Autun,[13] forced
Godomar to flee and occupied the whole of Burgundy.

12.   When Theuderic arrived in Clermont with his army, he
ravaged and destroyed the entire region.[14] Meanwhile Arcadius, who had been the original cause of the whole trouble
and through whose foolish behaviour this part of France was
now being laid waste, fled to the town of Bourges, which was
then under the rule of Childebert. Placidina, the mother of Arcadius, and Alchima, his father's sister, were arrested in the
town of Cahors. All their goods were seized and they were sent
into exile. King Theuderic entered the city of Clermont-Ferrand and quartered his troops in one of the suburbs. At that

13. A.D. 534.   14. A.D. 532.

time Saint Quintianus was the Bishop. The army ran riot through the whole region, attacking everything, destroying everything. Some of Theuderic's troops came to the church of Saint Julian: they destroyed the locks, broke open the doors, stole the possessions of the poor inhabitants which had been put there for safety and did as much damage as they could. Those responsible for these crimes were seized by an unclean spirit. 'Why do you torture us in this way, holy martyr?' they shouted, as they tore themselves to pieces with their own foul teeth. I have described all this in my book about the miracles of Saint Julian.[15]

13. The troops stormed the fortress of Vollore. The priest Proculus, who had once done wrong to Saint Quintianus,[16] was cruelly cut down in front of the altar of his own church. I should not be surprised if it were his fault that the fortress was allowed to fall into enemy hands, for until this moment it had always been inviolate. Theuderic's soldiers were not able to capture it and they were already preparing to return to wherever they had come from. When the besieged heard of this they were lured into a false sense of security and happiness, as the Apostle foretold: 'For when they shall say, Peace and safety; then sudden destruction cometh upon them.'[17] In the end the inhabitants, who thought themselves safe, fell into the enemy's hands, no doubt because of this earlier crime of the priest Proculus. The fortress was destroyed. As the inhabitants were led away into slavery, it rained in torrents, although not a drop had fallen for the previous thirty days.

The people of Chastel-Marlhac were besieged, but they retained their liberty, for they bribed the invaders not to take them captive. It was only because of their own stupidity that they had to pay anything at all. The place was a natural fortress, for it was surrounded not by man-made walls, but by cliffs which rose sheer for a hundred feet or more. In the middle there was a great pool of excellent drinking water, and elsewhere there were springs which never seemed to fail, so that a river of

15. *Liber de passione et virtutibus Sancti Juliani martyris* (*VSJ*), 13.
16. *VP*, 4, 1–2.   17. I Thessalonians 5, 3.

fresh water ran through the whole place. This natural strong-point was so extensive that the inhabitants farmed land and reaped an abundant harvest inside their walls. When they were besieged the people of Chastel-Marlhac felt so secure inside their natural fortification that they even dared to make a sally, thinking that it was they who could seize the goods of the Frankish soldiers and then rush back once more into their en-closure. About fifty of them were captured by the enemy. Their hands were tied behind their backs, they were dragged to a spot where their relatives could see them and the Franks drew their swords ready to kill them. Those inside Chastel-Marlhac con-sented to pay the third of a gold piece as ransom for each man, rather than let them be slaughtered.

In the end Theuderic marched out of Clermont-Ferrand, but he left behind one of his relations called Sigivald to garrison the town.

At that time there was a local official called Lytigius who kept plotting against Saint Quintianus. The holy Bishop went so far as to demean himself at this man's feet, but even then Ly-tigius showed him no deference. In fact he once went so far as to make fun of the Bishop to his wife. She had more sense than her husband. 'Quintianus may be humbled today,' said she, 'but that will never do you any good.' Only three days later mess-engers arrived from the King's court. Lytigius was bound and dragged off with his wife and children. He disappeared and was never seen again in Clermont.

14.   A man called Munderic, who pretended to be of royal blood, was so swollen with pride that he said: 'What is King Theuderic to me? My right to the throne is as good as his. I will go out and gather my people together, and I will persuade them to swear an oath of fealty to me, so that Theuderic may realize that I am a king, too, just as he is.' He went out and began to harangue the people. 'I am a prince of the blood,' said he. 'Follow me and all will be well with you.' A crowd of peasants did follow him, as so often happens, for people are so gullible. They gave him an oath of fealty and did him honour as if he

really were their king. Theuderic heard of this and sent a message to Munderic. 'Come to see me,' said Theuderic, 'and if any part of my kingdom is rightly yours, then take it.' When he said this, Theuderic was trying to trick Munderic: had he gone to the King he would have been killed. Munderic refused. 'Go and tell Theuderic,' said he to the messengers, 'that I am a king, too, just as he is.' Theuderic then assembled his army to quell Munderic and punish him. When Munderic learned this, he decided that he was not strong enough to resist Theuderic. He took refuge with all his possessions inside the walls of the fortress of Vitry-le-Brûlé: and there he prepared to defend himself, with all those whom he had won over to his cause. The army which Theuderic had assembled surrounded the fortress and besieged it for seven days. Munderic and his men resisted stoutly. 'Let us stand firm,' said he, 'and fight to the death together, for we must never submit to our enemies.' The besieging troops hurled their javelins from their lines, but they made no progress. Theuderic was informed of this. He sent one of his men called Aregisel to Vitry. 'You see how this traitor is succeeding in his rebellious behaviour,' he told him. 'Go to him and promise him on oath that he can come out safely. When he comes out, kill him, so that his very memory may be obliterated from my kingdom.' Aregisel set off and did as he was told. He had first of all arranged a signal with his men. 'As soon as I have said such and such,' he told them, 'rush at him and kill him.' Aregisel entered Vitry and said to Munderic: 'How long do you propose to remain here like someone out of his senses? How long do you think that you can resist the King? Your supply-lines are cut. As soon as your rations fail you will have to come out. You will fall into the hands of your enemies and then you will die like a dog. Listen to what I say and submit to the King. Your life will be spared and that of your sons, too.' Munderic was swayed by what Aregisel said. 'If I come out,' he answered, 'I shall be captured and the King will have me killed, me and my sons and all my friends who have gathered here under my command.' 'Don't be afraid,' said Aregisel. 'If you agree to come out, you have my word that your treason will be forgiven and that you will be safe as far as the King is concerned. Don't be afraid, I say: your relationship with Theuderic will be just what it was before.' 'As long as I am safe,' replied Munderic, 'and my life is assured!' Aregisel laid his hands on the holy altar and swore that he should have safe-conduct. When he had sworn this oath, Munderic came out of the gateway of the fortress, holding Aregisel's hand. The enemy troops watched him from afar, keeping their eyes fixed on him. Aregisel then spoke the words which were the prearranged signal: 'Men,' said he, 'why are you staring at Munderic so closely? Have you never seen him before?' Without more ado they rushed straight at him. Munderic understood what had happened. 'I see clearly,' said he, 'that when you said that it was a signal for your troops to kill me. My answer is this, that no one shall see you alive again, even if you have tricked me by your false promise.' He dashed his javelin between Aregisel's shoulders and pierced him through. Aregisel fell dead to the ground. Munderic then drew his sword and with his own men around him slew one after another of the enemy troops. As long as there was breath in his body he continued to cut down every man within his reach. He was killed and his property passed to the King's treasury.

15.   Theuderic and Childebert made a treaty. They swore an oath that neither would attack the other, and they each took hostages to ensure that their promises would be kept. Many sons of senatorial families were handed over in this exchange of hostages. Then a new quarrel arose between the two Kings, and the hostages were reduced to state labour, or became the slaves of those in whose custody they had been placed. Many escaped from their masters and made their way home; but quite a few remained in bondage. Among these last was Attalus, a nephew of Saint Gregory, Bishop of Langres; he was reduced to state labour and was set to groom horses.[18] He lived somewhere near Trier and had a certain Frank as his master. Saint Gregory sent some of his men to see what was happening to his nephew.

18. Attalus was thus a kinsman of Gregory himself, which explains the length and detail of the narrative. See the family tree on p. 11.

When they located him, they tried to buy his freedom, but the Frank refused their offer. 'A man of such family should be worth at least ten pounds of gold,' said he. When they reported this to Gregory, one of his cooks called Leo said to his master: 'Let me try. I shall be able to free him from slavery.' Gregory was delighted. Leo set off immediately to the place in question and tried to rescue Attalus by some subterfuge or other, but he failed. Then he plotted with one of his companions. 'Come with me,' he said, 'and sell me to the household of this Frank. What you receive for me you can keep as your own reward, for all I want myself is a freer opportunity of carrying out what I have planned.' They swore an oath to each other. The man went off and sold Leo for twelve pieces of gold. Then he disappeared. The Frank who had bought him asked his new slave what he could do. 'I am highly skilled in preparing all dishes which are fit to be eaten at a rich man's table,' replied Leo, 'and I am prepared to assert that no one can find my equal in the culinary science. Indeed, I tell you this: if you want to prepare a banquet for a king, I can cook such royal dishes for you, and none can do it better than I can.' 'Well,' said the Frank, 'tomorrow is Sunday' – for that is what the Franks call the Lord's Day – 'and on that day I shall invite my neighbours and relations to my house. I want you to prepare a meal at which they will marvel and exclaim: "Why, we have not seen better food in the King's palace!" ' 'My master has only to order a good supply of chickens,' answered Leo, 'and I will do what you command.' Everything which he had asked for was made ready. Sunday dawned, and he cooked a magnificent meal, with every imaginable delicacy. When they had all eaten their fill, the Frank's relations said how much they had enjoyed their meal and then went off home. The master thanked his slave. Leo was put in charge of the Frank's entire establishment: his master came to love him dearly, and he was given the task of preparing all the food eaten by those in the household.

By the time a whole year had passed, his master had come to trust Leo completely. He went off one day into a meadow which was near the house, together with Attalus, the slave who had charge of the horses. The two of them lay down on the grass, some distance apart, with their backs to each other, so that no one could see that they were talking to each other. 'The time has come,' said Leo to the young man, 'for us to be thinking of going home. Listen to what I say. Tonight, when you have brought the horses in and shut them in the stable, make sure that you don't fall asleep. Be ready as soon as I give you the word, and we will set off on our journey.' The Frank had invited many of his relations to dinner. Among them was his son-in-law, the husband of his daughter. At midnight they got up from the table and went off to bed. Leo followed his master's son-in-law to his bedroom with a drink. As Leo handed it to him, this man said to Leo: 'Tell me, you whom my father-in-law trusts so completely, now that you have the chance, why don't you steal his horses and set off home with them?' He was in a good humour and he said this as a joke. Leo replied in the same jesting vein, but he was telling the truth: 'This very night I will think about it, for it may indeed be God's will.' 'Well,' said the other, 'I only hope that my servants will guard me carefully, to make sure that you don't take anything of mine!' They had a good laugh over this and then separated. When the Franks were all asleep, Leo called Attalus. The horses were saddled. Leo asked Attalus if he had a sword. 'No,' replied Attalus, 'I don't need one. All I have is a small spear.' Leo went back into his master's house and took his shield and spear. The Frank asked him who he was and what he wanted. 'I am your slave Leo,' said he. 'I am waking up Attalus. He should get up quickly and take the horses to pasture. He is sunk in a drunken stupor.' 'Do as you wish,' said the Frank, and went off to sleep again. Leo went out once more and handed the weapons over to Attalus. By a miracle he found the gates of the courtyard unfastened, although at nightfall he had secured them with wedges which he had driven home with a mallet, to keep the horses in. For this he thanked God. Then they set off, taking the other horses with them, together with a bundle which contained their clothes.

They came to the River Moselle, which they had to cross. They were held up by the locals, so they abandoned their horses and their clothes and ferried themselves across the river on their shield. They reached the opposite bank and in the darkness of the night hid in the woods. It was now the third night which they had spent on their journey without anything to eat. By the grace of God they came upon a tree loaded with fruit. These were plums: they ate some, felt a little stronger and set off for Champagne. As they journeyed on, they heard the sound of galloping horses. 'Lie down on the ground,' they said to each other, 'so that these men who are coming can't see us.' Fortunately there was a big bramble-bush just at this spot. They rushed round behind it and threw themselves on the ground, drawing their swords, so that, if they were spotted, they could immediately defend themselves from their enemies. The riders came up and paused by the bramble-bush to let their horses empty their bladders. 'The devil take it!' said one of them. 'These swine are well away and we shall never catch them! Upon my soul I swear it, if they were caught I would send one to the gallows and have the other cut to ribbons, not with one sword but with half a dozen!' It was the Frank himself who was saying this, their own master, who had just ridden out from the city of Rheims, looking for them everywhere, and he would have found them if the darkness had not prevented him. The Franks stuck spurs into their horses and moved on again.

That same night the two fugitives reached the city of Rheims. They went in and found a man, whom they asked to tell them where the priest Paulellus lived. He gave them the necessary directions. As they crossed the city square the bell rang for morning prayer, for it was the Lord's Day. They knocked at the priest's door and went in. Leo explained whose servant he was. 'My vision has come true, then,' said the priest. 'This very night I dreamed that two doves flew in and perched on my head. One was white and the other black.' Leo said to the priest: 'May the Lord grant us indulgence for His holy day.[19] We beg you to give us something to eat. The fourth day is now dawning since we last tasted bread or meat.' The priest concealed them and gave them some bread soaked in wine. Then he went off to

19. On Sunday no food was eaten before one had attended Mass.

morning prayer. Later the Frank put in an appearance, still looking for his two slaves. The priest told him a lie, and he went off once more. The priest was an old acquaintance of Saint Gregory. When they had eaten the two slaves felt stronger. They stayed two days in the priest's house. Then they went on again and were brought before Saint Gregory. The Bishop was delighted when he saw them both. He wept on the neck of his nephew Attalus. He made Leo a freedman, and all his progeny, too, and he gave him a piece of land of his own on which he lived in freedom with his wife and children all the days of his life.

16. As long as Sigivald stayed in Clermont-Ferrand he did a great amount of harm there. He made off with the personal property of many people, while his dependants committed a long series of thefts, murders, assaults and other crimes, but no one dared to complain openly. A climax was reached when Sigivald dared to seize the villa of Bonghéat, which the saintly Bishop Tetradius had bequeathed to the church of Saint Julian. As soon as he set foot in the house he had a fit and collapsed on a bed. His wife was warned by the priest: she had him lifted on to a litter and carried to another villa, where he recovered. She joined him there and told him what had happened. As soon as he heard the story he made a vow to the blessed martyr and restored the double of all that he had taken. I have described all this in my book *Miracula Sancti Juliani*.[20]

17. When Bishop Dinifius died in Tours, Ommatius held the see for three years. He was ordained at the command of Chlodomer, about whom I have already told you. Ommatius died in his turn and Leo was Bishop for seven months. He was an active man and greatly skilled at carpentry. On the death of Leo, two Bishops called Theodorus and Proculus, who came from somewhere in Burgundy, were ordained at the wish of Queen Clotild and governed the diocese of Tours for three years. After their death the senator Francilio replaced them. In the

20. *VSJ*, 14.

third year of his episcopate, one Christmas night when all the world was rejoicing at the birth of our Lord, he asked for a drink before going off to vigils. A servant stepped forward and handed him a cup. He had no sooner drunk than he dropped down dead. There seems little doubt that he was poisoned. After his death one of the Tourangeaux called Injuriosus mounted the episcopal throne as the fifteenth successor to Saint Martin.

18.   While Queen Clotild was living in Paris, Childebert observed that his mother was lavishing all her affection on the sons of Chlodomer, whom I have already mentioned. This made him jealous, for he was afraid that this favour which the Queen was showing them might bring them into the line of succession. He sent a secret message to his brother, King Lothar: 'Our mother keeps the children of our brother close by her side and is planning to give them the throne. You must come to Paris without delay. We must take counsel together and make up our minds what is to be done about them. Ought we to cut off their hair and so reduce them to the status of ordinary individuals? Or should we have them killed and then divide our brother's kingdom equally between us?' Lothar was delighted when he received this message. He came to Paris. Childebert spread the rumour among the people that he and his royal brother were holding a meeting to plan the coronation of the young princes. When they had conferred together, they sent a message to the Queen, who was then resident in Paris. 'Send the princes to us,' they said, 'so that they may be raised to the throne.' This pleased Clotild very much, for she knew nothing of their plotting. She fed the boys and gave them something to drink. 'Once I see you succeed him on the throne,' she said, 'I shall forget that I have lost my son.' Off they set, but they were immediately seized and separated from their household and their tutors; for they were all locked up in different places, the household attendants here and the young princes there. Then Childebert and Lothar sent Arcadius to the Queen, the man about whom I have already told you, with a pair of scissors in one hand and a naked

180

sword in the other. When he came into the Queen's presence, he held them out to her. 'Your two sons, who are our masters, seek your decision, gracious Queen, as to what should be done with the princes. Do you wish them to live with their hair cut short? Or would you prefer to see them killed?' Clotild was terrified by what he had said, and very angry indeed, especially when she saw the drawn sword and the scissors. Beside herself with bitter grief and hardly knowing what she was saying in her anguish, she answered: 'If they are not to ascend the throne, I would rather see them dead than with their hair cut short.' Arcadius took no notice of her distress, and he certainly had no wish to see if on due reflection she would change her mind. He hurried back to the two Kings. 'You can finish the job,' said he, 'for the Queen agrees. It is her wish that you should do what you have planned.' Lothar did not waste a minute. He seized the older boy by the wrist, threw him to the ground, jabbed his dagger into his armpit and so murdered him with the utmost savagery. As he died the boy screamed. The younger lad threw himself at Childebert's feet and gripped him round the knees. 'Help me! Help me! dearest uncle,' he cried, 'lest I perish as my brother has done!' The tears streamed down Childebert's face. 'My dear brother,' said he, 'I beg you to have pity on him and to grant me his life! I will give you anything you ask in exchange, if only you will agree not to kill him.' Lothar shouted abuse at him. 'Make him let go,' he bellowed, 'or I will kill you instead! It was you who thought of this business! Now you are trying to rat on me!' When Childebert heard this, he pushed the child away and tossed him to Lothar. Lothar seized him, thrust his dagger in his ribs and murdered him just as he had murdered his brother. Then they slew all the attendants and the tutors. When all lay dead Lothar climbed on his horse and rode away, showing no remorse for the slaughter of his two nephews. Childebert skulked off to the outskirts of Paris. Queen Clotild placed the two small corpses on a bier and followed them in funeral procession to the church of Saint Peter, grieving her heart out as the psalms where sung. There she buried them side by side. One was ten years old and the other only seven. There was a third boy,

Chlodovald: him they could not catch, for those who guarded
him were brave men. Chlodovald had no wish for earthly dominion, but devoted himself to God.[21] With his own hands he
cut his hair short. He became a religious, devoted himself to
good works and was still a priest when he died. The two Kings
divided Chlodomer's lands equally between them. Queen Clotild earned the respect of all by her bearing. She gave alms to the
poor and spent her nights in prayer. In chastity and virtue she
lived out her blameless life. She endowed churches, monasteries
and other holy places with the lands necessary for their upkeep;
her giving was so generous and so eager that already in her
lifetime she was looked upon not as a Queen but as the handmaiden of God whom she served with such zeal. Neither the
royal status of her sons nor her worldly goods nor earthly am-
bition could bring her to disrepute. In all humility she moved
forward to heavenly grace.

19.   At this time in the city of Langres there lived Saint Gregory, that priest of God, famed far and wide for his miracles and
virtuous deeds.[22] While I am talking about this Bishop, I
thought that you would like me to tell you something of the
town of Dijon, where he greatly loved to spend his time. It is a
fortress girded round with mighty walls and set in the centre of
a pleasant plain. Its lands are fertile and so productive that,
after a single ploughing, when the fields are sown, a rich harvest
soon follows. On its southern side it has the River Ouche, which
teems with fish. A smaller stream runs down from the north,[23]
entering through one gateway, running under a bridge and then
flowing out again through another gate. This stream washes all
the fortifications with its gentle waters and turns the mill-wheels
round at wondrous speed outside the gate. The four entrances
to the town are placed at the four quarters of the compass, and
thirty-three towers adorn the circuit of the walls, which are

21. This young Prince who became a priest was later canonized and he is
known in France as Saint Cloud.
22. He was the great-grandfather of Gregory of Tours.
23. The River Suzon.

made of squared stones rising to a height of twenty feet, with smaller stones placed above to reach in all some thirty feet, the whole being fifteen feet thick. Why Dijon is not elevated to the dignity of a bishopric I cannot imagine. Round about are excellent springs of water. To the west the hills are covered with fruitful vines, which yield so noble a Falernian-type wine that the inhabitants have been known to scorn a good Mâcon. The ancients say that Dijon was built by the Emperor Aurelian.

20.   Theuderic had betrothed his son Theudebert to Wisigard, a king's daughter.[24]

21.   Since the death of Clovis the Goths had occupied much of the territory which he had conquered. Theuderic now sent his son Theudebert to win this back and Lothar sent his eldest son Gunthar. I do not know why, but Gunthar advanced as far as Rodez and then turned back. Theudebert went on as far as Béziers. He captured the fortress of Dio and sacked it. Next he sent messengers to a fortress called Cabrières to say that, unless the inhabitants surrendered, the whole place would be burnt to the ground and they themselves made captive.

22.   There was living in Cabrières at this period a married woman full of energy and resource whose name was Deuteria. Her husband had gone off to Béziers. She sent messengers to Theudebert to say: 'No one can resist you, noble prince. We accept you as our ruler. Come to our town and do with it what you will.' Theudebert marched to Cabrières and entered the township. He saw that the inhabitants were offering no resistance, and so he did them no harm. Deuteria went to meet him. He found her attractive, fell in love with her, persuaded her to go to bed with him and had intercourse with her.

23.   Next Theuderic drew his sword and killed his relative Sigivald. He sent a secret message to Theudebert to tell him to do away with Sigivald's son, who was then serving with him. Theu-

24. Wacho, King of the Longobards.

debert had held this young man at the font at his baptism and he was unwilling to kill him. Instead he gave him his father's letter to read. 'You must escape from here,' said Theudebert, 'for I have received this order from my father to kill you. When he dies and you learn that I am reigning in his place you can return to me safe and sound.' Sigivald's son thanked Theudebert for telling him this. He said good-bye and went on his way. The Goths had recently occupied the town of Arles, from which Theudebert held hostages. It was to Arles that the younger Sigivald fled. He soon realized that he was still in danger there, so he crossed into Italy and hid in that country. Meanwhile Theudebert learned that his father was seriously ill. He knew that unless he hurried home and reached his father before his death he would be cut off from his inheritance by his uncles and would never be able to return. As soon as he heard the news he abandoned everything and turned back. He left Deuteria and the daughter whom she had borne him in Clermont-Ferrand. A few days later, while Theudebert was still on his way, Theuderic died in the twenty-third year of his reign.[25] Childebert and Lothar joined forces against Theudebert and did what they could to seize his kingdom. He bought them off and with the help of his *leudes*[26] established himself on the throne. He then sent for Deuteria, who was still in Clermont, had her brought home and married her.

24.　When Childebert realized that he could not overcome Theudebert, he sent an embassy to him and told him to come on a visit. 'I have no children of my own,' he said, 'and I should like to adopt you as my son.' When Theudebert arrived, Childebert gave him so many presents that everyone was astonished. He gave him three pairs of everything which a king could need, arms, clothes and ornaments, with some silver dishes and a team of horses.

As soon as Sigivald heard that Theudebert had succeeded to his father's throne, he returned to him from Italy. Theudebert was delighted. He embraced Sigivald and gave him a third of all

25. A.D. 534.　　26. For *leudes*, see p. 157, note 64.

the gifts which he had received from his uncle. He ordered that
all Sigivald's property which his father had confiscated should
now be restored to him.

25. Once he was firmly established on the throne, Theudebert
proved himself to be a great king, distinguished by every virtue.
He ruled his kingdom justly, respected his bishops, was liberal
to the churches, relieved the wants of the poor and distributed
many benefits with piety and friendly goodwill. With great generosity he remitted to the churches in Clermont-Ferrand all the
tribute which they used to pay to the royal treasury.

26. When Deuteria saw that her daughter was a grown-up
woman, she was afraid that the King might desire her and take
advantage of her. She put her in a cart drawn by untamed bulls
and had her tipped over a bridge: she fell into the river and was
drowned. This happened in the city of Verdun.

27. Seven years had passed since Theudebert had become engaged to Wisigard, but he would not marry her because of Deuteria. The Franks all agreed that it was a scandalous situation
that he should have abandoned his fiancée. Theudebert gave in,
deserted Deuteria by whom he had a young son called Theudebald, and married Wisigard. He did not have her for long,
for she soon died. He refused to take Deuteria back and married another woman.

28. Childebert and Theudebert assembled an army and prepared to march against Lothar. When he heard of this he
realized that he was not strong enough to resist their combined
forces. He took to the woods, built a great circle of barricades
among the trees and put his trust in the mercy of God.[27]
Queen Clotild learned what had happened. She went to the
tomb of Saint Martin, where she knelt in supplication and spent

27. According to the *Chronicle* of Fredegar this happened in the Forest
of Arelaunum, which has been identified as the Forêt de Brotonne on the
south side of the River Seine opposite Caudebec.

the whole night praying that civil war might not break out between her sons. Childebert and Theudebert advanced with their troops, surrounded Lothar's position and made plans to kill him in the morning. When day dawned a great storm blew up over the spot where they were encamped. Their tents were blown down, their equipment was scattered and everything was overturned. There was thunder and lightning, and they were bombarded with hailstones. They threw themselves on their faces on the ground where the hail already lay thick, and they were severely lashed by the hailstones which continued to fall. They had no protection except their shields and they were afraid that they would be struck by the lightning. Their horses were scattered far and wide: some were recovered two or three miles away, but many of them were never found at all. The two Kings were cut about by the hailstones as they lay on the ground. They did penance to God and begged Him to forgive them for having attacked their own kith and kin. No drop of rain fell on Lothar, no clap of thunder was heard, no winds blew where he was. Childebert and Theudebert sent messengers to him to sue for peace and concord. This was granted and they all went home. None can doubt that this miracle was wrought by Saint Martin through the intercession of the Queen.

29. Next King Childebert set off for Spain. He and Lothar arrived there together. They attacked and laid siege to the city of Saragossa. The inhabitants turned in great humility to God: they dressed themselves in hair-shirts, abstained from eating and drinking, and marched round the city walls singing psalms and carrying the tunic of Saint Vincent the martyr. Their women-folk followed them, weeping and wailing, dressed in black garments, with their hair blowing free and with ashes on their heads, so that you might have thought that they were burying their dead husbands. The city pinned its hope on the mercy of God. It could have been said to fast as Nineveh fasted,[28] and it was quite unimaginable that God in His compassion would not be swayed by the prayers of these people.

28. Cp. Jonah 3, 5.

The besiegers were nonplussed to see them behave in this way: as they watched them march round the walls they imagined that it was some curious kind of black magic. They seized hold of a peasant who lived in Saragossa and asked him what in the world they were doing. 'They are marching behind the tunic of Saint Vincent,' he told them, 'and with this as their banner they are imploring God to take pity on them.'[29] This scared the troops and they withdrew from the city. However, they succeeded in conquering a large part of Spain and they returned to Gaul with immense booty.

30.   After Amalaric, Theuda was chosen as King of Spain.[30] He was assassinated, and then they raised Theudegisel to the kingship. When Theudegisel was feasting with his friends at supper and was very merry, the candles were blown out and he was struck by a sword as he lay on his couch, thus dying in his turn.[31] After him Agila became King.[32] The Goths had adopted the reprehensible habit of killing out of hand any king who displeased them and replacing him on the throne by someone whom they preferred.

31.   Theodoric, King of Italy, who had married Audofleda, the sister of Clovis, died and left his wife with a small daughter called Amalasuntha.[33] When she grew up Amalasuntha soon showed what little sense she had, for, ignoring the advice of her mother, who wanted her to marry a king's son, she took as lover one of her own slaves called Traguilla and eloped with him to a neighbouring city, where she thought she would be free to do as

29. Childebert brought this relic home with him and placed it in a church which he founded in Paris and which he dedicated to Saint Vincent. Later, when Saint Germanus was buried there, this church became Saint-Germain-des-Prés.

30. Theuda was King of the Visigoths from A.D. 531 to 548. He was assassinated in Seville.

31. Theudegisel was assassinated in Seville in A.D. 549.

32. Agila was assassinated in Merida in A.D. 554.

33. Both Theodoric and his wife Audofleda, sister of Clovis, died in *A*.D. 526. Amalasuntha had then been married for some ten or eleven years.

she liked. Her mother was very angry with her and begged her not to disgrace her royal blood any longer, but to marry the man of equal social status whom she had herself proposed. Amalasuntha would have none of this. Her mother became even more angry and sent a band of armed men to take her into custody. These soldiers came upon the two lovers, killed Traguilla, gave Amalasuntha a good beating and brought her back to her mother's home. Mother and daughter both belonged to the Arian sect, whose custom it is, when they come to the altar for communion, for those of royal blood to drink from one cup and lesser mortals from another. Amalasuntha popped some poison into the chalice from which her mother was to drink next. Audofleda drank from the cup and dropped down dead. There can be no doubt at all that such a crime as this was the work of the Devil. What can these miserable Arian heretics say, when the Devil is present even at their altar? We Catholics, on the contrary, who believe in the Trinity, co-equal and all-powerful, would come to no harm even if we were to drink poison in the name of the Father, the Son and the Holy Ghost, one true Godhead. The Italians were furious with Amalasuntha for what she had done, and they summoned Theudat, King of Tuscany, to rule over them. When he heard of the deeds of this meretricious woman, who had murdered her own mother for the sake of a slave who had been her lover, Theudat had a hot steam-bath prepared and ordered her to be shut up inside it with one of her maids. As soon as she was in the scalding steam she fell to the stone floor and died immediately.[34] When her cousins, the three Kings Childebert, Lothar and Theudebert, learned that Amalasuntha had died such a shameful death, they sent messengers to Theudat to upbraid him for having killed her. 'If you do not agree to pay lavishly for what you have done,' said they, 'we will seize your kingdom and submit you to the same treatment.' Theudat was afraid and sent them fifty thousand pieces of gold.[35] Childebert, that crafty man, who

34. None of this is true. Amalasuntha was a virtuous woman. She was murdered at the instigation of the Empress Theodora.
35. This was the *wergeld*.

was always jealous of King Lothar, conspired with his nephew Theudebert to divide the gold equally between them and give nothing to Lothar. Lothar thereupon seized the treasury of Chlodomer and deprived them both of much more than they had stolen from him.

32. Next Theudebert marched into Italy and laid hands on a great amount of booty.[36] Those regions are apparently very unhealthy: Theudebert's army was greatly harassed by a series of epidemics and many of his soldiers died there. When he saw what was happening, Theudebert returned home, he and his troops carrying vast riches which they had stolen. He is said to have advanced as far as Pavia. Later on he sent Buccelin back there.[37] Buccelin conquered Upper Italy and subjected it to the rule of King Theudebert. Then he marched against Lower Italy, where he fought many battles against Belisarius and beat him repeatedly. When the Emperor saw that Belisarius was being beaten time and time again, he dismissed him and appointed Narses to his command. To humiliate Belisarius, he reduced him to his old post of Count of the Stables.[38] Buccelin fought a series of great battles against Narses. He conquered the whole of Italy and pushed forward to the sea. From Italy he dispatched a great store of treasure to Theudebert. When Narses reported this to his master, the Emperor hired an army of foreign mercenaries and sent them to support Narses, who took the field again, but he was beaten once more. In the end Buccelin occupied Sicily,[39] where he exacted great tribute, which he again sent home to the King. He was most successful in his campaigns.

33. Asteriolus and Secundinus enjoyed great credit with King Theudebert. They were both of them educated men, well-

36. A.D. 539.

37. Buccelin's expedition took place in A.D. 553–4, long after Theudebert's death.

38. In effect Belisarius was made Commander of the Imperial Bodyguard. a most important function.

39. This is not true.

trained in the humanities. Secundinus had led several embassies
to the Emperor as the representative of Theudebert, and this
had made him boastful and often outrageous in his behaviour.
As a result he quarrelled bitterly with Asteriolus. Things came
to such a pitch that they grew tired of insulting each other and
resorted to fisticuffs. The King did his best to pacify them, but,
while Secundinus was still black and blue from his first beating,
another row started between the two of them. King Theudebert
supported Secundinus and put Asteriolus in a subordinate position under him. Asteriolus was disgraced and deposed from his
high position; but thanks to Queen Wisigard he was restored to
grace. When the Queen died, Secundinus renewed his attacks
and killed Asteriolus. At his death Asteriolus left a son who
grew to man's estate and made ready to avenge the wrong done
to his father. Secundinus was panic-stricken and fled from one
villa to another to escape him, but, when he realized that he
could not avoid the attentions of this pursuer who followed him
so closely, he is said to have killed himself with poison rather
than fall into the hands of his enemy.

34. King Theuderic had done much harm to Desideratus,
Bishop of Verdun. After long disgrace, ill-treatment and
sorrow, Desideratus regained his liberty with God's help and
again took possession of his bishopric, which was in the city of
Verdun, as I have said. He found the inhabitants of the city
poor and destitute, and he grieved for them. He had been deprived of his own property by Theuderic and had no means of
succouring his townsfolk. When he observed the charity of
King Theudebert and his generosity towards all men, Desideratus sent messengers to him. 'The fame of your charity has
spread throughout the whole world,' he said, 'for your generosity is so great that you even give to people who have asked
nothing of you. If in your compassion you have any money to
spare, I beg you to lend it to me, so that I may relieve the
distress of those in my diocese. As soon as the men who are in
charge of the commercial affairs in my city have reorganized
their business, as has been done in other cities, I will repay your

loan with interest.' Theudebert was moved to compassion and made a loan of seven thousand gold pieces. Desideratus accepted this and shared it out among his townsfolk. As a result the business-people of Verdun became rich and they still remain so today. The Bishop eventually returned the borrowed money to the King, but Theudebert replied: 'I have no need to take this money. It is enough for me that, when you asked that I should make a loan, those who were poor and in dire distress were returned to prosperity.' By taking no payment Theudebert restored the citizens of Verdun to affluence.

35. Eventually this famous Bishop of Verdun died and Ageric, who was a native of the city, replaced him on the episcopal throne. The son of Desideratus, a certain Syagrius, who could not forget the wrongs suffered by his father, who had been denounced to King Theuderic by Syrivald, deprived of his possessions and even submitted to torture, lay in wait for Syrivald with a band of armed followers and killed him. Early one morning, when the mist lay thick and visibility was very limited as the night gave way to day, he came to a villa of Syrivald's in the Dijon neighbourhood at a spot called Fleury-sur-Ouche. A friend of his came out of the house and they killed him, thinking that he was Syrivald. They set off for home, under the impression that they had dealt with their enemy, but one of Syrivald's slaves revealed that they had killed not the master of the household but one of his dependants. They turned back to look for Syrivald and made their way to the bedroom where he usually slept. They made repeated efforts to force the door, but had no success at all. In the end they knocked down the wall, burst in and killed Syrivald. This murder occurred after the death of Theuderic.

36. While this was going on, King Theudebert fell seriously ill. His doctors did all that they possibly could for him, but it was of no avail, for God was already summoning him. He lay ill for a long time: then his strength gradually failed and he died.[40]

40. A.D. 548.

The Franks hated Parthenius bitterly, for in the time of the late King it was he who had levied the taxes. Now was their moment to take vengeance. Seeing what danger he was in, he fled from the city and begged two bishops to help him. He asked them to escort him to the town of Trier and to quell the riot of the enraged citizens by their sermons. They set off: but one night while he was asleep in his bed he had a nightmare and shouted out: 'Help! Help! You who are there, come to my assistance, bring me your aid, for I am dying!' They were awakened by his cries and asked him what was the matter. He replied: 'My dear friend Ausanius and my wife Papianilla, both of whom I had murdered, were summoning me to atone for my sins. "Come and face judgement," they kept saying, "for you must reply to the indictments which we propose to bring before the Lord God." ' Some years before he had become jealous of his wife and his friend, and, although the woman was innocent, he had murdered them both. The two bishops reached Trier, but they could do nothing to quell the riot of the howling mob, and they had to hide Parthenius in a church. They put him in a chest and covered him over with church vestments. The people rushed in and poked about in every corner of the church. They found nothing and left again in a fury. Then one man more perspicacious than the others said: 'What about the chest? What about the chest? We haven't looked in the chest yet, to see if our enemy is there!' The churchwardens maintained that the chest contained nothing but church vestments. The people demanded the key. 'Open it quickly,' they bellowed, 'or we will break it open ourselves!' The chest was unlocked, and when they had moved the vestments to one side they discovered Parthenius and dragged him out. They clapped their hands and shouted: 'The Lord God has delivered our enemy into our hands!' They struck him with their fists and spat at him. Then they bound his hands behind his back, tied him to a pillar and stoned him to death. He was a voracious glutton: he used to eat aloes to give himself an appetite and to aid his digestion; and he would fart in public without any consideration for those present. Such was the manner of his death.

37. That year the winter weather was harsh and more bitter than usual. The mountain torrents were frozen solid and people walked across them as if they were dry ground. The snow lay deep and the birds were numbed with cold and famished with hunger, so that they could be taken by hand without any need of snares.

Thirty-seven years elapsed between the death of Clovis and the death of Theudebert. Theudebert died in the fourteenth year of his reign. Theudebald, his son, reigned in his place.

HERE ENDS BOOK III

BOOK IV

HERE BEGIN THE CHAPTER-HEADINGS OF BOOK IV

1. The death of Queen Clotild.
2. How King Lothar wanted to appropriate one third of the Church revenues.
3. The wives and children of Lothar.
4. The Counts of the Bretons.
5. Saint Gall the Bishop.
6. The priest Cato.
7. The episcopate of Cautinus.
8. The Kings of Spain.
9. The death of King Theudebald.
10. How the Saxons rebelled.
11. How at the King's bidding the Tourangeaux sought Cato for their bishopric.
12. The priest Anastasius.
13. The frivolity and wickedness of Chramn. Cautinus and Firminus.
14. How Lothar marched a second time against the Saxons.
15. The episcopate of Saint Eufronius.
16. Chramn and his supporters, and the evil which he did; how he came to Dijon.
17. How Chramn went over to Childebert.
18. Duke Austrapius.
19. The death of Saint Medard the Bishop.
20. The death of Childebert and the killing of Chramn.
21. The death of King Lothar.
22. The dividing up of Lothar's kingdom between his sons.
23. How Sigibert marched against the Huns and how Chilperic attacked Sigibert's cities.
24. How Celsus became a patrician.
25. Guntram's wives.

195

26. Charibert's wives.
27. How Sigibert married Brunhild.
28. Chilperic's wives.
29. The second war of Sigibert against the Huns.
30. How on the order of King Sigibert the men of Clermont-Ferrand marched against the city of Arles.
31. The fortress of Tauredunum; and other miraculous events.
32. The monk Julian.
33. Abbot Sunniulf.
34. The monk of Bordeaux.
35. The episcopate of Avitus of Clermont-Ferrand.
36. Saint Nicetius of Lyons.
37. Saint Friard the hermit.
38. The Kings of Spain.
39. The suicide of Palladius of Clermont-Ferrand.
40. The Emperor Justin.
41. How Alboin and the Longobards invaded Italy.
42. The wars of Mummolus against the Longobards.
43. The Archdeacon of Marseilles.
44. The Longobards and Mummolus.
45. How Mummolus came to Tours.
46. How Andarchius was killed.
47. How Theudebert captured certain cities.
48. The monastery of Latte.
49. How Sigibert came to Paris.
50. How Chilperic made a treaty with Guntram; and the death of Chilperic's son Theudebert.
51. The death of King Sigibert.

HERE ENDS THE LIST OF THE CHAPTER-HEADINGS

HERE BEGINS BOOK IV

1.   Queen Clotild died, full of days and rich in good works, in the city of Tours, in the time of Bishop Injuriosus.[1] With a great singing of psalms her body was carried to Paris and her two royal sons, Childebert and Lothar, buried her in Saint Peter's church at the side of her husband, King Clovis. She herself had this church built. Saint Geneviève is also buried there.[2]

2.   King Lothar had ordained that all the churches in his kingdom should pay a third part of their revenues to the treasury. All the other bishops had agreed to this and had signed documents saying so, with the greatest unwillingness, let it be admitted, but Saint Injuriosus would not sign and had the courage to refuse to pay. 'If you have made up your mind to seize what belongs to God, then the Lord will soon take your kingdom away from you,' he said, 'for it is criminal for you, who should be feeding the poor from your own granary, to fill your coffers with the alms which others give to them.' Injuriosus was so angry with the King that he went off without saying good-bye. Lothar was disturbed by this, for he was afraid that Saint Martin would punish him for what he had done. He sent messengers laden with presents after Injuriosus, to beg his pardon, cancel what he had done and beg that he would pray to Saint Martin for help.

3. King Lothar had seven sons by his various wives. By Ingund he had Gunthar, Childeric, Charibert, Guntram, Sigibert and a daughter called Chlothsind; by Aregund, who was the sister of Ingund, he had Chilperic; and by Chunsina he had Chramn. I had better tell you how he came to marry the sister

1. A.D. 544.
2. As a result the church took the name of Sainte Geneviève.

of his own wife. When he had already married Ingund and loved her with all his heart, she made the following suggestion to him: 'My lord, you have already done what you wished with me, your handmaiden, and you have taken me to bed with you. To complete my happiness, listen now to what I have to say. I ask you to choose for my sister, who is also a member of your household, a competent and wealthy husband, so that I need not be ashamed of her, but rather that she may be a source of pride to me, so that I may serve you even more faithfully.' Lothar was too much given to woman-chasing to be able to resist this. When he heard what Ingund had to say, he was filled with desire for Aregund. He went off to the villa where she lived and married her. When he had slept with her, he came back to Ingund. 'I have done my best to reward you for the sweet request which you put to me,' he said. 'I have looked everywhere for a wealthy and wise husband whom I could marry to your sister, but I could find no one more eligible than myself. You must know, then, that I myself have married her. I am sure that this will not displease you.' 'You must do as you wish,' answered Ingund. 'All I ask is that I may retain your good favour.' Gunthar, Chramn and Childeric died during their father's lifetime. I shall describe Chramn's death in a later chapter.[3] Alboin, King of the Longobards, married Lothar's daughter Chlothsind.

Injuriosus, Bishop of Tours, died in the seventeenth year of his episcopate. Baudinus, who had been in the King's service, replaced him as the sixteenth Bishop since the death of Saint Martin.

4.   A Breton Count called Chanao killed three of his brothers. He seized the fourth brother Macliaw and kept him chained up in prison while he was summoning up courage to kill him, too. Felix, Bishop of Nantes, saved him from certain death. Macliaw swore to his brother Chanao that he would be faithful to him. For some reason or other he decided to break his oath. Chanao heard of this and pursued him a second time. When

3. *HF*, IV, 20.

Macliaw realized that he could not escape he took refuge with another Breton Count called Chonomor. When Chonomor discovered that Macliaw's enemies were approaching, he hid him in a hole in the ground. He constructed a barrow on top, as their habit is in Brittany, but he left a little air-hole, so that Macliaw could breathe. Those who were pursuing Macliaw duly arrived. 'Macliaw is dead,' they were told. 'We buried him here.' They were so delighted at the news that they sat down on the tumulus and had a drink. When they returned home they told Chanao that his brother was dead. As soon as he heard it, he took over the entire kingdom; for from the death of King Clovis onwards the Bretons remained under the domination of the Franks and their rulers were called counts and not kings. Macliaw emerged from his hole in the ground and fled to Vannes. There he had himself tonsured and was consecrated as Bishop. When Chanao died, Macliaw renounced his vows, grew his hair again and took charge of both the wife whom he had deserted when he became a religious and his brother's kingdom. For this he was excommunicated by the other bishops. I shall describe his violent end in a later chapter.[4]

Bishop Baudinus died in the sixth year of his episcopate. Abbot Gunthar was appointed in his place, the seventeenth since the death of Saint Martin.

5.*   When the time finally came for Saint Quintianus to die, Saint Gall replaced him on his episcopal throne, with the full approval of the King, as I have already said.[5] In Saint Gall's time the plague raged in various parts of Gaul, causing great swellings in the groin. It was particularly bad in the province of Arles, and Saint Gall was anxious not only for himself but more especially for his flock. He prayed to God night and day that he might not live to see his diocese decimated. One night the Angel of the Lord appeared to him in a vision, with his hair and raiment as white as driven snow. 'You do well, Lord Bishop,' said the Angel, 'to pray to God in this way for your people. Your prayer has been heard. As long as you live, you and your flock

4. *HF*, V, 16.   5. *VP*, 6.

will be free of the plague and no one in this region will die because of it. At the moment you have, then, no need to be afraid; but when eight years have passed the time will really come for fear.' It was clear from this that Saint Gall would die eight years later.[6] He awoke and returned thanks to God for giving him this reassurance and for having deigned to comfort him by sending a message from on high. Saint Gall then instituted the Rogations for which all journeyed on foot in the middle of Lent to the church of Saint Julian the martyr, singing psalms as they went. The church is about sixty-five kilometres from Clermont-Ferrand. Suddenly before men's very eyes signs appeared on the walls of houses and churches. The inscription was recognized by the country-folk who saw it as a tau. As I have explained,[7] the plague raged through other parts of Gaul, but thanks to the prayers of Saint Gall it claimed no victims in Clermont-Ferrand. In my opinion it was no small grace which was able to bring it to pass that the shepherd who stayed to watch did not see his sheep devoured, because God preserved them.

The moment came for Saint Gall to die and his earthly remains were washed clean and carried into his church. A priest called Cato received the nomination to the episcopate of the local clergy, and he promptly assumed control of all church property as if he were already inducted as bishop, replacing the superintendents, dismissing the church officials and ordering everything on his own authority.

6.* When they had buried Saint Gall the bishops who had come to his funeral said to the priest Cato: 'We observe that the majority of the people in the diocese have voted for you. Come, then, agree with us, and we will give you our blessing and consecrate you as bishop. The King is only a child. If anyone criticizes you, we will protect you and we will deal with the princes and leaders of King Theudebald's court, if they bring any accusation against you. You may trust implicitly in us, for we give you our support in all this, and if you suffer loss of any sort we

6. Saint Gall died A.D. 551.   7. *GM*, 50.

will make it good from our own resources.' Cato was a man
filled with self-esteem and silly self-admiration. 'You will
know,' he answered, 'for it is common knowledge, that all my
life through I have lived as a religious, fasting, taking pleasure
in almsgiving and enduring long vigils. I have stood the whole
night through fervently chanting the psalms. The Lord my God
will not now permit me to be deprived of my proper induction,
for I have shown such zeal in His service. I have been promoted
through all the ranks of clerical preferment according to canonical precept. I was a lector for ten years; for five years I
performed the duties of subdeacon; for fifteen years I served as
deacon; and I have held the dignity of the priesthood for the
last twenty years. What is left but that I should be ordained
bishop as the reward for my faithful service? As for you, you
may return to your dioceses. If there is anything which you
really think that you are capable of doing for me, then please
do it. For myself, I propose to be inducted into this bishopric in
the proper canonical way.' When they heard this the bishops
went on their way, cursing the pride of this man Cato.

7.*   With the consent of all his clergy, Cato was elected to the
episcopate. Long before being inducted he started to take
charge of all chapter business. He began, for example, to
shower threats on his Archdeacon, one Cautinus. 'I will dismiss
you,' he kept saying, 'I will disgrace you,' even 'I will have you
killed in this way, in that way, in some other way.' 'Gracious
lord,' answered Cautinus, 'all I ask is your approval of what I
am doing. If I have it, I will offer you a service. To spare you
the trouble, and with no ulterior motive of my own, I will go to
the King and ask his approval of your elevation to the episcopate. For myself I ask nothing, except perhaps your gratitude.'
Cato took no notice of this offer, for he suspected Cautinus of
planning to deceive him. When Cautinus saw himself slighted
and calumniated, he pretended to be ill. One night he escaped
from Clermont-Ferrand. He made his way to King Theudebald
and announced to him the death of Saint Gall. When the King
and his officials heard the news, they summoned a council of

bishops in the city of Metz. Cautinus the Archdeacon was elected to the episcopate. By the time messengers reached the priest Cato, Cautinus was already ordained Bishop. At the King's command all the local clergy and all matters appertaining to the church were submitted to his jurisdiction. They sent him back to Clermont-Ferrand with the bishops and chamberlains who had been appointed to accompany him. He was received favourably by the clergy and the townsfolk and was accepted as Bishop of Clermont. There ensued a great feud between him and the priest Cato, for no one could ever persuade Cato to submit to his Bishop. Two parties were formed among the clergy, those who accepted Cautinus as bishop and those who wanted Cato. This was a great source of disappointment to Cato's partisans. Bishop Cautinus saw clearly that nothing could bend Cato's will or induce him to submit. He therefore removed all church benefits from Cato, his friends and all who supported him, and left them empty and destitute. Any who changed sides and came over to him had what they had lost restored to them.

8. Agila now reigned in Spain and oppressed the people beneath the heavy yoke of his tyranny.[8] An army sent by the Emperor Justinian marched into Spain and captured several cities. Agila was assassinated and Athanagild took over the kingship. Athanagild subsequently fought several battles against the Emperor's troops and beat them on a number of occasions. He managed to free from their occupation some of the cities which they had wrongfully captured.

9. When he came to man's estate Theudebald married Vuldetrada.[9] From all accounts he was a malicious person. One day when he was upbraiding a man whom he suspected of rob-

8. Agila was King of the Visigoths A.D. 549–54.

9. Vuldetrada was a daughter of Wacho, King of the Longobards. Her sister Wisigard had married Theudebert, the father of Theudebald, *HF*, III, 27, so that she would have become Vuldetrada's mother-in-law had she lived long enough!

bing him, he told him the following fable: 'A snake came across a jar full of wine. It slid in through the mouth of the jar and greedily drank all the wine. The wine swelled the snake up, so that it could not get out again through the neck of the jar. As it was struggling to squeeze its way out, without any success at all, the owner of the wine came up. "Spew up what you have swallowed," said he to the snake, "and then you will get out easily enough." ' This story made the man fear Theudebald, and hate him, too. During his reign Buccelin, who had brought the whole of Italy under Frankish domination, was killed by Narses.[10] Italy now came under the rule of the Emperor, and from this time on no one was able to wrest it free.

In the same reign we saw the phenomenon of grapes growing on an elder tree, without grafting, that is; for the blossoms of this tree, which normally produce black berries, as you know very well, yielded grapes instead. At this time, too, a fifth star, moving in the opposite direction, was seen to enter the circle of the moon. It is my belief that these portents presaged Theudebald's death. He had a stroke and could not move from the waist downwards. He gradually became worse and died in the seventh year of his reign.[11] King Lothar took over his kingdom; he also began to have intercourse with his widow Vuldetrada, but he stopped when the bishops complained and he handed her over to Garivald, Duke of Bavaria.

Lothar sent his son Chramn to Clermont-Ferrand.

10.   In this year the Saxons revolted. King Lothar mobilized an army against them and wiped out a great number of them. He invaded Thuringia and ravaged the whole province, for the Thuringians had supported the Saxons.

11.*   Bishop Gunthar died in the city of Tours. At the suggestion, or so it was said, of Bishop Cautinus, the priest Cato was invited to take over the diocese. As a result a deputation of clergy, led by Abbot Leubast, the guardian of martyrs' relics in the diocese, set out for Clermont-Ferrand with great pomp.

10. A.D. 555.   11. A.D. 555.

When they had explained the King's wishes to Cato, he kept
them waiting for an answer for a few days. They were very
keen to return home. 'Tell us your decision,' they said, 'so that
we may know what to do. Otherwise we shall go back to Tours.
It was not our idea that we should come to seek you out, for we
were told to do so by the King.' Cato was vainglorious as usual.
He assembled a crowd of poor people and ordered them to
shout: 'Why are you leaving us, good father, when you have
cared for us until now? Who will provide us with food and
drink, if you go away and leave us? We beg you not to desert
us, but to stay and feed us daily!' Cato then turned to the clergy
from Tours. 'You see, my dear brethren, how much this crowd
of poor folk loves me. I just can't desert them and go with you.'
Having received their answer, they went back to Tours. Cato
had ingratiated himself with Chramn, who had promised him
that, if King Lothar should chance to die in the foreseeable
future, Cautinus should be deposed from his episcopate and
Cato himself should be put in charge of the diocese. The man
who had despised the throne of Saint Martin was not, however,
elevated to the one which he wanted: and the words which
David sang were true of him: 'As he delighted not in blessing,
so let it be far from him.'[12] He was so above himself in his vain
conceit that he imagined that no one was more holy than he.
Once he bribed a woman to behave in church as if she were
possessed and to shout out that he, Cato, was a great saint and
very dear to God, whereas Bishop Cautinus had committed
every crime in the calendar and was unworthy to have been
ordained a priest.

12.*   Once he had taken possession of his bishopric, Cautinus
began to behave so badly that he was soon loathed by
everybody. He began to drink heavily. He was often so completely fuddled with wine that it would take four men to carry
him from the table. Later on, no doubt because of his excesses,
he became subject to epileptic fits. All this often occurred in full
public view. What is more, he was so avaricious that it was a

12. Psalms 108, 18.

source of great anguish to him if he failed to transfer to himself some part of any territory which was adjacent to his own. If the owners were persons of some standing, Cautinus did this by law-suits and calumny; but if they were people of no great importance he would just take the land by main force. As our own Sollius[13] wrote: 'He disdained to pay for what he took from these people, and yet he was in despair if they did not surrender the title-deeds.'[14]

There was at that time in Clermont-Ferrand a priest called Anastasius, a man of free birth, who owned a certain property which had been granted to him by Queen Clotild of glorious memory. Bishop Cautinus summoned him several times and asked him to surrender the title-deeds given by Queen Clotild and to make the property over to him. Anastasius refused to submit to the demands of his Bishop. Cautinus first tried what he could do by flattery, then he resorted to threats. In the end he ordered Anastasius to be brought into the city against his will, he had him locked up in the most outrageous manner and he went so far as to command that he should be beaten and starved to death if he would not hand over the title-deeds. Anastasius had the courage to resist and he refused steadfastly to produce the papers, saying that he preferred to waste away for lack of food rather than leave his children destitute. Then Bishop Cautinus ordered that he should be guarded closely and that if he did not hand over the documents he should die of hunger. In the church of Saint Cassius the Martyr there was a crypt which had been there for centuries and where no one ever went. It contained a great sarcophagus of Parian marble, in which, so it seems, lay the body of some person dead these many years. In this sarcophagus, on top of the body which was mouldering away there, they buried Anastasius alive. The stone slab which they had removed was put back and guards were posted at the crypt door. These guards were convinced that Anastasius must have been crushed to death by the slab. It was winter time, so

13. Sidonius Apollinaris, whose full name was Caius Sollius Sidonius Apollinaris.
14. *Epistolae*, 2, 1.

205

they lit a fire, warmed some wine and fell asleep after they had
drunk it. Meanwhile our priest, like some new Jonah, from the
confines of his tomb, as if from the belly of hell, was praying
for God's compassion.[15] The sarcophagus was quite big, as I
have told you. Anastasius could not turn over completely, but
he could stretch out his hands in all directions. Years afterwards
he used to describe the fetid stench which clung about the dead
man's bones, and tell how this not only offended his sense of
smell but turned his stomach over. If he stuffed his cloak into
his nostrils he could smell nothing as long as he held his breath;
but whenever he removed his cloak, for fear of being
suffocated, he breathed in the pestilential odour through his
mouth and his nose and even, so to speak, through his ears! To
cut a long story short, God finally took pity on him, for that is
what I think must have happened. Anastasius stretched out his
right hand to touch the edge of the sarcophagus and discovered
a crowbar. When the lid had been lowered on top of him, this
had been left between the stone slab and the edge of the sarcophagus. He levered the crowbar to and fro until, with God's
help, he felt the lid move. Once it was edged far enough along
for the priest to be able to stick his head out he was able to
make a bigger opening and so creep out of the tomb. The
shades of night were falling fast, but it was not yet completely
dark. Anastasius made his way to another door of the crypt. This
was secured by heavy locks and enormous nails, but it was not
so well fitted together that one could not peer out between the
planks. The priest knelt down and through one of these chinks
he saw a man pass by. Anastasius called out to him in a low
voice. The man heard him. Without more ado he grasped his
axe, cut through the wooden planks to which the locks were
attached and made a way out for the priest. Anastasius emerged
into the night and found his way home, having first impressed
upon the man that he must not tell anyone what had happened.
Once safe and sound inside his house, he looked out the title-
deeds which Queen Clotild had given to him. He took them to

15. Cp. Jonah 2, 1.

King Lothar and told him how he had been buried alive by his bishop. All those present were astounded: not even Nero or Herod, they declared, had committed such a crime as to bury a man alive. Cautinus appeared before King Lothar, but when Anastasius taxed him with this crime he left immediately, for he had no answer and he was confused. King Lothar gave Anastasius new title-deeds, which confirmed him in the possession of his property and prevented anyone from taking it away. He bequeathed the land to his descendants.

Nothing was sacred to Cautinus and he respected nothing. He had no time for literature, either sacred or profane. He was on familiar terms with the Jews and was much influenced by them, not for their conversion, which ought to be the preoccupation of a priest, but because he bought goods from them. He was easily flattered: and they knew how to keep in his good books, and so sold things to him at a higher price than they were worth.

13.   At this time Chramn was living in Clermont-Ferrand. He was extremely ill-advised in nearly everything that he did, and his premature death was a direct result of this. He was hated by the townsfolk of Clermont. Among all his associates there was not one capable of giving him good and useful advice. He collected round him a band of young and dissolute people from the lower classes. He cared for no one else and it was to their advice only that he listened, notably when, by royal decree, he ordered the daughters of certain senators to be abducted forcibly for their entertainment. He insulted Firminus and dismissed him from the countship of the city, appointing in his place Salustius, the son of Evodius. Firminus and his sister-in-law took sanctuary in the cathedral. It was Lent and Bishop Cautinus had made plans to go in procession to the parish of Brioude, to conduct the Rogations instituted by Saint Gall and which I have described in an earlier chapter.[16] He set off from

16. *HF*, IV, 5.

his city in great agony of spirit, for he was afraid that he himself
would be attacked on the way. He, too, was being threatened by
King Chramn.[17] While Cautinus was processing to Brioude,
the King sent Imnachar and Scapthar, two of the ring-leaders of
the gang around him. 'Go and drive Firminus and his sister-in-
law Caesaria out of the cathedral,' he told them. At the very
moment when the Bishop was walking in procession, as I have
already told you, the messengers whom Chramn had sent entered the cathedral and did all they could to allay the fears of
Firminus and Caesaria by telling them various lying tales. They
all walked up and down the cathedral for a long time, talking of
this and that. While the two who had fled to the cathedral for
sanctuary were focusing all their attention on what the others
had to say, they all came close to the doors of the sacred building, which at that time of day were unlocked. At the right
moment Imnachar seized Firminus in his arms and Scapthar
laid hold of Caesaria. They then bustled the two of them out of
the church to where their men were waiting to seize them. They
were immediately sent into exile. The next day, when their
guards were sleeping, they took the opportunity to make their
escape and fled to the church of Saint Julian, thus saving themselves from exile, but their goods were confiscated. Bishop Cautinus, who suspected that he, too, would be molested as he
followed this same road, kept a horse ready saddled at his side.
Looking round he saw horsemen coming up behind him.
Indeed, they were about to catch up with him. 'May God help
me!' he exclaimed. 'Those men have been sent by Chramn to
take me!' He leapt on the horse, broke away from the procession
and rode off alone to the gateway of the church of Saint Julian,
digging both spurs into his steed and arriving half-dead. As I tell
you this story I cannot help thinking of what Sallust said about
those who criticize historians: 'Arduum videtur res gestas scrib-
ere: primum quod facta dictis exaequanda sunt; deinde quia
plerique quae delicta repraehenderis malevolentia et invidia

17. All the sons of the Merovingian kings used this title. In a memorable
passage the nun Clotild, daughter of King Charibert, called herself a Queen,
HF, X, 15.

dicta putant.'[18] But let me press on with what I have begun.

14.   After the death of Theudebald,[19] Lothar took over the lands of the Ripuarian Franks. As he was touring his new territory, he was informed by his men that the Saxons were once more in wild ferment and were rebelling against him, for they were refusing to hand over the tribute which they had to pay each year. He was angry at what he heard and he marched against them. As soon as he came near to their territory, the Saxons sent messengers to meet him. 'It is not that we lack respect for you,' said they, 'nor are we refusing to pay the tribute which we have given to your brothers and nephews.[20] Indeed, we will pay more, if you insist. What we want is this, that there should be peace, and that your army and our people should not be embroiled in bloody warfare.' When he heard this, King Lothar said to his men: 'What these people say is good sense. We must not attack them, for that would be a sin against God.' 'We know what liars they are,' answered his men, 'for they never do what they have promised. We must attack them.' A second time the Saxons sent to sue for peace, offering in return one half of all they possessed. Lothar said to his men: 'Hold back, I tell you, do not attack the Saxons, for if we do we shall incur the wrath of God.' Still his men would not agree. A third time the Saxons came forward, offering all their clothes, their cattle and the whole of their property. 'Take all this,' they said, 'with half of all the territory which we hold, only leave our wives and little children free and let there be no war between us.' Once more the Franks would not agree. 'Hold back, I tell you,' said King Lothar yet again, 'and give up the idea of attacking them. There is no justice in what you are planning to do. You must not march into battle, for we shall be beaten if

18. 'Writing history seems a difficult job: in the first place because what you put down has to correspond exactly to the facts; and secondly because if you permit yourself to criticize any wrongdoing, most of your readers think that you are being malevolent, or even envious.' *Catilina*, 3.

19. A.D. 555.

20. In effect, to Lothar's brother Theuderic, to Theudebert his nephew and to Theudebald his great-nephew, all Kings of the Ripuarian Franks.

you do. If you insist upon advancing, then advance without me!' The Franks were furious with Lothar: they rushed at him, tore his tent to pieces, heaped insults upon him, dragged him out with great violence and swore that they would kill him if he refused to accompany them. When he saw how matters stood, King Lothar marched against his will. The battle was joined, vast numbers of the Franks were killed by their adversaries, and so many men were slaughtered on both sides that no one could count the bodies or even make a rough estimate of their number.[21] Lothar was beside himself: he sued for peace, maintaining that he had not marched of his own free will. Peace was patched up and Lothar returned home.

15.* When the citizens of Tours heard that King Lothar had come back from this battle against the Saxons, they sought an audience with him to tell him that they all agreed that they wanted the priest Eufronius as their Bishop. They put their proposal to him, but he answered: 'I decreed that the priest Cato should be ordained Bishop of Tours. Why was my order not carried out?' 'We asked him to come,' they replied, 'but he refused.' While they were speaking, the priest Cato suddenly appeared and asked the King to dismiss Cautinus from the bishopric of Clermont and to appoint him instead. The King laughed at this suggestion. Cato then asked that he might be made Bishop of Tours after all, although he had previously scorned this appointment. 'My original decision was that they should consecrate you Bishop of Tours,' said the King, 'but now that I have learnt that you have refused that diocese you must give up all hope of ever being appointed to it.' Cato then withdrew in great confusion. The King made inquiries about Saint Eufronius, and he was told that he was a nephew of Saint Gregory,[22] whom I have already mentioned to you. 'That is one of the noblest and most distinguished families in the land,' said Lothar.[23] 'Let God's will be done, and that of Saint Martin. I

21. A.D. 555.

22. Saint Gregory, Bishop of Langres, *c.* 506–*c.* 539. See *HF*, III, 19.

23. The family was, of course, that of Gregory of Tours himself. See the family tree on p. 11 of the Introduction.

order him to be elected.' The necessary papers were signed and
Saint Eufronius was appointed as Bishop of Tours, the eighteenth after Saint Martin.

16.   As I have already told you, Chramn committed a long
series of crimes in Clermont-Ferrand.[24] He remained bitterly
hostile to Bishop Cautinus. Then he became seriously ill with a
high fever and all his hair fell out. In his entourage he had a
citizen of Clermont called Ascovindus, an admirable person
who was circumspect in all his behaviour. Ascovindus did all in
his power to prevent Chramn from behaving so badly, but he
failed in his attempt. Chramn had another retainer called Leo
of Poitiers who encouraged him in his evil living, a man aptly
named, for he raged like a lion as he strove to satisfy his every
passion. It was Leo who was said to have alleged that Saint
Martin and Saint Martialis left nothing of any value to the royal
treasury. He was immediately struck deaf and dumb by the
miraculous power of the two saints and he died a raging lunatic.
In his misery he came to the church of Saint Martin in Tours
and kept vigils there and presented gifts, but the usual miraculous power did him no good, for he went away just as ill as
he was when he came.

Chramn left Clermont-Ferrand and went to the city of Poitiers. He lived there in great state. He was led astray by the
advice of the evil men around him and made up his mind to
go over to his uncle Childebert and to betray his father. Childebert agreed to listen to him, but he did so with every intention
of betraying him in his turn, whereas it was his Christian duty to
warn him not to revolt against his own father. They sent secret
messengers to each other and conspired together and plotted
against Lothar. Childebert seemed to have forgotten that every
time he conspired against Lothar he came off worse in the
end.

Once he had made this arrangement with Childebert Chramn
went off to the Limousin. All this territory, which was part of
his father's realm but which Chramn himself had once visited,

24. *HF*, IV, 13.

he now submitted to his own rule. At that time the people of
Clermont-Ferrand were shut up inside their city walls and were
dying off like flies, for they were attacked by one epidemic after
another. King Lothar sent his two sons, Charibert and Guntram, to deal with Chramn. When they reached Clermont they
learned that he was in the Limousin. They marched as far as the
hill called Nigremont and there they found him. They pitched
their tents and set up their camp directly opposite his. Then they
sent messengers to say that he must either restore all the possessions of his father which he had usurped or else come out to
fight. Chramn pretended to submit to his father. 'I am in no
position', said he, 'to give up all the land through which I have
marched, but I am willing to hold it under my own command
but in tenure from my father.' Charibert and Guntram insisted
that the issue should be put to the test of battle. The two armies
were drawn up and stood face to face with all their weapons
and ready for battle but a storm suddenly arose with violent
thunder and lightning, and this prevented them from making
contact. They marched back to their camps. With his usual
guile Chramn sent a stranger to report to his two brothers that
their father had been killed. This was on the occasion of the
war with the Saxons, about which I have told you.[25] In their
anxiety Charibert and Guntram retired as fast as they could to
Burgundy. Chramn marched after them with his army. He came
to the city of Chalon-sur-Saône, which he captured after a siege.
He then pushed on to Dijon, where he arrived on a Sunday.
What happened there I will tell you later.

At that time the Bishop of Langres was Saint Tetricus, about
whom I have told you in an earlier book.[26] His priests placed
three books on the altar, the Prophets, the Epistles and the
Gospels.[27] They prayed to the Lord that in His divine power
He would reveal to them what would happen to Chramn,
whether he would ever prosper and whether or not he would
come to the throne. At the same time they agreed among themselves that each should read at Mass whatever he found when he

25. *HF*, IV, 14.   26. *VP*, 7.
27. The *Sortes Biblicae*, cp. *HF*, V, 14.

first opened the book. The Book of the Prophets was opened first. There they found: 'I will take away the hedge thereof, and it shall be eaten up. When I looked that it should bring forth grapes, it brought forth wild grapes.'[28] Then the Book of the Apostle was opened and they found this: 'For yourselves know perfectly that the day of the Lord so cometh as a thief in the night. For when they shall say, Peace and safety; then sudden destruction cometh upon them, as travail upon a woman with child; and they shall not escape.'[29] Finally the Lord spoke through the Gospel: 'And every one that heareth these sayings of mine, and doeth them not, shall be likened unto a foolish man, which built his house upon the sand: And the rain descended, and the floods came, and the winds blew, and beat upon that house; and it fell: and great was the fall of it.'[30] Chramn was welcomed in his churches[31] by the Bishop whom I have named and he was allowed to take communion: then he went to meet Childebert. He was not permitted to go inside the walls of Dijon.

While this was happening King Lothar was fighting against the Saxons: for the Saxons, so they learned, had been stirred up by Childebert and incensed against the Franks the previous year, and were now marching out of their own territory into the land of the Ripuarian Franks and had laid waste as far as the city of Deutz, where they were doing immense damage.

17. Chramn married Wilichar's daughter.[32] He travelled to Paris, where he became the close ally of Childebert, showing himself loyal and affectionate towards the King. He swore that he would always be the most bitter enemy of his own father. While Lothar was fighting against the Saxons, King Childebert marched to the district round Rheims. He pushed on as far as the city, pillaging far and wide and burning as much as he could. He had been told that his brother had been killed by the

28. Cp. Isaiah 4, 4–5.   29. I Thessalonians 5, 2–3.
30. Matthew 7, 26–27.
31. The churches of Saint Paschasia and Saint Benignus, *extra muros*.
32. Chalda.

Saxons, and he imagined that the whole country would now
come under his rule. He therefore occupied as much of it as he
could.

18.   Duke Austrapius had good reason to fear Chramn and he
therefore sought sanctuary in the church of Saint Martin. God
did not fail to help him in his distress. In order that he might
more easily be forced by hunger to emerge of his own free will
from the sacred building, even though he faced certain death,
Chramn ordered him to be so closely watched that no one
should dare to offer him food and so closely guarded that no
one should give him water to drink. As he lay half-dead someone came with a cup of water and offered him a drink. He
took it, but the local judge rushed forward, snatched it from his
hand and poured it on the ground. The vengeance of God and
the miraculous power of the saintly Bishop were not slow in
punishing this deed. That very day the judge who had acted in
this way fell ill of a fever and by midnight he was dead, for he
was not even permitted to survive until that same hour on the
following day when he had dashed the cup from the fugitive's
hand in Saint Martin's church. After this miracle everyone
hastened to provide Austrapius with the necessities of life.
When King Lothar returned to his kingdom, he showed great
favour to the Duke. During his reign Austrapius was admitted
to the priesthood, and later on he was ordained Bishop of
Champtoceaux, which is in the diocese of Poitiers, it being
understood that, on the eventual death of Saint Pientius, who
held the episcopate of Poitiers, Austrapius should succeed him.
King Charibert would not agree to this. When Bishop Pientius
died, by a decree issued by King Charibert in Paris, Pascentius,
who was then Abbot of the monastery of Saint Hilary, succeeded him. Austrapius appealed against this decision, maintaining that the bishopric should be given to him, but his
protestations were not listened to. He returned to his own diocese. The Theifali[33] revolted against him, for he had always

33. The Theifali were a tribe of Goths who still lived in Poitou. The
place-name Tiffauges near Clisson (Loire-Atlantique) commemorates them.

been their enemy, and he died a cruel death from a blow from a spear. The diocese of Poitiers took back the parishes which had been allocated to Austrapius.

19.*   At this time, while Lothar was still reigning as King, Saint Medard the Bishop ended a lifetime of good works and died full of days and famous for his holiness. King Lothar had him buried with great pomp in the city of Soissons, and began to build over his remains the church which his son Sigibert later completed and embellished. At Medard's holy tomb I myself have seen the chains and shackles of prisoners burst asunder and lie broken on the ground;³⁴ and to this day they are preserved there as a proof of his miraculous power. Now I must return to what I was telling you.

20.   King Childebert fell ill: for a long time he lay bed-ridden in Paris and then he died.³⁵ He was buried in the church of Saint Vincent, which he himself had built.³⁶ King Lothar took over his kingdom and his treasury. He sent Queen Ultrogotha and her two daughters into exile. Chramn had an audience with his father, but he once more showed that he could not be trusted. When he saw that he could not escape his father's vengeance, he fled to Brittany and there he himself, his wife and his daughters went into hiding with Chanao, the Count of the Bretons. The priest Willichar sought sanctuary in the church of Saint Martin. Through the sins of the people and because of the wanton behaviour which used to take place there, this holy edifice was set on fire by Willichar and his wife, a misfortune which it grieves me greatly to have to relate. The previous year much of the city of Tours had been burnt down and many of its churches had been left desolate. Now King Lothar decreed that Saint Martin's church should be roofed with tin and restored to its former glory.

Two swarms of locusts appeared at this time. They passed through Auvergne and the Limousin and are said to have pen-

34. *GC*, 93.   35. A.D. 558.
36. Later Saint-Germain-des-Prés.

etrated as far as the plain of Romagnat. There they fought a
great battle and many were killed.

King Lothar was furious with Chramn and marched into
Brittany against him with his army.[37] Chramn had no compunction about fighting against his father. The two armies stood face
to face on the battlefield and Chramn, who was backed by the
Bretons, had already drawn up his line of attack facing his
father when night fell and the order to engage had to be deferred. During the night Chanao, Count of the Bretons, talked
things over with Chramn. 'In my opinion', said he, 'it would be
completely wrong for you to fight against your own father.
Why don't you let me attack him during the night? I could beat
him, and all his army, too.' Chramn would not agree to this, and
it is my belief that it was God's miraculous power which
stopped him. Morning dawned: the two armies moved forwards
and made contact. King Lothar advanced to do battle with his
own son, like some new David advancing against Absalom.
'Look down from heaven, O Lord,' he cried, weeping as he did
so, 'and judge my cause, for I suffer injury unjustly at the hands
of my son. Look down, O Lord, and make a fair decision, and
pass again that judgement which You passed between Absalom
and his father.'[38] Battle was joined on both sides. The Count of
the Bretons turned in flight and was killed. Chramn himself fled
soon afterwards. On the sea-coast he had ships ready to sail at a
moment's notice. He lost time trying to rescue his wife and
daughters: as a result he was overrun by his father's army,
made prisoner and bound. When this was announced to King
Lothar, he ordered Chramn to be burnt alive with his wife and
daughters. They were imprisoned in a poor man's hut. Chramn
was held down at full length on a bench and strangled with a
piece of cloth. Then the hut was burnt down over their heads.
So perished Chramn with his wife and daughters.

21. In the fifty-first year of his reign King Lothar went on a
pilgrimage to the entrance to Saint Martin's church, taking with
him many gifts.[39] When he reached Tours he visited the Saint's

37. A.D. 560.   38. Cp. II Samuel 15–18.   39. A.D. 561.

tomb and confessed to all the evil deeds which he had committed in his thoughtlessness. With many a groan he prayed to the blessed Saint to implore God's indulgence for his sins and by his intercession to gain pardon for his foolish actions. Then he went home again. In the fifty-first year of his reign, while he was hunting in the forest of Cuise, he fell ill with a high temperature and took to his bed in his villa in Compiègne. There he lay, suffering from a high fever. 'Well! Would you believe it?' he asked. 'What manner of King can be in charge of heaven, if he is prepared to finish off great monarchs like me in this fashion?' While he was in this agony of spirit he died.[40] His four sons bore him with great pomp to Soissons and buried him there in the church of Saint Medard. He died on the first anniversary of the killing of Chramn.

22. Once his father had been buried Chilperic took possession of his treasury, which was kept in his villa at Berny. Chilperic sought out the more influential of the Franks and won them over to his side with bribes. Soon after this he entered Paris and occupied Childebert's throne; but he was not to hold it for long, for his brothers leagued against him and drove him out. These four, Charibert, Guntram, Chilperic and Sigibert, then divided things up fairly between themselves. The kingdom of Childebert, with Paris for its capital, fell to Charibert. Guntram received the kingdom of Chlodomer, with Orleans as his chief city. Chilperic inherited the kingdom of his father Lothar, which he ruled from Soissons. Sigibert took over the kingdom of Theuderic, and established himself in Rheims.

23. The Huns attacked Gaul after the death of King Lothar.[41] Sigibert marched against them with his army, engaged them in battle, beat them and put them to flight. After this their King sent envoys and made overtures of friendship. Sigibert had other preoccupations while he was busy with the Huns. His brother Chilperic attacked Rheims and captured a number of other cities which were Sigibert's by right of inheri-

40. A.D. 561.   41. A.D. 562.

tance. What is worse, civil war then broke out between the two of them. When he came back as victor over the Huns, Sigibert occupied the city of Soissons. There he found Theudebert, King Chilperic's son: he took him prisoner and sent him into exile. Next he marched against Chilperic and fought a battle against him. Sigibert beat Chilperic, forced him to flee and brought his own cities once more under his dominion. He ordered Chilperic's son, Theudebert, to be imprisoned for a whole year in the villa of Ponthion. Sigibert was a clement man and, when the year was up, he sent Theudebert back safe and sound to his father, with many presents. He made Theudebert swear an oath that he would never fight against him again. Theudebert later broke his oath, which was a dishonourable thing to do.

24.   When King Guntram, like his brothers, had received his share of Lothar's dominions, he dismissed the patrician Agricola and gave the dignity of the patriciate to Celsus instead. Celsus was a tall man, broad of shoulder, strong of arm, haughty in speech, quick in his reactions and learned in law; but in course of time he had become so rapacious that he would often seize the possessions of the churches and make them his own property. One day in church he heard a passage being read from the prophet Isaiah: 'Woe unto them that join house to house, that lay field to field, till there be no place.'[42] He is said to have replied: 'This is a poor look-out! Woe then to me and to my children!' He left a son, who himself died childless and bequeathed the greater part of his possessions to the churches from which his father had stolen them.

25.   The good King Guntram first made Veneranda his mistress and took her to bed with him. She was the servant of one of his subjects. By her he had a son called Gundobad. Later on Guntram married Marcatrude, the daughter of Magnachar. He packed his son Gundobad off to Orleans. Marcatrude had a son of her own. She was jealous of Gundobad and encompassed his death. She sent him poison in a drink, so they say, and killed

42. Isaiah 5, 8.

him. Soon after Gundobad's death she lost her own son by the judgement of God. As a result the King was estranged from her and he dismissed her. She died not long afterwards. Then Guntram married Austrechild, also called Bobilla. He had two sons by her, the elder called Lothar and the younger Chlodomer.

26.   King Charibert married a woman called Ingoberg. He had by her a daughter, who eventually married a man from Kent and went to live there.[43] At that time Ingoberg had among her servants two young women who were the daughters of a poor man. The first of these, who wore the habits of a religious, was called Marcovefa, and the other Merofled. The King fell violently in love with the two of them. As I have implied, they were the daughters of a wool-worker. Ingoberg was jealous because of the love which the King bore them. She made a secret plan to set their father to work, in the hope that when Charibert saw this he would come to despise the two girls. When the man was working away Ingoberg summoned the King. Charibert came, hoping to see something interesting, and, without approaching too near, watched the man preparing wool for the royal household. He was so angry at what he saw that he dismissed Ingoberg and took Merofled in her place. He had another woman, the daughter of a shepherd who looked after his flocks. Her name was Theudechild and he is said to have had a son by her, but the child was buried immediately after his birth.

In the time of King Charibert Leontius assembled the bishops of his province in the city of Saintes and expelled Emerius from his see, for he maintained that he had not been appointed according to canon law. Emerius had been granted a charter by King Lothar which permitted him to be consecrated without the approval of his Metropolitan, who was away at the time. Emerius was expelled and they decided to choose instead Heraclius, who was then a priest in the city of Bordeaux. They signed a document to this effect and sent it to King Charibert by the hand of Heraclius himself. He reached Tours and ex-

43. This was Adelberg, known as Ethelberg and Bertha, who married Ethelbert, King of Kent.

plained to Saint Eufronius what had happened, asking him to be so good as to add his signature to the document. This the Bishop steadfastly refused to do. The priest Heraclius entered the gates of the city of Paris and sought an audience with the King. 'Hail, glorious King!' said he. 'I bring the warmest wishes to your Majesty from the apostolic see.' 'What?' said Charibert. 'Have you been in the city of Rome, that you bring me greetings from the Pope?' 'It is Leontius, your father in God, together with the bishops of his province, who sends this greeting to you,' answered Heraclius. 'He writes to tell you that he has expelled Cymulus from his see' – for that was the name of Emerius before he entered the church – 'because he accepted the episcopate of the city of Saintes without the sanction of canonical law. They notify you of their decision that he should be replaced by someone else, to the end that those who transgress the canons should be duly admonished and that the glory of your royal dominion should be handed down to later ages.' The King lost his temper when he heard Heraclius say this. He ordered the priest to be removed forcibly from his presence and to be driven into exile in a car filled with thorns. 'Do you really think that none of the sons of King Lothar lives to uphold the decisions of his father, and that, without even waiting for my approval, these men have the power to expel a bishop whom in his wisdom he elected?' Without more ado he despatched some of his ecclesiastics to restore Bishop Emerius to his see. With them he sent some of his chamberlains to exact a thousand pieces of gold from Leontius and to fine the other bishops as much as their circumstances permitted. In this way the insult done to the King was avenged.

Next King Charibert married Marcovefa, the sister of Merofled. They were both excommunicated as a result by Saint Germanus the Bishop. The King refused to give up Marcovefa: but she was struck by the judgement of God and died. Not long afterwards the King himself died in his turn.[44] After his death Theudechild, one of his queens, sent messengers to King Guntram, offering her hand in marriage. The King replied

44. A.D. 567.

in these terms: 'She may come to me and bring her treasure with her. I will receive her and I will give her an honourable place among my people. She will hold a higher position at my side than she ever did with my brother, who has died recently.' Theudechild was delighted when she heard this. She collected all her possessions together and set out to join Guntram. When he saw her, Guntram said: 'It is better that this treasure should fall into my hands than that it should remain in the control of this woman who was unworthy of my brother's bed.' He seized most of her goods, left her a small portion and packed her off to a nunnery at Arles. Theudechild bore ill the fasts and vigils to which she was subjected. She sent messengers in secret to a certain Goth, promising him that, if he would carry her off to Spain and marry her there, she would escape from the nunnery with what wealth remained to her and set off with him without the slightest hesitation. He immediately promised to do what she asked. She once more collected her possessions together and made them into bundles. As she was about to make her escape from the nunnery, she was surprised by the vigilant abbess. The abbess, who had caught her red-handed, had her beaten mercilessly and locked her up in her cell. There she remained until her dying day, suffering awful anguish.

27. King Sigibert observed that his brothers were taking wives who were completely unworthy of them and were so far degrading themselves as to marry their own servants. He therefore sent messengers loaded with gifts to Spain and asked for the hand of Brunhild, the daughter of King Athanagild. This young woman was elegant in all that she did, lovely to look at, chaste and decorous in her behaviour, wise in her generation and of good address. Her father did not refuse to give her to Sigibert, but sent her off with a large dowry. Sigibert assembled the leading men of his kingdom, ordered a banquet to be prepared and married Brunhild with every appearance of joy and happiness. She was, of course, an Arian, but she was converted by the bishops sent to reason with her and by the King who begged

her to accept conversion. She accepted the unity of the blessed Trinity and was baptized with the chrism. In the name of Christ she remains a Catholic.[45]

28.   When he saw this, King Chilperic sent to ask for the hand of Galswinth, the sister of Brunhild, although he already had a number of wives. He told the messengers to say that he promised to dismiss all the others, if only he were considered worthy of marrying a King's daughter of a rank equal to his own. Galswinth's father believed what he said and sent his daughter to him with a large dowry, just as he had sent Brunhild to Sigibert. Galswinth was older than Brunhild. When she reached the court of King Chilperic, he welcomed her with great honour and made her his wife. He loved her very dearly, for she had brought a large dowry with her. A great quarrel soon ensued between the two of them, however, because he also loved Fredegund, whom he had married before he married Galswinth. Galswinth was converted to the Catholic faith and baptized with the chrism. She never stopped complaining to the King about the insults which she had to endure. According to her he showed no respect for her at all, and she begged that she might be permitted to go back home, even if it meant leaving behind all the treasures which she had brought with her. Chilperic did his best to pacify her with smooth excuses and by denying the truth as convincingly as he could. In the end he had her garrotted by one of his servants and so found her dead in bed. After her death God performed a great miracle. A lamp suspended on a cord burned in front of her tomb. One day, without anyone touching it, the cord broke and the lamp fell to the stone floor. The hard stone withdrew at the point of impact and the lamp penetrated it just as if it had been made of soft material, and there it stood embedded up to its middle without anything being broken. Everyone who saw this knew that a miracle had occurred. King Chilperic wept for the death of

45. Queen Brunhild long outlived Gregory, dying a shameful ueath in A.D. 613. Lothar II, the son of Chilperic and Fredegund, had her dragged along the ground by an untamed horse until she expired.

Galswinth, but within a few days he had asked Fredegund to
sleep with him again. His brothers had a strong suspicion that
he had connived at the murder of the Queen and they drove
him out of his kingdom. Chilperic had three sons by one of his
earlier consorts, Audovera: these were Theudebert, about
whom I have told you already,[46] Merovech and Clovis. I must
return now to what I was describing to you.

29.   Once again the Huns tried to invade Gaul.[47] Sigibert
marched against them with his army, taking with him a large
force of brave warriors. Just as they were about to join battle,
the Huns, who were highly skilled in necromancy, made a
number of phantom figures dance before their eyes and so beat
them easily. Sigibert's army fled from the battlefield. He himself was surrounded by the Huns and made prisoner. However,
he was cunning and astute, and, although he could not beat
them in battle, he managed to suborn them later on by bribery.
He gave a great number of presents to their King and made a
treaty with him, with the result that there was peace between
the two peoples for the rest of his lifetime. This was greatly to
his credit, rather than something for him to be ashamed of. The
King of the Huns was called the Khan. All the rulers of the
Huns are given this title.

30.   King Sigibert wanted to take over Arles and he ordered
the men of Clermont-Ferrand to attack that city. At this time
Firminus was the Count of Clermont-Ferrand and it was he
who set out at their head. Meanwhile Audovarius marched on
the city with his army from the opposite direction. They entered
Arles and exacted oaths of fealty in the name of King Sigibert.
When King Guntram heard of this, he in his turn sent the patrician Celsus with an army. Celsus came to Avignon and captured the city. Then he, too, marched on Arles, surrounded the
place and began to assault Sigibert's army, which was shut up
inside the walls. Bishop Sabaudus delivered a speech to Sigibert's men. 'Make a sally,' said he, 'and engage the enemy, for

46. *HF*, IV, 23.   47. A.D. 566.

if you remain penned up inside the city walls you will have no chance of defending either us or the territory which belongs to Arles. If God is on your side and you beat your enemies, we will keep the promises which we have made to you. If on the contrary they defeat you, you will find the city gates open for you and you will be able to come in and save your lives.' Sigibert's men were deceived by the lies which Sabaudus told them. They sallied forth and prepared to fight. They were duly beaten by the army of Celsus and they turned in flight; but when they reached the city they found the gates closed against them. Their army was assailed by javelins from the rear and showered with rocks by the townsfolk. They made their way to the River Rhône, used their shields to support them in the water and tried to reach the opposite bank. The strength of the current carried many of them away and drowned them; and indeed the Rhône now did to the Auvergnats what we read that the Simois once did to the Trojans:

> . . . correpta sub undis
> Scuta virorum galeasque et fortia corpora volvit . . .
> Apparent rari natantes in gurgite vasto.[48]

Some were able to swim to the flat ground on the opposite bank, but only with the greatest difficulty and with the help of their shields. These made their way back home, stripped of all their equipment, deprived of their horses and thoroughly ashamed of themselves. Firminus and Audovarius were permitted to withdraw. Many of the leading men of Auvergne were carried away by the force of the current or else knocked on the head by blows from their enemies' swords. When he had received his own city back, King Guntram, with his usual magnanimity, restored Avignon to his brother's rule.

31.   A great prodigy appeared in Gaul at the fortress of Tauredunum, which was situated on high ground above the River

---

48. *Aeneid*, I, 100–101, 118. 'Beneath its waves it rolls the men's shields and helmets, and their strong bodies. A few appear, swimming in the great whirlpool.'

Rhône.[49] Here a curious bellowing sound was heard for more than sixty days: then the whole hillside was split open and separated from the mountain nearest to it, and it fell into the river, carrying with it men, churches, property and houses. The banks of the river were blocked and the water flowed backwards. This place was shut in by mountains on both sides, for the stream flows there through narrow defiles. The water then flooded the higher reaches and submerged and carried away everything which was on its banks. A second time the inhabitants were taken unawares, and as the accumulated water forced its way through again it drowned those who lived there, just as it had done higher up, destroying their houses, killing their cattle, and carrying away and overwhelming with its violent and unexpected inundation everything which stood on its banks as far as the city of Geneva. Many people maintained that the volume of water was so great that it flowed right over the walls of Geneva: and this is doubtless possible, for, as I have told you, at this spot the Rhône runs through mountainous defiles and, once its course was blocked, there was nowhere for it to turn on either side. It burst through the mountain which had fallen into it and washed everything away.

When all this had happened, thirty monks made their way to the spot where the fortress had collapsed, dug into the earth beneath where the landslide had occurred and found there bronze and iron. While they were busy at their task, they once more heard the bellowing of the mountain. So strong was their lust for gain that they took no notice: and a part of the hillside which had not previously collapsed now fell on top of them. It buried them completely and their dead bodies were never recovered.

Before the great plague which ravaged Auvergne prodigies terrified the people of that region in the same way.[50] On a number of occasions three or four great shining lights appeared

49. Les Evouettes, near Chessel. This disaster is described by Marius of Avenches in his *Chronicle, sub anno* 563.
50. A.D. 571.

round the sun, and these the country folk also called suns. 'Look!' they shouted. 'There are now three or four suns in the sky!' Once, on the first day of October, the sun was in eclipse, so that less than a quarter of it continued to shine, and the rest was so dark and discoloured that you would have said that it was made of sackcloth. Then a star, which some call a comet, appeared over the region for a whole year, with a tail like a sword, and the whole sky seemed to burn and many other portents were seen. In one of the churches of Clermont-Ferrand, while early-morning matins were being celebrated on some feast-day or other, a bird called a crested lark flew in, spread its wings over all the lamps which were shining and put them out so quickly that you would have thought that someone had seized hold of them all at once and dropped them into a pool of water. It then flew into the sacristy, under the curtain, and tried to extinguish the candle there, but the vergers managed to catch it and they killed it. In the same way another bird put out the lamps lighted in Saint Andrew's church.

When the plague finally began to rage, so many people were killed off throughout the whole region and the dead bodies were so numerous that it was not even possible to count them. There was such a shortage of coffins and tombstones that ten or more bodies were buried in the same grave. In Saint Peter's church alone on a single Sunday three hundred dead bodies were counted. Death came very quickly. An open sore like a snake's bite appeared in the groin or the armpit, and the man who had it soon died of its poison, breathing his last on the second or third day. The virulence of the poison made the victim unconscious. It was then that the priest Cato died. Many fled from the plague, but Cato never moved from the city of Clermont, burying the dead and with great courage continuing to say Mass. This priest was a person of great humanity and devoted to the poor. He was a proud man, it is true, but what he did at this moment excused everything. Bishop Cautinus, on the contrary, hurried from town to town to avoid the plague, but in the end he returned to Clermont, caught the infection and died on Good Friday, on the same day and at the same hour as his cousin

Tetradius. Lyons, Bourges, Chalon-sur-Saône and Dijon were
decimated by this plague.

32.* At that time there lived in the monastery of Randan near
the city of Clermont-Ferrand a priest called Julian who had
extraordinary miraculous power. He was most temperate in his
personal habits, never drinking wine, never eating meat, always
wearing a hair-shirt under his tunic, constant in his vigils, perpetually at prayer. To him it was a simple thing to cure those
possessed of a devil, to restore their sight to the blind and to
heal all other infirmities by calling on the name of our Lord or
by making the sign of the Holy Cross. Through long standing
his feet were swollen with dropsical fluid, but when he was
asked why he stood longer than his bodily strength permitted he
used to answer wittily enough: 'As long as life is in me, my feet
will serve me well enough, and by God's grace they will not fail
to support me.' Once in the church of Saint Julian the martyr I
myself saw him heal a man possessed of a devil by uttering a
single word. Often he would relieve quartan fevers and other
such diseases by prayer. At this time of plague he was taken
from this world to his rest, full of days and famous for his
miracles.

33.* At the same time the abbot of this monastery died. A man
called Sunniulf, who was of great simplicity of heart and
brotherly love, succeeded to him. He would often wash the feet
of visitors himself and then dry them with his own hands. He
had one weakness, that he sought to rule the monks under his
care not by commands but by entreaty. He used himself to tell
how once he was shown in a vision a certain river of fire, into
which men, assembling together on one part of the bank, were
plunging like so many bees entering a hive. Some were submerged up to the waist, some up to the armpits, some even up
to the chin, and all were shouting out that they were being
burned very severely. A bridge led over the river, so narrow that
only one man could cross at a time, and on the other side there
was a large house all painted white. Then Sunniulf asked those

who were with him what they thought this meant. 'From this
bridge will be hurled headlong anyone who is discovered to
have been lacking in authority over those committed to his
charge,' they answered. 'Anyone who has kept good discipline
may cross without danger and will be welcomed joyfully in the
house which you see opposite.' As he heard these words, Sunniulf awoke. From then on he was more severe with his monks.

34.*   I will now tell you something which happened in another
monastery at about the same time.[51] I do not propose to give
the name of the monk concerned, for he is still alive, and if he
should read what I have written he might be filled with vainglory and so lose virtue. A certain youth came to the monastery
and asked the abbot to let him join the brothers, for he wanted
to spend his life in God's service. The abbot was not very keen
to do this, for he said that the service was hard in that house and
that he did not think that the young man would be able to do
all that would be asked of him. The youth promised that, with
God's help, he would do everything that was expected of him,
and he was accepted. He turned out to be humble and God-
fearing in all that he did. A few days later it happened that the
monks carted three bushels or more of their grain out of their
barn and set it to dry in the sun, telling the young novice to
watch over it. They went off to rest and he was left in charge of
the grain. Suddenly the sky became overcast, a great wind blew
up and it looked as if a downpour of rain might fall on the heap
of grain. When the young monk saw what was happening he did
not know what to do. Even if he called the others, it was clear
that they could never cart all this grain back into the barn again
before the rain fell. He therefore gave up the attempt and con-
centrated on praying to God that no drop of rain might fall on
the corn. He threw himself on the ground as he prayed. The
cloud divided, the rain poured down all round the corn, but not a
single grain was wetted, if what I have heard is true. The other
monks, with the abbot at their head, came running to collect in
the grain, for they realized what was about to happen. This was

51. In Bordeaux; cp. the chapter-heading on p. 196.

the miracles which they saw, and, when they looked for the monk in charge of the corn, they found him prostrate in prayer a few yards away. When the abbot perceived what had occurred, he lay down in prayer beside the monk. The rain passed over and the abbot finished his prayer. He then told the youth to get up and ordered him to be seized and beaten. 'It is for you, my son,' said he, 'to grow more and more humble in the fear and service of God, not to puff yourself up with prodigies and miracles.' He had him shut in his cell for a whole week and made him fast in expiation of his sin, to prevent him from becoming too pleased with himself and so that he might learn to mend his ways. Today, and this I have learnt from reliable sources, this monk is so abstinent in his behaviour that he will not even eat bread in Lent and he will only drink a cup of barley water every third day. Let us pray to the Lord to deign to watch over him to the very end of his life, if He so wishes.

35.* Now when, as I have told you,[52] Bishop Cautinus died in Clermont-Ferrand, many put themselves forward for the episcopate, offering much and promising more. The priest Eufrasius, son of the late Evodius, who was of a senatorial family, despatched to the King, by the hands of his relative Beregisil, many precious gifts which he had obtained from the Jews, hoping to gain by bribery that which he could not hope to earn by his personal merit. His conversation was agreeable, but he was loose in his private life; he would ply the Franks with drink, but he very rarely gave refreshment to the poor. He tried to win this honour at the hands of men instead of through God, and this, in my opinion, was what prevented him from receiving it. The pronouncement which God had made through the mouth of Saint Quintianus could not be changed: 'No one descended from the family of Hortensius shall rule God's Church.' The clergy held a meeting in the cathedral of Clermont. Although he made no promises to them, the Archdeacon Avitus received their nomination and petitioned the King. Firminus, who had been appointed to the countship in that city, was deter-

52. *HF*, IV, 31.

mined to stand in his way. He did not go to court himself, but friends of his asked the King to allow one Sunday to pass before the consecration of Avitus. They promised to give the King a thousand pieces of gold if this delay were agreed to, but he refused. Thus it came about that Saint Avitus, who, as I have told you, was at that time archdeacon, was elected both by the clergy and by the people of Clermont, who had held their own meeting, and he mounted the episcopal throne. The King thought so highly of him that to do him honour he was prepared to forgo the strict observance of canonical rule, for he ordered Avitus to be consecrated in his own presence. 'May I be worthy to receive the gift of blessed bread at his hands,' said he. He made this special arrangement so that Avitus could be consecrated in Metz. Once Avitus had become Bishop, he made his magnanimity clear to all, ruling his flock justly, giving alms to the poor, solace to the widowed and every possible help to the orphaned. To this day, when a stranger comes to him, he is so warmly welcomed that he finds in Avitus at once a father and a fatherland.[53] May he prosper in the possession of his great virtues and preserve with all his heart whatever is pleasing in God's sight! May he reform all those given to loose-living and turn them towards that chastity which God ordains!

36.*   Sacerdos, Bishop of Lyons, died in Paris after the synod which deposed Saffarac.[54] As I have said in the book of his life,[55] Saint Nicetius, whom Sacerdos had himself chosen, received the bishopric. He was remarkable for his saintliness and chaste in his behaviour. He offered to all men, as far as in him lay, that loving kindness which the Apostle told us to show to everyone wherever possible.[56] In his heart was to be seen the Lord Himself, who is true love. If ever he was angry with anyone for some misdeed which he had committed, as soon as the offender had mended his ways, Nicetius would treat him as if nothing had ever gone wrong between them. He chastised those who had erred, but he forgave the penitent. He gave alms

---

53. Saint Avitus died in 594, just before Gregory of Tours.
54. A.D. 551 or 552.   55. *VP*, 8, 3.   56. Romans 12, 18.

freely and he himself worked very hard. He gave his full attention to the erection of churches and the building of houses, to
the sowing of his fields and the planting of his vines; but none of
these things distracted him from prayer. He died after holding
his bishopric for twenty-two years:[57] and now great miracles
are wrought at his tomb by those who come to pray there. By
means of the oil in the lamp which burns daily at his tomb he
gives back their sight to the blind; he drives out evil spirits from
the bodies of those possessed; he restores health to paralysed
limbs; and in our time he is considered to be a ready source of
help to all who are infirm.

Bishop Priscus, who succeeded Nicetius, began, with his wife
Susanna, to persecute and even put to death many of those who
had been the close associates of this godly man, not through any
sin which they had committed, not because they were guilty of
any crime, not for some theft for which they had been apprehended, but through the envy which burned within him, for he
was jealous of their loyalty to his predecessor. Priscus and his
wife did all they could to calumniate the Saint. Although it had
been a rule long observed by earlier bishops that no woman
should go into the church-house, Susanna and her young
women used to enter the very cell in which Nicetius had slept.
In the end God in His majesty took vengeance on the family of
Bishop Priscus for these sins. His wife Susanna was possessed of
a devil. In her madness she ran through the whole city, with her
hair loose about her shoulders, confessing that this holy man of
God, whom she had denied while she still had her wits, was in
fact Christ's friend, and calling upon him to spare her. The
Bishop was seized with a quartan ague and began to shake.
When he recovered from his ague, he continued to tremble
and was dull-witted. His son and his whole household
became white in the face and lost their wits, too, and it was
clear to all that Saint Nicetius had struck them with his miraculous power. Bishop Priscus and the members of his family
had constantly criticized the holy man of God, maintaining that
anyone who was prepared to spread scandal about him was

57. A.D. 573.

their friend. At the beginning of his episcopate he had ordered a storey to be added to the church-house. There was a deacon who, during his lifetime, God's Saint had not only deprived of communion for the sin of adultery, but had often caused to be flogged, without ever being able to reform him. This deacon now climbed to the roof of the church-house and began to take the tiles off. 'I thank you, Jesus Christ,' said he, 'that I have been permitted to walk on this roof now that that wicked man Nicetius is dead.' He had hardly finished speaking when the beam on which he was standing collapsed beneath his feet, and he fell to the ground and was crushed to death.

While the Bishop and his wife were misconducting themselves in this perverse way, Saint Nicetius appeared in a dream to a certain man. 'Go,' said he, 'and tell Priscus to stop behaving so badly and to mend his ways. Also say this to the priest Martin: "Since you support Priscus in what he is doing, you, too, will be punished; and if you do not give up your evil way of life, you will die." ' When he awoke this man went to a deacon of his acquaintance and said to him: 'You are well received in the Bishop's house. I beg you to tell what I have seen either to the Bishop himself or to the priest Martin.' The deacon promised to take the message, but he changed his mind and would not do it. That night when he had fallen asleep the Saint appeared to him. 'Why have you not reported what the priest told you to say?' he asked. Then Nicetius began to hit him in the throat with his clenched fists. When day dawned, the deacon's throat was painfully swollen. He went off to the two men concerned and told them all that he had heard. They made light of what they had been told and pretended that it was all empty dreams. The priest Martin immediately became ill with a high temperature, but he recovered from his sickness. He continued to flatter the Bishop, supporting him in his evil deeds and the abuse which he heaped on Saint Nicetius. He fell ill a second time with a fever and so died.

37.*   Saint Friard died, full of days, at exactly the same time as Saint Nicetius. He was famed for his holy life, admirable in all that he did and noble in his conduct. I have related some of his miracles in the book which I have written about his life.[58] Bishop Felix visited him just as he was dying and the whole cell shook. I have no doubt that he was being visited by an angel, which made the place tremble as he died. The Bishop washed his body, wrapped it in seemly clothing and buried it.

38. Now I must return to my story. When Athanagild died in Spain, his brother Leuvigild inherited his kingdom.[59] Leuva died next, and Leuvigild added his kingdom to what he already held.[60] When his wife died, Leuvigild married Goiswinth, the mother of Brunhild. He had two sons by his first wife, one of whom[61] had married the daughter of Sigibert[62] and the other[63] the daughter of Chilperic.[64] He divided his kingdom equally between these two sons, killing off everyone who might be planning to assassinate those who occupied the throne and 'left not one that pisseth against a wall'.[65]

39. Palladius, son of Count Britanus, who had died, and of his wife Caesaria, inherited the office of count in Javols, with the permission of King Sigibert. A quarrel ensued between him and Bishop Parthenius, which caused consternation among the inhabitants. Palladius heaped obloquy upon the Bishop, abusing him and accusing him of all sorts of crimes. He seized the property of the church and robbed those who served in it. This quarrel became worse and worse. In the end they both rushed off to the King's court and brought various charges against each other. Palladius accused the Bishop of being a weak, effeminate man. 'Where are your darling boys,' cried he, 'with whom you live in shame and debauchery?' The vengeance of God soon brought to an end these attacks upon the Bishop. The following year Palladius lost his countship and returned to Clermont-

---

58. *VP*, 10.   59. A.D. 567–8.   60. A.D. 572.
61. Hermangild.   62. Ingund.   63. Recared.
64. Rigunth. These two never married, as Chilperic's death intervened in 584.
65. I Samuel 25, 22 and I Kings 16, 11.

Ferrand. Romanus did all he could to be made count in his place. It happened one day that the two met in Clermont. A dispute began on the subject of the countship and Palladius was informed that King Sigibert wanted to have him killed. This was untrue, for it was a rumour being put about by Romanus. Palladius was so terrified and reduced to such straits that he threatened to kill himself with his own hands. He was watched closely by his mother and by his brother-in-law Firminus, to prevent him carrying out what he had planned in the bitterness of his soul. After a while he escaped from his mother's vigilance and went to his bedroom. There he took advantage of being alone, unsheathed his sword and, holding the hilt firm with his feet, pointed the blade towards his chest. He leant forward on the sword, which pierced his chest and came out at the back through one shoulder-blade. He then held the sword a second time, pierced his chest on the other side, and fell to the ground dead. I find it hard to believe that this horrible deed could have been achieved without the help of the Devil: for the first wound was enough to kill him, unless the Devil came to his assistance to give him strength to carry his terrible plan through to the end. His mother rushed in, beside herself with grief, and fell in a faint on the body of the son whom she had lost, while the whole family bewailed his fate. He was carried to the monastery of Cournon and buried there. His body was not placed among the Christian dead and no Mass was sung for him. It is clear that this fate befell him only because he had wronged his Bishop.

40.   The Emperor Justinian died in the town of Constantinople and Justin took over the imperial power.[66] He was the most avaricious of men, giving nothing to the poor and bleeding his senators dry. His cupidity was so great that he ordered iron coffers to be made and in them he amassed his wealth in gold coin. He is said to have lapsed into the Pelagian heresy. Not long afterwards he became insane and had to have Tiberius co-opted as Caesar to protect his provinces. Tiberius was a just and charitable man, equitable in his dealings, successful in war and,

66. A.D. 565.

what is more important than all his other good qualities, a true
Christian. King Sigibert sent Warinar the Frank and Firminus
from Clermont-Ferrand to him as envoys to seek peace. They
went by sea and came to the town of Constantinople, where
they had audience with the Emperor and gained what they had
come to seek. They returned home to Gaul the following year.

After this the two great cities of Antioch in Egypt[67] and
Apamea in Syria were captured by the Persians and their people
led off into slavery.[68] It was then that the church of Saint
Julian, the martyr of Antioch, was burnt down by a great fire.
The Persarmenians[69] visited the Emperor with a great store of
unwoven silk, seeking his friendship and declaring themselves to
be the enemies of the Persion Emperor. Persian envoys had
come to them with this message: 'Our Emperor in his solicitude
sends to ask if you intend to preserve the treaty which you have
made with him.' When they had answered that they would keep
intact all the promises which they had made, the envoys had
replied: 'It will be made clear that you propose to keep the
terms of the treaty if you agree to worship fire as he does.' The
people had answered that they would never do this. Their
Bishop, who was present, added: 'What is there divine about
fire, that it should be worshipped? God created it for men to
use. It is lighted from tinder. If you put water on it, it goes out.
It burns as long as you add fuel, but if you neglect it, it loses its
heat.' The envoys were furious when they heard the Bishop
continue in this strain. They abused him roundly and hit him
with their sticks. When the people had seen their Bishop covered
with blood, they had attacked the envoys, seized hold of them
by main force and killed them. Then, as I have said, they went
to seek an alliance with the Emperor.

41.   Alboin, the King of the Longobards, who had married
Chlothsind, the daughter of King Lothar, abandoned his own
country and emigrated to Italy with all his Longobard

67. Antioch on the River Orontes, in Syria, now in Turkey.
68. A.D. 572 or 573.
69. The people of Greater Armenia, who were in revolt against Chosroes.

235

people.[70] They assembled their army and set off with their wives and children, for they intended to take up residence there. Once they had occupied the country, they wandered all over it for seven years, robbing the churches, killing the bishops and subjecting everything to their dominion. When his consort Chlothsind died Alboin married a second wife, a woman whose father he had only recently killed.[71] She loathed her husband as a result, and was only waiting for an occasion to avenge the wrongs done to her father. In the end she poisoned her husband, for she had become enamoured of one of his servants. As soon as Alboin was dead, she went off with this servant. They were caught and were both put to death. The Longobards then appointed another King to rule over them.[72]

42. Eunius, surnamed Mummolus, was made a patrician by King Guntram. I have decided to go into his early career in some detail. He was the son of a certain Peonius and he lived in the town of Auxerre. Peonius held the countship of this municipality. In the hope of having his appointment renewed he sent gifts to the King through the hands of his son, but when he had handed over the things sent by his father, Mummolus canvassed his own appointment to the countship: in effect he replaced the father whom he ought to have been supporting. He advanced steadily from this beginning and was appointed to a more important post. When the Longobards invaded Gaul, the patrician Amatus, who had recently succeeded Celsus, marched out to meet them. The two armies met in battle, but Amatus was forced to flee and he was killed. The Longobards are said to have slaughtered so many Burgundians that no one could count the dead. Heavily laden with their booty, the Longobards then returned to Italy. Eunius, or Mummolus, as he was called, was summoned by the King and given the high honour of being made a patrician. A second time the Longobards attacked Gaul and this time they pushed forward as far as Plan de Fazi, near the town of Embrun. Mummolus mobilized an army and set

70. A.D. 568.
71. Rosamund, daughter of Cunimund, King of the Gepids.
72. Cleph: he was assassinated in A.D. 574.

out with his Burgundians for the place in question. He surrounded the Longobards with his army, made a rampart of
trees which he had felled, and attacked them along the woodland pathways. He killed quite a few, captured others and sent
these last back as prisoners to the King, who had them distributed in various places under close guard. The small contingent which managed to escape reached home and announced
the news. Two brothers called Salonius and Sagittarius, both of
them Bishops, fought in this battle.[73] Instead of seeking protection in the heavenly Cross, they were armed with the helmet
and breastplate of this secular world and, what is worse, they
are said to have killed many men with their own hands. This
was the first victory of Mummolus in a pitched battle.

Next the Saxons, who had invaded Italy with the Longobards, made a sally into Gaul and pitched their camp in a villa
at Estoublon, in the neighbourhood of Riez.[74] Then they scattered through the villas of the near-by towns, seizing booty,
making prisoners and causing great destruction. As soon as
Mummolus heard of this, he again raised an army and attacked the Saxons, killing many thousands of them and continuing the slaughter until evening fell and darkness put an end
to it. These men were unprepared for his assault and did not
have the foresight to see what would happen. When morning
dawned the Saxons reorganized their troops and prepared for
battle; but messengers passed between the two sides and peace
was patched up. The Saxons gave presents to Mummolus,
abandoned all their captives and the booty which they had seized
in that neighbourhood, and set out for home. Before they left
they swore that they would return to Gaul to take an oath of
fealty to the Frankish king and to make an alliance with him.
They made their way back to Italy, collected their wives, children and all their movable possessions, and made preparations
to return to Gaul, where they were to be received by King
Sigibert and settle in the region from which they had originally
emigrated. They split themselves into two lines of march, so to

73. Bishops of Embrun and Gap: see the Index for further references.
74. A.D. 572.

speak: one passed through the town of Nice and the other through Embrun, following the same route which they had used the previous year. They linked up again somewhere near Avignon. It was harvest time and in those parts most of the corn was still in the open fields, for the local peasantry had not yet brought it home. As soon as they arrived on the scene, the Saxons divided the harvest between them. They gathered in the grain, ground it and ate it, leaving nothing for those who had laboured to produce it. Only when it was all consumed did they move on to the bank of the River Rhône. Their plan was to cross the river and march on into the territory of King Sigibert, but Mummolus came out to meet them. 'You shall not cross this river,' said he. 'You have laid waste the land of my lord the King, you have stolen the harvest, killed off the cattle, burnt down the houses and cut down the olive-groves and the vineyards. You shall not move upstream unless you first recompense those whom you have left behind in poverty. If you fail to do this, you will assuredly not escape from me, for I will put you to the sword, you and your wives and your children, and so avenge the injury which you have done to my lord King Guntram.' The Saxons were terrified at this. They handed over many thousands of gold coins in payment for what they had done. Then they were allowed to cross the river and move towards Clermont-Ferrand. It was springtime by now. They paid their way with stamped bars of bronze instead of gold. Any local who saw this had no doubt at all that it was gold, guaranteed and properly assayed, for it was coloured by some clever process or other. Many were deceived by this, ruining themselves by handing over their goods and receiving bronze in exchange. The Saxons reached King Sigibert's territory and were settled in the place from which they had originally set out.

43.* In the realm of King Sigibert the governor of Provence, called Jovinus, was deprived of his office and Albinus was appointed in his place. This was a cause of great enmity between them. Some ships from overseas put into the harbour of Marseilles and the men of the Archdeacon Vigilius stole seventy wine-jars of the type called *orcae* which were full of oil and liquor, without their master knowing what they had done. When the merchant concerned discovered that his goods had been taken, he began to look everywhere to find out where the stolen property had been concealed. In the course of his inquiries he was told by someone that the servants of Archdeacon Vigilius had committed the crime. The news came to the Archdeacon's ears. He made inquiries in his turn and discovered the goods. He did not admit it, but began to make excuses for his men. 'No one who is a member of my household would ever dare to do such a deed,' he maintained. When the merchant heard the Archdeacon's statement, he went to Albinus. He explained what had happened and accused the Archdeacon of being implicated in the robbery. On Christmas Day the Archdeacon put on his alb and, when the Bishop entered the church, invited him, as the custom is, to proceed to the altar and at the proper moment to celebrate Mass according to the ritual of this holy occasion. Albinus thereupon rose from his seat, seized the Archdeacon and dragged him out of the church, punching him and kicking him, and then locking him up in prison. Neither the Bishop, nor the townsfolk, not even the most important of them, nor the people present, who all agreed about this, could gain permision for the Archdeacon to give some surety and then celebrate Mass with the others, on the understanding that the case should be heard properly later on. Albinus had no respect for the rites of the church, for he dared to arrest a priest serving at the Lord's altar on such a day. What more can I tell you? He fined the Archdeacon four thousand pieces of gold. When the matter came before King Sigibert, Jovinus spoke against Albinus and the latter was forced to pay back four times that sum in retribution.

44. Soon after this three leaders of the Longobards, Amo, Zaban and Rodan, invaded Gaul.[75] Amo marched by way of

75. A.D. 574.

Embrun, advanced as far as the villa of Saint-Saturnin, near Avignon, which Mummolus had received as a present from the King, and pitched his tents there. Zaban passed through the town of Die, came to Valence, and camped there. Rodan reached the town of Grenoble and set up his headquarters there. Amo captured the province of Arles and all the towns in the region; he then marched as far as the stony area called La Crau, which is near Marseilles, and stripped the countryside of its herds and inhabitants. He made plans to besiege Aix, but he was bought off with twenty-two pounds of silver and marched on. Rodan and Zaban did the same in the districts which they had invaded. When Mummolus came to hear of this he raised an army and attacked Rodan, who was besieging Grenoble. The army of Mummolus had great difficulty in crossing the River Isère, but by the intervention of God an animal entered the water and showed them where the ford was. In this way Mummolus' troops were able to cross freely to the opposite bank. When they saw them coming the Longobards drew their swords and attacked them immediately. Battle was joined and many of the Longobards were killed. Rodan was wounded by a spear and fled to the near-by mountain-peaks. With five hundred men, who were all that remained to him, he made his way along the forest tracks and so came at length to Zaban, who was then besieging Valence. Rodan told Zaban all that had occurred. Together they pillaged the whole neighbourhood and then withdrew to the town of Embrun. Mummolus marched with an enormous army to encounter them there. The battle began and the Longobard battalions were cut to pieces and annihilated, their leaders seeking refuge in Italy with the few men left to them. They retreated as far as Susa and there they received a harsh welcome from the locals, the more so as Sisinnius, the Emperor's Master of the Troops, lived in that town. A lad who said that he was in the service of Mummolus delivered a letter to Sisinnius in the presence of Zaban, giving greetings in Mummolus' name and adding: 'He is not far away.' As soon as he heard this Zaban left the town immediately and made off. When Amo heard the news he retreated in his turn, looting every place he came to on his route. He was blocked by the snows and forced to abandon his booty, making his way through with great difficulty and with a very small escort. They were all terrified by the prowess of Mummolus.

45. Mummolus conducted many campaigns and was always victorious. When, after the death of Charibert,[76] Chilperic invaded Tours and Poitiers, which, by their agreement, had fallen to the share of King Sigibert, that King joined with his brother Guntram to appoint Mummolus as the man to restore these cities to their dominion. He came to Tours, drove out Clovis, the son of Chilperic, and made the people swear an oath of allegiance to King Sigibert. Then he marched on Poitiers. Two of the inhabitants of the city, Basilius and Sighar, collected a mob together and prepared to resist. Mummolus hemmed them in on all sides, overpowered them, conquered them and killed them. He then entered Poitiers and again insisted on an oath of fealty. Now I must leave Mummolus for the time being.

46. I will now tell you about the death of Andarchius. First I will describe his birth and where he came from. He was, so they say, a slave of Felix, who himself came of a senatorial family. Andarchius acted as personal servant to his master. He joined in the literary studies of Felix and he distinguished himself by his learning. He became extremely well informed about the works of Virgil, the books of the Theodosian code of laws and the study of arithmetic. He was proud of his knowledge and began to despise his masters. When Duke Lupus visited Marseilles on the order of King Sigibert, Andarchius placed himself under his patronage. When Lupus left Marseilles, he asked Andarchius to go with him: Lupus recommended him strongly to King Sigibert and found employment for him at court. The King sent him on missions to various places and used him in the public service. He already seemed a person to whom some honour was due. He came to Clermont-Ferrand and wormed his way into the friendship of a man called Ursus, who lived in that city. Andarchius had a keen eye to his own advantage and he decided

76. A.D. 567.

to marry the daughter of this Ursus. He placed a mail shirt in a
case in which legal documents were usually kept, and said to the
wife of Ursus: 'I have put in this case a quantity of gold coins
which belong to me, more than sixteen thousand of them, as a
matter of fact. I leave them in your charge. They might perhaps
become yours, if you were to let me marry your daughter.'

>   . . . Quid non mortalia pectora cogis
>   Auri sacra fames![77]

The woman was simple enough to be taken in by this and in the
absence of her husband she promised Andarchius that he
should marry the girl. He went back to see the King and then
returned once more with a royal licence, which he showed to
the local magistrate, saying that he was to marry her. 'I have
already paid a deposit for her,' he maintained. Ursus denied
this, saying: 'I do not know who you are, or where you came
from, nor have I received any of your property.' A quarrel
arose between them and became worse and worse, until Andarchius demanded that Ursus should appear before the King.
Andarchius went to the royal villa at Berny, where he produced
another man also called Ursus. He brought him secretly before
an altar and made him swear the following oath: 'By this holy
place and on the relics of the Saints I swear that if I do not give
you my daughter in marriage I will immediately repay you
sixteen thousand pieces of gold.' There were witnesses standing
in the sacristy, listening unobserved to what he said, but they
could not see who was making this oath. Then Andarchius
spoke reassuringly to the true Ursus and persuaded him to return
home without having had an audience with the King. After the
oath had been sworn, Andarchius showed a copy of it to the
King. 'Ursus has written this out and given it to me,' he said. 'I
therefore ask your Majesty to give me a licence which shall
make him let me marry his daughter. If not, I am to take possession of his property, and when I have my sixteen thousand
gold coins back I will withdraw from the affair.' Andarchius

77. *Aeneid*, III, 56–7. 'Accursed lust for money, to what do you not drive
the hearts of men!'

took the document and went off with it to Clermont, where he made public the King's decree. Ursus fled to Le Velay, but, as his property was sequestered to Andarchius, the latter followed Ursus there. He went into a house belonging to Ursus and ordered a meal to be prepared for him and water to be heated so that he could wash. The house-servants refused to obey the orders of so rude a person, but he beat some with sticks and others with rods, hitting them over the head until the blood flowed. The household was coerced by this: supper was prepared and Andarchius washed himself in the water which they heated. He then drank himself silly with wine and retired to bed. He had only seven servants with him. They, too, went to bed, where they slept soundly because of the wine which they had swallowed. The household then assembled and closed the doors, which were made of wooden planks. First they removed the keys, then they broke open the corn-ricks, which stood near by, and piled all round the house and even on top of it the stooks of corn, which was still in sheaves. When they had finished, the house was completely covered and you could not have told that it was there. They then set fire to it in a number of places. The charred fragments of the building fell in on the unhappy wretches within. They shouted for help, but there was no one to hear them. The whole house was burnt down and they were roasted alive. Ursus was terrified by what had happened and fled for sanctuary to the church of Saint Julian. In the end he received all his goods back, but only after giving the King a bribe.

47.   When he was driven out of Tours, Clovis, Chilperic's son, fled to Bordeaux.[78] He lived there for a while and no one took any notice of him. Then a certain Sigulf, who was one of Sigibert's men, suddenly launched an attack on him. Clovis fled, but Sigulf pursued him with horns and bugles, as if he were chasing a hunted deer. It was only with great difficulty that Clovis managed to return safely to his father. In the end he arrived back, having made his way via Angers.

78. A.D. 573.

A dispute now began between the two Kings Guntram and Sigibert. King Guntram called a council in Paris of all the bishops in his realm, to decide which of them was in the right. The two Kings, however, refused to listen to the bishops' advice and as a result of their sinful behaviour this civil war grew more and more bitter.

Chilperic was the next to fly into a rage. He sent his elder son Theudebert to invade the cities of Tours, Poitiers and others south of the Loire, despite the fact that this same Theudebert had sworn an oath of fealty to Sigibert, when that King held him prisoner.[79] Theudebert came to Poitiers and fought a pitched battle against Duke Gundovald. Gundovald's army fled from the scene of combat and Theudebert slaughtered many of the local people. He also burned much of the district round Tours, and, if the inhabitants had not quickly surrendered, he would have burnt it all. He continued to advance with his troops and invaded the Limousin, the district of Cahors and other territories near by, all of which he ravaged and sacked. He burned the churches, stole their holy vessels, killed the clergy, emptied the monasteries of monks, raped the nuns in their convents and caused devastation everywhere. There was even more weeping in the churches at this period than there had been at the time of Diocletian's persecution.

48.*   To this day one is still amazed and astonished at the disasters which befell these people. We can only contrast how their forefathers used to behave with how they themselves are behaving today. After the missionary preaching of the bishops, the earlier generations were converted from their pagan temples and turned towards the churches; now they are busy plundering those same churches. The older folk listened with all their heart to the Lord's bishops and had great reverence for them; nowadays they not only do not listen, but they persecute instead. Their forefathers endowed the monasteries and churches; the sons tear them to pieces and demolish them.

What can one say, for example, of the monastery of Latte, in

79. *HF*, IV, 23.

which the relics of Saint Martin are kept? A force of hostile troops approached and prepared to cross the river which runs by, so that they might loot this monastery. 'This is the monastery of Saint Martin!' cried the monks. 'You Franks must not cross over here!' Most of those who heard this were filled with the fear of God and so withdrew. Twenty of their number, who did not fear God and had no respect for the blessed Saint, climbed into a boat and crossed the river. Driven on by the Devil himself, they slaughtered the monks, damaged the monastery and stole its possessions, which last they made into bundles and piled on their boat. Then they pushed off into the stream, but their keel began to sway to and fro, and they were carried round and round. They had lost their oars, which might have saved them. They tried to reach the bank by pushing the butts of their spears into the bed of the river, but the boat split apart beneath their feet. They were all pierced through by the points of their lances, which they were holding against their bodies; they were all transfixed and were killed by their own javelins. Only one of them remained unhurt, a man who had rebuked the others for what they were doing. If anyone thinks that this happened by chance, let him consider the fact that one innocent man was saved among so many who were doing evil. After their death the monks retrieved the corpses from the bed of the river. They buried the dead bodies and replaced their own possessions in their monastery.

49.   While all this was going on King Sigibert alerted the tribes which live across the Rhine and made preparations for civil war.[80] His plan was to march against his brother Chilperic. As soon as he heard this, Chilperic sent messengers to his other brother Guntram. They agreed to a treaty by which neither of them would permit the other to suffer harm. Sigibert advanced at the head of his forces. Chilperic on the other hand stood firm and did not budge. In his onward march against his brother Sigibert could find no ford by which to cross the Seine. He sent a message to his brother Guntram. 'If you do not permit me to

80. A.D. 574.

pass through the lands which you have inherited so that I may cross this river, I will turn my whole force on you,' said the message. Guntram was afraid, so he came to terms with Sigibert and permitted him to cross the Seine. Chilperic realized that Guntram had deserted him and gone over to Sigibert. He thereupon moved his camp and retreated to Havelu, a village not far from Chartres. Sigibert pursued him and made a demand that they should meet on the battlefield. Chilperic was afraid that, if their two armies joined battle, each of their two kingdoms might be destroyed. He sued for peace and handed back Sigibert's cities which Theudebert had so savagely attacked, stipulating that the inhabitants should not be punished, for Theudebert had annexed them forcibly, coercing them with fire and sword.

At this time many of the villages round Paris were burnt to the ground. The houses and all other property were pillaged by the enemy, and some of the inhabitants were even led away into slavery. King Sigibert ordered his troops to stop doing this; but he could not control the savagery of the tribes which came from across the Rhine. He bore all this patiently, only waiting for the chance to return home. Some of these people from beyond the Rhine began to demonstrate, because he had not let them fight. Sigibert was a brave man: he leapt on his horse and rode out to meet them and tried to calm them. Later on he had many of them stoned to death. It is clear that these people could never have been induced to make peace and abjure battle had it not been arranged by the miraculous power of Saint Martin. On the very day when they agreed to a peace-treaty, three paralytics stood up in the Saint's church. With God's help, I have described this in some of my other books.[81]

50. It causes me great grief to have to describe these civil wars. When a year had passed Chilperic once more sent messengers to his brother Guntram. 'Come to me, dear brother,' said he. 'Let us meet to make peace, so that we can attack Sigibert, who is our enemy.' This was achieved: the two met and ex-

81. *VSM*, 2, 5–7.

changed presents. Chilperic raised an army and marched as far
as Rheims, burning and destroying everything in his way. When
Sigibert heard of this, he once more summoned the tribes from
across the Rhine about which I have told you. He came to Paris
and prepared to march against his brother Chilperic. He sent
despatches to the inhabitants of Châteaudun and Tours to
order them to march against Theudebert. They were loath to do
this, and the King sent Duke Godigisel and Duke Guntram
Boso to take over the command. They raised an army and attacked Theudebert. He was deserted by most of his troops, but
he made a stand with the few who remained. All the same he
did not hesitate to engage the enemy. Battle was joined; Theudebert was beaten and killed; his dead body was despoiled by
his enemies, which is sad to have to relate. It was later picked up
by a certain Aunulf, washed and wrapped in decent vestments.
Theudebert was buried in the city of Angoulême. When his
father Chilperic realized that Guntram had again made peace
with Sigibert, he took refuge with his wife and sons inside the
walls of Tournai.

51. In that year lightning was observed to flicker across the
sky, just as we saw it before Lothar's death.

Once he had invested the cities which are south of Paris,
Sigibert advanced as far as Rouen. He had intended to abandon
these cities to the tender mercies of their enemies, but his ad·
visers prevented him from doing this. Next he left Rouen and
returned to Paris. Brunhild came to join him there, bringing
their sons. Then those Franks who had once looked to the older
Childebert sent envoys to Sigibert, saying that they would abandon Chilperic if he, Sigibert, would come to them, and that they
would then appoint him as their king. When he heard this Sigibert sent troops to besiege his brother in Tournai, planning to
follow himself with all speed. Saint Germanus, the Bishop, said
to him: 'If you set out with the intention of sparing your
brother's life, you will return alive and victorious. If you have
any other plans in mind, you will die. That is what God an·
nounced through the mouth of Solomon: "Whoso diggeth a pit

(for his brother) shall fall therein." [82] The King in his sinfulness took no notice of Saint Germanus. He advanced to the royal villa of Vitry and assembled the entire army around him. They raised him on a shield and elected him as their king. Two young men who had been suborned by Queen Fredegund then came up to Sigibert, carrying the strong knives which are commonly called scramasaxes, and which they had smeared with poison. They pretended that they had something to discuss with him, but they struck him on both sides. He gave a loud cry and fell to the ground. He died soon afterwards.[83] His chamberlain Charegisel was killed at the same time and Sigila, who had joined him long before from the Goths, was seriously wounded. Later on Sigila was captured by King Chilperic, burned by red-hot irons and died a cruel death, for his body was torn limb from limb. Charegisel was frivolous in his conduct and only serious when it came to personal gain. He came from the most humble origins, but rose to high place by fawning on the King. He was avid for other men's possessions and took no notice of their testamentary provisions. His end was such that death came to thwart him in his own plans, after he had spent his life thwarting those of others.

Chilperic was in a desperate situation, not knowing whether he could escape alive or would be killed instead. At this moment messengers arrived to tell him that his brother was dead. He sallied forth from Tournai with his wife and sons, dressed Sigibert's corpse and buried it in the village of Lambres. Later on Sigibert was translated to the church of Saint Medard at Soissons, which he had himself constructed, and buried there by the side of his father, Lothar. He died in the fourteenth year of his reign, when he was forty years old. Twenty-eight years passed between the death of the older Theudebert and the death of Sigibert. Sigibert died eighteen days after his nephew Theudebert. After his death his son Childebert reigned in his place.

From the Creation to the Flood were two thousand, two hundred and forty-two years. From the Flood to Abraham were

82. Proverbs 26, 27.   83. A.D. 575.

nine hundred and forty-two years. From Abraham to the departure of the Children of Israel from Egypt were four hundred and sixty-two years. From the departure of the Children of Israel from Egypt to the building of Solomon's Temple were four hundred and eighty years. From the building of the Temple to its destruction and the exile in Babylon were three hundred and ninety years. From the exile to the Passion of our Lord were six hundred and sixty-eight years. From the Passion of our Lord to the death of Saint Martin were four hundred and twelve years. From the death of Saint Martin until the death of King Clovis were one hundred and twelve years. From the death of King Clovis to the death of Theudebert were thirty-seven years. From the death of Theudebert to the death of Sigibert were twenty-nine years. This makes five thousand, seven hundred and seventy-four years in all.

HERE ENDS BOOK IV

BOOK V

HERE BEGIN THE CHAPTER-HEADINGS OF BOOK V

1. How the younger Childebert began to reign, and what happened to his mother.
2. How Merovech married Brunhild.
3. The war with Chilperic and the hideous behaviour of Rauching.
4. How Roccolen came to Tours.
5. The Bishops of Langres.
6. Leunast, the Archdeacon of Bourges.
7. The recluse Senoch.
8. Saint Germanus, Bishop of Paris.
9. The recluse Caluppa.
10. The recluse Patroclus.
11. How the Jews were converted by Bishop Avitus.
12. Abbot Brachio.
13. How Mummolus ravaged Limoges.
14. How Merovech was tonsured and sought sanctuary in the church of Saint Martin.
15. The war between the Saxons and the Swabians.
16. The death of Macliaw.
17. Doubt about Easter. The church in Chinon. How King Guntram killed the sons of Magnachar, lost his own sons and made an alliance with Childebert.
18. Bishop Praetextatus; and the death of Merovech.
19. Tiberius and his charity.
20. The Bishops Salonius and Sagittarius.
21. Winnoch the Breton.
22. The death of Samson, Chilperic's son.
23. Signs and wonders; and how Chilperic attacked and occupied Poitiers.

24. How Guntram Boso removed his daughters from the church of Saint Hilary.
25. How Dacolen died and Duke Dragolen after him.
26. How the army marched into Brittany.
27. How Salonius and Sagittarius were deposed.
28. The taxes imposed by Chilperic.
29. How Brittany was ravaged.
30. The reign of the Emperor Tiberius.
31. The traps laid by the Bretons.
32. How the church of Saint Dionysius was defiled through a woman.
33. Great signs and wonders.
34. An epidemic of dysentery, which caused the death of Chilperic's sons.
35. Queen Austrechild.
36. Bishop Heraclius and Count Nantinus.
37. Martin, Bishop of Galicia.
38. How the Christians were persecuted in Spain.
39. The death of Clovis.
40. Bishops Elafius and Eunius.
41. Ambassadors come from Galicia. More portents.
42. Maurilio, Bishop of Cahors.
43. My dispute with a heretic.
44. The writings of Chilperic.
45. The death of Bishop Agricola.
46. The death of Bishop Dalmatius.
47. The countship of Eunomius.
48. The wicked behaviour of Leudast.
49. The traps which he laid for me and how he was humbled.
50. What Bishop Salvius prophesied about Chilperic.

HERE END THE CHAPTER-HEADINGS OF BOOK V

HERE, I AM GLAD TO SAY, BEGINS BOOK V. AMEN.

It gives me no pleasure to write of all the different civil wars which afflicted the Frankish people and their rulers; what is even worse, we now seem to see the moment draw near which our Lord foretold as the real beginning of our sorrows: 'The father shall rise up against the son, and the son against the father; brother shall rise up against brother, and kinsman against kinsman.'[1] The Franks ought, indeed, to have been warned by the sad fate of their earlier kings, who, through their inability ever to agree with each other, were killed by their enemies. How many times has Rome, the city of cities, the great head of all the world, been brought low by her civil dissensions, yet it is true that, when the strife was over, she rose once more as if out of the ground! If only you kings had occupied yourselves with wars like those in which your ancestors larded the ground with their sweat, then the other races of the earth, filled with awe at the peace which you imposed, might have been subjected to your power! Just think of all that Clovis achieved, Clovis, the founder of your victorious country, who slaughtered those rulers who opposed him, conquered hostile peoples and captured their territories, thus bequeathing to you absolute and unquestioned dominion over them! At the time when he accomplished all this, he possessed neither gold nor silver such as you have in your treasure-houses! But you, what are you doing? What are you trying to do? You have everything you want! Your homes are full of luxuries, there are vast supplies of wine, grain and oil in your store-houses, and in your treasuries the gold and silver are piled high. Only one thing is lacking: you cannot keep peace, and therefore you do not know the grace of God. Why do you all keep on stealing from each other? Why do you always want something which someone else possesses? I

1. Cp. Matthew 10, 21 and 24, 7.

beg you, listen to the words of the Apostle: 'But if you bite and devour one another, take heed that ye be not consumed one of another.'[2] Read carefully what those who lived in earlier times have written down for us: there you will see the dire effects of civil wars. Look up what Orosius wrote about the Carthaginians. When he is describing how their city and all their territory were overthrown after seven hundred years, he has added these words: 'What is it that preserved the city for so long? Concord. What destroyed it in the end? Discord.'[3] Beware, then, of discord, beware of civil wars, which are destroying you and your people. As things are, what else can you look forward to, except that your army will be beaten and that you yourselves will be left without support and will fall into ruin, conquered by enemy peoples. If internal discord pleases you, King, turn your attention to that struggle which, according to the Apostle, is being waged deep inside every man, so that your spirit may lust against the flesh,[4] and your vices be overcome by your virtues, and you yourself, as a free man, may serve your leader, which is Christ the Lord, you who were wont, in chains, to serve instead the root of all evil.[5]

1. At the moment when King Sigibert was killed in Vitry, Queen Brunhild was in residence with her children in Paris.[6] When the news was announced to her, she was prostrate with anguish and grief, and she hardly knew what she was doing. Duke Gundovald took charge of her little son Childebert and removed him from her in secret, snatching him from certain death. Gundovald assembled the people over whom Sigibert had reigned and proclaimed Childebert King, although he was barely five years old. Childebert began to reign on Christmas Day.

In the first year of Childebert's rule, King Chilperic came to Paris, seized hold of Brunhild, banished her to the city of Rouen and took possession of the treasure which she had brought to Paris. He ordered her daughters to be held in custody in

2. Galatians 5, 15.   3. Orosius, *Adversus Paganos*, 5, 2.
4. Galatians 5, 17.   5. I Timothy 6, 10.   6. A.D. 575.

Meaux.[7] Next Roccolen came to Tours with the men of Maine, plundered the city and committed many crimes there. I shall tell you later on how, in retribution for his many evil deeds, he was killed by the miraculous power of Saint Martin.[8]

2.   Chilperic sent his son Merovech to Poitiers with an army. Merovech disobeyed his father's orders and marched on Tours, where he spent the holy days of Easter. His army did great damage to the entire neighbourhood. Under the pretext of visiting his mother Audovera, he next moved to Rouen. There he joined Queen Brunhild and made her his wife. When Chilperic heard that in defiance of custom and canonical law Merovech had married his uncle's widow, he was bitterly angry and marched to Rouen quicker than I can say the word. As soon as Merovech and Brunhild learned that Chilperic had decided to separate them, they sought sanctuary in the church of Saint Martin, which is built of wooden planks high on the city walls. The King arrived and did all in his power to persuade them to come out. They knew that he was up to no good and they refused to believe him, but he swore that insofar as it was God's will he would not try to separate them. When they heard his solemn oath, they came out from the church. Chilperic kissed them both and received them according to their rank. He had a meal with them and set off for Soissons a few days later, taking Merovech with him.

3.   While they were still in Rouen, troops assembled in Champagne and marched on the town of Soissons: they drove out Queen Fredegund and Clovis, Chilperic's son, and did what they could to capture the city. King Chilperic came to hear of this and set out in that direction with his army, sending messengers ahead to warn them to do nothing to his disadvantage, for otherwise bloody slaughter would be the lot of both armies. They took no notice of what he said and made ready for battle. The fight began and Chilperic's force was victorious: he put the

7. Ingund and Chlodosind.
8. *HF*, V, 4.

enemy army to flight and killed many of their soldiers, strong, capable men. The remainder fled and Chilperic entered Soissons.

After all this the King began to entertain suspicions about his own son Merovech, in view of his marriage to Brunhild, for he alleged that all these insurrections must be the result of Merovech's plotting. Chilperic had Merovech deprived of his arms and guarded closely, ordering him to remain in custody although not actually a prisoner, while he, the King, decided what action to take in the future.

The real instigator of this war was Godin. This man had transferred his allegiance from Sigibert to Chilperic, by whom he had been given many gifts. Godin was beaten in battle and he was the first to run away. King Chilperic thereupon took back again the villas which he had granted to Godin from the crown lands in the Soissons area, and gave them instead to the church of Saint Medard. Not long afterwards Godin died suddenly. Rauching married his widow.

This Rauching was an extremely vain man, puffed up with pride, impudence and arrogance. He behaved towards those in his service as if he found it difficult to accept that they were human beings at all. He treated them infamously, and his savage brutality went far beyond the bounds of human cruelty and folly. Whenever, as the custom is, a serf stood before him with a lighted candle as he ate his meal, Rauching would make him bare his shins and grasp the candle between them until it burned out; and when a new candle was lighted, Rauching would repeat the trick, until the serf's legs were completely scorched. If the serf uttered a sound or tried to escape, a naked sword was held in front of him; and Rauching would be convulsed with merriment to watch the man weep. The story used to be told of how two of his servants, a young man and a maiden, fell in love with each other, as happens so frequently. This relationship continued for two years and more, and then they went off to church together and were married. When Rauching heard of this he visited the local priest and demanded that his two servants should come back to him, saying that he forgave them for what they had done. 'You know what respect you owe to the house of God,' answered the priest. 'You cannot have these two back unless you promise to let them live together as man and wife. What is more, you must give me your word that you will not punish them.' Rauching stood silent for a long time whilst he made up his mind what he would do. Then he turned towards the priest, put his hands on the altar and swore the following oath: 'I will never separate them. On the contrary I will make only too sure that they remain closely united. I admit that I was annoyed when they married without my permission, but I accept what they have done and I am delighted that the man has not married a woman belonging to someone else's household or the woman some other man's serf.' In his simplicity the priest accepted this crafty man's promise and he handed over the two serfs whom Rauching had promised to pardon. Rauching thanked the priest, took charge of the two serfs and went home. He immediately ordered his men to cut down a tree and then had a portion of the trunk split by wedges and hollowed out. Then he had a hole dug three or four feet deep in the earth and the hollowed-out tree trunk placed in it. He put the girl inside, as if she were already a corpse, had the young man thrown on top of her, fixed a lid over them and filled the grave with earth, burying them both alive. 'I have not broken my promise,' said he, 'for I swore that they should never be separated.' When the priest heard what had happened, he came running at full speed. He upbraided Rauching bitterly, but it was only with the greatest difficulty that he had the two dug up again. He got the man up alive, but when he brought the girl out she was suffocated. This was the sort of outrage Rauching delighted in. His death was a fitting and well-deserved end to the life which he lived; but about this I will tell you later.[9]

Siggo the Referendary,[10] who used to act as keeper of the privy seal to King Sigibert, had been appointed by King Chilperic to fill the same office which he had held in his brother's time.

---

9. *HF*, IX, 9.

10. The Referendaries were the legal secretaries of the king, and they had charge of the royal signet-ring, by which documents were signed.

Siggo deserted Chilperic and went over to King Childebert, Sigibert's son. Ansovald received Siggo's property, which was in
the Soissons area. About this time quite a few of those who had
emigrated from Sigibert's kingdom and joined Chilperic abandoned this latter King. Not long afterwards Siggo's wife died;
but he married a second time.

4.   Next Roccolen marched on Tours, having received orders
to do so from Chilperic. He was full of braggadocio as to what
he proposed to do there. He pitched his camp on the further
bank of the River Loire and sent messengers to me to say that I
must expel Guntram from my church, for he was accused of
having killed Theudebert. If I did not carry out his commands,
he would order the city and all its suburbs to be burnt to the
ground. As soon as I heard this I sent a deputation to Roccolen
to say that what he demanded had never been done down all the
centuries from ancient times, and that it was quite unthinkable
that the holy church could be violated; that if it were to happen
it would bring small profit to him or to the King who had sent
such orders; and that he would do better to shake in fear before
Saint Martin the Bishop, whose miraculous power only the day
before had made paralysed limbs straight.[11] Roccolen was no
whit abashed. He pulled to pieces the church-house on the opposite bank of the Loire, in which he had his quarters. The
building was nailed together: the men of Maine, who formed
Roccolen's army, put the nails in their pockets and sneaked off
with them, destroying the harvest and ruining everything else as
they went. While Roccolen was committing these outrages he
was punished by God, for he fell ill with jaundice, the King's
evil, and became bright saffron. He repeated his harsh demands.
'If you do not expel Duke Guntram from your church this very
day,' he said, 'I will so trample down every green thing around
your city that the place will be fit for nothing but the plough.'
The holy day of Epiphany came round. Roccolen was in ever
greater agony with his illness. He submitted to the advice of
those around him, crossed the river and entered the city. As the

11. *VSM*, 27.

procession came out of the cathedral and set off, chanting as it went, towards the holy church of Saint Martin, he was carried on his horse behind the cross, with his banners waving before him. As he was borne into the Saint's church his fury and his threats abated. On his way back to his camp from the cathedral he was so ill that he could take no food that day. As a result his strength drained away. He set out for Poitiers. We were then in the holy month of Lent: and he kept on eating baby rabbits. He had earlier drawn up for the first day of March certain ordinances by which he planned to mulct and ruin the people of Poitiers. Twenty-four hours before that he died; and with him died his overweening arrogance.

5.* It was at this time that Felix, Bishop of the city of Nantes,[12] wrote an abusive letter to me. In it he alleged that my brother Peter[13] had murdered his own bishop, whose office he coveted, and that this was how he himself came to be killed. The reason for his making this allegation was that Felix coveted some church land which belonged to my see. When I refused to give it up he made this venomous attack on me, as I have already said. He was really furious and he loaded me with insults. In the end I sent the following answer to him: 'Remember the words of the prophet: "Woe unto them that join house to house and lay field to field, that they may be placed alone in the midst of the earth!"[14] What a pity that it was not Marseilles which elected you as its bishop! Instead of bringing you cargoes of oil and other wares, its ships could have carried only papyrus, which would have given you more opportunity for writing libellous letters to honest folk like me. As it is, only lack of paper cuts short your long-windedness.' Felix was a man whose greed and arrogance knew no bounds. I will say no more about this, for fear that you begin to think I am much the same myself.

12. Felix, Bishop of Nantes, A.D. 549–82. Venantius Fortunatus thought highly of him and wrote a number of poems to him, *Carmina*, 3, 4–10. Gregory of Tours, who was his Metropolitan, had a marked antipathy to him and never once visited Nantes.

13. Peter was a deacon in Langres.

14. Isaiah 5, 8.

Instead I will tell you how my brother came to die, and how quickly God took vengeance upon the man who killed him.

When he was already an old man Saint Tetricus,[15] Bishop of the church in Langres, had occasion to dismiss his deacon Lampadius, who had held a position of trust under him. Lampadius was discovered to have been robbing the poor in a shameful way. My brother, who wanted to do all he could to help the poor, was a party to his degradation and so incurred his hatred. At this juncture Saint Tetricus had an apoplectic stroke. The doctors applied their poultices, but they did no good. Thereupon the local clergy became concerned, for they saw themselves without a bishop. They asked for Munderic. The King agreed to this: and Munderic was tonsured and consecrated as Bishop, with the proviso that, as long as Saint Tetricus remained alive, Munderic should remain in charge of the town of Tonnerre as archpriest, living there and only replacing Tetricus when he eventually died. While he was still resident in Tonnerre Munderic incurred the anger of King Chilperic. He was accused of having brought provisions and gifts to Sigibert when that King was leading an expedition against his brother Guntram. Munderic was dragged out of Tonnerre and held in exile in a narrow, roofless tower on the banks of the River Rhône. He remained there in great hardship for nearly two years. By the intercession of the Bishop, Saint Nicetius, he was allowed to go to Lyons, where he lived with Nicetius for some two months. However, he failed in his attempts to obtain the King's permission to be restored to the place from which he had been expelled. He therefore escaped at dead of night and made his way to the kingdom of Sigibert, where he was inducted as Bishop in the small town of Alais. He had in his charge some fifteen parishes only, which the Goths had occupied previously, but which Dalmatius, Bishop of Rodez, was administering at this time. Having lost Munderic, the inhabitants of Langres again asked for a bishop, naming Silvester, who was at once one of my relations and a connection of Tetricus. They did this with

15. Saint Tetricus, Bishop of Langres A.D. 539–72, was the brother of Gregory's grandfather.

the encouragement of my brother Peter. At this moment Saint
Tetricus died. When Silvester had been tonsured and ordained as
a priest, he was put in charge of the church property in Langres.
He made preparations to travel to Lyons, where he was to be
consecrated as Bishop. In the meantime Silvester had an epileptic fit, for he had long been subject to this malady. He lost
more and more control of himself, and lay bellowing and
moaning for two days. On the third day he died. Lampadius,
who, as I have already told you, had been deprived of his office
and his possessions, now joined Silvester's son in his hatred of
the deacon Peter, alleging and repeatedly maintaining that the
father had been killed by Peter's magic arts. The son, who was
young and impulsive, made a furious attack on Peter and accused him publicly of having committed murder. When he
heard this, Peter set out for Lyons, where his case was heard
before Saint Nicetius the Bishop, who was my mother's uncle.
In the presence of Syagrius, Bishop of Autun, many other
churchmen and the principal laymen of the diocese, Peter took
an oath that he had had nothing to do with the death of Silvester. Two years later Silvester's son was again stirred up by
Lampadius: he attacked the deacon Peter in the street and
wounded him mortally with his spear.[16] When Peter was dead,
his body was removed from the spot where it lay and carried to
the town of Dijon, where he was buried beside Saint Gregory,
our great-grandfather. The murderer fled to King Chilperic and
his possessions were confiscated by King Guntram and added
by him to the royal treasury. Because of the crime which he had
committed, he became a wanderer, with no fixed place of
abode. In the end, so I have been told, the innocent blood which
he had shed cried unto God from the ground;[17] and in some
place or other where his errant footsteps had taken him he drew
his sword and killed a man who had done him no harm. The
man's relations, infuriated at their kinsman's death, started a
riot, drew their own swords, cut Silvester's son to pieces and
scattered the fragments abroad. Such was the end of this unhappy man. God in His judgement punished him, and he who

16. A.D. 574.   17. Cp. Genesis 4, 10.

had murdered his innocent neighbour did not survive long after his crime, for the events which I have described happened before three years had passed.

After the death of Silvester, the people of Langres once again petitioned for a bishop, and they were given Pappolus, who had been Archdeacon of Autun. I have heard it said that his behaviour in Langres was extremely bad, but I will not record his evil deeds, for I do not wish to appear to be a denigrator of my fellow churchmen. I must, however, tell you the manner of his death. In the eighth year of his episcopate, when he was carrying out a visitation of his parishes and the villas belonging to his see, Saint Tetricus appeared before him one night as he slept. The Saint's face was threatening and he said: 'What are you doing here, Pappolus? Why do you befoul my diocese? Why do you rob the Church? Why do you scatter the flock which was entrusted to my care? Off with you, resign from your bishopric, leave this neighbourhood and go somewhere else far away!' As Tetricus said this he struck Pappolus a mighty blow on the chest with a staff which he held in his hand. Pappolus woke up. While he was wondering what all this meant, he had the impression that his chest had been pierced and he suffered excruciating pain. He could not bear the sight of food and drink, and he made ready for the death which he felt to be near. What more can I say? On the third day he vomited blood and died. He was carried to Langres and buried there.

The Abbot Mummolus, surnamed the Good, was elected Bishop in the place of Pappolus. Mummolus is highly praised by many people: they say that he is chaste, sober, moderate, always ready to do a kind deed, sound in judgement and charitable in all his actions. When he took over the diocese, he discovered that Lampadius had defrauded the church of much property and by appropriating the alms given for the poor had acquired lands, vineyards and slaves. Mummolus ordered him to be stripped of everything he possessed and to be driven from his presence. Now Lampadius lives in great poverty and maintains himself by manual labour. That must be enough on this subject.

6.* In this year, the year in which Sigibert died and his son Childebert began to reign, many miraculous cures were performed at the tomb of Saint Martin.[18] I have described these in the books which I have tried to write about his miracles.[19] My Latin may be provincial, but I could hardly pass over in silence the things which I have seen, or which I have been told by the faithful. Here I will simply add what happened to certain sceptics, who, after witnessing a God-sent miracle, would have recourse to earthly remedies, for Saint Martin's power is shown just as much by the punishment meted out to fools as it is by the grace accorded to those who have been cured.

Leunast, Archdeacon of Bourges, lost his sight through cataracts in both eyes. He sought the help of a number of doctors, but he did not recover his sight. Then he went to Saint Martin's church, where he stayed for two or three months, fasting continually and praying that he might be able to see again. When Saint Martin's feast-day came round, Leunast's eyes cleared and he began to see. He went off home and consulted a Jew, who bled his shoulders with cupping-glasses, the effect of which was supposed to be that his sight would improve. As soon as the blood had been drawn off, Leunast became as blind as he had been before. He thereupon returned once more to the holy shrine. There he stayed for a long time, but he never recovered his vision. In my opinion this boon was never granted to him because he had sinned, in accordance with our Lord's pronouncement: 'For whosoever hath, to him shall be given, and he shall have more abundance: but whosoever hath not, from him shall be taken away even that he hath';[20] and again, 'Behold, thou art made whole: sin no more, lest a worse thing come unto thee.'[21] Leunast would have retained his health, if he had not sought the help of a Jew after he had received God's grace. It is men like him that the Apostle rebukes and condemns: 'Be ye not unequally yoked together with unbelievers: for what fellowship hath righteousness with unrighteousness? And what communion hath light with darkness?

18. A.D. 576.   19. *VSM*.
20. Matthew 13, 12.   21. John 5, 14.

And what concord hath Christ with Belial? or what part hath he that believeth with an infidel? And what agreement hath the temple of God with idols? for ye are the temple of the living God. Wherefore come out from among them, and be ye separate, saith the Lord.'[22] Let this story be a warning to every Christian man, that when it has been granted to him to receive a cure from Heaven, he should not then seek earthly remedies.

7.* I must now record the names of the men who were summoned home by God this year; for I consider any man great and acceptable in the eyes of God whom He has added to the number of those whom He has removed from our earth and placed in Paradise. Senoch, the holy priest, who lived in Tours, thus passed away from the world. He was one of the Theifali.[23] He became a churchman in Tours, but withdrew from the world and lived in a cell which he had built for himself among the ancient ruins there. He gathered a number of monks around him and rebuilt an oratory which had long been in a dilapidated state. Senoch performed many miracles for the sick and these I have described in the Book of his Life.[24]

8. At the same time died Saint Germanus, Bishop of Paris.[25] The following miracle, which occurred at his funeral, has. confirmed the many others which he performed while still alive. Certain prisoners called upon him as his body was being carried by in the street: the corpse became heavy but, when the prisoners were released, it was lifted up again with ease. In their newly-found liberty the freed men followed the funeral procession into the church where Germanus was buried. By the grace of God true believers experience many miracles at his tomb, for any man whose petition is just receives without delay what he has sought. Anyone who really wishes to find out about the miracles which Saint Germanus performed in the flesh will read all he wants to know in the Book of his Life written by the priest Fortunatus.[26]

22. II Corinthians 6, 14–17.   23. See p. 214, note 33.
24. *VP*, 15.   25. A.D. 576.   26. The *Vita Sancti Germani.*

9.* In the same year the recluse Caluppa died. He had been a religious from his youth. He went to live in the monastery at Méallet, in the Clermont region. He behaved with great humility towards the monks there, as I have described in the Book of his Life.[27]

10.* In the neighbourhood of Bourges there lived a recluse called Patroclus. He had been ordained a priest and was a man of remarkable holiness and piety, and of great abstinence, too: he was always being plagued with this illness or that through his fasting. He would not drink wine, or cider, or anything else which could intoxicate, taking only water slightly sweetened with honey. He would eat no animal food. His staple diet was bread soaked in water and sprinkled with salt. His eyes were never closed in sleep. He prayed unceasingly, or, if he stopped praying for a moment, he spent the time reading or writing. By prayer he would often cure those suffering from fevers, boils or other maladies. He performed many other miracles which it would take me a long time to relate. He always wore a hair-shirt next to his body. He was eighty years old when he died and went to join Christ. I have written a short account of his life.[28]

11. Since our God is ever willing to give glory to His bishops, I will tell you what happened this year to the Jews in Clermont-Ferrand. Saint Avitus the Bishop[29] had often exhorted them to drop the veil of the Mosaic Law, to learn the real spiritual meaning of what they were reading and with a pure heart to discover in the Holy Scriptures Christ, the son of the living God, promised by the authority of the Law and the prophets. Nevertheless there remained in their breasts, I will not say the veil which covered the face of Moses, but rather a wall.[30] The

27. *VP*, 11.   28. *VP*, 9.

29. Avitus, Bishop of Clermont-Ferrand A.D. *c*. 572–*c*. 594, was the Archdeacon Avitus who had been largely responsible for Gregory's education: see Introduction, p. 9. Fortunatus wrote a poem on this conversion and dedicated it to Gregory: 'De Judaeis conversis per Avitum episcopum Arvernum', *Carmina*, 5, 5.

30. Cp. Exodus 34, 33–5.

Bishop prayed that they might be converted to the Lord, and that the veil of the Letter might be torn from before them. One of them asked that he might be baptized at the holy feast of Easter: born again in God through the sacrament of baptism, he walked in procession in a white gown, in company with the other newly-baptized people who were similarly robed in white. As the populace was processing through the city gate, one of the Jews, no doubt put up to this by the Devil, tipped some rancid oil on the head of this new convert. The people were so infuriated by this that they wanted to stone the offender, but the Bishop would not let them do so. On the blessed day on which our Lord ascended in glory into heaven after the redemption of man, while psalms were being sung and the Bishop was processing from the cathedral to one of the local churches, the crowd following him attacked the Jewish synagogue, destroyed it down to its very foundations and levelled it to the ground. On another occasion the Bishop sent this message to the Jews: 'I do not use force nor do I compel you to confess the Son of God. I merely preach to you and I offer to your hearts the salt of knowledge. I am the shepherd set to watch over the sheep of the Lord. It was of you that the true Shepherd, who suffered for us, said that He had other sheep, which are not of His fold, but which He must bring, so that there might be one flock, and one shepherd.[31] If you are prepared to believe what I believe, then become one flock, with me as your shepherd. If not, then leave this place.' They argued among themselves and hesitated for some time; but on the third day, persuaded by the Bishop, or so I believe, they gathered in a group and sent this answer to him: 'We believe that Jesus Christ is the son of the living God, promised to us by the pronouncements of the prophets.' The Bishop rejoiced at the news. He celebrated nocturns on the holy eve of Pentecost and then went out to the baptistery without the city wall. There the whole company of Jews lay prostrate before him, begging for baptism. Saint Avitus wept with joy. He washed them all in water, anointed them with chrism and brought them together into the bosom of the Mother Church.

31. John 10, 16.

Candles flamed, lamps burned and the whole city shone bright
with the white-robed flock. The joy felt in Clermont was no
whit less than that experienced long ago in Jerusalem when the
Holy Spirit descended on the Apostles. More than five hundred
were baptized. Those who refused to accept baptism left the city
and made their way to Marseilles.

12.* Not long afterwards died Brachio, Abbot of the
monastery of Ménat. He was a Thuringian by birth. He had
been a huntsman in the service of Duke Sigivald, as I have
related elsewhere.[32]

13. I must now return to my subject. King Chilperic sent his
son Clovis to Tours. Clovis assembled an army, marched
through the lands of Touraine and Anjou, and so came to
Saintes, which he occupied. Thereupon Mummolus, the patrician in the service of King Guntram, invaded the region of
Limoges and attacked Desiderius, King Chilperic's commander.
Five thousand of Desiderius' troops fell in this battle and Desiderius himself escaped only with difficulty. The patrician
Mummolus then turned back through Clermont which was laid
waste in parts by his army. In this way he crossed into Burgundy.

14. After this Merovech, who was being held in custody by his
father, was tonsured, had his clothes changed for those used by
clerics, was ordained a priest and was packed off to a monastery
in Le Mans called Anille, there to be instructed in the priestly
rule. Guntram Boso, who, as I have told you, was then living in
Saint Martin's church, heard of this. He sent the subdeacon
Riculf secretly to advise Merovech to seek sanctuary in the
same church. Merovech set out, and his servant Gailen advanced to meet him from another direction. Those in charge of
Merovech were few in number. He was rescued on the road by
Gailen: he covered his face, put on secular clothes and made his
way to the church of Saint Martin. He found the door open and

32. *VP*, 12.

walked in. I was celebrating Mass at the time. When the service
was over he asked me to give him some of the bread of oblation. Ragnemod, Bishop of Paris, who had succeeded Saint
Germanus, was with me at the time.[33] We refused, but Merovech made a scene and said that we had no right to suspend
him from communion without the consent of our fellow-
bishops. When we had listened to him, with the full approval of
my one brother-bishop present he received the bread from my
hands, although the case could be argued canonically. I was
afraid that by refusing to give communion to one man I might
cause the death of many, for Merovech threatened to kill some
of our congregation if he were not allowed to take communion
with us. The region round Tours suffered great devastation as a
result of what I had done. At about this time Nicetius, my
niece's husband,[34] went to King Chilperic on some affair of his
own; and he was accompanied by our deacon, who went and
revealed to the King the fact that Merovech had escaped. As
soon as Queen Fredegund saw the two of them, she cried:
'These men are spies. They have come to find out what the King
intends to do, and then report what they discover to Merovech.'
She had them stripped of all that they possessed and sent into
exile. They were not released until seven months later.

Thereupon Chilperic sent messengers to me to say: 'Expel
this apostate from your church. If you refuse, I will set your
whole countryside alight.' When I wrote back that it was impossible to do in Christian times what had not been done even in
the days of the heretics, he raised an army and sent it to attack
Tours.

In the second year of King Childebert's reign,[35] seeing that
his father was set upon his purpose, Merovech took Duke Guntram with him and made plans to visit Queen Brunhild. 'Far be
it from me,' said he, 'that I should allow Saint Martin's church

33. Ragnemod, Bishop of Paris A.D. 577–91.
34. Nicetius, husband of Eustenia, the second daughter of Gregory's
unnamed sister. The elder daughter was Justina, Prioress of Saint Radegund's nunnery in Poitiers. See Introduction, p. 8.
35. A.D. 577.

to suffer violence through my being here, or his countryside to be overrun because of me.' He came into the church during vigils, bringing with him everything that he possessed. He placed it all beside the tomb of Saint Martin and prayed that the Saint might succour him and grant him this favour that he might win the kingdom. Leudast, the Count of Tours, laid many snares for Merovech, hoping to gain the favour of Queen Fredegund. In the end he caught in an ambush some of Merovech's servants, who had set off across country, and he put them to the sword; if he could have come upon Merovech himself in a suitable spot he would have been only too pleased to kill him, too. To revenge himself, Merovech took the advice of Guntram and ordered that Marileif, the royal physician, should be seized when he was journeying home from the King's court. Marileif was cruelly beaten, his gold and silver and everything else which he had with him was confiscated, and he was left destitute. Merovech would have killed him, in his turn, but he escaped from the hands of his assailants and sought refuge in the cathedral. I fitted him out with clothes, obtained a safe-conduct for him and sent him home to Poitiers.

Merovech brought many charges against his father and his stepmother.[36] Some of these may well have been true, but in my opinion it is not acceptable in God's sight that one should make such revelations, and this was made clear to me in the sequel. One day I was summoned to have a meal with him and, as we sat side by side, he begged me to read some passages to him for the instruction of his soul. I opened the book of Solomon and read the first verse I found. It contained these words: 'The eye that mocketh at his father, the ravens of the valley shall pick it out.'[37] Merovech did not see the point of this, but it is my opinion that the verse was chosen by the Lord.

The next thing which happened was that Guntram Boso sent one of his servants to a certain woman who was supposed to have the power of prophecy. He had known this woman since the days of King Charibert. He asked her to tell him what was to happen in the future. He used to maintain that she had re-

36. Fredegund.   37. Proverbs, 30, 17.

vealed to him before the event not merely the year but the very
day and hour when King Charibert would die. She sent the
following prognostication back to Guntram through his servants: 'It shall come to pass that King Chilperic will die this
very year. Merovech will become King, for he will seize the
realm and exclude his brothers. For five years, you, Guntram,
will be the military leader of Merovech's kingdom. In the sixth
year, in a city situated on the right bank of the River Loire, you
will be made a bishop, with the full consent of the local inhabitants. When the time comes for you to die you will be an old
man and full of days.' Guntram's servants reported all this to
their master and he was very proud of what he had heard, for
he already saw himself sitting on the bishop's throne in Tours.
He came to tell me the story. I laughed at his stupidity and
said to him: 'It is God who grants these things. One should put
no reliance on the Devil's promises.' When he had gone off in
some confusion, I had a good laugh at this man who found such
things credible. One night when I lay sleeping in my bed after
having celebrated vigils in the saintly Bishop's church, I saw an
angel flying through the air. As he passed over the holy church,
he cried in a loud voice: 'Woe! and more woe! God has stricken
Chilperic, and all his sons. Of all those who have issued from his
loins not a single one has survived ever to rule over his kingdom.' Leaving his daughters on one side, he had at that moment
four sons by his various wives. When at a later date these words
were fulfilled, I realized just how false were the promises of
soothsayers.

While all these folk continued to find sanctuary in Saint
Martin's church, Queen Fredegund, who supported Guntram
Boso in secret because it was he who had killed Theudebert,
sent a message to him. 'If you can persuade Merovech to leave
the church,' she said, 'so that he can be killed, you will receive
from me a handsome gift.' Guntram imagined that the assassins
were already in position. 'Why do we stay cooped up here, as if
we were too idle or too timid to set foot out of doors?' he asked
Merovech. 'We slink about in this church as if we were half-
witted. Let us call for our horses! Let us take our hawks and go

hunting with our hounds! A ride through the open fields will do us good.' Of course, his cunning scheme was simply to manoeuvre Merovech out of the church. Guntram Boso was a good enough man in other ways, but he was too much given to breaking his word. He never made an oath to any of his friends without being prepared to break it at a moment's notice. As I have said, the two left the sanctuary of the church. They rode as far as Jonzac, a villa in the vicinity of Tours, but nothing untoward happened to Merovech.

In consequence of the fact, as I have told you, that Guntram Boso was accused of having killed Theudebert, King Chilperic wrote a letter and addressed it to the tomb of Saint Martin, asking that the Saint should write back to him to say whether or not he could have Guntram forcibly ejected from the church. The deacon Baudegil, who brought this letter, placed it on the Saint's tomb, with a blank piece of paper beside it. He waited three days, but he received no answer, so he returned to Chilperic. Then the King sent more messengers, who were to exact a promise from Guntram that he would not leave the church without informing Chilperic first. Guntram did not hesitate for a moment, but swore on the altar-cloth that he would never come out without the King's express permission.

Merovech had no faith in Guntram's female soothsayer. He placed three books on the Saint's tomb, the Psalter, the Book of Kings and the Gospels: then he spent the whole night in prayer, beseeching the holy confessor to show him what was going to happen and to indicate clearly whether or not he would be allowed to inherit the kingship. He spent three days and nights in fasting, vigil and supplication: then he went up to the tomb and opened the first volume, which was the Book of Kings. This was the first verse on the page which he opened: 'Because thou hast forsaken the Lord thy God and hast taken hold upon other gods and hast not walked uprightly before him, the Lord thy God will deliver thee into the hands of thy enemies.'[38] He found the following verse in the Psalms: 'Surely thou didst set them in slippery places: thou castedst them down into de-

38. I Kings 9, 9. This is the *Sortes Biblicae.* Cp. *HF*, IV, 16.

struction. How are they brought into desolation, as in a moment! they are utterly consumed because of their iniquities.'[39] This was what he found in the Gospels: 'Ye know that after two days is the feast of the passover, and the Son of man is betrayed to be crucified.'[40] Merovech was dismayed by these answers and for a long time he wept at the tomb of the holy Bishop. Then he took with him Duke Guntram Boso and five hundred men or more, and went on his way. Having emerged from the holy church he made his way through the region round Auxerre and there he was captured by Duke Herpo, one of King Guntram's leaders. He was held captive by Herpo, but by some means or other he escaped and sought sanctuary in the church of Saint Germanus. King Guntram was very angry when he heard this. He fined Herpo seventy pieces of gold and removed him from his office. 'My brother tells me that you captured my enemy,' said he. 'Once you had made up your mind to do this, you should have delivered him into my hands immediately. If you were not prepared to hold him, you should not have laid a finger on him.'

King Chilperic's army now advanced as far as Tours. He sacked the whole neighbourhood, setting fire to it and ravaging it, and not sparing even the things which belonged to Saint Martin. He seized whatever he could lay his hands on, and he showed no fear of God or respect for Him.

Merovech spent two months in the church of Saint Germanus. Then he escaped and made his way to Queen Brunhild, but the Eastern Franks would not receive him. His father sent an army against the people of Champagne, for he thought that Merovech was hiding there. He failed to find Merovech and so did him no harm.

15. When Alboin went off to Italy,[41] Lothar and Sigibert settled the Swabians and other peoples in the territory which he left vacant. In the lifetime of Sigibert the Saxons who had gone

39. Psalms 73, 18–19.   40. Matthew 26, 2.
41. A.D. 568–9. Lothar had died in 561.

with Alboin came back again and attacked these new arrivals, for they were determined to drive them out of their own land and destroy them. The settlers offered the Saxons a third part of the territory, saying: 'Surely we can live side by side without fighting each other.' The Saxons, who were furious with the Swabians because they themselves had previously held all the land, showed no inclination whatsoever to make peace. Then the Swabians offered half, and afterwards two thirds, keeping only one third for themselves. The Saxons still refused, and the Swabians then offered not only two thirds of the land but all the flocks and herds on it, if only the Saxons would refrain from war. The Saxons would not accept even this offer, for they were determined to do battle. They began to quarrel among themselves about how they should share out the women-folk and whatever else they might capture after the annihilation of the Swabians, whom they already looked upon as dead men. God in His compassion, which is the source of all justice, decided otherwise about them. The battle was joined, but out of twenty-six thousand Saxons who took part no fewer than twenty thousand were slain. There were only six thousand Swabians, and four hundred and eighty of them were killed, those who remained alive winning the victory. Those Saxons who survived swore to a man that they would not cut their hair or trim their beards until they had taken vengeance on their enemies. A second battle followed and the Saxons suffered an even more decisive defeat. That is how the war ended.

16. The following events occurred in Brittany. Macliaw and Bodic, two Breton chieftains, swore an oath to each other that whichever outlived the other would take care of the dead man's sons as if they were his own. Bodic died first, leaving a son called Theuderic. Macliaw broke his oath, drove Theuderic out of his patrimony and occupied the land which had been Bodic's. For a long time Theuderic wandered as an exile. Then God took compassion on him: for Theuderic gathered a band of Bretons, attacked Macliaw and killed both him and his son

Jacob. He then took command of that part of the land over which his father had ruled. Waroch, the son of Macliaw, managed to hold on to the remainder.

17. King Guntram killed the two sons of Magnachar, who himself had died some time before. His excuse was that they had made hateful and abominable remarks about Queen Austrechild and her children.[42] He seized their possessions and added them to the royal treasury. Later on Guntram lost his own two sons, who died of some sudden disease.[43] He was greatly distressed at their death, for it left him bereaved and childless.

In this year there was a dispute about Easter. We in Gaul, in common with many other cities, celebrate the holy feast of Easter on 18 April. Others have agreed with the Spaniards in keeping the feast on 21 March. It is true, however, or so they say, that those springs in Spain which are filled by the will of God have run with water on our Easter Day.[44]

At Chinon, a village in Touraine, the church shook while Mass was being celebrated on the day of our Lord's Resurrection. The congregation was terrified and all shouted out that the church was about to collapse about their heads. They broke down the doors and all rushed out in a body. Later on they were decimated by a terrible epidemic.

Soon after this King Guntram sent envoys to his nephew Childebert to sue for peace and to suggest a meeting. Childebert with his leaders came to meet Guntram. They met on the spot called the Stone Bridge.[45] When they had greeted each other and exchanged a kiss of peace, King Guntram said: 'For my

42. Magnachar was the father of King Guntram's second wife Marcatrude, which explains why his sons Guntio and Wiolich made hateful remarks about his third wife Austrechild.

43. Lothar and Chlodomer died of dysentery in A.D. 577.

44. The springs at Osser, near Seville, ran with water on 18 April. Cp. *GM*, 23, 'Insigne miraculum de fontibus Hispaniae'. Cp. *HF*, VI, 43.

45. '... ad pontem quem Petrium vocant' = Pompierre (Pons petrae), Neufchâteau, Vosges.

sins I have had the misfortune to be left childless. This, then, is my request, that you, my nephew, should be considered as my son.' He placed Childebert on his throne and made over to him his entire realm. 'Let one single shield protect us both,' said he, 'and a single spear defend us. Even if I still have sons, I will nevertheless contrive to look upon you as one of them, so that the same loving kindness which, as God is my witness, I promise you today, may remain between you and them.' Childebert's leaders made a similar promise on his behalf. They ate and drank together, and loaded each other with gifts suitable to the occasion, each then going his way in peace. They sent an embassy to King Chilperic to demand that he should restore all the territory which he had taken from their realm; for, unless he did this quickly, he had better choose a spot for battle. Chilperic took no notice of what they said: he was busy building amphitheatres in Soissons and Paris, for he was keen to offer spectacles to the citizens.

18.   While these things were happening Chilperic heard that Praetextatus, Bishop of Rouen, was bribing the people to act against his interests. He ordered that prelate to be summoned to his presence. In his possession Praetextatus was found to have property entrusted to him by Queen Brunhild. This was confiscated and Chilperic ordered Praetextatus to be banished from his see until his case should be heard by a council of bishops. Such a council was convoked and Praetextatus was made to appear before it. The bishops who attended met in the church of Saint Peter the Apostle in Paris. The King said to the accused: 'What was in your mind, Bishop, when you married my enemy Merovech, who should have been my son, to his own aunt, his uncle's widow? Surely you knew what the canons of the Church have prescribed for such a case? What is more, it is proved that you not only did wrong in this, but that you have conspired with Merovech to bribe certain people to encompass my death. You have encouraged a son to become his father's enemy, you have bribed the common people so that none should keep the faith which he had promised to me and you

275

have sought to betray my kingdom into another's hands.' As he said this, a great shout went up from the Franks outside, for they wanted to break down the church doors, drag the Bishop out and stone him to death, but this Chilperic forbade. Bishop Praetextatus swore that what the King had said was not true. Then there came forward false witnesses, holding precious objects in their hands and saying: 'This is what you gave us, and this, and this, and this, in your attempt to persuade us to swear loyalty to Merovech.' 'What you say is true,' answered Praetextatus, 'in that you have often received gifts from me, but this was not so that the King might be driven from his realm. You gave me fine horses and other gifts. What could I do except make similar presents to you in my turn?'

The King withdrew to his lodging. We remained seated in a group in the sacristy of Saint Peter's church. As we were conferring together there suddenly arrived Aetius, Archdeacon of the church of Paris. He saluted us and said: 'Listen to me, all you priests of the Lord who are assembled here! The moment has come when you will make your names famous and you will shine like bright lights because of the good reputation which you will have earned, or else you will abandon all claim to be called God's bishops because you will have behaved in a craven fashion and allowed your fellow-churchman to be destroyed.' That was what Aetius said, but not a single bishop dared to reply. They were afraid of the King who had raged at them, the King at whose instigation all this was being done. They all sat silent, with their fingers pressed to their lips. Then I rose and spoke. 'Listen carefully to what I have to say to you,' I said, 'saintly men all, God's bishops, and especially those among you who seem to be in the King's confidence. Make sure that the advice which you give him is holy advice, and worthy of your rank in the Church, for there is a danger that by turning his wrath against one of God's ministers he may destroy himself in his paroxysm and so lose both his good name and his kingdom.' They listened to what I said, but still they remained silent. As they sat there mute, I spoke again. 'My Lord Bishops,' I said, 'remember the words of the prophet: "If the watchman see the iniquity of man and the people be not warned, he shall be guilty for the soul that perisheth."[46] You must not remain silent. You must speak out and parade his sins before the King's eyes, lest some calamity should occur, in which case you will be responsible for his soul. Have you already forgotten the things which have happened recently? What of Chlodomer, who laid hold of Sigismund and then threw him into prison? When Avitus, the priest of the Lord, said to him: "Do not maltreat Sigismund, and then you will be victorious when you march into Burgundy," Chlodomer refused to take the Bishop's advice, for he murdered Sigismund and his wife and his sons. He duly marched into Burgundy and there he was beaten by the enemy army and killed.[47] What of the Emperor Maximus, who forced Saint Martin to live in daily contact with another bishop who had committed murder? Saint Martin did what this impious ruler ordered, for he hoped that by submitting to the Emperor's will he might the more easily free certain men who had been condemned to death. The vengeance of the Eternal King pursued Maximus: he was driven from his throne and condemned to a most cruel death.' That was what I said, but no one answered: instead they sat there as if stunned and petrified.

Among their number were two sycophants – it is sad to say this about bishops – who rushed off to the King to report all that had happened and to tell him that no one was more hostile to his cause than I. He thereupon sent one of his courtiers to summon me to appear before him. When I arrived the King was standing outside a little arbour made of the branches of trees. Bishop Bertram was on his right hand and Bishop Ragnemod on his left. In front of them stood a bench on which had been placed bread and various other things to eat. When he saw me the King said: 'As a bishop you are supposed to administer justice to all men. You are now behaving most unjustly towards me. It is quite clear to me that you are supporting this man in his criminal actions. You are a living example of the proverb: Corvus oculum corvi non eruit.'[48] 'My Lord King,' I answered,

46. Ezekiel 33, 6.   47. *HF*, III, 6.
48. 'A crow does not pick out another crow's eye.'

'if any one of our number has attempted to overstep the path of justice, it is for you to correct him. If, on the other hand, it is you who act unjustly, who can correct you? We can say what we think to you. If you wish to do so, you listen to us. If you refuse to listen, who can condemn you for it, except Him who has promised eternal justice?' Chilperic, who was incensed against me by his sycophants, gave me the following answer. 'All other men treat me fairly. You alone are unjust to me. I know what I will do, so that you may appear in your true colours before your own people, and so that they may all come to realize that you are incapable of administering justice. I will call a meeting of the inhabitants of Tours and I will say to them: "Here is a slogan for you to shout about Gregory: 'He is an unfair man, and he treats no one justly.' " As they shout this, I shall answer: "Even I, who am the King, can find no justice at his hands. Why do you lesser folk expect to find it?" ' 'It is not for you to say whether or not I am unjust,' I replied. 'God alone, to whom the secret places of all hearts are open, knows what is in my conscience. You can insult me, and you can persuade my people to shout untrue things about me. What does that matter to me? They will all know that they are shouting these things to please you. It is not I but you who will endure the obloquy of what they shout. I am wasting my breath on you. You have the law and the canons. You must study them diligently. If you do not carry out what they say, you will soon come to realize that the judgement of God hangs over your head.' At this Chilperic tried to propitiate me, apparently imagining that I would not see through his ingratiating behaviour. He turned towards a dish of soup which stood in front of him. 'I have had this broth cooked especially for you,' said he. 'There is nothing in it except chicken and some peas.' I, of course, realized that he was trying to win me over. 'My nourishment should not consist of such delicacies as these,' I replied, 'but rather in doing God's will and making sure that, whatever may befall, I do not transgress His commandments. As for you, who accuse others of injustice, promise first that you yourself will keep the law and the canons.' Chilperic stretched out his right

hand and swore by Almighty God that he would in no circumstances fail to observe the ordinances of the law and the canons.
Only then did I agree to eat a little bread, and even drink some
wine. Then I left him.

That night, when we had finished singing our hymns at nocturns, I heard a loud knocking on the door of my lodging. I sent
my boy down and discovered that messengers had arrived from
Queen Fredegund. I asked them to come in, and they gave me a
greeting from the Queen. These servants of hers then begged me
to stop opposing her interests. They promised me two hundred
pounds of silver if I would speak out against Praetextatus, so
that he might be condemned. 'We now have a promise from all
the other bishops,' they added. 'You are the only one to oppose
what we want.' 'If you were to give me a thousand pounds of
silver,' I answered, 'could I do anything else except what God
ordains? I promise you this, and only this: I will agree to what
the others decide, provided that it is in full accord with the
ordinances of the canons.' Although they did not understand
what I meant, they thanked me and went off. The next morning
some of the bishops came to me with a similar request; and I
gave them the same answer.

That same morning we reassembled in Saint Peter's church.
The King was present. 'If a bishop is found guilty of larceny,'
he said, 'it is decreed on the authority of the canons that he
should be removed from his episcopal office.' We countered this
by asking him who the bishop was who was accused of the
crime of larceny. 'You have seen the goods which he has stolen
from me,' Chilperic answered. Three days earlier the King had
shown us two bundles, filled with precious objects and all sorts
of jewels which were valued at more than three thousand gold
pieces, and a bag of coins which, to judge from its weight, must
have held some two thousand. According to Chilperic these had
been stolen from him by the Bishop. Praetextatus had given the
following explanation: 'I am sure that you remember', said he,
'that, when Queen Brunhild left the city of Rouen, I came to
you and told you that she had entrusted to me five bundles
containing her possessions. I also told you that her servants kept

calling on me to return these things, but that I was unwilling to
do so without your permission. Your answer was as follows:
"Hand these things over, and let the woman have her goods
back, for I do not want them to be the cause of a quarrel
between me and my nephew Childebert." I thereupon went
back to my city and handed over one bundle to Brunhild's
servants, for that was all that they could carry. They came back
once more and asked for the rest. A second time I consulted
your Majesty. A second time you advised me as follows: "Hand
the things over, Bishop, for otherwise they will be a cause of
disagreement." I gave them two more of the bundles. This
meant that only two remained in my possession. Why do you
now bring this false charge against me and accuse me of theft,
when this is clearly not a case of stealing, but one of custody?'
The King replied: 'If this property was only deposited in your
safe-keeping, why did you open one of the bundles and remove
a belt with threads of gold, which you then cut into pieces and
gave to certain men who were to drive me out of my kingdom?'
'I have already told you', answered Bishop Praetextatus, 'how I
had received gifts from them and, since I had nothing by me to
give them in return, I took out this belt and gave it to them as a
present. Since it belonged to Merovech, who is my own son in so
far as it was I who lifted him out of the baptismal font, it
seemed to me to be mine also.' King Chilperic realized that he
could not get the better of Praetextatus by false charges. He was
confused in his conscience and greatly puzzled, and he thereupon left us. He called some of his flatterers to him and said to
them: 'I confess myself beaten by what the Bishop has said, for
I know that he is telling the truth. What can I do next to ensure
that the Queen has her way concerning him?' Then he added:
'Go to Praetextatus and talk with him, as if you are giving him
your own private opinion. Say this to him: "You know that King
Chilperic is a God-fearing man, and tender-hearted, and
quickly moved to compassion. Humble yourself before him and
confess that you did indeed commit the crimes of which he has
accused you. Then we will all throw ourselves at his feet and
beg him to pardon you." ' Praetextatus was misled by what they

said and promised that he woud act as they had suggested.

The next morning we once again assembled in the usual place. The King came, and he said to the Bishop: 'If you were simply offering these men presents in exchange for what they had given to you, why did you ask them to swear an oath of fidelity to Merovech?' 'I confess that I sought their friendship for him,' answered Praetextatus. 'Had it been right to do so, I would have asked not only mortal man but even an angel from Heaven to come to his assistance. As I have told you repeatedly, he is my spiritual son, for I baptized him.' The argument went on and on, and then Praetextatus suddenly threw himself on the ground and said: 'Most merciful King, I have sinned against Heaven and before thee;[49] I am an evil murderer, for I wanted to kill you and to place your son on the throne.' As Praetextatus said this, the King knelt at the feet of the bishops and exclaimed: 'Most pious bishops, you hear this guilty man confess his execrable crime.' We wept as we raised the King from the ground. He ordered Praetextatus to leave the church.

King Chilperic went home to his lodging. He sent to us a book of the canons, with a newly-copied four-page insert, which contained what appeared to be apostolic canons, including the following words: 'A bishop convicted of murder, adultery or perjury shall be expelled from his bishopric.' While these were being read out, Praetextatus stood as if struck dumb. Bishop Bertram said: 'Listen, brother and fellow-Bishop. You have lost favour in the King's eyes. You can therefore expect no kindly treatment from us, unless you first gain the King's pardon.' When all was over, King Chilperic demanded that Praetextatus should have his tunic rent, or that Psalm 108, which contains the maledictions against Judas Iscariot,[50] should be recited over his head, or at least that he should be excommunicated for ever and that this verdict should be recorded in writing. I myself spoke against these conditions, for they were contrary to the King's promise that nothing should be done which was not in the canons. Praetextatus was removed from our presence and thrown into prison. One night he tried to

49. Luke 15, 18.   50. Psalm 109 in the Authorized Version.

The Death of Merovech

escape and was cruelly beaten as a result. He was sent in exile to an island off Coutances.[51]

It was rumoured that Merovech was again trying to seek sanctuary in Saint Martin's church. Chilperic had the church closely guarded and all the approaches blocked. The guards left one door free, so that my clergy could enter to perform the offices, but they kept the rest closed, which was no small inconvenience to the people. While we were still hanging about in Paris portents appeared in the sky. Twenty rays of light appeared in the north, starting in the east, and then moving round to the west. One of them was longer than the others and shone high above them: it reached right up into the sky and then disappeared, and the others faded away, too. In my opinion they were a presage of Merovech's death.

Merovech was hiding somewhere in the Rheims area, for he was afraid to risk entrusting himself to the Eastern Franks. He was led to his destruction by the people of Thérouanne, for they pretended that, if he would join them, they would throw off their allegiance to his father Chilperic and accept him as their leader. He chose a band of his most valiant followers and marched swiftly to join them. They thereupon set up the ambush which they had prepared and surrounded him in a certain country-house. They posted an armed guard all around and sent messengers to his father. As soon as he heard the news, Chilperic set out at speed. Merovech, who knew what they were up to and who was afraid that in their desire for vengeance his enemies would maltreat him in the most cruel way, called his servant Gailen to him. 'Until this day', said he, 'we two have always shared the same intent and the same thoughts. I beg you not to allow me to fall into the hands of my enemies. Take my sword and kill me.' Gailen did not hesitate for a moment. He killed Merovech with his own sword. When the King arrived Merovech was found dead.[52] There were some who said that the last words of Merovech, which I have set out above, were invented by the Queen, and that he was murdered in secret at her command. Gailen was seized: they cut off his hands, and

51. Probably Jersey.   52. A.D. 578.

his feet, and his ears, and his nose, tortured him cruelly and then despatched him in the most revolting fashion. Grindio was attached to the spokes of a wheel and then suspended on high. Ciuciolo, who had been Count of the Palace to King Sigibert, was slaughtered by having his head cut off. Many others who had accompanied Merovech were cruelly done to death. Some said at the time that Bishop Egidius and Guntram Boso had been the ringleaders in this ambush, the latter because he had enjoyed the secret favour of Queen Fredegund as the man who had killed Theudebert,[53] the former because he had long been one of her favourites.

19.   When the Emperor Justin went out of his mind and was realized to be insane, the Empire was ruled by the Empress Sophia, who assumed sole power. As I have told you in Book IV,[54] the people chose Tiberius as Caesar, a capable man, strong in body and in mind, full of charity and dedicated to the care of the needy. He distributed among the poor much of the treasure which Justin had amassed, and the Empress frequently rebuked him for reducing the state to bankruptcy. 'What I have taken so many years to save,' she used to say to him, 'you are busy squandering in a prodigal way, and without losing much time about it, either.' 'As long as the poor receive alms and those whom we capture are ransomed,' Tiberius would answer, 'our treasury will never be empty. This is the great treasure, as our Lord explained: "But lay up for yourselves treasures in heaven, where neither moth nor rust doth corrupt, and where thieves do not break through nor steal."[55] Let us indeed lay up for the needy in heaven a share of what God has given to us, so that the Lord may deign to give us increase in this world.' As I have told you, Tiberius was a great Christian and a faithful one: as long as he continued to take pleasure in distributing alms to the poor our Lord went on providing him with more and more to give. One day when he was walking through the palace he noticed on the paved floor a marble slab carved with the Cross of Christ. 'Your Cross, O Christ,' he cried, 'is marked

53. *HF*, IV, 50.   54. *HF*, IV, 40.   55. Matthew 6, 20.

on our foreheads and on our breasts as a sign of protection, and here we are walking on it.' He ordered the flagstone to be dug up immediately and removed from where it was. When they had prised it up and it stood on end, they found a second one underneath marked with the same sign. They told Tiberius what had happened and he had the second flagstone lifted. Underneath they found a third one, and Tiberius made them take that up, too. Beneath it they found a vast hoard of treasure, amounting to more than a hundred thousand pounds of gold. This was taken out of the ground and, as his custom was, Tiberius was able to make even more generous contributions to the poor. Because of his human charity, the Lord did not ever suffer Tiberius to be in want.

I must not fail to tell you what our Lord did for Tiberius on another occasion. Narses, the famous commander in the Italian campaigns, possessed a large house in a certain city. As he marched out of Italy carrying vast booty, he came to this city. He had a great underground chamber dug in his house without anyone knowing, and in it he buried many hundreds of thousands of pounds of gold and silver. Those who had helped him he murdered, and then he entrusted his secret to a single old man who had sworn never to divulge it. Narses died:[56] and his treasure lay hidden in the earth. The old man about whom I have told you observed the never-ending charity of Tiberius. He went to him one day and said: 'My Lord, there is not much that I stand to gain from doing so, but I will tell you a great secret.' 'Say on,' replied Tiberius. 'If you can tell me anything to my own advantage, it will profit you as well.' 'I know where the treasure of Narses is hidden,' was the answer, 'and now that I am reaching the end of my life I must not keep the secret any longer.' The Caesar Tiberius was delighted. He sent his servants to the spot. The old man marched ahead, and the servants followed behind, wondering what was going to happen next. They came to the underground chamber, they opened it up and they went in. They found so much gold and silver that those who were charged with clearing it spent many days in carrying it

56. A.D. 568.

away. In this way Tiberius was given the joy of distributing even more alms to the needy.

20.*   The people revolted against the Bishops Salonius and Sagittarius. These two had been brought up by Saint Nicetius, Bishop of Lyons. They were made deacons and, while Saint Nicetius was still alive, they were chosen as bishops, Salonius in Embrun and Sagittarius in Gap. They were no sooner raised to the episcopate than their new power went to their heads: with a sort of insane fury they began to disgrace themselves in peculation, physical assaults, murders, adultery and every crime in the calendar. One day when Victor, Bishop of Saint-Paul-Trois-Châteaux, was celebrating his birthday, they sent a mob to attack him with swords and arrows. The assailants tore Victor's clothes off his back, beat up his servants, stole his table silver and all the furnishings of the feast, and left him in a sorry state. This was reported to King Guntram and he ordered a council of inquiry to be convened in Lyons. The bishops met, with the aged Saint Nicetius in their number, and they heard the case. They found Salonius and Sagittarius clearly guilty of the charge laid against them, and they ordered the two to be deposed from their bishoprics as a consequence of their criminal behaviour. The two Bishops knew that the King still had a soft spot for them. They sought an audience with him, pleaded that they had been wrongly dismissed and asked his permission to take their appeal to the Pope in Rome. The King granted their petition, gave them a letter of introduction and let them leave. They appeared before Pope John III[57] and put forward the plea that they had been dismissed with no reasonable cause given. The Pope sent a letter to King Guntram, ordering them to be restored to their former positions. The King did as the Pope commanded, but not before he had administered a severe reprimand to Salonius and Sagittarius. The worst of the story is that from then onwards they behaved no better. It is true that they asked forgiveness of Victor and handed over the men whom they had sent to attack him. Victor remembered our Lord's exhortation:

57. John III, Pope 559–72.

'Recompense to no man evil for evil', for he did these men no harm and let them go free. For this he was afterwards suspended from communion, on the grounds that he had privately forgiven the enemies whom he had in public accused, and this without the approval of his brother bishops before whom he had arraigned them. Later on, with the approval of the King, he was received into communion once more. As day followed day Salonius and Sagittarius became involved in one new crime after another. As I have already told you, in the battles between Mummolus and the Longobards they armed themselves like laymen and killed many men with their own hands. They engaged in a quarrel with their own congregations and beat quite a few of them with wooden clubs, until in their rage they made the blood flow. As a result the people once again appealed to the King. He ordered the two to be brought to court. When they came, he refused to see them; for he said that they ought only to be allowed into his royal presence if and when their case had been heard and they had been proved innocent. This annoyed Sagittarius very much. He was a fatuous and empty-headed fellow, much given to garrulous talk, and he bore this decision ill. He began to spread silly tales about the King, saying, for example, that Guntram's sons could never succeed to the throne because when their mother[58] married him she had been one of Magnachar's servants. Sagittarius was overlooking the fact that, irrespective of their mother's birth, all children born to a king count as that king's sons. When Guntram heard this he was greatly incensed. He deprived them of their horses, their servants and all their possessions. He shut them up in two monasteries far removed from each other and there they were left to repent of their sins. He permitted them each one religious only as a servant, and he gave stern warning to the local counts that the two should be kept under armed guard and not allowed to receive any visitors.

In those days King Guntram's sons were still alive, but the elder was already beginning to ail. Some of Guntram's close associates went to him. 'Lord King,' they said, 'if you will only

58. Austrechild.

deign to listen to what we say, we have something to tell you.'
'You are free to say whatever you wish,' answered Guntram. 'It
is possible,' they replied, 'that the Bishops whom you dismissed
were innocent. You may well have sinned in what you did, and
that is why your son is dying.' 'Go and free them immediately,'
said Guntram, 'and entreat them to pray for my two young
sons.' They did as they were told and the two Bishops were
released. They emerged from the two different monasteries to
which they had been banished, met and exchanged the kiss of
peace, for it was a long time since they had seen each other.
They returned to their dioceses and were so filled with remorse
that they seemed to pass their whole time in singing psalms,
fasting and giving alms to the poor. All day long they recited
the Psalms of David, and all night long they sang hymns and
meditated on the Holy Scriptures. This unrelieved sanctity did
not last long, for they soon slipped back into their old habits.
They began to spend all and every night in feasting and car-
ousing, and when their clergy came to celebrate matins in their
cathedrals they would still be asking for clean goblets and pouring out yet more wine. God was never mentioned in their conversation and they seemed to have forgotten all about the
church services. When dawn stole across the sky, they would
rise from their feasting, wrap themselves in garments soft to the
skin, sink into an oblivion of sleepiness and liquor, and so slum-
ber on until half-way through the morning, usually in the arms
of some woman or other, with whom they had intercourse.
Then they would get up, have a bath, and sit down to another
meal. As evening fell they would rise from the table and begin
to count the minutes until it was time for supper, which, as I
have told you, would see them through to daybreak. Each day
they would spend in this way. In the end the wrath of God
descended on their heads; but about this I will tell you later on.

21. At this time a Breton called Winnoch, who practised
extreme abstinence, made his way from Brittany to Tours. His
plan was to go on to Jerusalem. He wore no clothes except
sheepskins from which the wool had been removed. He seemed

to me to be a most pious man and in the hope of keeping him with me I ordained him as a priest.

A certain religious called Ingitrude was in the habit of collecting the water used for washing Saint Martin's tomb. One day there was a shortage of water and Ingitrude asked if a jar of wine could be carried to the spot instead. As soon as the night had passed she ordered this wine to be brought to her at a moment when the priest Winnoch was standing near. The jar was placed before her and she said to Winnoch: 'Pour out some of the wine and replace it by a single drop of the holy water, for I still have a very small quantity left.' Winnoch did as he was told. It is a remarkable fact that, as he added the single drop, the jar, which stood half empty, was filled to the brim. Ingitrude emptied the jar two or three times, and on each occasion it was replenished by the addition of a single drop of water. This must surely have been a miracle performed by Saint Martin.

22.   At the same time died Samson, the younger son of Chilperic, who had been ill with a high temperature and diarrhoea. This child was born while King Chilperic was being besieged in Tournai. Fredegund, the boy's mother, who thought that her own end was near, rejected him and wanted to have him killed. She failed in her attempt. Under pressure from Chilperic, she ordered Samson to be baptized. This was done, the ceremony being performed by the Bishop himself, but Samson died before completing his fifth year. His mother Fredegund was herself seriously ill at the time, but she recovered.

23.   When I was celebrating Mass on Saint Martin's Eve, which is 11 November, a remarkable portent was seen in the middle of the night. A bright star was seen shining in the very centre of the moon, and other stars appeared close to the moon, above it and below. Round the moon stretched the circle which is usually a sign of rain. I have no idea what all this meant. This same year the moon often appeared in eclipse and there were loud claps of thunder just before Christmas. The meteors which country folk calls suns and which were seen before the plague in

Clermont-Ferrand, as I have told you in an earlier book, also appeared round the sun. I was told that the sea rose higher than usual, and there were many other signs and wonders.

24. Guntram Boso came to Tours with a small band of armed followers and carried off by force his daughters, whom he had left for safety in the holy church there. He took them to the city of Poitiers, which belonged to King Childebert. King Chilperic attacked Poitiers and his troops put his nephew's forces to flight. These same troops deposed Ennodius from his countship and took him off to appear before the King. He was banished and his goods were confiscated. A year later he was allowed to return home and his property was restored to him. Guntram Boso left his daughters in Saint Hilary's church and joined King Childebert.

25. In the third year of King Childebert's reign,[59] which was the seventeenth year of that of Chilperic and Guntram, Dacolen, the son of Dagaric, who had himself died some time previously, left the service of King Chilperic. While wandering from place to place, Dacolen was treacherously seized by Duke Dragolen, surnamed the Zealous. Dragolen tied Dacolen up and dragged him off to King Chilperic, who was at Berny-Rivière. Dragolen had sworn that he would persuade the King to spare Dacolen's life. He did not keep his oath, for instead he accused Dacolen of various acts of impiety and did all he could to encourage Chilperic to have him killed. Dacolen was kept tied up in prison and in the end he realized that he had no hope of escape. Without asking permission from the King, he sought absolution from a priest. As soon as he had received absolution he was murdered. Dragolen then hurried off home, just at the moment when Guntram Boso was busy removing his daughters from Poitiers. Dragolen heard of what was happening and blocked his route; but Guntram Boso's men were expecting trouble and they resisted Dragolen and did all in their power to fight him off. Guntram Boso sent one of his friends to Dragolen.

59. A.D. 578.

'Give him the following message,' he said: ' "You know very
well that you and I have a pact. I ask you to stop ambushing my
men. I can do nothing to prevent you from stealing my possessions. All I want is liberty to go wherever I wish, taking my
daughters with me, even if I lose all my property in the
process." ' Dragolen was a silly, thoughtless fellow. 'You see this
rope?' he asked. 'I have used it to tie up quite a few other
culprits, whom I have handed over to the King. Today I shall
tie up Guntram Boso with it and hand him over in his turn.' As
he said this he struck spurs into his horse and rode full tilt at
Guntram Boso; but he failed in his assault, for his lance shattered and his sword fell to the ground. When Guntram Boso
saw death staring him in the face, he prayed to our Lord and
invoked the miraculous power of Saint Martin. Then he raised
his pike and jabbed Dragolen full in the throat. Dragolen
lurched over in his saddle, whereupon one of Guntram Boso's
friends struck him in the side with his lance and finished him off.
Dragolen's men ran. Guntram Boso stayed to despoil the
dead man: then he himself made off unmolested, taking his
daughters with him.

Some time later Severus, Guntram Boso's father-in-law, had
a serious accusation brought against him before the King by
his own sons. When Severus heard of this, he set out to see the
King. He carried rich bribes with him, but on the road he was
attacked and his gifts were stolen. Severus was banished and
later met a miserable end. His two sons, Burgolen and Dolo,
were condemned to death on a charge of *lèse-majesté*. One
was killed out of hand by the soldiery. The other fled, but he
was captured and had his hands and feet cut off. Thus they both
perished. Their property was confiscated and that of their
father, too. They had possessed vast wealth.

26.   The next thing which happened was that the men of Touraine, Poitou, the Bessin, Maine and Anjou, with many others,
were ordered by King Chilperic to march into Brittany and to
pitch their tents along the River Vilaine, in readiness for an
assault on Waroch, son of the dead Macliaw. Waroch made a

surprise night-attack on the Saxons from the Bessin and killed a great number of them. Three days later he came to terms with King Chilperic's military commanders: he handed his son over as a hostage and swore that he would be faithful to the King. He also restored the city of Vannes, it being understood that Chilperic would permit him to keep command of the place, and that he, for his part, would continue to pay annual tribute as it fell due, without waiting for a demand. Once all these matters were settled, the army withdrew from the region. King Chilperic subsequently ordered his ban to be enforced against the poorer citizens and the young people of Tours cathedral and Saint Martin's church, because they had failed to march with the army, although it was not customary for them to do public service. Later on Waroch forgot his oath and decided to break his agreement, sending Eunius, Bishop of the city of Vannes, to Chilperic. The King was greatly incensed at this: he rebuked the Bishop and ordered him to be banished from his diocese.

27.   By command of King Guntram a council was held in the city of Chalon-sur-Saône in the fourth year of Childebert's reign,[60] which was the eighteenth of that of Guntram and Chilperic. There were many matters on the agenda, but after a while they turned to discussing yet again the old *cause célèbre* of Salonius and Sagittarius. A number of charges were levelled against them, and they were accused of adultery and of murder. The bishops present were all of the opinion that such peccadilloes as these could be purged by penitence, so that it was found necessary to add further charges of *lèse-majesté* and high treason. As a result Salonius and Sagittarius were stripped of their bishoprics and imprisoned in the church of Saint Marcellus, with a guard to watch over them. They managed to escape and became wanderers on the face of the earth. Meanwhile new bishops were elected in their dioceses.[61]

28.   King Chilperic decreed that a new series of taxes should be

60. A.D. 579.

61. Emeritus became Bishop of Embrun in place of Salonius and Aridius replaced Sagittarius in Gap.

levied throughout the kingdom, and these were extremely
heavy. As a result a great number of people emigrated from
their native cities or from whatever bits of land they occupied
and sought refuge elsewhere, for they preferred to go into exile
rather than endure such punitive taxation. The new tax laws
laid it down that a landowner must pay five gallons of wine for
every half-acre which he possessed. Many other taxes were
levied, not only on land but also on the number of workmen
employed, until it became quite impossible to meet them. When
they realized how they were to be mulcted by this taxation, the
people of Limoges called a meeting on 1 March and decided to
kill Mark, the tax-collector who had been ordered to put the new
laws into effect. They would have carried out their threat, too,
had not Bishop Ferreolus saved Mark from the danger which
threatened him. A mob gathered: the people seized the tax-
collector's demand-books and burned them to ashes. The King
was furious. He sent his officials to Limoges and inflicted terrible punishments on the populace, having them tortured and
even put to death out of hand. It is said that these officials sent
from the King's court falsely accused the abbots and priests of
having incited the people to burn demands during the riot, and
that they had them staked to the ground and then submitted
them to all sorts of torture. Then they demanded even more
punitive payments.

29.   The Bretons made a savage attack on the district round
Rennes, burning property, stealing everything that they could
lay their hands on and taking prisoners. They advanced as far as
the village of Corps-Nuds, destroying everything as they went.
Bishop Eunius was recalled from exile: he was packed off to live
in Angers, for they forbade him to take up residence in his own
city of Vannes. Duke Beppolen was sent against the Bretons. He
destroyed a number of places with fire and sword, but this
merely roused the inhabitants to greater fury.

30.   While these things were happening in Gaul, the Emperor
Justin completed the eighteenth year of his reign. He remained

insane until the day of his death.[62] As soon as Justin had been
buried, Tiberius the Caesar took charge of the Empire which
had in reality been his for some time. According to the local
custom the populace expected Tiberius to process in the hippodrome. They prepared an ambush for him there and planned
to replace him by Justinian, Justin's nephew, but Tiberius went
in procession to the holy shrines instead. He prayed there and
then called the Patriarch of Constantinople to his side and set
off to the palace with the prefects and those of consular rank.
Invested with the purple and crowned with the diadem he took
his seat on the imperial throne and so was made Emperor amid
tumultuous applause. When the conspirators who had been
waiting to attack him in the hippodrome learned what had happened they were covered with shame and confusion. Having
failed in their purpose, they withdrew, for this man who had put
his trust in God had no reason to fear his enemies. A few days
later Justinian came to court. He threw himself at the Emperor's feet and offered him fifteen hundred pounds of gold in
an attempt to gain his pardon. With his customary long-
suffering, Tiberius raised him to his feet and told him to take up
his residence in the palace. The Empress Sophia broke the
promise which she made long before to Tiberius and made
plans to lay a trap for him. While he was away on one of his
country estates, enjoying the wine-harvest for a month, as was
the custom of the Eastern Emperors, she secretly summoned
Justinian to her presence and plotted to raise him to the Imperial throne. When he heard what was happening, Tiberius returned with all speed to the city of Constantinople. He had the
Empress arrested and he deprived her of all her wealth, leaving
her only sufficient for her daily needs. He also took away her
personal servants, replacing them with others among whom
there were certain of his own faithful retainers; what is more he
gave orders that none of those dismissed should ever again have
access to her. He reprimanded Justinian and then took him
back into high favour. He even went so far as to promise his

62. Justin II was Emperor of Constantinople from A.D. 565 to 578, that
is for thirteen years only.

daughter in marriage to Justinian's son, asking in return that Justinian's daughter should marry his own son, but nothing came of this.

The troops of Tiberius beat the Persians in battle and came home victorious, carrying enough booty to satisfy the cupidity of any man, or so one would have thought. Twenty elephants which they had captured were paraded before the Emperor.

31. In this same year[63] the Bretons attacked the cities of Nantes and Rennes. They seized a vast amount of booty, ravaged the fields, stripped the vineyards of their grapes and captured the inhabitants. Bishop Felix sent a deputation to the Bretons: they promised to make good the damage, but they did not carry out their promises.

32.* In Paris a woman who had left her husband was accused by a number of people of living with another man. The husband's relations went to the woman's father and said: 'Either you must prove your daughter's innocence or else let her die, for we cannot permit her adultery to bring disgrace upon our family.' 'I know that my daughter is completely innocent,' answered the father. 'There is no truth at all in this rumour which is being spread by malicious people. I will prove her innocence by an oath and so stop the accusation going any farther.' 'If she really is innocent,' they replied, 'swear an oath to that effect on the tomb of Saint Denis, the martyr.' 'I will certainly do so,' said her father. Having agreed to this, they went off together to the holy martyr's church. The father raised his hands over the altar and swore that his daughter was not guilty. The husband's supporters declared that he had perjured himself. An argument ensued, in which they all drew their swords, rushed at each other and started killing each other in front of the altar. These men were of noble birth and among the leaders of Chilperic's court. Many received sword-wounds, the holy church was spattered with human blood, the portals were pierced with swords and javelins, and weapons were drawn in senseless anger at the very tomb of Saint Denis. Peace was

63. A.D. 579.

restored with great difficulty, but services could not be held in
the church until what had happened was brought to the notice
of the King. Both parties rushed off to court, but Chilperic
refused to exonerate any of them. He sent them to the local
bishop with orders that only if they were found not guilty were
they to be admitted to communion. They paid a fine for their
offences, and so were readmitted to communion by Bishop
Ragnemod, who had charge of the church in Paris. A few days
later the woman in question was summoned to trial, but she
strangled herself with a rope.

33. In the fifth year of King Childebert's reign[64] great floods
devastated parts of Auvergne. The rain continued for twelve
days and the Limagne was under such a depth of water that all
sowing had to cease. The River Loire, the River Allier (which
used to be called the Flavaris) and the mountain-streams which
run into this latter were so swollen that they rose higher above
the flood-level than ever before. Many cattle were drowned, the
crops were ruined and buildings inundated. The River Rhône,
at the spot where it meets the Saône, overflowed its banks and
brought heavy loss to the inhabitants, undermining parts of the
city walls of Lyons. When the rains stopped, the trees came out
in leaf once more, although by now it was September. In Touraine this same year, one morning before the day had dawned,
a bright light was seen to traverse the sky and then disappear in
the East. A sound as of trees crashing to the ground was heard
throughout the whole region, but it can hardly have been a tree
for it was audible over fifty miles and more. In this same year
again the city of Bordeaux was sadly shaken by an earthquake.
The city walls were in great danger of collapsing. The entire
populace was filled with the fear of death, for they imagined
that they would be swallowed up with their city unless they fled.
Many of them escaped to neighbouring townships. This terrible
disaster followed them to the places where they had sought
refuge and extended even into Spain, but there it was less
serious. Huge rocks came cascading down from the mountain-

64. A.D. 580.

peaks of the Pyrenees, crushing in their wake the local inhabitants and their cattle. Villages around Bordeaux were burned by a fire sent from heaven: it took so swift a hold that homesteads and threshing-floors with the grain still spread out on them were reduced to ashes. There was no other apparent cause of this fire, and it must have come from God. The city of Orleans blazed with a great conflagration. Even the richer citizens lost their all, and if anyone managed to salvage anything from the flames it was immediately snatched away by the thieves who crowded around. Somewhere near Chartres blood poured forth when a loaf of bread was broken in two. At the same time the city of Bourges was scourged by a hailstorm.

34. A most serious epidemic followed these prodigies. While the Kings were quarrelling with each other again and once more making preparations for civil war, dysentery spread throughout the whole of Gaul. Those who caught it had a high temperature, with vomiting and severe pains in the small of the back: their heads ached and so did their necks. The matter they vomited up was yellow or even green. Many people maintained that some secret poison must be the cause of this. The country-folk imagined that they had boils inside their bodies; and actually this is not as silly as it sounds, for as soon as cupping-glasses were applied to their shoulders or legs, great tumours formed, and when these burst and discharged their pus they were cured. Many recovered their health by drinking herbs which are known to be antidotes to poisons. The epidemic began in the month of August. It attacked young children first of all and to them it was fatal: and so we lost our little ones, who were so dear to us and sweet, whom we had cherished in our bosoms and dandled in our arms, whom we had fed and nurtured with such loving care. As I write I wipe away my tears and I repeat once more the words of Job the blessed: 'The Lord gave, and the Lord hath taken away; as it hath pleased the Lord, so is it come to pass. Blessed be the name of the Lord, world without end.'[65]

65. Job 1, 21.

In these days King Chilperic fell ill. When he recovered, his younger son, who had not yet been baptized in the name of the Holy Ghost, was attacked in his turn. They saw that he was dying and so they baptized him. He made a momentary recovery, but then Chlodobert, his older brother, caught the disease. When their mother Fredegund realized that he, too, was at death's door, she repented of her sins, rather late in the day, it is true, and said to the King: 'God in his mercy has endured our evil goings-on long enough. Time and time again He has sent us warnings through high fevers and other indispositions, but we have never mended our ways. Now we are going to lose our children. It is the tears of paupers which are the cause of their death, the sighs of orphans, the widows' lament. Yet we still keep on amassing wealth, with no possible end in view. We still lay up treasures, we who have no one to whom we can leave them. Our riches live on after us, the fruits of rapine, hated and accursed, with no one left to possess them once we are gone. Were our cellars not already over-flowing with wine? Were our granaries not stuffed to the roof with corn? Were our treasure-houses not already full enough with gold, silver, precious stones, necklaces and every regal adornment one could dream of? Now we are losing the most beautiful of our possessions! Come, then, I beg you! Let us set light to all these iniquitous tax-demands! What sufficed for King Lothar, your father, should be plenty enough for our exchequer, too.' As she said this, the Queen beat her breast with her fists. She ordered to be placed before her the tax-demands which had been brought back by Mark from her own cities,[66] and she put them on the fire. She spoke to the King a second time. 'What are you waiting for?' she asked. 'Do what you see me doing! We may still lose our children, but we shall at least escape eternal damnation.' King Chilperic was deeply moved. He tossed all the files of tax-demands into the fire. As soon as they were burnt, he sent mess-

66. On the morning after their first night together the Merovingian Kings made over to their Queens certain of their cities, with the revenues accruing from them. This was the *morgengabe*. Cp. *HF*, IX, 20 for the *morgengabe* which Chilperic gave to Galswinth.

engers to ensure that no such assessments should ever be made again. Meanwhile their youngest son wasted away before the onslaught of the disease and finally died. With broken hearts they carried him to Paris from their estate at Berny, and buried him in the church of Saint Denis. As for Chlodobert, they placed him on a stretcher and carried him to the church of Saint Medard in Soissons. They set him down before the Saint's tomb and made vows for his recovery. He died in the middle of the night, worn to a shadow and hardly drawing breath. They buried him in the church of the holy martyrs Crispin and Crispinian. The whole populace bewailed his death: they walked behind his funeral cortège, the men weeping and the women wearing widows' weeds as if they were escorting their own husbands to the grave. From this time onwards King Chilperic was lavish in giving alms to cathedrals and churches, and to the poor, too.

35. At the same time died Austrechild, King Guntram's Queen, and of the same disease.[67] Before this wicked woman breathed her last, she realized that there was no hope for her. She sighed deeply and as her last wish asked that others might die with her, for at her funeral she wanted to have the sound of others bewailing their dead. As Herod had done before her,[68] she is said to have made this last request to the King: 'I should still have some hope of recovery if my death had not been made inevitable by the treatment prescribed for me by these wicked doctors. It is the medicines which they have given me which have robbed me of my life and forced me thus to lose the light of day. I beseech you, do not let me die unavenged. Give me your solemn word, I beg you, that you will cut their throats the moment that my eyes have closed in death. If I have really come to the end of my life, they must not be permitted to glory in my dying. When my friends grieve for me, let their friends grieve for them, too.' As she said this, she died. When the fu-

67. A.D. 580.

68. Herod is supposed to have ordered that a number of Jewish leaders should be executed immediately after his own death.

neral ceremony was over, the King was forced by this dying wish of his evil consort to commit the foul deed which she begged of him. At his orders the two doctors who had lavished their skill upon her were duly executed.[69] All those who had any sense at all knew that this was a sinful act.

36.* Nantinus, Count of Angoulême, was another who wasted away with this disease and then died. I shall have to go back a little in time if I am to describe the damage which he did to God's bishops and His churches. His uncle Marachar had held the countship in that same city for many years. When his period of office was over, Marachar joined the church: he became a religious and was consecrated as a bishop. He devoted his energy to building and furnishing churches and church-houses. His death was a cruel one, for in the seventh year of his episcopate his enemies put poison in a fish's head, which he then ate without suspecting anything. God in His justice did not allow him to go long unavenged: for Frontonius, who had planned and carried out this murder, and who immediately seized the bishopric for himself, held it for one year only and then died by divine judgement. After his death they con-secrated as bishop a priest from Bordeaux called Heraclius, who had formerly been one of Childebert I's ambassadors. Nantinus canvassed for the countship of the city, his purpose being to avenge his uncle's death. Once he had been appointed he did all in his power to harass Heraclius. 'You are harbouring in your house the very murderers who were responsible for my uncle's death,' said he, 'and you receive at your table church-men who were involved in the affair.' The hostility between the two men became more and more bitter; and soon Nantinus began to occupy by force the estates which Marachar had left to the Church in his will, alleging as a pretext that the Church had no right to possess the property of a benefactor who had been killed by her clergy. A number of laymen met their death in this quarrel and then Nantinus went so far as to seize one of

69. According to Marius of Avenches their names were Donatus and Nicolaus.

the priests, tie him up and thrust him through with a javelin. The priest survived this maltreatment, so Nantinus bound his hands behind his back, hung him from a post and did all he could to make him confess that he had been involved in the murder. The priest denied it, but he died from loss of blood from his wound. The Bishop was greatly incensed by what had happened, and he forbade Nantinus to enter the church. At a council of bishops convened in the city of Saintes, Nantinus asked that peace be restored between himself and Heraclius, promising to do penance and to return all the church property which he had wrongfully seized. Heraclius gave in to the pressure of his brother-bishops and granted all that was asked of him. He commended to Almighty God the cause of the priest who had been murdered and only then would he receive Nantinus back into Christian charity. The Count went home to Angoulême and immediately set about looting, knocking down and destroying the buildings which he had occupied illegally. 'If this property really has to be returned to the Church,' he said, 'I will see to it that it is handed over in a sorry state.' Heraclius was furious and once more suspended Nantinus from communion. Not long after this the saintly Bishop reached the end of his earthly journey and went to join our Lord in Heaven. By the bribes which he distributed and by flattery Nantinus managed to persuade certain other bishops to readmit him to communion. A few months later he fell ill with dysentery. As his temperature rose higher and higher, he kept screaming: 'What torment this is! I am being burned by Bishop Heraclius! It is Bishop Heraclius who is torturing me! It is Bishop Heraclius who is summoning me to judgement! I confess my guilt! I admit that I wronged him in the most unpardonable way! I beseech him to stop tormenting me with this awful pain and let me die!' At the height of his fever he kept shouting these words. Then his bodily strength failed. As he breathed out his unhappy soul he gave incontrovertible proof that he was being punished to avenge the holy Bishop. In his dying hours his body became so black that you would have thought that it had been placed on glowing coals and roasted.

All should stand amazed and be filled with awe at what happened, and more especially all should take care not to offend their bishops, for the Lord will avenge His servants if they put their trust in Him.

37.* Saint Martin, Bishop of Galicia,[70] died at this time and was greatly lamented by his people. He was a native of Pannonia, but he left that region to travel in the East and to visit the holy places. He read so widely that he was held second to none among his contemporaries. Later he journeyed to Galicia and there he was consecrated as a bishop just at the moment when the relics of Saint Martin of Tours were being unloaded. He ruled his bishopric for more than thirty years and died full of good works. It was he who composed the verses over the southern portal of the church of Saint Martin of Tours.

38. In this same year the Christians in Spain suffered sad persecution. Many of them were driven into exile, deprived of their possessions, weakened by hunger, thrown into prison, beaten with sticks and tortured to death. The chief instigator of this horror was Goiswinth, the widow of King Athanagild, whom Leuvigild later married.[71] This woman who had brought such humiliation to God's servants was herself the victim of divine vengeance, for she was branded as infamous before all peoples. A white cataract blinded one of her eyes, and in this way her eye-lids lost the sense which had long before departed from her mind. Leuvigild already had two sons by a former wife. The elder of these married a daughter of King Sigibert[72] and the younger a daughter of King Chilperic.[73] Ingund, for that was the name of King Sigibert's daughter, was sent off to Spain with much pomp and circumstance. Her stepmother-in-law Goiswinth received her very warmly, but it was soon apparent that

70. Saint Martin, Bishop of Braga, died 580.
71. Goiswinth was the mother of Queen Brunhild.
72. Hermangild, who married Ingund, the daughter of King Sigibert.
73. Recared, who was betrothed to Rigunth, the daughter of King Chilperic and Fredegund. He did not marry her.

she had no intention of allowing her to remain a Catholic. She talked with her in a kindly way, and tried to persuade her to be rebaptized into the Arian heresy. Ingund had the courage to refuse. 'It is quite enough for me that I have been cleansed once and for all from original sin by a baptism which will save my soul, and that I have made clear my belief in the Holy Trinity one and indivisible,' she said. 'I hereby confirm that I believe this with all my heart and that I will never go back on this article of faith.' When she heard this the Queen lost her temper completely. She seized the girl by the hair and threw her to the ground: then she kicked her until she was covered with blood, had her stripped naked and ordered her to be thrown into the baptismal pool. There are many witnesses who can tell how Ingund refused to budge an inch from the faith which we share.

As their place of residence and seat of government Leuvigild handed over one of his cities to Ingund and his son Hermangild. As soon as they were installed, Ingund began to persuade her husband to give up his belief in the false Arian heresy and to accept instead the true Catholic faith. For a long time he resisted, but in the end he was persuaded by her arguments and was converted to the Catholic religion. He was anointed with the chrism and he took the name John. When Leuvigild heard of this he began to cast about to see how he could destroy his son. Hermangild knew what his father was about and he joined the party of the Emperor Tiberius, making overtures to the Emperor's army commander, who was then invading Spain. Then Leuvigild sent messengers to Hermangild to say: 'Come and see me, for there are matters which we must discuss.' 'I will not go,' answered Hermangild. 'He is hostile to me because I have become a Catholic.' Leuvigild bribed the Emperor's army commander with thirty thousand pieces of gold to withdraw his support from Hermangild: then he raised an army and marched against him. Hermangild called upon the Greeks to support him, left his wife in his capital and went out to fight his father. As soon as Leuvigild ordered his troops to advance Hermangild found himself deserted by the Greeks. He realized that he had no hope at all of winning and he sought sanctuary in a near-by church. 'My father does wrong to attack me,' he said. 'It is a sin for a father to be killed by a son, or a son to be killed by a father.' When this was reported to Leuvigild, he sent Hermangild's brother Recared to parley with him. Recared swore that Hermangild would suffer no humiliation. 'Go and throw yourself at your father's feet,' he said, 'and he will forgive you everything.' Hermangild told Recared to call their father in, and when Leuvigild came he threw himself at his feet. His father raised him up, kissed him, spoke to him kindly and led him off to his own camp. Then he made a sign to his men and, despite his promise, had Hermangild seized. He stripped him of his clothes and dressed him in rags. When he returned to Toledo, which was his own capital, he dismissed all Hermangild's men and sent him into exile with a single slave to wait on him.

39.   After the death of their sons, King Chilperic and his wife spent the month of October in mourning in the forest of Cuise. Then, at the suggestion of Fredegund, Chilperic sent his son Clovis to Berny, in the hope that he would die of the same disease. The epidemic which had killed Clovis' brothers was still raging there in all its intensity, but he did not catch it. The King moved to Chelles, his estate near Paris. After a few days he ordered Clovis to join him there. I will now tell you in full detail how Clovis met his death.

While Clovis was staying with his father on the estate at Chelles, he began to boast in a childish way. 'Now that my brothers are dead,' he kept saying, 'the entire kingdom comes to me. The whole of Gaul is mine to command; fate has made me heir to the entire country. My enemies are now in my power and I can do to them whatever I choose.' He also made unforgivable remarks about his stepmother, Queen Fredegund. She came to hear of this and was terrified. Not long afterwards someone approached the Queen and said: 'It is through Clovis' treacherous behaviour that you sit there deprived of your sons. He has fallen in love with the daughter of one of your women-servants, and it is through the mother's magic arts that he has

303

encompassed their death. I warn you, you can expect no better
fate yourself, now that you have lost the hope through which
you were to have reigned.' The Queen was greatly frightened.
She was still in a state of nervous depression because of her
recent loss, and she worked herself up into a fury. She took the
girl on whom Clovis had cast sheep's eyes and had her thrashed.
Then she ordered all her hair to be cut off, and had her tied to a
stake which was stuck up outside Clovis' lodging. The girl's
mother she had bound and subjected to torture, until she had
forced her to admit that the charges against her were true. All
this she reported to the King, adding a few details of her own.
Then she demanded her revenge on Clovis.

The King was just setting off for the hunt. He ordered Clovis
to be brought before him in secret. When he arrived, the King
commanded that he should be seized and manacled by Duke
Desiderius and Duke Bobo. He was stripped of his weapons and
his clothes, and paraded before the Queen in rags and with his
arms bound. She ordered him to be kept in custody, for she
wanted to find out if the events had really happened as she had
been told, whose advice Clovis had been following, at whose
encouragement he had acted as he did and who were his most
intimate friends. He denied everything else, but he admitted
that he possessed many close associates. Three days later the
Queen gave orders that he should be taken across the River
Maine, with his arms still bound. He was kept under close surveillance on an estate called Noisy-le-Grand. While he was a
prisoner there he was murdered by a stab with a knife. They
buried his body immediately. Messengers were sent off to the
King to announce that Clovis had stabbed himself with his own
hand; and they added the confirmatory detail that the knife
with which he had struck the blow was still in the wound.
Chilperic accepted their report: the Queen had kept egging him
on, but in my opinion it was the King who had delivered Clovis
up to death, and yet he wept no tear. The young prince's household was dispersed. His mother was murdered in the most cruel
fashion.[74] His sister was tricked by Fredegund's servants and

74. Audovera.

persuaded into entering a nunnery, where she has become a religious and where she remains to this day.[75] All their property was purloined by the Queen. The woman who had given evidence against Clovis was condemned to be burnt alive. As she was dragged off to the stake, the poor creature started to admit that she had lied. Her confession availed her nothing: she was bound to the stake and set alight while still alive. Clovis' treasurer was fetched back from Bourges by Chuppa, Master of the Stables to Chilperic, and handed over to the Queen. He was condemned to be subjected to various tortures. At my intervention Fredegund had his shackles struck off and absolved him from punishment. The King eventually gave him his liberty.

40.* While on a mission to Spain to attend to the affairs of Queen Brunhild, Elafius, Bishop of Châlons-sur-Marne, developed a very high temperature and died. His body was brought home to his own city and buried there.

Bishop Eunius, who, as I have related in an earlier chapter,[76] consented to act as legate for the Bretons and as a result was not permitted to return to his own diocese, was at the King's command maintained at the public expense in Angers. He visited Paris and was celebrating Mass one Sunday when he fell to the ground with a scream like a horse neighing. Blood poured from his mouth and his nostrils. The congregation carried him out and he recovered. He was much given to excessive drinking and was often so intoxicated that he could not walk.

41. Ambassadors were despatched to King Guntram's court from Mir, King of Galicia.[77] As they passed through the neigh-

75. Basina, who became a nun in Saint Radegund's nunnery in Poitiers, where, with Clotild, the daughter of King Charibert, she led the revolt against the Abbess Leubovera.

76. *HF*, V, 26 and *HF*, V, 29.

77. Mir, King of the Swabians in Galicia, died in A.D. 583. Cp. *HF*, VI, 43.

bourhood of Poitiers their presence was announced to King Chilperic, who at that time ruled over this region. He ordered them to be seized and brought before him, and then he locked them up in Paris.

At this time a wolf came out of the woods and made its way through one of the gates into the city of Poitiers. Thereupon all the gates were closed, and the wolf was cornered inside the city walls and killed. Some said that they saw the heavens aflame. At the point where the waters of the River Cher mingle with it, the River Loire was even higher than the previous year. A wind from the south raged with such great violence that it knocked down forest-trees, destroyed houses, carried off fences and blew men off their feet and killed them. This wind devastated an area some mile or more across, but no one ever discovered how far the damage continued. On a number of occasions, too, the cocks crowed at the beginning of the night. The moon was darkened and a comet appeared in the sky. A serious epidemic followed among the common people.

The Swabian ambassadors were held for a year; then they were dismissed and allowed to go home.

42.* Maurilio, Bishop of Cahors, suffered badly from gout. He added terrible tortures of his own to the pain which this affliction caused him, for he would occasionally apply a red-hot poker to his shins and feet in order to increase his suffering. There were many candidates for his bishopric, but he himself favoured Ursicinus, who had been Queen Ultrogotha's Referendary.[78] In his later years Maurilio used to pray that Ursicinus would be elected. Then he died. He was a man of great charity and extremely well-versed in the Holy Scriptures, to the point that he could recite from memory the list of genealogies set out in the Old Testament, which very few know by heart. He was just in his decisions and, as it is written in the Book of Job, he protected the poor of his diocese from the hand of unfair judges: 'Because I delivered the poor from the hand of the mighty, and him that had none to help him. The blessing of the

78. Queen Ultrogotha was the wife of King Childebert I.

widow came upon me, I was eyes to the blind, and feet was I to
the lame, I was father to the poor.'[79]

43.   As envoy to Chilperic King Leuvigild sent Agilan, a man
of low intelligence, untrained in logical argument, but distinguished by his hatred of our Catholic faith. Tours was on his
route and he took advantage of this to attack me concerning my
beliefs and to assail the dogmas of the Church. 'The bishops of
the early Church made a foolish pronouncement,' he said,
'when they asserted that the Son was equal to the Father. How
can He be equal to the Father, when He says: "My Father is
greater than I"?[80] It is not right that the Son should be considered equal to the Father when He Himself admits that He is
less, when it is to the Father that He complains about the miserable manner of His death, when at the very moment of His
death He commends His spirit to the Father, as if He Himself
were completely powerless. Surely it is quite obvious that He is
less than the Father, both in power and in age!' In reply to this,
I asked him if he believed that Jesus Christ was the Son of God,
and if he admitted that He was the wisdom of God, the light,
the truth, the life, the justice of God. Agilan answered: 'I believe that the Son of God was all those things.' Then I said: 'Tell
me now, when was the Father without wisdom? When was He
without light, without life, without truth, without justice? Just
as the Father could not exist without these things, so He could
not exist without the Son. These attributes are absolutely essential to the mystery of the Godhead. Similarly the Father could
hardly be called the Father if He had no Son. When you quote
the Son as having said: "My Father is greater than I," you must
know that He said this in the lowliness of the flesh, which He
had assumed so that He might teach you that you were redeemed not by His power but by His humility. You must also
remember, when you quote the words: "My Father is greater
than I," that He also says in another place: "I and my Father
are one." His fear of death and the fact that He commended
His spirit are a reference to the weakness of the flesh, so that,

79. Cp. Job 29, 12–13 and 15–16.   80. John 14, 28.

just as He is believed to be very God, so may He be believed to be very man.'[81] Agilan answered: 'He who does what another commands is less than that other: the Son is always less than the Father because He does the will of the Father, whereas there is no proof that the Father does the will of the Son.' 'You must understand', I replied, 'that the Father is the Son and that the Son is in the Father, each subsisting in one Godhead. If you want proof that the Father does the will of the Son, consider what our Lord Jesus Christ says when He comes to raise Lazarus – that is if you have any faith in the Gospel at all: "Father, I thank thee that thou hast heard me. And I knew that thou hearest me always: but because of the people which stand by I said it, that they may believe that thou hast sent me.'[82] When He comes to His Passion, He says: "And now, O Father, glorify thou me with thine own self with the glory which I had with thee before the world was."[83] Then the Father replies from Heaven: "I have both glorified it, and will glorify it again."[84] Therefore the Son is equal in Godhead, and not inferior, and He is not inferior in anything else. If you admit that the Son is God, you must agree that He is perfect and that He lacks nothing. If you deny that He is perfect, then you do not admit that He is God.' Agilan answered: 'It was after He was made man that He began to be called the Son of God: there was a time when He was not.' 'Listen to David speaking in the name of the Lord,' I replied: ' "Out of the womb have I borne thee, before the morning star."[85] John the Evangelist says: "In the beginning was the Word, and the Word was with God, and the Word was God. And the Word was made flesh and dwelt among us, by whom all things were made."[86] You are so blinded by your poisonous heresy that you do not understand the Godhead.' Agilan answered: 'Do you believe that the Holy Ghost is God and do you maintain that He is equal to the Father and the Son?' 'In the Three there is one will, one power, one action,' I replied, 'one God in Trinity and three Persons in unity. There are three Persons, but one kingdom, one majesty,

81. John 10, 30. 82. John 11, 41–2. 83. John 17, 5.
84. John 12, 28. 85. Cp. Psalms 110, 3. 86. John 1, 1, 14 and 3.

one power, one omnipotence.' Agilan answered: 'The Holy
Ghost, who is equal to the Father and the Son, according to
you, is clearly less than either, for we read that He was promised by the Son and sent by the Father. No one promises
anything which is not in his power, and no one sends any person
who is not his own inferior. Jesus himself says in the Gospel:
"If I go not away, the Comforter will not come unto you; but if
I depart, I will send him unto you." '[87] I replied: 'The Son does
well to say before His Passion that if He does not return in
victory to His Father, having redeemed the world with His own
blood and having prepared a habitation in the heart of man, the
Holy Ghost, which is God, cannot come down from Heaven
into a heart which is idolatrous and spotted with the stain of
original sin. As Solomon says: "The Holy Ghost will flee
deceit."[88] As you hope for resurrection, do not speak against
the Holy Ghost. As the Word of God puts it: "Whosoever
speaketh against the Holy Ghost, it shall not be forgotten him,
neither in this world, neither in the world to come." '[89] Agilan
answered: 'God is He who sends: he who is sent is not God.'
Then I asked him if he believed the doctrine of the Apostles
Peter and Paul. He answered: 'I do believe.' 'When the Apostle
Peter accuses Ananias of behaving fraudulently over the field
which he has sold,' I replied, 'he asks: "Why hath it seemed
good to thee to lie to the Holy Ghost? Thou hast not lied unto
men, but unto God."[90] When Paul is differentiating between
the dogmas of spiritual graces, he says: "But all these worketh
that one and the selfsame Spirit, dividing to every man severally
as he will."[91] The man who achieves what he has set out to do is
under an obligation to no one. As I have said already, you are
absolutely wrong about the Holy Trinity and, what is more, the
way your founder, Arius, met his end shows just how perverse
and wicked your sect is.' Agilan answered: 'You must not blaspheme against a faith which you yourself do not accept. You
notice that we who do not believe the things which you believe
nevertheless do not blaspheme against them. It is no crime for

87. John 16, 7.   88. Wisdom of Solomon, 1, 5.
89. Matthew 12, 32.   90. Acts 5, 3–4.   91. I Corinthians 12, 11.

one set of people to believe in one doctrine and another set of people to believe in another. Indeed, it is a proverbial saying with us that no harm is done when a man whose affairs take him past the altars of the Gentiles and the Church of God pays respect to both.' I realized what a fool the man was. 'You are, I perceive,' said I, 'at once a defender of the Gentiles and a champion of the heretics. You not only defile the dogmas of the Church, but you also advocate the worship of pagan abominations. You would do much better to arm yourself with the faith which Abraham found near the oak-tree, Isaac in the ram, Jacob in the stone and Moses in the bush; the faith which Aaron wore in the ephod, which David knew when he danced with the timbrel and which Solomon proclaimed by his wisdom; the faith which all the patriarchs and prophets, and the very Law itself, have celebrated in their oracular pronouncements and represented symbolically in their sacrifices; the faith which our own Martin, as is witnessed still today, possesses in his heart and manifests in his miraculous power. If you were converted to Catholicism, you would believe in the indivisible Trinity, you would be able to receive my blessing, your heart would be cleansed of the poison of false belief and your sins would be washed away.' Agilan lost his temper and ground his teeth, almost as if he was going off his head. 'May my soul leave the confines of my body,' he muttered, 'before I ever receive a benediction from a priest of your religion!' 'May the Lord never permit my religion or my faith to grow so tepid,' I answered, 'that I waste His blessing upon dogs, or cast the sacredness of His precious pearls before filthy swine!' At this Agilan gave up the discussion, rose to his feet and marched out. Some time later, when he was back again in Spain, he fell seriously ill: as a result he felt a compulsion to accept conversion to our religion.

44. At this same time King Chilperic published a decree that we should make no distinction of Persons in the Holy Trinity, but call it simply God, for he maintained that it was unseemly that we should speak of a Person in the case of God, as if He

were a man of flesh and blood. He affirmed that the Father was the same as the Son, and that the Holy Ghost was the same as the Father and the Son. 'That was how He appeared to the prophets and the patriarchs,' he said, 'and that is how He was considered in the Law.' He ordered these pronouncements to be read to me and he added: 'That is my decision, and you and the other doctors of the Church must make it an article of your own faith.' 'Most pious King,' I answered, 'you must give up this ill-founded belief, and follow that which the Apostles and after them the other Fathers of the Church have handed down to us, that which Hilary[92] and Eusebius[93] taught and which you yourself confessed at your baptism.' The King was very angry. 'It is clear,' he said, 'that what Hilary and Eusebius taught is the very opposite of what I believe.' My answer was as follows: 'You must make sure that your personal belief offends neither God Himself nor His saints. You must accept that in their Persons the Father is different from the Son and the Son different from the Holy Ghost. It was not the Father who was made man, nor the Holy Ghost, but the Son, who was the Son of God, so that for man's redemption He might be accepted as the Son of man and of the Virgin. It was not the Father who suffered the Passion, nor the Holy Ghost, but the Son, in order that He who was made flesh in the world might become a sacrifice for the world. What you say about the Persons must be interpreted spiritually, not physically. In these three Persons there is thus one glory, one eternity and one omnipotence.' King Chilperic was annoyed by what I said. 'I will put these matters to men who are more wise than you,' he answered, 'and they will agree with me.' 'Anyone who is prepared to accept your proposals will not be a wise man but a fool,' I replied. He gnashed his teeth, but said no more. A few days later Salvius, the Bishop of Albi, arrived at court. The King had his views propounded to him and begged him to say that he agreed with them. As soon as Salvius heard the proposals he rejected them with such violence that if he had been able to reach the paper

92. Hilary, Bishop of Poitiers, *c.* 350–*c.* 368.
93. Eusebius, Bishop of Vercelli, died 371.

on which they were written he would have torn it into shreds.
King Chilperic was forced to change his mind.

The King wrote a number of books of poetry[94] in which he
tried to imitate Sedulius,[95] but his poems observed none of the
accepted rules of prosody. He also added certain letters to our
alphabet,[96] the *w* of the Greeks, and the *ae, the* and *wi*, these
four to be represented by the characters ω, ψ, Z and Δ. He
sent instructions to all the cities in his kingdom, saying that
these letters should be taught to boys in school, and that books
using the old characters should have them erased with pumice-
stone and the new ones written in.

45.* Agricola, the Bishop of Chalon-sur-Saône, died at this
time.[97] He came of a senatorial family, and was known for his
wisdom and refinement. He was responsible for many building
projects in his own city, putting up private houses and erecting
the cathedral, which stands on columns, and is adorned with
marble and decorated with mosaics. Agricola practised extreme
abstinence: he never ate at midday but only at supper-time, and
even then he sat down to his meal so early that it was always
over while the sun was still in the sky. He was little versed in the
humanities, but he spoke with great eloquence. He died in the
forty-eighth year of his episcopate, when he was eighty-three
years old. Flavius, the Referendary of King Guntram, was
elected in his place.

46.* Dalmatius, Bishop of Rodez, was the next to die.[98] He
was a pious man, temperate in eating and free from the desires
of the flesh, extremely charitable, friendly to all, and steadfast
in his prayers and vigils. He built a cathedral, but he pulled so
much down in order to improve the new building that he never
finished it. As always happens, when he died there were many
candidates for his bishopric. A priest called Transobadus, who

94. None of the poems of King Chilperic has survived.
95. Sedulius was a Christian poet of the fifth century.
96. The Latin alphabet. Chilperic's new letters were soon abandoned.
97. A.D. 580.   98. A.D. 580.

had once been archdeacon under Dalmatius, had high hopes, trusting to the fact that he had placed his son in the household of Gogo, who at that time was King Childebert's governor. Bishop Dalmatius had left a will in which he made clear what gift he would like to receive from the King after his death. He adjured him with awful oaths not to permit the election of a stranger, or a covetous man, or of anyone who was married, but to find a man to replace him who should be free from these disadvantages and who passed his time in giving praise to God. The priest Transobadus gave a dinner for the churchmen of the city. When they were all seated at their meal, one of the priests began a most shameful attack on the late Bishop, going so far as to call him a fool and a madman. As he spoke, the cupbearer came to him to offer him wine. He took the cup and put it to his lips: as he did so he began to tremble and then dropped it from his hand, leaning his head against the priest next to him and dying on the spot. He was carried straight from the table to the grave, for they buried him immediately. The will of Bishop Dalmatius was read aloud to King Childebert and his adviser. Theodosius, who was Archdeacon of Rodez at the time, was consecrated Bishop.

47.* When Chilperic heard of all the crimes which Leudast[99] kept committing against the churches and, indeed, the entire population of Tours, he sent Ansovald to the city. He arrived on the feast of Saint Martin and gave me and the people a free choice. Eunomius was elected as the new Count. When he realized that he was deposed, Leudast sought an audience with Chilperic. 'Most pious King,' he said, 'I have held the city of Tours for you until this moment. Now that I have been removed from office, you had better be told how the place is governed. You must know, for example, that Bishop Gregory has every intention of handing it over to Sigibert's son.' When he heard this, Chilperic answered: 'That is not true. You only say it because you have been dismissed.' 'The Bishop has some

99. Leudast, Count of Tours.

pretty scandalous tales to tell about you,' continued Leudast. 'Among other things, he says that your Queen is having an affair with Bishop Bertram.' King Chilperic was furious: he ordered Leudast to be punched and kicked, and then had him loaded with chains and thrown into prison.

48.* It is about time that Book V came to an end. I will round `it off by describing some of Leudast's evil deeds, but first I must tell you about his family, his place of origin and his character. There is an island off Poitou called Gracina,[100] and it was there that Leudast was born. He was the son of a certain Leucadius, a slave who looked after the vines on one of the estates. The time came for Leudast to go into service and he was given a job in the royal kitchens. His eyes were weak when he was a young man and the acrid smoke was harmful to him. He was therefore promoted from the kitchen pestle to the baker's basket. He pretended to enjoy himself amidst the fermenting dough, but eventually he abandoned his service and ran away. Two if not three times he was dragged back after escaping, but, since it was impossible to hold him, he was punished by having one of his ears slit. As there was no possibility of his concealing this mark on his body, he fled to Queen Marcovefa, whom King Charibert had married in her sister's place and whom he loved very dearly. She received Leudast with great kindness, promoted him and put him in charge of the finest horses in her stable. In consequence his conceit and arrogance became so great that he applied for the post of Master of the Stables. In this new appointment he looked down on and slighted everyone. He was as proud as a peacock, he lived an extremely loose life and there was no limit to his covetousness. As the special favourite of his protectress, he hurried here, there and everywhere to see to the Queen's affairs. When she died, his purse was already well filled from his dishonest peculations and he was thus able to bribe King Charibert to allow him to retain his post. The sins of the people of Tours were immense, and Leudast was well chosen as Count of the city. Pride of place made him even more arrogant.

100. This island has not been identified.

He feathered his own nest in the most rapacious way, was always the loudest shouter in any brawl and simply wallowed in promiscuity. When Charibert died, the city of Tours was part of the land inherited by Sigibert, but Leudast threw in his lot with Chilperic, whereupon his ill-gotten gains were looted by Sigibert's adherents. Through Chilperic's son Theudebert, the city of Tours later fell into that King's hands. I myself had only recently come to Tours and Theudebert recommended me very strongly to reappoint Leudast to the countship which he had held earlier on. Leudast behaved towards me with great humility and submissiveness. Time and time again he swore on Saint Martin's tomb that he would always act rationally and that he would stay loyal to me not only in my own affairs but also in all the vicissitudes of the church. What he dreaded most was what actually came to pass, that King Sigibert would once again take over the city. When Sigibert died, Chilperic regained control of Tours and Leudast once more became Count. When Merovech came to Tours, he seized all Leudast's property, wherever he could lay hands on it. During the two years of Sigibert's occupation of the city, Leudast had remained in hiding in Brittany. Then he was made Count again, as I have told you, and he was so beside himself that he used to walk into the church-house in his cuirass and mail shirt, with his quiver hanging round him, his javelin in his hand and his helmet on his head. He could trust no one, for he himself was every man's enemy. When he sat in court with the senior citizens to support him, some of them laymen and others churchmen, he would fly into a rage and curse the inhabitants of Tours if any one came to seek justice. He would order priests to be dragged about in manacles and have soldiers whipped with sticks: his cruelty was so great that there are no words to describe it. When Merovech, who had robbed Leudast of much of his wealth, left Tours, the Count started to calumniate me, alleging that it was on my advice that the prince had carried off his property. Having done his best to injure me, he then renewed his oath, swearing by the cloak which lay on Saint Martin's tomb that he would never again oppose my wishes.

49.* It would be tedious to relate one by one all Leudast's perjuries and other misdeeds. Let me instead move on at once to his attempt to have me expelled from my bishopric by means of unjust and wicked calumnies[101] and to how he was punished by the vengeance of God, thus fulfilling the prophecy: 'Every man that supplanteth shall be supplanted',[102] and again: 'Whoso diggeth a pit shall fall therein.'[103]

Leudast did much harm to me and mine, and he stole a vast amount of church property, too. He conspired with the priest Riculf,[104] who was about as malicious a man as he was, to accuse me of having slandered Queen Fredegund. He alleged that, if my Archdeacon Plato and my close friend Galienus were put to the torture, they would admit that I had been guilty of this slander. It was then that the King lost his temper, as I have already told you, ordered Leudast to be punched and kicked, and then had him loaded with chains and thrown into prison. Leudast said that he had this information from a sub-deacon also called Riculf, who had told him about it. This Riculf was as wayward and unprincipled a man as Leudast himself. He had started plotting with Leudast the previous year. What he needed were some grounds for taking offence, so that, once embroiled with me, he might have a pretext for going over to Leudast. He soon found these grounds, and joined his patron. For some four months he laid all manner of traps and snares for me. Then he came to see me, bringing Leudast with him, and entreated me to forgive him and to take him back. I did so, I admit: I publicly took into my household this man who was my private enemy. When Leudast had gone off, Riculf the sub-deacon threw himself at my feet. 'Unless you help me quickly,'

101. It is surely a remarkable circumstance that no mention of this most perilous moment in Gregory's whole life, when he was in great danger of deposition and exile, if not worse, should have been made in the first version of the *Historiae*, and that he should then have changed his mind and recounted it in such detail in the second version.

102. Cp. Jeremiah 9, 4.   103. Proverbs 26, 27.

104. There seem to be two men called Riculf in the conspiracy, a priest and a subdeacon.

he said, 'I shall die. Egged on by Leudast, I have said certain things which I ought not to have said. You must send me away to one of the other kingdoms. If you refuse to do this, I shall be captured by the King's men and I shall pay the penalty with my life.' 'If you really have said anything foolish,' I answered, 'your words shall be upon your own head. I will certainly not send you away to any other kingdom, for if I did I should incur King Chilperic's suspicion.' It was subsequent to this that Leudast made his accusation against the subdeacon Riculf, declaring that he had heard him discussing these matters. Leudast was set free and Riculf the subdeacon was loaded with chains and thrown into prison in his place. Riculf the subdeacon then declared that both Galienus and the Archdeacon Plato had been present when I, the Bishop, had said these things.

As for the other Riculf, the man who had already been promised by Leudast that he should succeed me in my bishopric, he was so elated that he seemed as proud as Simon Magus. Although he had sworn loyalty to me three or more times on the tomb of Saint Martin, on the sixth day of Easter week he reviled me and even spat at me, and he had great difficulty in keeping his hands off me, so sure was he of the trap which he had prepared for me. On the next day, which was Easter Saturday, Leudast came to Tours, allegedly on some other business. He arrested Galienus and the Archdeacon Plato, loaded them with chains, and paraded them before the Queen, fettered and in their underclothes. The news reached me when I was in the church-house. I was grieved and vexed in spirit. I went into my oratory and picked up the book of the Psalms of David, hoping that when I opened it I might discover some text which would give me consolation. This is what I found: 'And he led them on safely, so that they feared not: but the sea overwhelmed their enemies.'[105] Meanwhile they had begun to cross the river at a point upstream from the bridge which used to be supported on two pontoon-boats. The ferry which was carrying Leudast sank, and he would have been drowned with his companions, had he not saved himself by swimming. With God's help the second

105. Psalms 78, 53.

boat, which was attached to the first and which carried the prisoners, remained afloat. They were thereupon taken in their chains into the King's presence and accused without more ado. They were due to receive the death penalty, but the King changed his mind. He had them liberated from their bonds, but kept them under guard, unharmed but under surveillance.

Meanwhile Duke Berulf and Count Eunomius spread a rumour in Tours that King Guntram was proposing to invest the city. Berulf was thus able to say that the place must be closely guarded, for fear that something untoward might happen. They craftily posted sentinels at the gates, allegedly to protect the city, but really so that they could keep their eyes on me. They went so far as to send messengers to advise me that I should do well to take the finest treasures in my church and to try to escape in secret to Clermont-Ferrand. I did not do as they wished.

The King now convened a council of all the bishops of his kingdom and ordered the affair to be investigated thoroughly. Riculf the subdeacon was several times interrogated in secret and he told many lies about me and mine. Modestus, a carpenter, said to him: 'What a wretched creature you are, to conspire and plot against your own Bishop in this contumacious way! You would do better to keep your mouth shut, to ask your Bishop's pardon and so once more to obtain his grace.' In reply Riculf the archdeacon began to shout: 'This fellow tells me to keep my mouth shut, instead of revealing the truth! He is an enemy of the Queen, for he wants to prevent us from investigating the charge brought against her.' This event was immediately reported to Queen Fredegund. Modestus was arrested, put to the torture, beaten, loaded with chains and locked up in prison. As he sat there in his chains, between two guards and fastened to the block, midnight arrived and his guards nodded off to sleep. Modestus prayed to the Lord that in His omnipotence He would deign to visit a poor wretch who was tied up without having deserved it, and arrange for him to be freed through the intervention of Saint Martin the Bishop and Saint

318

Medard. Thereupon the chains broke asunder, the block split open, the prison-door was unlocked and Modestus marched out and into the church of Saint Medard, where I myself was that night keeping vigils.

The bishops assembled in King Chilperic's villa at Berny-Rivière, where they were all ordered to take up residence in the same building. The King arrived, he saluted all those present, they gave him their blessing and he took his seat. Then Bertram, Bishop of the city of Bordeaux, against whom, in company with the Queen, the charge had been brought, outlined the case and interrogated me, declaring that I was the author of the accusation levelled against Queen Fredegund and himself. I denied in all truth having said anything of the sort: others might have listened to such talk; as for me, the idea had never even come into my head. Outside the house there now arose an uproar among the people assembled there. 'Why are these attacks being made on the priest of the Lord?' they shouted. 'Why does the King continue with this case? Surely the Bishop would not have made such allegations, even against a slave! Alas! Alas! Lord God, come, we pray you, to the help of your servant!' The King said: 'A charge levelled against my wife is a direct insult to me. If you consider that witnesses should be called against the Bishop, they are ready and waiting. If, however, you decide that this is out of order and that we should accept the Bishop's statement, then say so. I am here to listen to your decision.' All those present wondered at the King's wisdom and restraint. They agreed unanimously to the following decision: 'It is not right to accept the evidence of an inferior against a Bishop.' The final judgement was that I should say Mass at three different altars and clear myself of the accusation by a sworn statement. These conditions were contrary to the canons, but I fulfilled them out of consideration for the King's feelings. I must add that Princess Rigunth, in her sympathy for me and my sufferings, continued fasting with the whole of her household until one of the servants came to announce that I had carried out the conditions forced upon me.[106] The bishops now reassembled in the presence of the King. 'The Bishop has done all that he has been ordered to do,' they announced. 'It is now only just that you yourself should be cut off from communion, together with Bertram, who brought the charge against his fellow-Bishop.' King Chilperic answered: 'I only repeated what I had heard.' The bishops demanded to know who had said it. The King said that he had heard the slander from Leudast. The Count had already fled, for he was a man infirm of purpose and vacillating in judgement. Then the entire assembly of bishops decreed that this sower of scandal, this slanderer of the Queen, this man who had accused his own Bishop, should be banned from all churches as a punishment for having fled from the judgement-chamber. They sent a signed letter to this effect to all bishops who were not actually present. Then they returned home to their dioceses. When Leudast heard what had happened, he sought sanctuary in the church of Saint Peter in Paris. He later learned first that the King had decreed that no man in the entire kingdom should give him lodging in his house and then that his own son, whom he had left behind at home, had died. He made his way in secret to Tours and carried away the most valuable of his possessions to somewhere near Bourges. He was pursued by men sent by the King, but he once more managed to escape. His wife was seized and sent into exile in the Tournai area. Riculf the subdeacon was condemned to death. I managed to have him reprieved, but I could not save him from the torture. Nothing, not even metal, could bear such blows as this wretched creature had to endure. From the third hour of the day he hung suspended from a tree, with his hands tied behind his back. At the ninth hour he was taken down, racked with the rope and pulley, and then beaten with sticks and staves and double leather thongs, not by one man or by two, but everyone who could come within reach of his wretched limbs. Finally, when he was within an inch of death, he revealed the truth and publicly

106. Rigunth, the daughter of King Chilperic and Queen Fredegund, was to have married Recared. She seems to have degenerated somewhat after her disappointment. Cp. *HF*, IX, 34.

confessed his secret plotting. He admitted that the accusation
had been levelled at the Queen with the aim of forcing her to
flee the kingdom. Clovis' brothers were to have been assassinated and then Clovis himself would have been made King,
while Leudast would have received a dukedom. The priest
Riculf, who from the time of Saint Eufronius the Bishop had
been the close friend of Clovis, was to have asked for the
bishopric of Tours, and he himself, Riculf the subdeacon, had
been promised the appointment of archdeacon.

By the grace of God I returned home safe to Tours. I found
my church thrown into great confusion by the priest Riculf.
This man had been raised up from very humble beginnings by
Bishop Eufronius and had been made archdeacon. When he was
promoted to the priesthood, he showed his true nature. He was
always above himself, boasting and presumptuous. While I was
away answering these charges before the King, he had the impudence to enter the church-house as if he were already
bishop. He made an inventory of the church plate and took
charge of all church property. He gave valuable presents to the
senior clergy, handing over vineyards and meadows. The lesser
clergy he rewarded with blows from sticks and even cudgels,
which he administered with his own hand, saying as he did so:
'It is I who am in charge now, for I have overcome my enemies
and with masterly skill I have purged the city of Tours of the
rabble from Clermont.' The poor fool seems not to have realized that, apart from five, all the other bishops who held their
appointment in the see of Tours were blood-relations of my
family. He often used to say to his intimate friends that the only
way of deceiving a prudent person was to perjure oneself. When
I returned to Tours, he continued to treat me with contempt.
He did not come out to receive my greeting, as all the other
citizens did, but went on threatening me and saying that he
would kill me. I took the advice of my suffragan bishops and
ordered him to be taken to a monastery. He was kept there
under close surveillance, but he escaped by telling lies to the
Abbot and with the help of people sent by Bishop Felix, who
had supported the guilty party in the case which I have just

described to you. He went to join Felix, and this Bishop, who should have held him in execration, welcomed him warmly instead. Leudast fled to the Bourges area, taking with him the fortune which he had amassed by plundering the poor. Some time later the local judge and the inhabitants of the region launched an attack on him and took back all the gold and silver which he had stolen, leaving him nothing but what he had on his person. They intended to kill him, but he escaped once more. He gathered together a band of supporters, including some from Tours, and in his turn attacked those who had despoiled him. One man was killed, but Leudast recovered some of his lost property and made his way back to Touraine. When he heard of this, Duke Berulf despatched an armed force to capture him. When Leudast saw that he was on the point of being taken, he jettisoned everything and sought sanctuary in the church of Saint Hilary in Poitiers. Duke Berulf sent the property which he had seized to the King. From time to time Leudast emerged from the church to break into the homes of various citizens and to rob them quite brazenly. He was even seen to interfere with women in the porchway of the church. Queen Fredegund, who took exception to this desecration of a place consecrated to God, ordered Leudast to be expelled from the church. He was driven out and made his way to his friends in the Bourges region and begged them to hide him.

50. I meant to tell you earlier on of a conversation which I had with Saint Salvius, the Bishop.[107] I forgot to mention it, so perhaps you will not mind if I include it here. After the council which I have described to you, I had already taken my leave of the King and was about to set off home when it occurred to me that I could not depart without saying good-bye to Salvius and exchanging an embrace with him. I looked for him in the entrance-hall of the house where he was staying in Berny-Rivière and in the end I found him. I told him that I was on the point of setting out for home. We walked a little way out of the house

107. Saint Salvius, Bishop of Albi, c. 571–84, a friend of Gregory and a very forthright person: cp. *HF*, V, 44 and VII, 1.

and stood chatting together. 'Look at the roof of that building,' said Salvius. 'Do you see what I see?' 'I see only the new tiling which the King has had put there fairly recently,' I answered. 'Can you see nothing else?' he asked. 'No,' I answered, 'I see nothing.' I was beginning to think that he was making fun of me. 'If you yourself can see anything else, tell me,' I added. He sighed deeply and said: 'I see the naked sword of the wrath of God hanging over that house.' He was not wrong in his prophecy. Twenty days later died the two sons of King Chilperic, as I have told you already.[108]

Here ends Book V, which I finished in the fifth year of King Chilperic.[109]

108. *HF*, V, 34.   109. A.D. 580.

BOOK VI

HERE BEGIN THE CHAPTER-HEADINGS OF BOOK VI

1. How Childebert formed an alliance with Chilperic. The flight of Mummolus.
2. How Chilperic's ambassadors came back from Eastern Europe.
3. How Childebert sent envoys to Chilperic.
4. How Lupus was expelled from Childebert's kingdom.
5. My dispute with a Jew.
6. Saint Hospicius the recluse: his abstinence and the miracles which he performed.
7. The death of Ferreolus, Bishop of Uzès.
8. Eparchius, the recluse of the city of Angoulême.
9. Domnolus, Bishop of Le Mans.
10. How Saint Martin's church was broken into.
11. Bishop Theodore and Dynamius.
12. An army is sent to attack Bourges.
13. How Lupus and Ambrosius, two citizens of Tours, were killed.
14. Signs and wonders.
15. The death of Bishop Felix.
16. How Pappolen rescued the woman he wanted to marry.
17. How the Jews were converted by King Chilperic.
18. How King Chilperic's ambassadors came back from Spain.
19. King Chilperic's troops on the banks of the River Orge.
20. The death of Duke Chrodin.
21. More signs and wonders.
22. Bishop Charterius.
23. How a son was born to King Chilperic.
24. How new traps were laid for Bishop Theodore. Gundovald.

25. Signs and wonders.
26. Guntram Boso and Mummolus.
27. How King Chilperic entered Paris.
28. Mark the Referendary.
29. The nuns in their convent in Poitiers.
30. The death of the Emperor Tiberius.
31. The great damage which was done to his brother's cities on the orders of King Chilperic and the devastation which he wrought himself.
32. The terrible death of Leudast.
33. Locusts, epidemics and other prodigious happenings.
34. The death of Theuderic, Chilperic's son.
35. How the Prefect Mummolus was tortured to death, after the execution of a number of housewives.
36. Bishop Aetherius.
37. The murder of Lupentius, Abbot of Javols.
38. The death of Bishop Theodosius, and the man who succeeded him.
39. The death of Bishop Remigius; his successor.
40. My dispute with a heretic.
41. How King Chilperic went off to Cambrai, taking his treasure with him.
42. Childebert's invasion of Italy.
43. The kings of Galicia.
44. More portents.
45. The engagement of Rigunth, Chilperic's daughter.
46. How King Chilperic was assassinated.

HERE END THE CHAPTER-HEADINGS

HERE BEGINS BOOK VI, WHICH GOES ON FROM THE SIXTH YEAR OF CHILDEBERT'S REIGN

1. In the sixth year of his reign[1] King Childebert broke the peace which he had made with King Guntram and formed an alliance with Chilperic. Gogo died soon afterwards and Wandelen was appointed in his place.[2] Mummolus fled from Guntram's kingdom and took refuge inside the walls of Avignon. A council of bishops was convened in Lyons: it settled a number of matters which were in dispute and punished certain people who had proved unsatisfactory. This council then went to confer with the King: for it had many decisions to make about the flight of Mummolus, and quite a few, too, about the dissensions which had arisen.

2. Meanwhile King Chilperic's ambassadors, who had set off to visit the Emperor Tiberius II[3] three full years before, came back home. They had suffered serious hardship and considerable loss on their return journey. They had not dared to put in to the port of Marseilles because of the state of war between the two Kings Guntram and Chilperic, but had steered instead for the town of Agde, which is in Visigothic territory.[4] Just as they were about to land, their ship was caught by a squall and driven ashore, where it broke up. As soon as the ambassadors and their servants realized their danger, they seized hold of some planks and so struggled to reach land. Most of them survived, but quite a few of the servants were drowned. The local inhabitants stole such of their effects as were washed

1. A.D. 581.
2. Gogo was governor or nutritor of the young King Childebert II. Cp. *HF*, V, 46.
3. In Constantinople.
4. In Septimania.

327

ashore, but the ambassadors managed to salvage the more precious objects and bring them safe to King Chilperic. The Agathais kept quite a few things for themselves.

It happened that I had recently been summoned to visit the King at his manor in Nogent-sur-Marne. He showed us a great salver, which he had had made of gold encrusted with gems and which weighed fifty pounds. 'I have had this designed for the greater glory and renown of the Frankish people,' he said. 'If it is granted to me to live, I propose to have other objects made.' Then he showed us a number of gold medallions, each weighing a pound, which the Emperor had sent to him. On the obverse side was portrayed the Emperor's bust with TYBERII CONSTANTINI PERPETVI AVGVSTI[5] in relief round the edge; on the reverse there was a chariot and a charioteer, with the legend GLORIA ROMANORVM.[6] He let us see many other precious things which the ambassadors had brought back with them.

3. While King Chilperic was still in residence at Nogent-sur-Marne, Egidius, Bishop of Rheims, arrived on an embassy, with the chief notables of Childebert's court. A conference was arranged and they made plans to deprive King Guntram of his kingdom and to draw up a treaty of alliance between Childebert and Chilperic. 'My sins have grown so great that my sons have been taken away from me,' said Chilperic. 'I have no heir left, except King Childebert, the son of my brother Sigibert. I confirm that Childebert shall inherit everything that I manage to keep under my control. All I ask is that for the term of my natural life I may be left to enjoy these things in peace and quiet.' They thanked him, ratified all that had been said and signed a treaty. They then went back to Childebert, carrying with them many gifts. King Chilperic in turn sent Bishop Leudovald[7] to Childebert, and with him the leading men of his own

5. 'Belonging to Tiberius, Emperor of Constantinople, who will live for ever.'

6. 'The fame of the Romans.'

7. Leudovald, Bishop of Bayeux.

kingdom. The treaty was confirmed, promises were sworn, and they, too, came back loaded with gifts.

4.   Lupus, Duke of Champagne, had long been harassed and despoiled by those who were hostile to him, especially Ursio and Berthefried.[8] These two now made a pact to have him killed, and they sent an army against him with that end in view. When Queen Brunhild learned of this, she was greatly incensed at the wrongs being done to her faithful supporter. With a vigour which would have become a man she rose in her wrath and took her stand between the two enemy forces. 'Stop!' she shouted. 'Warriors, I command you to stop this wicked behaviour! Stop harassing this person who has done you no harm! Stop fighting each other and bringing disaster upon our country, just because of this one man!' 'Stand back, woman!' answered Ursio, when he heard her. 'It should be enough that you held regal power when your husband was alive. Now your son is on the throne, and his kingdom is under our control, not yours. Stand back, I say, or you will be trodden into the ground by our horses' hoofs!' For some time they shouted orders at each other, but in the end the Queen prevailed and stopped the conflict. No sooner had they left the scene than the two broke into the houses belonging to Lupus and stole all his property. They made a pretence of handing this over to the King's treasury, but in effect they carried it off to their own homes. They kept threatening Lupus. 'He won't escape alive from our forces,' they said. Lupus saw his peril: he left his wife safe inside the walls of Laon and himself took refuge with King Guntram, who received him kindly. He remained there in hiding with the King, only waiting for the time when Childebert should come of age.

5.   King Chilperic, who was still at Nogent-sur-Marne, sent his

8. Lupus, Duke of Champagne, was a faithful supporter of King Childebert II, his mother Queen Brunhild and their party. Ursio and Berthefried were leaders of the aristocratic party, which was determined to permit no increase in the royal power.

baggage on ahead and made plans to travel to Paris. I had gone
to take leave of him, when there came in a Jew called Priscus,
who was on familiar terms with the King, having acted as his
agent for scme of the purchases which he had made. The King
put his hand on the Jew's head in a kindly way and said to me:
'Come along, Bishop, put your hand on him, too.' The man
drew back. 'O faithless and perverse generation,'[9] said the
King, 'why can you not comprehend what has been promised to
you by the words of the prophets? You cannot accept that the
mysteries of the Church were foreshadowed in the sacrifices of
your own race.' The Jew replied: 'God has no need of a Son, He
has not provided Himself with a Son and He does not brook
any consort in His kingdom, for He said through the mouth of
Moses: "See now that I, even I, am he, and there is no god with
me: I kill, and I make alive; I wound, and I heal." '[10] 'God
brought forth from the womb of the spirit His own eternal
Son,' answered the King, 'no younger than Himself in time, and
no less than Himself in power, of whom He said: "From the
womb of the morning have I begotten thee."'[11] This Son, born
before all ages, He sent in later times to heal the world, as your
own prophet said: "He sent his word, and healed them." As for
your own statement, that He did not provide Himself with a
Son, listen now to another of your own prophets, who puts
these words into God's mouth: "Shall I bring to the birth, and
not cause to bring forth?"'[12] This He said of the people which is
born in Him by faith.' The Jew replied: 'How should God be
made man, or be born of woman, or submit to stripes, or be
condemned to death?'

At this the King was silent, so I took up the debate in my
turn. 'The fact that God, the Son of God, was made man', I
said, 'resulted from our own necessity, not His. For had He not
been made flesh, He could not have redeemed man from the
captivity of sin, or from his servitude to the Devil. Just as we
read that of old David slew Goliath, so will I pierce you with
your own sword, producing my proof not from the Gospels, nor

9. Matthew 17, 17.   10. Deuteronomy 32, 39.
11. Cp. Psalms 110, 3.   12. Isaiah 66, 9.

from an apostle, neither of which you believe, but from your own Scriptures. Listen to one of your own prophets foretelling that God should be made man: "He is both God and man," he says, "and who has known Him?" In another place we read: "This is our God, and there shall none other be accounted in comparison with Him, for He hath found out all the way of knowledge, and hath given it unto Jacob His servant, and to Israel His beloved. Afterwards did He show Himself upon earth, and conversed with men."[13] As proof that He was born of the Virgin, listen to the statement by another of your prophets: "Behold, a virgin shall conceive and bear a son, and shall call his name Immanuel, which being interpreted is, God with us."[14] Another prophet makes it clear that He must submit to stripes, be pierced with nails and endure other insults: "They pierced my hands and my feet; they parted my garments among them,"[15] and so on. Elsewhere the same prophet says: "They gave me also gall for my meat; and in my thirst they gave me vinegar to drink."[16] To make clear that through the gibbet of the Cross He should restore to His kingdom the world which was sinking beneath the Devil's rule, David then says: "The Lord hath reigned from the Cross."[17] Not that He had not reigned before, in company with the Father, but now He accepted a new and unaccustomed domination over the people whom He had delivered from their servitude to the Devil.' The Jew replied: 'What need was there for God to suffer these things?' 'I have told you already,' I answered, 'that man was innocent when God created him. Man was ensnared by the serpent's guile and encouraged to break God's command. That is why he was cast out of Paradise and condemned to all the travails of this earth. By the death of Christ, the only Son of the Father, he was reconciled with God.' The Jew replied: 'Could not God have sent prophets or apostles to recall man to the way of salvation, without being Himself humbled in the flesh?' 'The

13. Baruch 3, 36 and 3, 38.　　　14. Isaiah 7, 14 and Matthew 1, 23.
15. Psalms 22, 16, 18.　　16. Psalms 69, 21.
17. Cp. Psalms 96, 10. These words 'from the Cross' were the subject of never-ending disputes between Christians and Jews.

human race was given to sin from the very beginning,' I answered. 'The Flood did not frighten man, nor the burning of Sodom, nor the plagues of Egypt, nor the miracle of the sea and the Jordan dividing their waters. He continued to resist God's commandment and he refused to believe the prophets; more than that, he not only disbelieved but he actually put to death all those who preached repentance. If God Himself had not come down from heaven to redeem him, by no other means could this redemption have been accomplished. We were reborn by His baptism, cured by His wound, raised up by His resurrection, glorified by His ascension. As your own prophet says, there was every need for Him to come to heal our infirmities: "And with his stripes we are healed."[18] He goes on: "He shall bear the sin of many, and make intercession for the transgressors."[19] Then he says: "He is brought as a lamb to the slaughter, and as a sheep before her shearers is dumb, so he openeth not his mouth. He was taken from prison and from judgement: and who has declared his generation? The Lord of hosts is his name."[20] It is about Him that Jacob speaks, that same Jacob from whom you proudly claim your descent, when he blesses his son, Judah, as if he were addressing Christ, the Son of God, in person: "Thy father's children shall bow down before thee. Judah is a lion's whelp: from the seed, my son, thou art gone up: thou stooped down, thou couched as a lion, and as a young lion; who hath raised him up? His eyes shall be fairer than wine and his teeth whiter than milk. Who", he asks again, "hath raised him up?"[21] Although Christ Himself has said: "I have power to lay my life down, and I have power to take it again,"[22] the Apostle Paul maintains: "Who shall not believe in his heart that God hath raised him from the dead, shall not be saved." '[23]

Despite all my arguments, this wretched Jew felt no remorse and showed no sign of believing me. Instead, he just stood there in silence. The King realized that he could not be moved to compunction, whatever we said. He turned to me and told me

18. Isaiah 53, 5.   19. Isaiah 53, 12.   20. Isaiah 53, 7–8 and 54, 5.
21. Genesis 49, 8–9 and 12.   22. John 10, 18.   23. Romans 10, 9.

that he must go, but he asked my blessing first. 'Bishop,' he said, 'I will say to you what Jacob said to the angel who spoke with him: "I will not let thee go, except thou bless me."[24] As he said this, he ordered water to be brought. We washed our hands, and I said a prayer. I then took bread, gave thanks to God, received it myself and gave it to the King. We drank the wine and parted, saying farewell to each other. King Chilperic climbed on his horse and set off for Paris, with his wife, his daughter and all his household.

6. At this time there lived near the town of Nice a recluse called Hospicius.[25] He was a man of great abstinence, who had iron chains wound round his body, next to the skin, and wore a hair-shirt on top. He ate nothing but dry bread and a few dates. In the month of Lent he fed on the roots of Egyptian herbs, which merchants brought home for him. Hermits are greatly addicted to these. First he drank the water in which they were boiled, and then he would eat the herbs themselves. The Lord deigned to perform remarkable miracles through the agency of Hospicius. Once the Holy Ghost revealed to him the coming of the Longobards into Gaul. His prophecy went as follows: 'The Longobards', he said, 'will invade Gaul and they will destroy seven cities, because the wickedness of those cities has grown great in the eyes of the Lord. No one in them understands God, no one seeks Him, no one does good in order to appease the wrath of God. The entire populace is without faith, given to perjury, prone to theft, quick to commit murder: and no justice can be seen to flourish among them. They do not pay their tithes, they do not feed the poor, they do not clothe the naked: no hospitality is offered there to strangers, and they are not even given enough to eat. As a result disaster is on its way to these people. I therefore tell you: Collect all your property together inside your walls, for otherwise the Longobards will steal it. Fortify yourselves in the strongest places you can find.' Every-

24. Genesis 32, 26.
25. His name is preserved in Pointe de Saint-Hospice, a promontory near Nice.

one was amazed at what Hospicius said. They bade him farewell and hurried off home in great perturbation. Then he spoke
to his monks. 'Leave this place immediately,' he said, 'and take
all your possessions with you. The people about whom I have
told you are already approaching.' 'We cannot abandon you,
holy father,' they answered. 'Have no fear for me,' he said.
'They will do me harm, it is true, but they will not kill me.' The
monks ran off and the Longobards arrived. They destroyed
everything that they could lay their hands on, and came eventually to the spot where the holy man of God lived as a recluse.
He showed himself to them through a window in his tower.
They marched round and round the tower, but they could find
no entrance through which they could come to him. Two of
them climbed up and tore a hole in the roof. When they saw
Hospicius wrapped round with chains and wearing a hair-shirt,
they exclaimed: 'Why, this is a criminal! He must have murdered someone. That is why he has chains tied round him.' An
interpreter was called and they asked Hospicius what he had
done to merit such punishment. He confessed that he had committed murder and that he was guilty of every crime in the
calendar. One of the Longobards drew his sword and made
ready to cut off the recluse's head. His right hand was paralysed in mid air as he dealt the blow, and he was unable to draw
it back to his side. He dropped his sword and let it fall to the
ground. At the sight of this his comrades gave a great shout,
beseeching the holy man to tell them what they should do next.
Hospicius made the sign of the Cross over the soldier's arm and
it became whole again. The man was converted on the spot: his
head was tonsured, and he became one of Hospicius' most
faithful monks. Two of the Longobard leaders, who had
listened to what he said, returned home to their country safe
and sound. The others, who had nothing but scorn for his warnings, died miserably in Provence. Many of them were possessed
by demons and kept shouting: 'Holy man, most blessed man,
why do you torture and burn us in this way?' He laid his hand
upon them and cured them.

Some time afterwards there was an inhabitant of Angers who

developed a very high temperature and lost the power of speech and hearing. He recovered from his fever, but he remained deaf and dumb. A deacon was about to set out for Rome from this region, to bring back relics of the blessed Apostles and other saints who watch over that city. When the sick man's parents heard of this, they asked the deacon to be so good as to take their son with him on his journey, for if only he could visit the tombs of the blessed Apostles he would immediately be cured. The two set off together and came at length to the spot where Saint Hospicius lived. The deacon saluted him and gave him the kiss of peace. He explained the reasons for their journey and said that he was on his way to Rome. He asked the holy man to give him an introduction to any local sailors whom he might know. Just before they left, Hospicius felt miraculous powers rising in him through the Spirit of our Lord. He said to the deacon: 'Show me, please, this afflicted person who is travelling with you.' The deacon hurried off to his lodging and found the invalid, who was once more suffering from a high temperature. The man made signs that there was a tremendous ringing in his ears. The deacon seized his arm and rushed him off to the Saint. Hospicius laid his hand on the man's hair and pulled his head in through the window. He took some oil, consecrated it, held the man's tongue tight in his left hand and poured the oil down his throat and over the top of his head. 'In the name of my Lord Jesus Christ,' he said, 'may your ears be unsealed and your mouth opened, by that miraculous power which once cast out the evil spirit from the man who was deaf and dumb.' As he said this, he asked the man what his name was. 'I am called so-and-so,' he answered, enunciating the words clearly. When the deacon saw what had happened, he said: 'I thank you from the bottom of my heart, Jesus Christ, for having deigned to reveal such a miracle by the hand of your servant. I was on my way to Peter, I was going to Paul and Lawrence, and all the others who have glorified Rome with their blood. I have found them all here, in this very spot I have discovered them.' As he said this, he wept and was filled with wonder. The man of God took no empty credit to himself. 'Be quiet, dear brother,' he said. 'It is not I who do this, but He who created the world out of nothing, who was made man for our salvation, He who makes the blind to see, the deaf to hear, the dumb to speak, who restores the skin which they have lost to the leprous, and finds a soothing remedy for all who are sick.' The deacon bade Hospicius farewell and went on his way rejoicing with his companions.

When they had gone, a man called Dominicus – and this time I give you his real name – who had been blind from birth, came to put to the test this miraculous power. He stayed in the near-by monastery for two or three months, spending all his time in prayer and fasting. Then Hospicius summoned him. 'Do you wish to gain your sight?' he asked. 'It has always been my wish to learn about things which are unknown to me,' answered Dominicus. 'I do not know what light is. One thing I am sure of, and that is that everyone who sees it praises it highly. As for me, from the day I was born until now I have never possessed the power of sight.' Hospicius consecrated some oil, and made the sign of the Cross over his eyes with it. 'May your eyes open,' he said, 'in the name of Jesus Christ our Redeemer.' The man's eyes opened immediately, and he stood lost in admiration as he gazed on the wonderful works of God, which he was seeing for the first time in this world.

Some time later there was brought to Hospicius a woman who, on her own admission, was possessed of three devils. He laid his hand on her and blessed her, marking the sign of the Cross on her brow with consecrated oil. The devils were driven out and the woman went away cured. By his blessing he cured another girl who was harassed by an unclean spirit.

As the day of his death drew near, Hospicius called the prior of the monastery to him. 'Bring a crow-bar,' he said, 'break through the wall, and send messengers to the Bishop of the city of Nice, so that he may come and bury me. Three days from now I shall leave this world and go to my appointed rest, which the Lord has promised to me.' As Hospicius said this, the prior of the monastery sent his men to the Bishop of Nice to give him the news. Meanwhile a certain Crescens came to the window. When he saw the chains round Hospicius' body, which was alive with worms, he said: 'My lord, how can you bear such terrible torments?' Hospicius replied: 'He in whose name I endure these sufferings offers me comfort. I tell you, I am being released from these chains and I am going to my rest.' On the third day he removed the chains which were bound round him and knelt in prayer. When he had prayed and wept for a long time, he lay down upon a bench, stretched out his feet, raised his hands to heaven, rendered thanks to God and so gave up the ghost. All the worms which had eaten into his saintly limbs immediately disappeared. Bishop Austadius came[26] and committed the Saint's body to the grave. I heard all this from the mouth of the deaf and dumb man who, as I have told you, was cured by Hospicius. This man told me many other stories about the miracles performed by Hospicius, but I decided not to set them down, because I heard that his life had been written by many others.[27]

7.* At this time died Ferreolus, Bishop of Uzès, a man of great sanctity. He was a learned person, given to intellectual pursuits, and he had composed a number of volumes of Letters,[28] in the style of Sidonius,[29] one might say. After the death of Ferreolus, the ex-Governor Albinus took over the bishopric, with the backing of Dynamius, who had become Governor in his place, but without the approval of the King. Albinus was Bishop for three months only. A move was being made to eject him, when he died. Next Jovinus, who was another ex-Governor of Provence, received the King's nomination to the see. The deacon Marcellus, son of Felix, who was of a senatorial family, forestalled him. The bishops of the diocese assembled and, with the full approval of Dynamius, Marcellus was consecrated. He was attacked by Jovinus, who wanted to have him deposed. He was besieged in his own city, where he defended himself valiantly. He was not strong enough to beat Jovinus, so he bought him off with bribes.

26. Austadius, Bishop of Nice.
27. No *Vita Sancti Hospicii* has come down to us.
28. These letters have not been preserved.
29. Sidonius Apollinaris, Bishop of Clermont-Ferrand, A.D. 472–c. 488

8.* Eparchius, the recluse of Angoulême, was the next to die.[30] He, too, was a person of great sanctity, and God performed many miracles through his agency. He was originally an inhabitant of Périgueux, but, after his conversion and his ordination as a priest, he went to Angoulême and built himself a cell there. He collected a few monks around him and passed his time in continuous prayer. Whenever gold or silver was offered to him, he would spend it in suppying the needs of the poor or in freeing people from prison. As long as he lived bread was never baked in his cell, for, as need arose, it was supplied by those who came there to worship. Eparchius arranged for the freeing of a great number of prisoners by using the alms and oblations of the faithful. By making the sign of the Cross over them he would destroy the poison in malignant boils, by prayer he would cast out evil spirits from bodies which were possessed, and many a time he persuaded judges to pardon the accused, more by his power of sweet reasonableness than by violent pleading. He begged so charmingly that when he asked for leniency they could refuse him nothing.

Once a man was being led off to be hanged for theft, an habitual criminal, who was considered by the locals to be guilty of many other offences, robberies, and murders, too. Eparchius heard all this and he sent one of his monks to beg the Count concerned to grant him the man's life, however guilty he might be. The mob began to demonstrate: if this man were freed, they shouted, it would be the end of law and order in the district and the Count would lose all authority. It was therefore not possible to free him. He was tortured on the rack, beaten with sticks and cudgels, and condemned to be hanged. The monk returned and sadly reported this to Eparchius. 'Back you go,' he said. 'Don't approach too near, but stay there. The Lord in His loving kindness will grant me this fellow-creature whom man has refused to surrender. When you see him fall, pick him up and bring him back to me in the monastery.' The monk did as he was told. Eparchius knelt in prayer and for a long time addressed himself to God, weeping as he did so. Thereupon the gibbet collapsed,

30. Cp. *GC*, 98.

the chains were broken and the hanged man fell to the ground. The monk picked him up and took him back safe and sound to the abbot. Eparchius gave thanks to God. Then he had the Count summoned. 'My dear son,' said he, 'you have always listened sympathetically to what I have had to say. Why were you so adamant today, when you refused to pardon the man whose life I asked you to save?' 'I am always ready to listen to you, saintly priest,' replied the Count, 'but today the mob staged a demonstration and I could not do what you asked, for I had a riot on my hands.' 'You did not listen,' answered Eparchius, 'but God deigned to listen. The man whom you handed over for execution He restored to life. You see him there, where he stands unharmed.' As Eparchius said this, the condemned man flung himself at the feet of the Count, who was quite stupefied when he saw still alive one whom he had last seen suffering execution. This story was told to me by the Count himself.

Eparchius did many other things which I have no space to relate to you. When he had been a recluse for forty-four years he fell ill of a fever and died. They carried him out of his cell and buried him. A great crowd of people whom he had freed from the clutches of the law, as I have told you, walked in his funeral procession.

9.* Soon after this Domnolus, the Bishop of Le Mans, fell ill.[31] During the reign of King Lothar he had been the head of a monastic community in Saint Lawrence's church in Paris. As long as Childebert I lived, Domnolus remained faithful to Lothar, and he often concealed the emissaries which that King sent to Paris to find out what was happening there. To reward him, Lothar wanted to find a diocese to which Domnolus would accept election as bishop. The Bishop of Avignon died, so Lothar planned to offer him that see. Domnolus heard of it, and made his way to the church of Saint Martin, where King Lothar had come to worship. Domnolus himself spent the whole night there in prayer and vigil, and then intimated to the King,

31. Domnolus, Bishop of Le Mans, A.D. c. 559–81.

through some of his leading courtiers, that he had no wish whatsoever to be banished from his presence, as if he had done something wrong; he looked upon being sent to Avignon as a humiliation rather than an honour, and he begged the King not to submit him, a simple man, to the boredom of having to listen to sophisticated arguments by old senatorial families, or to counts who spent all their time discussing philosophic problems.[32] Lothar agreed, and when Innocentius, Bishop of Le Mans, died, he appointed Domnolus to that diocese instead. From the day he took over the bishopric, he revealed himself as a man distinguished by extreme holiness, restoring the use of his limbs to a lame man and his sight to one who was blind. When he had occupied the bishopric for twenty-two years, he realized that he was seriously ill with jaundice and stone in the kidneys, and he chose Abbot Theodulf as his successor. The King agreed to this, but later on he changed his mind and had Badegisil,[33] Mayor of the Palace,[34] elected instead. Badegisil was tonsured and promoted through the various ranks of the church, so that, when Domnolus died some six weeks later, he could be ordained Bishop.

10.* About this time Saint Martin's church was broken into by thieves. They took a railing which was over the tomb of someone who had died, set it against a window in the apse, climbed up, broke the glass and made an entrance. They stole a deal of gold and silverware, with some silken cloths, and then made off, having gone so far as to walk on the Saint's tomb, which we ourselves hesitate to touch even with our lips. In his miraculous power Saint Martin made a terrible example of these reckless men. After committing their crime they fled to the city of Bordeaux, where they quarrelled and one was killed

32. Cp. Introduction, p. 47.
33. Cp. *HF*, VIII, 39.
34. This is supposed to be the first mention of the functionary called Mayor of the Palace, Domus regiae Maior. Pepin the Short was Mayor of the Palace when he deposed Childeric III, the last of the Merovingians, in 754, and so had been his father Charles Martel and his grandfather Pepin of Herstal.

by a comrade. In this way the outrage became public knowledge and the stolen goods were discovered: for the silken cloths
were found in their lodging, and the silverware, too, although it
had been broken up. King Chilperic heard of this and he
ordered the malefactors to be bound and brought before him. I
was afraid that these men might be put to death because of the
very Saint who while he was on earth had so often begged for
the life of condemned criminals: so I sent a letter to the King
beseeching him not to have them executed, and saying that we,
who must make the charge, proposed not to do so. He accepted
what I said and spared their lives. The stolen goods had been
scattered, but he had them collected together with great care
and ordered them to be restored to the church.

11.* In the town of Marseilles Dynamius, the Governor of
Provence, began to lay traps for Bishop Theodore.[35] The
Bishop was on the point of hurrying off to King Childebert
when he was arrested by the Governor and locked up inside his
own city. In the end he was released, but only after he had been
gravely insulted. The clergy of Marseilles plotted with Dynamius to have Theodore expelled from his diocese. When he was
on his way to King Childebert, he was detained on the order of
King Guntram, and the ex-Governor Jovinus with him. The
clergy of Marseilles were delighted when they heard this news,
for if their Bishop was apprehended, he would no doubt be sent
into exile, and things had come to such a pass that he would
never return to the city. They took command of the church-
houses, drew up an inventory of the plate, broke open the
chests, pillaged the strong-rooms and made free with all church
property, just as if the Bishop were already dead. They levelled
a great number of criminal charges against Theodore, but, with
the help of Jesus Christ, these were later proved false.

Now that he had made peace with Chilperic, Childebert sent
envoys to King Guntram to say that he must return that half of
Marseilles which Childebert had given to him after the death of
his father. If Guntram would not agree, he must know that

35. Theodore, Bishop of Marseilles, A.D. 566–94.

holding on to this half of the city would cost him dear. Guntram refused. He had the roads blocked, so that no one should
find the way open to cross his kingdom. When Childebert
learned this, he sent to Marseilles Gundulf, a man of senatorial
family, who had once held a lowly position in the royal household but who had been made a Duke. Gundulf was afraid to
make his way through Guntram's kingdom, so he came to
Tours. I received him kindly, the more so as I realized that he
was my mother's uncle. I put him up for five days, provided him
with all that he needed, and then let him go on his way. He
continued his journey, but he was not able to enter Marseilles,
for Dynamius stood in his way. Bishop Theodore joined Gundulf, but he, too, could not return to his cathedral. With the
support of the clergy Dynamius blocked the city gates, jeering
at the two of them, Bishop and Duke alike, and pouring scorn
on them. In the end Dynamius was summoned to a conference
with Duke Gundulf, and came to Saint Stephen's church, which
is just outside Marseilles. The church doors were guarded by
bedels, who had instructions to close them the moment Dynamius went in. This was done, so that the troop of armed men
who accompanied him was shut outside and could not get in.
Dynamius was unaware of what had happened. They discussed
their various problems at the altar, and then drew back and
passed into the sacristy. Dynamius, who had none of his supporters at hand to protect him, was fiercely assailed as he went
in. Meanwhile his troops, who were cut off from their leader,
marched up and down outside and made a show of using their
weapons, but they were driven off. Duke Gundulf assembled
the more important among the citizens and prepared to enter
Marseilles in company with the Bishop. When he saw this,
Dynamius sought their pardon, loading the Duke with presents
and swearing that in future he would be loyal to the Bishop and
to the King. They gave him back all his equipment. The city
gates were opened once more, and the church doors, too. Duke
Gundulf and Bishop Theodore entered Marseilles, with the
bells ringing, the crowd shouting and the flags waving in their
honour. The local clergy, who had been involved in this revolt,

with their ringleaders, Abbot Anastasius and a priest called
Proculus, took refuge in Dynamius' house, seeking help from
the man who had egged them on. Many of them were pardoned,
but only after paying considerable fines, and even then they
were ordered to go and explain themselves to the King. Once he
had returned the city to Childebert's jurisdiction and restored
the Bishop to his see, Gundulf made his way back to the King's
court.

Dynamius soon forgot that he had sworn to remain loyal to
King Childebert. He sent envoys to Guntram to say that
through the machinations of Bishop Theodore the King would
surely lose that part of Marseilles which belonged to him, and
that he could never hope to hold the city in his power unless he
first expelled this prelate. Guntram was furious. He behaved in
the most impious way. He had this high priest of the Lord God
bound and brought before him. 'This enemy of my kingdom
must be driven into exile,' he said, 'and so prevented from doing
me any more harm.' The Bishop knew what they were planning
to do, and it was clearly going to be no easy matter to force him
out of his city. Then came the dedicatory ceremony of a rural
oratory outside the city walls. Theodore had emerged from
Marseilles, and was leading the procession towards this festival,
when with a great hue and cry a band of armed men suddenly
appeared from an ambush and surrounded him. They knocked
him off his horse, put all his companions to flight, tied up his
servants, beat his clergy, and then placed him on a miserable old
nag and set off with him to King Guntram's court, forbidding
any of the others to follow them. As they passed by Aix, the
Bishop of that city, whose name was Pientius, took pity on his
fellow-churchman and sent his own clergy out to succour him.
He provided Theodore with all that he lacked and only then let
him continue on his way. While all this was going on, the clergy
in Marseilles once more invaded the church-houses, pried into
all the church secrets, made inventories of some of what they
found and carried the rest off to their own homes. Bishop Theodore was brought before King Guntram, but he was found not
guilty. He was allowed to return home and he was again wel-

comed joyfully by his people. As a result a great quarrel arose between King Guntram and his nephew Childebert. They broke off their alliance, and began to set traps for each other.

12. When King Chilperic saw how frequently these disagreements kept occurring between his brother and his nephew, he summoned Duke Desiderius and ordered him to launch a particularly savage attack upon King Guntram. Desiderius put an army into the field, beat Duke Ragnovald and made him seek safety in flight, and then occupied Périgueux. He exacted an oath of loyalty from the Périgourdins and then marched on Agen. As soon as Ragnovald's wife realized that, now that her husband had been forced to flee, this city in its turn must fall into the hands of King Chilperic, she sought sanctuary in the church of the martyr Saint Caprasius.[36] She was forced to come out, they robbed her of all her possessions, took away her servants, and only allowed her to set out for Toulouse when she had paid over a sum of money as a surety. She took up residence in the church of Saint Saturninus in that city. Desiderius captured all the other cities which owed allegiance to King Guntram in the region and handed them over to Chilperic.

Duke Berulf learned that the men of Bourges were planning to invade the district round Tours. He marched his army in that direction and occupied the area. The territory round Yzeures and Barrou, which are near the city of Tours, was completely devastated. Later on all those who had not been able to take part in Berulf's expedition were cruelly punished.

Duke Bladast marched into Gascony and lost the greater part of his army.

13.* Lupus, a citizen of Tours, who had lost both his wife and his children, wanted to enter the church. His brother Ambrosius was against this, for he was afraid that, once Lupus had joined it, he might leave all his goods to the Church of God. This brother who was so ready with wrong advice found a second wife for Lupus and fixed a day on which they should meet to

36. Saint Caprasius, martyred in Agen with Sainte Foy in A.D. 303.

exchange wedding-presents. The two of them went off to the town of Chinon, where they had a house. The wife of Ambrosius, who hated him and was consoling herself by having an adulterous relationship with another man, laid a trap for her husband. The two brothers had supper together, and then spent the rest of the evening in a drinking-bout, with the result that they became completely intoxicated. They lay down to sleep in the same bed. In the night, when everyone was fast asleep, and completely drunk into the bargain, the lover of Ambrosius' wife came creeping in. He lit a handful of straw, so that he could see what he was doing. Then he drew his sword and hit Ambrosius over the head. The blow struck him straight across the eyes and severed his head from his neck. Lupus was awakened by the impact and found himself wallowing in blood. 'A terrible thing has happened!' he shouted. 'Come quickly! My brother has been murdered!' The lover, who had completed his crime, was already making himself scarce, but when he heard this he came back to the bed and attacked Lupus. Lupus tried to fight him off, but his assailant was too much for him and gashed him in a great number of places. In the end he dealt Lupus a blow from which he could not possibly recover, and left him more dead than alive. No one in the household heard anything. Day dawned and they were terrified at the crime which it revealed. Lupus was found still alive: he told them what had happened and then breathed his last. The unfaithful wife did not waste too much time in mourning. A few days later she joined her lover and they left the neighbourhood.

14. In the seventh year of King Childebert's reign,[37] which was the twenty-first of both Chilperic and Guntram, there were torrential downpours in the month of January, with flashes of lightning and heavy claps of thunder. The trees suddenly burst into flower. The star which I have described as a comet appeared again, and the sky seemed particularly black where it passed across the heavens. It shone through the darkness as if it were at the bottom of a hole, gleaming so bright and spreading

37. A.D. 582.

wide its tail. From it there issued an enormous beam of light, which from a distance looked like the great pall of smoke over a conflagration. It appeared in the western sky during the first hour of darkness.

In the city of Soissons on Easter Sunday the whole sky seemed to catch fire. There appeared to be two centres of light, one of which was bigger than the other: but after an hour or two they joined together to become one single enormous beacon, and then they disappeared.

In the Paris region real blood rained from a cloud, falling on the clothes of quite a number of people and so staining them with gore that they stripped them off in horror. This portent was observed in three different places in that city. In the Senlis area a man woke up one morning to find the whole of the inside of his house spattered with blood.

This year the people suffered from a terrible epidemic; and great numbers of them were carried off by a whole series of malignant diseases, the main symptoms of which were boils and tumours. Quite a few of those who took precautions managed to escape. We learned that a disease of the groin was very prevalent in Narbonne this same year, and that, once a man was attacked by it, it was all up with him.

15.* Felix, Bishop of the city of Nantes, contracted this disease and became gravely ill. He summoned the other bishops of the region to him and begged them to put their signatures to the proposals which he had drafted in favour of his nephew Burgundio. When they had signed, they sent Burgundio to me. He was then about twenty-five years old. He arrived with a request that I should travel all the way to Nantes, give him the tonsure and consecrate him as bishop in succession to his uncle, who was still alive. I refused to do anything of the sort. It contravened the canons, anyway. I gave Burgundio the following advice: 'It is set out here in the canons, my dear boy, that no one can be consecrated as a bishop until he has first passed through the various ranks of the Church in the normal way. You had better go back to Nantes and ask the person who is spon-

soring you to give you the tonsure. Once you have been found
worthy of admission to the priesthood, apply yourself seriously
to all that the Church asks of you. When God decides that the
moment has come to remove your uncle the Bishop to a better
world, it may well be that you yourself will be given episcopal
rank.' Burgundio went back home. He made no attempt to
follow my advice, probably because Bishop Felix seemed to be
recovering somewhat from his illness. His fever abated, but as
the result of his low state of health his legs were covered with
tumours. He applied a plaster of cantharides, but it was too
strong. His legs festered and so he died in the thirty-third year
of his episcopate, when he was seventy years old. At the King's
command, his cousin Nonnichius succeeded him.

16. When Pappolen heard that Felix was dead, he came to
seek the Bishop's niece, from whom he had been separated.
Some time earlier she had become engaged to him, but, as
Bishop Felix did not approve of the proposed marriage, Pappolen suddenly appeared with a great number of his supporters,
abducted the girl from an oratory, and took sanctuary with her
in the church of Saint Albinus. This annoyed Bishop Felix very
much. By some trick or other he managed to separate the girl
from the man she wanted to marry. He made her put on the
habit of a religious and shut her up in a nunnery at Bazas. She
thereupon sent some of her servants to Pappolen in secret,
asking him to rescue her from where she was locked up and to
make her his. He was only too willing to do this. He organized
her escape from the nunnery, and married her. He had the
King's formal approval, so that she was able to disregard the
threats of her relations.

17. In this year King Chilperic ordered a great number of
Jews to be baptized. He went so far as to help some of them out
of the baptismal pool himself. Washed clean as they were in a
bodily sense, some of them were not cleansed in their hearts,
and they clung to the beliefs to which they had always sub-
scribed. They lied to God, for they still observed the Jewish

Sabbath while appearing to honour the Lord's Day. Priscus in particular could not by any persuasion be induced to accept the truth. The King was furious and ordered him to be locked up, saying that if he would not believe of his own free will he should be compelled to listen and to believe despite himself. By handing over bribes, Priscus managed to gain a respite until his son had married a Jewess in Marseilles, promising that he would then do as the King ordered, although he had no intention of giving in. Meanwhile a great quarrel arose between Priscus and a certain Phatyr, one of the converted Jews, who was godson to the King in that Chilperic had sponsored him at his baptism. One Jewish Sabbath Priscus was on his way to the synagogue, with his head bound in a kerchief and carrying no weapon in his hand, for he was about to pray according to the Mosaic law. Phatyr appeared from nowhere, drew his sword, cut Priscus' throat and killed his companions. When they all lay dead, Phatyr took refuge in the church of Saint Julian, together with his servants who had been waiting in a near-by square. There they remained in sanctuary, but they heard that the King, while prepared to spare their master's life, had given orders that they themselves should be dragged out of the church and executed. One of them drew his word. Phatyr immediately fled, but the man killed all his associates and rushed out of the church, with his weapon still in his hand. The mob fell upon him and he was cruelly done to death. Phatyr received permission to return to Guntram's kingdom, whence he had come. A few days later he was killed in his turn by some of the relations of Priscus.

18. Ansovald and Domigisel, King Chilperic's ambassadors, who had been sent to Spain to look into the question of the dowry promised to Princess Rigunth, arrived back home. At this time King Leuvigild was leading his army against his own son Hermangild, from whom he captured the city of Merida.[38] I have already told you how this prince had made an alliance with the generals of the Emperor Tiberius. All this delayed the ambassadors and they came back later than was expected.

38. A.D. 582.

When I met them I was keen to discover whether there was still any zeal for the Christian faith among the few Catholics who still remained in that country. Ansovald gave me the following information: 'Those Catholics who still exist in Spain keep their faith unimpaired. The King has a new trick by which he is doing his utmost to destroy it. In his cunning way he pretends to pray at the tombs of the martyrs and in the churches of our religion. Then he says: "I accept without question that Christ is the Son of God and equal to the Father. What I cannot believe is that the Holy Ghost is God, for that is written in none of the Scriptures." ' How depressing this is! What a wicked argument! What a poisonous belief! How depraved his mind must be! What of the saying of our Lord: 'God is a Spirit'?[39] What of the words of Peter to Ananias: 'Why hath Satan filled thine heart to lie to the Holy Ghost? Thou hast not lied unto men, but unto God.'[40] What also of the words of Paul, when he reminds us of the mystical gifts of God: 'But all these worketh that one and the selfsame Spirit, dividing to every man severally as he will?'[41] Anyone who does exactly what he wishes is plainly in subjection to none. After Ansovald had come home and reported to King Chilperic, there arrived a party of Spanish envoys. They came to Chilperic first and then visited Childebert. After this they went back to Spain.

19. King Chilperic had guards posted on the bridge over the River Orge, near the city of Paris. His purpose was to prevent infiltrators from his brother's kingdom from coming to do him harm. Asclepius, who was once a Duke, knew about the guards. He made a night attack and killed every one of them, doing great damage to the region round the bridge. This was announced to King Chilperic, and he sent messengers to his counts, dukes and other representatives, telling them to collect an army and invade his brother's kingdom. On the advice of certain of his wiser counsellors, he was persuaded to change his plan. 'These men have acted foolishly,' they said, 'but you should be more sensible. Send envoys to your brother to say

39. John 4, 24.   40. Acts 5, 3–4.   41. I Corinthians 12, 11.

that if he is prepared to make good this damage you will not attack in return; but if he refuses, then you will take such action as you think fit.' Chilperic listened to what they said. He recalled his troops and sent an embassy to King Guntram, who made complete amends and asked for his brother's friendship.

20. Chrodin died in this year.[42] He gave alms to all and was a man of great virtue and piety. He relieved the wants of the poor, endowed churches most lavishly and supported the clergy. He would lay out new estates, plant vineyards, build houses and prepare land for cultivation. Then he would call in those bishops whose revenue was small, give them a good meal and share all the buildings among them, with the farm-workers and the land which he had cleared, adding money, hangings, utensils, servants and slaves, in the most affable way. 'These are for the Church,' he would say. 'They must be used to relieve the needs of the poor. They will gain me grace in the eyes of God.' I have heard many other good reports about Chrodin, but I have no space for them here. He was seventy or more when he died.

21. The portents appeared again this year. The moon was in eclipse. In the neighbourhood of Tours real blood flowed from the broken bread. The walls of the city of Soissons collapsed. There was an earthquake in Angers. Wolves found their way inside the walls of the town of Bordeaux and ate the dogs, showing no fear whatsoever of human beings. A great light was seen to move across the sky. The city of Bazas was burned down by a great conflagration, the church and the church-houses being destroyed. I was told that all the sacred vessels were saved.

22.* King Chilperic appointed new counts to the cities which he had taken from his brother and ordered all the taxes from these cities to be paid to him. I know for a fact that this was done. About this time two men were arrested by Nonnichius,

42. A.D. 582.

Count of Limoges: they were found to be carrying letters signed by Charterius, Bishop of Périgueux, which contained many abusive attacks on the King. Among other things the Bishop bewailed the fact that he had fallen from heaven to hell when he was transferred from the jurisdiction of Guntram's kingdom to that of Chilperic. The Count despatched these letters and the men themselves to the King under close guard. Chilperic behaved with some restraint: he sent some of his men to summon the Bishop to his presence, so that he could find out whether or not the allegations made against him were true. Charterius arrived, and the King confronted him with the men and the letters. Chilperic questioned Charterius closely as to whether or not he had sent the letters. Charterius denied it. The men were asked who had given them the letters. They said that it was the deacon Frontinus. Bishop Charterius was asked about the deacon. He answered that Frontinus was his implacable enemy and that without any doubt at all the whole villainous plot was of his contriving, for he had often made malicious attacks on him. Thereupon Frontinus was led in. He was interrogated by the King and made admissions which involved the Bishop. 'It was I who wrote this letter,' he said, 'but only because the Bishop told me to do so.' The Bishop protested and said that the deacon was constantly plotting to have him removed from his bishopric. Chilperic was moved to compassion and left the decision to God. He stopped interrogating them, asked the Bishop to pardon Frontinus and begged him to pray for his King. Charterius returned with honour to his diocese. Two months later Count Nonnichius, who had started all this scandal, died of a stroke. He had no children, so the King handed his property over to various people.

23. Some time later a son was born to King Chilperic, who had buried so many sons.[43] In honour of the event, the King ordered all the prisons to be opened, those incarcerated to be freed and all fines owing to the treasury to be cancelled. Later on this child was to be the cause of great grief.

43. Theuderic: he died two years later, cp. *HF*, VI, 34.

24.   Fresh attacks were now made on Bishop Theodore. Gundovald, who gave it out that he was the son of King Lothar, arrived from Constantinople and landed in Marseilles. I must tell you a few brief facts about him.

Gundovald was born in Gaul and educated with great care. He wore his hair long and down his back, as is the custom of the Frankish kings. He was taught to read and write. His mother presented him to King Childebert I. 'This is your nephew,' said she, 'the son of King Lothar. He is hated by his father, so you take him, for he is of your blood.' King Childebert had no sons of his own, so he took the boy and kept him at his side. When King Lothar heard the news, he sent messengers to his brother to say: 'Let my boy go, and send him to me.' Childebert immediately sent the boy to Lothar, who took one look at him and ordered him to have his hair cut. 'This is no son of mine,' he said. After the death of King Lothar, Gundovald was taken up by King Charibert. Later on Sigibert summoned him and had his hair cut off a second time, sending him to Colonia Claudia Agrippinensis, which is now known simply as Cologne. Gundovald escaped from there, let his hair grow long again and made his way to Narses, who was at that time in charge of Italy. There he married, became the father of sons and then moved to Constantinople. Many years later he was invited by a person who shall be nameless to return to Gaul. He landed in Marseilles and was received by Bishop Theodore. The Bishop provided him with horses and he set off to join Duke Mummolus who, as I have already told you, was then in the city of Avignon.[44]

Count Guntram Boso arrested Bishop Theodore and threw him into prison for doing this, charging him with having introduced a foreigner into Gaul, with the intention of subjecting a Frankish kingdom to the Imperial rule. They say that Theodore was able to produce a letter signed by Childebert's more important leaders.[45] 'I have not acted of my own volition,' he

44. *HF*, VI, 1.
45. Guntram Boso himself was the person who had invited the pretender Gundovald to Gaul. Behind him were the other nobles who wished to diminish the power of the Frankish kings.

said, 'and I have only obeyed the commands of our lords and masters.' Nevertheless he was locked up in a cell and not allowed to go near his own cathedral. One night, when he was praying to our Lord, a great light appeared in the cell, so that the count who was guarding him was terrified. For the space of two hours an immense luminous globe shone over his head. When morning came the count related what had happened to the others who were with him. Theodore was brought before King Guntram, together with Bishop Epiphanius,[46] who had fled from the Longobards and was living at this time in Marseilles, he being implicated in the same affair. They were interrogated by the King, but they were found not guilty. All the same, Guntram ordered them to be kept in custody, where Bishop Epiphanius died after long suffering. Gundovald withdrew to an island in the Mediterranean, there to await the issue of the matter. Count Guntram Boso shared out Gundovald's property with one of King Guntram's dukes, and then, so they say, retired to Clermont-Ferrand with an immense treasure of silver, gold and other precious objects.

25. In the city of Tours on 31 January in the eighth year of the reign of King Childebert,[47] this day being Sunday, the bell had just rung for matins. The people had got up and were on their way to church. The sky was overcast and it was raining. Suddenly a great ball of fire fell from the sky and moved some considerable distance through the air, shining so brightly that visibility was as clear as at high noon. Then it disappeared once more behind a cloud and darkness fell again. The rivers rose much higher than usual. In the Paris region the River Seine and the River Marne were so flooded that many boats were wrecked between the city and Saint Lawrence's church.[48]

26. Count Guntram Boso went back to Clermont-Ferrand with the treasure about which I have told you, and then paid a

46. Epiphanius, Bishop of Fréjus.   47. A.D. 583.
48. There still exists in Paris a church dedicated to Saint Laurent, faubourg de Strasbourg.

visit to King Childebert. When he returned home once more
with his wife and daughters, he was seized by King Guntram
and locked up. 'It was your invitation which brought Gundovald to Gaul,' said the King, 'and it was to arrange this that
you went to Constantinople a few years ago.' 'It was your
leader Mummolus', answered Guntram Boso, 'who received
Gundovald and gave him hospitality in Avignon. Let me go and
fetch Mummolus, and bring him to your court. This will clear
me of the charges levelled against me.' 'You shall not go', replied the King, 'until you have first paid the penalty for the
wrongs which you have done.' Guntram Boso realized that his
life was threatened. 'Here is my son,' he said. 'Take him and let
him be a surety for this promise which I make to you, my lord
and King: if I do not bring Mummolus to you, I shall lose my
young son.' The King gave him permission to depart, and held
the boy as hostage. Guntram Boso took with him a supporting
force from Clermont-Ferrand and Le Velay, and set out for
Avignon. By a cunning trick thought out by Mummolus, rickety
boats were drawn up on the banks of the River Rhône. Guntram Boso and his men clambered on board, foreseeing no
danger; when they were halfway across the river, the boats
filled with water and sank. All on board were in great danger:
some escaped by swimming, others reached the bank by seizing
hold of loose planks from the boats. Quite a few, who had less
presence of mind, were drowned in the river. Count Guntram
Boso reached Avignon safely. When Mummolus had first entered the town, he had realized that there was a section of the
city boundary which was not protected by the River Rhône: he
had a channel dug from the main stream, so that the entire
circuit of the town should be protected by the river-bed. He had
great pits dug deep into the bottom of the river at this spot, and
then the water concealed this booby-trap as it flowed in. When
Guntram Boso appeared, Mummolus stood on the city-wall and
shouted: 'If he comes in good faith, let him advance from one
bank and I will move forward from the other, and then he can
say what is on his mind.' As soon as they were both in position,
with this particular arm of the river flowing between them,

Guntram Boso shouted back: 'I will come over, if you don't mind, for there are certain matters which we ought to discuss in private.' 'Come on then,' answered Mummolus. 'There's nothing to be afraid of.' Guntram Boso stepped into the river, with one of his close friends, who was weighed down by a heavy mail shirt. The moment he reached the first of the pits in the river-bed, this friend vanished under the water and was never seen again. Guntram Boso was just being submerged by the swiftly-flowing current when one of his men on the bank stretched out his lance and pulled him back to land once more. Mummolus and Guntram Boso exchanged a few insults, and then each drew back. Guntram Boso laid siege to Avignon with the help of the troops provided by King Guntram, but then Childebert came to hear of what was happening. He was incensed because Guntram Boso was doing all this without his permission, and he sent to the spot Gundulf, whom I have mentioned earlier.[49] The siege was raised and Gundulf took Mummolus to Clermont-Ferrand. A few days later Mummolus returned to Avignon.

27. On Easter Eve King Chilperic set off for Paris.[50] In order to avoid the curse pronounced in the pact between his brothers and himself on whichever of them should enter Paris without the agreement of the others, he sent the relics of a great number of saints on ahead, and then marched into the city himself.[51] He celebrated the feast of Easter with great joy and happiness, and brought his son to be baptized. The boy was lifted from the baptismal pool by Ragnemod, Bishop of Paris, and was named Theuderic, in compliance with the King's wish.[52]

28. Mark the Referendary, about whom I have already told you, had amassed vast wealth by keeping for his own use part

49. The uncle of Gregory's mother Armentaria: cp. *HF*, VI, 11.
50. A.D. 583.
51. The treaty of division entered into between Kings Guntram, Sigibert and Chilperic on the death of King Charibert in A.D. 567.
52. Theuderic was to die of dysentery a year later, cp. *HF*, VI, 34.

of the taxes which he collected. He was suddenly seized with a pain in his side. He had his head tonsured, confessed his sins and then gave up the ghost. His property was transferred to the public treasury. A vast hoard of gold and silver was discovered, and many other precious objects, too. When he died he took nothing with him on his journey, except the eternal damnation of his soul.

29.* The ambassadors sent to Spain came back home with nothing precise to report,[53] for Leuvigild was still with the army, leading a campaign against his eldest son.[54]

In the nunnery ruled over by the blessed Radegund[55] there died a girl called Disciola, who was the niece of Salvius, the saintly Bishop of Albi. The circumstances of her death were as follows. When she began to feel ill, the other nuns nursed her with great care. The day came when she was on the point of death. At about nine o'clock, she said to the nuns: 'I seem to be lighter in body than I was. My pain has gone. Please do not worry about me any more, or nurse me with such care. Perhaps you will leave me now, so that I can manage to sleep for a while.' When the other nuns heard this, they left her cell. Later on they returned and stood there at her bedside, wondering if she would have the strength to speak to them. She spread her hands wide and seemed to be asking a benediction of someone. 'Give me your blessing, holy messenger from God on high,' she whispered. 'This is the third time today that you have taken the trouble to visit me. Why, holy one, do you take such pains for a poor, feeble woman?' The nuns asked her whom she was speaking to, but she did not answer. Some time passed and then she laughed aloud. Just as she did so, she died. A man possessed of a devil, who had come there to be cured by the wondrous relic

53. These were the envoys whom King Chilperic had sent to Leuvigild, King of the Visigoths, to make plans for the betrothal of his own daughter Rigunth and Leuvigild's second son Recared.

54. Hermangild.

55. The nunnery of the Holy Cross, founded in Poitiers by Saint Radegund. It was there that the revolt of Clotild and Basina was to cause such a stir, *HF*, IX, 39–43, X. 15–17.

of the True Cross,[56] dragged at his hair and collapsed on the ground. 'What a terrible loss we have just suffered!' he shouted. 'What a disaster! To think that this soul should have been snatched from us, without those on our side being able to look into matters first!' The nuns who were there asked him what on earth he meant. 'The Archangel Michael has just received that sister's soul,' said he, 'and he is even now carrying it off to heaven. My own master, he whom you call the Devil, has no share in her at all!' Those who washed Disciola's body said that it shone with a snow-white purity, and that the Abbess could not find in her cupboard a winding-sheet which was whiter than she was. They wrapped her in clean linen and committed her to the grave.

Another woman in this nunnery saw a vision which she described to her sisters. She seemed to be on a journey, she said. As she walked along, she was filled with a great desire to find her way to a certain spring of living water. She did not know the way. She saw a man coming to meet her. 'If you want to visit the well of living water,' said the man, 'I will lead you there.' She thanked him and he went on ahead, leaving her to follow. They walked a long distance and then they came to a great spring. Its water shone like gold and the grass around it glowed as if with the sparkling light of myriad gems. The man said to her: 'This is the well of living water, for which you have been looking so long and so hard. Drink your fill of its stream, so that it may become for you a well of living water, springing up into everlasting life.'[57] She drank thirstily from the stream. Then her Abbess arrived from the opposite direction. She stripped the nun naked and dressed her in a queenly robe, which shone so clear with light and gold and jewels that it could scarcely be conceived. The Abbess said: 'It is your husband who sends you this gift.' When she saw this vision, the nun was deeply moved. A few days later she asked the Abbess to prepare a cell and to shut her up there for ever. The Abbess wasted no time in doing

56. The fragment of the True Cross, sent to Saint Radegund by the Emperor Justin II and his consort, the Empress Sophia.

57. John 4, 14.

so. 'There it is!' she said. 'Now what more do you want?' The nun asked permission to live there as a recluse. This was granted. All the other nuns assembled, with their lamps lighted. They sang psalms together and then their sister was taken in procession to the spot, the blessed Radegund leading her by the hand. They all bade her farewell and she gave to each the kiss of peace. Then she was enclosed in her cell and the door through which she had entered was bricked up. There she now passes her days in prayers and holy reading.

30.   It was in this same year that the Emperor Tiberius died.[58] His death caused great sorrow to the races over which he ruled. He was a man of the utmost goodness, ready in charity, just in his decisions, most cautious in making up his mind, looking down on no man, but including all in his kindly benevolence. He loved all men, and by all men was he loved. When he began to feel ill and realized that he might soon die, he called the Empress to him. 'I feel,' he said, 'that the days of my life have run their full course. With your help I will choose a man to rule the state in my stead. We must find a strong man to inherit all this power from me.' The Empress proposed a certain Maurice.[59] 'He is a strong man,' she said, 'and a wise one, too. He has often fought for the state against its enemies, and he has always won.' Sophia said this because she saw herself marrying Maurice as soon as Tiberius should be dead. Tiberius agreed to the proposal which the Empress had made. Then he ordered his own daughter to be decked with all the rich adornments which become an Imperial princess. He called Maurice to him and said: 'You have been nominated Emperor, with the complete agreement of the Empress Sophia. I give you the hand of my daughter, so that you may sit the safer on your throne.' The princess came in, and her father gave her to Maurice. 'With this young woman,' said Tiberius, 'I give you my imperial power. Enjoy it to the full, but always remember to make equity and justice your first concern.' Maurice accepted the hand of the

58. A.D. 583, but the Emperor Tiberius II had died in 582.
59. The Emperor Maurice Tiberius.

princess and took her to his home. They were married, and soon afterwards Tiberius died. When the period of public mourning was over, Maurice put on the diadem and the purple and the imperial robes, and walked in procession to the hippodrome. There he was received with acclamation. He distributed the customary gifts among the populace, and he was confirmed in possession of the Empire.

31. King Chilperic was visited by ambassadors from his nephew Childebert, the embassy being led by Egidius, the Bishop of Rheims. They were shown into the King's presence and given permission to speak. 'Our master, your nephew, wishes to preserve in all its details the pact which you have signed with him,' they said. 'He finds it impossible, however, to keep peace with your brother Guntram, because, after their father's death, Guntram took from him part of Marseilles, and now he is harbouring fugitives from his kingdom, and refusing to hand them over. For this reason your nephew Childebert is particularly keen to preserve in its entirety the friendly relationship which he has with you.' Chilperic answered: 'My brother is clearly guilty of many crimes. If my adopted son Childebert will look into the sequence of events, he will soon discover that his father Sigibert was killed with Guntram's connivance.' Bishop Egidius listened to what Chilperic said and then he replied: 'If you will now join forces with your nephew and he with you, and if the two of you will march together against him, Guntram will soon be punished for what he has done.' An agreement was sworn to between them to that effect, hostages were exchanged, and then the envoys went off home.

Trusting in the promises which they had given to him, Chilperic assembled his own army and entered Paris. His stay there cost the inhabitants a pretty penny. Duke Berulf marched into the Bourges area, with the men of Tours, Poitiers, Angers and Nantes. Desiderius and Bladast attacked Bourges from the other side, at the head of the combined troops from the province under their command,[60] causing great devastation in the

60. South Aquitaine.

districts through which they marched. Chilperic ordered the
soldiers whom he had called up to pass through Paris. As soon
as they had marched through the city, he himself advanced and
came to the fortified township of Melun, setting fire to everything there and causing great devastation. His nephew's
troops had not yet shown up, but their leaders and messengers were in his camp. Chilperic sent despatches to Desiderius
and Bladast, saying: 'March on Bourges, advance as far as the
city itself, and insist upon their making oaths of allegiance to
me.' The men of Bourges assembled an army of fifteen thousand
men, took the field near Melun and met Duke Desiderius in
pitched battle. The slaughter was immense, more than seven
thousand being killed from the two armies. With what remained
of their force the leader pushed on to Bourges itself, ravaging
and destroying everything. The devastation there was greater
than anything described in ancient times: not a house remained
standing, not a vineyard, not an orchard; everything was razed
to the ground and utterly ruined. They stole the communion
vessels from the churches and set fire to the churches themselves. Then King Guntram marched with his army to meet his
brother, putting all his hope in the judgement of God. One day,
just as the evening shadows were falling, he ordered his forces
to make contact and he destroyed the greater part of Chilperic's
army. The next morning messengers hurried to and fro, and
the two Kings made peace, each promising the other that his
bishops and leading subjects should agree as to how far the
bounds of law had been exceeded, and that then they would
both pay compensation. With peace restored, they each went
home. King Chilperic found it impossible to keep his troops
from plundering, and he had to have the Count of Rouen
executed on the spot. He returned to Paris, after abandoning all
his booty and liberating all his prisoners. When the troops who
were besieging Bourges received the order to withdraw and
return home, they stole so much booty that, as they evacuated it,
the entire region seemed empty of inhabitants and cattle. As
they passed through the Tours area, the men led by Desiderius
and Bladast set fire to everything, stole everything that they

could lay their hands on, and murdered the inhabitants out of hand, just as if they were in an enemy country. They captured those whom they did not kill, returning them, or most of them, it is true, but only after stripping them of all that they had. After this disaster came an outbreak of disease among the herds, so that scarcely a head of cattle survived, and it was quite a rare thing to see a horse or set eyes on a heifer.

While all this was going on, King Childebert remained encamped with his army in one spot. In the end, when he ordered his troops to advance by a night march, the lower ranks raised a great outcry against Bishop Egidius and the King's other advisers. 'King Childebert should dismiss those who are betraying his kingdom!' they shouted, not caring who heard them. 'Down with those who are handing his cities over to an enemy power! Down with those who are selling Childebert's subjects into foreign slavery!' When morning dawned the demonstration was still going on. The men seized their weapons and rushed to the King's tent, determined to lay violent hands on the Bishop and Childebert's senior advisers, to savage them, hit them over the head and gash them with their swords. As soon as he realized what was happening, Egidius leapt on a horse and fled. He set off at full speed for his own city, with the mob following at his heels, shouting their heads off, hurling stones and bellowing insults. The one thing that saved him was that they had no horses to hand. Even as it was, his comrades' horses flagged and the Bishop was the only one to win through, in such a state of panic that he had no time to fasten one of his riding-boots, which fell off as he galloped along. In this state he reached his city of Rheims and shut himself up within its walls.

32. A few months earlier Leudast had turned up again in the Tours area. He brought with him a written order from the King, saying that his wife should be restored to him and that he should be allowed to take up residence in the city. He also brought a letter signed by several bishops, asking that he should be admitted to communion again. It was largely because of Queen Fredegund that he had been excluded, and so, as I saw no

note from her, I put off making a decision. 'When I receive an
order from the Queen,' I said, 'I will then readmit him without
more ado.' Meanwhile I sent word to her and she wrote back.
'I was under such pressure from a great number of people,' ran
her answer, 'that there was nothing else that I could possibly do,
except let him go. I ask you not to make your peace with him
and not to give him the consecrated bread, until I have had time
to see clearly what my future action should be.' When I read
this I was afraid that the Queen was planning to have Leudast
killed. I asked his father-in-law to come to see me and I told
him what had happened, begging him to put Leudast on his
guard, until such moment as the Queen's anger should be as-
suaged. This advice, which I had given to him in all sincerity
and for the love of God, was received by Leudast with deep
distrust, for he was still hostile to me and unwilling to accept
any suggestion which came from me. This is a good example of
the proverb which I once heard an old man say: *Amico inimicoque bonum semper praebe consilium, quia amicus accepit,
inimicus spernet.*[61] Leudast rejected my advice and went off to
see the King, who at that moment was with his troops in the
neighbourhood of Melun. He asked the army to intercede for
him with King Chilperic and to gain him an audience. They all
gave him their support and the King agreed to see him. He
threw himself at Chilperic's feet and begged his forgiveness.
'You must hold yourself in patience for a while,' said Chilperic,
'until I have discussed this matter with the Queen and found
some way of restoring you to her good grace, for you have
done everything you could to antagonize her.' Leudast, who
was still as improvident and reckless as ever, was full of
confidence because the King had given him an audience. He
went off with Chilperic to Paris and the next Sunday threw
himself at Fredegund's feet in the cathedral, begging her for
forgiveness. She was furious, for she hated the sight of him. She
burst into tears and thrust him aside. 'I have no son left to take
up my cause,' she sobbed. 'I therefore commit it to You, Lord

61. 'Give the same good advice to him who loves you and him who hates
you: your friend has accepted it, even if your enemy will scorn it.'

Jesus.' It was now her turn to throw herself at the King's feet. 'Things have come to a sorry pass,' she said, 'when I see my enemy face to face and I am powerless to do anything!' Leudast was ejected from the cathedral and they began to celebrate Mass. When the King and Queen came out of church, Leudast followed them along the street, not realizing what was going to happen to him. He went round the shops, looking at what they had for sale, counting how much money he had in his purse and asking to be shown various pieces of jewellery. 'I will buy this, and that, too,' he said, 'for I have sufficient gold and silver with me.' Almost as he spoke, some of the Queen's men caught up with him and tried to secure him with a chain. Leudast drew his sword and hit one of them. Thereupon the others were roused to fury. They seized their own swords and their shields, and made a concerted attack upon him. One of them struck him on the head, cutting away most of his hair and scalp. He started to run across the city bridge, but he caught his foot between two of the planks of which the bridge is constructed and broke his leg. They bound his hands behind him and threw him into gaol. King Chilperic ordered that he should receive medical attention until his wounds were cured, and then that he should be submitted to lingering torture. He was dragged off to one of the royal manors. The wounds inflicted on him by his torturers began to fester and it was clear that he could not last much longer. At the personal command of the Queen he was placed flat on his back on the ground, a block of wood was wedged behind his neck and then they beat him on the throat with another piece of wood until he died. His life had been one long tale of perfidious talk: so that he met a fitting end.

33. In the ninth year of Childebert's reign,[62] King Guntram of his own volition restored the second half of Marseilles to his nephew.

King Chilperic's ambassadors returned home from Spain and announced that Carpitania,[63] the district round Toledo, had

62. A.D. 584.

63. Carpitania was the district round Toledo, the capital of the Visigoths in Spain.

been ravaged by locusts, so that not a single tree remained, not a vine. not a patch of woodland: there was no fruit of the earth, no green thing, which these insects had not destroyed. The ambassadors also reported that the enmity which had developed between Leuvigild and his son had now reached a sorry pitch.

The plague was decimating a number of districts, but it raged most fiercely in the city of Narbonne.[64] Some three years had passed since it first gained a hold, and then it seemed to die out. The populace which had fled now came back, but they were wiped out once more by disease. The city of Albi was suffering very greatly from this same epidemic.

At this time there appeared at midnight in the northern sky a multitude of rays which shone with extreme brilliance. They came together and then separated again, vanishing in all directions. The sky towards the north was so bright that you might have thought that day was about to dawn.

34. Once again legates arrived from Spain. They brought gifts, and in conference with King Chilperic they arranged that his daughter Rigunth should marry Recared, the son of King Leuvigild, according to the agreement made some time earlier. The contract was confirmed, all the details were settled and the ambassador set off for home. King Chilperic then left home and travelled some way towards Soissons, but on the journey he suffered yet another bereavement. His son, who had been baptized only the year before, fell ill with dysentery and died.[65] This is what the ball of fire presaged. the one I described above as emerging from a cloud. They were all prostrate with grief. They turned back to Paris and buried the child there. They sent after the ambassador and called him back, for clearly what they had just planned would now have to be deferred. 'I can hardly think of celebrating my daughter's wedding when I am in mourning because I have just buried my son,' said Chilperic. For a time he considered the idea of sending another daughter to Spain instead, Basina, whom he had shut away in the nun-

64. Narbonne was in Septimania, which belonged to the Visigoths.
65. Theuderic.

nery in Poitiers, her mother having been Audovera. She was
unwilling, and the blessed Radegund backed her up. 'It is not
seemly', she said, 'for a nun dedicated to Christ to turn back
once more to the sensuous pleasures of this world.'

35.   While these things were going on, it was announced to the
Queen that her little son Theuderic, who had just died, had been
taken from her by witchcraft and incantations, and that Mummolus the Prefect,[66] whom she had long hated, was involved in
this. The truth seems to have been that, when Mummolus was
at supper in his own home, someone from the court was lamenting that a child very dear to him had recently died of dysentery.
The Prefect answered: 'I always keep by me a certain herb
which has this property, that, if anyone who is attacked by
dysentery drinks a concoction of it, he is immediately cured,
however desperately ill he may be.' This was reported to Queen
Fredegund, and she was furious. She had a number of Parisian
housewives rounded up, and they were tortured with the instruments and the cat, and so compelled to act as informers. They
confessed that they were witches and gave evidence that they
had been responsible for many deaths. They then added something which I find quite incredible: 'We sacrificed your son, O
Queen, to save the life of Mummolus.' Fredegund then had
these poor wretches tortured in an even more inhuman way,
cutting off the heads of some, burning others alive and breaking
the bones of the rest on the wheel. She went to stay with King
Chilperic for a while in their manor at Compiègne, and while
there she revealed to him all that she had been told about the
Prefect. Chilperic immediately sent his men to seize the person
of Mummolus. He was interrogated, loaded with chains and put
to the torture. Then his hands were tied behind his back, he was
suspended from a rafter and he was questioned about these
sorceries. He denied that he knew anything of them. He did
admit one thing: that he had often received from these women
unguents and potions which were supposed to bring him into the
good favour of the King and Queen. As they took him down, he

66. This is not Mummolus, Count of Auxerre.

called one of the torturers to him and said: 'Tell the King, my master, that what you keep doing to me causes me no pain.' When the King heard this, he said: 'It must be true then, that he is a sorcerer, if the punishment which we are giving him does not hurt him.' Mummolus was extended on the rack and then flogged with treble thongs until the torturers were quite exhausted. After this splinters were driven beneath the nails of his fingers and toes. So things continued: finally, at the very moment when the sword was about to cut off his head, Queen Fredegund granted him his life. There followed an indignity which was perhaps worse than death itself. All his property was sequestered; and he was placed on a cart and packed off to Bordeaux, which was his native city. On the way he had a stroke. He had just enough strength to reach his destination, but he died almost immediately afterwards.

The Queen now collected together anything that had belonged to her dead son and burned it, all his clothes, some of them silk and others of fur, and all his other possessions, whatever she could find. It is said that all this filled four carts. Any object in gold or silver was melted down in a furnace, so that nothing whatsoever remained intact to remind her of how she had mourned for her boy.

36.*Aetherius, Bishop of Lisieux, about whom I have already told you,[67] was expelled from his diocese and then restored to it again in the following circumstances. There lived in the town of Le Mans a certain priest, who was fond of fine living and who was always having affairs with women, a gluttonous man, much given to fornication and other forms of immorality. There was one particular woman with whom he had intercourse regularly. He persuaded her to have her hair cut short, dressed her up as a man and went off with her to another city, thinking that when he was among strangers he would not be suspected of immorality. She was a woman of free birth and she came from a good family. A long time passed, but eventually her relations came to realize what had happened. They hastened to avenge the

67. He has not been mentioned before.

dishonour done to their family. They laid hands on the priest, tied him up and had him thrown into prison. The woman they burned alive. The lust for gain, which afflicts us all, is so irresistible that they eventually tried to sell the priest for ransom, thinking that someone would assuredly pay something to bail him out. Had they failed, they would have had him killed. As it was the news reached Aetherius. He was moved to compassion and paid over twenty pieces of gold to save the priest from immediate execution.

Thus restored to life, the priest explained to Aetherius that he was highly skilled in the humanities. He promised his Bishop that, if he would entrust pupils to his care, he would do all in his power to give them a good training in the humane letters. Aetherius was delighted. He collected the boys of Lisieux together and handed them over to this priest, so that he could teach them. The townsfolk thought highly of the tuition which he gave. The Bishop rewarded him with a plot of land and a vineyard, and he was often invited to their homes by the parents of his pupils. He came to forget his earlier misdeeds, and, like some dog which had returned to its vomit, he made advances to the mother of one of the boys; but he had chosen a virtuous woman, and she told her husband what he was up to. The other members of the family banded together, they made a serious assault on the priest and they would have killed him if they could. Aetherius was again moved to compassion: he had the priest freed, grumbled at him in a mild way and then restored him to his post.

By now the priest had become so addicted to his evil ways that there was no hope of his ever learning how to behave. The reverse happened, for he soon began to hate the very man who had twice saved him from destruction. He conspired with an archdeacon of Lisieux and together they plotted their Bishop's death, the priest having the gall to see himself as a possible replacement. They even managed to find a cleric who was prepared to hit Aetherius over the head with an axe. They themselves went about plotting, whispering in corners, entering into secret conspiracies, and promising rewards if their Bishop should die and the priest should take his place. God in His mercy prevented their miserable plan from succeeding, for by His ever-loving kindness He swiftly blocked the cruel designs of these wicked men. One day Aetherius was out in the fields with his farm-workers, who were busy with their ploughs. The cleric about whom I have told you dogged his footsteps, with his axe ready in his hand. Aetherius had no idea what he was up to, and in the end he said to him: 'Why do you keep following me all over the place with that axe of yours?' The cleric lost his nerve and threw his arms round the Bishop's knees. 'Don't be alarmed, good Bishop,' he stammered. 'You must know that I have been deputed by the archdeacon and that schoolmaster of yours to hit you over the head with this axe. I have several times steeled myself to do it, but each time I raised my right arm ready to strike the blow, my eyes went dim, there was a buzzing in my ears, and my whole body shook and trembled. My hands lost their grip and I was powerless to do the deed; but the moment I lowered my arms I felt all right again. I have come to realize that the Lord is with you, and that I am powerless to do you any harm.' Aetherius wept when he heard this. He swore the cleric to secrecy, and then he walked off home to supper. After his meal he went to lie down for a while on his bed. All around his own couch were the beds of his clergy.

The conspirators realized that their precious cleric had failed them and they made fresh plans to achieve their evil design by their own unaided efforts. They thought up a new plot to destroy Aetherius, or at least to bring against him some new charge which should be so irrefutable that he would have to give up his bishopric. About midnight, when everyone was fast asleep, they burst into the Bishop's bedroom and began shouting at the top of their voices that they had seen a woman come out of the door, but that in their haste to catch him at it they had let her escape. Only the Devil could have put into their heads this idea of bringing such a charge against the Bishop, for he was nearly seventy years old! Without more ado they called in the same cleric who had helped them before. Thereupon the Bishop was bound with chains by the hands of the very priest whose neck he had saved on a number of occasions, and he was placed under strict guard by the very man whom he had rescued from a series of insanitary prison-cells. When Aetherius saw that his enemies had prevailed over him by force and that he was securely chained up, he wept and prayed to our Lord for succour. The prison-guards dropped off to sleep, and immediately with God's help the Bishop's chains came undone. He, the sinless, who had so often set free the sinful, now escaped from his prison: he slipped away unseen, and made his way to King Guntram's kingdom. As soon as he was gone, the conspirators, now free from all constraint, rushed off to King Chilperic to ask for the bishopric. They accused Aetherius of every crime in the calendar and ended with this final charge: 'You can judge the truth of what we say, most glorious King, from the fact that he has now fled to your brother's kingdom in fear of his life because of the crimes which he has committed.' Chilperic did not believe them. He told them to go back home to Lisieux.

Meanwhile the citizens were sad at the loss of their shepherd. They were quite sure that everything which had happened had been the result of jealousy and greed. They laid hands on the archdeacon and the priest, his fellow-conspirator, and gave them both a good beating. Then they petitioned King Chilperic to send their Bishop back to them. The King sent messengers to his brother to say that he had never found anything to complain of in the behaviour of Aetherius. Thereupon King Guntram, kindly as ever, and swift to pity, loaded the Bishop with presents. At the same time he wrote round to all the bishops in his own kingdom, telling them for the love of God to do what they could for this exile. Aetherius stayed in their cities, one after the other, and so much wealth was showered upon him by their bishops, both in clothing and in money, that he had difficulty in carrying home all that he received. Thus the words of the Apostle were fulfilled: 'All things work together for good to them that love God.'[68] His journeying brought him riches and his exile great plenty. He finally reached Lisieux and there he was received with great honour by his flock. They wept with joy

68. Romans 8, 28.

and gave thanks to God, who in the end had given back to their church this worthy Bishop.

37.*   Lupentius, Abbot of the church of the martyr Saint Privatus in Javols, was summoned by Queen Brunhild and appeared before her. They say that he had been accused by Innocentius, Count of that city, of making libellous remarks about the Queen. His case was discussed, but he was found not guilty of the charge of *lèse-majesté* and ordered to return home. On the journey he was seized by the Count, dragged off to the manor of Ponthion and grievously maltreated. Once more they let him go. As he continued on his way he pitched his tent on the bank of the River Aisne, and there his enemy attacked him yet again. Rude hands were laid on him. Innocentius cut off his head, put it in a sack weighted with stones and threw it into the river. He tied the body to a rock and threw that, too, into the water. A few days passed, and then the body was discovered by some shepherds, who pulled it out of the river and prepared to bury it. While they were making plans for the funeral, not knowing who it was from Adam, the more so as the severed head had not been found, there suddenly appeared an eagle, which fished the sack out from the bottom of the river and placed it on the bank. The shepherds stood stock still in amazement. They picked up the sack, wondering what could possibly be in it, and then found inside the head belonging to the body. The two were buried together. They say that even now a celestial light still shines above the burial-place; and that if a sick man prays in faith over the tomb, he goes on his way whole.

38.*   Theodosius, Bishop of Rodez, died. He had been the successor to Saint Dalmatius. The lobbying and scandalous rivalries which ensued for the bishopric of this diocese reached such a pitch that it was more or less stripped of its sacred vessels and its more important possessions. The priest Transobadus was rejected and Innocentius, Count of Javols, was elected to the episcopate, he being the candidate whom Queen Brunhild supported. No sooner had he been consecrated as Bishop than he began to harass Ursicinus, Bishop of Cahors, alleging that he had sequestered certain parishes belonging to the diocese of Rodez. The dispute dragged on from day to day. When it had lasted some years, the Metropolitan Bishop convened a council of the bishops of the province of Clermont-Ferrand. It was decreed that Ursicinus should keep possession of the parishes, for they had never belonged to Rodez in the history of man. This was done.

39.* Remigius, Bishop of Bourges, died. After his death, a fire destroyed the greater part of the city. All those quarters which had survived enemy action now perished in the flames. Sulpicius, who had the support of King Guntram, was elected to the bishopric. Many tried to bribe the King to elect them to the vacant see. Guntram is said to have replied: 'It has not been my custom since I became King to put up bishoprics for sale, nor should you yourselves expect to purchase them with bribes. I have no intention of incurring the shame of accepting filthy lucre, nor do I want you to be compared with Simon Magus. As God has always intended, Sulpicius shall be your Bishop.' He was admitted to the priesthood and then elected to the bishopric. He is a man of very noble birth, descended from one of the foremost senatorial families in Gaul. He is extremely learned in the humanities, and second to none as a poet. It was he who summoned the council about which I have just told you, to make a decision concerning the parishes belonging to Cahors.

40. There arrived from Spain an envoy called Oppila, who brought with him many presents for Chilperic. Leuvigild, the King of Spain, was afraid that Childebert might march against him to avenge the insult done to his sister Ingund. He had seized hold of his son Hermangild, who had married Childebert's sister,[69] and he had locked him up in prison, leaving his wife to the good graces of the Greeks. The envoy arrived in Tours in time for Easter Sunday, and I asked him if he was a member of our faith. He replied that he believed what Catholics believe.

69. Ingund.

Thereupon he accompanied me to the cathedral and was present at Mass. He did not exchange the kiss of peace with the congregation, nor did he take communion. It was quite clear that he was lying when he said that he was a Catholic. I invited him to have supper with us and he came. I asked him exactly what his beliefs were. He replied: 'I believe that the Father, the Son and the Holy Ghost are equal in power.' My answer to this was: 'If you really believe this, what made you refuse to take communion with us?' 'I did this,' he said, 'because you use the word glory wrongly. We follow Saint Paul and say: "Glory be to God the Father, and to the Son." You say: "Glory be to the Father, and to the Son, and to the Holy Ghost." The main authorities of the Church teach that the Father was revealed to the world through the Son, as Saint Paul himself says: "Now unto the King eternal, immortal, invisible, the only God, be honour and glory for ever, through Jesus Christ our Lord."[70] 'No Catholic, I think,' I answered, 'is ignorant of the fact that the Father was proclaimed through the Son; but the Son proclaimed the Father in this world in a way which proved by His miracles that He, too, was God. God the Father had no recourse but to send His Son to earth to reveal the Godhead, so that the world, which had refused to believe the prophets, the patriarchs and the very Giver of the Law Himself, might at least believe the Son. It is therefore necessary for glory to be given to God under distinction of Persons. That is why we say: "Glory be to God the Father, who sent the Son; glory be to God the Son, who by His blood redeemed the world; glory be to the Holy Ghost, who sanctified man redeemed." When you say: "Glory be to the Father through the Son," you take away glory from the Son, as if He were not equal to the Father in glory because He proclaimed the Father in the world. As I have said, the Son proclaimed the Father in the world, but many did not believe, as John the Evangelist says: "He came unto his own, and his own received him not. But as many as received him, to them gave he power to become the sons of God, even to them that believe on his name."[71] Observe, you

70. I Timothy 1, 17.   71. John 1, 11–12.

who do less than justice to the Apostle Paul and who really do
not understand his meaning at all, observe, I say, how carefully
he speaks, according to the intelletual level of the person
whom he is addressing, observe his way of preaching to unbelievers, and how he never asks too much of anyone. To some he
says: "I have fed you with milk, and not with meat: for hitherto
ye were not able to bear it, neither yet now are ye able.[72] But
strong meat belongeth to them that are of full age."[73] To others
he says: "I have preached nothing among you, save Christ, and
him crucified."[74] What do you make of that, you heretic? Because Paul preached only Christ crucified, do you refuse to
believe that Christ rose from the dead? Observe his caution, and
how clever he was, and what he said to others whom he knew to
be stronger in faith: "Yea," he says, "though we have known
Christ crucified, yet now henceforth know we him no more."[75]
Deny then, if you dare to do anything so foolish, you who
criticize Saint Paul, deny that Christ was ever crucified. I beg
you to give up these false ideas and to listen to better advice.
Wash away the blindness from your eyes with some unguent or
other, and observe the true revelation of the Apostle's preaching. Paul used simple words so that men could understand him,
and so that he might raise them up to the higher pinnacles of
faith. Elsewhere he says: "I am made all things to all men, that I
might by all means save all."[76] Shall mortal man not give glory
to the Son, whom the Father Himself glorified from Heaven,
not once, but twice and even three times? Hear the words which
He spoke from Heaven, when the Holy Ghost came down and
the Son was baptized by the hand of John: "This is my beloved
Son, in whom I am well pleased."[77] If your ears are so blocked
that you cannot hear these words, believe the words which the
Apostles heard on the mount, when Jesus was transfigured in
glory and talked with Moses and Elisha, and the Father spoke
out of the bright cloud: "This is my beloved Son; hear ye
him." [78]

72. I Corinthians 3, 2.   73. Hebrews 5, 14.   74. I Corinthians 2, 2.
75. II Corinthians 5, 16.   76. Cp. I Corinthians 9, 22.
77. Matthew 3, 17.   78. Matthew 17, 5.

To these arguments the heretic replied: 'In these passages which you have quoted the Father says nothing of the glory of the Son. He simply reveals Him as His Son.' 'If that is how you interpret it,' I answered, 'I will give you another testimony, in which the Father glorifies the Son. When our Lord came to His Passion, He said to His Father: "Father, glorify thy Son, that thy Son also may glorify thee."[79] What answer did the Father then make from Heaven? Did He not say:"I have both glorified Thee and will glorify Thee again?"[80] You see, the Father glorifies His Son with His own voice. Do you propose to try to take His glory away from Him? You have no power to do this, even if you have the will. Listen to Saint Paul speaking, or rather to Christ speaking through Saint Paul, you who are prepared to criticize the Apostle: "And that every tongue should confess that Jesus Christ is Lord, to the glory of God the Father."[81] If He now shares the glory of the Father, and if He is now in that glory where the Father himself is, how can you dishonour Him as one without glory? Why should He not be glorified among men, when He reigns in Heaven with the Father in equal glory? That is why we confess that Christ, the Son of God, is very God, and why, since the Godhead is one, so also shall the glory be.'

We had no more to say to each other and our dispute came to an end. He went to see King Chilperic, handed over the gifts sent by the King of Spain, and then returned home.

41. When King Chilperic heard that his brother Guntram had made peace with his nephew Childebert, and that they proposed to win back the cities which he had occupied by force of arms, he withdrew to Cambrai with all his treasury, carrying with him everything that was easily portable. He sent messengers to his dukes and counts to tell them to repair the walls of their cities, and then to shut themselves up inside these fortifications together with their property and their wives and children. If need be, they must be prepared to offer stout resistance and to prevent the enemy from doing any harm. 'If you suffer any

79. John 17, 1.   80. John 12, 28.   81. Philippians 2, 11.

loss,' he added, 'it will be repaid to you more than amply when I come to take vengeance.' He never managed to understand that victory lies in the hand of God.

He several times ordered his army to advance, but he never allowed it to cross his own frontiers.

About this time a son was born to Chilperic.[82] He had the child brought up in the manor of Vitry, for he was afraid that, if he appeared in public, some harm might befall him and he might even be killed.

42. Next King Childebert marched into Italy.[83] As soon as the Longobards heard of this, they submitted to his authority, for they were afraid that they might be cut to pieces by his troops. They gave him many gifts and promised to be his faithful subjects. As soon as he had achieved all that he intended, Childebert returned to Gaul. A little later he conscripted an army with the intention of invading Spain, but he never took the field. Some years before he had received fifty thousand pieces of gold from the Emperor Maurice to rid Italy of the Longobards. When Maurice learned that Childebert had made peace with the Longobards, he asked for his money back; but Childebert was so sure of his power that he did not even send an answer.

43. Extraordinary events now occurred in Galicia. I must go back to the beginning to explain these. As I have already told you, Hermangild quarrelled with his father. He took refuge with his wife in one of the cities of Spain, relying upon support from the Emperor and from Mir, King of Galicia. When he learned that his father was marching with his army to attack him, he made plans to repel the invader and even to kill him if necessary. Poor prince, he did not realize that the judgement of God hangs over anyone who makes such plans against his own father, even if that father be a heretic. He debated what he could best do, and then picked out three hundred armed men from the many thousands under his command and stationed

82. Lothar, later King Lothar II.　　83. A.D. 584.

them inside the fortress of Osser,[84] where the springs in the church are made to flow at God's will. His idea was that his father would be alarmed and weakened when this band attacked him and then would concede victory to the bulk of Hermangild's troops, who were numerous but not well trained. When King Leuvigild heard of this stratagem, he hesitated as to what he could best do. 'If I attack with my entire army,' he said, 'this solid mass of soldiery will suffer cruelly from the enemy's javelins. If, on the other hand, I advance with only a few men, I shall find it impossible to overcome a force of defenders hand-picked for their fighting qualities.' In the end he marched his entire army forward, attacked the fortress, defeated the garrison and burned the place down, as I told you in a previous chapter.[85]

No sooner had Leuvigild won this victory than he discovered that King Mir was waiting to attack him with his army. He surrounded Mir's forces and made him swear loyalty for the future. They exchanged presents and each went home. Mir returned to his own country, but immediately took to his bed and died. His health had been undermined by the bad water and the unwholesome air of Spain. After his death, his son Euric sought to renew the pact with Leuvigild. He took the same oaths as his father had done and succeeded to the kingship of Galicia.

In this same year his relation Andica, who had married his sister, led an army against Euric. He captured him and forced him to enter the Church, having him consecrated first as a deacon and then as a priest. Andica then married the widow of his father-in-law and seized the kingship of Galicia.

Leuvigild captured his son Hermangild and carried him off as prisoner to Toledo. Later he exiled him. He was unable to force the Greks to hand over Hermangild's wife.[86]

44.   The locusts which had ravaged the district round Toledo for five long years now moved forward along the public highway and invaded another near-by province. The swarm covered an area fifty miles long and a hundred miles broad.

84. The springs of Osser: cp. *HF*, V, 17.
85. *HF*, V, 38.   86. Ingund.

In this same year many strange portents appeared in Gaul and the sufferings endured by the population were very harsh. Roses flowered in January. A great circle of many colours appeared round the sun, rather like what one sees in a rainbow when the rain pours down. Frost nipped the vineyards, doing serious damage: then came a terrible storm which battered down the vines and the crops. What was left after this hailstorm was destroyed by a fierce drought. A few grapes remained on some vines, on others none at all. Men were so furious with God that they left the gates of their vineyards wide open and drove in their cattle and horses. In their misery they called down ruination upon themselves and were heard to shout: 'We don't care if these vines never bear shoots again until the end of time!' Trees which had borne apples in July had a second crop in September. One epidemic after another killed off the flocks, until hardly any remained alive.

45. On 1 September[87] a great embassy of Visigoths came to see King Chilperic. He took up residence in Paris once more. Then he ordered a great number of families of serfs to be rounded up from various royal estates and carted off in wagons. They wept bitterly and refused to go. He had them guarded closely, ready for the day when he could send them abroad with his daughter Rigunth. They say that quite a few of the serfs hanged themselves in their distress, dreading to be carried off from those near and dear to them. Sons were torn from fathers, mothers were separated from daughters. They parted with groans and curses. The mourning in the city of Paris could only be compared with that in Egypt. Quite a few of them were of good birth. Those who were forced to emigrate made their wills, leaving all their property to the churches and stipulating that, as soon as it was known that the Princess had reached Spain, these wills should be acted upon at once, as if they themselves were dead and buried.

Meanwhile envoys from King Childebert came to Paris, warning King Chilperic to remove nothing from the cities

87. A.D. 584.

which he had taken from his brother's kingdom and forbidding him to dare to lay a finger on any slaves, or horses, or pairs of bulls or anything else of that sort. They say that one of these envoys was murdered in secret, but no one knows by whom, although suspicion turned on the King. Chilperic promised that he would touch none of these things. He invited the Frankish leaders and all his loyal subjects to celebrate the engagement of his daughter. Then he handed her over to the Visigothic envoys, providing her with a tremendous dowry. Her mother added a vast weight of gold and silver, and many fine clothes. When he saw this, King Chilperic thought that he had nothing left at all. Queen Fredegund realized that he was upset. She turned to the Franks and said: 'Do not imagine, men, that any of this comes from the treasures amassed by your earlier kings. Everything you see belongs to me. Your most illustrious King has been very generous to me, and I have put aside quite a bit from my own resources, from the manors granted to me, and from revenues and taxes. You, too, have often given me gifts. From such sources come all the treasures which you see in front of you. None of it has been taken from the public treasury.' The King calmed down when he heard this. There was such a vast assemblage of objects that the gold, silver and other precious things filled fifty carts. The Franks themselves all brought wedding-presents, gold, silver, horses and clothing, each giving according to his means. At length the time came for the Princess to say good-bye. The tears streamed down her face as she kissed her parents. As she drove through the city gate, one of the axles of her carriage broke. 'An unlucky omen!' people muttered, for some saw it as poor promise for the future.

As she left Paris, Rigunth ordered her tents to be pitched by the eighth milestone. That night fifty of her escort got up, stole a hundred of the best horses, with their golden bridles, and two great salvers as well, and slipped away in flight to King Childebert. All the way along the route anyone who saw the chance of escaping made off, taking with him whatsoever he could lay his hands on. Vast supplies were stockpiled along the road, at the expense of the cities through which they passed. The King made no provision whatsoever from the public purse, everything being requisitioned from the poor inhabitants. Chilperic had a suspicion that his brother or his nephew might set an ambush for his daughter, so he ordered her to be escorted by a force of soldiery. Many men of great distinction went with her: Duke Bobo, the son of Mummolen, who was to give away the bride, took his wife with him; Domigisel, Ansovald and Waddo, major-domo of the Princess's household and onetime Count of Saintes, also went; and there were more than four thousand ordinary folk. All the other dukes and chamberlains who had set out with Rigunth turned back at Poitiers; but those whom I have mentioned, who were to complete the journey, pressed on as best they could. As they advanced they robbed and plundered to an extent which beggars all description. They stole from the cottages of the poor, ruined the vineyards by cutting off whole branches with the grapes hanging on them, made off with the cattle and took everything they could lay their hands on, leaving desolation along the roads where they passed. Thus was the saying of the prophet Joel fulfilled: 'That which the locust hath left hath the cankerworm eaten; and that which the cankerworm hath left hath the caterpillar eaten; and that which the caterpillar hath left hath the blight eaten.'[88] What actually happened at this time was as if a great storm blew down what the hoar-frost left, and a drought burned up what the great storm left and then a hostile army carried off what the drought left.

46. While these people were proceeding on their way with all their plunder, Chilperic, the Nero and Herod of our time, went off to his manor of Chelles, which is about a dozen miles from Paris. There he spent his time hunting. One day when he returned from the chase just as twilight was falling, he was alighting from his horse with one hand on the shoulder of a servant, when a man stepped forward, struck him with a knife under the armpit and then stabbed him a second time in the stomach. Blood immediately streamed both from his mouth and through the gaping wound, and that was the end of this wicked man.[89]

88. Joel 1, 4.   89. A.D. 584.

The evil which Chilperic did has been set out in this book. Many a district did he ravage and burn, not once but many times. He showed no remorse at what he did, but rather rejoiced in it, like Nero of old who recited tragedies while his palace was going up in flames. He frequently brought unjust charges against his subjects with the sole object of confiscating their property. In his day churchmen were rarely elected to bishoprics. He was extremely gluttonous, and his god was in his belly. He used to maintain that no one was more clever than he. He wrote two books, taking Sedulius as his model, but the verses were feeble and had no feet to stand on: he put short syllables for long ones, and long syllables for short ones, not understanding what he was doing. He composed some other short pieces, hymns and sequences for the Mass, but it was impossible to use them. He hated the poor and all that they stood for. He never ceased his attacks on those who served our Lord and, when he was among his intimate friends, the bishops were the constant butt of his ridicule and facetiousness. One he would accuse of levity, another of superbia, a third of excess and a fourth of luxuria. How empty-headed was this bishop, according to him, how pompous that! There was nothing that he hated so much as he hated the churches. He was perpetually heard to say: 'My treasury is always empty. All our wealth has fallen into the hands of the Church. There is no one with any power left except the bishops. Nobody respects me as King: all respect has passed to the bishops in their cities.' With this in his mind he made a practice of tearing up wills in which property had been bequeathed to the bishops. He trampled underfoot the royal decrees of his own father, thinking that there was no one left alive who was interested in seeing that they should be carried out. It is impossible to imagine any vice or debauchery which this man did not practise. He was always on the watch for some new way of torturing his subjects. Whenever any were judged guilty of some crime or other, he would have their eyes torn out of their heads. In the instructions which he issued to judges for the maintenance of his decrees, he would always add the sentence: 'If anyone disobeys my orders, he must be punished by having his eyes torn out.' He himself cared for no one, unless he had some ulterior motive for doing so; and in return he was loved by none. When his time came to die, he died deserted by all.

Only Mallulf, Bishop of Senlis, who had been encamped for three days in a tent at Chelles, waiting in vain to have an audience, came forward when he heard that Chilperic had been assassinated. He washed the body and dressed it in more seemly garments. He passed the night singing hymns and then put the corpse in a boat and buried it in the church of Saint Vincent,[90] which is in Paris. Meanwhile Queen Fredegund remained all alone in the cathedral.

HERE ENDS BOOK VI OF GEORGIUS FLORENTIUS,
OTHERWISE KNOWN AS GREGORY, BISHOP OF TOURS
THANKS BE TO GOD

90. Later Saint-Germain-des-Prés.

BOOK VII

HERE BEGIN THE CHAPTER-HEADINGS OF BOOK VII

1. The death of Saint Salvius the Bishop.
2. The conflict between the men of Chartres and the men of Orleans.
3. How Vedast, surnamed Avius, met his end.
4. How Fredegund sought sanctuary in the cathedral and how her treasure was handed over to Childebert.
5. How King Guntram came to Paris.
6. How this same King took command of the lands which were formerly Charibert's.
7. Envoys from Childebert demand the surrender of Fredegund.
8. How King Guntram asked the people not to kill him as they had killed his brothers.
9. How Rigunth was robbed of her treasure and imprisoned by Desiderius.
10. How Gundovald was raised on the shield. The action taken by King Chilperic's daughter Rigunth.
11. Signs and wonders.
12. How part of Tours was burnt down. The miracles performed by Saint Martin.
13. How Poitiers was burnt and looted.
14. Legates are sent by King Childebert to King Guntram.
15. The evil behaviour of Fredegund.
16. The return of Bishop Praetextatus.
17. Bishop Promotus.
18. How King Guntram was warned of the danger of his being assassinated.
19. How Queen Fredegund was ordered to withdraw to a country manor.
20. How Fredegund sent an emissary to assassinate Brunhild.

21. How Eberulf fled and then was kept under guard.
22. The evil behaviour of Eberulf.
23. How a Jew came to be murdered and his companions with him.
24. How the city of Poitiers was looted.
25. How Marileif was robbed.
26. How Gundovald made a progress through certain cities.
27. The outrage done to Bishop Magnulf.
28. The advance of the army.
29. How Eberulf was murdered.
30. The envoys sent by Gundovald.
31. The relics of Saint Sergius the martyr.
32. How Gundovald sent envoys a second time.
33. How Childebert visited his uncle Guntram.
34. How Gundovald made his way to Comminges.
35. How the church of Saint Vincent the martyr of Agen was looted.
36. How Gundovald parleyed with the besiegers.
37. The assault on the city of Comminges.
38. How Gundovald was killed.
39. How Mummolus and Bishop Sagittarius were killed.
40. The treasure of Mummolus.
41. A giant.
42. The miracle performed by Saint Martin.
43. Desiderius and Waddo.
44. A sorceress.
45. The famine which befell this year.
46. The murder of Christopher.
47. The civil discord between the townsfolk of Tours.

HERE END THE CHAPTER-HEADINGS

1. Although I have every intention of picking up the threads of this history of mine from the point which I reached in the preceding books the feeling of reverence which I have for him compels me to begin by saying something about Saint Salvius, who, as everyone knows, died in this year.[1]

Salvius used often to tell the story of how, during his long years as a layman and while he was busying himself with worldly affairs, he never permitted himself to be ensnared by the carnal desires which so frequently fill the minds of young people. When the spirit of the Holy Ghost finally found a place in his heart, he gave up the struggle of secular existence and entered a monastery. As one now dedicated to Almighty God, he came to understand that it was better to serve the Lord in poverty and to humble oneself before Him, rather than to keep striving after the wealth of this transient world. He spent long years in his monastery and observed the rule instituted by the Fathers. When the time came for the abbot of the house in question to die, Salvius took over the charge of feeding the flock, for he had by then reached the full force of his physical and intellectual powers. Once he had been given this appointment, it was his duty to mix more freely with the brethren, in order to maintain discipline among them, but instead he became even more withdrawn. He chose for himself a cell which was still more remote, although, as he often used to tell, in his former cell he had become so weak as the result of continuous fasting that he had cast his skin nine times or more. Now that he had been elected Abbot, he lived just as frugally as before, devoting all his time to reading and to prayer. He became convinced that it suited him better to remain hidden away among his monks rather than to appear in public and be addressed as Abbot. Having once

1. A.D. 584.

come to this conclusion, he said good-bye to the monks and in turn received their farewells. He became a recluse: and in the loneliness of his cell he submitted himself to even greater abstinence than before. At the same time he took good care to observe the law of Christian charity, offering up prayers for all who came to visit the monastery, and giving them the bread of oblation with grace abounding. Time and time again those who arrived with grave afflictions went away cured.

One day when Salvius lay on his bed, gasping for breath and weakened by a high temperature, his cell was suddenly filled with a bright light and the walls seemed to shake. He stretched forth his hands to heaven, and as he gave thanks he breathed forth his spirit. The monks, and his own mother with them, carried his dead body out of the cell, lamenting as they did so; then they washed it, dressed it in the last vestments and placed it upon a bier. They passed the long night in weeping and singing psalms. When morning dawned and all was ready for the funeral office, the corpse began to move on the bier. Salvius' cheeks flushed red again, he stirred himself as if awakened from a deep sleep, opened his eyes, raised his hands and spoke. 'Merciful Lord,' he said, 'why have You done this to me? Why have You decreed that I should return to this dark place where we dwell on earth? I should have been so much happier in Your compassion on high, instead of having to begin once again my useless life here below.' Those around him were nonplussed. When they asked him the meaning of the miracle which had occurred, he made no reply. He rose from the bier, feeling no ill effects from the illness which he had suffered. For three days he remained without food or drink. On the third day he summoned the monks and called his mother in, too. 'My dearest friends,' said he, 'listen to what I have to say. You must understand that all you see in this world is quite without value. "All is vanity",[2] exactly as the prophet Solomon proclaimed. Happy is he who manages to behave in such a way in this earthly existence that he is rewarded by seeing God in His glory in heaven.' As he said this he began to wonder whether he should speak more fully or

2. Ecclesiastes 1, 2.

leave it at that. He remained silent for a while, but the monks
begged him to tell them what he had seen. 'When my cell shook
four days ago,' he went on, 'and you saw me lying dead, I was
raised up by two angels and carried to the highest pinnacle of
heaven, until I seemed to have beneath my feet not only this
squalid earth of ours, but the sun and the moon, the clouds and
the stars. Then I was led through a gate which shone more
brightly than our sunshine and so entered a building where all
the floor gleamed with gold and silver. The light was such as I
cannot describe to you, and the sense of space was quite beyond
our experience. The place was filled with a throng of people
who were neither men nor women, a multitude stretching so
far, this way and that, that it was not possible to see where it
ended. The angels pushed a way for me through the crowd of
people who stood in front of me, and so we came to a spot to
which our gaze had been directed even while we were still a
long way off. Over it hung a cloud more luminous than any
light, and yet no sun was visible, no moon and no star: indeed,
the cloud shone more brightly than any of these and had a
natural brilliance of its own. A Voice came out of the cloud, as
the voice of many waters.[3] Sinner that I am, I was greeted with
great deference by a number of beings, some dressed in priestly
vestments and others in everyday dress: my guides told me that
these were the martyrs and other holy men whom we honour
here on earth and to whom we pray with great devotion. As I
stood in the spot where I was ordered to stand there was wafted
over me a perfume of such sweetness that, nourished by its
delectable essence, I have felt the need of no food or drink until
this very moment. Then I heard a Voice which said: "Let this
man go back into the world, for our churches have need of
him." I heard the Voice; but I could not see who was speaking.
Then I threw myself flat on the ground and wept. "Alas! Alas!
Lord," I said. "Why have You shown me these things only to
take them away from me again? You cast me out today from
before Your face and send me back again to a worldly existence
which has no substance, powerless as I am ever to return on

3. Cp. Revelation 14, 2.

high. I entreat You, Lord, do not turn Your mercy aside from me. Let me stay here, I beseech You, lest, falling once more to earth, I perish." The Voice which spoke to me said: "Go in peace.[4] I will watch over you, until I bring you back again to this place."[5] Then my guides left me and I turned back through the gate by which I had entered, weeping as I went.'

As he said this, all those who were with him were amazed. The holy man of God wept. Then he said: 'Woe is me that I have dared to reveal such a mystery! The perfumed essence which I breathed in from that holy place, and by which I have been sustained for three whole days without taking food or drink, has already left me. My tongue is covered with sores and so swollen that it seems to fill my entire mouth. It is only too clear to me that it has not been pleasing in the eyes of my Lord God that these mysteries should be revealed. You know well, Lord, that I did that which I did in the simplicity of my heart, and in no spirit of vainglory. Have mercy on me, I beseech You, and do not forsake me, according to Your promise.' When he had said this, Salvius fell silent: then he began to eat and drink.

As I set down these words, I am afraid that my story may seem quite incredible to certain of my readers; and I am mindful of what the historian Sallust wrote: 'When we record the virtue or glory of famous men, the reader will readily accept whatever he considers that he might have done himself; anything which exceeds these bounds of possibility he will look upon as untrue.'[6] I call Almighty God to witness that I have heard from the lips of Salvius himself everything which I have related here.

Many years later the saintly Salvius was forced to leave his cell, so that he might be elected Bishop and then consecrated against his will. According to my reckoning, he had held this position for ten years when there was an outbreak of plague at Albi and the greater part of the population died as a result. Only a few of the citizens remained alive, but Saint Salvius, that good shepherd, refused to leave his city. There he remained, exhorting

---

4. I Samuel 1, 17.   5. Cp. Genesis 28, 15.
6. *Catilina*, 3. Cp. p. 209, note 18.

those still in the land of the living to pray unceasingly, not to relax in their vigils and to concentrate their minds and their bodies on doing only what was good. 'Always act in such a way,' he used to say, 'that if God should decide to recall you from this world, you may enter not into His judgement but into His peace.' When the time came for God to reveal to Salvius that his own death was near, he prepared his own coffin, and, so I believe, washed himself carefully and put on his shroud. He died in blessed contemplation, with his thoughts turned towards heaven. He was an extremely holy man. He had no wish whatsoever for possessions and simply refused to accept money: if anyone ever forced it upon him, he would immediately hand it over to the poor. During his period as Bishop, the patrician Mummolus carried off many of the inhabitants of Albi as his prisoners, but Salvius followed him and managed to persuade him to free them all. The Lord gave him such influence over these people that those who had captured the Albigeois accepted a reduction in the ransom which they had asked and even gave presents to Salvius. In this way he liberated the townsfolk of his own diocese and restored them to their former state.

I have heard many other improving stories told about him; but I must not tell you any more, for I want to press on with the History which I have begun.

2. No sooner was Chilperic dead, he having met the fate for which he had been asking so long, than the men of Orleans joined forces with the inhabitants of Blois and attacked the citizens of Châteaudun out of the blue and beat them. Dwelling-houses, stocks of corn and anything else which could not be moved they set light to; then they made off with the cattle and stole everything which was portable. They had not gone far when the Dunois, supported in this by other people from the Chartres neighbourhood, followed in their tracks and meted out to them the same treatment which they themselves had received: they left nothing inside the houses and nothing outside the houses, and then they knocked the houses down. The two sides pressed on with the struggle, starting new quarrels among

themselves. The men of Orleans were on the point of taking up arms for a counter-attack when the Counts came between them and peace was enforced until the case could be heard. Once the affair had been submitted to arbitration and a legal decision had been reached, the side which had attacked the other with no reason given was made to pay compensation. In this way an end was made to the fighting.

3.   At this time Vedast, commonly known as Avius, was committing many crimes in the district round Poitiers. It was he who, some years earlier, had murdered Lupus and Ambrosius for love of the latter's wife, and then had married the woman, although she was said to be his cousin.[7] By pure chance Avius met Childeric the Saxon somewhere or other, whereupon each heaped insults on the other and in the end one of Childeric's supporters ran Avius through with his spear. He fell to the ground, where he was wounded by a number of other blows, and so with his blood poured out his wicked soul. In this way God in His majesty avenged the innocent blood which this man had shed with his own hand. The miserable creature had committed one crime after another, robberies, murders and adulteries, but I prefer not to give you details. All the same, the Saxon had to compound with the sons of Avius over his killing.

4.   Meanwhile the widowed Queen Fredegund arrived in Paris. She took with her that part of her treasure which she had secreted within the city walls, and she sought sanctuary in the cathedral, where she was given protection by Bishop Ragnemod. The remainder of her treasure, which had been left behind in Chelles and which included the golden salver which Chilperic had recently had made,[8] was confiscated by the treasury officials, who lost no time in joining King Childebert, he being in Meaux at the time.

5.   Queen Fredegund took the advice of her supporters and sent messengers to King Guntram. 'Let my lord come and take charge

7. Cp. *HF*, VI, 13.   8. Cp. *HF*, VI, 2.

of his brother's kingdom,' she said. 'I have a tiny baby, whom I long to place in his arms. At the same time I shall declare myself his humble servant.' King Guntram wept bitterly when he heard of his brother's death. As soon as his mourning was over, he summoned his army and marched on Paris. He had already taken up his quarters within the city walls when his nephew, King Childebert, arrived from another direction.

6.   The Parisians refused to allow Childebert to enter the city. He thereupon sent messengers to King Guntram. 'I know, my dearest uncle,' he said, 'that it will not have escaped your pious comprehension that until this moment we have both been the object of the attacks of a hostile party, with the result that neither of us could have justice in respect of what was owing to him. For this reason I beg you to continue to observe the treaty which has bound us together since my father's death.' King Guntram gave the following reply to the envoys: 'You are a miserable band of liars, with no touch of truth in what you say, for you never keep the pledges which you give. You have broken every single promise which you made to me, for you drew up a new pact with King Chilperic to expel me from my kingdom and to divide my cities between him and Childebert. Look! Here is the very document, signed with your own names and confirming your own connivance in what I have said! How can you have the effrontery to ask me to make friends with my nephew Childebert, that same Childebert whom, in your perversity, you wanted to make my enemy?' 'If you are so carried away by your evil temper,' answered the envoys, 'that you refuse to grant to your nephew the things which you have promised to him, at least do not withhold from him that part of Childebert's kingdom which is his by right.' 'Here is the pact to which we agreed,' answered King Guntram. 'It stipulates that, if one of us should enter the city of Paris without the prior agreement of his brother, he should thereupon forfeit his share; and it nominates Polyeuctes the martyr, with the support of Saint Hilary and Saint Martin, to judge the circumstances and to punish the offender. Not long after this my brother Sigibert entered Paris:

he died by the judgement of God and so forfeited his share. Next Chilperic entered Paris. By breaking the terms of the pact they both lost their claim to a share. They both incurred the vengeance of God and the malediction promised in the pact. Without breaking the law in any way I therefore propose to take under my own jurisdiction the whole kingdom of Charibert and his entire treasure: none of this will I hand over to anybody, except as a completely voluntary act on my part. Off you go, now, you liars and hypocrites, for that is the answer which you can take back to your King.'

7. The envoys departed. A second set of messengers then arrived from Childebert to ask King Guntram to surrender the person of Queen Fredegund. 'Hand over the murderess,' they said, 'the woman who garrotted my aunt,[9] the woman who killed first my father[10] and then my uncle,[11] and who put my two cousins to the sword.'[12] 'We will consider all these matters at an assembly which we propose to hold,' answered King Guntram, 'and so decide what is to be done.' He had taken Fredegund under his protection, inviting her frequently to eat with him, and promising that he would see that she came to no harm. One day, when they were eating at the same table, the Queen rose and begged to be excused, but Guntram asked her to stay. 'Won't you have something more to eat?' he asked. 'You must excuse me,' answered Fredegund. 'I beg you to do so, my lord, for what happens so frequently to women has happened to me, and I am pregnant again.' Guntram was astonished when he heard this, for he knew that four months earlier she had borne a son. All the same, he let her go.

The chief men of Chilperic's kingdom, Ansovald and the others, rallied round his son, who, as I have just said, was four months old. They decided to call him Lothar. From all the cities which had hitherto owed allegiance to Chilperic they exacted an oath of loyalty to King Guntram and his nephew Lothar. King Guntram, as an act of justice, made restitution to a number of

9. Galswinth.   10. King Sigibert.   11. King Chilperic.
12. Merovech and Clovis, the sons of Chilperic.

people of all those possessions which King Chilperic's adherents had wrongly sequestered; he also gave many gifts to the churches. What is more, he honoured the wills of certain persons, now departed this life, who had left their goods to the churches, which wills Chilperic had refused to ratify. He behaved with great kindness to many of his subjects and made considerable grants to the poor.

8. Guntram was still unwilling to trust his person to the Parisians around him and he never went anywhere without an armed escort. Even when he went to church, or to any other place which he wished to visit, he was always surrounded by a band of guards. It happened one Sunday that, after the deacon had requested the congregation to stop speaking, in order that the Mass might be celebrated, the King turned to them and said: 'Men and women, all people present, I ask you to remain loyal to me, instead of assassinating me, as only recently you assassinated my brothers. Give me three years at least in which to bring up these two nephews of mine, who are my adopted sons,[13] for otherwise it might well happen – and this I beg everlasting God not to permit – that I should be killed while they were still small children, and then you, too, would perish, for there would be no full-grown man of my line to protect you.' When they had heard what the King had to say, the entire population prayed to God for his safety.

9. While these things were going on in Paris, Rigunth, the daughter of Chilperic, reached Toulouse, carrying with her the treasures which I have described to you.[14] When she realized that she was already very close to territory held by the Goths,[15] she began to contrive reasons for delay; what is more, her retainers impressed upon her the need to halt for a while in that city, saying that they were exhausted by the journey, their clothes were shabby and their shoes torn to pieces. The furnishings for the horses and the carriages, which were being con-

13. King Childebert II and King Lothar II.
14. *HF*, VI, 45.   15. Septimania.

veyed in the waggons, had still to be assembled. It would be better, they said, to give some attention to these matters now and not to resume their journey until they were in good shape: for in that way they would look their best when they appeared before her bridegroom, instead of meeting the Goths in their present travel-stained condition, thus offering themselves to ridicule. While they were being held up by these considerations, the news of King Chilperic's death began to be whispered into the ears of Desiderius. He collected together some of his most formidable warriors and entered the city of Toulouse. He discovered the whereabouts of the treasure and took it out of the hands of the Princess. He placed it in one of the buildings there, sealed the doors and left a strong force of men on guard. He doled out a meagre allowance to the Princess, this to last her until he should come back to the city.

10.   Desiderius then hurried off to find Mummolus, with whom he had made a pact two years earlier. At this time Mummolus was living inside the walls of Avignon, in company with Gundovald, about whom I told you in an earlier book.[16] Accompanied by the two Dukes Desiderius and Mummolus, Gundovald set off for the district of Limoges, coming to Brives-la-Gaillarde, where is to be found the tomb of Saint Martin, a disciple of our own Martin, or so they say. There Gundovald was raised up as King on a shield. As they carried him round for the third time, he stumbled and had great difficulty in remaining upright, even with the helping hands of those standing round him. Then he made a progress through the neighbouring cities.

Rigunth took up residence in Saint Mary's church in Toulouse, where, as I have told you earlier, Ragnovald's wife had sought sanctuary when she had reason to fear Chilperic. Ragnovald now returned from Spain and took charge once more of his wife and his property. He had gone to Spain on an embassy at the command of King Guntram.

As the army marched in, Saint Martin's church in Brives-la-

16. *HF*, VI, 24 and 26.

Gaillarde was burnt down by a terrible conflagration. The heat was so great that the altar and even the pillars, constructed of different kinds of marble, were destroyed in the fire. However, the building was restored for posterity by Bishop Ferreolus, with such skill that no one could see that it had been damaged. The local inhabitants worship and venerate this Saint Martin of theirs with great devotion, for time and time again they have received proof of his miraculous powers.

11. All this happened in the tenth month of the year.[17] New shoots appeared on the vine-stocks, misshapen grapes formed and the trees blossomed a second time. A great beacon traversed the heavens, lighting up the land far and wide some time before the day dawned. Rays of light shone in the sky, and in the north a column of fire was seen to hang from on high for a space of two hours, with an immense star perched on top of it. There was an earthquake in the district of Angers and many other portents appeared. In my opinion all this announced the coming death of Gundovald.

12. King Guntram thereupon sent his counts to invest the cities which Sigibert had previously taken over from the kingdom of his brother Charibert. Guntram ordered them to demand oaths of loyalty and to subject the cities to his authority. The inhabitants of Tours and Poitiers wanted to transfer to Sigibert's son Childebert; but Guntram called to arms the men of Bourges, who made ready to march against them and began setting light to buildings in the Tours area. Next they burned down the church of Mareuil in that neighbourhood, in which the relics of Saint Martin were preserved. The miraculous power of the Saint made itself felt, for, despite the fierceness of the flames, the cloths which were lying on the altar were not consumed by the fire. More remarkable still, certain herbs, which had been gathered long before and placed on the altar, were not burnt at all. When they saw those conflagrations, the men of Tours sent envoys, for they declared that it was better for them

17. The year began on 1 March, so that the tenth month was December.

to submit to King Guntram for the time being, rather than to have all their possessions destroyed by fire and sword.

13. Immediately after the death of Chilperic, Duke Gararic came to Limoges and received oaths of allegiance in the name of Childebert. From there he moved to Poitiers, where he was received and allowed to take up residence. When he heard what the inhabitants of Tours were suffering, he despatched messengers to us to say that if we wished to further our own interests we should not go over to King Guntram's party, but rather that we should remember Sigibert, whose son was Childebert. We sent back this message in reply to the Bishop and the citizens: that unless they submitted to King Guntram for the time being, they would suffer the same fate as we had. Guntram now stood in the place of father to the two sons of Sigibert and Chilperic, whom he had adopted; and it followed from this that he held sway over the entire kingdom, as his father Lothar had done before him. They did not agree with this; and Gararic rode out from Poitiers, planning to return with an army, but leaving Ebero, King Childebert's Treasurer, behind in the city. With the help of Willachar, Count of Orleans, whom Tours had accepted as its Count, Sichar now led an armed force against the people of Poitiers. In this way the men of Tours could advance on one side and the men of Bourges on the other, and lay waste the whole territory. As soon as they had entered the neighbourhood of Poitiers and begun to burn the houses, the Poitevins sent messengers to them. 'We beg you to desist,' they said, 'until the conference which the two Kings Guntram and Childebert have called. If it is then agreed that King Guntram should take us over in peace, we shall not resist. If not, we recognize as our overlord whichever King we may be called upon to serve.' 'This has nothing to do with us,' the invaders answered. 'We are here to obey our ruler's commands. If you refuse, we shall go on as we have begun and destroy everything.' As things had come to such a pass that all their possessions must otherwise be burnt, or stolen or carried away as loot, the people of Poitiers ordered Childebert's men to leave and gave an oath of allegiance to

King Guntram. They were not destined to keep it for long.

14.   When the time came for the conference, Bishop Egidius, Guntram Boso, Sigivald and a great number of others were sent as representatives to King Guntram by King Childebert. As they came into his presence, the Bishop said: 'Most pious King, we give thanks to Almighty God for having restored you to your kingdom and your territories after so many hazards.' 'Our thanks are indeed due to Him who is King of Kings and Lord of Lords, and who has deigned in His mercy to bring these things to pass,' replied the King; 'but none is due to you, by whose double-dealing and broken promises my lands were sent up in flames this last year, to you who have never kept faith with any man, whose underhand behaviour is common knowledge on all sides, who present yourself not as a bishop but as the sworn enemy of my kingdom.' The Bishop was furious when he heard this, but he did not answer. 'Your nephew Childebert asks that you should order the return of the cities which his father held,' said one of the envoys. 'I have already told you,' replied Guntram, 'that the agreement between us gives these cities to me, and I therefore refuse to return them.' Then another of the envoys said: 'Your nephew asks that you should hand over that witch Fredegund, as the result of whose malpractices so many royal personages have met their end, so that vengeance may be sought for the deaths of his own father, his uncle and his cousins.' 'She has a king as her son,' answered Guntram, 'and she therefore cannot be surrendered into Childebert's hands. What is more, I do not believe the allegations which you have made against her.' It was now Guntram Boso's turn to go up to the King, as if he, too, had something to put forward, but as the rumour had gone round that Gundovald had been publicly raised on the shield as king, Guntram cut him short. 'You enemy of my country and of my kingdom!' he shouted. 'You who many years ago went off to the East for this express purpose of smuggling into my realm a Ballomer!'[18] – for that

18. Ballomer is a Frankish word which is supposed to have meant Pretender.

397

was what King Guntram called Gundovald. 'You traitor, who have never been known to keep your word!' 'You are a ruler' answered Guntram Boso, 'and you sit as king upon a royal throne. That is why no one dares to reply to what you say. For all that, I declare myself innocent of this accusation. If any person of my own rank should dare to bring such a charge secretly, let him now step forward and speak out. Then, most pious King, put the issue to the judgement of God, so that He may decide when He sees us do battle together face to face in the field.' All stood silent, but King Guntram answered: 'All of us present should now have one single cause at heart, to ensure that this adventurer, whose father used once to be a mill-over-seer, should be driven out of our lands. Not to make too nice a point of it, his father sat at a weaver's loom and carded wool.' Although it is possible for a single artisan to exercise both these trades, one of the envoys made the following reply to the King's allegation: 'According to you, then, this man had two fathers, a weaver and a miller! It becomes you ill, King, to talk so fool-ishly. It has never been heard that a man could have two fathers, unless one is speaking of spiritual matters.' At this they all burst out laughing, and another of the envoys added: 'We take our leave of you, King. Since you have refused to hand these cities over to your nephew, we are mindful of the fact that the axe is still ready and waiting which split open the heads of your brothers.[19] One day soon it will split open your head, too.' Thereupon they departed, mad with anger. The King was furious at what they had said. He ordered decaying horse-dung to be flung over their heads as they went, wood-chips, straw and hay which had gone mouldy, and even stinking mud from the town-gutters. They were spattered all over with what was thrown at them, and they went their way beyond measure out-raged and insulted.

15. While Queen Fredegund was still living in the cathedral in

19. This was a fanciful way of speaking, as both Sigibert and Chilperic were stabbed to death. A blow on the head from an axe was the normal Frankish method of execution.

Paris, her servant Leunard, who had just come back from the town of Toulouse, called upon her and began to tell her the wrongs being done to her daughter and the various humiliations which she was suffering. 'According to the orders which you gave me,' he said, 'I accompanied the Princess Rigunth. I witnessed the treatment which she received, and I saw her despoiled of her treasure and of all her possessions. I myself escaped, and I have hurried here to tell my mistress what has happened.' Fredegund went nearly mad when she heard this. She ordered Leunard to be stripped of his possessions there and then in the cathedral. She had his clothes torn off his back and she took away the baldric which Chilperic had given to him. Then she ordered him to get out. The cooks, too, and the pastrycooks, and anybody else whom she recognized as having returned from this expedition, she had mutilated, stripped of their goods and manacled. By making the most wicked charges against him and alleging that he had made off with large sections of the dead King's treasure, she tried to destroy the influence at court of Bishop Badegisil's brother, Nectarius. She declared that he had stolen vast quantities of hides and of wine from the storehouses, and she demanded that he should be bound and cast into the darkest dungeon. The brother of Nectarius spoke up for him and the King was too tolerant to permit this to be done. Fredegund had no fear of God, in whose house she had sought sanctuary, and she was the prime mover in many outrages. At this time she had with her the judge Audo, who, during the lifetime of King Chilperic, had been her accomplice in much evil-doing. With the support of the prefect Mummolus, this Audo had, in the time of King Childebert, exacted taxes from many Franks who had been free men. When that King died, these men stripped and despoiled Audo of everything, so that nothing remained to him except the clothes that he stood up in. They burned his house to the ground; and they would have killed him, too, had he not sought sanctuary with the Queen in the cathedral.

16. Praetextatus, whom the inhabitants of Rouen had recalled

from exile after the death of King Chilperic, returned to his
diocese and was restored to his city with great acclamation.
After his return he visited the city of Paris and sought an audience of King Gunthram, begging him to make a thorough investigation of his case. Queen Fredegund maintained that he ought
not to be restored, in that he had been deposed from his office as
Bishop of Rouen by the decision of forty-five bishops. The
King wanted to summon a council to look into the matter, but
Ragnemod, Bishop of Paris, spoke up for all the others and
said: 'You must know that he was sentenced by these bishops to
do penance, not to be removed from his bishopric.' Praetextatus
was received by the King and invited to have a meal with him;
then he went back to his own city.

17.   Promotus had been installed as Bishop of Châteaudun at
the command of King Sigibert. When that King died he had
been removed from his see, on the argument that Châteaudun
was in the diocese of Chartres. Judgement was given against
him and it was decreed that he should serve merely as a priest.
He sought an audience of the King to ask that he might be
installed once more as bishop in Châteaudun. Pappolus, Bishop
of Chartres, opposed the petition. 'This is my diocese,' said he,
and he came himself to present the decision made by the
bishops.[20] Promotus gained no other dispensation from the
King than that he might have restored to him the private
property which he owned in the region of Châteaudun and
might live there with his mother, who was still alive.

18.   While King Guntram was still in residence in Paris, a poor
man came to him and said: 'Listen, King, to what I have to say.
You should know that Faraulf, who used to be your brother's
chamberlain, is planning to assassinate you. I have heard what
he is plotting: when you are on your way to church for matins,
he plans to attack you with a dagger or transfix you with a
spear.' The King was nonplussed, and he ordered Faraulf to
appear before him. Faraulf denied everything, but the King was

20. At the Council of Paris, A.D. 573.

afraid and surrounded himself by an armed guard. He never
again went to church or, indeed, anywhere else, unless he was
protected by guards and men carrying their weapons. Not long
after this Faraulf died.

19. A great outcry arose against the men who had held positions of great power while Chilperic was King. They were accused of having misappropriated by main force villas and all
sorts of property belonging to others. As I have already told
you, the King ordered that everything which had been seized
unjustly should be handed back.[21] He told Queen Fredegund
to return to the manor of Rueil, which is in the Rouen area.
With her went all the chief men of King Chilperic's realm.
There they left her in the care of Bishop Melanius, who had
been deposed from the episcopate of Rouen.[22] Then they
transferred their allegiance to her son Lothar, promising that he
should be brought up with the greatest care.

20. When Queen Fredegund had been packed off to the manor
about which I have told you, she was very depressed, because
much of her power had been brought to an end, and yet she
considered herself a better woman than Brunhild. In secret she
sent a cleric of her household who was to gain Brunhild's
confidence by trickery and then assassinate her. If only he could
on some pretence or other be accepted as one of her retainers
and so gain her confidence, she could then be despatched when
no one was about. The cleric went off to Brunhild and by the
lies which he told made his way into her good graces. 'I am a
fugitive from Queen Fredegund,' he said, 'and I seek your
protection.' He began by behaving in a most humble manner to
everyone and so gave himself out as the obedient and trusty
servant of the Queen. Not long afterwards they realized on
what a treacherous errand he had been sent. He was bound and
flogged until he confessed his secret plan; then he was permitted
to return to the Queen who had sent him. When he told Frede-

21. *HF*, VII, 7.
22. The reinstatement of Praetextatus made this necessary.

gund what had happened and confessed that he had failed in his mission, she punished him by having his hands and feet cut off.

21. While these things were happening, King Guntram set off for Chalon in an attempt to find out the truth concerning his brother's death. Queen Fredegund tried to put the blame on the Treasurer, Eberulf. After the death of King Chilperic, she had asked him to come to live with her, but he had refused. A bitter enmity had resulted between them, and the Queen now alleged that it was he who had killed Chilperic, that he had stolen much of the treasury and had then gone off with it to Touraine. If the King wished to avenge his brother's death, let him know that this was the ringleader in the crime. King Guntram swore before all his leaders that he would destroy not only Eberulf himself but his children down to the ninth generation, so that by their death an end might be put to an abominable habit and no more kings be assassinated. As soon as Eberulf heard of this, he sought sanctuary in the church of Saint Martin, whose property he had often made off with. It was thought necessary to set up a guard over him, and the men of Orleans and Blois took it in turns to keep watch. They duly arrived, but, when they had stayed fifteen days, they set off home again, taking with them a vast amount of loot, carrying off pack-animals, cattle and whatever they could lay their hands on. These men who had stolen Saint Martin's animals then quarrelled among themselves and started thrusting each other through with their spears. Two of them, who were driving off the mules, came to the house of one of the local inhabitants and began to ask for a drink. The man said that he had none, so they levelled their spears and were about to transfix him. Thereupon he drew his sword and pierced them both. They fell to the ground and died on the spot. Saint Martin's beasts arrived home safe. So many crimes were committed on this occasion by the men of Orleans that it is impossible to tell them all.

22. In the meantime Eberulf's possessions were distributed

among a number of people. The gold, silver and other precious objects which he kept with him the King ordered to be put on display. The lands granted to him for life were sold by public auction. His herds of horses, his pigs and beasts of burden were taken from him. His house inside the city walls, which he had sequestered from church property, and which was filled with corn, wine, fowls and all sorts of other things, was completely ransacked, until nothing remained but the bare walls. Despite the fact that I had been most punctilious in my attention to his affairs, he held me more responsible for this than anyone else, and he threatened that, if he ever returned to royal favour, it was from me that he would exact vengeance for all that he was suffering. God, to whom all secrets of the heart are known, is well aware that with a clear conscience I gave him every assistance which was in my power. Although he had treated me very badly over property which belonged to Saint Martin, I had good reason to overlook his evil actions, for it was I who had held his son at the baptismal font. In my opinion the cause of his unhappy downfall was that he had no reverence for the saintly Bishop Martin. He often committed manslaughter in the very vestibule which led towards the Saint's tomb, and he behaved there in a drunken and stupid way. Once he flung a priest on a bench, beat him with his fists and belaboured him with blows, to the point that he nearly breathed his last, simply because he had refused to give Eberulf wine when he was obviously drunk. The priest would have died if the doctors had not arrived with their cupping-glasses.

In his fear of the King, Eberulf took up residence in the sacristy of the holy church. When the priest who had charge of the door-keys had locked everything up and gone off, Eberulf's young women and his men-servants used to come in through the sacristy entrance and stand gaping at the frescoes on the walls or pry about among the decorations on the Saint's tomb, all of which was a desecration of religious feeling. When the priest realized what was happening, he nailed up the top of the door and had locks fitted to it. After supper, when he was sodden with wine, Eberulf noticed what had been done. In a mad

frenzy he came up to me inside the church, where I was chanting psalms at the service held at nightfall, and began loading me
with curses and insults, reproaching me, among other things,
with having cut off his access to the fringes which hang round
the Saint's tomb.[23] I was amazed to hear him start such insane
ravings, but I tried to soothe him by talking to him quietly.
When I was unable to appease him by speaking to him in this
gentle fashion, I made up my mind to remain silent. As soon as
he saw that I was determined to say no more, he turned on my
priest and cursed him roundly. He assailed him with wanton
insults, and submitted me to every vilification to which he could
lay his tongue. When we realized that Eberulf was harassed by
a devil, so to speak, we marched out of the church and put an
end both to this scandalous episode and to our own evening
prayers, bearing it very ill that he had permitted himself this
shameful behaviour without any respect for the Saint and just
in front of his tomb. About this time I had a vision, which I
related to Eberulf in the holy church itself. 'I saw myself in this
consecrated building, celebrating the sacred rite of Mass,' I told
him. 'When the altar, with the holy offerings upon it, was
already covered with a silken cloth, I suddenly saw King Guntram come rushing in. "Drive out this enemy of my family!" he
shouted. "Remove this murderer from God's sacred altar!"
When I heard him, I turned to you and said: "Hold tight, miserable wretch, to the altar cloth which covers the holy offerings,
for otherwise you will be expelled from the church." You seized
hold of it, but with a feeble hand, instead of grasping it firmly. I
spread my own hands wide and pressed my chest against that of
the King. "Do not dare to drag this man out of the sacred
building," I cried, "on peril of your life, lest the saintly Bishop
slay you with his miraculous power! Do not encompass your
own death with your own weapon, for if you do so you will
forfeit not only your earthly life but also the life to come!" The
King resisted me, and you let go the altar-cloth and came up
behind me. I was very angry with you. Then you went back to

23. If he were molested he would hold on to these as proof that he was
in sanctuary.

the altar and seized hold of the cloth a second time, but a second time you let it go. While you were holding it in a feeble way, and I was manfully resisting the King, I woke up in fear and trembling, not knowing what the vision meant.' When I had told Eberulf all this, he said, 'The vision which you saw is true, for it tallies completely with my intentions.' 'What are your intentions, then?' I asked. 'I had made up my mind,' he answered, 'that, if the King ordered me to be thrown out from this place, I would hold the altar-cloth in one hand and draw my sword with the other. First I would kill you and then I would slay as many churchmen as I could lay my hands on. It would mean nothing to me if I had to die next, if I had taken vengeance on the clerics of this Saint of yours.' I was amazed when I heard this and I wondered how such a thing could be, for the Devil was speaking through his mouth. He had never shown any reverence for God. As long as he had his freedom, his horses and flocks were sent to ravage the crops and the vines of the poor. If those animals were driven out again by the men whose labours were being ruined, he would have them struck down by his servants. Even in the sorry straits in which he found himself, he would boast of what he had stolen from the saintly Bishop. Only the year before he had stirred up some foolish fellow from among the townsfolk and ordered him to molest the church bailiffs. Then, setting all justice at naught, by a spurious purchase-order he had sequestered certain property belonging to the church and rewarded the man concerned by giving him a golden ornament from his own baldric. To the last day of his life, which I shall later describe to you, he went on acting in this wicked way.

23. In this same year[24] a Jew called Armentarius, accompanied by a man of his own religion and two Christians, came to Tours to collect payment on some bonds which had been given to him on the security of public taxes by Injuriosus, who had been Vice-Count at the time, and by Eunomius, who had then been Count. Armentarius had an interview with the

24. A.D. 584.

two men and they agreed to repay the money with the accrued interest. They told him that they would go on ahead. 'If you follow us to our house,' they said, 'we will pay you what we owe, and in addition we have some gifts to give to you, as is only right in the circumstances.' Armentarius made his way there and was received by Injuriosus. He sat down to dinner. When the meal was over and night had begun to fall, they moved from this house to another. Then, so they say, the Jews and the two Christians were killed by the servants of Injuriosus and their bodies were thrown into a well which was near the house. Their relations heard what had happened and travelled to Tours. From information received from certain persons, they identified the well and recovered the bodies. Injuriosus hotly denied that he had played any part in the crime. He was prosecuted; but, as I have said, he denied his guilt vehemently, and the plaintiffs had no evidence on which he could be convicted. He was sentenced to clear himself by oath. The dead men's relations were not satisfied with this, and they demanded that the case should be brought before King Childebert's court. The money and the bonds of the dead Jew were never found. Many said that Medard, the assistant of Injuriosus, was mixed up in this crime, for he, too, had borrowed money from the Jew. Injuriosus attended the court before King Childebert, and sat there waiting three days in succession until the setting of the sun. The plaintiffs never came and no one put in an appearance to prosecute Injuriosus, so he returned home.

24. In the tenth year of King Childebert's reign[25] King Guntram called up all the men in the realm who were liable for service and brought together a vast army. The greater part of this force, including the men of Orleans and Bourges, marched on Poitiers, the inhabitants of which city had broken the oath of allegiance which they had made to the King. The invaders sent envoys ahead of them to ask whether or not the Poitevins would admit them, but Maroveus, the Bishop of Poitiers, gave these

25. A.D. 585.

envoys a hostile reception. The troops then invaded the lands
belonging to Poitiers, looted them, set light to the buildings and
massacred the inhabitants. On their return journey they
marched through the Tours region with their plunder, and there
they did the same damage, although the Tourangeaux had
sworn the oath of allegiance. They even burned the churches
and they carted off everything on which they could lay their
hands. They ravaged the region of Poitiers several times, and in
the end the inhabitants had to recognize the King, although they
did it with an ill grace. When the invading armies came close to
the city itself and most of the neighbourhood had been ravaged,
they sent representatives who were to declare their loyalty to
King Guntram. Once the soldiers were admitted inside the city
walls, they attacked the Bishop and accused him of disloyalty.
When he saw that he was at their mercy, Maroveus broke up a
chalice which he had among his church vessels, melted it down
into coins and so ransomed himself and his people.

25. The troops also attacked Marileif, who had been the chief
physician at the court of King Chilperic. He had already been
robbed once by Duke Gararic; and now he was stripped a
second time, so that nothing remained to him of all his property. They took his horses, his gold and silver, and all his
precious possessions, of which he had a vast store, and reduced
him once more to service to the church. That had been his
father's position, for he had been in charge of the church mills,
while his brothers, cousins and other relations had been employed in the royal kitchens and bakery.

26. Gundovald now planned to move to Poitiers, but he was
afraid to do so. He had heard that an army was being raised
against him. He demanded an oath of allegiance to King Childebert from all the cities which had belonged to King Sigibert.
The others, which had belonged either to Guntram or to Chilperic, had to swear an oath to Gundovald himself. Then he moved
to Angoulême, received the oath there and gave bribes to the

chief citizens. After that he went to Périgueux, where he persecuted the Bishop[26] for not having received him with due
honour.

27. Gundovald next marched on Toulouse. He sent messengers to Magnulf, who was Bishop in the city, to order him to
receive him. Magnulf had not forgotten the ill-treatment which
he had suffered earlier on at the hands of Sigulf, who had also
aspired to the kingship. 'We know that Guntram and his
nephews are kings,' said he to the citizens. 'Where this man
comes from we have no idea. Be on your guard, then. If Duke
Desiderius intends to inflict a similar disaster on us, let him die
the same death as Sigulf died. This must be an example to all
men that no foreigner must dare to violate the Frankish realm.'
They prepared to resist and made ready for war, but Gundovald
arrived with a vast army. When the Toulousains saw that resistance was impossible, they admitted Gundovald.

Some time later, when the Bishop was sitting at table with
Gundovald, he said to him: 'You maintain that you are the son
of King Lothar, but we have no way of telling whether or not
this is true. It seems incredible to me that you can carry out
what you have planned.' Gundovald replied: 'I am indeed the
son of King Lothar and I am determined to take over my share
of the kingdom without any more delay. I shall march on Paris
with all speed and there I shall establish the seat of my government.' 'If you succeed in carrying out what you say,' answered
Magnulf, 'then it is indeed true that no prince of the Frankish
royal line remains alive.' When Mummolus heard this altercation between the two of them, he raised his hand and boxed
the Bishop's ears. 'It is not right,' he said, 'for so stupid and
debased a man as you to give such an answer to a great King!'
When Desiderius understood what the Bishop was thinking and
saying, he in his turn laid hands on him. They both prodded
Magnulf with their spears, punched him and kicked him. Then
they bound him with a rope and banished him from his city.
They stole all his possessions and those of his church, too.

26. Charterius; cp. *HF*, VI, 22.

Waddo, who had been major-domo to Princess Rigunth, joined them in what they were doing. The others who had set out from Paris with Waddo had already dispersed and sought safety in flight.

28. The next thing which happened was that the army ended its occupation of Poitiers and set out in pursuit of Gundovald. Many of the inhabitants of Tours marched behind it, hoping to share in the plunder. In effect the Poitevins waylaid these camp-followers and killed some of them, leaving the others to return home stripped of everything they had. At the same time the contingent of Tourangeaux who had joined the army in the first place decided to desert. The main body of the army advanced as far as the River Dordogne and there awaited news of Gundovald. As I have already told you, Duke Desiderius had joined him, with Bladast and Waddo, Princess Rigunth's major-domo. The allies he thought most of were Bishop Sagittarius and Mummolus. Sagittarius had been promised the bishopric of Toulouse.

29. In the meantime King Guntram sent a certain Claudius with these instructions: 'If you will go and drag Eberulf out of Saint Martin's church, and then either kill him with your sword or load him with chains, I will reward you richly; but, whatever else you do, I enjoin you not to damage the sacred building itself.' Claudius set out for Paris immediately. He was an empty-headed and greedy fellow. His wife came from the Meaux area. He debated with himself whether or not he should go to see Queen Fredegund. 'If I do see her, she, too, may give me some reward. After all, I know very well that she is the personal enemy of the man whom I am sent to kill.' He did visit the Queen and he was immediately loaded with presents. What is more, he elicited from her the promise of much more, if only he would drag Eberulf out of the church and kill him, or capture him by some subterfuge or other and load him with chains, or, indeed, even cut him down in the vestibule of the church. Claudius went back to Châteaudun and ordered the Count to

put three hundred men under his command to garrison the gates of the city of Tours. In effect, once he reached Tours, he was going to use these men to destroy Eberulf. The local Count called up three hundred of his men and Claudius made his way to Tours. While he was riding along he began to look out for auguries, as the barbarous Franks always do, and his conclusion was that they were unfavourable. He also questioned a number of people as to whether or not Saint Martin had recently exercised his miraculous power against those who had broken faith, and especially as to whether vengeance was exacted immediately from anyone who did wrong to those who put their hopes in the Saint. He rode on ahead of the men who were supposed to give him support and came to the church. Without more ado he went up to the ill-fated Eberulf. He gave Eberulf his solemn word, and swore by all that he held holy, and even by the miraculous power of the saintly Bishop whose remains lay just beside them, that no one could be more faithful to his cause and no one could represent that cause so well to the King. The pathetic creature had formed this plan in his mind: 'I shall never get the better of him unless I trick him by swearing these oaths to him.' When Eberulf heard Claudius promise these things and swear oaths about them in the church itself and in the portico and in the other venerated parts of the vestibule, the poor fool believed the man who was perjuring himself. The next day, when I myself was staying in a country manor some thirty miles away from the city, Eberulf was invited to a meal in the church-house. Claudius and a number of the citizens were present. Claudius would have struck Eberulf down there and then with his sword, if the man's servants had not been so close. Eberulf was unobservant and he noticed nothing. When the meal was over, Eberulf and Claudius walked up and down the forecourt of the church-house, swearing faith and friendship to each other, with a running exchange of oaths. As they were chatting, Claudius said to Eberulf: 'It would give me great pleasure to come and have a drink in your lodging, if the wine were mixed with spices, or if you, my noble friend, would order up a stoup of stronger drink.' Eberulf was delighted when he

heard this. He said that he had exactly what Claudius was thinking of. 'You will find all that you want in my lodging,' he said,
'provided, my noble lord, that you will deign to enter the poor
hovel in which I live.' He then sent his servants, first one and
then another, to fetch more potent wines, those of Latium and
Gaza. When Claudius saw that all Eberulf's servants had gone
off and that he was left alone, he lifted up his hand in the direction of the church and said: 'Holy Martin, bring it about that I
soon may see my wife and my relations again!' The wretched
man was now on the horns of a dilemma: he was planning to
murder Eberulf in the vestibule and he feared the miraculous
power of the saintly Bishop. One of the servants of Claudius
who was stronger than the rest seized Eberulf from behind,
clasped him tight in his powerful arms, and held him
with his chest stuck out so that his throat could the
more easily be cut. Claudius drew his sword from his baldric and aimed a blow at Eberulf. Although he was gripped
so tight, Eberulf drew a dagger from his belt and prepared to
strike Claudius. Claudius raised his right hand high in the air
and stuck his knife into Eberulf's chest. With a great effort
Eberulf planted his own dagger under Claudius' armpit and
then withdrew it and with a lunging blow cut off Claudius'
thumb. Claudius' servants then came running back from all
directions with their swords drawn and stabbed Eberulf in a
number of places. He slipped out of their hands and started to
run, although he was already mortally wounded. They struck
him a mighty blow on the head with a naked sword. He fell
down, with his brains scattered. It was too much for him to
expect to be saved by Saint Martin, for he had never known
what it was to pray to the Saint with a contrite heart. Claudius
was terrified by what had happened and sought refuge in the
Abbot's cell, seeking protection from one whose patron he had
never had the sense to reverence. The Abbot was there and
Claudius said to him: 'A frightful crime has been committed
and if you do not help me I shall be killed!' As he said this
Eberulf's men rushed up with their swords and spears at the
ready. They shattered the glass panes and hurled their spears

through the windows in the wall. Claudius was already half dead and they transfixed him with one of the blows. His own men were hiding behind the doors and under the beds. Two of the churchmen present seized hold of the Abbot and dragged him out more dead than alive through the line of naked swords. The doors were opened wide and the band of armed men marched in. Some of the beggars who regularly received alms at the church and a number of other poor folk were so incensed at the crime that they tried to pull the roof off the cell. Then certain men who were possessed of devils and a number of other wretched creatures seized sticks and stones and rushed to avenge the violence done to their church, bearing it ill that such atrocities as had never been witnessed before should now have been perpetrated there. What more can I tell you? Those who had taken refuge were dragged from their hiding-places and cruelly put to death. The floor of the Abbot's cell reeked with blood. The dead bodies were pulled out and left to lie naked on the ground. The killers seized what loot they could and disappeared into the darkness which had now fallen. The vengeance of God was not slow to fall on those who had defiled His holy house with blood; but the wrong-doing of the man Eberulf, whom Saint Martin had permitted to endure all this, was certainly very great.

King Guntram was furious at what had happened, but he calmed down when he learned the full details. All the property of this unhappy man, his personal possessions and the real estate which he had inherited from his ancestors, Guntram distributed among his own supporters, who left Eberulf's wife, now reduced to penury, to the care of Saint Martin's church. Their near relations carried away the corpses of Claudius and the others, and buried them in their own country.

30. Gundovald then sent two messengers, both of them churchmen, to his supporters. One of the two, the Abbot of Cahors, carried a letter which he had hidden under the wax of his hollowed-out wooden tablets. He was captured by King Guntram's men and the letter was discovered. He was taken

before the King, severely beaten and thrown into prison.

31. At this time Gundovald was in the city of Bordeaux, where he had the support of Bishop Bertram. He was looking out for anyone who could further his cause. Somebody told him that a certain king in Eastern parts had obtained possession of the thumb of Saint Sergius the martyr, and that he had attached this to his own right arm. Whenever he needed help to drive back his enemies, he would put his trust in this support; for when he raised his right arm the enemy troops would immediately turn in flight, as if they had been vanquished by the martyr's miraculous power. As soon as Gundovald heard of this, he began to inquire very urgently whether there was anybody in the neighbourhood who had managed to acquire any relics of this martyr Saint Sergius. The name of a merchant called Eufronius was put forward by Bishop Bertram. Bertram hated Eufronius, because he had once had him tonsured against his will, hoping to obtain control of his possessions, but Eufronius had treated the whole matter with ridicule, going off to live in another town until his hair grew, and then returning. 'There is a certain Syrian living in this city,' said Bertram. 'His name is Eufronius and he has turned his house into a shrine. In this house he has placed relics of the Saint whom you have just mentioned: through their influence, and with the help of the supernatural power of the martyr, he has witnessed many miracles. There was a time, for instance, when the city of Bordeaux was being burnt in a great fire, but Eufronius' house was not touched, although it was enveloped in flames.' When Bertram said this, Mummolus immediately set off at full speed for the Syrian's house, taking the Bishop with him. They stood on either side of the man, and Mummolus demanded that the holy relics be shown to him. Eufronius refused to do so. Thinking that some trap was perhaps being laid for him, in view of the malice which the Bishop bore him, he said: 'I am an old man. Do stop harassing me and insulting the Saint. Here are a hundred gold pieces. Take them and go.' Mummolus repeated that he wanted to see the holy relics. Eufronius then offered him two hundred gold

pieces, but he could not persuade him to leave until the relics
had been shown to him. They were hidden in a casket high up in
the wall near the altar. Mummolus ordered a ladder to be set up
against the wall, and then he told one of Bishop Bertram's
deacons to climb up. The man clambered up the steps of the
ladder and took hold of the casket, but he trembled so violently
that it seemed impossible that he could reach the ground again
alive. Anyway, as I have said, he took the casket in his hand,
from where it was hanging against the wall, and brought it
down. Mummolus examined it and found in it one of the
bones of the Saint's finger. He had the nerve to give it a knock
with his knife. He hit it with this knife, first on one side and then
on the other. After giving it a number of such blows, he managed with great difficulty to break it. The little bone broke into
three pieces and the fragments dropped out of sight in different
directions. What had happened can hardly have pleased the
martyr, or so I imagine. Eufronius wept bitterly and all three
knelt in prayer, beseeching God of His grace to deign to reveal
to them the fragments which had disappeared from human
sight. When they had finished their prayers, they discovered the
pieces of bone. Mummolus took one of them and went off with
it, but not with the approval of the martyr, as the remainder of
the story has made clear.

While Gundovald and Mummolus were still in Bordeaux,
they ordered the priest Faustianus to be installed as Bishop of
Dax. The local prelate had recently died, and Nicetius, Count
of the city, who was brother of Rusticus, the Bishop of Aire,
had obtained written permission from Chilperic for him to be
tonsured and made Bishop of the diocese. Gundovald went out
of his way to nullify every decree which Chilperic issued. He
summoned the bishops and ordered them to give their blessing
to Faustianus. Bishop Bertram, the Metropolitan, was afraid
of what might happen, so he told Palladius, Bishop of Saintes,
to give the blessing. It is true that his eyes were troubling him at
the time. Orestes, Bishop of Bazas, was also at the consecration,
but he denied it later on when he was summoned before the
King.

32.   After this Gundovald once more sent two messengers to
King Guntram. They carried consecrated wands, according to
the Frankish custom, so that they should not be molested by
anybody, but might return with the answer once they had explained the purpose of their mission. Even before they had
been given an audience by the King, they were foolish enough
to reveal to quite a number of people what they were trying to
achieve. This was immediately reported to King Guntram: and
they were brought into his presence in chains. They did not dare
to deny what they had come to ask, whom they were seeking or
by whom they had been sent. 'Gundovald, who has only recently arrived from the East, maintains that he is the son of
King Lothar, your own father,' they said. 'He has sent us to
demand that portion of Lothar's kingdom which is his due.
You must know that unless you hand it over he will come to
attack you at the head of an army. All the most powerful men
of that region of Gaul which lies beyond the Dordogne have
rallied to his standard. This is the message which he sends to
you: "When we meet on the battlefield, God will make it clear
whether or not I am King Lothar's son." ' King Guntram was
furious. He ordered the men to be stretched on the rack, so that
they might give further proof as to whether or not they were
speaking the truth. If they were keeping back any more secrets
in the depths of their hearts, the terrible torture would force
them to confess it, whether they wanted to or not. As their
agony increased they confessed that Guntram's niece, the
daughter of King Chilperic,[27] had been sent into exile with
Magnulf, the Bishop of Toulouse, and that the whole of her
treasure had been seized by Gundovald, who had been asked to
accept the kingship by all King Childebert's leaders. Things had
come to a head a few years earlier when Guntram Boso had
visited Constantinople with the express purpose of inviting
Gundovald to come to Gaul.

33.   The messengers were flogged and thrown into prison. King
Guntram then ordered his nephew Childebert to be summoned,

27. Rigunth.

415

for it was clearly desirable that they should both in each other's presence hear the evidence of the messengers. The two Kings therefore questioned the prisoners together, and the men repeated to them both what King Guntram had already heard alone. They continued to assert that this conspiracy, as I have already told you, was common knowledge to all the more senior people in King Childebert's realm. That was the reason why some of King Childebert's leaders had been afraid to come to this conference, for they were suspected of being implicated in the plot. King Guntram placed his spear in King Childebert's hand and then he said: 'This is a sign that I have handed the whole of my realm over to you. Go now, and by this token take under your own rule all my cities, just as if they were yours. As a consequence of the sins which I have committed, no male of my own line remains alive, except you who are my brother's son. I exclude all others from the succession. It is you who are my heir and you must inherit my whole kingdom.' Then Guntram dismissed all the others present and took the boy on one side so that he might speak with him in private, adjuring him most earnestly never to reveal to any man the secrets of their conversation. He then told Childebert which men he should choose to share his counsel and which he must exclude from all his secret plans – those whom he might trust, those whom he should avoid, those whom he might well honour with gifts and those whom he must degrade from their offices. Above all he warned Childebert never to trust Bishop Egidius, or even to permit him to come near, for he had always been Guntram's enemy, and time and time again he had perjured himself to him and to his father. Later on they appeared together at the feast and King Guntram addressed his assembled warriors in the following terms: 'Men, you observe that my son Childebert is already a grown man. See to it that you are careful not to take him any longer for a child. The time has come for you to abandon your doubts and any feelings of superiority which you may still have towards him. He is now a king and you must serve him as such.' That is what he said and he went on for some time in the same strain. They kept the feast going for three days, making merry together and exchanging many gifts. Then they parted in peace. On this occasion King Guntram restored to Childebert everything that his father Sigibert had held. He warned him not to visit his mother, and not to give her any opportunity of writing to Gundovald or of receiving communications from him.

34. When Gundovald heard that Guntram's army was marching in his direction, he crossed the Garonne and made for Saint-Bertrand-de-Comminges. Duke Desiderius had deserted him, but he was still supported by Bishop Sagittarius, the two Dukes Mummolus and Bladast, and Waddo. The town of Comminges is built on the top of a high hill, with no other elevated spot near. At the foot of the hill a great spring gushes forth, enclosed by a strongly fortified tower: the inhabitants go down to the spring by a covered way, so that when they draw water they are not exposed to view. Gundovald invested the town at the beginning of Lent. He addressed the townsfolk and said: 'You know that I have been elected King, with the backing of all those who dwell in Childebert's realm. What is more, I have a strong force of men with me. However, my brother, King Guntram, is moving up an immense army to attack me. You must therefore bring all your food-supplies and all your equipment inside the circuit of your walls, so that you may not die of famine while waiting for God in His compassion to bring me reinforcements.' They believed what he said and moved all their possessions inside the town, making ready to resist. King Guntram then sent a letter to Gundovald in the name of Queen Brunhild, advising him to disband his troops and order them to return home, while he himself took up winter-quarters in Bordeaux without letting anyone know where he was. This letter was a trick, so that Guntram could find out what Gundovald planned to do. Gundovald remained in Comminges. He addressed the inhabitants a second time. 'The enemy army is approaching,' he said. 'You must sally forth and fight.' They marched out to do battle. Gundovald's men then seized the gates, slammed them to and so shut out the people of Com-

minges and their Bishop.[28] They thereupon took possession of everything which they could find in the town. They discovered such a vast quantity of corn and wine that, had they resisted like men, they would have had supplies to last them many years.

35. By now King Guntram's leaders had learnt that Gundovald was ensconced on the opposite bank of the Garonne, with a huge force of enemy troops and having in his possession the entire treasure of Rigunth, which he had stolen. They advanced until they reached the Garonne and then swam across with their horses, some of the soldiers being drowned in the process. The remainder reached the opposite bank. In their search for Gundovald they came upon camels and horses, still carrying huge loads of gold and silver, which his men had abandoned along the roads because the animals were exhausted. Then they learned that Gundovald's troops had taken up their position inside Comminges. They left their waggons and baggage train behind in the charge of the less able-bodied, and sent on ahead the stronger men, who had already crossed the Garonne, to launch the attack. These advanced at great speed and came to the great church of Saint Vincent, inside the boundaries of the town of Agen, on the spot where the martyr is said to have ended his fight in the name of Christ. They found the church filled with all sorts of treasures belonging to the local inhabitants. Their hope was that the shrine of so great a martyr would never be violated by men calling themselves Christians. The doors were heavily padlocked. As soon as they realized that they could not unlock the church doors, the advancing troops promptly set light to them. Once the doors were burnt down, the soldiers looted all the property and all the equipment which they found there, and stole the church plate as well. The vengeance which God exacted gave them a severe fright. Many of their hands caught fire supernaturally and gave forth a great smoke, like the pall which rises from a conflagration. Some were possessed by a devil and rushed about screaming the martyr's name. Others fought with each other

28. Rufinus.

and wounded themselves with their own javelins. A vast horde of troops continued to advance, but with fear in their hearts. What more is there to tell? They came to Comminges, for, as I have told you, that was the name of the township. The entire force pitched camp in the countryside immediately round the town, and there they remained in the tents which they had put up. They ravaged the whole region, but some of the soldiers, more avid for booty than their comrades, wandered too far afield and were killed by the peasants.

36. They kept climbing up the hill to taunt Gundovald and to hurl insults at him. 'You are that painter-fellow, aren't you,' they would ask, 'who, in the days of King Lothar, used to slap whitewash on the walls and cellars of oratories? Aren't you the chap whom the inhabitants of Gaul used to call Ballomer?[29] Surely it is you who, because of the fairy-tales which you keep telling about yourself, had your hair cut short every now and again by the Frankish kings, and were sent into exile? Tell us, you wretched creature, who it was who sent you here! Who put the rash idea into your head to presume to set foot in the domain of our lords and masters? If someone did invite you here, don't be afraid to tell us his name! The death you must die surely stares you in the face! You can see before you the pit of destruction for which you have been asking for so long and into which you will be flung headlong! Tell us the names of your confederates! Let us know who it really was who invited you here!' When he heard all this, Gundovald appeared in person on top of the town-gate. 'Everybody knows that my father Lothar hated me,' he answered. 'It is common knowledge that I had my hair cut short on a number of occasions, both by him and by my brothers. That is why I went over to Narses, the military leader in Italy. There I married and became the father of two sons. When my wife died, I took my children with me and went off to Constantinople. I was welcomed warmly by the Eastern Emperors, and there I lived until recently. A few years ago Guntram Boso came to Constan-

29. Cp. p. 397, note 18.

tinople. I questioned him closely about the fate of my brothers
and I was told that our line had almost died out. Of all our
house none remained except the two Kings Childebert and
Guntram, my brother and my brother's son. The sons of King
Chilperic had died with him, leaving only one small child alive.
My brother Guntram had no sons.[30] My nephew Childebert
had no following. Guntram Boso told me all this in detail.
"Come!" he said. "You are invited by all the leaders of King
Childebert's realm, for not one has dared to speak against you.
We all know that you are Lothar's son. If you refuse to come,
there is nobody in Gaul who can rule over his kingdom." I
rewarded him richly. In twelve sacred places I made him swear
to me that I should be safe if I set foot in this realm. I landed in
Marseilles, where the Bishop welcomed me warmly. He showed
me letters from the leaders of my nephew's kingdom. From
there I rode to Avignon, on the advice of the patrician Mummolus. Guntram Boso broke his oath and his promises, for he
stole my treasure and took it for himself. You must therefore
recognize that I, too, am a King, just as much as my brother
Guntram is. If the hatred which you bear me burns too fiercely
in your hearts, take me to your King and, if only he will accept
me as his brother, he may do with me what he will. If you
refuse to do this, let me return to the place from which I set
out. I will go willingly and I will do harm to no man. Ask
Radegund of Poitiers and Ingitrude of Tours, and you will find
that what I say is true.' As he spoke the mob capped his words
with taunts and insults.

37. The fifteenth day of the siege dawned. Leudegisel[31] spent
this time in preparing new machines with which to destroy the
city. He constructed wagons, which he fitted with battering-
rams and protected with wattle-work, old leather saddles and
planks of wood, so that the troops could rush forward under

30. These circumstances were true in 585, when Gundovald was speaking.
When he had arrived in Gaul in 582 Chilperic was still alive.
31. Leudegisel was King Guntram's Count of the Stables. He was in
charge of the siege of Comminges.

cover to knock down the walls. The moment they came near, rocks were dropped on their heads, so that all who approached the city walls were killed. The defenders hurled down on them flaming barrels of pitch and fat, as well as boxes filled with stones. Once nightfall had brought the struggle to an end, the besiegers returned to their camp.

Among Gundovald's supporters was a certain Chariulf, a wealthy man and an important one. The city was full of his store-houses and granaries, and it was from his supplies that Gundovald's troops were for the most part fed.

When Bladast observed the way in which things were going, he was very frightened, for he foresaw that Leudegisel would capture the city and put them all to death. He set light to the church-house and, when all the beleaguered soldiers ran to put it out, he took to flight and got away. As soon as morning came, the besiegers launched a second assault. They prepared fascines from bundles of sticks, and tried to fill in the deep ravine which lies on the eastern side. This device did no harm to anyone. Bishop Sagittarius walked round and round the ramparts fully-armed, and with his own hand kept tossing rocks on to the heads of the besiegers.

38.   When they saw that all their efforts were in vain, those who were attacking the city sent messengers in secret to Mummolus. 'Acknowledge your true overlord,' they said, 'and even at this late hour withdraw from this senseless revolt. How can you be so foolhardy as to serve this unknown man? We have captured your wife and your children. No doubt by this time your sons have been put to death. What earthly purpose is there in what you are doing? All you can expect is your own destruction.' When he received this message, Mummolus said: 'I am well aware that we are at the end of our tether, and that we have no more power to resist. For me there is only one course open. If only I had your assurance that my life would be saved, I would spare you further efforts.' The messengers returned to their camp. Bishop Sagittarius made his way to the cathedral, taking with him Mummolus, Chariulf and Waddo. Once there,

they swore an oath to each other that, if only their lives were promised to them, they would break their alliance with Gundovald and hand him over to his enemies. The messengers came back once more, with an assurance that their lives would be spared. Mummolus answered: 'If this is done, I will hand Gundovald over to you. For my part, I will acknowledge that King Guntram is my overlord, and I will seek an audience with him immediately.' The messengers swore that, if Mummolus kept his word, they would receive him in peace. If they failed to persuade the King to give him pardon, they would make it possible for him to seek sanctuary in some church, so that he might escape the punishment of death. They gave him their solemn word and then they departed.

Mummolus, with Bishop Sagittarius and Waddo, went off to interview Gundovald. 'You who stand there before us', they said, 'are only too well aware of what promises of loyalty we all made to you. Now, here is some good advice for you. Go forth from this city and seek an audience with your brother, as you have repeatedly said you wished to do. We have just had a conference with these men. They have told us that the King does not wish to lose that support which you can give him, seeing that so few members of your generation remain alive in his family.' Gundovald knew that he was being tricked, and he burst out sobbing. 'It was at your invitation that I came to Gaul,' he cried. 'Half of my treasure, which included an immense weight of gold and silver, and many precious objects, lies blocked in Avignon, and the other half has been stolen by Guntram Boso. Next to God's help, I placed all my hope in you. I gave you my full confidence. Through you I hoped to become King. If you have deceived me, you must explain your actions to God, for it is He who must judge my case.' Mummolus listened to him and then replied: 'There is nothing treacherous in what we have said. You see those fully-armed men who stand there at the city gate. It is for you that they are waiting. Take off my golden baldric, which you have round your middle. You don't want to go out as if you are proud of what you have done. Take your own sword and give me back mine.' 'I am not such a fool that I cannot see through your words,' answered Gundovald, 'now that these things which I have worn as symbols of our friendship are about to be taken from me.' Mummolus repeatedly assured him that nothing unpleasant would happen to him.

They went out through the city gate. Gundovald was received by Ullo, Count of Bourges, and by Boso.[32] Mummolus drew back into the city with his supporters and closed the gate fast. When Gundovald saw that he was betrayed into the hands of his enemies, he raised his hands to heaven. 'O God,' he cried, 'Eternal Judge, true Avenger of the innocent, from whom all justice must proceed, whom no deceit can ever please, in whom can be no treachery, no craft and no maliciousness, it is to You that I, Gundovald, commend my cause. I ask You to avenge me with all speed on those who have betrayed me in my innocence into the hands of these, my enemies.' As he said this he crossed himself and then proceeded on his way with those whom I have named to you. When they had gone some distance from the city gate, they came to the steep ravine which surrounds Comminges on all sides.[33] Ullo pushed Gundovald over and, as he fell, the Count shouted: 'There goes your Ballomer,[34] who pretends that he is the son of one king and the brother of another.' He thrust his lance at Gundovald and tried to transfix him. The rings of Gundovald's hauberk withstood the lance and he was not wounded. He picked himself up and tried to scramble to the top of the cliff. Boso threw a rock at him and hit him full in the head. Gundovald fell and as he fell he died. The mob surrounded him and prodded him with their spears. They tied his feet together with a rope and dragged him through the whole army encampment. They pulled out his hair and his beard. Then they left his body unburied on the spot where he had met his death.

The next night the leading men of Comminges took into safe-

32. This is not Guntram Boso. Boso was one of King Guntram's military leaders, cp. *HF*, IX, 31.
33. Senuvia, the place where this happened, is the modern Chenove.
34. Cp. p. 397, note 18.

keeping all the treasure which they could lay hands on and all
the church plate. When day dawned the gates were flung open
and the army was allowed in. All the common people were put
to the sword, and all the priests of the Lord God, with those
who served them, were murdered where they stood at the
church altars. When they had killed every living soul, so that
there remained not one that pisseth against a wall,[35] the troops
burned the whole city, with all the churches and every single
building, leaving there nothing but the bare earth.

39. When Leudegisel returned to his camp, he took Mummolus, Sagittarius, Chariulf and Waddo with him. Without letting anyone know what he was doing, he sent messengers to the
King to ask what he wanted done with them. The King ordered
that they should be put to death. Waddo and Chariulf left their
sons behind as hostages and deserted the other two. The news
went round that they were slain. When he heard this, Mummolus put on full armour and went to beard Leudegisel in his
hut. As soon as Leudegisel saw him he asked: 'Why do you
come here looking as if you were about to run away?' 'As far as
I can see,' answered Mummolus, 'no attempt is being made to
keep the promise which you made to me. It is clear to me that
you are planning my death.' 'I will come out and settle this
business,' replied Leudegisel. He emerged and immediately
ordered the hut to be surrounded, so that Mummolus might be
killed. For a long time Mummolus resisted his assailants, but in
the end he came to the door. As he stepped out they ran him
through from both sides with their lances. He fell dead to the
ground.

When Bishop Sagittarius saw this, he was terrified. A by-
stander said to him: 'You see with your own eyes, Bishop, what
is going on here. Cover your head to stop them recognizing you,
and make a dash for the forest. Hide there for a while and when
tempers cool you may escape.' Sagittarius took the man's
advice. He covered his head and ran for it. Someone drew a
sword and cut off the Bishop's head, and his hood with it. All

35. I Samuel 25, 22 and I Kings 16, 11.

the soldiers then returned to their quarters, looting as they went and killing everyone they met.

At this time Fredegund sent Chuppa into the Toulouse area to bring home her daughter Rigunth by hook or by crook. Many people said that the real reason why he was sent was to entice Gundovald away with many promises, provided that Chuppa found him alive, and to bring him to the Queen. This, of course, he could not do, so he took Rigunth, humiliated and insulted as she was, and brought her home instead.

40.   Duke Leudegisel set off to meet King Guntram with all the treasures which I have described. Later on the King distributed them among the poor and the churches. The wife of Mummolus[36] was brought in as a captive, and the King began to question her about all the wealth which she and her husband had amassed. She knew that her husband had been killed and that all their pride was humbled to the ground. She was forced to reveal everything. She admitted that a vast hoard of gold and silver, of which the King knew nothing, lay hidden in Avignon. The King immediately sent men to fetch it, with a trusted servant of Mummolus, in whose care the treasure had been left. They made their way to Avignon and took charge of everything which Mummolus had left in the city. They say that there were two hundred and fifty talents of silver and more than thirty talents of gold. According to the story, Mummolus had stolen this from some hoard of treasure which he had discovered. King Guntram shared the treasure with his nephew, King Childebert. Most of his own portion he gave away to the poor. To the widow of Mummolus he gave nothing, except what she had inherited from her own relations.

41.   One of the servants of Mummolus was brought to the King. He was a giant of a man, so immense that he was reckoned to be two or three feet bigger than the tallest men ever known. He was a carpenter by trade. He died soon afterwards.

36. Sidonia, according to Fredegar, *Chronicle*, 4, 4.

42. Some time later a decree was issued by the judges that anyone who had shown unwillingness to join this military expedition should be fined. The Count of Bourges sent his representatives into one of the religious houses belonging to Saint Martin in that region, with orders that the churchmen there should pay the fine. The steward of the house resisted vehemently. 'These men serve Saint Martin,' he said. 'They are not in the habit of taking part in military manoeuvres.' 'This Martin of yours, whom you keep quoting in such a fatuous way, means absolutely nothing to us,' they replied. 'These men must pay the fine, and so must you, too, for disobeying the King's command.' As he said this, one of them marched into the courtyard of the house. He immediately fell to the ground in great pain and became extremely ill. He turned to the steward and said in a feeble voice: 'Make the sign of the Cross over me, I beg you, and call upon the name of Saint Martin. I fully recognize how great is his miraculous power. As I walked into the courtyard of this house, I saw an old man holding in his hand a tree, the branches of which spread out until they soon covered the whole yard. One of the branches of that tree touched me, and I was so affected by the contact that I collapsed.' The steward made a sign to his men and threw the interloper out. From where he stood outside the building, he began to call fervently upon Saint Martin's name. He soon felt better and was cured.

43. Desiderius sought safety for himself and his possessions inside his own walled encampments. Waddo, Rigunth's former major-domo, fled to Queen Brunhild, and she received him graciously. She gave him presents and then let him go. Chariulf sought sanctuary in Saint Martin's church.

44. At this time there was a woman who had the gift of prophecy. She gained much profit for her masters by her prowess in divination. She so won their favour that they set her free and let her live as she wished. If anyone had been the victim of a robbery or any other disaster, she would immediately announce where the thief had fled, to whom he had handed over his ill-

gotten gains, or what else he had done with them. Every day she acquired more and more gold and silver, and she would walk about so loaded with jewellery that she was looked upon by the common people as a sort of goddess. When this reached the ears of Ageric, Bishop of Verdun, he sent to have her arrested. She was seized and brought before him, and, in accordance with what we read in the Acts of the Apostles,[37] he realized that she was possessed by an unclean spirit which had the gift of prophecy. When Ageric had pronounced over her the prayer of exorcism and had anointed her forehead with holy oil, the devil cried out and revealed his identity to the Bishop. However Ageric was not successful in freeing the woman of this devil, and she was allowed to depart. She realized that she could no longer live in that neighbourhood, so she made her way to Queen Fredegund and sought refuge with her.

45. In this year almost the whole of Gaul suffered from famine. Many people made bread out of grape-pips or hazel catkins, while others dried the roots of ferns, ground them to powder and added a little flour. Some cut green corn-stalks and treated them in the same way. Many others, who had no flour at all, gathered grasses and ate them, with the result that they swelled up and died. Vast numbers suffered from hunger to the point that they died. The merchants took sad advantage of the people, selling a bushel of corn or half a measure of wine for the third of a gold piece. The poor sold themselves into slavery in order to obtain something to eat.

46. A certain merchant called Christopher travelled to the city of Orleans, because he had heard that a large quantity of wine had been delivered there. When he reached the city he bought the wine and had it transported in boats. He himself travelled on horseback, with two Saxon servants, carrying a large sum in money which he had borrowed from his father-in-law. These servants had long hated their master and had often run away from him, because on a number of occasions he had had them

37. Acts 16, 16.

flogged unmercifully. They entered a certain wood. The master rode ahead. One of the servants hurled his lance with all his strength and transfixed his master. He fell to the ground and the other servant cut him about the head with his javelin. Hacked to pieces by them both, he was left for dead. They stole his money and ran away. Christopher's brother buried his body and sent his men to pursue the servants. The younger was caught and tied with a rope, but the older disappeared with the money. On their way back, the men left their captive too loosely tied up: he seized a lance and killed one of the men who had arrested him. He was taken by the others to Tours, submitted to various tortures and mutilated: then his corpse was hanged from a gibbet.

47. A most serious civil discord now arose between the citizens of Tours. When Sichar, the son of John, was enjoying himself in the village of Manthelan, as part of the Christmas festivities, with Austregesil and a number of other local folk, the village priest sent one of his servants to invite some of the men to come and have a drink in his house. When the servant arrived, one of the men who were invited drew his sword and hit him. He fell down dead. Sichar was a personal friend of the priest. As soon as he heard that the priest's servant had been killed, he seized his weapons and went to the church to wait for Austregesil. When Austregesil was informed of this, he snatched up his own weapons and went to look for Sichar. A pitched battle ensued. In the end a number of people slipped away on both sides, and Sichar was brought safely out by some of the clerics. He sought refuge in the country estate where he lived. In the priest's house he left behind four of his servants who had been wounded, together with some money and some of his effects. Once Sichar had fled, Austregesil launched a second attack, killed the four servants, and stole the gold and silver with the other things. The two parties were called up before a tribunal of citizens. Their verdict was that Austregesil, who had committed murder, killed Sichar's servants and removed his goods without having any right to them, was guilty in the eyes of the law. A few days after the case had been tried, Sichar

heard that the goods which Austregesil had stolen were now in the hands of a man called Auno, Auno's son, and his brother Eberulf. Sichar thereupon dismissed the tribunal from his mind as if it had never been, sought the help of a certain Audinus and started an affray by attacking those three in the middle of the night with a gang of armed men. He broke into the house where they were sleeping, murdered Auno, his son and his brother, killed their servants and stole not only all their portable property but also their herds. When I came to hear of this I was greatly disturbed. In conjunction with the judge I sent a message to them, summoning them to appear before me to see if the matter could be settled rationally, so that they might part in peace without the feud going any further. They duly arrived and a number of townsfolk with them. 'Men,' said I, 'you must stop this riotous behaviour and not let the wrong which has been done spread any wider. I have already lost several sons of the Church, and I have reason to fear that I may well lose others in this feud. I ask you to keep the peace. Whichever of you has done wrong, let him pay for it in brotherly love, and then all of you make peace, so that, if God grants, you may be worthy to receive the kingdom of heaven. He Himself has said: "Blessed are the peacemakers: for they shall be called the children of God."[38] If he who is ordered to pay a fine lacks the wherewithal, the Church will provide it, rather than see any man lose his soul.' When I had finished speaking, I offered money belonging to the Church. The supporters of Chramnesind, who was there to demand justice for the killing of his father, brother and uncle, refused to accept it. When they had all gone off, Sichar made ready to go to see the King. With this in mind he set off first for Poitiers to visit his wife. There he was exhorting one of his slaves to get on with his work, and had just taken hold of a stick and was belabouring him with it, when the slave dragged Sichar's sword from his belt and had the effrontery to wound his master with it. Sichar fell to the ground. His friends ran up. The slave was seized, he was cruelly beaten, his hands and feet were cut off, and he was hanged from

38. Matthew 5, 9.

the gallows. Meanwhile the news reached Tours that Sichar was dead. When Chramnesind heard of this, he sent word to his friends and relations, and hurried off to Sichar's house. He stole everything that he could lay his hands on, killed a few slaves, burned down not only Sichar's house but also those of his neighbours who lived in the same estate, and carried off with him all the cattle and every other movable object. The parties concerned were summoned to appear before the judge in the city to plead their cases. The judgement of the court was that Chramnesind, who had refused to accept the compensation offered and had then proceeded to burn down the houses, should forfeit half of the sum previously awarded to him. This decision was made against the letter of the law, in an attempt to persuade them to make peace. It was further decreed that Sichar should pay the remaining half of the compensation. In effect the money was provided by the Church. Thus the compensation which the judges had demanded was duly paid over, and securities were lodged in court. Both parties swore an oath that they would never make further trouble against each other. So the feud came to an end.

HERE ENDS BOOK VII

BOOK VIII

HERE BEGIN THE CHAPTER-HEADINGS OF BOOK VIII

1. The visit made by King Guntram to Orleans.
2. How the bishops were presented to him and how he had a banquet prepared.
3. The singers there; and the silver plate of Mummolus.
4. Praise of King Childebert.
5. The visions of Chilperic which the King and I had seen.
6. Those whom I presented to the King.
7. How Bishop Palladius said Mass.
8. Signs and portents.
9. The oath concerning Chilperic's son.
10. What happened to the corpses of Merovech and Clovis.
11. The door-keepers. How Boantus was killed.
12. Bishop Theodore and the misfortune which befell Rathar.
13. How Guntram sent messengers to Childebert.
14. The accident which I met with on the river.
15. The conversion of the deacon Vulfolaic.
16. The account which Vulfolaic gave of the miracles performed by Saint Martin.
17. How I saw more portents.
18. How Childebert sent an army into Italy. The dukes and counts whom he appointed and those whom he dismissed.
19. The death of Abbot Dagulf.
20. The transactions of the Council of Mâcon.
21. The tribunal at Breslingen and the violation of a tomb.
22. The death of certain bishops and that of Wandelen.
23. The floods.
24. The islands in the sea.
25. The island where blood appeared.
26. Berulf, who was once a Duke.

27. How Desiderius went to see the King.
28. Hermangild and Ingund, and how messengers were sent secretly by the Spaniards to Fredegund.
29. How Fredegund sent assassins to murder Childebert.
30. How the army marched into Septimania.
31. How Bishop Praetextatus was murdered.
32. The murder of Domnola, wife of Nectarius.
33. The fire in the city of Paris.
34. The hermits who were tempted.
35. Envoys are sent from Spain.
36. How Magnovald was killed.
37. A son is born to Childebert.
38. How the Spaniards invaded Gaul.
39. The death of certain bishops.
40. Pelagius of Tours.
41. The men who murdered Praetextatus.
42. How Beppolen was given a dukedom.
43. How Nicetius was appointed Governor of Provence. What Antestius did.
44. The man who tried to assassinate King Guntram.
45. How Duke Desiderius was killed.
46. The death of King Leuvigild.

HERE END THE CHAPTER-HEADINGS OF BOOK VIII
THANKS BE TO GOD

1. In the twenty-fourth year of his reign,[1] King Guntram set out from Chalon-sur-Saône and travelled to the city of Nevers. He was on his way to Paris, for he had been invited there to receive from the holy baptismal font Chilperic's son, whom they called Lothar. From Nevers he turned aside and visited Orleans, where he made a great attempt to establish friendly relations with the townsfolk. When he was invited to their houses he accepted and he greatly enjoyed the meals which they offered him. He received many gifts from them and gave them presents in return with lavish generosity. The day of his entry into Orleans was the feast of Saint Martin, that is 4 July. A vast crowd of citizens came out to meet him, carrying flags and banners, and singing songs in his praise. The speech of the Syrians contrasted sharply with that of those using Gallo-Roman and again with that of the Jews, as they each sang his praises in their own tongue. 'Long live the King!' they all shouted. 'May he continue to reign over his peoples for more years than we can count!' The Jews played a full part in these acclamations. 'Let all peoples continue to worship you and bow the knee before you and submit to your rule!' they kept shouting. The only result of this was that, after Mass had been celebrated and the King had taken his place at the banquet, he was heard to say: 'Woe to the Jewish people, evil, treacherous and full of deceit in all that they do! They sang my praises in this flattering way today, calling upon all peoples to submit to me as their overlord, in the hope that I should give an order that their synagogue, which was destroyed some time ago by the Christians, should be rebuilt from public funds. This I will never do, for it is contrary to the Lord's will.' One cannot fail to wonder at the wisdom of the famous King. He saw through the cunning of

1. A.D. 585.

433

the unbelievers, with the result that, when the time came for
them to petition for this very thing, they failed to take advantage of him. When the banquet finally came to an end, King
Guntram spoke to the bishops who were present. 'I ask this
boon of you,' he said, 'that you will give me your blessing in
my own lodging tomorrow, so that your coming there may
assure my salvation and that, as the words of this blessing are
pronounced over me, I may, in all humility, find safety in your
benediction.' As he said this we all thanked him and rose from
our seats, and so ended the banquet.[2]

2.   When morning dawned the King went to say his prayers in
the places where the Saints had dwelt. He visited my lodging.
This was near to the church of Saint Avitus the Abbot,[3] about
whom I have written in my Book of Miracles.[4] I rose
to welcome him and I must admit that I was delighted to see
him come. I said a prayer and then I begged him to deign to
receive in my house Saint Martin's bread of oblation. He did
not refuse what I had to offer. He came in and behaved in a
most friendly fashion. He accepted a drink, invited me to have a
meal with him, and went away happy.

At this time Bertram, Bishop of Bordeaux, with Palladius of
Saintes, had greatly incensed the King by receiving Gundovald,
as I have already told you.[5] Bishop Palladius in particular had
incurred the King's anger, for he had several times done all he
could to deceive him. Some time earlier these two had been
interrogated by their fellow-bishops and the King's notables as
to why they had supported Gundovald and why they had consecrated Faustianus when Gundovald made this stupid request.
Bishop Palladius tried to take the blame from his Metropolitan
Bertram and to accept the responsibility himself. 'My Metro-

2. '. . . omnes gracias agentes . . . surreximus'. Once again one is impressed by Gregory's modesty: had he written *surrexerunt*, we should never
have known, from this chapter at least, that he was present at King Guntram's entry into Orleans on 4 July 585.

3. Saint Avitus, died 527, was Abbot of Piciacus = La Perche and of
Miciacus = Saint-Mesmin-de-Micy.

4. *GC*, 97.   5. Cp. *HF*, VII, 31.

politan's eyes were almost closed with pain,' he said, 'and, despoiled and derided as I was, I was dragged to the scene against my will. I had no choice but to accept the orders of this man who claimed to be the ruler of all Gaul.' When this statement was reported to the King, he was very angry and it was with the greatest difficulty that he was persuaded to invite them to eat with him, the more so as he had not yet received them. When Bertram came in, the King asked: 'Who is this man?' It was a long time since he had last seen him. 'It is Bertram, Bishop of Bordeaux,' they replied. 'I am grateful to you', said Guntram, 'for the loyalty which you have shown to your own house. You should have remembered, dear father, that you were my kinsman on my mother's side, and you should not have introduced into your own family this pestilential person from overseas.' Bertram had to listen to this and to more in the same strain. Then the King turned to Palladius. 'I have little to thank you for either, Bishop Palladius,' he said. 'Three times you have lied to me, sending me reports which were full of untruths, and that is an evil thing to say of a bishop. You wrote me letters in which you denied that you were doing anything wrong, and at the same time you were sending other letters of invitation to my brother. God has been judge of my cause. I have constantly done all in my power to further your interests as father of the Church, but for your part you have always behaved most treacherously towards me.' To the two Bishops Nicasius[6] and Antidius[7] he said: 'Tell me now, holy fathers, what have you ever done for the benefit of your country or for the safety of my realm.' They had no answer to make. The King washed his hands, received a benediction from the bishops, and sat down to table with a smiling face and a contented look, as if he had never said a word about the scurvy treatment which he had received.

3.   When the meal was more than half-way over, the King ordered me to tell my deacon to sing. This was the man who had

---

6. Nicasius, Bishop of Angoulême.
7. Antidius, Bishop of Agen.

chanted the Responsorium at Mass the previous day.[8] While he was singing, Guntram gave me a second commission. I was to be responsible personally for seeing that each of the other bishops present should in turn provide a deacon from his own church to sing before the King. I communicated this order to the bishops. Each of the deacons chosen chanted the Responsorium to the best of his ability, with the King listening.

As one particular course was being handed round, the King said: 'All the plate which you see here belonged to the traitor Mummolus. By the grace of God, it has now passed into my possession. I have had fifteen other dishes out of the set broken up, all as large as the one which you see before you. I have kept only this plate, with a second one which weighs one hundred and seventy pounds. It is a sad thing that I have no other son but Childebert. For his part he must be satisfied with the treasure which his father left to him, and with what I have just recently sent to him as his share of this wretched man Mummolus' treasure, which we discovered in Avignon. I shall have no choice but to hand over everything else for the benefit of the poor and your churches.'[9]

4. He went on: 'One thing only I ask of you, who are God's representatives here below: and that is to pray for the Lord's compassion on my son Childebert. He is a wise man and an able one, and for many a long year past no one as prudent and energetic as he has come to the fore. If God designs to spare him to rule over Gaul, there is some hope that my family, which is now on the point of dying out, may through him gather strength once more. I have no doubt at all that by God's grace this may be brought about, for such was the augury when the boy was born. It was on Easter Sunday itself, that holy day, that my brother Sigibert stood in church, and the deacon stepped

8. In the Gallican Mass in Merovingian times the *Responsorium* or *Psalmus responsorius* came immediately after the *Benedictio*. It was usually sung by the choir-boys and not, as here, by a deacon. After it, the deacon processed to the ambo and read the Gospel.

9. Cp. Introduction, p. 45.

forward with the sacred text of the Gospels. A messenger arrived to see Sigibert, and both he and the deacon who was reading the lesson said exactly the same thing: "Unto you a son is born." The result was that the whole congregation present was able to answer them both in a single sentence: "Glory be to God on high." The child was baptized on Whit Sunday. He was crowned King on Christmas Day. If, then, your prayers attend him, he may well rule the kingdom one day, provided only that God so ordains.' As King Guntram said this, we all prayed to God that in His mercy He might protect the two Kings. 'It is true enough', added Guntram as an afterthought, 'that his mother Brunhild threatened to murder me, but as far as I am concerned that is a matter of small moment. God who snatched me from the hands of my other enemies also delivered me from the snares of Brunhild.'

5. On the same occasion Guntram said a great number of hostile things about Bishop Theodore. If Theodore had come to this council, the King maintained, he would have been driven into exile once more. 'I am well aware', he went on, 'that it was he who had my brother Chilperic murdered, and that he did it in collusion with these men.[10] If I do not succeed in avenging Chilperic's death before this year is up, I ought no longer to be held a man.' This was the answer which I gave to him. 'Who is it, then, who should be held responsible for Chilperic's death, if it is not he himself in his wickedness and you yourself in your prayers? He behaved in the most outrageous fashion and placed many a snare for you, but it was those very snares which brought about his death. Let me tell you, moreover, that everything which subsequently happened I saw in a dream. In my vision I saw Chilperic with his head tonsured, as if he were being ordained as a bishop. I saw him carried in on a throne, which was quite unadorned except that it was covered with a plain black cloth. Lighted lamps and tapers were being borne before him.' That is what I said, and the King answered: 'I, too, saw a vision in

10. In that he was a supporter of the pretender Gundovald and the Austrasian nobles who backed him.

which Chilperic's death was announced. Three bishops led him into my presence and he was bound with chains: the first was Tetricus,[11] the second Agricola[12] and the third Nicetius of Lyons.[13] Two of them said: 'Undo his fetters, we beseech you, give him a good beating and let him go." Bishop Tetricus, on the contrary, opposed them with great bitterness. "That is not what you must do!" he said. "For his sins this man must be cast into the flames." They went on arguing among themselves like this for a long time, and then far off I perceived a cauldron which was boiling fiercely, for there was a fire lighted beneath it. Poor Chilperic was seized: they broke his limbs and they threw him into the cauldron. I wept to see what happened. He was dissolved away and quite melted in the steaming water, and soon no trace at all of him remained.' As the King said all this to our great astonishment, the meal came to an end and we rose from our seats.

6. The next morning King Guntram went off hunting. When he returned, I brought Garachar, Count of Bordeaux,[14] and Bladast to have an audience. As I told you earlier on, they had sought sanctuary in Saint Martin's church, because they had belonged to Gundovald's party. At first I had no success at all when I made my intercession on their behalf. I persevered all the same. 'Listen, mighty King!' I said. 'I have been sent by my master to give you a message. What answer shall I carry back to him who sent me, seeing that you refuse to give me a reply?' Guntram was astonished at what I said. 'Who is this master who sent you?' he asked. I answered with a smile: 'It was Saint Martin who told me to come.' At that he ordered the men to be brought in. No sooner did they appear than he reproached them for their many acts of perjury and treason, calling them

11. Tetricus, Bishop of Langres, A.D. 539–72. He was the brother of Gregory's grandfather.

12. Agricola, Bishop of Chalon-sur-Saône, *c.* 532–80. Cp. *HF*, V, 45.

13. Nicetius, Bishop of Lyons, A.D. 552–73. He was the brother of Gregory's grandmother.

14. Garachar has not been mentioned before.

repeatedly cunning foxes. In the end he restored them to his favour and gave them back all that had been taken from them.

7. Sunday came round and the King went to church to hear Mass. My fellow-bishops and the other churchmen who were present gave Palladius the honour of saying the office. As soon as he began the Benedictus,[15] the King asked who he was. When they told him that it was Palladius who had begun the service, Guntram was very angry. 'Shall this man who has always been disloyal to me and dishonest now preach the sacred word before me?' he cried. 'I will leave this church immediately rather than hear my enemy preach!' As he said this he began to walk out. The other bishops were greatly disturbed to see their colleague humiliated. 'We have seen him present at your table,' they said. 'We have watched you accept a blessing at his hand. Why should you, the King, spurn him now? If we had realized that you hated him, we would have chosen some other bishop to conduct the service. Seeing that he has begun, let him celebrate Mass. If you have anything against him, it should be decided afterwards, according to the tenet of the canons.' Meanwhile Bishop Palladius, who was deeply humiliated, had retired into the sacristy. The King ordered him to be fetched out again, and he went on with the service which he had started. Palladius and Bertram were invited to present themselves once more at the King's table, but they began to quarrel, accusing each other in turn of adultery and fornication, and heaping lies on each other. Many present thought this a great joke, but others, quicker on the uptake, were grieved to see the Devil's tares grow rank among the Bishops of the Lord. As they left the King's presence, they gave bond and surety that they would attend a council on 23 October.

8. Portents appeared. Rays of light were seen in the northern sky, although, indeed, this happens often. A flash of lightning

15. In the Gallican Mass in Merovingian times, once the celebrant had entered, three canticles were sung, the *Aios*, the *Kyrie Eleison*, by three choir-boys, and then the *Prophetia* or *Benedictus*, by the bishop, as here.

was observed to cross the heavens. Flowers blossomed on the trees. It was the fifth month of the year.

9. The King then travelled to Paris and there he made a speech in public. 'When my brother Chilperic died,' he said, 'he is reported to have left behind a son. At the mother's behest, those in charge of bringing up the boy asked me to receive him from the sacred font on Christmas Day. They did not come. They made a second proposal, that he should be baptized on Easter Sunday. On that occasion, too, he was not produced. Then they made a third suggestion, that he should be presented on Saint John's Day. Once again, he was not there. Now they have obliged me to leave my home in this sultry season. I have come, but the boy is still kept hidden from me and I do not see him. As far as I can tell, there is nothing in this promise which they have made to me. I am beginning to think that he is the son of one of my *leudes*.[16] If he had really been a member of my own family, he would surely have been presented to me. You must know that I shall not acknowledge him, unless I am given incontrovertible evidence in his favour.' When Queen Fredegund heard this, she assembled the leading men of her husband's kingdom. Three bishops came and some three hundred of the more important leaders. They all swore an oath that King Chilperic was the boy's father. This put an end to King Guntram's suspicions.

10. The King still grieved for the death of Merovech and Clovis, bewailing the fact that he did not know where their bodies had been thrown after they were slain. One day a man came to him and said: 'If I can be sure that it will not be held against me in the future, I will show you where the body of Clovis lies.' The King swore that no harm should come to the man, but that on the contrary he should be richly rewarded. 'My lord King, the events as they occurred will vouch for the truth of what I say,' he answered. 'When Clovis was killed, he was buried beneath the eaves of a certain oratory. The Queen

16. See p. 157, note 64.

was afraid that the body might one day be discovered and receive honourable burial. She therefore ordered it to be thrown into the bed of the River Marne. I had constructed a trap there for catching fish, and in it I found the corpse. At first I was not sure who it was, but when I saw the long hair I knew that it was Clovis. I put the body on my shoulders and carried it to the bank, and there I buried it under a heap of turves. The limbs have not been harmed. It is now for you to do with the corpse what you will.' As soon as the King heard all this, he set out as if on a hunting expedition. He located the grave and uncovered the body, which was intact and unharmed. Part of the hair, which was underneath the head, had disintegrated, but the rest of the corpse, with its long flowing locks, remained untouched. It was obvious enough that this was the man whom King Guntram had sought so intently. He summoned the bishop of the city and had the body carried to Saint Vincent's church[17] and buried there, with a cortège of clergy and people, and with so many candles that it was not possible to count them. He wept for his dead nephews as bitterly as when he had seen his own sons buried. Later on he sent Pappolus, Bishop of Chartres, to ask for Merovech's body, and this he had buried next to the grave of Clovis.

11.   One of the church door-keepers made the following accusation against a colleague: 'My lord King, this man has accepted a bribe and has promised to assassinate you.' The second door-keeper, against whom the accusation had been levelled, was arrested, flogged and subjected to a whole series of tortures. Nothing came to light of the plot about which he was being interrogated. Many people said that this was all done for reasons of jealousy and foul play, simply because the door-keeper against whom the charge was brought was a particular favourite with the King.

Ansovald, who nourished some suspicion the details of which are unknown to me, left the King without taking leave.

The King returned to Chalon and ordered Boantus, who had

17. Later Saint-Germain-des-Prés.

always been disloyal to him, to be put to the sword. His house was surrounded and he was killed by the King's soldiery. His property was confiscated by the state.

12.   King Guntram continued to do all he could to persecute Bishop Theodore. Marseilles had by now been restored to King Childebert's jurisdiction. Rathar was therefore sent to Marseilles in his position as Duke and as representative of King Childebert, with orders to investigate the matter. He rejected the action which the King had recommended to him. Instead he surrounded the Bishop's house, demanded sureties and despatched Theodore to King Guntram so that he might be sentenced by the bishops at the council which was to be held at Mâcon. However, the vengeance of God never fails and He always defends His servants from the jaws of ravening dogs. The moment the Bishop had left his city, Rathar pillaged the possessions of the church, keeping some for himself and locking up the remainder under seal. No sooner had he done this than a mortal illness attacked his servants, so that they developed a high temperature and died. Rathar's own son succumbed to the disease, and he himself buried the boy in a suburb of Marseilles, weeping bitterly as he did so. There was such an epidemic among his household that when he left the city it was thought unlikely that he would reach his home alive.

Bishop Theodore was held prisoner by King Guntram, but no harm was done to him. He is a man of great sanctity and assiduous in his prayers.[18] Magneric, the Bishop of Trier,[19] told me this story about him. 'Some years ago,' he said, 'when Theodore was being carried off to appear before King Childebert, he was kept under so close a guard that when he came to a city he was not allowed to see the bishop or any of the townsfolk. He reached Trier and it was announced to the bishop there that he had already been taken on board a ship and was being carried

18. Theodore, Bishop of Marseilles, A.D. 566–94, died a few months before Gregory.

19. Saint Magneric, Bishop of Trier, A.D. 570–96.

off in secret. The bishop was greatly saddened by what he had heard. He set out immediately, followed on behind as quickly as he could and caught up with Theodore on the river-bank. He sought an interview with the guards and asked them why they were treating their captive in this inhuman way and not even allowing him to be spoken to by a fellow-bishop. In the end, he was given permission to see Theodore: he embraced him, gave him some clothes and then left him. He made his way to the church of Saint Maximinus,[20] lay down by the tomb and meditated on the words of the Apostle James: "Pray one for another, that ye may be healed."[21] He prayed and wept for a long time, beseeching God to vouchsafe to succour his brother, and then he went out. As he did so a woman who was possessed of an evil spirit began to shout at him. "You wicked man, grown old in sinfulness," she said, "you who petition the Lord for our enemy Theodore, surely you realize that no day passes without our begging that this man who unceasingly fans the flames which consume us should be exiled from Gaul. All the same, you go on praying for him! You would be wiser to concentrate on the affairs of your own church and to ensure that the poor lack nothing, instead of using up all your energy in praying for Theodore." Then she added: "This is a sorry day for us, for we are powerless to destroy him!" ' We ought not to put credence in anything which devils say. All the same, it is quite clear what sort of a man this Bishop Theodore was, seeing that a devil attacked him in this way and failed against him. Now I must return to my book.

13. King Guntram sent messengers to his nephew Childebert, who was at that time living in Coblenz, so named because at this spot the two rivers Moselle and Rhine flow together and unite. It had previously been agreed that the bishops of the two kingdoms should hold an assembly at Troyes, the town in Champagne, but this had not suited those of Childebert's kingdom. The head of the mission, Felix, saluted King Childebert

20. Saint Maximinus, Bishop of Trier, died A.D. 349.
21. James 5, 16.

and presented a letter to him. 'Your uncle, noble King,' he said, 'wishes to know who has caused you to break your promise, with the result that the bishops of your realm have refused to come to the assembly which you and he called. Is it possible that ill-wishers have sown some seed of discord between the two of you?' Childebert made no answer. 'It is not to be wondered at,' I said, 'if tares are sown between the two peoples, but none exists which can take root between the two Kings. Everyone knows that King Childebert has no father except his uncle, and that King Guntram has no son except his nephew. This very year we have heard Guntram say it. Heaven forbid, then, that any seed of discord should take root between them, seeing that they have such good reason to support and love each other.' King Childebert asked to speak to the messenger Felix in private. 'I entreat my lord and father not to harm Theodore,' he said. 'If he does harm him, trouble will immediately arise between the two of us, a quarrel will ensue, and we who have such cause to regard each other with affection and to live in peace will be divided.' When he had received this answer and a reply to his other question, the messenger started for home.

14. I myself stayed for some time with King Childebert in Coblenz. One night I was obliged to remain at his table until it was quite dark. When the meal was over, I rose from my seat and went down to the river. I found waiting on the bank a boat which had been made ready for me. I went on board, but a motley crowd of individuals followed me. As the boat filled with men it also filled with water. God in His omnipotence performed a miracle, for, though the boat had water up to its gunwale, it could not sink. With me I had some relics of Saint Martin, and of other Saints, too. It was to their miraculous power that I owed my preservation. The boat was steered back to the bank which we had just left. The men got out and the boat was emptied of water. None of the interlopers was allowed in again and I crossed the river without incident. The next morning I said good-bye to the King and set out on my return journey.

15. As I travelled along I came to the town of Carignan and there I was welcomed kindly by the deacon Vulfolaic,[22] who took me to his monastery. This is situated about eight miles from the town, on the top of a hill. Vulfolaic had built a large church on the hillside and made it famous for its relics of Saint Martin and other saints. While I was there I asked him to tell me about the happy event of his conversion and how he, a Longobard by birth, had come to enter the service of the Church. At first he was unwilling to tell me his story, for he was very sincere in his desire to avoid notoriety. I adjured him with terrible oaths, begging him not to keep back anything of what I was asking him, and promising never to reveal what he told me to a living soul. He resisted me for a long time, but in the end he gave in to my prayers and my entreaties.

'When I was a small boy,' he said, 'I came to hear tell of the name of Saint Martin. I did not even know whether he was a martyr or just a famous churchman, what good he had done in this world, or which place had been honoured by receiving his sacred body for burial. Nevertheless I used to keep vigils in his name, and whenever I had any money I would give it as alms. When I grew a little older I made a great effort to learn to write. I first taught myself just to copy out the letters, and then I discovered what they meant when they were put in proper order. I became a disciple of Abbot Aredius[23] and with his encouragement I visited the church of Saint Martin. When the time came for us to leave, he gathered a little dust from the sacred tomb as a holy relic. He put it in a small box and hung it round my neck. On our arrival at his monastery near Limoges, he put this box away in his oratory. The dust increased in quantity until it not only filled the box but forced its way through the joints wherever it could find an opening. Inspired as I was by this miracle, my heart was filled with joy, with the result that all my hope for the future was placed in the Saint's miraculous power. I then moved to the neighbourhood of Trier, and on the

22. He is known in France as Saint Walfroy.

23. Saint Aredius, Abbot of Limoges, died A.D. 591. He is known in France as Saint Yrieix.

hillside where you are now standing I built with my own hands
the dwelling which you see before you. I found here a statue of
Diana, which the credulous locals worshipped as a god. I myself
set up a column, on which I remained standing with bare feet,
no matter how much it hurt me. When winter came in its season,
it so froze me with its icy frost that the bitter cold made my
toenails fall off, not once but several times, and the rain turned
to ice and hung from my beard like the wax which melts from
candles. This district is famous for its harsh winters.'

I was very curious to know what food and drink he took, and
how he succeeded in destroying the idols on the hillside. 'All I
had to eat and drink was a little bread and green vegetables,
with some water,' he answered. 'Crowds began to flock to me
from the manors in the region, and I kept telling them that
Diana was powerless, that her statues were useless, and that the
rites which they practised were vain and empty. I made it clear
that the incantations which they chanted when they were drunk
and in the midst of their debaucheries were quite unworthy of
them. Instead they should make a seemly offering of worship to
God Almighty, who had made heaven and earth. Night and day
I prayed that the Lord would vouchsafe to cast down the statue
and free these people from their false idolatry. God in His
mercy moved their rustic minds, with the result that they began
to listen to what I had to say, to forsake their images and to
follow the Lord. Then I called an assembly of some of their
number and with their help I was able to destroy it myself. I
had already overthrown the smaller idols, which were easier to
deal with. A great crowd collected by Diana's statue: they tied
ropes round it and began to pull, but all their efforts were of no
avail. I hurried off to the church and lay prostrate and weeping
on the ground, praying to God for help, that in His divine
power He would destroy what human strength was powerless to
overturn. When I had finished praying I came out again, went
up to the workmen and took hold of the rope. At the very
first heave which we gave the idol crashed to the ground. I
had it broken to pieces with iron hammers and then reduced to
dust.

'When I went home for some food I found my whole body from the top of my head to the soles of my feet covered with malignant sores, so that it was not possible to find the space of a single finger-tip which was free from them. I went into the church by myself and stripped myself naked by the holy altar. It was there that I kept a flask full of oil which I had brought home with me from Saint Martin's church. With my own hands I anointed my whole body with this oil, and then I went to sleep. It was nearly midnight when I awoke. As I rose to my feet to say the appointed prayers, I found my body completely cured, just as if I had never had any ulcers at all. Then I realized that these pustules had been caused by the hatred which the Devil bore me. He is so full of spite that he does all he can to harm those who seek God.

'There came to me certain bishops whose plain duty it was to exhort me to press wisely on with the task which I had begun. Instead they said to me: "It is not right, what you are trying to do! Such an obscure person as you can never be compared with Simeon the Stylite of Antioch![24] The climate of the region makes it impossible for you to keep tormenting yourself in this way. Come down off your column, and live with the brethren whom you have gathered around you." Now, it is considered a sin not to obey bishops, so, of course, I came down and went off with those brethren and began to take my meals with them. One day a certain bishop persuaded me to go off to a manor which was some distance away. Then he sent workmen with wedges, hammers and axes, and they dashed to pieces the column on which I used to stand. When I came back the next morning I found it completely destroyed. I wept bitterly, but I have never dared to set up again the column which they broke, for that would be to disobey the commands of the bishops. As a result I have been content to live among the brethren, and here I have remained until this day.'

24. Saint Simeon the Stylite, who died A.D. 460, stood on the top of a tall column in Antioch for some thirty years. As the bishops pointed out to Vulfolaic, this sort of thing was no doubt all right in the Middle East, but the climate of Northern Gaul was hardly suited to it.

16. When I asked Vulfolaic to tell me about the miracles which Saint Martin had performed there, he related the following stories. 'A certain Frank, who came from a very noble family among his own people, had a son who was deaf and dumb. The boy was brought by his parents to this church, and I ordered him to sleep on a bed in the building itself, at the side of my deacon and another of my priests. All day long he busied himself with prayer, and at night time, as I have told you, he slept in the church. God took pity on him and Saint Martin appeared to me in a vision. "You can now move your protégé out of the building," he said, "for he is cured." The next morning, as I was thinking about the vision which I had seen, the boy came up to me and spoke. His first words were to give thanks to God for what had happened. Then he turned to me and said: "I am thanking Almighty God for having given to me my speech and my hearing." He then went back home, for he was completely cured.

'A certain man, who was frequently implicated in thefts and other crimes, made a habit of clearing himself by swearing false oaths. He was accused by certain persons of having committed a robbery. "I will go to Saint Martin's church," he said, "and prove my innocence by the oaths which I will swear there." As he came in through the door, his axe slipped from his hand and he himself fell to the floor, with a severe spasm in his heart. Thereupon the miserable wretch confessed his crime in the very speech in which he planned to swear that he was innocent.

'Another man was accused of having burnt down his neighbour's house. "I will go to Saint Martin's church," he said, "and swear that I am innocent, and so come home again exonerated from this charge." There was no doubt at all that he actually had burnt the house down. As he made to come in to take the oath, I went to meet him. "Your neighbours assert that, whatever you say, you cannot be absolved from this crime," I said. "Now, God is everywhere, and His power is just as great outside the church as it is inside. If you have some misguided conviction that God and His Saints will not punish you for perjury, look at His holy sanctuary which stands before you.

You can swear your oath if you insist; but you will not be allowed to step over the threshold of this church." He raised his hands to heaven and cried: "By Almighty God and the miraculous power of His priest Saint Martin, I deny that I was responsible for this fire." As soon as he had sworn his oath, he turned to go, but he appeared to be on fire himself! He fell to the ground and began to shout that he was being burnt up by the saintly Bishop. In his agony he kept shouting: "As God is my witness, I saw a flame come down from heaven! It is all around me and it is burning me up with its acrid smoke!" As he said this, he died. This was a warning to many folk not to dare to perjure themselves in this place.'

The deacon told me of many other miracles, but I cannot repeat them all here.

17. While I was staying in Carignan,[25] I twice during the night saw portents in the sky. These were rays of light towards the north, shining so brightly that I had never seen anything like them before: the clouds were blood-red on both sides, to the east and to the west. On a third night these rays appeared again, at about seven or eight o'clock. As I gazed in wonder at them, others like them began to shine from all four quarters of the earth, so that as I watched they filled the entire sky. A cloud gleamed bright in the middle of the heavens, and these rays were all focused on it, as if it were a pavilion the coloured stripes of which were broad at the bottom but became narrower as they rose, meeting in a hood at the top. In between the rays of light there were other clouds flashing vividly as if they were being struck by lightning. This extraordinary phenomenon filled me with foreboding, for it was clear that some disaster was about to be sent from heaven.

18. King Childebert, who was being pressed by envoys from the Emperor to return the gold which had been given to him the previous year, sent an army into Italy. There was a rumour that

25. Carignan, on the River Chiers, near to its confluence with the Meuse, in the Ardennes, was called Yvois until 1662, when Louis XIV decided to change its name.

his sister Ingund had been transferred to Constantinople. His
military commanders quarrelled with each other and came back
home without having gained any material advantage.

Duke Wintrio[26] was driven out by the people who lived in
his province: he lost his dukedom and would have lost his life,
too, had he not sought safety in flight. Later on the people
came to terms with him and he returned to his dukedom.

Nicetius was demoted from his position as Count of
Clermont-Ferrand and Eulalius was sent to replace him. Nicetius asked the King to make him a duke and paid over immense
sums in bribes. As a result he was appointed Duke of Clermont,
Rodez and Uzès. He was a young man but he had great ability,
and he kept the peace in Auvergne and the other districts under
his jurisdiction.

Childeric the Saxon, who had lost favour with King Guntram
for reasons which I have already explained to you,[27] causing
others to run away, himself sought sanctuary in Saint Martin's
church, leaving his wife behind in Guntram's territory. The
King had adjured her not to presume to visit her husband until
such time as he had been restored to royal favour. I sent a series
of messengers to Guntram on Childeric's behalf, and in the end
I obtained permission for him to be joined by his wife and to go
off to live on the other side of the River Loire, it being understood that he should not take advantage of this to join King
Childebert. Once he had received his wife back, Childeric
secretly went over to Childebert. He was given the appointment
of Duke of those cities beyond the Garonne which were under
Childebert's jurisdiction, and he made his way there.

King Guntram wished to take under his personal government
the kingdom of his nephew Lothar, son of Chilperic, so he made
Theodulf Count of Angers. Theodulf entered the city, but he
was ignominiously driven out again by the townsfolk, who were
led by Domigisel.[28] He hurried back to the King, had his

26. Wintrio, Duke of Champagne, died in 597.
27. Cp. *HF*, VII, 3.
28. The nobles of the late King Chilperic took great exception to the
attempts of King Guntram to rule them through his own nominees.

appointment confirmed and, once he had been established there
by Duke Sigulf, managed to exercise his authority as Count in
Angers.

Gundovald, who had been appointed as Count of Meaux in
the place of Werpin, entered the city and began to carry out his
functions. While he was on tour through the territory belonging
to the city, he was murdered by Werpin in a manor where he
was staying. His relations joined forces and attacked Werpin,
shutting him up in a bathroom in the manor and killing him
there. Death thus deprived them each in turn of their countship.

19.   Abbot Dagulf had been convicted time and time again for
his crimes, for he was guilty of a great number of robberies and
murders, and he frequently committed adultery. He lusted after
the wife of a man who lived near by, and he kept having intercourse with her. On a number of occasions he sought some way
of killing his paramour's husband, who occupied land which
belonged to his monastery. In the end the husband swore that
the Abbot would pay dearly for it if he came near his wife again.
He had occasion to leave home for a while, and the Abbot came
in the night with one of his clergy and was allowed into the
woman's house. For a long time they sat drinking until they
were quite tipsy, and then they lay down together in one bed. As
they slept the husband returned home. He lighted some straw,
raised his axe and killed them both. Let this story be a warning
to all clergy not to break the statutes of the canons by seeking
the company of women not related to them, for the canon law
itself and all the Holy Scriptures forbid such relationships,
except with those women concerning whom it can hardly be
considered a crime.[29]

20.   Meanwhile the day of the council came round and by the
order of King Guntram the bishops assembled in the town of

29. A man who was married and then entered the Church was allowed to
continue to live with his wife, as long as sexual relations ceased between
them and they treated each other as brother and sister.

Mâcon. Faustianus, who had been inducted as Bishop of the town of Dax at the express command of Gundovald, was deposed, on condition that Bertram, Orestes and Palladius, who had given him the benediction, should supply him with food and should pay him a hundred gold pieces every year. Nicetius, who was a layman, took over the position of Bishop in that town. Ursicinus, the Bishop of Cahors, was excommunicated, because he openly confessed that he had welcomed Gundovald. It was decreed that he should do penance for three years, during which time he must refrain from cutting his hair or his beard, and from eating meat or drinking wine; what is more, he must not presume to celebrate Mass, to ordain clergy, to bless churches or the holy chrism, or to present the consecrated bread. However, the day-to-day business of the church could be carried out under his direction in the usual way.

There came forward at this council a certain bishop who maintained that woman could not be included in the term 'man'. However, he accepted the reasoning of the other bishops and did not press his case: for the holy book of the Old Testament tells us that in the beginning, when God created man, 'Male and female created he them, and called their name Adam,'[30] which means earthly man; even so He called the woman Eve, yet of both He used the word 'man'. Similarly our Lord Jesus Christ is called the Son of man, although He was the son of the Virgin, that is to say of a woman. When He was about to change the water into wine, He said to her: 'Woman, what have I to do with thee?'[31] and so on. They supported their argument with many other references, and he said no more.

Praetextatus, Bishop of Rouen, recited in front of his fellow-bishops the prayers which he had composed when sent into exile. They pleased some who were present, but they were criticized by others because Praetextatus had given too little attention to literary form. Here and there the style was appropriate and worthy of a churchman.

A great quarrel arose between the servants of Bishop Priscus[32]

30. Genesis 5, 2.   31. John 2, 4.
32. Priscus, Bishop of Lyons, A.D. 573–*c*. 586.

and those of Duke Leudegisel. Bishop Priscus offered a large sum of money to buy peace.

At this same time King Guntram became so seriously ill that it was thought by some that he could never recover. In my opinion this was God's providence, for he was planning to send a great number of the bishops into exile.[33]

Bishop Theodore returned to his own city, where he was received with approval and, indeed, acclamation by his entire flock.

21. While this council was sitting, King Childebert arranged a meeting with his leaders on his estate at Breslingen,[34] which is in the middle of the forest of the Ardennes. There Queen Brunhild pleaded with all the nobles on behalf of her daughter Ingund, who was still detained in Africa, but she received little sympathy. Then a case was brought against Guntram Boso. A few days earlier a relative of his wife had died childless. She was buried in a church near Metz, together with much gold and a profusion of ornaments. It so happened that a short time later there was celebrated the feast-day of Saint Remigius, which is held on the first day of October. A great crowd of the local inhabitants went out of the city with their Bishop[35] and they were accompanied by the Duke and the leading men of the place. Thereupon Guntram Boso's servants made their way to the church where the woman had been buried and went in. As soon as they were inside they shut the doors behind them, opened the tomb and stole as many of the precious objects from the dead body as they could lay their hands on. The monks attached to the church heard what they were at and came to the door. They were not allowed in, so they went off to tell their Bishop and the Duke what they had discovered. Meanwhile the servants pocketed their gains, jumped on their horses and fled. Fearing that they might be captured in their flight and subjected to divers punishments, they then returned to the church. They

33. These were the bishops who had supported Gundovald.
34. Breslingen is now in the Grand Duchy of Luxembourg, near Diekirch.
35. The church of Saint Remi at Metz was *extra muros*.

put the things back on the altar, but they were afraid to come out again. 'We were sent by Guntram Boso!' they began to shout. With his leaders Childebert convened a court of inquiry in the manor which I have named. Guntram Boso was closely questioned, but he had no answer to give. Later he fled in secret. All the property which he held in Clermont-Ferrand in gift was taken from him. In his hurry he left behind goods which he had sequestered from a number of people.

22.   It was in this year that Laban, Bishop of Eauze, died. Desiderius, a layman, succeeded him, despite the fact that the King had sworn an oath that he would never appoint a layman as bishop; but to what will not the cursed lust for gold persuade the hearts of men?[36] On his return home from the council, Bertram developed a high fever. He summoned the deacon Waldo, who had also been given the name of Bertram when he was baptized, handed over to him the authority of his episcopal office, and made him responsible for carrying out all the conditions of his will and of his charitable bequests. No sooner had Waldo left him than Bertram died. The deacon immediately came back again and then hurried off to the King with gifts and the full support of the townsfolk, but he achieved nothing. The King issued a diploma ordering Gundegisel, the Count of Saintes, surnamed Dodo, to be ordained as Bishop, and this was done. Since many of the clergy of Saintes, with the connivance of Bertram, had before the council written a series of attacks on their Bishop Palladius in order to humiliate him, they were arrested by their Bishop after Bertram's death, severely beaten and fined.

Wandelen, King Childebert's tutor, died at this time. No one was appointed to replace him, for the Queen Mother herself wanted to have charge of her son. Whatever Wandelen had held from the state now returned to the administration of the treasury. At the same time Duke Bodigisil died, at an advanced age, and his sons inherited his estate without having to forfeit any of it. Saius replaced Faustus as Bishop of Auch. On the death of

36. *Aeneid*, III, 56–7. Cp. p. 242, note 77.

Saint Salvius, in the same year, Desiderius was appointed as Bishop of the Albigeois.

23. There was heavy rain this year and the rivers were so swollen with water that many boats were wrecked. They overflowed their banks, covered the near-by crops and meadows. and did much damage. The Spring and Summer months were so wet that it seemed more like Winter than Summer.

24. This same year two islands in the sea were consumed by fire which fell from the sky. They burned for seven whole days, so that they were completely destroyed, together with the inhabitants and their flocks. Those who sought refuge in the sea and hurled themselves headlong into the deep died an even worse death in the water into which they had thrown themselves, while those on land who did not die immediately were consumed by fire. All were reduced to ash and the sea covered everything. Many maintained that all the portents which I have said earlier that I saw in the month of October, when the sky seemed to be on fire, were really the reflection of this conflagration.

25. In another island, which lies just off the city of Vannes, there was a large pond full of fish. This was turned into blood to the depth of a yard or more. Day after day vast packs of dogs and flocks of birds assembled there to drink the blood, returning home at nightfall completely satiated.

26. Ennodius was made Duke of Tours and Poitiers. Berulf, who had earlier been appointed to these two cities, was looked upon with suspicion, as was also his associate Arnegisel, because the two of them had in secret made off with King Sigibert's treasure. On his way to take over the dukedom of the two cities, Berulf was captured by Duke Rauching by some trick or other and bound with ropes, and his confederate with him. Servants were immediately despatched to Berulf's house. They dragged everything out, most of it his own property, but

some of Sigibert's treasure was discovered. All these objects were taken to King Childebert. It was thereupon decreed that Berulf and Arnegisel should have their heads cut off, but at the intervention of the Bishop[37] their lives were spared and they were freed. However, none of the property which had been taken from them was ever returned.

27. Duke Desiderius hurried off to see King Guntram, taking with him Antestius, Abbot Aredius and a number of bishops. The King was at first unwilling to receive him, but he allowed himself to be persuaded by the entreaties of the bishops and took him into favour. At this same time Eulalius was also there, for he was preparing to bring a lawsuit about his wife, who had left him and gone to live with Desiderius. However, he became the subject of so much ridicule and humiliation that he decided to remain silent. Desiderius received presents from the King and came back home in good grace.

28. As I have told you several times,[38] Ingund had been handed over to the Imperial army by her husband. While she was on her way under escort to the Emperor himself, with her little son, she died in Africa[39] and was buried there. Leuvigild encompassed the death of his own son Hermangild, who had been Ingund's husband. Inflamed by these events, King Guntram planned to send an army into Spain. It was first to subject Septimania to Guntram's rule, for that region is still considered to be within the boundaries of Gaul; then it was to advance further. At the very moment when this army was about to take the field, a document was discovered in the possession of certain peasants. They sent it to King Guntram so that he might read it, for it seemed as if Leuvigild had written it to Fredegund, enjoining her, by whatever stratagem she could think of, to prevent the army from marching into Spain. 'Kill our enemies,' it said, 'that is, Childebert and his mother, as quickly as you can. Make peace with Guntram; buy this peace at whatever price you can.

37. Was this not Gregory himself? Once again he is being very modest.
38. See *HF*, VI, 40 and 43.   39. In Carthage.

If, as may well be, you are short of money, we will send you some in secret, so that we may be sure that we achieve our purpose. Once we have taken vengeance on our enemies, reward Bishop Amelius[40] and the Lady Leuba, through whose good offices our envoys have access to you.' Leuba was the mother-in-law of the Duke Bladast.

29. Despite the fact that these despatches had been handed over to King Guntram and brought by him to the notice of his nephew Childebert, Fredegund still had two iron daggers made, which she ordered to be deeply grooved and smeared with poison so that, even if no mortal thrust should sever vital tissues, the infection caused by the poison would quickly be a cause of death. She handed these daggers over to two clerics, and then gave them the following instructions: 'Take these two poignards and make your way with all speed to King Childebert, pretending that you are mendicants. As soon as you have cast yourselves at his feet, as if you have come to beg for alms, stab him on both sides, so that at long last Brunhild, whose arrogant behaviour is encouraged by the support which he gives to her, may fall as he falls and so cease to be my rival. If the boy is so closely guarded that you cannot come close to him, kill Brunhild instead, that woman whom I hate. For doing this you will receive the following reward: if you are killed as you carry out your task, I will give recompense to your relations, endowing them richly and raising them to the highest rank in my realm. Cast all fear aside, then, and let no dread of death enter your minds, for you know full well that all human beings are but mortal. Steel your hearts like men and remember that, if many brave soldiers have died in battle, the outcome has been that their relatives have risen to high place in the state, overstepping others in their vast wealth and holding precedence over all men.' As she said this, the two churchmen began to shiver and shake, for they realized how difficult it was going to be to carry out her orders. When she saw how hesitant they were, she drugged them with a potion and packed them off on their

40. Amelius, Bishop of Bigorra, Tarbes.

mission. Their courage rose immediately and they swore that they would do what she had asked of them. She ordered them to carry with them a phial filled with the same potion. 'On the day when you are due to carry out my command,' she said, 'swallow this potion early in the morning, before you set out to do the deed. It will give you courage to see things through to the end.' As soon as she had given them all these instructions, she dismissed them. They set out on their journey and came to Soissons. There they were captured by Duke Rauching. They were questioned closely and they revealed everything, whereupon they were bound and thrown into prison. A few days passed and then Fredegund, who was quite convinced that her orders had been carried out, sent a servant to inquire whether there was any rumour circulating among the people, and to see if he could find anyone who would admit to him that Childebert had been assassinated. He left her presence and made his way to Soissons. Having heard rumours that the two churchmen had been thrown into prison, he went to the city gate, but the moment he started talking to the gate-keeper he, too, was seized and placed under arrest. All three of them were sent to King Childebert. When they were interrogated they told the truth, saying that they had been sent by Queen Fredegund to assassinate the King. 'The Queen ordered us to disguise ourselves as beggars,' they said. 'We were to throw ourselves at your feet and beg for alms, and then we intended to stab you through and through with these daggers. Even if the thrust had been so weak that each dagger failed to do its work, the poison with which the blade is smeared would soon have caused your death.' When they had made these admissions, they were submitted to a number of tortures, their hands, ears and noses were cut off, and they were put to death each in a different way.[41]

41. 'The decree said that the authorities would slice off a thief's ear after the first offence, his other ear after the second offence, and his right hand after the third. A fourth offence would bring public execution.' The Merovingians were bloodthirsty. Is this Childebert II and Brunhild again? Or is it Fredegund? No, it is a dispatch from one of the enlightened native republics of central Africa, as reported in *The Times* of 1 August 1972. The offences are petty thieving, not the attempted assassination of a King.

30. King Guntram then ordered his army to march against
Spain. 'First subdue to my rule the province of Septimania,' he
said, 'seeing that it is so near to Gaul; for it is a shameful thing
that the territory of these horrible Goths should extend into
Gaul.' Thereupon the entire armed forces of his kingdom were
put into the field and marched in that direction. The people
dwelling beyond the Saône, the Rhône and the Seine joined
the Burgundians and ravaged the banks of the Saône and the
Rhône until they had completely destroyed the crops and the
herds. They killed many men, burned buildings and seized booty
even in their own territory, stripping the churches, slaughtering
the clergy, with their bishops and the civil population, before
the altars consecrated to God. They came eventually to the
town of Nîmes. The men of Bourges, Saintes, Périgueux and
Angoulême, with the inhabitants of the other towns ruled over
by King Guntram, committed similar atrocities, pushing on
eventually to the town of Carcassonne.[42] When they reached
this town they found the gates left open for them by the citizens
and they marched in without meeting resistance. A quarrel arose
between them and the Carcassonnais, so they marched out
again. At this juncture Terentiolus, one-time Count of Limoges,
was struck by a stone thrown from the walls and killed. The
enemy revenged themselves on him by cutting off his head and
taking it back into the town. Thereupon the entire army was
stricken with panic and the men made up their minds to return
home. They abandoned everything that they had captured on
the march, and even the things which they had brought with
them. The Goths set a number of ambushes for them, stole their
goods and killed them. The rest fell into the hands of the people
of Toulouse, whom they had treated very badly during their
advance: they were robbed and knocked about to the point that
they had great difficulty in reaching their homes alive. Those
who had attacked Nîmes ravaged the entire neighbourhood,
burning the houses and the crops, cutting down the olive-groves
and destroying the vineyards, but they were unable to harm the

42. Nîmes and Carcassonne were in Septimania and thus under Visigothic rule.

beleaguered townsfolk and so marched on to other towns. These, too, were heavily fortified and well provided with food and other necessities, so the invaders laid waste the surrounding countryside, not being strong enough to break into the towns themselves.

Duke Nicetius, who had set out on this expedition at the head of the men of Clermont-Ferrand, besieged these cities with the others. He gained no profit from his actions. He made his way to a certain fortified town, gave his word, and those inside opened the gates of their own free will, in their innocence welcoming Nicetius and his men as if they really came in peace. Once they were inside Nicetius forgot his promise, and his men plundered all the stores and made the inhabitants prisoners. After this they conferred together and then all returned home. On the way they committed so many crimes, murders, robberies and seizures of property, even in their own region, that it would take too long for me to tell you all the details. As the result of their having burnt all the crops in Provence, as I have described to you, they themselves died of hunger and want on the march, leaving their dead behind them, while some were drowned in the rivers and many were killed by the locals who rose against them. People said that more than five thousand met their end in these disasters; but their fate did not deter the others who remained alive. The churches round about Clermont which were near the public highway were stripped of their plate. There was no end of the evil done until the very last of these men arrived home.

On their return King Guntram was bitterly angry. Those who had led the army sought sanctuary in the church of Saint Symphorian the martyr.[43] When the King visited the church for the Saint's feast-day, they were allowed to appear before him, on condition that they should explain their actions on some later occasion. Four days afterwards he summoned the bishops and the more highly born of the laity, and began to criticize his army commanders. 'How can we expect to win a victory nowa-

43. Saint Symphorian was martyred in Autun *c*. 180. King Guntram was in Autun at this moment.

days,' he asked, 'when we no longer keep to the conventions of our forefathers? They used to build churches, for they placed all their hope in God, doing honour to His martyrs and respecting His priesthood: the result was that, with God's help, they won victories and were frequently able to conquer hostile peoples with sword and shield. Not only do we not fear God, but we lay waste His holy places, we slaughter His ministers, and in our contempt we scatter far and wide the relics of His Saints and so allow them to be destroyed. As long as such deeds are being done, we can never expect to be victorious: there is no strength in our hands, our swords lose their bite, our shields no longer defend and protect us as they used to do. If it is I who am in the wrong in this, may God bring vengeance down upon my head; but if it is you who are disobeying my royal commands and failing to carry out my orders, it is in your skulls that the axe should be buried. It will be an example to the whole army if one of its leaders is executed. We must here and now make up our minds what is to be done. If any of you has it in his heart to act according to the law, well and good, let him do so; as for him who scorns such action, let the law bring vengeance on his head. It is better that the one or two who are disobedient should perish rather than that the wrath of God should hang over a whole realm of innocent men.' When the King had finished speaking, the leaders made their reply. 'Gracious King,' they said, 'it is impossible to describe in detail your goodness and your magnanimity, the extent to which you fear God, the love which you have for your churches, your reverent behaviour towards your bishops, your pity for the poor and the charity which you show to the needy. All that you say, gracious lord, is clearly right and proper; but what can we do when the entire population is steeped in vice and all delight in doing evil? No man fears the King, no man has any respect for his duke or his count. If it happens by chance that one of us disapproves of all this and tries to put things right, in the hope of lengthening your life, the people immediately revolt and an uprising immediately begins. Everyone reviles this person in charge so savagely that he can scarcely expect to escape with his life unless he is prepared to swallow his words.' 'If anyone among you is prepared to observe the law, let him live,' answered the King. 'As for him who has no respect for the law and for my own commands, let him die, and by dying put an end to this blasphemous behaviour of ours.'

Just as Guntram said this, a messenger came in. 'Recared, the son of Leuvigild, has come out of Spain,' he announced. 'He has captured the castle of Cabaret, he has ravaged the greater part of the land round Toulouse and he has led off a number of captives. He has attacked the castle of Beaucaire near Arles,[44] made off with all the inhabitants and their property, and shut himself up inside the walls of Nîmes.' When he heard this, the King appointed Leudegisel as army commander in place of Calumniosus, surnamed Egilan, put the whole of the Arles region in his charge and posted more than four thousand men as frontier-guards. In addition, Nicetius, Duke of Clermont, marched forward with a protecting force and went off to patrol the border.

31. While these things were happening, Fredegund was living in the town of Rouen. A bitter exchange of words took place between the Queen and Bishop Praetextatus. She told him that the time would come when he would have to return to the exile from which he had been recalled. 'In exile and out of exile I have always been a Bishop,' replied Praetextatus, 'but you will not always enjoy royal power. With God's help I myself have come back from exile and have returned to my diocese; but when you give up your role as Queen you will be plunged into the abyss. It would be better for you to abandon your stupid, malicious behaviour, and to turn your mind to higher things. If you were to give up the boastful pride which burns within you, you might gain eternal life and be able to bring up to man's estate this young boy whose mother you are.' That was what Praetextatus said. The Queen bore his words ill. She was extremely angry when she left him.

44. This is the little township in which Aucassin wooed Nicolette, 'sa tresdouce amie que tant amoit'.

The day of our Lord's Resurrection came round. Early in the morning Bishop Praetextatus hurried off to church to perform the holy offices. He began to intone the antiphons in their proper order according to the use. During the chanting he reclined on a bench. As Praetextatus rested on this bench, there appeared a cruel assassin who drew a dagger from his belt and struck the Bishop under the armpit.[45] He cried out to the clergy who were present for help, but of all those standing near not one came to his assistance. As he prayed and gave thanks to God the hands which he stretched out over the altar dripped with blood. Then he was carried into his cell by his faithful followers and placed on his bed. Fredegund lost no time in coming round to see him. She was accompanied by Duke Beppolen and Ansovald. 'Holy Bishop,' she said, 'your flock and I should never have lived to see the day when such a crime as this should be committed, and while you were performing the office, too. I can only hope that the man who has dared to do such a thing will be discovered, and that he will be properly punished for his evil action.' The Bishop knew that she was lying. 'Who else has done this thing,' he answered, 'but the person who has killed our kings, caused innocent blood to be shed not once but many times, and been responsible for so much evil behaviour in this realm?' 'I have experienced doctors in my household who can cure the wound,' said Fredegund. 'Do let them come to take care of you.' 'God has decreed that I must be recalled from this world,' answered Praetextatus. 'As for you, who are the prime mover in these crimes, as long as you live you will be accursed, for God will avenge my blood upon your head.' As soon as the Queen had left him, the Bishop put his affairs in order and then gave up the ghost.

Romachar, Bishop of Coutances, came to bury Praetextatus.[46] All the inhabitants of Rouen were greatly grieved and especially the Frankish leaders in the town. One of these leaders went to Fredegund and said: 'You have been the cause of much evil in this world, but you have never done anything worse than

45. Bishop Praetextatus was murdered on 24 February 586.
46. Romachar, Bishop of Coutances, died later in this same year A.D. 586.

this, when you ordered one of the Lord's bishops to be murdered. May God be quick to avenge his innocent blood! We all propose to inquire closely into this crime, to prevent you from committing any more atrocities of the sort.' As he said this he left the Queen's presence, but she sent after him to invite him to take a meal with her. He refused. She then begged that, if he would not eat with her, he would at least have a drink, rather than leave the royal household without taking anything. For this he stopped. He was given a glass and swallowed some absinth mixed with wine and honey, which is a favourite drink of the barbarians. It was poisoned. Even as he drank it he felt a great pain in his chest, as if he were being stabbed inside. 'Fly!' he shouted to his companions. 'Fly, miserable wretches, from this horror, lest you all perish with me!' They refused to drink and fled at full speed. As for him, his eyes went blank, he clambered on to his horse, rode for less than half a mile and then fell dead to the ground. Thereupon Bishop Leudovald[47] sent a letter to all his fellow-bishops and with their assent closed the churches of Rouen so that the people could attend no more divine services in them until such a general outcry should arise that the author of this crime would be discovered. Leudovald apprehended certain individuals. They were put to the torture and he extracted a confession from them that these deeds had been done at the instigation of Fredegund. She denied everything, so that she could not be punished. It was said that assassins pursued Leudovald himself, because he was so determined to look closely into the matter, but he was guarded closely by his own men and they failed to do him any harm.

Once these matters were brought to the notice of King Guntram, especially the accusation which was being levelled at Fredegund, he sent three Bishops to the young man who was supposed to be the son of Chilperic and who, as I have already told you, bore the name of Lothar. These were Arthemius of Sens, Veranus of Cavaillon and Agricius of Troyes. They were ordered to confer with the men who were bringing up Lothar,

47. Leudovald, Bishop of Bayeux.

and then to seek out the individual responsible for this crime
and bring him before the King. The Bishops explained their mission to Lothar's governors. 'What has happened here certainly
gives us no pleasure,' they answered, 'and, as time passes, we are
more and more determined to exact vengeance. All the same,
given that the perpetrator is discovered, we cannot accept that
he should appear before your King. We are quite capable of
punishing local misdemeanours ourselves, under the general jurisdiction of the King, of course.' 'You must know,' answered
the Bishops, 'that if the person who has done this deed is not
brought to book, our King will march here with his army and
put this whole region to the sword and lay it waste with fire. It is
quite obvious that the miscreant who ordered the Frank to be
murdered is the same person who had the Bishop stabbed to
death.' When they had said their say, they went home. They had
received no reasonable reply, but at least they had made it
abundantly clear that Melantius, who had already been appointed to replace Praetextatus, could never perform the office
of bishop in the cathedral there.

32.   Many evil deeds were done at this time.[48] Domnola, the
daughter of Victorius, the Bishop of Rennes, who was the
widow of Burgolen and the wife of Nectarius, had an argument
with Bobolen, Fredegund's Referendary, about a vineyard.
When Bobolen learned that Domnola had visited the vineyard,
he sent messengers to her to tell her that she was not to have the
presumption to enter the estate. Domnola took no notice of
this. The vineyard had belonged to her father, she said, and she
went in. Bobolen started an affray and attacked Domnola with
a band of armed men. He had her murdered, claimed that the
vineyard was his and stole all the movable property. All the men
and women who were with Domnola were put to the sword:
none was left alive, except a few who ran away.

33.   About this time a woman resident in the town of Paris
made the following pronouncement to the townsfolk: 'You

48. A.D. 585.

must know that the whole of this town is about to be destroyed by a conflagration. You had better evacuate it.' They mostly laughed at her, saying that she had had her fortune told, or that she had dreamed it, or that she had been possessed by the noontide demon.[49] 'None of what you say is true,' she answered. 'What I tell you is what is really going to happen. I saw in a vision a man coming out of Saint Vincent's church,[50] radiant with light, holding a wax candle in his hand and setting fire to the merchants' houses one after another.' Three nights after she had given this warning, just as twilight was falling, a worthy citizen lit a light, went into his storehouse to fetch some oil and other things which he needed, and then came out again, leaving the light behind quite near to the cask of oil. The house was the first one inside the city-gate, which was left open in the daytime. It caught fire from the light and was burnt to ashes. The flames spread to the other houses. Soon the town gaol was alight: but Saint Germanus appeared to the prisoners, broke the great wooden beam and the chains by which they were held fast, undid the prison gateway and made it possible for those who had been locked up to escape. As soon as they were out they fled into Saint Vincent's church, where the tomb of Saint Germanus is to be found. The wind veered this way and that, so that the flames were carried through the whole city and the conflagration raged completely out of control. Soon it moved near to another city-gate, the one which had an oratory of Saint Martin, put up some time ago to commemorate the fact that it was there that he had cleansed the leprosy of some diseased individual by means of a kiss. The man concerned had constructed this oratory out of wattle-work. Putting his trust in God and his hope in Saint Martin's miraculous power, he now moved all his worldly goods inside the oratory walls. 'It is my firm belief,' he said, 'and to this I pin my faith, that he who more than once overruled the flames and who on this very spot cleansed the skin of a leper with his healing kiss will drive the

49. This is the *daemonium meridianum*, 'the destruction that wasteth at noonday', Psalms 91, 6.
50. Later Saint-Germain-des-Prés.

fire back from this place.' The flames came nearer and nearer, and great gobbets of fire were borne on the wind, but as they struck against the oratory walls they immediately lost their heat. The townsfolk shouted to the man and his wife: 'Run, poor wretches, and escape while there is still time! Look! A great mass of fire is coming straight at you! Can't you see? The burning sparks and red-hot embers are spreading towards you like some great shower of rain. Come out of the oratory! If you don't, you will be burnt to a cinder, and your oratory, too!' They took no heed of what was being said to them, but continued in prayer. The woman stood firm at the window, through which the flames kept entering, for she was protected by her invincible faith in the miraculous power of the saintly Bishop. This was so great that not only did he save the oratory and the house of his servant but he prevented any harm from being done by the relentless flames to the dwellings which stood all round it. The conflagration, which had begun to rage at one end of the bridge, stopped at this spot. On the other side it burned everything completely, so that only the river put an end to it. However, the churches and the houses belonging to them were not burned.

It used to be said that this town of Paris was, as it were, hallowed from antiquity, so that no fire could overwhelm it, and no snake or rat appear there. Only a short time before, when a drain by the bridge was being cleaned out and the mud which blocked it was being taken away, they discovered a snake and a rat made of bronze. They removed them both: and from this time onwards an inordinate number of rats and snakes made their appearance. Subsequently the city began to be plagued with fires.

34. Since the Prince of Darkness has a thousand ways of doing us harm, I will relate what happened recently to certain hermits dedicated to God. In an earlier book I mentioned Winnoch the Breton, who was ordained a priest.[51] The abstinence which he practised was so great that he wore only animal skins as cloth-

51. *HF*, V, 21.

ing and as food ate only the uncooked herbs of the field. As far as wine was concerned, he would merely lift the cup to his mouth, appearing to touch it with his lip instead of drinking it. However, his followers were so open-handed in offering him goblets filled to the brim that he fell into the habit, which is a very bad one, of drinking immoderately, and he was often so far gone in liquor that on more than one occasion he was obviously drunk. The result of this was that, as time passed, his intemperance became worse and worse. He was possessed by a devil, and he became so unbalanced that he would pick up a knife or whatever weapon he could lay his hands on, sometimes a stone, sometimes a stick, and chase after people in insane fury. There was nothing for it but to chain him up and lock him in his cell. Condemned to this fate, he continued to rave for a couple of years, and then he gave up the ghost.

Then there was the case of Anatolius, a boy who lived in Bordeaux, only twelve years old, or so they say. He worked for a merchant, but he sought permission to become a hermit. For a long time his master refused, thinking that he would lose enthusiasm for the idea and that in any case at his age he would not be able to carry out what he seemed so keen to do. In the end the merchant submitted to his servant's entreaties and gave him leave to do what he appeared to want so much. In the town there was a crypt, covered over with a vaulted roof by the ancients, and not without a certain elegance in its construction. In the corner of this crypt there was a tiny cell, walled in with squared stones, inside which it was only just possible for one man to stand upright. The boy entered this cell and there he remained for eight years or more, content with very little food and drink, and spending all his time in vigils and prayers. A great panic then seized him and he began to shout that he was being tortured internally. The next thing which happened, or so I believe, was that, with the help of some of Satan's legions, he moved the squared stones which formed his prison, knocked down the wall, and then clapped his hands together and shouted that he was being burned through and through by the holy men of God. He suffered from this madness for a long time, calling frequently on the name of Saint Martin and saying that he was being tortured more by that Saint than by the others. As a result he was brought to Tours. There the evil spirit was unable to harm him: in my opinion it was held in check by the miraculous power of Saint Martin. He stayed in Tours for about a year without suffering further harm and then went home, but the trouble from which he had recovered soon began again.

35. Messengers loaded with gifts arrived from Spain to see King Guntram. They came to seek peace, but nothing definite was offered to them in reply. The previous year,[52] when his army was attacking Septimania, certain ships which were sailing from Gaul to Galicia had been looted on the orders of King Leuvigild, their cargo stolen, their crews wounded or even killed, and some of their men taken captive. A few of these last managed to escape in boats and came home to their own country to announce what had happened.

36. For some reason which was never revealed Magnovald was killed at the court of Childebert on the King's own orders. It happened in the following way. As the King, who was in residence at his palace in Metz, was watching some wild beast which was being harried from all sides by a pack of hounds, Magnovald was summoned to his presence. Without having been told the reason for the summons, Magnovald came and stood watching the animal, laughing loudly with the others. A man who had been told what he was to do came up to the group and, when he saw that Magnovald was intent upon the sport, pulled out his axe and split his skull. Magnovald fell to the ground dead and was thrown out of the window of the house. He was buried by his men. His property was seized immediately, and all that was found was handed over to the public treasury. Some maintained that the reason for his execution was that, after his brother's death, he had murdered his own wife, after cruelly maltreating her, and had then slept with his brother's wife.

52. A.D. 585.

37. Some time later a son was born to King Childebert. He was baptized by Magneric, Bishop of Trier, and given the name Theudebert.[53] King Guntram was so pleased with what had happened that he immediately sent envoys loaded with gifts and bearing this message: 'Through this child, God, by the loving kindness of His divine majesty, will exalt the kingdom of the Franks, if only his father will live for him and he will live for his father.'

38. In the eleventh year of King Childebert's reign, envoys once more came from Spain to sue for peace.[54] They were given no definite answer and they went off again. Recared, the son of Leuvigild, advanced as far as Narbonne and captured a certain amount of booty inside Frankish territory, but he returned home unobserved.

39. Many bishops died in this year. One was Badegisil, Bishop of Le Mans, who was a very savage shepherd of his flock, unlawfully seizing and carrying off the goods of many people. His wife, who was even more fierce than he was, had the same morose and harsh temper as her husband. By constantly nagging at him she egged him on to commit the most detestable crimes. No day passed and, indeed, no part of a day, in which he did not occupy himself in plundering his citizens or in quarrelling with them about something or other. Every day in his life he would argue law-cases with the judges, meddle with secular affairs, lose his temper with someone or other, ill-treat some, hit others with his fists, bring about the ruin of quite a few. 'Just because I am a priest,' he would say, 'it does not follow that when wrong is done to me I may not seek my rights.' However, I have no need to quote instances outside the family. He behaved extremely badly towards his own brothers and sisters, and,

53. Theudebert was the son of a concubine. He was murdered, with his two young children, by his half-brother Theuderic, in A.D. 612. According to the *Chronicle* of Fredegar, 4, 27, his father was really one of Childebert II's gardeners, so that his blood was not all that royal.

54. A.D. 586.

indeed, despoiled them even more than other people. They never succeeded in establishing with him their rights over what they should have inherited from their own mother and father. Then, when the fifth year of his episcopate was completed and he was about to enter upon the sixth, he prepared a feast for his townsfolk and great joy was to reign, but he fell ill of a fever and his death intervened, so that he ended abruptly the year which he had only just begun. Bertram, Archdeacon of Paris, was appointed in his place. He is known to have had many disputes with the widow of the man who had just died, the reason being that she retained as if they were her own certain objects which had been given to the church during Badegisil's episcopate. 'That was part of my husband's stipend,' she would say. However unwilling she may have been to do so, she restored everything. Her malice and cruelty were quite beyond words. On more than one occasion she cut off a man's penis with part of the skin of his stomach, and she burned the more secret parts of women's bodies with metal plates which she had made white-hot. She was responsible for many other iniquities, but about these I have preferred to remain silent.

Sabaudus, Bishop of Arles, died; and Licerius, the Referendary of King Guntram, took his place. Next a serious epidemic ravaged Provence. Evantius, Bishop of Vienne, died, and Virus, a priest belonging to a senatorial family, was chosen by the King to take over his see. Many other bishops passed away that year, but I have decided to leave them out, because each one of them has left memorials of himself in his own city.

40. In the town of Tours there lived a man called Pelagius, well versed in all manner of evil-doing and who revered no judge, insofar as the guardians of the royal horses were under his control. As a result he was responsible for endless robberies, attacks, assaults, woundings and crimes of all sorts, on land and down the rivers. I frequently called him up and tried by means of threats and gentle rebukes to make him put an end to his evil conduct, but all I got from him was hatred instead of any furtherance of the ends of justice, in accordance with the prov-

erb in the Wisdom of Solomon: 'Reprove not a fool, lest he hate thee.'[55] His dislike for me was so great that he would cut down the servants of our holy Church and leave them for dead, being always on the look-out for excuses to do harm to the cathedral or the church of Saint Martin. On one occasion it happened that a group of my men came along carrying some sea-urchins in pots, and Pelagius knocked them down and went off with the pots. When I heard what had happened, I suspended him from communion, not to punish him for any wrong done to me, but the better to cure him of his madness. He chose twelve men and came to me to swear his innocence in this matter. I was unwilling to receive his oath. He argued with me and I was urged on by our citizens, so in the end I sent the twelve away, took his oath alone and ordered him to be readmitted to the sacrament. This was the first month of the year. When the fifth month came round and the time for mowing the hay arrived, he trespassed on a meadow belonging to some nuns, which happened to be adjacent to a field of his own. As soon as he began to wield his sickle he was seized by a fever, and on the third day he died. He had constructed a tomb for himself in Saint Martin's church in the village of Candes, but when his men went to look at it they found it broken in pieces. In the end he was buried in the porch of that same church. The pots which had contained the sea-urchins, concerning which he had perjured himself, were removed from his storehouse after his death. Thus was made manifest the miraculous power of the Blessed Mary, in whose church this miserable liar had proffered his oath.

41. The rumour ran throughout the entire country that Bishop Praetextatus had been murdered by Fredegund, and so she tried to clear herself of the charge by ordering one of her servants to be seized and beaten. 'It is you who have brought this infamous charge upon me,' said she with great vehemence, 'for it was you who attacked Praetextatus, Bishop of Rouen, with your sword.' She handed the man over to the Bishop's nephew, and when he

55. Proverbs 9, 8.

was put to the torture he admitted everything. 'I received a
hundred golden pieces from Queen Fredegund for what I did,'
he said. 'From Bishop Melanius I received another fifty and
from the archdeacon of the city fifty more. In addition to this,
I had a promise from them that I should be given my freedom
and that my wife, too, should be freed.' As soon as he heard
this, Bishop Praetextatus' nephew drew his sword and cut the
accused man to pieces. Fredegund appointed Melantius to the
cathedral, the candidate whom she had proposed in the first
place.

42. Duke Beppolen was very badly treated by Fredegund. In
all the time that he served her he never received the honour
which was due to him. Realizing that he was being slighted, he
went off to King Guntram. From that King he received the
appointment of duke to the cities which belonged to Lothar,
King Chilperic's son. He set out with a vast retinue, but the
people of Rennes refused to receive him. He moved on to
Angers and there he did much harm, destroying the corn, hay,
wine and whatever else he could lay his hands on in such houses
of the townsfolk as he came to, breaking down the doors without waiting for the keys. He knocked many of the local inhabitants about and maltreated them. Even Domigisel was afraid of
him, but in the end the two made peace. Beppolen went into
Angers, but while he was feasting with a group of people in an
upper room there, the roof of the house suddenly fell in. He
himself escaped more dead than alive, and many of his men
were injured. This did not stop him from going on with the evil
deeds which he had been doing. Thereupon Fredegund sequestered many of Beppolen's possessions in her son's kingdom.
He turned back to Rennes. His plan was to bring the Rennais
under the jurisdiction of King Guntram and to that end he left
his son in the city. A short time later the locals attacked the boy
and he was killed, together with a number of nobles.

Many portents appeared in this year. In the month of September the trees were seen to blossom, and many which had
already borne fruit now had a second crop, which remained on

the trees until Christmas. A flash of lightning was observed to run across the sky in the shape of a serpent.

43.   In the twelfth year of King Childebert's reign[56] Nicetius of Clermont-Ferrand was made governor of the province of Marseilles and of the other towns in those parts which belonged to the King.

Antestius was sent to Angers by King Guntram. He punished severely all those who had been involved in the death of Domnola, wife of Nectarius. The goods of Bobolen, who had been the ringleader in this outrage, were confiscated to the public treasury. Antestius then moved to Nantes and began to harass Bishop Nonnichius. 'Your son was implicated in this crime,' he said, 'and justice demands that he should pay the penalty for the crimes which he has committed.' The young man in question fled to Lothar, Chilperic's son, for he was terrified by all that he had on his conscience. Antestius moved on to Saintes, but only after he had obtained sureties from Nonnichius that he would appear before the King.

Soon after this a rumour went the rounds that Fredegund had dispatched secret messengers to Spain and that these men had been received by Palladius, Bishop of this same town of Saintes, in a clandestine way, and had then been sent on again. It was Lent and the Bishop had gone off to pray on an island in the sea.[57] As he was on his way back to his church for the celebration of the Lord's Supper, according to the custom, and his flock was there waiting for him, he was waylaid by Antestius. Without making sure of the truth of the accusation, he said to Palladius: 'You shall not enter your city. In granting an audience to these envoys you acted contrary to the interests of our King and you will therefore suffer banishment.' 'I don't know what you are talking about,' answered Palladius. 'Let me go into my city, for the feast-days of the Church are about to begin. As soon as these religious ceremonies are over, bring whatever charge you wish against me and then listen to my

56. A.D. 587.
57. In all probability one of the Channel Islands is meant.

defence. There is nothing in what you say.' 'You will certainly not set foot over the threshold of your cathedral,' answered Antestius, 'for there seems little doubt that you have betrayed our King.' What further details do you want to hear? The Bishop was arrested while still in transit. An inventory was made of the church-house. The citizens of Saintes were not even able to persuade Antestius to defer the inquiry until the Easter ceremonies were over. They begged him to do this, but he refused. In the end he revealed what was really festering in his mind. 'I will grant what you ask,' he said, 'only if your Bishop will make over to me, with a proper conveyance, to have and to hold, the house which he is known to possess in the Bourges area. Unless he does this, he shall not escape from my hands, but will be sent into exile.' The Bishop was afraid to say no. He wrote out the conveyance, signed it and made over the property. He gave sureties that he would appear before the King, and only then was he allowed to enter his own city. When the Easter ceremonies were over, Palladius made his way to the King. Antestius put in an appearance, but he was not able to substantiate the charges which he had made against the Bishop. Palladius was ordered to return to Saintes and the case was held over until some future council, just in case new information might be forthcoming about the charges which had been laid. Bishop Nonnichius was there: and he, too, was sent home, but only after handing over a great number of gifts.

44. Fredegund sent envoys to King Guntram in the name of her son. They presented their petition, received their reply, said good-bye and withdrew. For some reason or other which I do not understand, they hung about for some time in their lodging. The next day came and the King set off for early-morning communion. As a candle was being carried before him, a man was observed sleeping in a corner of the oratory, just as if he were drunk, his sword girt round him and his spear resting against the wall. When he saw this, the King exclaimed aloud. It was not natural, he said, for a man to be asleep in such a place in the dread horror of the night. The man was seized, he was

bound with leather thongs and then he was put to the question to discover what he meant by his behaviour. As soon as they began to torture him, he confessed that he had been sent by the envoys who had come and that his orders were to kill the King. Fredegund's messengers were then taken into captivity, but they would not confess to any of the things about which they were interrogated. 'We were sent for no other purpose than to bring to you the message which we have delivered,' they said. The King ordered the man to be cut about in various ways and then had him thrown into prison. He had the envoys banished to a number of different places. It was quite obvious that they had been sent by Fredegund to have the King assassinated, but God in His mercy had not permitted this. Baddo was one of the senior members of the party.

45. Envoys had come a number of times to King Guntram from Spain, but they had obtained no promise of peace. On the contrary, the rift had become even deeper.

King Guntram gave the town of Albi back to his nephew Childebert.[58] Now Duke Desiderius had transferred the greater part of his worldly goods to this town and the neighbouring district. When he saw what the King had done, he was afraid that Guntram might be planning to seek vengeance for the old quarrel between them, for in that same city he, Desiderius, had once inflicted a serious defeat on the army of King Sigibert of glorious memory. He therefore crossed into the territory of Toulouse, with all his property and with his wife Tetradia, whom he had taken from Eulalius, then Count of Clermont. He raised an army and made preparations to march against the Goths, having first, or so they say, divided all that he possessed between his sons and his wife. He set out for Carcassonne, taking Count Austrovald with him. The Carcassonnais got wind of this, for the news reached them early, and they made their preparations, being determined to resist. The battle began, the Goths turned in flight and Desiderius with Austrovald at his side attacked their rear. As the Goths con-

58. A.D. 587.

tinued their retreat Desiderius came near to the town, accompanied by only a handful of his troops, for his men's horses were exhausted. As he rode up to the town-gate, he was cut off by the inhabitants, who had been lurking inside their walls. Desiderius was killed, together with all the men who had kept up with him. Hardly a man escaped to carry the news of what had happened. When he heard that Desiderius was slain, Austrovald withdrew and made his way to the King. He was later appointed Duke in Desiderius' place.

46. Soon after this Leuvigild, King of Spain, fell ill.[59] There are some who say that he repented of his heretical errors and embraced the Catholic faith, giving orders that from then on Arianism should be strictly forbidden.[60] When he had wept for seven days for the wrongs which he had done against God, he gave up the ghost. His son Recared reigned in his place.

59. King Leuvigild died in A.D. 586.
60. This is thought to be untrue; it is certainly unlikely.

BOOK IX

HERE BEGIN THE CHAPTER-HEADINGS OF BOOK IX

1. Recared and his envoys.
2. The death of Saint Radegund.
3. The man who went up to King Guntram with a dagger.
4. How a second son was born to Childebert.
5. Signs and wonders.
6. Impostors and soothsayers.
7. Ennodius is deprived of his office. The Gascons.
8. Guntram Boso is brought into the King's presence.
9. The killing of [Ursio and] Rauching.
10. How Guntram Boso was killed.
11. The two Kings face to face.
12. How Ursio and Berthefried were killed.
13. How Baddo, who had been sent on a mission, was imprisoned and then released two [years] later. An epidemic of dysentery.
14. Peace is made between Bishop Egidius and Duke Lupus.
15. [The conversion of Recared.]
16. [The embassy which he sent to our Kings.]
17. The famine which occurred this year.
18. About the Bretons; and how Bishop Namatius died.
19. The murder of Sichar, who was a townsman of Tours.
20. How [Childebert] sent me to King Guntram to help keep the peace.
21. The charity and goodness of this King.
22. An epidemic in the town of Marseilles.
23. The death of Bishop Ageric and who succeeded him.
24. The episcopate of [Pronimius.]
25. How Childebert's army marched into Italy.
26. The death of Queen Ingoberg.
27. The death of Amalo.

28. The valuable gifts dispatched by Queen Brunhild.
29. How the Longobards sought peace from King Childebert.
30. The tax-collectors come to Poitiers and Tours.
31. How King Guntram sent an army into Septimania.
32. Enmity between Childebert and Guntram.
33. How the nun Ingitrude went to Childebert to make accusations against her daughter.
34. The ill-feeling between Fredegund and her daughter.
35. How Waddo met his death.
36. How King Childebert sent his son Theudebert to Soissons.
37. Bishop Droctigisel.
38. How certain men conspired against Queen Brunhild.
39. The revolt which occurred in the nunnery of Poitiers through Clotild and Basina.
40. How the revolt first began.
41. Blood is shed in the church of Saint Hilary.
42. The text of the letter sent to the bishops by Saint Radegund.
43. The priest [Theuthar] comes to put an end to the revolt.
44. The weather this year.

THE END

1. After the death of Leuvigild, King of Spain,[1] his son Recared came to terms with Goiswinth, his father's widow,[2] and agreed to acknowledge her as his own mother. In reality she was the mother of Queen Brunhild, who was the mother of Childebert II. Recared was the son of Leuvigild by another wife.[3] He took counsel with his stepmother and then sent envoys to King Guntram and to Childebert. 'Make peace with us,' said these envoys, 'and let us sign a treaty by which we may rely on your backing should necessity arise, and by the terms of the same alliance, we may in our turn give you support.' The messengers who had been sent to King Guntram arrived eventually. They were ordered to halt in the town of Mâcon. The King refused to give them an audience, but he sent some of his own men to find out why they had come. As a result great enmity arose between the two Kings, and these people refused to allow anyone from Guntram's realm to enter the cities of Septimania. The envoys who came to King Childebert were received kindly: gifts were exchanged, peace was made and they went back home loaded with presents.

2. In the same year Saint Radegund passed away.[4] Her death was the cause of great lamentation in the nunnery which she had founded. I myself was present at her funeral. She died on 13 August and was buried three days later. In my *Book of*

1. A.D. 586.
2. Queen Goiswinth was married to Athanagild, King of the Visigoths, and by him she had Brunhild, who was to marry King Sigibert. When Athanagild died in A.D. 567, Goiswinth married his brother, King Leuvigild. According to John of Biclar she died in 589.
3. The mother of Recared was Theodosia.
4. A.D. 587.

Miracles I have described at some length the wonders which occurred that day and the circumstances of her burial.[5]

3.   Meanwhile the feast of Saint Marcellus came round and was celebrated in the town of Chalon-sur-Saône in the month of September.[6] King Guntram was present. Mass was over and the King had stepped forward to the holy altar to receive communion when a man came up to him as if he had something to say. As this man walked quickly towards the King, a knife slipped out of his hand. He was immediately seized and they found a second unsheathed dagger in his hand. Without delay he was taken out of the holy church, bound and tortured. He confessed that he had been sent to assassinate the King. 'That was the object of the person who sent me,' he said. 'The King is well aware of the fact that there are many who hate him; he is suspicious of attack and has ordered his guards to protect him on all occasions. It is not possible to come close to him, and we certainly could not approach his person with our weapons in our hands, except in church, where he is deemed to be safe and may stand without incurring danger, or so it is thought.'[7] Those to whom the man referred were apprehended; a great many were executed, but the man himself was given a severe beating and then Guntram set him free, for he held it to be impious to kill a man who had been taken prisoner in a church.

4.   That same year a second son was born to King Childebert.[8] Veranus, Bishop of Cavaillon,[9] received him at the altar and gave him the name of Theuderic. This Bishop was at that time famous for the miracles which he had performed. By making the sign of the Cross over them he had, with God's aid,

5. *GC*, 104.

6. Saint Marcellus was martyred near Chalon *c.* A.D. 178.

7. This is a curiously composed and complex speech for an assassin, who must have expected a hideous death and who had just been submitted to merciless torture.

8. The mother was Queen Faileuba.

9. Saint Veranus, Bishop of Cavaillon, A.D. 585–9.

immediately restored the sick to health on a number of occasions.

5.   Many portents appeared at this time. In the homes of a number of people vessels were discovered inscribed with unknown characters which could not be erased or scraped off however hard they tried. This phenomenon began in the neighbourhood of Chartres, spread to Orleans and then reached the Bordeaux area, leaving out no township on the way. In the month of October new shoots were seen on the vines after the wine-harvest was over, and there were misshapen grapes. On other trees new fruits were seen, together with new leaves. Flashes of light appeared in the northern sky. Some said that they had seen snakes drop from the clouds. Others maintained that an entire village had been destroyed and had vanished into thin air, taking the houses and the men who lived in them. Many other signs appeared of the kind which usually announce a king's death or the destruction of a whole region. That year the wine-harvest was poor, water lay about everywhere, there was torrential rain and the rivers were greatly swollen.

6.   That same year[10] there appeared in Tours a man called Desiderius, who gave it out that he was a very important person, pretending that he was able to work miracles. He boasted that messengers journeyed to and fro between himself and the Apostles Peter and Paul. I myself was not there, so the country folk flocked to him in crowds, bringing with them the blind and the infirm. He set out to deceive them by the false art of necromancy, rather than to cure them by God's grace. Those who were paralysed or disabled by some other infirmity he ordered to be stretched forcibly, as if he could restore by his own brute strength men whom he was unable to cure by the intervention of divine power. Some of his helpers would seize a patient's hands and some would tug at other parts of his body, until it seemed that his sinews must snap. Those who were not cured his servants sent away half dead. The result was that many

10. A.D. 587.

gave up the ghost under his treatment. The wretched man was so above himself that he gave it out that Saint Martin had less power than he: for he imagined himself to be the equal of the Apostles. It is no wonder that this man Desiderius should say that he was the Apostles' equal, when the author of all evil, he from whom all wrongs proceed, will, at the Last Trump, pretend that he is Christ. It is quite clear from what I have just told you that Desiderius practised the foul arts of necromancy. Those who actually saw him said that, if anyone had spoken ill of him secretly and in his absence, he would gather the people round him and reprove the man in question. 'The things which you have said about me ill become the divinity which is mine,' he would say. How else could he know what had been said, unless his familiar demons had reported it to him? He wore a tunic and a hood of goat's hair, and when anyone was present he was most sparing in his food and drink. When he was in private and had come to his lodging, he would stuff so much into his mouth that his servant could not keep pace with his demands. However, it became obvious that he was an impostor and, once the bogusness of his behaviour was comprehended by my people, he was expelled from the city boundaries. I have never discovered where he went. He used to say that he came from Bordeaux.

Seven years before there appeared another great impostor, who deceived many folk with his tricks. He came dressed in a short-sleeved tunic, with a mantle of fine muslin on top, and he carried a cross from which hung a number of phials, containing, or so people said, holy oil. He gave it out that he had come from Spain and that he had in his possession relics of the two most blessed martyrs, Felix and Vincent the deacon. He turned up at Saint Martin's church in Tours just as night was falling and I was having my supper. He sent in a message: 'Come quickly and look at my holy relics.' As the hour was so late, I replied: 'Let the holy relics be placed upon the altar, and in the morning I will come out to look at them.' At first light the man rose from his bed and, without waiting for me to appear, arrived with his cross and marched straight into my cell. I was quite dumbfounded and flabbergasted at his impudence. I asked him what he meant by behaving in this way. He answered me very insolently, shouting at the top of his voice: 'You should have given me a much warmer welcome. I shall tell King Chilperic what has happened. He will avenge this insult which has been done to me.' Then he walked into my oratory, without asking my permission, and recited first one verse, then another, then a third. He began to say the morning prayer and went right on to the end. When he had finished he picked up his cross and went away again. He spoke the language of the common people, his accent was poor and the words he used vulgar. It was not easy to follow what he was trying to say.[11] He made his way to Paris, where he arrived just as public Rogations were being celebrated, as the custom is before the feast of our Lord's Ascension. As Bishop Ragnemod was processing to the holy places with his flock, this man put in an appearance with his cross, wearing his strange clothes, which the people had never seen before. He gathered round him a mob of ruffians and peasant-women, formed up his own procession, and prepared to visit the holy places with his own crowd of followers. As soon as he perceived this, the Bishop sent his archdeacon with a message. 'If you have some holy relics to show me,' he was to say, 'deposit them for the time being in the church, and celebrate these holy days with us. When the feast is over, go on your way.' The man paid no attention to what the archdeacon was saying, but began to curse the Bishop and insult him. Ragnemod realized that he was an impostor and had him locked up in a cell. His stock in trade was examined. He carried with him a big bag filled with the roots of various plants; in it, too, were moles' teeth, the bones of mice, bears' claws and bear's fat. The Bishop had all this thrown into the river, for he recognized it as witchcraft. The man's cross was taken away from him and Bishop Ragnemod ordered that he should be expelled from the Paris region. The only result was that the fellow made a new cross and began to carry on with the same practices as before. He was seized by the archdeacon, who had him chained up and then committed him to prison.

11. See Introduction, p. 40.

Just about this time I had occasion to come to Paris myself and I was put up in the church-house of Saint Julian the martyr.[12] The very next night this poor wretch broke out of his prison and, with his chains wrapped round him, made his way to Saint Julian's church, where he collapsed on the stone floor on the exact spot where I was due to stand. Exhausted and sodden with wine, he fell asleep where he lay. In the middle of the night I got up to say my prayers to God, quite unaware of what had happened. There I found him sleeping. He smelt so foul that compared with the stench which rose from him the noisome fetor of lavatories and sewers quite pales into insignificance. I was quite unable to step into the church for this odour. One of the junior clergy ventured forward holding his nose and tried to rouse the man. He was unable to do so, for the poor wretch was completely drunk. Four other priests went up to him, lifted him up in their hands and threw him into a corner of the church. Water was brought, the stone floor was washed clean and then strewn with sweet-smelling herbs, and so eventually I came in to perform the office. Even my singing failed to wake him. When daylight returned to the world and the sun's bright lamp climbed up the sky,[13] I handed the man back to Bishop Ragnemod and asked that he might be pardoned. There were a number of bishops in Paris for a council-meeting, and when we sat down to supper I told this tale. I gave orders that the man should appear before us, so that I could tell him what I thought of him. As he stood there, Amelius, Bishop of Bigorra, looked him up and down and recognized him as one of his own servants who had run away. He forgave him all that he had done and took him back home with him.

There are quite a number of these people who go in for impostures of this sort and keep on leading the common folk astray. In my opinion it is of them that Our Lord Himself speaks in the Gospel when He says that in later times 'there shall

12. See Introduction, pp. 15–16.
13. *Aeneid*, VIII, 148–9:
> Postera cum prima lustrabat lampade terras
> Orta dies. . .

arise false Christs, and false prophets, and shall show great signs
and wonders; insomuch that, if it were possible, they shall deceive the very elect'.[14] That is enough of this sort of thing. I
must now return to my proper subject.

7.   Although he was already Duke of the towns of Tours and
Poitiers, Ennodius was now given command of Aire and Lescar.
The Counts of Tours and Poitiers went to King Childebert and
succeeded in having Ennodius withdrawn from their own
towns. As soon as he learned that he had been superseded in
Tours and Poitiers, Ennodius hurried off to the two other places
which I have named. While he was in Aire and Lescar, he received an order to withdraw from them, too. His occupation
gone, he returned home and busied himself with his own private
affairs.

The Gascons made a sortie from their mountains and clambered down to the plains below.[15] They ravaged the vineyards

14. Cp. Matthew 24, 24.
15. In A.D. 582 Bladast attacked the mountain strongholds of the Basques
and 'lost the greater part of his army', *HF*, VI, 12. Here the Basques made
a sortie from their mountains and Austrovald was 'unable to inflict any
punishment worth talking about'. One is reminded of the Battle of Ronce-
vaux, 15 August 778, and of the death of Roland. 'At a moment when
Charlemagne's army was stretched out in a long column of march, as the
nature of the local defiles forced it to be, these Basques, who had set their
ambush on the very top of one of the mountains, came rushing down on the
last part of the baggage train and the troops who were marching in support
of the rearguard and so protecting the army which had gone on ahead. The
Basques forced them down into the valley beneath, joined battle with them
and killed them to the last man. They then snatched up the baggage, and,
protected as they were by the cover of darkness, which was just beginning to
fall, scattered in all directions without losing a moment. In this feat the
Basques were helped by the lightness of their arms and by the nature of the
terrain in which the battle was fought. On the other hand, the heavy nature
of their own equipment and the unevenness of the ground completely
hampered the Franks in their resistance to the Basques. In this battle died
Eggihard, who was in charge of the King's table, Anshelm, the Count of
the Palace, and Roland, Lord of the Breton Marches, along with a great
number of others. What is more, this assault could not be avenged there
and then, for, once it was over, the enemy dispersed in such a way that no

and the open fields, set fire to houses, and led off into captivity quite a few of the local farmers and their flocks. Duke Austrovald organized several expeditions against them, but he was unable to inflict any punishment worth talking about.

In revenge for the devastation caused by King Guntram's army in Septimania the previous year, the Goths attacked the province of Arles, captured a deal of property and led the locals off into slavery, this right up to the tenth milestone from the city. They sacked the stronghold of Beaucaire, and returned home with the property which they had seized, and with some of the inhabitants, too, for no one offered resistance.

8.   Guntram Boso, who was loathed by the Queen, began to visit the bishops and nobles one after the other, in order to sue for forgiveness, which he had previously scorned. During the minority of King Childebert, he had never ceased to heap abuse and insults on Queen Brunhild; and he had encouraged her enemies, too, to behave towards her in the most hostile fashion. The King was now determined to avenge the wrongs done to his mother; and he ordered Guntram Boso to be pursued and killed. As soon as he realized what peril he was in, Guntram Boso sought sanctuary in Verdun cathedral, confident that he could obtain pardon through the good offices of Bishop Ageric, who had been the King's sponsor at his baptism. Ageric hurried off to King Childebert and interceded for Guntram Boso. The King found it hard to refuse the Bishop this boon, but he said: 'He must appear before me in person, and give sureties. Then he must go before my uncle. I will take whatever action King Guntram ordains.' Guntram Boso was brought to the place where the King was in residence. He was stripped of his arms and then manacled. In this state Bishop Ageric led him into the King's presence. He threw himself at Childebert's feet and said: 'I have sinned before you and before your mother, I have refused to obey your commands, and I have acted against your

one knew where or among which people they could be found.' Einhard, *Vita Caroli*, I, 9, my translation, *Two Lives of Charlemagne*, Penguin Classics, 3rd edition, 1972, pp. 64–5.

will and against the public weal. For all that, I now entreat you
to forgive me all the wrong that I have done to you.' King
Childebert told him to get up off the ground. He then handed
him over to Ageric, saying: 'He must remain in your charge,
Bishop, until the times comes for him to appear before King
Guntram.' Then he ordered him to withdraw.

9. The next thing that happened was that Rauching conspired
with the leading men of the kingdom of Lothar, Chilperic's son.
He gave it out that his object was peace and that he was determined to make sure that there would be no more quarrels and
frontier-incidents between the territories of the two kings, but
their real plan was to assassinate King Childebert. Rauching
would then be given command of Champagne, with control of
Theudebert, Childebert's elder son, while Ursio and Berthefried
would seize the King's younger son, called Theuderic, who had
been born only recently, take command of the rest of the kingdom, and see that King Guntram did not intervene. They were
full of hostility towards Queen Brunhild and determined once
more to humiliate her, as they had done during the early days of
her widowhood.

Rauching was greatly elated by the power which was to be
his. Glorying in his almost regal position, if I may call it that, he
made preparations for his journey: his plan was to seek an
audience with King Childebert, so that he might carry out his
plot. By the grace of God the conspiracy came almost immediately to the ears of King Guntram. In secret he sent messengers
to King Childebert and revealed the whole enterprise to him.
'Come quickly,' was his message, 'for we must take counsel
together. We must decide what is to be done.' Childebert lost no
time in looking into the matter which had been reported to him.
He discovered that it was true, and then he summoned Rauching to appear before him. Rauching came, but before Childebert gave orders for him to be admitted he wrote letters and
sent his servants off post-haste in the King's name to sequester
all his property wherever it might be found. Only then did he
order Rauching to be shown into his private room. The King

talked with him about this and that, and then commanded him to withdraw. As he walked out the two guards at the door grabbed his feet. He fell over on the threshold, part of his body lying inside the room and the other part outside. The men who had been ordered to do the deed then fell upon him with their swords. They cut and sliced his head this way and that until the whole of his brains were exposed. He died immediately. He was stripped naked and flung out through the window. Then his body was dispatched for burial. Rauching was loose in his habits, greedy beyond human measure and covetous of the belongings of others. His wealth made him so overweening that at the time of his death he was giving it out that he was the son of King Lothar. A great amount of gold was found on his person.

As soon as Rauching had been dispatched, one of his servants dashed off at full speed to tell his wife what had happened. At that moment she was on horseback and being carried along a street in the city of Soissons, bedecked with fine jewels and precious gems, bedizened with flashing gold, having a troop of servants in front of her and another one behind, for she was hurrying off to the church of Saint Crispin and Saint Crispian, where she proposed to hear Mass, it being the feast-day of the two blessed martyrs.[16] As soon as she saw the messenger, she turned down another street, flung all her ornaments on the ground and sought sanctuary in the church of Saint Medard the Bishop. Her idea was that she would be safe under the pro-

---

16. 25 October. The Battle of Agincourt was to be fought just eight hundred and twenty-eight years later, on 25 October 1415:

> This day is call'd the feast of Crispian: ...
> And Crispin Crispian shall ne'er go by,
> From this day to the ending of the world,
> But we in it shall be remembered;
> We few, we happy few, we band of brothers ...
>
> *Henry V*, Act IV, Scene 2

The two brothers Crispinus and Crispinianus, by birth inhabitants of Rome and shoemakers by trade, were martyred in Soissons under Diocletian in A.D. 289 by being thrown into a cauldron of molten lead.

tection of this holy man. Those who had been sent by the King to sequester Rauching's property discovered more things in his coffers than they could have expected to see in the public treasury of the King. All this they carried back for King Childebert to inspect. On this particular day when Rauching was killed quite a number of Tourangeaux and Poitevins were in attendance on the King. The plot was that, if the assassination had succeeded, these men would have been put to the torture and the conspirators would have said: 'It was one of you who killed the King.' Then they would have been executed by continued torture, and the conspirators would have boasted that they had avenged the King's death. Almighty God confounded their plans, because they were evil, and fulfilled that which is written: 'You who will dig a pit shall fall therein.'[17] Magnovald was sent as Duke to replace Rauching.

Ursio and Berthefried, quite convinced that Rauching had been able to carry out the plan which they had concerted together, collected an army and began to march. When they learned the manner of his death, they gathered an even greater crowd of men around them, partisans who supported their cause, and shut themselves up with all their possessions inside a strong-point on the Woëvre, which was near Ursio's estate. They were only too conscious of their guilt, but they considered that, if King Childebert made any move against them, they would be strong enough to resist his troops. It was Ursio who was their ringleader and the cause of all the trouble. Queen Brunhild sent a message to Berthefried. 'Break off your relations with that evil man,' she said, 'and you shall have your life. Otherwise you and he will die together.' The Queen had stood sponsor to Berthefried's daughter at her baptism, and she therefore felt a certain compassion for him. 'I will never abandon Ursio,' answered Berthefried, 'until death comes to tear me from him.'

10.   While all these things were happening, King Guntram sent once more to his nephew Childebert. 'There can be no more

17. Cp. Proverbs 26, 27.

excuse for these delays,' went the message. 'Come, and let me
see you. The need for us to meet is most urgent, both on your
own personal account and for our public business.' As soon as
he heard this, Childebert took his mother, sister and wife[18] with
him, and set off to meet his uncle. Magneric, Bishop of Trier,
was also at the meeting, and Guntram Boso, for whom Ageric,
Bishop of Verdun, was surety. Although he had agreed to stand
surety for Guntram Boso, Bishop Ageric himself was not actually present. It had been decided that Guntram Boso should not
have anyone to defend him, so that, if the King were to decree
that he should be executed, no plea for pardon could be advanced by the Bishop. If, on the other hand, the King granted
him his life, he would be set free. The two Kings concurred in
their judgement, which was that Guntram Boso was guilty on a
number of counts. Their verdict was that he must die.

The moment he learned what had happened, Guntram Boso
ran at full speed to Magneric's lodging. He fastened all the
doors, shut out all the clergy and the servants, and then said to
Magneric: 'Most saintly Bishop, I know that you have great
influence with the two Kings. It is to you that I flee as a suppliant, in my hope of escaping from them. Those deputed to
murder me are already outside your door. I want you to understand this clearly: either you help me to escape, or I will kill
you where you stand, and then go out to meet my own death.
This you must get clearly into your head: if I am to die, you
die with me; and you have just about the same hope of survival
as I have. Holy Bishop, I know that you are as much a father
to the King's son as is the King himself, and that whatever boon
you seek of the King is granted to you, for he is unwilling to
refuse your holiness anything that you ask. Ask for me to be
pardoned, then, or else we die together.' As Guntram Boso said
this, he drew his sword. The Bishop was terrified by what he had
just heard. 'What can I do as long as I am shut up here?' he
asked. 'Only let me out and I will go to the King and beseech
him to take pity on you. It is possible that he will show
compassion.' 'Not on your life,' answered Guntram Boso.

18. Brunhild, Chlodosind and Faileuba.

'Send some of your abbots and others in your confidence, with orders to pass on what I have just said.' The account which reached the King's ears was not this, however – not what was really happening. They reported instead that Guntram Boso was being harboured by the Bishop. The result was that the King lost his temper. 'If the Bishop refuses to come out,' he said, 'he can sacrifice his own life with this traitor.' When Magneric heard this, he sent more messengers to the King, who told the truth of the matter. 'Set light to the house,' replied King Guntram. 'If the Bishop is unable to come out, they can go up in smoke together!' This was reported to Magneric's clergy. They burst down the door and dragged him out. When he saw that he was surrounded on all sides by the raging flames, the unhappy Guntram Boso girded on his sword and edged towards the exit. The moment he crossed the threshold and put one foot outside, a man in the crowd threw a javelin and hit him full in the forehead. He was thrown off his balance by this blow and driven almost berserk. He tried to draw his sword, but he was wounded by lance after lance as the mob closed in. They stuck the points of their spears into his ribs and propped him up with the shafts, so that his body could not even fall to the ground. The few who supported him were killed out of hand and their bodies were exposed in the open with his. After some argument the two Kings gave permission for them to be buried.

Guntram Boso was an unprincipled sort of man, greedy and avaricious, coveting beyond all measure the goods of other people, giving his word to all, keeping his promises to none. His wife was sent into exile, with his sons. His possessions were confiscated for the public treasury. In his treasure-house was discovered a vast hoard of gold, silver and precious objects. When his conscience pricked him for his many sins, he buried quite a lot in the ground, but these items, too, were discovered. It was his habit to consult fortune-tellers and to put his trust in sorcery, in an attempt to foresee the future, but this gave him little solace.

11. King Guntram signed a treaty with his nephew and the

Queens. They gave each other gifts. Once they had established affairs of state on a firm footing, they all sat down to a banquet. As they did so, King Guntram gave thanks to the Lord. 'Almighty God,' he said, 'I thank You for having considered my eyes worthy to have seen the children of Childebert, who is to me as a son. Now that You have permitted me to look upon my own son's sons, I no longer need consider myself to be abandoned entirely by You in your almighty power.' On this occasion Dynamius and Lupus came over to Childebert's side once more, and the King received them in audience. Childebert gave Cahors back to Brunhild.[19] They signed the treaty, gave each other gifts and exchanged the kiss of peace; then each returned to his own city in joy and amity, thanking God again and again.[20]

12.   King Childebert assembled an army and ordered it to proceed to the place where Ursio and Berthefried were still taking refuge. This was an estate in the Woëvre region, dominated by a high hill. On the top of this hill there had been built a church in honour of the blessed Saint Martin. In former times, or so they say, there used to be a strong-point here; but nowadays the site is protected more by nature than by art. In this church, then, the two men whom I have named had shut themselves up, together with their wives and families and all their possessions. As I have told you, King Childebert raised an army and ordered it to march there. On their way to the church the troops who had been conscripted looted and then burned to the ground every building they came to which belonged to Ursio and Berthefried, stealing all their goods. Eventually the men reached the spot in question, clambered up the hill and brandished their weapons as they encircled the church. As leader they had Godigisel, the son-in-law of Duke Lupus. They found it impossible to drive the besieged men out of the church, so they tried to set

19. This had been part of Chilperic's *morgengabe* to Galswinth.
20. The Treaty of Andelot, 28 November 587, the text of which is given on pp. 503–7.

fire to it. When Ursio saw what was happening, he girded on his sword and made a sortie. He killed so many of the besiegers that of all those who came within range of him not one was left alive. Trudulf, Count of the Royal Palace, died in this skirmish, and many of the troops were killed. Only then was it realized that Ursio was quite out of breath from the slaughter. Someone managed to strike him in the thigh and, weakened by this, he fell to the ground. They made a concerted rush, and that was the end of Ursio. Godigisel saw what had happened. He said to those around him and then began to shout: 'Let us make peace now! The main enemy of our master lies dead! Berthefried can have his life!' As soon as he made this announcement, all his men turned their attention towards looting the goods which were piled up in the church. Thereupon Berthefried leapt on a horse and rode off to the town of Verdun, thinking that he would be safe in the oratory inside the church-house there, the more so as Bishop Ageric had his residence in this same house. When it was reported to King Childebert that Berthefried had escaped, he was furious. 'If Berthefried does escape with his life,' he said, 'I will hold Godigisel instead.' Childebert was unaware that Berthefried had sought sanctuary in the church-house, for he understood that he had fled the country. Godigisel was frightened by what he heard. He re-formed his troops and put a cordon of armed men round the church-house. The Bishop refused to hand Berthefried over and did what he could to protect him. The soldiers climbed on the roof, tore off some of the tiles and other building materials which covered the oratory, dropped them down on Berthefried, and killed him and three of his men. The Bishop was greatly grieved by what had happened, for not only had he proved powerless to protect Berthefried, but now he saw the very spot on which he was accustomed to say his prayers, the place moreover where the relics of the saints were kept, polluted with human blood. King Childebert sent some men with presents, in the hope of distracting Ageric from his grief, but the Bishop refused to be consoled.

At this time a great number of men emigrated to other

regions, for they were greatly afraid of the King. Certain dukes were demoted from their dukedoms, and others were promoted to replace them.

13. King Guntram ordered Baddo to appear before him and then to be moved to Paris. As I told you earlier on,[21] Baddo had been taken into custody for the crime of high treason. 'If Fredegund can clear him of the charge which is brought against him, and have the support of men of good repute in doing so,[22] Baddo may go free and take himself off wherever he wishes,' said the King. Baddo was brought to Paris, but no one put in an appearance to represent Fredegund and to establish his innocence. He was bound and loaded with chains, and then taken back under close surveillance to the town of Chalon-sur-Saône. Later on messengers passed to and fro, especially from Leudovald, Bishop of Bayeux, and in the end Baddo was released and went home.

There was a serious epidemic of dysentery in the town of Metz. As I was hurrying off to have an audience with the King, I met on the road, near Rheims, a citizen of Poitiers called Wiliulf, who was in a high fever and suffering from this disease. He was already seriously ill with dysentery when he set out, accompanied by his wife's son. He reached the Paris area, but died in the villa of Rueil, having just time to make his will. The boy, who was suffering from the same disease, died in his turn. They were both carried back to Poitiers and there they were buried. As her third husband Wiliulf's wife married Duke Beppolen's son. It is common knowledge that he had already deserted two wives who were still living. He was loose in his habits and libidinous. Whenever his desire for intercourse drove him to it, he would leave his wife and go to bed with the servant-girls. His first marriage irked him, and he sought a second union. He treated his second wife in the same way, and then he did the same to this woman whom he had married *en troisièmes*

---

21. *HF*, VIII, 44.
22. They would merely have to swear that he was innocent.

noces. 'Neither doth corruption inherit incorruption'[23] was a statement beyond his comprehension.

13. Egidius, Bishop of Rheims, was suspected of this same high treason for which others of whom I have told you lost their lives.[24] He was the next to visit King Childebert to sue for pardon, bringing rich gifts with him. Before he set out he received a sworn assurance in the church of Saint Remigius that no harm should come to him on the way. He was given an audience by the King and then he departed in peace. He also made his peace with Duke Lupus, who, as I told you earlier on,[25] had been dismissed from the dukedom of Champagne at his instigation. King Guntram was bitterly angry about this, for Lupus had promised him that he would never come to terms with Egidius, as one well known to be the King's enemy.

15. About this same time[26] in Spain King Recared was moved by the grace of God to call a meeting of the bishops of his own church and to make the following pronouncement: 'Why does this schism continue on both sides between you and the bishops who call themselves Catholics? How is it that they perform numerous miracles, while you are incapable of doing anything of the sort? I want you to meet together to debate the doctrines of the two sects. Only in this way shall I discover where the truth lies. Either they must accept our faith and believe what you profess, or else you must recognize the truth of what they believe and subscribe to the tenets explained in their preaching.' This was done. The bishops of the two sects came together. The heretics put forward the arguments which I have often described as being their profession of faith. In the same way the bishops of our own church reiterated in their turn the articles by which, as I have shown in my previous books, this sect of schismatics had so often been confuted.[27] In particular the King maintained that no miracle for the healing of the sick

23. I Corinthians 15, 50.
24. Rauching, Ursio and Berthefried.   25. *HF*, VI, 4.
26. A.D. 587.   27. *HF*, V, 43.

had ever been performed by the heretic bishops. He called to mind how, in his father's time, a certain bishop, who was in the habit of boasting that he could restore sight to the blind through his false faith, laid his hands on a blind man, condemned him to lifelong blindness by doing so, and then went on his way confounded – a story which I have related in more detail in my *Book of Miracles*.[28] Recared then summoned to him the bishops of the Lord and questioned them closely. He was instructed that the one God is to be worshipped under the distinction of Three Persons, the Father, the Son and the Holy Ghost; that the Son is not less than the Father or the Holy Ghost, and that the Holy Ghost is not less than the Father or the Son; but that he should confess this Trinity, equal and omnipotent, to be the true God. Recared perceived the truth of what he had heard. He put an end to the dispute and submitted to the Catholic faith. He received the sign of the blessed Cross with unction of holy chrism, and confessed his belief in Jesus Christ, the Son of God, equal to the Father and the Holy Ghost, reigning world without end, Amen. He then sent messengers to the province of Narbonne[29] to explain what he had done, so that the people of those parts might join him in his conversion.

There was at that time a bishop of the Arian sect called Athaloc,[30] who by his empty pronouncements and false interpretations of the Scriptures kept causing so much trouble to the churches of God that he might have been taken for Arius himself, who, according to the historian Eusebius, lost his entrails in the lavatory.[31] Athaloc tried to prevent the people of his sect from accepting this conversion. Only a few flatterers sided with him, and this made him very bitter. He went to his cell, laid his head on his pillow, and breathed out his perverse spirit. Thus this people of heretics who lived in that province

28. *GC*, 13.

29. Septimania, the former Gallia Narbonensis.

30. According to John of Biclar, Bishop Athaloc and two Counts of Septimania, Granista and Wildigern, revolted against the newly converted Recared.

31. *Historia Ecclesiastica*, 10, 4.

gave up their false belief and confessed the Trinity, one and
indivisible.

16.   Recared now sent envoys to Guntram and to King Childebert to sue for peace. He was one with them in faith, or so he
asserted, and he would like to be united with them in friendship.
For his part Guntram sent the envoys packing. 'How can they
suggest that I should trust them, and how can they hope to be
believed, when it was they who delivered my niece Ingund into
captivity, when it was as the result of their treachery that her
husband was murdered, and when she herself died on her long
journey?[32] I will receive no envoys from Recared until God has
granted me revenge on this people who are my enemies.' When
the messengers heard this, they went off to Childebert. He on
the contrary received them in a friendly way. 'Our master Recared, who is your brother,' ran their message, 'wishes to
clear himself of the charge laid upon him that he was in any
way inculpated in your sister's death. He is prepared to prove
his innocence by oath, if you so wish, or by any other means
whatsoever. In addition he proposes to pay your Majesty ten
thousand gold pieces. He greatly desires your alliance, so that
he may have your support in time of need and you may have
his.' Childebert and his mother listened to what the envoys had
to say: then they promised that they would maintain unbroken
peace and friendship with Recared. Presents were exchanged.
The legates then added a further item. 'Our master orders us to
whisper a word in your ear about Chlodosind, the sister of one
of you and the daughter of the other. He suggests that if she
were to marry him, the peace which is promised between you
might the more easily be maintained.' 'As far as we are concerned,' answered Brunhild and Childebert together, 'we will
readily agree to the engagement, but we do not dare to do so
without the approval of our uncle King Guntram. We have
promised him that we would make no major decision without
asking his advice.' As soon as they had received this answer, the
envoys returned home.

32. *HF*, VIII, 18, 21 and 28.

17. This year[33] it rained very heavily throughout the Spring, and then, when the trees and the vines were already in leaf, a fall of snow buried everything. There followed such a frost that the vine-shoots were withered, together with any fruit which was already showing. The weather was so bitter that even the swallows, birds which fly to us from foreign parts, were killed by the extreme cold. A curious feature of all this was that the frost destroyed everything in places where it usually did no harm, and yet it did not reach the spots where it usually caused most damage.

18. The Bretons invaded the Nantes region. They stole property, attacked country estates and led off a number of captives. As soon as this came to the notice of King Guntram, he ordered an army to be raised. Then he sent a messenger to parley with the Bretons and to say that they must make good all the damage which they had caused, for otherwise they could rest assured that they would be put to the sword by his troops. They were frightened and swore that they would make amends for all the wrong which they had done. When this news was reported to him, the King sent envoys to the Bretons, to wit, Namatius, Bishop of Orleans, Bertram, Bishop of Le Mans, and a few counts and other illustrious persons. There were also present notables from the kingdom of Lothar, King Chilperic's son. The envoys made their way to the Nantes region, where they delivered all the King's injunctions to Waroch and Vidimael. 'We, too, are well aware that these cities belong to the sons of King Lothar,' answered the Bretons, 'and we know that we should show allegiance to those princes. Without more ado, we will pay for the damage which we have so wantonly done.' They appointed sureties and signed agreements, by which they promised that they would pay a thousand pieces of gold to King Guntram and Lothar in compensation, and that they would never again invade the territory of the cities in question. Once this settlement was agreed to, the envoys went home and told the King what they had done.

33. A.D. 587.

Bishop Namatius remained behind in Nantes, for he had had restored to him certain estates which his relatives had lost in times gone by on the outskirts of the city. Three malignant boils grew on his head. He felt extremely ill as a result and decided to return to his own city as quickly as he could. As he was passing through Angers he died. His body was carried to his own city and he was buried in the church of Saint Anianus the Bishop.[34] Austrinus, the son of Pastor, was elected to his see.

Waroch soon forgot the oath and the pledge which he had given. He failed to do any of the things which he had promised. He seized the vineyards of the Nantais, harvested the grapes and carted the wine off to Vannes. King Guntram was once more roused to fury by this and ordered an army to be put into the field, but afterwards he calmed down.

19. The civil discord between the townsfolk of Tours, which I described above as having spent its force,[35] broke out once more with renewed fury. After having murdered Chramnesind's relatives, Sichar formed a great friendship with him, and they became so devoted to each other that they often had meals together and even slept in the same bed. One day as twilight was falling Chramnesind ordered his supper to be prepared and then invited Sichar round to eat with him. He came, and they both sat down to table. Sichar drank far more wine than he could carry and began to boast at Chramnesind's expense. He is reported to have said: 'Dear brother, you ought to be grateful to me for having killed off your relations. There is plenty of gold and silver in your house now that I have recompensed you for what I did to them. If it weren't for the fact that the fine which I've paid has restored your finances, you would still today be poor and destitute.' When he heard Sichar's remarks, Chramnesind was sick at heart. 'If I don't avenge my relatives,' he said to himself, 'they will say that I am as weak as a woman, for I no longer have the right to be called a man!' Thereupon he blew

34. Saint Anianus, Bishop of Orleans, died A.D. 453.
35. *HF*, VII, 47.

the lights out and hacked Sichar's skull in two. Sichar uttered a low moan as life left his body, then he fell dead to the floor. The servants who had come with him lost no time in making off. Chramnesind stripped Sichar's corpse of its clothes and hung it from a post in his garden-fence. He then climbed on a horse and went off to find the King. He entered a church and threw himself at Childebert's feet. 'Mighty King!' he said, 'I come to plead for my life. I have killed the man who in secret destroyed my relations and then stole all their possessions.' He explained what had happened, point by point. Queen Brunhild took it very ill that Sichar, who was under her protection, should have been killed in this way, and she began to rage at Chramnesind. When he saw that she was against him, he fled to the village of Bouges in the Bourges area, where his people came from, this being under the jurisdiction of King Guntram. Tranquilla, Sichar's wife, abandoned her children and her husband's property in Tours and Poitiers, and went off to join her own relations in the village of Pont-sur-Seine. There she married again.

Sichar was only about twenty when he died. He was a loose-living young man, drunken and murderous, causing trouble to all sorts of people when he was in liquor. Chramnesind went to the King a second time. The judgement was that he must prove that he had taken life in order to avenge an affront, and this he did. In view of the fact that she had taken Sichar under her protection, Queen Brunhild ordered Chramnesind's property to be sequestered. Eventually his goods were handed back by Flavinius, one of the Queen's retainers. Chramnesind rushed off to Count Aginus and obtained a letter of restitution from him. It was to Flavinius that the Queen had made over his possessions.

20. In the thirteenth year of Childebert's reign,[36] just as I had hurried off to Metz to meet the King, I received a command to go to King Guntram on an embassy. I found him in the town of Chalon-sur-Saône. 'Noble King,' said I, 'your illustrious nephew Childebert sends to you his sincerest

36. A.D. 588.

greetings. He thanks you warmly for your loving kindness and the constant encouragement which you give to him to do that which is pleasing in God's sight, which is acceptable to you and in the best interests of his own people. He promises to carry out everything that was agreed between you, and he pledges himself not to contravene any article of the treaty signed by you both.' 'As far as I am concerned,' replied the King, 'I have little reason to feel grateful to Childebert. Why, he has already broken the promises which he made to me! He has not made over to me my part of the town of Senlis. He has not returned to me those men who, for my own well-being, I wished to summon back from his kingdom, seeing that they were hostile to my interests. How then can you stand there and say that this precious nephew of mine is determined in no way to contravene any article of the treaty signed by us both?'

To this I made the following reply: 'Childebert has no intention of contravening any of the provisions. On the contrary, he really is determined to see that they are all carried out. As for the one to which you refer, if you wish to proceed to a partition of Senlis, it can be made immediately and you can take over your third of the town without delay. As far as the men to whom you have referred are concerned, give me their names in writing and you will see that all the promises made in the treaty will be honoured.'

When I had finished my speech, the King ordered the treaty to be read aloud once more in the hearing of all who were present.

Text of the Treaty. When, in the name of Christ, the most noble Lords King Guntram and King Childebert, and the most renowned Lady Queen Brunhild, met at Andelot to reaffirm their friendship and, after full debate, to put an end to any circumstance whatsoever which might prove to be a cause of dispute between them, it was settled, approved and mutually agreed, by the grace of God, and with the approval of their bishops and their military leaders that, for as long as Almighty God should preserve them in their lives here below, they should maintain good faith one with another, in pure loving kindness and singleness of heart.

§. Insofar as King Guntram, according to the terms of the alliance into which he had entered with King Sigibert of blessed memory, has claimed as his own the entire domain which King Sigibert had inherited from the lands ruled over by Charibert, and in so far as King Childebert has wished to recover from all this that portion which his own father had possessed, it is agreed between them and after full debate decided that the third part of the city of Paris, with its territory and its inhabitants, which came to King Sigibert by signed treaty from the lands ruled over by Charibert, together with the castles of Châteaudun and Vendôme, and all that the aforesaid King possessed with right of free passage in the region of Etampes and Chartres, with the lands concerned and the people who lived there, shall remain in perpetuity under the jurisdiction and dominion of King Guntram, this in addition to what he, Guntram, had already inherited from the lands ruled over by Charibert during the lifetime of King Sigibert.

§. It is further agreed that from this day forward King Childebert shall hold under his dominion the city of Meaux, two thirds of Senlis, and the cities of Tours, Poitiers, Avranches, Aire, Couserans, Labourd and Albi, with their territories.

§. The following condition shall be observed, that whichever of the aforesaid Kings may by God's decree survive the other, given that that other has passed away from the light of this world without male issue, shall inherit the kingdom of that other, in its entirety and in perpetuity, and, by God's grace, hand it down to his own descendants.

§. It is further most specifically agreed, and it shall be observed come what may, that whatsoever King Guntram has donated to his daughter Clotild, or may, by God's grace, in the future donate, in property of all kinds, in men, cities, lands or revenues, shall remain in her power and under her control. It is agreed that if she shall decide of her own free will to dispose of any part of the lands or revenues or monies, or to donate them to any person, by God's grace they shall be held by that person in perpetuity, and they shall not be taken from him at any time or by any other person. Moreover, she herself shall, under the protection and guardianship of King Childebert, hold secure, in all honour and dignity, everything of which she shall stand possessed at the death of her father.

§. In addition to this and under the same terms, King Guntram promises that if, in the light of human frailty, it should come to pass, and may God in His compassion not permit this, for Guntram himself would certainly not wish to live to see the day, that King Childebert should pass away from the light of this world leaving Guntram still alive, he, Guntram, will take under his own guardianship and protection, in the guise of a loving father, Childebert's sons, the princes Theudebert and Theuderic, and ensure that they inherit their father's kingdom in all security.

§. In addition King Guntram promises that he will take under his own guardianship and protection, with all loving-kindness, her Majesty the Queen Brunhild, mother of King Childebert, Brunhild's daughter Chlodosind, the sister of King Childebert, as long as she remain in the land of the Franks, and Childebert's Queen, Faileuba, as if she were his own dear sister, and her daughters, too; and he will ensure that they may hold in all security and peace, and in all honour and dignity, such men and such goods, such cities, lands, revenues, rights of all sorts and wealth of all kinds, as at this present time they are seen to hold, or as, in the future, with Christ to guide them, they are able lawfully to acquire. If of their own free will they wish to dispose of or to grant to any person any part of their lands, revenues or monies, this shall be secured in safe possession in perpetuity, and their wish shall not be annulled at any time by any other person.

§. As to the cities of Bordeaux, Limoges, Cahors, Lescar and Cieutat, which, as is unquestioned, Galswinth, sister of the Lady Brunhild, acquired as dowry, or as *morgengabe*,[37] that is as a morning-gift, on her first coming to the land of the Franks, and which the Lady Brunhild is recognized to have inherited, by the decree of King Guntram and with the agreement of the Franks, during the lifetime of Chilperic and King Sigibert, it is agreed that the Lady Brunhild shall forthwith receive into her possession the city of Cahors, with its lands and all its inhabitants, but that King Guntram shall hold the other cities named above as long as he lives, on this condition, that after his death they shall pass, God willing, in all security, into the possession of the Lady Brunhild, it being understood that, as long as King Guntram lives, they shall not under any pretext or at any time be claimed by the Lady Brunhild, or by her son King Childebert, or by his sons.

§. It is furthermore agreed that King Childebert shall hold in its entirety the town of Senlis, but that, by the transfer to his lands of that third part of Ressons which is in King Childebert's possession,

37. For the *morgengabe*, see p. 297, note 66.

compensation shall be given to King Guntram for that third part of Senlis which is rightly claimed by him.

§. It is furthermore agreed that in accordance with the treaty made between King Guntram and King Sigibert of blessed memory, those *leudes*[38] who, on the death of King Lothar, first took oaths of loyalty to King Guntram, but who can be shown since then to have transferred their allegiance elsewhere, shall be brought back from the places in which they are known to have taken up residence. In the same way those *leudes* who, after the death of King Lothar, are known first to have taken oaths of loyalty to King Sigibert, and then to have transferred their allegiance elsewhere, shall be brought back.

§. Furthermore, whatsoever the afore-mentioned Kings have conferred upon the churches or upon their own faithful subjects, or may in future, by God's grace, and in lawful fashion, wish to confer upon them, shall be held by them in all security.

§. Whatsoever any faithful subject, in either of the two kingdoms, may justly and legally hold in his possession, shall in no way be open to question, for he shall be permitted to retain the things which are his. If, during interregna, anything is taken away from anyone through no fault of his own, an inquiry shall be held and restoration shall be made. Whatsoever, through the munificence of earlier kings, down to the death of King Lothar of blessed memory, any man has possessed, let him continue to possess it in security. Whatsoever has been taken away from our faithful subjects since then must be restored immediately.

§ Insofar as one single unequivocal treaty has now been accepted in God's name by the aforesaid Kings, it is agreed that, in both kingdoms and for the faithful subjects of both kingdoms, the right of free passage shall at no time be refused to any person who may wish to travel on public affairs or on private business. It is furthermore agreed that neither King shall invite the *leudes* of the other King to join him, and that, if they should come, he shall not receive them. If, as the result of some misdemeanour, the *leudes* of one King seek refuge in the territory of the other King, they shall be handed back and punished in accordance with their crime.

§. It is further resolved to add to the treaty that, if at any time, on any pretext, any one of the parties concerned should fail to observe its provisions, he must forfeit all benefits conferred in the present or promised for the future, to the advantage of him who shall have

38. For the *leudes*, see p. 157, note 64.

carried out all the provisions in full detail, this latter then being
absolved in all respects from being bound by his oath.

§.   Now that agreement has been come to on all these points, the
parties concerned swear in the name of God Almighty, and by the
inseparable Trinity, by all things divine and by the awful Day of
Judgement, that they will observe, in full detail, without fraud
or treachery or wish to deceive, each and every provision as it is
written above.

This treaty was made on 28 November, in the twenty-sixth year of
the reign of King Guntram and in the twelfth year of the reign of
King Childebert.

When this treaty had been read aloud, the King said: 'May I
be struck by the judgement of God, if I break any of the provisions contained in that!' Then he turned to Felix, who had
come with me. 'Tell me, Felix,' he said, 'is it really true that you
have established warm friendly relations between my sister
Brunhild and that enemy of God and man, Fredegund?' Felix
said that it was not. I spoke up and said: 'The King need not
question the fact that the "friendly relations" which have
bound them together for so many years are still being fostered
by them both. That is to say, you may be quite sure that the
hatred which they have borne each other for many a long year,
far from withering away, is still as strong as ever. Noble King, it
is a great pity that you cannot bring yourself to be less kindly
disposed towards Queen Fredegund. We have so often remarked
that you receive her envoys with more consideration than you
give to ours.' 'You may be quite sure in your turn, Bishop,' answered King Guntram, 'that I receive Fredegund's envoys in this
way simply in order to maintain friendly relations with my
nephew Childebert. I can hardly be offering ties of genuine
friendship to a woman who on more than one occasion has sent
her men to murder me!'

As soon as the King stopped speaking, Felix said: 'I believe
that it has come to your august ears that Recared has sent envoys to your nephew to ask for the hand in marriage of
Chlodosind, your own niece and your brother's daughter.
Childebert has, however, refused to give any promise without

507

your express approval.' 'It cannot be a good thing,' answered the King, 'that my niece should set out for a land in which her sister met her end. I cannot accept it as right that my niece Ingund's death should go unavenged.' 'They are very keen to prove themselves guiltless of this,' said Felix, 'either by swearing oaths, or by any other means which you may propose. Only give your consent that Chlodosind may be betrothed to Recared as he asks!' 'If my nephew carries out all that has been written into the treaty, and that with his full approval,' answered Guntram, 'I, for my part, will agree to what he wishes in this other matter.' We promised that Childebert would fulfil all the conditions.

'Childebert further asks of you, in your loyalty to your own kith and kin,' went on Felix, 'that you send him help against the Longobards, so that he may drive them out of Italy and win back the territory which his father claimed during his lifetime. Then, with your assistance, the rest of Italy can be restored to Imperial rule.' 'I will never send my troops into Italy,' answered the King, 'for in doing so I should encompass their certain death. A terrible epidemic is raging in that country at this moment.'

'You have put the request to your nephew,' said I in my turn, 'that all the bishops of his realm should meet together, since there are so many other matters which need to be settled. Your nephew has always been of the opinion, and in this he follows the canonical use, that each metropolitan should hold a meeting of the bishops of his own province, and then anything which is wrong in his own diocese can be put right as they may decide. What reason can there be for calling such a huge council together in one place? No threat is being made to the doctrine of the Church. No new heresy is being spawned. What need can there be for so many bishops to meet together in a single council?' 'There are many matters which need to be settled,' answered Guntram. 'Many evil deeds are being committed, there is a decline in personal morality, for instance, and there are many other things which we need to discuss together. Above all, and more important than all the rest, for the issue concerns God Himself, you need to discover how Bishop Prae-

textatus came to be struck down in his own cathedral. Then
there should be an inquiry into the case of those who are accused of the crime of *luxuria*. If they are proved guilty, they
should be punished as their fellow-bishops decide, but if they
are found to be innocent, the injustice of the accusation should
be made public.' He then ordered the council to be deferred
until the first day of June.

As soon as our interview was over, we processed to the
cathedral. It was the feast-day of our Lord's Resurrection. When
Mass was over, Guntram asked us to eat with him. The abundance of dishes on the table was only rivalled by the full contentment which we felt in our hearts. The King talked of God,
of building new churches, of succouring the poor. From time to
time he laughed out loud, as he coined some witty phrase,
thereby ensuring that we shared his happiness. Among the other
things which he said, he kept returning to this: 'If only my
nephew keeps his promises! All that I have is his! If he takes
offence because I grant an audience to my nephew Lothar's
envoys, am I such a fool that I cannot mediate between them
and so stop their quarrel from spreading? I am quite sure that it
is better to end that quarrel, instead of letting it drag on. If I do
recognize Lothar as my nephew, I will give him two or three
cities in some part or other of my dominions, so that he may not
feel that he is disinherited from my kingdom. Childebert has no
reason to take offence if I make these gifts to Lothar.' He also
said a number of other things. He was extremely friendly
towards us and loaded us with gifts. Then he bade us farewell,
exhorting us always to give Childebert such counsel as would
make his life easier.

21. As I have often told you, King Guntram was well known
for his charity and much given to vigils and fasting.

At this time[39] it was reported that Marseilles was suffering
from a severe epidemic of swelling in the groin and that this
disease had quickly spread to Saint-Symphorien-d'Ozon, a village near Lyons. Like some good bishop providing the remedies

39. A.D. 588.

by which the wounds of a common sinner might be healed, King Guntram ordered the entire people to assemble in church and Rogations to be celebrated there with great devotion. He then commanded that they should eat and drink nothing else but barley bread and pure water, and that all should be regular in keeping the vigils. His orders were obeyed. For three days his own alms were greater than usual, and he seemed so anxious about all his people that he might well have been taken for one of our Lord's bishops, rather than for a king. He put his hope in the compassion of our Lord, directing all his prayers towards Him, for through His agency he believed with perfect faith that his wishes would be realized.

The faithful had a story which they used to tell about Guntram. There was a woman whose son was seriously ill of a quartan ague. As the boy lay tossing on his bed, his mother pushed her way through the vast crowds and came up behind the King. Without his noticing she cut a few threads from his cloak. She steeped these threads in water and then gave the infusion to her son to drink. The fever left him immediately and he became well again. I accept this as true, for I have often heard men possessed of a devil call upon Guntram's name when the evil spirit was in them, and through his miraculous powers confess their crimes.

22. As I have just said, the city of Marseilles was suffering from a most serious epidemic. I want to tell you exactly how this came about. At the time Bishop Theodore had gone to see King Childebert, for he had some complaint or other to make against the patrician Nicetius. The King paid little attention to what Theodore had to say, so the Bishop prepared to return home. In the meantime a ship from Spain put into port with the usual kind of cargo, unfortunately also bringing with it the source of this infection. Quite a few of the townsfolk purchased objects from the cargo and in less than no time a house in which eight people lived was left completely deserted, all the inhabitants having caught the disease. The infection did not spread through the residential quarter immediately. Some time passed

and then, like a cornfield set alight, the entire town was suddenly ablaze with the pestilence. For all that Bishop Theodore came back and took up residence in Saint Victor's church,[40] together with seven poor folk who remained at his side. There he stayed throughout the whole of the catastrophe which assailed his city, giving up all his time to prayers and vigils, and imploring God in His mercy to put an end to the slaughter and to allow the people some peace and quiet. At the end of two months the plague burned itself out. The population returned to Marseilles, thinking themselves safe. Then the disease started again and all who had come back died. On several occasions later on Marseilles suffered from an epidemic of this sort.

23. Ageric, Bishop of Verdun, fell seriously ill. Day after day he tortured himself with the thought that it was his fault that Guntram Boso had been killed, in that he had stood surety for him. The fact that Berthefried had been slain in the oratory of his church-house was another cause of chagrin to him. Then there was this last straw, that he faced the daily reminder of having Guntram's sons living with him. 'It is my fault that you are left orphans,' he kept saying to them. As I have told you, these things weighed heavily upon him. He suffered from black depression, virtually giving up eating, and so died and was buried. Abbot Buccovald put in for the bishopric, but he had no success. By royal decree the Referendary Charimer was appointed, this also being the wish of the people. Abbot Buccovald was passed over; but they used to say that he was a proud man, hence his nickname, Buccus Validus.

Licerius, Bishop of Arles, died. With the backing of Bishop Syagrius, Virgil, Abbot of Autun, replaced him in his cathedral.

24. Deutherius, Bishop of Vence, died, and Pronimius was appointed in his place. This Pronimius once lived in Bourges. For some reason or other he moved to Septimania. After the

40. Saint Victor, a Christian soldier in the Roman army, was martyred in A.D. 303.

death of King Athanagild, he was received in great honour by Leuva, that King's successor, and made Bishop of Agde. Leuva died in his turn and then came Leuvigild, who was steeped in the depravity of the Arian heresy. As I have told you previously, King Sigibert's daughter Ingund was brought to Spain on the occasion of her marriage and it came to Leuvigild's ears that Bishop Pronimius had advised her not to get mixed up with this poisonous heresy. Leuvigild hated Pronimius from that moment onwards and was always trying to catch him out by some trick or other, so that he might expel him from his bishopric. However often he tried he never succeeded, and so he sent a man with a sword to deal with the Bishop. Pronimius was warned by informants. He escaped from Agde and fled to Gaul. He was given hospitality by a number of bishops and they started a fund for him. He made his way to King Childebert. A place fell vacant and, nine years after his flight from Agde, the King appointed him Bishop in the town of Vence.

In this year the Bretons ravaged Nantes, Rennes and the neighbourhood. They stole the wine-harvest, destroyed the cultivated fields and carried off as slaves those who lived on the country estates. They kept none of the promises which they had made. Not only did they break their pledges, but they even stole property belonging to our Kings.

25. King Childebert had received gifts from the Longobards, when they had come to ask if his sister could marry their King, and he had given his promise.[41] When envoys arrived from the Visigoths, he promised her to them, recognizing them as a people converted to the Catholic faith. He also sent an embassy to the Emperor, undertaking now what he had failed to do before, that is to attack the Longobards and, with the Emperor's help, to drive them out of Italy. Next he sent his troops to occupy their lands. His military leaders marched into Italy at the head of an army and engaged the enemy. Our people were cut to pieces: quite a few were slain, some were captured, the

41. King Childebert II had previously promised his sister Chlodosind in marriage to Authari, King of the Longobards.

remainder turned in flight and made their way home, but not without difficulty. The slaughter of the Frankish army was such that nothing like it could be remembered.

26. In the fourteenth year of King Childebert's reign[42] there died Queen Ingoberg, the widow of Charibert, a woman of great wisdom, devoted to the religious life, constant in her vigils, her prayers and her alms-giving. Warned of her approaching death by God in His providence, or so I believe, she sent messengers to me to ask me to help her to carry out what she wanted to do for the salvation of her soul. She said that she would wait until I arrived and then, when we had talked it over, she would set down in writing what she wanted to be done. I went to her, of course. I found a woman who feared God. She received me most kindly, called a notary and then, after she had discussed her plan with me, as I have told you, left a legacy to Tours cathedral, another to Saint Martin's church and a third to the cathedral of Le Mans. A few months later she was suddenly taken ill and died. By deeds of enfranchisement she freed many serfs. I think that she was in her seventieth year. She left a daughter, who had married the son of a King of Kent.[43]

27. Duke Amalo sent his wife away to one of his other estates to look after his affairs. Then he was seized with desire for a young girl of free birth. One night when he was completely drunk he sent his servants to seize the girl and put her in his bed. She resisted, but she was carried to Amalo's house by main force. They punched her until her nose bled, so that Duke Amalo's bed was stained red with her blood. In his turn he, too, punched her and hit her and slapped her; then he took her in his arms. Just at this moment he fell asleep. The girl stretched out her hand above his head, took hold of his sword, eased it out of its scabbard and, just as Judith did to Holofernes, dealt him a mighty blow. He gave a loud scream and his servants came running. They were about to kill the girl, but Amalo shouted:

42. A.D. 589.   43. Cp. p. 219, note 43.

'Stop, stop, I tell you! It is I who have sinned, for I tried to rape this girl! She only did this to preserve her virginity. You must not hurt her.' As he said this he died. While all Amalo's family stood there lamenting, the girl escaped with God's help and ran home. She then made her way to the city of Chalon-sur-Saône, which is about thirty-five miles from the place where this happened. She went into the church of Saint Marcellus, threw herself at the King's feet and told him all that had occurred. He was filled with compassion. Not only did he grant her her life, but he ordered a royal edict to be drawn up to the effect that she was under his protection and must not be molested by any of the dead man's relations. I later learned that with God to guard her she did not lose her virginity at the hands of her brutal ravisher.

28.   Queen Brunhild had a great salver of incredible size made out of gold and precious gems. This she dispatched to the King in Spain, together with a pair of wooden dishes, commonly called basins, which were also decorated with gold and jewels. She entrusted the commission to Ebregisel, for he had often been sent on missions to Spain. It was announced to King Gun-tram that Ebregisel had set out, for someone reported to him that Queen Brunhild was sending presents to Gundovald's sons. As soon as he heard it, Guntram had all the roads in his kingdom closely guarded, so that no one could pass through without being searched. Even the clothes and shoes of travellers were examined, and all their possessions, too, to see if a letter were hidden in them. Ebregisel came to Paris, carrying the precious gifts. He was seized by Duke Ebrachar and brought before the King. 'You miserable wretch!' shouted Guntram. 'Is it not enough that you had the effrontery to summon the Ballomer,[44] him whom you call Gundovald, to marry Brunhild – the man whom I destroyed because he wanted to take over the government of my kingdom? Now you are carrying presents to his sons and no doubt inviting them back to Gaul to cut my throat! You shall never reach your journey's end! You must die

44. Cp. p. 397, note 18.

the death, for your mission is a challenge to me and my race!'
Ebregisel protested that he did not know what Guntram was
talking about, for the gifts were being sent to Recared, who was
to marry King Childebert's sister Chlodosind. The King believed what he said and let him go. He set out once more on his
journey, taking the presents with him.

29.   King Childebert decided to accept the invitation of Sigimund, Bishop of Mainz, to celebrate Easter Day in that town.
Theudebert, his elder son, was suffering from a nasty tumour in
his throat, but he recovered.

In the meantime King Childebert raised an army and made
ready to set out into Italy at its head to attack the Longobards.
When they heard the news, the Longobards sent envoys and
gifts. 'Let there be peace between us,' said the messengers.
'Rather than perish we will pay tribute to you and your government. If ever you have need of our help against your enemies,
we shall not be slow to come.' King Childebert sent representatives to King Guntram to report what he had heard and to
inform him of the offer made by the Longobards. Guntram was
in favour of the agreement and advised Childebert to make
peace. King Childebert ordered his troops to remain where they
were, but he sent envoys to the Longobards to say that his army
would return home if they would confirm what he had heard. In
effect things turned out differently.

30.   At the request of Bishop Maroveus King Childebert sent
tax inspectors to Poitiers: Florentianus, Mayor of the Queen's
Household, and Romulf, Count of his own Palace. Their orders
were to prepare new tax-lists and to instruct the people to pay
the taxes which had been levied from them in the time of Childebert's father. Many of those who were on the lists had died,
and, as a result, widows, orphans and infirm folk had to meet a
heavy assessment. The inspectors looked into each case in turn:
they granted relief to the poor and infirm, and assessed for
taxation all who were justly liable.

After this they came to Tours. When they announced that

they were about to tax the townsfolk, and that they had in their possession tax-lists showing how the people had been assessed in the time of earlier kings, I gave them this answer: 'It is undeniable that the town of Tours was assessed in the days of King Lothar. The books were taken off to be submitted to the King. Lothar had them thrown into the fire, for he was greatly overawed by our Bishop, Saint Martin. When Lothar died, my people swore an oath of loyalty to King Charibert, and he swore in his turn that he would not make any new laws or customs, but would secure to them the conditions under which they had lived in his father's reign. He promised that he would not inflict upon them any new tax-laws which would be to their disadvantage. Gaiso, who was Count at that time, took the tax-lists, which, as I have said, had been drawn up by earlier tax inspectors, and began to exact payment. He was opposed by Bishop Eufronius, but he went off to the King with the money which he had collected illegally and showed to him the tax-lists in which the assessment was set down. King Charibert sighed, for he feared the miraculous power of Saint Martin, and he threw the lists into the fire. The money which had been collected he sent back to Saint Martin's church, swearing that no public taxation should ever again be forced upon the people of Tours. King Sigibert held this city after Charibert's death, but he did not burden it with taxation. In the same way Childebert has made no demands in the fourteen years during which he has reigned since his father's death. The city has not had to face any tax-assessment at all. It lies in your power to decide whether or not tax should be collected; but beware of the harm which you will do if you act contrary to the King's sworn agreement.' When I had finished speaking, they made the following reply: 'You see that we hold in our hands the book which lists the tax-assessment for your people.' 'That book was not issued by the King's treasury,' I answered. 'For all these long years it has been in abeyance. I would not be at all surprised if it had been kept carefully in someone's house out of hatred for these townsfolk of mine. God will surely punish the individuals who have produced it after such a long passage of time, just to despoil my citizens.' That very day the son of Audinus, the man who had produced the inventory, caught a fever. He died three days later. We then sent representatives to the King, to ask that he send instructions and make clear just what his orders were. An official letter came back almost immediately, confirming the immunity from taxation of the people of Tours, out of respect for Saint Martin. As soon as they had read it, the men who had been sent on the mission returned home.

31. King Guntram raised an army to attack Septimania. Duke Austrovald had gone on ahead to Carcassonne to exact an oath of allegiance and to subject the people to the King's rule. Guntram then sent Boso and Antestius to subdue the other cities. When Boso arrived he behaved most arrogantly. He sneered at Duke Austrovald and reprimanded him for having entered Carcassonne without waiting for him. Then he marched on Carcassonne with men of Saintes, Périgueux, Bordeaux, Agen and even Toulouse. While he was moving up in this overweening way, the Goths came to hear of it and laid an ambush for him. He pitched his camp on the banks of a small river[45] which flows hereabouts, sat down to supper, drank more than was good for him, and was heard taunting and abusing the Goths. This was the moment which the Goths chose to attack, taking Boso and his men unawares and at their meal. They sounded the alarm and sprang up to resist. The Goths immediately withdrew and pretended to run away. Boso and his men chased after them, whereupon those in ambush leapt out at them and caught them between two fires. The Frankish force was almost wiped out. It was a case of *sauve qui peut*: some scrambled on their horses and managed to escape, leaving all their equipment behind on the battlefield and abandoning all their personal effects, for, indeed, they thought themselves lucky to get away with their lives. The Goths pursued them. They captured all their gear, pillaged their camp and took all

45. The River Aude.

the foot-soldiers prisoner. Nearly five thousand men died in this engagement. The enemy seized more than two thousand. Many were freed later and found their way home.

32. King Guntram was greatly alarmed. He ordered all the roads through his realm to be closed, in order to prevent the passage of all persons from Childebert's kingdom through his territory. 'It is because of his wickedness in making an alliance with the King of Spain that my army has been wiped out,' he complained. 'It is at his instigation that these cities have refused to accept my rule.' He had another reason for bitter resentment. Childebert was planning to send his elder son Theudebert to Soissons, and this aroused suspicion in Guntram's mind. 'My nephew is only sending his son to Soissons so that he may next enter Paris and so seek to deprive me of my kingdom,' he alleged. If I may say so, no such idea had ever entered Childebert's head. Guntram also made a number of wild accusations against Brunhild, maintaining that it was she who was advising Childebert, and adding that she had once wanted to marry one of Gundovald's sons. As a result Guntram ordered a council of bishops to be convened for the first day of November. Quite a few of them set out for this council from the uttermost ends of Gaul. However, Queen Brunhild cleared herself of the accusation on oath, and they all went home again. The roads were opened once more and Guntram gave free passage to anyone who wanted to visit King Childebert.

33. About this time Ingitrude, who had founded a nunnery[46] in the forecourt of Saint Martin's church, went to the King to complain about her daughter (Berthegund). This was the nunnery in which also lived Berthefled, King Charibert's daughter. The moment Ingitrude set out, Berthefled left in her turn and moved to Le Mans. She was a woman who ate and slept a lot, and she had no interest at all in the holy offices.

I propose to tell you the tale of Ingitrude and her daughter from the beginning. Years before, when, as I have explained to

46. This nunnery later took the name of Sainte Maria de Scriniolo.

you, Ingitrude first founded her convent for young women inside the forecourt of Saint Martin's church, she sent a message to her daughter, saying: 'Leave your husband and come, so that I can make you Abbess of the community which I have brought together.' As soon as Berthegund received this stupid message, she came to Tours with her husband. She entered her mother's nunnery, saying to her husband: 'Go back home and look after the children, for I don't propose to return with you. No one who is married will ever see the Kingdom of Heaven.' The husband came to me and told me what his wife had said to him. I went to the nunnery and read aloud the relevant portion of the Nicene Creed,[47] which runs as follows: 'If any woman abandons her husband and scorns the married state in which she has lived honourably, saying that no one who is married will ever see the Kingdom of God, let her be accursed.' When Berthegund heard this, she was afraid of being excommunicated by God's bishops, so she left the convent and went back home again with her husband.

Three or four years passed. Then Ingitrude sent another message to her daughter, asking her to come back. One day when he was away from home, Berthegund loaded some boats with her own possessions and those of her husband, and set out for Tours with one of her sons. Her mother was unwilling to keep her there, because the husband kept asking her to return. She was worried, too, about the charge to which Berthegund had exposed them both by her illegal act. She therefore packed her off to Bertram, Bishop of Bordeaux, who was Berthegund's brother and Ingitrude's son. The husband followed Berthegund to Bordeaux, but Bertram said to him: 'You married her without her parents' consent, and therefore she is no longer your wife.' This was when they had been married for nearly thirty years! The husband visited Bordeaux several times, but Bishop Bertram refused to give his sister up. When King Guntram came to the town of Orleans, as I have told you in a previous book,[48] the husband sought an audience and made a bitter

47. In effect this is Canon 14 of the Council of Gangres, A.D. 340.
48. *HF*, VIII, 2.

attack on Bishop Bertram. 'You have taken away my wife and her servants,' he said. 'What is more, and this ill becomes a bishop, you have seduced some of my women-servants and my wife has had intercourse with some of your men.' The King was very angry and forced Bishop Bertram to promise to give Berthegund back to her husband. 'She is a relation of mine,' the King said. 'If she has done anything wrong in her husband's home, it is for me to punish her. If she has done nothing wrong, why should her husband be humiliated in this way by having his wife taken away from him?' Bishop Bertram gave his promise. 'I admit that my sister came to me after many years of married life,' he said. 'It was out of brotherly love and affection that I kept her with me as long as she wished to stay. Now she has left me. He can come to fetch her and take her away whenever he wishes, for I shall not stand in his way.' That is what he said, but in secret he sent a messenger to Berthegund, telling her to take off her secular clothes, do penance and seek sanctuary in Saint Martin's church. All this she did. Then her husband arrived with a number of his men to force her to leave the church. She was wearing the habit of a nun and refused to go with her husband, for she said that she had taken a vow of penitence.

Meanwhile Bishop Bertram died in Bordeaux. Berthegund then came to her senses. 'What a fool I have been,' she said, 'to listen to the advice of my stupid mother! Now my brother is dead, my husband has left me and I am cut off from my children! How unhappy I am! Where shall I go, and what shall I do?' She thought things over for a while and then she went to Poitiers. Her mother wanted to keep her with her, but she was unable to do so. A quarrel then arose between them, and they kept on appearing before the King, Berthegund trying to establish a claim to what her father had left and Ingitrude asking for the estate of her late husband. Berthegund produced a deed of gift from her brother Bertram, saying: 'My brother gave me this, and that, too.' Her mother would not recognize the deed and tried to claim everything for herself. She sent men to break into her daughter's house and steal everything, including the deed of gift. By doing this Ingitrude put herself in the wrong, and at her daughter's request she was forced to restore what she had taken. Maroveus, one of my fellow-Bishops, and I received letters from the King, ordering us to try to pacify the two of them. Berthegund came to Tours and appeared in our court, and we did all we could to make her listen to reason. Her mother took no notice of us. She went off to the King in a raging temper, determined to disinherit her daughter from all share in her father's property. She pleaded her case in the King's presence, without her daughter being there, and the judgement given was that one quarter should be restored to Berthegund, but that Ingitrude should receive three quarters, to share with her grandchildren, whom she had from another son. The priest Theuthar, who had been one of King Sigibert's Referendaries but had since entered the Church and joined the priesthood, came at King Childebert's command to make the division. However, Berthegund refused to accept the judgement, and so the division was not made and the quarrel continued.[49]

34. Rigunth, Chilperic's daughter, was always attacking her mother (Fredegund), and saying that she herself was the real mistress, whereas her mother ought to revert to her original rank of serving-woman. She would often insult her mother to her face, and they frequently exchanged slaps and punches. 'Why do you hate me so, daughter?' Fredegund asked her one day. 'You can take all your father's things which are still in my possession, and do what you like with them.' She led the way into a strong-room and opened a chest which was full of jewels and precious ornaments. For a long time she kept taking out one thing after another, and handing them to her daughter, who stood beside her. Then she suddenly said: 'I'm tired of doing this. Put your own hand in and take whatever you find.' Rigunth was stretching her arm into the chest to take out some more things, when her mother suddenly seized the lid and slammed it down on her neck. She leant on it with all her might and the edge of the chest pressed so hard against the girl's throat

49. See *HF*, X, 12.

that her eyes were soon standing out of her head. One of the
servant-girls who was in the room screamed at the top of her
voice: 'Quick! Quick! Mistress is being choked to death by her
mother!' The attendants who had been waiting outside for them
to emerge burst into the strong-room, rescued the princess from
almost certain death and dragged her out of doors. The quarrels
between the two were even more frequent after this. There were
never-ending outbursts of temper and even fisticuffs. The main
cause was Rigunth's habit of sleeping with all and sundry.

35.   When she was dying, Beretrude appointed her daughter as
her heiress. She made a few bequests to the nunneries which she
had founded, and to the cathedrals and churches of the blessed
Saints. Then Waddo, of whom I have told you in an earlier
book,[50] made a complaint that some of his horses had been
stolen by Beretrude's son-in-law. He made up his mind to pay a
visit to one of Beretrude's country estates, which she had left to
her daughter, somewhere near Poitiers. 'This man, who came
here from another country anyway, stole my horses,' said
Waddo. 'All right! I will take his villa!' He thereupon sent word
to the bailiff to make all ready for his coming. When the bailiff
heard this he lined up all the other servants of the household
and prepared to do battle. 'Waddo will never enter my master's
villa,' he exclaimed, 'except over my dead body!' When
Waddo's wife heard that such a hostile reception was being
prepared for her husband, she said to him: 'Don't go, dearest
husband! You will be killed if you do! Then I, and my children,
too, will be left destitute.' She stretched out her hand and tried
to restrain him. One of the boys said: 'If you go, father, we shall
die! You will leave my mother a widow and my brothers
orphans!' No matter what they said, they could not dissuade
Waddo. He flew into a mad rage with his son, upbraiding him as
a coward and a weakling, throwing his axe at him and nearly
killing him. The boy jumped to one side and avoided the
blow.

Then Waddo and his men leapt on to their horses, and off they

50. *HF*, VII, 27 and 43.

rode, sending another messenger on ahead to the bailiff to tell him to sweep the house out and to put covers on the benches. The bailiff took no notice whatsoever of these orders, but stood firm outside his master's gate, with all the household, men and women, lined up beside him to await Waddo's coming. Waddo rode up and marched into the house, 'Why are there no covers on the benches?' he demanded. 'Why hasn't the house been swept clean?' He raised his hand, struck the bailiff on the head with his dagger and knocked him down dead. When the murdered man's son saw what had happened, he hurled his javelin at Waddo and then rushed at him. The javelin hit him full in the stomach and stuck out behind his back. He fell to the ground and the crowd which stood all around began to stone him. Then one of the men who had come with Waddo pushed his way forward through the shower of stones and covered his master with a cloak. The crowd calmed down. Waddo's son, who was sobbing his heart out, put him on a horse and carried him back home still alive. To the great grief of his wife and children, he died almost immediately. Thus he ended his life in misery. His son went to the King and obtained possession of his estate.

36. In this same year[51] King Childebert went to stay with his wife and mother near a town called Strasbourg.[52] Some of the more important citizens of Soissons and Meaux visited him there and said: 'Send us one of your sons, so that we may serve him. If we have a member of your family resident among us as a pledge, we shall resist your enemies with all the greater zeal and have more reason to protect the lands round your city.' The King was very pleased with the suggestion. He promised to send his elder son Theudebert to them. He appointed counts, personal servants, major-domos and tutors to serve him, and everyone else necessary for his royal household. In the month of August he sent the prince, thus meeting the wishes of these men who had asked their King that he might come. The people re-

51. A.D. 589.
52. This is the first record of the new name, Strateburgus, of the Roman township Argentoratum. Cp. *HF*, X, 19.

ceived Theudebert with great joy and prayed that God in His goodness might prolong his days and those of his father, too.

37.   At this time Droctigisel was Bishop of Soissons. He had been out of his mind now for nearly four years, through drinking to excess. Many of the citizens maintained that this was brought about by witchcraft, through the action of an archdeacon whom he had dismissed from his post. He was certainly more mad when he was inside the city walls, whereas whenever he ventured outside he behaved fairly normally. Although Droctigisel was better when the young prince came to Soissons, he was not allowed inside the city because of the royal entry. Everyone agreed that he ate and drank far more than is seemly for a bishop, but no accusation of concupiscence was ever levelled against him. A council of bishops was later convened in a villa at Sorcy, and there it was decreed that Droctigisel might return to his see.

38.   King Childebert's consort Faileuba had a child, who died almost immediately. While she was recovering from the birth, it came to her ears that there was a conspiracy afoot against Queen Brunhild and herself. As soon as she was strong enough, she went to Childebert and told him and his mother all that she had learnt. To cut a long story short, Septimima, nurse to the royal children, was to persuade the King to banish his mother, desert his wife and marry another woman. In this way the conspirators hoped to do with the King what they wished and to obtain from him what they asked. If the King refused to agree to what Septimima was to press upon him, he was to be killed by witchcraft, his sons were to be trained to succeed him, and in the meantime the conspirators would take over the government, the young princes' mother and grandmother being banished all the same. The informers said that those privy to the plot were Sunnegisil, the Count of the Stables, the Referendary Gallomagnus and Droctulf, who had been deputed to help Septimima in bringing up the royal children. These last two, Septimima and Droctulf, were taken into custody. They were

immediately put to the torture by being stretched upon the rack, whereupon Septimima confessed that she had killed her husband by witchcraft because she was in love with Droctulf, whose mistress she had then become. The two confessed to all the charges which I have set out above and confirmed that the men whom I have mentioned were implicated in the plot. A search was at once made for them, but they had guessed what was happening and had sought sanctuary in various churches. The King visited the buildings in person. 'Come out and stand your trial,' he shouted. 'Then we shall discover whether the charges brought against you are true or false. It seems to me that you would never have sought sanctuary in church unless your conscience had been pricking you. All the same, you have my promise that your lives will be saved, even if you are proved guilty. I am a Christian and I deem it wrong to punish people convicted of a crime if I have to drag them out of a church to do so.' They were taken out of the churches and they appeared before the King to be tried. When they were questioned they pleaded not guilty. 'It was Septimima and Droctulf who tried to embroil us in this plot,' they protested. 'We refused and took to our heels, for we would not be party to such a crime.' 'If you really were unwilling to join the conspiracy,' answered the King, 'you would have told me what was happening. Is it really true that you took no part in the plot, seeing that you failed to inform me of it?' He ordered them to leave his presence and they again sought sanctuary in a church. Septimima and Droctulf were both severely beaten. Septimima's face was disfigured with red-hot irons. All that she had was taken from her, and she was packed off to the country estate of Marlenheim to turn the mill and grind the corn each day to feed the women who worked in the spinning and weaving room there. They cut off Droctulf's ears and hair, and he was sent to labour in the vineyards. A few days later he escaped. He was discovered by the bailiff and once more brought before the King. He was flogged and sent back again to the vineyard which he had left. Sunnegisil and Gallomagnus were stripped of all the property which they held for life from the King and then sent into exile. King Guntram sent messengers, among them some bishops, to plead for them, and they were recalled from exile. Nothing was left to them, except their own personal property.

39.   A great scandal arose in the convent in Poitiers.[53] Clotild, who used to pretend that she was Charibert's daughter, gave in to the blandishments of the Devil. Relying upon the ties which she claimed with the royal family, she bound the nuns by oath to bring charges against Leubovera the Abbess, to expel her from the convent and then to choose herself, Clotild, as Mother Superior. She walked out of the convent with forty or more of the nuns, including her cousin Basina, Chilperic's daughter. 'I am going to my royal relations,' she said, 'to tell them about the insults which we have to suffer, for we are humiliated here as if we were the offspring of low-born serving-women, instead of being the daughters of kings!' How little mindful was this unhappy woman of the humility shown by Saint Radegund who founded the convent!

Clotild had not gone far on her journey when she arrived in Tours. She came to pay her respects to me and then added: 'Do me a favour, saintly Bishop, and keep an eye on these nuns, who have been greatly humiliated by their Abbess in Poitiers. You might also see that they have regular meals. I am going off to visit my royal relations and to explain to them what we have to put up with. I will be back soon.' 'If the Abbess has transgressed,' I answered, 'or broken the canonical rule in any way, let us go to my fellow-Bishop, Maroveus, and explain the situation to him together. When we have put things right, you must all go back to your convent. What Saint Radegund built up by her fasts and never-ending prayers and constant acts of charity must not now be dispersed in this wanton way.' 'That I will never do,' replied Clotild. 'I am off to see my royal relations.' 'Why do you refuse to listen to reason?' I asked her. 'Why do you reject the advice which I give to you as Bishop? I am

53. The Nunnery of the Holy Cross, founded by Saint Radegund. Cp. p. 164, note 9.

afraid, you know, that if the bishops come together in council, they may well exclude you from communion.'

This is what my predecessors wrote in a letter which they sent to Saint Radegund, when she first founded her convent. I think that it is a good thing to quote the letter in full at this point.

Text of a Letter. To the most blessed Lady Radegund, daughter of the Church in Christ, Bishops Eufronius, Praetextatus, Germanus, Felix, Domitianus, Victorius and Domnolus.

Almighty God in His ever-loving care watches constantly over the human race. In no place and at no time does that loving care cease to bestow its benefits upon us. On every side the holy Judge of all things sends forth men to foster the faith of the Church from generation to generation. With great zeal these men turn the sods of the Lord's field with the ploughshare of their keen conviction, so that, with help from Heaven, Christ's harvest may bring forth an hundred-fold. In this loving-kindness God pours forth unceasingly His healthful dispensation, never refusing what He knows to be of profit to so many. Through the blessed example of these men, when He comes to judge us there will be many worthy of the crown.

In the early days of the Christian religion, when the first beginnings of the faith which we venerate had just begun to make themselves felt in the lands of Gaul, and when the ineffable mysteries of the Holy Trinity were as yet known only to a few, in His compassion He deigned to send Saint Martin, born of a foreign race, to bring light to our fatherland, so that He might not here win less than, by the preaching of the Apostles, He had gained elsewhere in neighbouring cities. It is true that Saint Martin was not alive in the days of the Apostles, but for all that he did not lack apostolic grace. What he lost by the lateness of his coming, he made up for by the gains which he made for Christ. It was no disadvantage to him to follow in the steps of others, for by his merits he eclipsed them.

For this we give you thanks, our daughter most revered, that, by God's grace, the example of celestial love is now once more in you to be renewed. In these last days, with the whole world long past its prime, by the hot yearning of your heart the buds of faith burst once more into flower; and what in the long winter of old age had grown so chill now finds its warmth rekindled in the ardour of your fervent soul. In that you came to us from well-nigh that same region whence Saint Martin came, for so we learn, it is no marvel if in your work you seem to mirror him whom we believe to have been your guide. You followed in his footsteps and now by this happy vow you follow his example. As you renounce your claim to any share of worldly wealth, you choose as your associate that most saintly man. The bright gleam of his doctrines shines forth again from you. You suffuse with heavenly light the hearts of all who hear you. The minds of your nuns receive their inspiration from you and so are lit with a clear spark of heavenly fire. Burning with the love of Christ, they hasten in their zeal to quench their thirst at your soft bosom's fountain. They leave their families and choose you as their mother, their mother in God's grace, if not by nature. When we consider the zeal of their devotion, we give thanks to God Almighty, who in His mercy unites the will of mortal men with His own will, for we are sure that He will hold conjoined with you all those who wish to seek their safety in His embrace.

We learn that, by Divine Providence, a number of women from our dioceses have with great enthusiasm flocked to accept your Rule. We have considered the petition contained in your letter, and it has given us great pleasure. In the name of Christ our Maker and our Redeemer, we ordain that all those, without exception, who come together there to live their life in the charity of God must observe and keep inviolate the Rule which they have explicitly accepted of their own free will. It is not meet to break a promise made to Christ and sworn with Heaven as a witness, nor is it a light crime to pollute the temple of the Lord, which God forbid, in such a way that in His wrath He may think fit to destroy it. Moreover, we most specifically decree that if a woman comes, as we have said already, from the parts committed by God's Providence to our episcopal safe-keeping, and is considered worthy to be chosen as an inmate of your nunnery in Poitiers, according to the Rule of Caesarius, Bishop of Arles, of blessed memory,[54] she shall never have the right to leave it, it being clear that she has entered of her own free will, as ordered by the Rule, for otherwise what seems so honourable a state in the eyes of all may by the shameful sin of one be turned into dishonour. If therefore any nun, driven insane by the prompting of a mind diseased, shall seek to bring the shame of such opprobrium upon her vows, her glory and her crown, and, at the Devil's urging, like Eve expelled from Paradise, shall venture forth from the clois-

54. Saint Caesarius, Bishop of Arles, A.D. 502–42. The Rule of Saint Caesarius was in general use until it was replaced by that of Saint Benedict a few years later.

ters of her convent, as if from the Kingdom of Heaven itself, to visit this place and that, to be bustled and trodden under foot in the vile mud of our public streets, she shall be cut off from our communion and shall be stricken with the awful wound of anathema. If then perchance such a woman, having forsaken Christ and being deceived by the blandishments of the Devil, shall desire to marry a man, not only she who has eloped, but also the man who is joined to her, shall be considered as a shameful and sacrilegious adulterer rather than as a spouse. Any person who, in bringing about this union, has served her poison rather than good counsel, shall, by the judgement of God and by our express decree, be visited by the same vengeance as falls to her, until, when the two have been separated, and after such penance as may fit her execrable offence, she may deserve to be received once more in the house from which she has escaped and there restored to fellowship. We further add that all bishops who come after us shall hold themselves bound to make a like condemnation. If any shall desire, and this we cannot believe, to relax any part or parcel of what we have decreed, let them know that it will be for them to defend their actions before us on the day of the Last Judgement, for it is the general law of our salvation that any promise made to Christ must be preserved inviolate.

In order that what we have decided and decreed may have full authority, we have thought fit to confirm it by signing it with our own hands. In this way it may be observed for evermore, with Christ to watch over it.

When I had read this document to her, Clotild replied: 'None of these agreements shall prevent me from seeking an audience with the Kings who, as I know full well, are my own relations.' She and her fellow-nuns had come on foot from Poitiers. They had no horses to ride on. They were quite exhausted and worn out. No one had offered them a bite to eat on the journey. They reached our city on the first day of March. The rain was falling in torrents and the roads were ankle-deep in water.

40. They also made some very critical remarks about their own Bishop,[55] alleging that it was by his incompetent handling of the situation that they had been upset and that this was the real

55. Maroveus, Bishop of Poitiers, A.D. 584–90.

reason for their leaving the nunnery. The best thing now, I think, is for me to tell you the whole story of the revolt.

In King Lothar's days, when Saint Radegund founded the nunnery, she herself and all her community were submissive and obedient to the bishops of the period. In the days of Sigibert, by which time Maroveus had succeeded to the bishopric, Saint Radegund, inspired by her faith and led on by her devotion, sent churchmen to Eastern lands to search for pieces of wood from the True Cross, and for relics of the holy Apostles and other martyrs. She had King Sigibert's written permission to do this. The churchmen set out and eventually they brought back some relics.[56] As soon as these arrived, the Queen asked Bishop Maroveus if he would deposit them in her nunnery with all due honour and a great ceremony of psalm-chanting. He refused point-blank: instead, he climbed on his horse and went off to visit one of his country estates. Then the Queen wrote a second time to Sigibert, begging him to order one of his bishops to deposit the relics in the nunnery with all the honour due to them, in compliance with her vow. Sigibert deputed Saint Eufronius, Bishop of Tours, to do what Radegund had asked. Eufronius came to Poitiers with his clergy. Maroveus deliberately stayed away, but Eufronius deposited the sacred relics in the nunnery with much chanting of psalms, with candles gleaming and with a great burning of incense.

Down the years Radegund had frequent occasion to seek the help of the Bishop, but she received none, and she and the Mother Superior whom she had appointed[57] were forced to turn instead to Arles. There they received the Rule of Saint Caesarius and the blessed Caesaria. They put themselves under the protection of the King, for they aroused no interest or sup-

56. The Emperor Justin II and the Empress Sophia gave a piece of the wood of the True Cross to Saint Radegund's envoys when they arrived in Constantinople. This was set in a small gold triptych, $2 \cdot 15'' \times 2 \cdot 25''$, which still exists in the nunnery. See Sir Martin Conway, 'St Radegund's Reliquary at Poitiers', *Antiquaries Journal*, 1923, pp. 1–12, with a coloured reproduction.

57. Agnes.

port in the man who should have been their pastor. When the time approached for Saint Radegund to die, the disagreement between them was daily becoming worse instead of better. Radegund died, and the Mother Superior once again begged her own Bishop to take the nunnery under his care. The first reaction of Maroveus was to refuse, but those around him persuaded him with some difficulty to promise that he would be as a father to them, as was only right and proper, and that he would do all that he could to foster their interests if they ever had occasion to seek his help. Maroveus went to King Childebert and obtained from him a written statement by which he was put in charge of the nunnery in the normal way, just as he was in charge of everything else in the diocese. All the same, or so it seems to me, Maroveus still harboured some resentment against the nuns, and, indeed, they declared that this was one of the causes of their revolt.

As I have said, they were determined to seek an audience with the King. I gave them the following advice: 'What you are doing is extremely unwise. If you persist, you will lay yourselves open to criticism, no matter how you proceed. However, if you refuse to listen to reason, as I said just now, and will not take the good advice which I am giving to you, at least get this into your heads. Wait until this wintry spell which we are experiencing in the midst of Spring is over. Stay here until the winds blow warm again, and then you will be able to go wherever your fancy takes you.' They saw the sense of what I said. Summer came round once more and Clotild set out from Tours, leaving the nuns in the charge of her cousin (Basina). She paid her visit to King Guntram. He gave her an audience and honoured her with gifts. Then she returned to Tours, leaving behind in the nunnery at Autun Constantina, the daughter of Burgolen. In Tours she awaited the bishops who had been ordered by the King to come to investigate the matters at issue between the nuns and their Abbess. However, long before she arrived back from her mission, a number of the nuns had given in to circumstances which seemed to be against them, and had accepted the offers of marriage which were made to them. The others

531

awaited the arrival of the bishops, but no bishops ever came. In the end they returned to Poitiers and took refuge in Saint Hilary's church. There they gathered around them a gang of burglars, murderers, adulterers and criminals of all sorts. They were determined to continue their resistance. 'We are of royal blood,' they said, 'and we will not set foot inside our nunnery until the Mother Superior has been dismissed.'

At this time there lived in the nunnery a certain recluse who, a few years before, had lowered herself from the wall and fled to Saint Hilary's church, accusing her Mother Superior of many transgressions, all of which I discovered to be false. Later on she had herself pulled up into the nunnery again by ropes at the very spot from which she had previously lowered herself down. She asked permission to shut herself up in a secret cell, saying: 'I have greatly sinned against our Lord and against my Lady Radegund' – she still being alive at that time. 'I want to cut myself off from all contact with the community and to do penance for my wrongdoings. I know that our Lord is merciful and that He forgives the sins of all who make confession.' As she said this she entered the cell. When the revolt started, she broke down the door of her cell in the middle of the night, escaped from the nunnery, found her way to Clotild and, as she had done on the previous occasion, made a series of allegations against her Mother Superior.

41.   While these things were going on, Gundegisel, the Bishop of Bordeaux, accompanied by Nicasius of Angoulême, Safarius of Périgueux and Maroveus, the Bishop of Poitiers, went to Saint Hilary's church in his position as Metropolitan to censure the nuns, hoping presumably to persuade them to return to their nunnery. They were very stubborn and refused to do so. Gundegisel and the other Bishops, in accordance with the terms of the letter quoted above, announced their excommunication. Thereupon the mob of ruffians about whom I have told you profaned the church of Saint Hilary by attacking the Bishops physically and knocking them to the ground, so that it was only with great difficulty that they got up again. The deacons and

other churchmen present were covered with blood and emerged from the church with their heads broken. The Devil himself took a hand in all this, or so I believe: and the clergy were so terrified by what had happened that, when they came out of the church, they all rushed off home by the shortest route, without saying good-bye to each other. Desiderius, who was the deacon of Syagrius, Bishop of Autun, was present at this fiasco. He did not wait to find a ford, but jumped into the River Clain at the spot where he reached the bank, forced his horse to swim across and so escaped to the low ground on the other side.

Thereupon Clotild appointed her own stewards and took over the estates belonging to the nunnery. By main force she compelled all the men employed by the nunnery whom she could lay hands on to work for her instead. She threatened that, if she could only make her way into the building, she would toss the Mother Superior over the wall. When Childebert heard what had happened, he lost no time in sending dispatches to Count Macco, instructing him to do all in his power to put down the revolt. As I have told you, Gundegisel left the nuns cut off from communion, having first gained approval for his action from the other bishops who were with him. Then he wrote a letter in his own name and that of his fellow-churchmen to the bishops who were at that moment sitting in council with King Guntram. From them he received this answer:

Copy of the Reply (sent to Gundegisel). To their dear Lords Gundegisel, Nicasius and Safarius, worthy occupants of their apostolic sees, Bishops Aetherius, Syagrius, Aunacharius, Hesychius, Agricola, Urbicus, Felix, Veranus, the second Felix and Bertram (send greetings).

We have received the letter which your messenger brought and we congratulate you on your escape. At the same time we are distressed beyond measure to read of the insult which you say has been done to you. The Rule has been broken and great outrage has been done to the Church. You have told us how the nuns who, at the prompting of the Devil, had escaped from the nunnery of Radegund, of blessed memory, refused to listen to your admonition and also refused to go back inside the walls of their institution. Then they profaned the church of Saint Hilary by doing violence there to

533

you yourself and your attendant clergy. As a result you have decided to excommunicate them. Now, for what it is worth, you ask for our advice in this matter. Insofar as we are quite sure that you have consulted the canonical statutes, and as the Rule ordains expressly that those who are caught in such misdemeanours must be punished not only by excommunication but also by doing full penance, and as a token of the respect and warm brotherly love which we feel for you, we declare that we are unanimously in agreement with what you have decided to do. When we sit side by side at our next Council of Bishops, which is to meet on 1 November, we will discuss with you how best to bridle the temerity of such offenders, to the end that it may never happen again that anyone may be led by overweening pride to commit a crime of this nature.

Forasmuch as the Apostle Paul repeatedly enjoins us in his epistles, in season and out of season and in all our preaching, to admonish those who transgress,[58] making it clear that godliness will find a remedy for all our problems,[59] we urge you to pray unceasingly for the merciful intervention of Almighty God, that He may deign to visit these nuns with the spirit of contrition and that in penance they may make true amends for the sin which they have committed, that by your preaching these souls, which are well on the way to perdition, may, by Christ's grace, be brought back to their nunnery, and that He who carried home to the fold one lost sheep upon His shoulders may now rejoice that the outcome of their transgression is that He has regained a whole flock. We ask above all that you remember us always in your prayers, and this we are sure that you will do. I, Aetherius, the sinner, your close friend, venture to send you greetings. I, Hesychius, your humble servant, presume in all reverence to send you greetings. I, Syagrius, who love you dearly, greet you in all reverence. I, Urbicus the sinner, your admirer, send humble greetings. I, Bishop Veranus, with all respect, send you my dutiful greetings. I, Felix, your humble servant, venture to greet you. I, Felix, your humble servant and admirer, presume to greet you. I, Bishop Bertram, your humble and obedient servant, venture to send you greetings.

42.   The Mother Superior also read out the letter which Saint Radegund addressed to the bishops of her own time. Then she sent new copies of this letter to the bishops of all the neighbouring cities. It ran as follows:

58. Cp. II Timothy 4, 2.   59. Cp. I Timothy 4, 8.

Copy of the Letter (originally sent by Radegund). To the holy fathers in Christ and to the Lord Bishops, worthy occupants of their apostolic sees, Radegund of Poitiers (sends greetings).

In its first beginnings a new project such as this can only move forward towards fruition with any hope of success if it is explained in full detail to the common fathers, the physicians and the shepherds of the flock, and if it then gains their support. It can only be realized if in their loving kindness they are prepared to cooperate, if they give it the benefit of their valuable advice, if they support it in their prayers.

Some time ago, when I found myself freed from earthly cares, with Divine Providence and with God's grace to inspire me, I turned of my own volition, under Christ's guidance, to the religious life. I asked myself, with all the ardour of which I am capable, how I could best forward the cause of other women, and how, if our Lord so willed, my own personal desires might be of advantage to my sisters. Here in the town of Poitiers I founded a convent for nuns. Lothar, my lord and King of glorious memory, instituted this and was its benefactor. When it was founded, I made over to it by deed of gift all the property which the King in his munificence had bestowed upon me. For the community which, with Christ to help me, I had myself assembled, I accepted the Rule in accordance with which Saint Caesaria had lived, and which in his loving care Saint Caesarius had drawn up from the writings of the holy Fathers to suit her very needs. With the full approval of the Bishop of this city and of his fellow-prelates, all of them holy men, and after proper election by our community, I appointed as Mother Superior the Lady Agnes, who became like a sister to me, and whom I have loved and brought up as if she were my daughter from her childhood onwards. I submitted myself in regular obedience to her authority, after God. The other nuns and I followed the example of the Apostles in making over to her by deed whatever earthly property we possessed at the moment we entered the nunnery, reserving nothing at all for ourselves, for we feared the fate of Ananias and Sapphira.[60] However, since the affairs of human beings are unpredictable, and because our times and our circumstances are always changing, for the world is running to its end and some people now prefer to follow their own desires rather than the dictates of God, while I am still alive, and in full devotion, in Christ's name and with

60. Cp. Acts 5, 1–11.

God to guide me, I send to you, apostolic fathers, this document in which I have set out all my plans.

Seeing that I have not been able to come to you in person, I make obeisance to you vicariously through this letter, throwing myself at your feet. I conjure you, in the name of the Father, the Son and the Holy Ghost, and by the awful Day of Judgement, just as if I stood before you, to ensure that no tyrant may stand in my way, but that the rightful king may crown my wishes. If perchance after my death any person whatsoever, either the bishop of this city, or some representative of the king, or any other individual, should attempt, in a spirit of malevolence or by some legal subterfuge, to disturb the community, or to break the Rule, or to appoint any Mother Superior other than Agnes, my sister in God, whom Saint Germanus, in the presence of his brother churchmen, consecrated with his benediction; or if the community should rise in revolt, which is surely impossible, and wish to make a change; or if any person, possibly even the bishop of the diocese, shall wish to claim, by some newfangled privilege, jurisdiction of any sort over the nunnery, or over the property of the nunnery, beyond that which earlier bishops, or anyone else, have exercised during my lifetime; or if any nun shall wish to break the Rule and go out into the world; or if any prince, or bishop, or person in power, or even individual from among the nuns themselves, shall attempt with sacrilegious intent to diminish or to appropriate to his or her own personal possession any part or parcel of the property which our most noble Lothar and the most glorious kings his sons have bestowed upon me, and which I, with his express permission and injunction, have made over to the nunnery, for which conveyance I obtained confirmation by letters from our noble lords and Kings Charibert, Guntram, Chilperic and Sigibert, by the swearing of an oath and the subscribing of their sign manual, or which others have donated for the saving of their souls, or which the nuns themselves have made over from their own property, may that person incur the wrath of God and that of your holiness and of those who succeed you, and may all such persons be shut off from your grace as robbers and despoilers of the poor. With you to block the way, may no change ever be brought about in our Rule and may no alienation of the nunnery's property ever be permitted. This also do I pray, that when it shall be the will of God that the holy Agnes, our aforesaid sister, must leave this earthly life, a Mother Superior shall be appointed to replace her from among our own community, who shall find favour in God's sight, and who shall guard the Rule and shall nowise sanction a decline in holy living, never permitting her own will or that of any other individual to run counter to it. If any person whatsoever, in defiance of the will of God and of the king's authority, thus contravening the conditions here set out and before our Lord and His Holy Saints commended in my prayers to your protection, shall do aught to harm any individual or to despoil any property, which God forbid, or shall attempt in any way to harass the aforesaid Abbess Agnes, my sister, may he incur the wrath of God and of the Holy Cross and of the Blessed Mary, and may he be assailed and pursued by Saint Hilary and Saint Martin, to whose especial care, after God, I have entrusted these nuns, who are my sisters.

You, too, saintly Bishop, and those who come after you, whom I hasten to appoint as my patrons in God's cause, if any be found who shall try to act contrary to these my dispositions, which God forbid, do not be slow to make your appeal to the king who at that time shall rule over this place, or to the city of Poitiers, on behalf of this institution which is commended to your care before the Lord; and do not shrink from the vital labour of pursuing and defending the ends of justice, even in the face of the injustice of others: for only thus will you repel and confute the Enemy of God. No Catholic king shall brook in any wise such infamy in his time, nor shall they permit to be torn down what has been builded up, by God's will and by my own intent and by the wishes of the several kings. At the same time I conjure the princes whom God shall see fit to order to rule the people after my own death, through that King whose reign shall have no end and at whose nod all earthly realms subsist, and who has granted to them the very breath of life and their own royal power, to ensure that the Mother Superior Agnes and this nunnery, which, with the express permission and the approval of the kings their fathers and grandfathers, I have thought fit to build, order according to the Rule and endow, be ever guarded by their sovereign power and rule. May it never be allowed to come about that our Mother Superior, whom I have named several times, shall be molested or harassed by any man, or that anything pertaining to this nunnery should in any wise be alienated or changed. On the contrary may they be given every protection and assurance. With God to watch over me, on bended knee I commend my cause to those rulers and to those princes of the Church, in the name of Him who redeemed all peoples. May they dwell for ever in the Kingdom which has no end, together with the Defender of the poor and the

Husband of all cloistered nuns, in whose name they protect the handmaidens of God.

I also beseech you, saintly bishops, and you, lords and kings omnipotent, and the whole Christian people, by that Catholic faith in which you are baptized, that, when God shall ordain that the time has come for me to die, my poor body shall be buried here, in this church which I have begun to build in honour of the Blessed Mary, Mother of God, where so many of my nuns have been laid to rest, no matter whether that church is finished or not. If anyone wishes or attempts anything to the contrary, may he incur the wrath of God, through the mediation of the Cross of Christ and of the Blessed Mary. I pray that I may be held worthy, with you to intervene for me, to find a resting-place in this church, with the nuns of my own community all around me.

With my face suffused with tears, I beg that this petition, which I have signed with my own hand, may be preserved in the archives of our cathedral church. If the Mother Superior, Agnes, my sister in God, or her community, should ever seek your help in time of trouble, because they have been molested by their enemies, I pray that they may be able to rely upon the God-given solace of your sympathy and the pastoral care which in your loving kindness you give to them. God has promised them the protection of your grace. May they not live to say that I have left them destitute!

All this I put before you, in the name of Him who from the Cross did commend His own Mother, the Blessed Virgin, to Saint John. Just as the Apostle John fulfilled our Lord's request, so may you fulfil all that which, humble and unworthy though I be, I commend to you, the elders of my Church, my masters and my apostolic fathers. If you keep the trust which I hand on to you, you will be worthy sharers of the example set by Him whose apostolic mandates you perform.

43. When Bishop Maroveus heard the hateful things which they were saying about h.m, he sent Porcarius, the Abbot of the church of Saint Hilary, to Bishop Gundegisil and the other prelates of his province to ask if they would permit him to administer communion to the nuns, and then appear before them and be heard. This was refused. King Childebert, who was becoming tired of the never-ending stream of complaints, first from this side, then from that, from the nunnery and from the

nuns who had left the nunnery, sent the priest Theuthar to stem the tide of recriminations which they kept up between them. Theuthar summoned Clotild and the other nuns to appear before him. 'We will not come,' they answered. 'You see, we have been excommunicated. If we are received back into the Church, we will agree to appear.' When he heard this, Theuthar went off to see the bishops. He put his problem before them, but he made no progress on the subject of the nuns' excommunication. Back he went to Poitiers. The nuns were separated. Some went back to their own homes, others to their relations, and quite a few returned to the religious houses where they had previously lived. They could no longer live as a community, because lack of fuel made them unable to bear the winter cold. However, one or two remained behind with Clotild and Basina. Even these few kept on quarrelling with each other, for each one of them wanted to lord it over her companions.

44. Just after Easter this year it rained and hailed very heavily. Within the space of two or three hours great rivers began to flow along even the smallest windings of the valleys. The fruit-trees flowered a second time in Autumn and gave a second crop as heavy as the first. Roses bloomed in November. The rivers ran unusually high. They broke their banks and flooded areas which they had never reached before, doing great damage to the sown fields.

HERE ENDS BOOK IX

BOOK X

HERE IN CHRIST'S NAME BEGIN
THE CHAPTER-HEADINGS OF BOOK X

1. Gregory, the Pope in Rome.
2. The return of the envoy Grippo from his mission to the Emperor Maurice.
3. How King Childebert's army marched into Italy.
4. How the Emperor Maurice despatched to Gaul the men who had killed the envoys.
5. How Chuppa made a raid on Touraine.
6. The gaol-birds of Clermont-Ferrand.
7. How King Childebert remitted the taxes of the clergy of that city.
8. Eulalius and his wife Tetradia.
9. How King Guntram's army marched into Brittany.
10. The execution of Chundo, King Guntram's Chamberlain.
11. The illness of Prince Lothar.
12. The malicious behaviour of Berthegund.
13. A disputation about the resurrection.
14. How Theudulf the deacon met his death.
15. The revolt in the nunnery at Poitiers.
16. The judgement given against Clotild and Basina.
17. How they were excommunicated.
18. The men who were sent to assassinate King Childebert.
19. The dismissal of Egidius, Bishop of Rheims.
20. How the nuns described in an earlier chapter were reconciled with the Church at our council.
21. The execution of [one of] Waddo's sons.
22. How Childeric the Saxon met his death.
23. Portents. Doubt about Easter.
24. The destruction of the town of Antioch.

25. How a man calling himself Christ was put to death.
26. The death of Bishop Ragnemod and of Bishop Sulpicius.
27. The men whom Fredegund had killed.
28. The baptism of her son Lothar.
29. The conversion, miracles and death of Saint Aredius, Abbot of Limoges.
30. The weather this year.
31. A complete list of the Bishops of Tours.

HERE END THE CHAPTER-HEADINGS

IN THE NAME OF OUR LORD JESUS CHRIST
HERE BEGINS BOOK X

1. In the fifteenth year of King Childebert's reign,[1] on his
return from the city of Rome with relics of the Saints,[2] my
deacon (Agiulf) told me that the previous year, in the month
of November, the River Tiber had covered Rome with such
flood-water that a number of ancient churches had collapsed
and the papal granaries had been destroyed, with the loss of
several thousand bushels of wheat. A great school of water-
snakes swam down the course of the river to the sea, in their
midst a tremendous dragon as big as a tree-trunk, but these
monsters were drowned in the turbulent salt sea-waves and their
bodies were washed up on the shore. As a result there followed
an epidemic, which caused swellings in the groin. This started in
January. The very first to catch it was Pope Pelagius,[3] thus
fulfilling what is written in the prophet Ezekiel: 'And begin at
my sanctuary',[4] for he died almost immediately. Once Pelagius
was dead a great number of other folk perished from this disease. The people then unanimously chose as Pope the deacon
Gregory,[5] for the Church could not be left without a leader.
He was descended from one of the leading senatorial families.[6]
From his youth upwards he had been devoted to God's service.
He founded six monasteries in Sicily from his own resources,[7]

1. A.D. 590.

2. On the sea-journey from Portus, the port of Rome, to Marseilles, the
relics which Agiulf was bringing home were instrumental in saving the boat
from being wrecked. Cp. *GM*, 82.

3. Pope Pelagius II, A.D. 578–90.   4. Ezekiel 9, 6.

5. The Pope was served by seven deacons, one for each of the seven
districts into which Rome was divided for church administration. Gregory,
so soon to become Pope Gregory the Great, was the least of these.

6. The gens Anicia.

7. His mother Silvia possessed large estates near Palermo.

and he established a seventh inside the walls of the city of Rome.[8] He endowed them with sufficient land to provide the monks with their daily sustenance; then he sold the rest of his possessions, including all his household goods, and gave the proceeds to the poor. He who until then had been in the habit of processing through the city in silken robes sewn with glittering gems[9] now served at the Lord's altar in a fustian gown. He was appointed as seventh among the deacons who served the Pope. His abstinence in taking food, his vigils and his prayers, the severity of his fasting, were such that his weakened stomach could scarce support his frame. He was so skilled in grammar, dialectic and rhetoric that he was held second to none in the entire city. He wanted very much to avoid the highest honour, lest as a result of his being elected the worldly pomp which he had renounced should invade once more his public life. As an earnest of this he sent a letter to the Emperor Maurice, whose son he had held at the font,[10] conjuring him and with humble prayers entreating him never to sanction his being chosen by the people, or to permit his elevation to this position of power and glory. Germanus, Prefect of the City of Rome, intercepted the messenger, seized him, tore up the letter, and then sent him on to the Emperor to make known the people's unanimous choice. The Emperor, who loved the deacon dearly, gave thanks to God that he could now promote Gregory to such a place of honour. He issued a diploma ordering Gregory to be enthroned. While preparations were still in train for his enthronement, this epidemic came to devastate the city. Thereupon Gregory exhorted his flock to do penance in the following words:

POPE GREGORY'S ADDRESS TO THE PEOPLE: Dearly beloved brethren, those scourges of God which we fear when they are still far off must terrify us all the more when they are come among us and we have already had our taste of them. Our present trial must open the way to our conversion. The afflictions which we suffer must soften the hardness of our hearts, for, as was foretold by the prophet: 'The

8. This was in his palace on the Mons Caelius.
9. He was then Prefect of the City.
10. Gregory had been nuncio in Constantinople from A.D. 579 to 585.

sword reacheth unto the soul.'[11] Indeed, I see my entire flock being
struck down by the sword of the wrath of God, as one after another
they are visited by sudden destruction. Their death is preceded by
no lingering illness, for, as you know, they die before they even
have time to feel ill. The blow falls: each victim is snatched away
from us before he can bewail his sins and repent. Just think in what
state he must appear before the Implacable Judge, having had no
chance to lament his deeds! Our fellow-citizens are not, indeed,
taken from us one at a time, for they are being bustled off in droves.
Homes are left empty, parents are forced to attend the funerals of
their children, their heirs march before them to the grave. Every one
of us, I say, must bewail his sins and repent, while there is still time
for lamentation. We must pass in review all those things we have
done which we ought not to have done, and we must weep as we
think of our trespasses. 'Let us come before His presence with confession.'[12] As the prophet adjures us: 'Let us lift up our heart with
our hands unto God'[13] To lift up our heart with our hands unto
God means to enhance the fervour of our prayer with the merit of
our good works. In our anguish He gives us renewed hope, in truth
that is what He gives us when He makes the prophet say: 'I have no
pleasure in the death of the wicked; but that the wicked turn from
his way and live.'[14] None of you must despair because of the enor-
mity of your sins. A penance lasting only three days wiped away the
long-lived sins of the men of Nineveh! The thief who repented won
the reward of life at the very moment when he had received the
sentence of death! We must have a change of heart and pray that
we have already been granted our request. The judge is the more
quick to pardon if the suppliant has already repented of his sin. The
sword of this dire punishment hangs over us already: we must then
be the more importunate in our prayers. That very importunity
which so often proves unwelcome to our fellow-men pleases the
Judge of truth: for God is full of mercy and compassion, and it is
His will that we should win His pardon through our prayers. He will
not be angry with us, however much we deserve it. Through the
psalmist He tells us: 'And call upon me in the day of trouble: I will
deliver thee, and thous shalt glorify me.'[15] He thus bears witness of
Himself that He wishes to show mercy to them who call upon Him,
and He asks us to address our prayers to Him. Therefore, dearly

11. Jeremiah 4, 10.   12. Cp. Psalms 95, 2.
13. Jeremiah 3, 41.   14. Ezekiel 23, 11.   15. Psalms 50, 15.

beloved brethren, with contrite hearts and with all our affairs in order, let us come together, to concentrate our minds upon our troubles, in the order which I will explain in a minute, as day dawns on the Wednesday of this week, to celebrate the sevenfold litanies. When He sees how we ourselves condemn our own sins, the stern Judge may acquit us of this sentence of damnation which He has proposed for us.

Let the clergy go in procession from the church of the holy martyrs Cosmas and Damian, with the priests of the sixth region. Let all the Abbots with their monks process from the church of the holy martyrs Protasius and Gervasius, with the priests of the fourth region. Let all the Abbesses and their assembled nuns walk from the church of the holy martyrs Marcellinus and Peter, with the priests of the first region. Let all the children go from the church of the holy martyrs John and Paul, with the priests of the second region. Let all the laymen go from the church of the protomartyr Stephen, with the priests of the seventh region. Let all the widows go from the church of Saint Euphemia, with the priests of the fifth region. Let all the married women go from the church of the holy martyr Clement, with the priests of the third region. Let us all process with prayers and lamentations from each of the churches thus appointed, to meet together at the basilica of the blessed Virgin Mary, Mother of our Lord Jesus Christ, so that there we may at great length make our supplication to the Lord with tears and groans, and so be held worthy to win pardon for our sins.

When he had finished speaking, Gregory assembled the different groups of churchmen, and ordered them to sing psalms for three days and to pray to our Lord for forgiveness. At three o'clock all the choirs singing psalms came into church, chanting the *Kyrie eleison* as they passed through the city streets.[16] My deacon,[17] who was present, said that while the people were making their supplication to the Lord, eighty individuals fell dead to the ground. The Pope never once stopped preaching to

16. 25 April 590. As the procession reached the bridge over the River Tiber, the Archangel Michael appeared on the dome of Hadrian's mausoleum with a flaming sword in his hand. He sheathed his sword and so put an end to the plague; hence the new name given to the mausoleum, Castel S. Angelo.

17. Agiulf. This is an eye-witness account.

the people, nor did the people pause in their prayers. It was from Gregory himself, while he was a deacon, that, as I have told you, my own deacon received the relics of the saints. Just as he was preparing to go into hiding, he was seized, carried along, brought to the basilica of Saint Peter, consecrated ready for his pontifical duties and then given to the City as Pope. My deacon could not resist turning back from Portus[18] to witness the enthronement, for he wanted to see with his own eyes how the ceremony was carried out.

2. Grippo arrived back home from a mission to the Emperor Maurice. He reported that, after having set out by ship the year before with his companions, he had landed at a port in North Africa and had made his way to Carthage. There they were delayed for some time while they awaited the permission of the Prefect[19] to continue their journey to the Emperor.

A servant whom Evantius had taken with him snatched some valuable object or other from the hand of a shopkeeper and ran off with it to his lodging. The owner of the object followed him home and demanded the return of his property. The servant refused, and the result was a quarrel which grew steadily more acrimonious as the days passed. Then a moment came when the merchant met the servant by chance in the street, seized hold of him by his sleeve and refused to be shaken off. 'I will not let go,' he shouted, 'until you give me back what you have stolen.' The servant struggled to free himself from the merchant's grasp, and then he was fool enough to draw his sword and kill him. After this he went back again to his lodging, but he did not tell the others what had happened.

There were three men sent on this mission which I have described to you: Bodegisil, the son of Mummolen, who came from Soissons; Evantius, the son of Dynamius, from Arles; and this Grippo, who was a Frank. They had just risen from the table and had stumbled off to bed for a siesta. In the meantime

18. Gregory says Ostia, which was on the opposite bank of the River Tiber and is now a bathing-beach.
19. The Prefect of Africa was based on Carthage.

what their servant had done was reported to the Prefect of
Carthage. This official summoned a squad of soldiers, enlisted
the help of such passers-by as were bearing arms, and dispatched this force to their lodgings. To their great stupefaction
they were suddenly aroused from their slumbers to find pan-
demonium raging outside. 'Put down your weapons!' shouted
the man in charge. 'Out you come, now! Gently does it! We'll
soon find out how this fellow-me-lad came to be done for!'
When those inside heard this, they were thunder-struck, for they
still had not the slightest idea of what had happened. They
asked for an assurance that, if they came out without their
weapons, they would not be assaulted. The men swore that they
would not hurt them, but in the excitement of the moment it
proved impossible to avoid it. Bodegisil emerged first and
promptly received a sword-cut which put paid to him. The same
thing happened to Evantius. Grippo seized his weapons and
went out to face the mob, accompanied by the other members
of his party and stepping over the dead bodies outside the door
of their lodging as he went. 'I haven't the remotest idea what all
this is about,' he said. 'My two fellow-envoys, on their way to
make representations to your Emperor, have been cut down
and murdered. God will surely judge the wrong which you have
done to us and avenge their death by encompassing your own
destruction. Those whom you have murdered were men of
peace, who had journeyed here in all innocence. There can
never be peace between our King and your Emperor after this!
We travelled here in the cause of peace, to further friendly
relations with the Empire. Now I call God to witness that the
understanding between our leaders may well come to an end,
for this act of yours has murdered peace.' As Grippo said this,
and then went on to drive his point home, the Carthaginian
squad melted away, each man present slipping off to see to his
own affairs. Then the Prefect came to Grippo. He did what he
could to mollify him concerning what had happened and he
made arrangements for him to have an audience with the Emperor. On his arrival, Grippo explained what he had come for
and then lodged a complaint about the murder of his com-

panions. The Emperor Maurice was greatly displeased by what he heard. He promised to see that those who had killed the envoys should be punished and to agree to any other suggestion which King Childebert might put forward. The Emperor gave Grippo a number of presents, and he then returned home without further incident.

3. When King Childebert received Grippo's report, he immediately ordered his troops to march into Italy, instructing twenty of his dukes to lead them in a war against the Longobards. I have not thought it necessary to give the full list of their names. Duke Audovald, supported by Wintrio, raised a contingent in Champagne, advanced as far as Metz, which was on his line of march, and stole so much booty there, killing so many men and doing so much destruction, that you might have imagined that he had been sent to attack his own country. The other dukes did much the same with the troops under their command, first ravaging their own regions and despoiling the people who lived in them, and only then making an effort to beat the enemy.

As soon as they came to the Italian frontier, Audovald turned to the right with six of the other dukes, and advanced as far as the town of Milan. From there he moved into the open countryside, where they all pitched camp. Duke Olo was foolish enough to approach Bellinzona, a strong-point belonging to Milan, in the Canini lowlands.[20] There he was hit in the chest by a javelin and fell dead. Those of his men who were plundering the countryside for supplies were attacked by the Longobards and cut down where they stood. Not far from the town of Milan there is a lake called Lugano, out of which runs a stream which is narrow but very deep. The Franks learned that the Longobards were encamped on the bank of this stream. They marched towards it, but, before they could cross the watercourse which I have described to you, a Longobard stood up on the opposite bank, wearing a cuirass and with his helmet on his head, and waved a spear at them. He issued a challenge to the

20. This is where the River Ticino flows into Lake Maggiore.

Frankish army. 'Today we shall find out which side God intends to be victorious!' he shouted. I imagine that this was a signal which the Longobards had agreed upon. A few of the Franks managed to cross. They fought with this Longobard and killed him. Then, lo and behold, all the Longobard army wheeled round in retreat and marched away. The main force of the Franks crossed over, but not a single Longobard could they discover. All they found were the traces of their encampment, where their fires had been lit and where they had pitched their tents. The Franks returned to their own camp, having failed to take a single prisoner. Envoys then arrived from the Emperor to announce that a support-group was on its way. 'In three days,' said these messengers, 'we will march our forces back, and this will be the sign: when you see the houses of that village going up in flames, the one up there in the mountains, and the smoke of the conflagration rises up in the sky, you will know that we have come as promised at the head of our army.' In accordance with the terms of this truce the Franks waited six days. As far as they could see not a single man ever came.

Cedinus, with thirteen other dukes, turned left on entering Italy. He captured five strong-points and extracted oaths of allegiance. His army suffered greatly from dysentery, for the climate was new to the troops and did not suit them. Many died as a result: then the wind changed and rain fell, which brought the temperature down a little, so that those who were ill became well once more. There is little more to tell. For nearly three months the troops wandered about in Italy, but they achieved nothing and inflicted no losses on the enemy, who had shut themselves up in strongly fortified places. They failed to capture the King and avenge themselves on him, for he was safe inside the walls of Pavia. As I have told you, the soldiers suffered very much from the heat and lacked proper food. In the end they turned homewards, having subjected to King Childebert's authority those parts which his father had held before him. In these they took oaths of allegiance. They also brought back some booty and a number of prisoners from where they had been. On their journey home their supplies were so short that before they reached their native land they had to sell their weapons and even their clothes to buy food.

Aptachar, the King of the Longobards,[21] sent envoys to King Guntram. 'It is our wish, noble King,' went the message, 'to be true and obedient to yourself and your people, as we were to your predecessors. We have not broken the oath which our forefathers swore to yours. Give up attacking us. Let there be peace and concord between us. We will give you support against your enemies as occasion shall arise, so that the safety both of your people and of ours may be assured, and that the adversaries who prowl about our frontiers may have cause to fear because they see us in agreement, rather than reason to rejoice in our discord.' King Guntram received this message graciously and sent the envoys on to his nephew King Childebert. However, while they were still at King Childebert's court, after delivering their dispatch, other messengers arrived to say that King Aptachar was dead and that Paul had taken his place.[22] They brought the same protestations of peace which I have set out above. King Childebert agreed to a truce and then dismissed them, saying that he would later on announce what his detailed plans were.

4. Maurice now sent to King Childebert the men who had murdered his envoys the previous year. Twelve of them appeared before the King, loaded with chains and with their hands bound. It was understood that if Childebert wished to have them executed he was free to do so. If, on the other hand, he preferred to release them in exchange for a ransom, he should receive three hundred golden pieces for each man and say no more about it. Childebert was to make his own decision, provided only that no more should be heard of the unfortunate event and that it should not be allowed to become a lasting cause of enmity between the two rulers. King Childebert refused to accept the manacled men without looking further into

21. He is usually known as Authari.
22. Aptachar or Authari, King of the Longobards, died A.D. 590. He was succeeded by Agilulf, Duke of Turin. Nothing is known of Gregory's Paul.

the matter. 'We cannot be sure that they really are the murderers,' he said. 'Have you really brought the right men? These
may be completely different people, someone's slaves perhaps,
whereas those men of mine who were murdered in your country
were both of noble birth.' It happened that Grippo was present,
he who had been sent on the same embassy as those who were
killed. 'The Prefect of the town sent to attack us two or three
thousand men whom he had collected,' he said, 'and that was
how he managed to kill my fellow-envoys. I, too, would have
been cut down in that same fracas, had I not had the courage to
defend myself like a man. If I were to go back to Carthage now,
I might recognize the individuals responsible. If he really wants
to remain at peace with our King, as you say, those are the men
whom your Emperor ought to punish.' Childebert dismissed the
prisoners, having made up his mind that he would send another
embassy to follow them home to their Emperor.

5.   About this time Chuppa, who was formerly Count of the
Stables to King Chilperic, made a raid on the district round
Tours, hoping to drive off the flocks and seize other property as
his booty. When the local inhabitants realized what he was
doing, they collected together a force of men and made after
him. He was forced to give up his ill-gotten gains and he escaped only by abandoning everything. Two of his followers
were killed and two were captured. The locals tied these up and
sent them to Childebert. The King had them thrown into prison.
He ordered them to be questioned closely, for he wanted to find
out by whose intervention Chuppa had managed to escape and
to avoid falling into the hands of those who were pursuing him.
They revealed that it was Animodius who had contrived this,
the local representative of the Count, who was responsible for
the administration of justice in those parts. The King immediately sent a letter to the Count of Tours, ordering him to have
Animodius bound and sent to appear before him. If Animodius
attempted to resist, the Count was to overpower him and kill
him, if he valued the goodwill of his sovereign. In effect, Animodius offered no resistance; he found sureties and went where

he was bidden. He reported to Flavianus, a court official, and appeared before him for trial with his confederate (Chuppa). He was found not guilty and the case against him was dismissed. Chuppa, too, was pardoned. He was ordered to go home, but not before he had given bribes to the court official (Flavianus).

On another occasion this same Chuppa assembled some of his men and tried to carry off as his bride the daughter of Badegisel, the late Bishop of Le Mans. With a band of followers he broke into a country house at Mareil to accomplish his design, but when the girl's mother, Dame Magnatrude, came to hear of his plans, she assembled her servants and sallied forth against him. Several of Chuppa's men were killed. He himself escaped, but it was a pretty discreditable affair.

6. One night in the gaol at Clermont-Ferrand the chains holding the prisoners came undone by the intervention of God, the gates of the lock-up were unfastened, and they all rushed out to seek sanctuary in a church. Count Eulalius had them loaded with fresh chains, but no sooner had these been placed in position than they snapped asunder like brittle glass. Bishop Avitus pleaded for the prisoners to be released, and they were given their liberty and sent home.

7. In this same city King Childebert, with open-handed charity, remitted all (arrears of) tax due from churches, monasteries, clergy who were attached to a given parish, and, indeed, anyone who was employed by the Church. The tax-collectors had for some time been finding it very difficult to call in this money, the passing of the years, the replacement by other individuals of those who were assessed and the division of the property concerned through a number of sub-leases making the levy virtually impossible. Inspired perhaps in this by God, the King ordered the system to be overhauled, so that what was owing on the assessment should not stand as a loss to the tax-collector and at the same time no servant of the Church could be held liable for arrears due from the office to which he had succeeded.

8. A council of bishops was convened on the borders of Clermont, the Gévaudan and the Rouergue to judge the case of Tetradia, the widow of Desiderius, in a law-suit brought against her by Count Eulalius for the restitution of the property which she had taken with her when she left him. I shall now have to trace this case farther back and tell you how Tetradia left Eulalius and went to live with Desiderius.

As young men often do, Eulalius used to behave in an irresponsible fashion. The result was that his mother frequently had reason to chide him, and in the end he came to hate her whom he ought to have loved. After the servants had retired to bed, it was his mother's habit to go off to pray in her oratory and to keep the night vigils there, making her tearful supplications to God. She was found garrotted, still wearing the hair-shirt which she put on when she prayed. No one knew who had done this, but her son was strongly suspected of having murdered his mother. As soon as Cautinus, the Bishop of Clermont,[23] came to hear of this, he cut Eulalius off from communion. On the feast of Saint Julian, the blessed martyr, when his flock assembled before their Bishop, Eulalius threw himself at the feet of Cautinus and complained that he had been excluded from communion without a proper hearing. The Bishop gave him permission to remain in the congregation and to attend the Mass. When the moment came for Eulalius to receive communion and he went up to the altar, Cautinus said to him: 'It is common talk among the people that you killed your own mother. I do not know whether or not you really committed this crime. I therefore leave it to God and to the blessed martyr Julian to judge this matter. If you really are innocent, as you maintain, draw near, take your portion of the consecrated bread and place it in your mouth. God will be looking into the deepest confines of your heart.' Eulalius took the consecrated bread, communicated and went his way.

He had married Tetradia, through her mother a young woman of noble blood, but of humbler origin on her father's

---

23. As Bishop Cautinus died in A.D. 571, Gregory is looking back some twenty years.

side. He was in the habit of sleeping with the women-servants in
his household. As a result he neglected his wife. He used to
knock her about when he came back from these midnight ex-
ercises. As a result of his excesses, he ran into serious debt, and
to meet this he stole his wife's jewellery and money. In the
appalling straits in which she found herself, Tetradia gradually
lost all standing in the marital home. Eulalius had occasion to
go off to see the King. During his absence a man called Virus,
who was her husband's nephew, fell in love with Tetradia. He
had lost his own wife and wanted to marry her. He was afraid of
what his uncle would do to them both, so he sent Tetradia off to
Duke Desiderius, still hoping to marry her later on. She took
with her all her husband's property, gold, silver, clothing, everything in fact which she could carry. She also took her elder son,
leaving her younger boy behind. When Eulalius came back from
his journey he discovered what they had done. For a while he
took no action, nursing his resentment. Then he attacked his
nephew Virus and killed him in one of the narrow defiles of the
Auvergne. In the meantime Desiderius had lost his own wife.
When he heard that Virus had been killed, he married Tetradia
himself. Then Eulalius abducted a nun from a convent in Lyons
and made her his wife. The other women with whom he was
having relations were jealous, or so it is said, and by witchcraft
they cast a spell over him. A little later Eulalius assaulted
Emerius, who was the nun's cousin, and killed him. Then he
killed Socratius, the brother of his own half-sister, which half-
sister his father had had by one of his mistresses. He committed
a number of other crimes which I have no space to relate. His
son John, who had gone off with his mother, left the house of
Desiderius and came back to Clermont. At the time when
Innocentius was canvassing for the bishopric of Rodez, Eulalius
sent a message to him, asking his help in the recovery of certain
property which he claimed in that city and the vicinity. 'I will do
what you say,' answered Innocentius, 'if you will give me one of
your sons, so that I may make a priest of him and keep him
among my clergy.' Eulalius sent his son John, and received in
exchange the property which was his. When he had become

Bishop, Innocentius received the youth, had his head tonsured and handed him over to the archdeacon of his diocese. The young man practised such abstinence that he ate barley-bread instead of wheat, drank water instead of wine, rode about on a donkey instead of a horse and wore the shabbiest clothes.

The bishops and the leading laymen met, then, as I have told you, at the spot where three districts come together. Tetradia was represented by Agin, and Eulalius pleaded his own case against her. He demanded restitution of the property which she had taken when she went off to Desiderius. The verdict was that Tetradia should repay fourfold all that she had taken. The sons which she had borne to Desiderius were declared illegitimate. It was then agreed that if she paid back to Eulalius all that she had been ordered to pay, she might return to Clermont without let or hindrance and have there the free use of what she had inherited from her father. All this was done.

9.　While these things were happening the Bretons were busy ravaging the open country round Nantes and Rennes. King Guntram put Duke Beppolen and Duke Ebrachar in charge of an army, and ordered them to march against the Bretons. Ebrachar had an idea in his head that if he and Beppolen were to win a victory, Beppolen would usurp his dukedom. He therefore started a quarrel, and the two enlivened the whole march by abusing, taunting and cursing each other. Wherever they passed they burned, slew and sacked, committing every crime in the calendar. They came to the River Vilaine, crossed it and reached the River Oust. There they destroyed all the houses near the bank and constructed bridges over the river, so that the entire army crossed. At this juncture a certain priest sought an interview with Beppolen. 'If you will follow me,' he said, 'I will lead you to Waroch and show you the Bretons all assembled in one place.' When Fredegund learned that this expedition was being led by Beppolen, whom she had hated for many a long year, she ordered the Saxons settled in Bayeux[24] to

24. This was a tribe of one-time Saxon pirates who had settled in the district known as the Bessin round Bayeux.

cut their hair in the Breton way, to rig themselves out in clothes in the Breton fashion, and then to march in support of Waroch. Beppolen advanced with all his followers, joined battle and for two whole days caused great slaughter among the Bretons and the Saxons about whom I have told you. Ebrachar had already withdrawn with the greater part of the army. He refused to take any part in the offensive until news should reach him that Beppolen was killed. The third day came. All the men with Beppolen were killed, and he himself was wounded, but he still defended himself with his spear. Then Waroch made a concerted attack on him with his troops and slew him. Waroch had managed to shut the Frankish soldiers in between the marshes and narrow lanes, with the result that more perished in the bogs than were ever killed by the sword.

Ebrachar then advanced to the town of Vannes. Bishop Regalis sent his clergy out to meet him, carrying crosses and chanting psalms, and they led the Frankish troops into their town. The rumour went that Waroch was trying to reach the islands,[25] and that he had put out to sea in ships which were heavily laden with gold and silver, and with all his other possessions. A storm blew up, the ships foundered and he lost the entire cargo. However this might be, he now came to Ebrachar, sued for peace, handed over a number of hostages and many valuable presents, and then swore that he would never again do anything to the disadvantage of King Guntram. When Waroch had gone, Bishop Regalis swore a similar oath, and so did his clergy and his townsfolk. 'We have nothing whatsoever to reproach ourselves with in our relations with our lords and masters,' he said, 'nor have we ever been foolish enough to do anything to their disadvantage. We have to do as the Bretons tell us, and this irks us very much.' When peace was concluded between Waroch and Ebrachar, the Breton leader made the following speech: 'Go back now and report to your King that I will carry out his commands to the letter. As a pledge of my good intentions, I will hand over my own nephew as a hostage.' This he

25. He was escaping to Belle-Ile and the smaller islands off the coast of Morbihan.

did, and so the campaign came to an end. The casualties had been very heavy, both in the King's army and among the Bretons.

The troops marched out of Brittany. The stronger men crossed the river, but those less strong and the camp-followers with them were not able to wade through. There they had to stay on the far bank of the River Vilaine. Waroch promptly forgot his oath and the hostage whom he had handed over, and sent his son Canao with an army to seize these stragglers. Canao tied up with ropes all he could find on the river bank, and those who resisted he killed. Some who tried to swim their horses across the river were carried down to the sea by the strong current. Later on many were freed by Waroch's wife by taper and tablet,[26] and these were allowed to make their way home. Ebrachar's army, which had crossed over earlier on, was afraid to go home by the route which it had followed on the outward journey, lest it receive the same treatment which it had meted out. Instead the troops made for Angers, hoping to cross the River Mayenne by the bridge there. The small advance-guard which moved up to this bridge was stripped, knocked about and subjected to every indignity. As they passed through the Tours region they are said to have collected a deal of booty and to have robbed a great number of people, for they caught the local inhabitants unawares. Many of those who took part in this expedition went to King Guntram and alleged that Duke Ebrachar and Count Willachar had been bribed by Waroch to lead their troops to disaster. When Ebrachar appeared at court the King reproached him bitterly and ordered him to leave his presence. Count Willachar fled and went into hiding.

10. In the fifteenth year of King Childebert[27] and the twenty-ninth of King Guntram, when this latter King was out hunting in the forest of the Vosges, he came across the tracks of an aurochs which had been killed. He questioned the forester

26. This was one form of manumission. The slave held a lighted candle in his hand and was led three times round the altar by a priest. He was then given a document which certified that he was free.

27. A.D. 590.

closely to discover who had dared to do this in the royal forest.
The forester told him that it was Chundo, his own royal
Chamberlain. Relying upon what the man had said, Guntram
ordered Chundo to be arrested, and to be loaded with chains
and taken to Chalon-sur-Saône. When they appeared before
Guntram, the two had a bitter argument, Chundo denying that
he had ever committed the presumptuous act with which they
were charging him. The King decided upon trial by combat.
The Chamberlain appointed a nephew of his to do battle in his
stead. When the two stood face to face on the battlefield, the
young man hurled his spear at the forester and pierced his foot,
so that he fell over backwards. Then he drew the dagger which
hung at his belt and tried to cut the fallen man's throat. Instead
he himself was wounded in the stomach by a knife-thrust. In
short they were both laid low and died. As soon as Chundo
saw what had happened, he made a dash for the church of
Saint Marcellus. The King shouted that he must be captured
before he set foot on the holy threshold. They caught him. He
was tied to a stake and stoned to death. Afterwards the King
was sorry that he had lost his temper and that for such a
trifling offence he had recklessly killed out of hand a faithful
servant whom he could ill spare.

11. Lothar, the son of Chilperic, our former King, fell
seriously ill. His life was so far despaired of that it was actually
announced to King Guntram that he was dead. The King set
out to travel to Paris from Chalon-sur-Saône and reached
the neighbourhood of Sens, but there news reached him that the
boy had recovered, so he turned back. When Fredegund, the
mother of Lothar, saw how desperately ill he was, she vowed
that she would donate a great sum of money to the church of
Saint Martin. That was why he recovered. In another attempt to
save his life, she sent messengers to Waroch, ordering him to set
free the prisoners from King Guntram's army whom he was
still holding in Brittany. Waroch did as he was told. This is
proof enough that this woman was in some way responsible for
the killing of Beppolen and the destruction of his army.

12. Ingitrude, the religious, who, as I have told you in my earlier books,[28] had founded a convent of nuns in the court-yard of Saint Martin's church, now began to be ill. As Mother Superior she appointed her niece, but the community com-plained about this. I had to speak to them and then they stopped. Ingitrude was on bad terms with her daughter Berthegund, because the latter had taken so much of her prop-erty. She now swore that Berthegund should never be allowed to offer prayers either in the nunnery which she had founded or at her tomb. Ingitrude was in her eightieth year, I think, when she died. She was buried on 8 March. Her daughter Berthegund came to Tours, but she was not allowed into the nunnery. She thereupon sought an audience with King Childebert and peti-tioned him to allow her to replace her mother in the nunnery. The King forgot the decision in Ingitrude's favour which he had made some time previously. He now gave Berthegund a new document signed with his own hand and saying that she might inherit all the property which her mother and father had left, and even go as far as to take everything which Ingitrude had be-queathed to her nunnery. Armed with this order she came back and removed all the furniture from the building, leaving nothing behind but the bare walls. Then she assembled a band of ruffians who were prepared for any lawless act, and stole all the produce from such other estates as devout people had do-nated to the nunnery. She did so many evil things that I find it impossible to set them all down in order for you. When she had taken everything that she could lay her hands on she returned to Poitiers. She had nothing but abuse for the Mother Superior, who was her close relation.

13. One of my priests revived once more the pernicious doc-trine of the Sadducees and expressed his disbelief in the resurrection of the body. When I argued that it was foretold in the Holy Scriptures and that it had the full support of apostolic tradition, he replied: 'I do not deny that many people believe in it, but we can't be sure whether it is true or not, the more so

28. See *HF*, V, 21, VII, 36 and IX, 33.

as, when God was angry with the first man, whom he had fashioned with His own divine hand, He said to him: "In the sweat of thy face shalt thou eat bread, till thou return unto the ground; for out of it wast thou taken: for dust thou art, and unto dust shalt thou return."[29] What do you say to that, you who preach the resurrection to come? You see that, in actual fact, God does not promise that man, become dust, shall rise again.' 'Well,' I answered, 'I don't think that any Catholic can be ignorant of the words spoken by our Lord and Saviour on this point, and, indeed, by the fathers who were before us. In Genesis, when the Patriarchs died, God used to say: "You will be gathered to your people. You will be buried in a good old age."[30] To Cain He says: "The voice of thy brother's blood crieth unto me from the ground."[31] From this it is obvious enough that souls live on after they have left the body and that they eagerly await the resurrection to come. Of Job it is written that he will rise again in the resurrection of the dead. Though he spoke in God's own name the prophet David foresaw the resurrection when he said: "And now he that lieth, shall he rise up no more?"[32] What he meant to ask was whether or not he who has succumbed to death's long sleep will rise again. Isaiah tells us that dead men will rise again from the tomb.[33] The prophet Ezekiel was most clearly announcing the resurrection to come when he described how dry bones would be covered with skin, joined together with sinews, threaded through and through with veins and brought to life once more with the breath of the spirit, and how man would become one again.[34] It was also a manifest sign of the resurrection when a dead body miraculously came to life again at the touch of Elisha's limbs.[35] Our Lord, who is the first begotten of the dead,[36] Himself gave proof of the resurrection when from the dead He destroyed death and from the tomb gave life back to the dead.' To this the priest replied: 'I do not doubt that our Lord Himself was made man,

29. Genesis 3, 19.   30. Cp. Genesis 25, 8.   31. Genesis 4, 10.
32. Psalms 41, 9.   33. Cp. Isaiah 26, 19.   34. Ezekiel 37, 6.
35. Cp. II Kings 4, 34.   36. Revelation 1, 5.

that He died and rose again; but I can't accept that all the other dead will rise.' 'What need was there, then,' I asked him, 'for the Son of God to come down from heaven, to be incarnate, to suffer death and to descend into Hell, if it were not that He would not permit man, whom He had Himself created, to be condemned to death eternal? The souls of the just, who, until His Passion, remained imprisoned in the lock-up house of Hell, were set free at His coming. When He descended into Hell, suffusing the darkness with a new light, He led forth those souls with Him, for when He rose He did not wish their anguish to continue. "For the dead rise in their graves,"[37] He said.' 'Can bones which have been reduced to ashes really be given new life, then, and make once more a living man?' asked my priest. 'We believe,' I answered, 'that even if a man were reduced to very fine dust and then scattered over the land and sea in the face of a keen wind it would still not be difficult for God to restore that dust to life.' 'In my opinion,' replied the priest, 'you are quite wrong in what you say. You put it very smoothly, but you are trying to prove something very hard to believe when you say that a body torn about by wild beasts, or immersed in water and then perhaps snapped up in the jaws of fishes, or reduced in the process of digestion and then deposited as excrement, or cast up by running water, or simply destroyed by decomposition in the earth, can ever come to resurrection.' 'It seems to me,' said I, 'that you have forgotten what John the Evangelist, who was our Lord's most intimate associate and who was familiar with all the secrets of the divine mystery, said in the Apocalypse. "Then the sea shall give up the dead which are in it"[38] were his words. It is clear from this that although a fish may have swallowed part of a body, or a bird torn sections of it away, or a wild animal devoured it, it will still be joined together again and restored by our Lord for the resurrection. He who created man as yet unborn from nothing at all will not find it difficult to replace any lost portions. He will restore our physical attributes in their entirety and just as they were before,

37. This quotation has not been traced.
38. Cp. Revelation 20, 13.

so that according to its deserts the actual body which existed on earth may be punished or pass to glory. This is what our Lord says in the Gospel: "For the Son of man shall come in the glory of His Father with his angels: and then he shall reward every man according to his works."[39] When she had doubts about the immediate return to life of her brother Lazarus, Martha said: "I know that he shall rise again in the resurrection at the last day."[40] Our Lord answered her and said: "I am the resurrection and the way, the truth and the life." '[41] 'What about the passage in the psalm?' replied my priest. ' "The ungodly shall not stand in the judgement".'[42] 'They will not rise again that they may judge,' I answered, 'but they will rise again that they may be judged. The Judge cannot sit with the wicked to give an account of His judgements.' 'In the Gospel our Lord said: "He that believeth not is condemnedalready",'[43] replied the priest; 'and that means that he will not rise at the resurrection.' He is condemned to eternal punishment,' I answered, 'because he did not believe in the only-begotten Son of God. Nevertheless, he will rise in the flesh so that he may be punished in that body in which he has sinned. There cannot be a Judgement Day unless the dead have risen first. Just as we believe that heaven awaits those who have died in sanctity, and that as they emerge from the tomb a miracle will be performed by which the blind will see, the lame will walk, the lepers will be made clean and all the sick who seek it will be granted the full benefit of health, so we believe that sinners will be held in the prison-house of Hell until the Day of Judgement.' 'We read in the psalm,' replied the priest: ' "For the wind passeth over him, and he is gone; and the place thereof shall know him no more." '[44] 'That is what our Lord said in the parable of the rich man, who was tormented in the flames of Hell,' I answered. ' "Thou in thy lifetime receivest thy good things, and likewise Lazarus evil things."[45] When the rich man was tortured in the flames, he knew no more his purples and his fine linen, nor the delights of the table which

39. Matthew 16, 27.   40. John 11, 24.   41. John 11, 25.
42. Psalms 1, 5.   43. John 3, 18.   44. Psalms 103, 16.
45. Luke 16, 25.

the air and the earth and the sea afforded him; whereas Lazarus, when he rested in Abraham's bosom, knew no more the wounds and the putrid sores which he had endured when he lay at the rich man's gate.' 'We read in another psalm,' went on the priest: ' "Their breath goeth forth, they returneth to their earth; in that very day their thoughts perish." '[46] 'That was well said,' I answered. 'When the breath has left a man's body and that body lies dead, he will think no more of the things which he has left behind on earth. As you imply, he no longer thinks of building, planting, cultivating the soil; he no longer thinks of amassing gold and silver, or the riches of this world. That sort of preoccupation has no place in a body which is dead, for the spirit has left it. Why do you have doubts about the resurrection, when the Apostle Paul, through whom Christ spoke, as he himself tells us, says quite clearly: "Therefore we are buried with him by baptism into death: that like as Christ was raised up from the dead, even so we also should walk in newness of life."[47] He also says: 'We all shall rise, but we shall not all be changed. The trumpet shall sound, and the dead shall be raised incorruptible, and we shall be changed."[48] Again he says: "One star differeth from another star in glory. So also is the resurrection of the dead."[49] He goes on: "It is sown in corruption: it is raised in incorruption,"[50] and so on. Later on he says: "For we must all appear before the judgement seat of Christ: that everyone may receive the things done in his body, according to that he hath done, whether it is good or bad."[51] He refers most clearly to the resurrection to come when he speaks to the Thessalonians: "But I would not have you to be ignorant, brethren, concerning them which are asleep, that ye sorrow not, even as others which have no hope. For if we believe that Jesus died and rose again, even so them also which sleep in Jesus will God bring with him. For this we say unto you by the word of the Lord, that we which are alive and remain unto the coming of the Lord shall not prevent them which are asleep. For the Lord

46. Psalms 146, 4.   47. Romans 6, 4.
48. I Corinthians 15, 51–2.   49. I Corinthians 15, 41–2.
50. *ibid.*   51. II Corinthians 5, 10.

himself shall descend from heaven with a shout, with the voice of the archangel, and with the trump of God: and the dead in Christ shall rise first: then we which are alive and remain shall be caught up together with them in the clouds, to meet the Lord in the air: and so shall we ever be with the Lord. Wherefore comfort one another with these words."[52] There is much testimony of these matters and arguments to confirm our belief. I do not know why, but you have doubts about the resurrection, to which the saints look through their good deeds, but which sinners fear because of their guilt. All natural things which we see about us give further proof of the resurrection. The trees which are covered with leaves in the Summer season are laid bare when Winter comes. When Spring follows fast behind, they rise again, as it were, and are clad once more in a garment of leaves just as they were before. The seeds which lie in the earth give us further proof: they are cast into the furrows, and there they lie as if dead, but they rise again and bear fruit a thousandfold, just as the Apostle Paul tells us: "Thou fool, that which thou sowest is not quickened, except it die."[53] All these things bear witness to the world, that we may have faith in the resurrection. If there is to be no resurrection, what will it profit the just that he has done well, how will it harm the sinner that he has behaved ill? If there is no Judgement Day to come, all men can follow their own petty desires, each of us can do exactly as he wishes. You wicked man, do you not fear what the Lord Himself said to the blessed Apostles? "When the Son of man", He says, "shall come in his glory, and before him shall be gathered all nations: and he shall separate them one from another, as a shepherd divideth his sheep from the goats: And he shall set the sheep on his right hand, but the goats on his left. Then shall he say unto them on his right hand, Come, ye blessed, inherit the kingdom. Then shall he say also unto them on the left hand, Depart from me, ye that work iniquity."[54] The same Scriptures also say: "And these shall go away into everlasting punishment: but the righteous into life eternal."[55] Do you really think that there will be no

---

52. I Thessalonians 4, 13–18.   53. I Corinthians 15, 36.
54. Matthew 25, 31–4 and 41.   55. Matthew 25, 46.

resurrection of the dead and no judgement of their works, when the Lord will do these things? Let the Apostle Paul give you your answer, just as he did to other unbelievers: "And if Christ be not risen, then is our teaching vain, and your faith is also vain." '[56]

When I had said all this, my priest was contrite. As he left me, he promised to believe in the resurrection, according to the passages from the Holy Scriptures which I have quoted above.

14. At this time there was living in Paris a deacon called Theudulf, who considered himself to be extremely well informed and who as a result was always becoming involved in arguments. He left Paris and went to Angers, where, in view of their old friendship, for they had lived together in Paris, he placed himself under the orders of Bishop Audioveus. Theudulf was excommunicated time and time again by Ragnemod, Bishop of Paris, for refusing to return to the church to which he had been appointed as deacon. He stuck so closely and so devotedly to Audioveus that the Bishop, who was a kindly person and loyal to his friends, was unable to shake off his importunities. The Bishop had conceived the idea of building himself a solarium high up on the city walls. One evening after supper, as he was making his way down from this solarium, he rested his hand upon his deacon's shoulder. Theudulf was so drunk with the wine which he had taken that he could scarcely stand on his feet. A servant walked in front of them with a light, and for some reason which I do not know Theudulf chose to strike this man on the back of the neck with his fist. The force of the blow was such that Theudulf lost his balance, lurched forward and fell headlong from the wall. The Bishop would have gone over with him, if a priest who was present had not immediately seized hold of his feet; even so, as he fell, Theudulf snatched away a cloth which was hanging from the Bishop's belt. He landed on a rock, broke a number of bones and stove in his ribs. He died on

56. I Corinthians 15, 14.

the spot, after vomiting blood and bile. He was a drunkard and a fornicator.

15. Meanwhile the revolt which, at the instigation of Satan, had broken out in the nunnery in Poitiers, became more and more serious as day followed day. I have told you how Clotild was set upon rebellion and had gathered round her a band of cut-throats, evil-doers, fornicators, fugitives from justice and men guilty of every crime in the calendar. These she ordered to break into the nunnery and to drag out the Abbess. However, the Abbess heard them coming and asked to be carried to the shrine of the Holy Cross.[57] She was suffering from an attack of gout at the time and she hoped that she would be safe in the shrine. By the light of a taper these men burst into the nunnery and wandered about all over the place, brandishing their weapons. They looked everywhere for the Abbess and in the end they entered the shrine, where they discovered her lying on the ground in front of the reliquary which held the Holy Cross. Thereupon one of them, even more ferocious than his fellows, and who had come there with the express intention of committing the crime of murdering the Abbess with his sword, was, by the intervention of divine providence, or so I believe, knifed by one of his companions. He failed to carry out his mad design, but lay on the ground, bleeding profusely. At that moment Justina, the Prioress,[58] blew out the taper and, with the help of her sister-nuns, covered the Abbess with a cloth from the altar which stood before the Cross of our Lord. The other men rushed forward with their javelins at the ready and their swords drawn. They slit the nuns' dresses and were prepared to slit their hands, too. They laid hands on the Prioress, in the darkness taking her for the Abbess, tore off her veil, let down her hair, dragged her out and carried her off in the midst of a mob to Saint Hilary's church, where they proposed to guard her closely. As they approached the church, the sky began to

57. Cp. p. 530, note 56.
58. Gregory's niece: cp. the family tree on p. 11 of the Introduction.

lighten momentarily and they realized that she was not the Abbess. They ordered her to return to her nunnery. They themselves went back the way they had come, seized the Abbess, dragged her out in her turn and locked her up in a house not far from Saint Hilary's church where Basina had her lodging. They placed guards on the door to prevent her being rescued. Then they once more made their way to the nunnery through the darkness. They were unable to find a light, so they took from the storehouse a cask which had once contained pitch but which was now dry. They set light to this cask. As it burned it formed a great beacon, so that they were able to loot all the contents of the nunnery, leaving nothing behind which they could carry. These events occurred only seven days before Easter.

Bishop Maroveus bore all this very ill. Realizing that he himself could not cope with such a diabolical revolt, he sent a message to Clotild. 'Free your Abbess from her imprisonment and let her go,' he said. 'You know what season it is. Unless you order her to be released from the prison in which she is locked up, I shall refuse to celebrate our Lord's Easter ceremony, and no one being given instruction for baptism will receive it in this town. If you refuse to do what I say, I will rouse the townsfolk and free her myself.' When she received this message, Clotild lost no time in singling out one of her assassins and giving him the following order: 'If anyone tries to free the Abbess by force, hit her with your sword without wasting a moment.' It happened that Flavianus, who had only recently been appointed as one of the King's officials, was in Poitiers at this time, and with his help the Abbess was released and carried into Saint Hilary's church. Meanwhile men were being killed before Saint Radegund's tomb and others were cut down in a riot outside the shrine of the Holy Cross. As day followed day Clotild in her arrogance egged them all on to further fury. Those in revolt committed murder after murder and kept up the assaults which I have described to you. Clotild's overweening insolence reached the point at which she even sneered at her cousin Basina. The upshot of it all was that Basina began to regret what she had done. 'I committed a sin when I behaved in the same arrogant way as Clotild,' she said to herself. 'I am in revolt against my Abbess all right, but that doesn't seem to stop me being despised by Clotild.' She put an end to her evil behaviour and humbled herself before the Abbess, in the hope of being forgiven. They patched up an agreement with each other and made peace. However, a fresh quarrel arose almost immediately. While the servants of the Abbess were trying to put down an affray organized by Clotild's gang, they struck one of Basina's servants and the man fell down dead. They then sought refuge with the Abbess in Saint Hilary's church, whereupon Basina broke once more with the Abbess and went off. Later on these same servants escaped from the church. Basina and the Abbess made peace a second time, but their rival bands of supporters never stopped squabbling. Scarcely a day passed without someone being murdered, scarcely an hour without some quarrel or other, scarcely a minute without some person or other having cause for sorrow. Who could possibly set down in words all this violence, all this slaughter, all this evil?

When King Childebert heard what was happening, he sent messengers to King Guntram to suggest that a group of bishops from the two kingdoms should meet together, in an attempt to end the revolt by canon law. As his own representatives Childebert chose Ebregisel, Bishop of Cologne, Maroveus, Bishop of Poitiers, and my own unworthy self. King Guntram chose Gundegisel, Bishop of Bordeaux, together with the bishops of his province, for he was the Metropolitan of the city in question. I objected to the terms of our appointment. 'I will not set foot in Poitiers,' I said, 'until the local Count has used his authority to put down this bloodthirsty rebellion which Clotild has stirred up.' As a result, Macco, who was then Count, received a written order to suppress the revolt, using force if he met with resistance. When she heard the news, Clotild ordered her cutthroats to stand to their arms outside the nunnery gate and to be ready to meet violence with violence if the Count should resort to force. Macco had no option but to march on the nunnery with a band of armed men. He crushed the rising, knocking some of the dissidents over the head with staves, running others through with spears and using swords to cut down those who were really determined to resist. Clotild watched all this. Then she picked up the Holy Cross, which until then she had held in small esteem, and sallied forth to face the foe. 'I warn you!' she shouted. 'Do not lay a finger on me! I am a queen, the daughter of one king and the niece of another! If you touch me you can be quite sure that the day will come when I shall have my revenge.' However, the assembled mob took little notice of what she said. Macco's men closed in on all those who offered any resistance, tied them up and bundled them out of the nunnery. Some they roped to posts and then gave them a good beating. Some had their hair cut off, others their hands, some even their ears and noses. So the revolt petered out.

Then we Bishops appeared and took our seats on the tribunal of the cathedral. Clotild was called before us. She showered abuse on her Abbess and made a number of accusations against her. She maintained that the Abbess kept a man in the nunnery, dressed in woman's clothing and looking like a woman, although in effect there was no doubt that he was a man. His job was to sleep with the Abbess whenever she wanted it. 'Why! There's the fellow!' cried Clotild, pointing with her finger. Thereupon a man stepped forward, dressed in woman's clothing as I have told you. Everyone stared at him. He said that he was impotent and that that was the reason why he dressed himself up in this way. He maintained that he had never set eyes on the Abbess, although, of course, he knew her by name. He had never spoken to her in his life, and, in any case, he lived more than forty miles out of Poitiers. Clotild failed to prove her Abbess guilty on this count.

She then made a second accusation. 'The Abbess has a very odd way of proving her sanctity!' she said. 'She has men castrated and then keeps them around her as eunuchs, just as if this were the Imperial court!' The Abbess was questioned and she replied that she did not know what Clotild was talking about. Thereupon Clotild gave the name of one of the servants who was a eunuch. Reovalis, who was a doctor, then stepped forward and made the following statement: 'When this servant was a young lad,' he said, 'he had terrible pains in the groin. Nobody could do anything for him. His mother went to Saint Radegund and asked her to have the case looked into. I was called in and she told me to do what I could. I cut out the lad's testicles, an operation I had once seen performed by a surgeon in the town of Constantinople. Then I handed him back to his mother. To my knowledge the Abbess knew nothing about this.' On this second count Clotild again failed to gain a conviction.

She then proceeded to make many more savage attacks on her Abbess. All these accusations and the replies of the defence are set out in the judgement made against the nuns, so that the best thing is for me to give you a transcript of it.

16. Text of the Judgement. To their noble lords the Kings in question[59] the Bishops present (send their greetings). With God agreeing the Church has never sought to conceal her judgements from the pious and Catholic Kings who have been set over the people and to whom sovereign power has been granted; and this is only right and proper. The Church recognizes that, with the help of the Holy Ghost, she is confirmed and strengthened in her authority by the jurisdiction of those in power.

At your specific command we met together in the city of Poitiers to consider what was happening in the nunnery founded there by Radegund of pious memory. We were to investigate the dispute between the Abbess and the nuns who were at loggerheads with her, they having been ill-advised enough to leave the community.

We summoned the parties to appear before us. We questioned Clotild and Basina as to why they had so rashly broken their Rule, forced open the nunnery gates and quitted their community, with the result that this order of nuns was now split up.

Clotild and Basina made the following reply. They said that they could no longer endure the poor food, the lack of clothing and, indeed, the harsh treatment. They disapproved of the fact that other people shared their bathroom. The Abbess played backgammon. Lay visitors ate with her. Occasionally engagement-parties were held in the nunnery. She was so lacking in reverence that she made dresses for her niece out of a silken altar-cloth. Without consulting anyone, she had cut some gold leaf from the edge of this same altar-

59. King Guntram and King Childebert II.

cloth and made a necklace with it for her niece, which was again quite incommensurate with the occasion.

The Abbess was then ordered to answer the charges made. As to the poor food about which they complained, she denied that they had ever gone short, especially if one considered what hard times these were. As far as their clothing was concerned, if their boxes were examined they would be found to possess far more than was necessary. The complaint about the bathroom arose, she went on, from something which had happened in Lent: the building had just been put up, the plaster was new and the Lady Radegund, afraid that their health might suffer if they washed in it, had decided that the nunnery servants could use it until the unpleasant smell disappeared. It was therefore given over to the servants during Lent and until Whitsun. 'Quite a lot of them went on using it long after that,' said Clotild. The Abbess replied that, if what they said was true, she certainly disapproved of it, but it was news to her. If they had seen it happen, it was very wrong of them not to have reported it to her. As to the backgammon, she used to play during the lifetime of the Lady Radegund, she saw nothing wrong in it, and it was not expressly forbidden in the Rule, or in the canons. If the Bishops now forbade it, she would bow to their authority and do any penance which they might impose. As far as the meals were concerned, she had done nothing new, but had acted just as they used to do under the Lady Radegund: she had offered the bread of oblation to Christian souls, but it could not be shown that she had ever eaten with them. Then there was the matter of the engagement-party. She had received a marriage-portion for her orphaned niece, but the Bishop himself, the clergy and some of the town notables had been present. If there was anything wrong in what she had done, she was prepared to ask forgiveness with everyone listening. There had certainly been no entertainment in the nunnery itself. An allegation had been made about a silken cloth. The Abbess produced in court a nun from a noble family who had made her a present of a silk mantle which her parents had given to her. She had cut off a small portion of this for her own use. From what was left she had handed over as much as was necessary to make a suitable cloth for the altar. The piece which she had cut off was not needed for the altar-cloth, so she had made a purple edging for her niece's tunic with it. The length which she had handed over had been placed where it was of most use to the nunnery. Didimia, the nun who had presented the silk mantle, confirmed what the Abbess had said in every detail. As for the gold leaf and the fillet which she had made with it, she called Macco, your own representative, to witness that he himself had handed over to her twenty gold pieces which were a present from the fiancé of the niece about whom we have told you. With these she had bought the fillet as an ordinary public purchase, and no money belonging to the nunnery had been involved in any way.

Clotild and Basina were then asked if they wished to prefer any charge of sexual promiscuity against their Abbess, which God forbid, or one of homicide perhaps, or of witchcraft, or of any other major crime for which she should be punished. Their answer was that they had no such charge to make and that their case rested on what they had already said about her having broken the Rule. They concluded by pointing out that several of the nuns were now pregnant. In our opinion this was not their fault. The poor girls had been left to their own devices for so many months, with their nunnery gates broken down and no control possible by their Abbess, and as a result they had sinned.

We investigated all these points one by one, and our decision was that no charge could be made against the Abbess. We gave her some paternal advice on the small points which had been raised, and we suggested that she take care not to expose herself to such criticism in future. We then turned our attention to the accusations levelled against the other party. The crimes which they were said to have committed were extremely serious. They had taken no notice when their Bishop visited the nunnery and exhorted them not to leave. They had treated their Bishop with the greatest possible contumely, and actually trodden him underfoot before they left him behind in the nunnery. They had broken locks, burst open gates, started a revolt, and then escaped from the nunnery, encouraging others to go with them and share in their sin. More serious by far, when Bishop Gundegisel had come to Poitiers with the other bishops of his province, having been ordered by the Kings to look into this matter, and had summoned them to appear before him in their own nunnery, they had disobeyed his order. When the Bishops then went in person to Saint Hilary's church, where the nuns had taken up residence, and remonstrated with them there, thus carrying out their pastoral duty, they had again started a riot, belabouring the Bishops and their attendant clergy with sticks and shedding the blood of deacons inside the church. When our royal masters sent the venerable priest Theuthar to look into the case and a day had been chosen for the hearing, they had refused to wait. Instead they forced their way back into the nunnery with the utmost violence, built a fire with casks in the courtyard, knocked down the door-posts with crowbars and axes, and then set light to them in their turn. They knocked the nuns about and wounded some of them inside the building and even in their oratories, they sacked the nunnery, they tore off the Abbess's veil and let down her hair, dragged her through the streets as a laughing-stock, and then shut her up in a house where, if she was not actually tied up, she was certainly not free. When Easter Day came round, with its eternal feast, the Bishop offered to pay over a sum of money as a surety if the Abbess were allowed at least to watch the baptismal ceremony, but no persuasion or entreaty had been of any avail. At this point Clotild intervened to say that this outrage was done without their knowledge and certainly without their approval. She added that it was only at a sign from her that her men were prevented from killing the Abbess out of hand. From all this it is quite clear what their intentions were. Furthermore they had most cruelly done to death one of the nunnery servants, who had sought refuge at the tomb of Saint Radegund. Their evil behaviour had gone from bad to worse and, however many times they were asked, they refused to stop. On the contrary, when they had occupied the nunnery buildings, they steadfastly refused to hand over to justice the more seditious members of their gang, even when they were ordered to do so by the Kings. In the face of the Kings' commands, they persisted in their armed rebellion, and they fought against the Count and the townsfolk with their arrows and their javelins in the most reprehensible way. When they came out of the nunnery for their public trial, they carried with them, secretly and irreligiously, the most hallowed Holy Cross, which they had since been forced to hand back in the cathedral.

There is no denying that these were all misdemeanours of a most serious nature; and even then they had not stopped, for they had gone on committing one crime after another. When we ordered them to beg forgiveness of their Abbess for the wrong which they had done, and to make good the damage caused by their evil behaviour, they had refused to do so. Instead they pressed on with their plan to kill her, as they had now confessed in public.

We have opened the canons and we have consulted them. Our decision is that these two must in all justice be cut off from communion until they have done proper penance. The Abbess must be restored to her position permanently.

We maintain that in all these matters we have acted in accordance with your orders, with due respect for the Church's authority and after having consulted the canons. What is more, we have acted without respect for persons. For the rest, it lies within your piety and power, if you are prepared to exert your royal authority, to order restitution to its proper place of all property belonging to the nunnery, as set out in the deeds of gift of our royal masters, your own ancestors, which has been stolen and carried away. They have admitted in public, that they have taken away this property; but so far they have ignored our request that they should hand it back of their own volition. If you give the order, your own benefactions and those of earlier kings will endure for ever. You have, then, to decide whether or not you will allow them to entertain some hopes of returning eventually, or if you will forbid them ever to be re-admitted to the place which they have ransacked so wickedly and profanely, for fear that even worse things may happen.

By the grace of our Lord, once everything has been restored to its original state, may all that is His be rendered unto God, with our Catholic Kings to rule us, and may our faith suffer no loss. May the Rule of the Fathers and of the canons be preserved, to be of profit to us in our worship and of advantage to you in its outcome. May Christ our Lord guide you and watch over you, may He permit you to rule over us for many years and may He grant you life eternal.

17. Our verdict was made public, and soon afterwards Clotild and Basina were suspended from communion, while the Abbess was restored to her nunnery. The two sought an audience with King Childebert, and there they made one evil accusation after another. They gave the King the names of a number of men who were supposed to be having sexual relations with the Abbess and who, according to them, were also carrying messages daily to his enemy Fredegund. When he heard this the King ordered the persons concerned to be bound and brought before him. The case against them was investigated, but they were found to have done nothing wrong and they were sent home again.

18.   Some days earlier, just as King Childebert was going into
the oratory in his house in Marlenheim, his servants saw an unknown man standing on one side. 'Who are you? Where do you
come from? What are you doing here?' they asked him. 'We do
not recognize you.' 'I am one of you,' he answered. They immediately dragged him outside the oratory and put him to the
question. This did not take long, for he soon admitted that he
had been sent by Queen Fredegund to assassinate Childebert.
'She sent a dozen of us,' he said. 'Six came here. The other six
stayed behind in Soissons to kill the young prince.[60] I was just
taking up my position here to strike King Childebert down in his
oratory, but I was absolutely terrified and really quite incapable
of carrying out my mission.' As soon as he said this he was
tortured unmercifully until he gave the names of his accomplices. They were looked for everywhere. Some were thrown
into prison, some had their hands amputated and were afterwards released, some had their ears and noses cut off and were
then let out as a subject of ridicule. Several of them killed themselves with their own daggers while they were still in prison; for
they could not face all these different tortures; still others died
while they were actually being questioned. In one way and
another the King certainly had his revenge.

19.   Sunnegisil was tortured again and again. He was flogged
daily with sticks and leather thongs. His wounds festered. As
fast as the pus oozed away and the places began to mend, they
were opened once more by this constant maltreatment. While
he was being tortured he not only confessed that he had planned
to assassinate King Childebert, but also revealed that he had
committed all sorts of crimes. To his other admissions he added
the fact that Bishop Egidius had been implicated in the plot
made by Rauching, Ursio and Berthefried to kill King Childebert. The Bishop was immediately seized and dragged off to
the town of Metz, although he had been ill for a long time and
was very low in health. There he was kept in prison while the
King ordered a council of his fellow-bishops to be convened for

60. Theudebert.

his trial. They were to meet in Verdun at the beginning of October. The other bishops complained to the King that he had ordered Egidius to be removed from his diocese and thrown into prison without a hearing. Thereupon Childebert gave him permission to return to his own city. Meanwhile, as I have told you, the King sent letters to all the bishops of his realm, ordering them to meet in the city of Metz in the middle of November to take part in the trial. It rained continually and in torrents, and it was unbearably cold, the roads were deep in mud and the rivers overflowed their banks; nevertheless they were unable to disobey the King's orders. The bishops met together and then they were compelled to go on to Metz, where Egidius was now awaiting trial.

The King declared Egidius his own personal enemy and a traitor to the state. He ordered Ennodius, who had once been a Duke, to undertake the prosecution. The first question which Ennodius put was this: 'Tell me, Bishop, why you decided to desert our own King, in one of whose cities you were enjoying the dignity of episcopal rank? Why did you debase yourself by accepting favours from King Chilperic, who is well-known to have been the constant enemy of King Childebert, whose father he killed,[61] whose mother he sent into exile[62] and whose kingdom he invaded? How did it come about that in the very cities on which, as I have said, he forced his overlordship by wrongful violence and invasion, you choose to receive at his hands a grant of crown lands?' 'I cannot deny that I was King Chilperic's friend,' answered Egidius, 'but this friendship was certainly never to the disadvantage of King Childebert. The estates of which you have spoken I received by proper deeds of conveyance from King Childebert himself.' As he said this he produced the deeds for all to see, but the King denied that he had ever granted them. Otto, who was Referendary at the time and who was supposed to have written the studied signature,[63] was

61. King Sigibert.   62. Queen Brunhild.

63. A studied signature, *subscriptio meditata*, was a signature ornately written, with many flourishes, so that it could not be imitated easily. Cp. the figures at the bottom of modern cheques.

ordered to appear. He came, but he said that the signature was not his. His handwriting had been imitated when the document was copied. The Bishop was thus found guilty of forgery on the very first charge.

Next letters were produced in court which he had addressed to Chilperic and in which many insulting remarks were made about Brunhild. There were other letters from Chilperic to the Bishop, which contained statements like the following: 'The stalk which emerges from the soil will not wither until its root is severed.' It was quite clear from what was written that Brunhild was to be destroyed first and her son killed afterwards. The Bishop said that he had not sent these letters or signed them, and that he had not received the replies from Chilperic. However, there appeared in court one of Egidius' own servants, who kept shorthand copies of letters for the Bishop's files, and from his evidence there could be no doubt at all in the minds of those sitting in judgement that the messenger had actually been dispatched by Egidius.

Copies of agreements were then produced, signed by both King Childebert and King Chilperic, in which it was expressly stated that these two Kings would first expel Guntram and then share his kingdom and his cities between them. Childebert denied that he had ever given approval to any agreement of this sort. 'It was you, Egidius, who set my uncles against each other and stirred up civil war between them,' he said. 'An army was put into the field, and the troops attacked and laid waste the city of Bourges, the district round Etampes and the town of Châteaumeillant. Many men died in this war, and their souls, I imagine, are only waiting for the moment when God will sit in judgement on you.' Egidius was in no position to say that this was not true, for the papers concerned had been discovered in one of King Chilperic's dispatch-cases. They had passed into Childebert's possession when Chilperic died and his treasures were removed from Chelles, his country estate near Paris, and handed over to his nephew.

The legal argument about these charges and others of the same nature went on for a long time. Then Epiphanius, the

Abbot of the church of Saint Remigius, appeared in court and gave evidence that Egidius had received two thousand pieces of gold and many other sums of money to encourage him to maintain his connection with King Chilperic. There also appeared the messengers who had gone with the Bishop to Chilperic. 'He left us,' they said, 'and spent a long time conferring alone with the King. We know nothing of what was said, but soon afterwards we learned of the invasion and slaughter which have already been mentioned.' The Bishop denied that all this was true. However, the Abbot, who had always been kept closely informed of Egidius' secret plans, gave the name of the man who had conveyed the pieces of gold about which I have told you and of the actual place where they had been handed over. He described in full detail the plans which they had made for the devastation of the region concerned, for the killing of King Guntram and for all that had happened subsequently.

Egidius was convicted on these charges. He thereupon confessed his guilt. When the prelates who were present heard this and realized that one of our Lord's bishops had been involved in plotting so many evil deeds, they were greatly troubled. They asked for three days' respite in which to consider the case together. They hoped that Egidius might be able to pull himself together and find some way of exculpating himself from all the charges brought against him. When the third day dawned they went in a body to the church and questioned Egidius, saying that if he had any excuse to offer he must declare it. He was in great distress. 'I am guilty,' he replied. 'I ask you to announce your verdict immediately. I confess that I deserve death for the crime of high treason. I have repeatedly conspired against the interests of the King and his mother. It is as the direct result of my plotting that many battles have been waged and many districts of Gaul devastated.' When they heard this the bishops were greatly saddened by the disgrace which had befallen their brother. They succeeded in saving Egidius' life, but when they had read the relevant passages in the canons they removed him from the priesthood. He was taken to the town of Argentoratum, now called Strasbourg, and he was condemned to

exile. Romulf, the son of Duke Lupus, who had already been
made a priest, was enthroned as Bishop in his place. Epiphanius
was deposed from his position as Abbot of the church of Saint
Remigius. A vast amount of gold and silver was discovered in
the coffers of Egidius. Everything that had come to him as the
result of his evil conspiracies was handed over to the royal
treasury; but all that had accrued from the proper dues and
incomes of the Church was left untouched.

20.   At this same council Basina, the daughter of King Chilperic, who, as I have told you, had recently been excommunicated
in company with Clotild, threw herself at the bishops' feet and
begged for forgiveness. She promised to return to her nunnery,
to live there in peace with her Abbess and to observe all the
provisions of the Rule. Clotild, on the other hand, swore that
she would never go back to the nunnery as long as Leubovera
remained there as Abbess. The King asked that they might both
be pardoned. They were received once more into communion
and ordered to return to Poitiers. Basina went back into her
nunnery, as I have said. The country estate which I have described as having belonged formerly to Waddo was conveyed to
Clotild in gift by the King and she went to live there.

21.   Waddo's sons were now living a wandering life in the Poitiers region, committing various crimes, including robbery and
murder. A short time before they had attacked a group of merchants, put them to the sword under the cover of darkness and
made off with all their property. They ambushed another man
who had an appointment as tribune, killed him and stole all his
goods. Count Macco tried to put them down, but they sought
an audience with the King. When the Count went to court in the
normal course of his duties to pay in the money due from him
to the treasury, they appeared in their turn and handed over a
huge baldric decorated with gold and precious stones, and a
marvellous sword the pommel of which was made of gold and
Spanish jewels. The King inquired into the crimes which had
been reported to him and made sure that they really had com-

mitted them. Then he had them chained up and submitted to torture. While the torture was being applied, they revealed the whereabouts of the hoard which their father had stolen from Gundovald's treasure, as I told you earlier on. Men were immediately sent to look for this. They discovered an enormous quantity of gold and silver, and all sorts of precious objects decorated with gold and gems. They brought all this in to the royal treasury. The elder brother had his head cut off, but the younger they sent into exile.

22. After committing a great number of crimes, among them murders, public affrays and misdemeanours of all sorts, Childeric the Saxon betook himself to the town of Auch, where his wife had a property. All his misdeeds came to the ears of the King and he gave orders that Childeric should be killed. However, one night he became so completely sodden with wine that he choked himself and was found dead in his bed. It was said that he was the ringleader in the crime described earlier on, when the Bishops were knocked about in Saint Hilary's church on the order of Clotild. If that was true, God took vengeance for the wrong done to his servants.

23. In the same year so bright a light illumined a wide spread of lands in the middle of the night that you would have thought that it was high noon. On a number of occasions fiery globes were also seen traversing the sky in the night-time, so that they seemed to light up the whole earth.

A dispute arose about the date of Easter, because Victorius, in his cycle,[64] had written that Easter should be celebrated on the fifteenth day after the full moon. To prevent Christians holding the feast on the same day after the full moon as the Jews, Victorius added: 'The Church of Rome celebrates on the twenty-second day.' As a result many people in Gaul held Easter on the fifteenth day,[65] but I myself kept the feast on the

64. This is a reference to the *Cursus Paschalis*, drawn up in A.D. 541 by Victorius of Aquitaine at the request of Pope Hilary I. Cp. *HF*, Preface to Book I.

65. A.D. 590, 26 March.

twenty-second day.[66] I made careful inquiries and discovered that the Spanish Springs, which flow by divine agency, began to run on the day which I had chosen for Easter.[67] There was a great earthquake very early in the morning on Wednesday, 14 June, just as the day began to dawn. There was an eclipse of the sun in the middle of October. The sun's rays were so diminished that it gave no more light than the horned moon when five days old. It rained in torrents, there were violent thunder-storms in Autumn and the river-waters rose very high. There was a serious outbreak of bubonic plague in the towns of Viviers and Avignon.

24. In the sixteenth year of King Childebert's reign[68] and the thirtieth year of King Guntram's, a Bishop called Simon travelled to Tours from foreign parts. He gave us news of the overthrow of Antioch[69] and described how he himself had been led away captive from Armenia into Persia. The King of the Persians had invaded Armenia, sacking the country, burning down the churches and, as I have said, taking this Bishop away into captivity with his flock. It was on this occasion that they had tried to burn down the church of the Forty-eight Saints and Martyrs, who met their death in that region, as I have described in my *Book of Miracles*.[70] They piled the church high with heaps of wood soaked in pitch and pigs' fat, and then set blazing torches to it. Despite all their efforts this inflammable material would not catch fire, and when they saw this miracle performed by God they left the church. One of his fellow-prelates came to hear of how Bishop Simon had been led off into captivity, and he sent his men with ransom-money to the

66. A.D. 590, 2 April.

67. The springs at Osser, near Seville, always began to run on Easter Day. Cp. *HF*, V, 17 and VI, 43.

68. A.D. 591.

69. The city of Antioch on the River Orontes was captured and partially destroyed in A.D. 573 by Adarmaanes, the general of Chosroes. It is now Antakya, since the referendum of 23 June 1939 just inside Turkey. As Bishop Simon was telling his story in 591, he must have been held captive in Persia for a great number of years.

70. *GM*, 95.

King of the Persians. The King accepted the ransom, unchained Simon and released him from slavery. The Bishop then left that region and travelled to Gaul, where he sought help from the faithful. That was how he came to tell me his story, just as I have set it down above.

In Antioch there lived a man who had a wife and children, and who was much given to acts of charity. In all his life no day passed, from the time when he first had some property of his own that is, without his inviting a poor man in to eat at his table. One day he searched the whole city until nightfall without finding a single needy person whom he could invite to share his meal. As darkness began to fall he went outside the city gate, and there he saw a man in a white robe who was standing with two other men. As he looked at him he was filled with awe, just like Lot in the tale of long ago.[71] 'My lord,' he said, 'you seem to be a stranger here. Would you care to come to my humble home and have a meal with me and then retire to bed to rest? In the morning you can go on your way, wherever you wish.' The oldest of the three men, who held a cloth in his hand, gave him the following answer: 'Were you not able, then, O man of God, even with the help of Simeon,[72] to save this city from destruction?' He raised his hand and waved the cloth which he was holding over one half of the town. Immediately all the buildings came crashing to the ground and nothing at all was left standing. Old men and young children were crushed to death, hundreds were killed with their wives, men and women together.[73] When he saw this the man was so dazed by the presence of the stranger and by the din made by the houses as they collapsed that he fell to the ground as if he were dead. The stranger raised the hand in which he held the cloth and was about to wave it over the other half of the town, but he was stopped by the two companions who stood at his side. They begged him with terrible oaths to spare this second half from destruction. His fury abated and he stayed his hand. He picked up the man who had fallen to the

71. Cp. Genesis 19.
72. Saint Simeon the Stylite: cp. p. 447, note 24.
73. No doubt this was really the earthquake of A.D. 589.

ground and said to him: 'Go home. You have no reason to fear.
Your sons are safe and so is your wife. None of them has
perished, and your household, too, is unharmed. You have been
saved by your habit of praying regularly and by your daily acts
of charity to the poor.' As he said this, he and his companions
disappeared from the man's sight and they were never seen
again. The man went back into the town. Half of it he found
completely destroyed and overthrown, together with the inhabitants and their flocks. Later on many of them were taken out of
the ruins dead, those few who were still alive being badly hurt.
The promises made by the Angel of the Lord, if I may call him
that, were fulfilled. When the man reached his own home he
found everybody there unharmed; but they were mourning the
death of their neighbours, who had met their end in all the
houses round about. The right hand of the Lord had protected
him and all his household in the midst of the unrighteous, and
he was saved from the peril of death, just as they tell of Lot in
Sodom long ago.

25. In Gaul the bubonic plague which I have so often had
occasion to mention attacked Marseilles. A terrible famine
afflicted Angers, Nantes and Le Mans. These were the beginning of sorrows, as our Lord said in the Gospels: 'And there
shall be famines, and pestilences, and earthquakes, in divers
places.'[74] For false Christs and false prophets shall rise, and
shall shew signs and wonders in the sky, to seduce, if it were
possible, even the elect.'[75] That is exactly what happened at this
time.

As he himself explained later on, a man from Bourges went
into a forest glade to cut down some wood, which he needed for
a job which he had undertaken. He was attacked by a swarm of
flies, and as a result he became insane and remained so for two
whole years. One can well imagine that this was some evil
machination of the Devil. He wandered through the neighbouring towns and so made his way to the province of Arles. There
he dressed himself up in animal skins and spent his time in

74. Matthew 24, 7.   75. Mark 13, 22.

prayer as if he were a religious. In order to encourage him in his
deception, the Devil gave him the power of prophesying the
future. As a result, he left Arles and moved on from that province, with the intention of practising even greater deceptions.
He came eventually to the Javols area, and there he announced
himself as someone of great importance, eventually going so far
as to pretend that he was Christ. With him he took a woman
who pretended to be his sister and whom he called Mary. Great
crowds of people flocked to see him and brought out their sick.
He laid hands upon them, to restore them to health. Those who
gathered round him gave him clothes, and gifts of gold and
silver. All this he handed over to the poor, which helped him in
his deception. He would lie on the ground, saying prayer after
prayer, with the woman about whom I have told you: then he
would rise to his feet and tell those who stood round to begin
worshipping him again. He foretold the future, prophesying
that some would fall ill and that others would suffer affliction,
while to a few he promised good fortune. All this he did by
devilish arts and by tricks which I cannot explain. A great
number of people were deceived by him, not only the un-
educated, but even priests in orders. More than three thousand
people followed him wherever he went. Then he began to rob
and despoil those whom he met on the road, giving to the poor
and needy all that he took. He moved to the neighbourhood of
Le Velay and then made his way to Le Puy. There he encamped
round the local churches with his army of camp-followers. He
drew up a sort of battle-line and made ready to attack Aurelius,
who was at that time Bishop of the diocese. He sent messengers
ahead to announce his coming, men who danced naked and
capered about. The Bishop was quite put out. He chose some of
the toughest of his servants and told them to go and find out
what it all meant. One of them, the man in charge, bowed low as
if to kiss the man's knees and then held him tight. He ordered
him to be seized and stripped; then he himself drew his sword
and cut him down where he stood. So fell and died this Christ,
more worthy to be called an Antichrist. All his followers were
dispersed. Mary was submitted to torture and she revealed all

the man's hallucinations and tricks. Those whose mind he had so far deranged by his devilish devices that they believed in him never recovered their full sanity. They continued to profess that he was Christ and that Mary had a share in his divinity.

Quite a number of men now came forward in various parts of Gaul and by their trickery gathered round themselves foolish women who in their frenzy put it about that they were saints. These men acquired great influence over the common people. I saw quite a few of them myself. I did my best to argue with them and to make them give up their inane pretensions.

26.   Ragnemod, Bishop of Paris, died.[76] His brother Faramod, who was a priest, put his name forward for the bishopric. Eusebius, who was a merchant and a Syrian by race, was, however, elected in Ragnemod's place, but only as the result of bribery. Once he had been enthroned as Bishop, Eusebius dismissed the entire household of his predecessor and replaced them by a number of other Syrians.

Sulpicius, Bishop of Bourges, died. Eustasius, a deacon of Autun, was elected to take over his diocese.

27.   An altercation now arose between certain Franks in Tournai. The immediate cause was that the son of one of them angrily and repeatedly rebuked the son of another, who had married his sister, for neglecting his wife and going after loose women. The young man at fault took no notice. The ill-feeling reached such a pitch that the girl's brother attacked his brother-in-law and killed him, with some of his relations. Then the brother in his turn was murdered by those who had supported his brother-in-law. In the end not a single member of either family remained alive, except one survivor for whom there was no opponent left. The next thing which happened was that relations of each of the two families started quarrelling with each other. They were warned by Queen Fredegund on a number of occasions to give up their feud and to make peace once more, for if the dispute continued it would become a public nuisance of

76. A.D. 591.

considerable dimensions. This attempt at reconciliation by soothing talk was not a success, and in the end Fredegund silenced both sides by the axe. She invited a great number of people to supper and she made the three survivors sit on the same bench. The meal lasted a long time, until darkness fell. The table was then removed, as is the Frankish custom, but the three sat on, still occupying the same bench on which they had been placed. They kept on drinking wine until they were completely tipsy. Their servants were as drunk as their masters, and each of them soon fell asleep in the corner of the room where he had collapsed. Three men with three axes were lined up by the Queen behind the three enemies and, as they went on chatting, these swung their weapons and decapitated them with one blow, so to speak. Everyone then went home. The men were called Charivald, Leudovald and Waldin. When the news reached their other relations, they set a close watch on Fredegund. Then they sent messengers to King Childebert to say that she should be arrested and executed. As a result the Champenois were called out, but they delayed so long that, with the help of her supporters, Fredegund escaped and found refuge somewhere else.

28. The next thing which Fredegund did was to send messengers to King Guntram. 'Will my lord the King please come to Paris?' she asked.'My son is his nephew. He should have the boy taken there and arrange for him to be baptized. It is for the King to receive him from the baptismal font, and he should deign to treat him as his own son.' When he heard this, King Guntram summoned some of his Bishops, Aetherius of Lyons, Syagrius of Autun, Flavius of Chalon-sur-Saône and a few others whom he wanted to have with him. He told them to set off for Paris and promised that he would soon follow. At this ceremony there were also to be present many of Guntram's officials, the counts and the household officers needed to provide all that was necessary for the King's coming. The King had no sooner decided that he must be present in person than he developed gout in his feet. However, he recovered and set off for

Paris. He made his way straight to his country estate at Rueil outside the city. He had the boy brought to him there and he ordered preparations to be made for the baptism in the village of Nanterre.

Just as these arrangements were being completed, envoys arrived from King Childebert. 'This was not what you promised to your nephew Childebert only a short time ago,' ran their message. 'You are busy establishing friendly relations with his enemies. As far as I can see, you are not keeping your promises at all. On the contrary, you are breaking them all, for what you are doing is confirming this child in his right to the royal throne in the city of Paris. God will sit in judgement on you for having forgotten all your pledges, which were, moreover, freely given.'[77] 'I shall certainly not break the treaty which I made with my nephew, King Childebert,' answered Guntram. 'He ought not to take offence just because I receive from the holy font my brother's son, who is, moreover, his own cousin. This is a request which no Christian can refuse. As God knows full well, I am performing this act in no deceitful spirit, but in all the simplicity of a pure heart, for I tremble to think what divine anger I should incur if I did otherwise. No indignity is being done to our race when this child is received by me at the holy font. If a master can receive his own household dependants, why cannot I receive my own close blood-relation and make him my own son by the spiritual grace of baptism? Back you go now and say this to your master: "The treaty which I have made with you I shall observe in its smallest detail. As long as you continue to keep your side of it, it will certainly not be broken by me." '

As he said this King Guntram dismissed the messengers, stepped forward to the holy font, and presented the boy for baptism. He received him back in his arms and said that he wished him to be called Lothar. 'May he grow to man's estate,' he added, 'and be a living embodiment of this name.[78] May he

77. The envoys are referring to the terms of the Treaty of Andelot.

78. The proper name Lothar is cognate with the *MG* adjective *lauter* = clear.

one day enjoy such power as the King who bore the name before him.' When the ceremony was over, Guntram invited the small boy to a banquet and gave him many gifts. The King then received a similar invitation from the young prince, and was given many presents in his turn. When he left he decided to return to Chalon-sur-Saône.

29. Here begin the miracles and the death of Abbot Aredius,[79] who in this year[80] ended his life here below and went to heaven at our Lord's command. He came originally from Limoges, a man of free birth, being descended from quite important people in those parts. He was sent to King Theudebert and joined the group of noble youths attached to the royal household. At that time Nicetius, a man of great sanctity, was Bishop of the town of Trier. He was considered by his flock to be a remarkably eloquent preacher, and he was famed far and wide for his good works and his miracles. He noticed the young man in the King's palace. He perceived some divine quality in his face, and he ordered Aredius to follow him. He left the King's palace and joined Nicetius. They went together to the Bishop's cell and talked of those matters which are the concern of God. The young Aredius asked the saintly Bishop to correct him in his errors, to be his teacher and to give him instruction in the Holy Scriptures. He was full of burning zeal for his studies. He passed some time with Bishop Nicetius and then he had his head tonsured. One day when the clergy were chanting psalms in the cathedral, a dove flew down from the ceiling, fluttered gently round Aredius and then alighted on his head. This was in my opinion a clear sign that he was filled with the grace of the Holy Ghost. He was embarrassed by what had happened and tried to drive the dove away. It flew round for a while and then settled down again, first on his head and then on his shoulder. Not only did this happen in the cathedral, but when Aredius went off to the Bishop's cell the dove accompanied him. This was repeated day after day, to the great surprise of Nicetius.

Aredius' father and brother both died, and this man of God,

79. Aredius is the French Saint Yrieix.   80. A.D. 591.

filled, as I have said, with the Holy Ghost, went back home to console his mother Pelagia,[81] who had no one to look after her except her one remaining son. He was by now devoting all his time to fasting and to prayers, and he asked his mother to go on being responsible for all the household duties, to be in charge of the servants, the tilling of the fields and the culture of the vines, so that nothing should come between him and his praying. There was only one commitment for which he wanted to remain responsible, and that was that he should have control of the building of churches. What more can I tell you? He built churches to the glory of God's saints, collected relics for them and tonsured as monks his own family retainers. He founded a monastery[82] in which was observed the Rule of Cassain, Basil and the other abbots who had regulated the monastic life. His saintly mother provided food and clothing for all the monks. She did not allow this heavy responsibility to interrupt her prayers to God. No matter what she was doing she continued to pray and her words rose up like fragrant incense, finding favour in God's sight. Meanwhile the sick began to flock from all sides to the saintly Aredius. He restored them to health by making the sign of the Cross on each with his hand. If I tried to write all their names down one by one, I should never be able to list them all or to give you a complete record. One thing I know, that no sick man ever came to him without going away cured. Here are a few details of the more important miracles which he performed.

One day he was on a pilgrimage with his mother to the church of Saint Julian the martyr. That evening they reached a spot which was dry and sterile, for no water ran there. 'Son,' said his mother to him, 'we have no water. We cannot possibly spend the night here.' Aredius prostrated himself in prayer and continued to supplicate our Lord for a very long time. Then he stood up and stuck the stick which he was holding in his hand in the ground. He twisted it round in a circle two or three times and then with a happy smile pulled it out. So much water

81. Pelagia died in A.D. 572; cp. *GC*, 104.
82. The monastery of Saint Yrieix in the Limousin.

gushed out that not only was there enough for their own present needs but they were able to water their animals.[83]

Not so long ago, when Aredius was on a journey, great rain clouds began to blow up. As soon as he saw this, he bowed his head a little over the horse which he was riding and raised his hand to God. He had no sooner finished his prayer than the cloud split into two parts: all round them the rain poured down in torrents, but not a single drop fell on them.

A citizen of Tours called Wistrimund, commonly known as Tatto, was suffering terribly from toothache. His whole jaw was swollen. He went off to find this saintly man. Aredius placed his hand on the bad place, whereupon the pain immediately stopped and never plagued the man again. Wistrimund himself told me this story. As for the miracles which our Lord performed at his hands through the power of Saint Julian the martyr and the blessed Saint Martin, I have recorded most of them in my *Book of Miracles* just as he himself told them to me.[84]

When with Christ's help he had performed these miracles, and many others like them, he came to Tours just after the feast of Saint Martin. He stayed with me for a while, and then he told me that he was not long for this world and that his death was assuredly near. He said good-bye and then went on his way, giving thanks to God that he had been permitted before his death to kiss the tomb of the holy Bishop. He returned to his cell, made his will and set all his affairs in order, appointing the two Bishops, Saint Martin and Saint Hilary, as his heirs. Then he fell ill of dysentery and began to ail. On the sixth day of his illness, a certain woman, who had long been possessed of an unclean spirit of which the Saint had not been able to cure her, and whose hands were bound behind her back, began to shout: 'Run, citizens! Leap for joy, you people! Go out to meet the saints and martyrs who are gathering together for the passing of Saint Aredius! Here is Julian of Brioude, and here Privatus of Mende. Martin has come from Tours and Martial from Aredius' own city. Here come Saturninus of Toulouse, Denis of

83. This is an early example of water-divining.
84. Cp. *VP*, 17; *VSJ*, 41; *VSM*, 2, 39; 3, 24; 4, 6; *GC*, 9 and 102.

Paris and all the others now in heaven to whom you are wont to pray as God's saints and martyrs.' She began to shout all this just as night was falling. Her master had her tied up, but he was unable to hold her. She broke her bonds and hurried off to the monastery, shouting as she went. Only a short time later the saintly man breathed his last, there being considerable evidence that he was taken up by angels.

During his funeral, just as the grave was closing over him, Aredius cleansed this woman from the curse of the devil who infested her, together with another woman possessed by an even more evil spirit. It is my belief that it was by God's will that he was unable to cure them while in the body, so that his funeral might be glorified by the miracle. When the ceremony was over, a third woman who was dumb and suffered from a gaping rictus, came to his tomb and kissed it, whereupon she received the gift of speech.

30. In the April of this year[85] a terrible epidemic killed off the people in Tours and in Nantes. Each person who caught the disease was first troubled with a slight headache and then died. Rogations were held and there was fasting and strict abstinence, while alms were given to the poor. In this way the wrath of God was turned aside and things became better.

In the town of Limoges a number of people were consumed by fire from heaven for having profaned the Lord's day by transacting public business. This day is holy, for in the beginning it first saw light created and it gleamed bright in witness of our Lord's Resurrection: it must therefore be observed punctiliously by Christians, and no public business should then be done. Some people were also burnt by this fire in Tours, but not on a Sunday.

There was a terrible drought which destroyed all the green pasture. As a result there were great losses of flocks and herds, which left few animals for breeding purposes. As the prophet Habakkuk foretold: 'The flock shall be cut off from the fold, and there shall be no herd in the stalls.'[86] This epidemic

85. A.D. 591.   86. Habakkuk 3, 17.

not only afflicted the domestic cattle, but it also decimated the various kinds of wild animals. Throughout the forest glades a great number of stags and other beasts were found lying dead in places difficult of access. The hay was destroyed by incessant rain and by the rivers which overflowed, there was a poor grain harvest, but the vines yielded abundantly. Acorns grew, but they never ripened.

31. HERE IN CHRIST'S NAME BEGINS THE LIST OF THE BISHOPS OF TOURS.

In my earlier books I have mentioned them in passing, but it seems a good idea to run over the list in correct order, and with length of service, from the moment when the first preacher of the Gospel came to Tours.

The first Bishop, Gatianus, was sent by the Pope of Rome in the first year of the Emperor Decius.[87] At that time a vast number of pagans addicted to idolatry lived in the city. By his preaching Gatianus managed to convert some of them to the Lord. He often had occasion to hide from the attacks of those in high place who, when they found him, subjected him to insults and abuse. He used to celebrate the holy mysteries secretly on Sunday in crypts and other hiding-places, with the handful of Christians whom, as I have told you, he had converted. He was a very pious and God-fearing man; had he not been so, he would never have abandoned his home, his relations and his fatherland for the love of our Lord. In such circumstances and of his own free will, or so they say, he lived in the city for fifty years. Gatianus died in peace and was buried in the cemetery in the Christian quarter. The see then remained vacant for thirty-seven years.

In the first year of the Emperor Constans,[88] Litorius was

87. Saint Gatianus died *c.* 301. Decius was Emperor from A.D. 249 to 251, so that Saint Gatianus held the bishopric of Tours for some fifty-two years.

88. Constans became co-Emperor with his brother Constantinus in A.D. 337.

consecrated as the second Bishop. He was one of the townsfolk of Tours and a man of great piety. It was he who built the first church inside the town of Tours, for the Christians were now numerous. He converted this first church from the house of one of the senators. It was during the lifetime of Litorius that Saint Martin began to preach in Gaul. Litorius held the see for thirty-three years. He died in peace[89] and was buried in the church mentioned above, which today is named after him.

Saint Martin, the third Bishop,[90] was consecrated in the eighth year of Valens and Valentinian. He came from the town of Sabaria in Pannonia.[91] In his love of God he first of all founded a monastery in the Italian town of Milan. He was beaten with sticks and driven out of Italy by heretics because he had the courage to preach the Holy Trinity. As a consequence he came to Gaul, converted a great number of pagans, and knocked down their temples and idols. He performed many miracles among the people: before he was made Bishop he raised two men from the dead, but after his consecration he raised only one. He translated the body of Saint Gatianus and buried him beside the tomb of Saint Litorius, in the church named after this latter. He persuaded Maximus against the war which he was planning in Spain in an attempt to wipe out the heretics, considering it sufficient for them to be expelled from Catholic churches and from Catholic communion. When his earthly course was run, he died in Candes, a village in his own diocese, in his eighty-first year. From that village he was carried by boat and buried in Tours on the spot where his tomb is now venerated. I have read a life of Saint Martin in three books written by Sulpicius Severus.[92] He manifests himself still today by many miracles. In the monastery now called Marmoutier[93] he built a church in honour of the Apostles Saint Peter and

89. Presumably in A.D. 370.

90. Saint Martin, Bishop of Tours, A.D. 371–97.

91. Sabaria is now Szombathely in Hungary.

92. The *De vita Beati Martini* by Sulpicius Severus, who died in A.D. 410.

93. Later the great Benedictine house of Marmoutier (Maius Monasterium) at Sainte-Radégonde, near Tours.

Saint Paul. He destroyed pagan shrines, baptized the heathen and built churches in a number of villages, Langeais, Sonnay, Amboise, Ciran-la-Latte, Tournon and Candes. Martin occupied the see for twenty-six years, four months and seventeen days. It remained vacant for twenty days.

Bricius, the fourth Bishop, was consecrated in the second year of Arcadius and Honorius, when they were reigning together.[94] He was a citizen of Tours. In the thirty-third year of his episcopate he was accused by his fellow-citizens of the crime of fornication. They drove him out and consecrated Justinian. Bricius made his way to the Pope of Rome. Justinian went after him, but he died in the town of Vercelli. The Tourangeaux remained hostile to Bricius and they elected Armentius. Bricius stayed seven years with the Pope, and then he was found innocent of any crime and ordered to return to his city. He had a small church constructed over Saint Martin's body and there he himself was buried. As he re-entered his city through one gate, Armentius, who had died, was carried out by another. As soon as Armentius was buried, Bricius was enthroned again in his diocese. They say that he built churches in the villages of Clion, Brèches, Ruan, Brizay and Chinon. When the two periods are added together, his episcopate lasted forty-seven years. When Bricius died he was buried in the church which he had built over Saint Martin.

Eustochius was consecrated as the fifth Bishop.[95] He was a pious, God-fearing man, descended from a senatorial family. He is said to have built churches in the villages of Braye, Yzeures, Loches and Dolus. He also built a church inside the city of Tours, and there he deposited the relics of the martyrs Saint Gervasius and Saint Protasius. It was Saint Martin who brought these relics from Italy, as Saint Paulinus tells us in one of his letters. Eustochius held the see for seventeen years. He was buried in the church which Bishop Bricius had built over Saint Martin.

94. A.D. 397. Saint Bricius was Bishop of Tours from A.D. 397 to 443. He is known in France as Saint Brice.

95. Saint Eustochius was Bishop of Tours from A.D. 443 to 460.

Perpetuus was consecrated as the sixth Bishop.[96] He, too, was of a senatorial family, or so they say, and a relative of his predecessors. He was a man of some wealth and he had property in quite a few cities. He pulled down the church which Bishop Bricius had earlier constructed over Saint Martin, and built another of greater size and wonderful workmanship. He translated the blessed body of the venerable Saint to the apse of this new church. It was he who instituted the fasts and vigils which are still observed in Tours throughout the course of the year. I possess a written list of these. It runs as follows:

Fasts

At Whitsun, the fourth and sixth days of the week, until the Nativity of Saint John.[97]
From 1 September to 1 October, two fasts each week.
From 1 October until the Burial of Saint Martin,[98] three fasts each week.
From the Burial of Saint Martin until Christmas, three fasts each week.
From the Nativity of Saint Hilary[99] until the middle of February, three fasts each week.

Vigils

At Christmas, in the cathedral.
At Epiphany, in the cathedral.
On the Nativity of Saint John, in Saint Martin's church.
On the anniversary of the Episcopate of Saint Peter,[100] in Saint Peter's church.
On the Resurrection of Jesus Christ our Lord, 27 March, in Saint Martin's church.
At Easter, in the cathedral.
On Ascension Day, in Saint Martin's church.

96. Saint Perpetuus was Bishop of Tours from A.D. 460 to 490.
97. 14 June.   98. 11 November.   99. 13 January.
100. 22 February.

On Whit-Sunday, in the cathedral.

On the Passion of Saint John,[101] in the baptistery of Saint John's church.

On the Feast of the Apostles Saint Peter and Saint Paul,[102] in their own church.

On Saint Martin's Day,[103] in Saint Martin's church.

On Saint Symphorian's Day,[104] in Saint Martin's church.

On the Day of Saint Litorius,[105] in the church of Saint Litorius.

On Saint Martin's Day,[106] in Saint Martin's church.

On the Day of Saint Bricius,[107] in Saint Martin's church.

On Saint Hilary's Day,[108] in Saint Martin's church.

Perpetuus built Saint Peter's church, into which he incorporated the vaulted roof of Saint Martin's old church, this roof being still there today. He also built Saint Lawrence's church at Mont-Louis. During his episcopate churches were built in the villages of Esvres, Mougon, Barrou, Balesmes and Vernou. When he drew up his will he bequeathed all his property in a number of cities to these churches, leaving quite a considerable sum to Tours. Perpetuus occupied the see for thirty years and was buried in Saint Martin's church.

Volusianus was consecrated as the seventh Bishop.[109] He was of a senatorial family, very pious and very rich, a close relative of Bishop Perpetuus, his predecessor. In his day Clovis was already reigning in some of the other towns of Gaul. As a result the Bishop was suspected by the Goths of wishing to subject them to Frankish rule. He was exiled to the town of Toulouse and there he died. In his day the village of Manthelan was constructed, as was also Saint John's church in Marmoutier. Volusianus occupied the see for seven years and two months.

101. 29 August.   102. 29 June.   103. 4 July.
104. 22 August.   105. 13 September.
106. 11 November. There are two feasts of Saint Martin.
107. 3 November.   108. 13 January.
109. Saint Volusianus was Bishop of Tours from A.D. 491 to 498.

Verus was consecrated as the eighth Bishop.[110] He, too, was suspected by the Goths of being committed to the same cause as Volusianus, and he was sent into exile, where he died. He left all his property to the churches and to deserving people. Verus occupied the see for eleven years and eight days.

Licinius came ninth.[111] He was a citizen of Angers. For the love of God he travelled in the East and visited the Holy Places. When he returned he founded a monastery of his own on land which he possessed in the Angers area. Later on he was appointed Abbot of the monastery in which Saint Venantius had been buried. Then he was elected Bishop. In his time King Clovis came back to Tours as victor, after having defeated the Goths. Licinius occupied the see for twelve years, two months and twenty-five days. He was buried in Saint Martin's church.

Theodorus and Proculus came tenth, being appointed to the see at the command of the pious Queen Clotild.[112] They had followed her from Burgundy, where they were already consecrated as Bishops, but they had been expelled from their cities because they had incurred hostility there. They were both very old men. They governed the Church in Tours together for two years and then they were buried in Saint Martin's church.

Dinifius was the eleventh Bishop.[113] He, too, came from Burgundy. It was at the wish of Queen Clotild that he succeeded to the bishopric. She endowed him with a certain property from the royal domain, and then empowered him to do with it what he wished. He bequeathed most of it to his own cathedral, which was a wise decision. The rest of it he left to deserving people. Dinifius occupied the see for ten months. He was buried in Saint Martin's church.

Ommatius came twelfth.[114] He was descended from a sena-

110. Verus was Bishop of Tours from A.D. 498 to 508.

111. Saint Licinius was Bishop of Tours from A.D. 508 to 520. He is known in France as Saint Lézin.

112. Saint Clotild married King Clovis I in A.D. 493. She died in Tours in 545. Theodorus and Proculus presumably were co-Bishops of Tours from A.D. 520 to 521.

113. Dinifius was presumably Bishop of Tours in A.D. 521.

114. Ommatius was Bishop of Tours from A.D. 521 to 525.

torial family and was a native of Clermont-Ferrand. He possessed a great amount of land. When he drew up his will, he distributed his property among the churches near which the land lay. He restored the church consecrated to the relics of Saint Gervasius and Saint Protasius, inside Tours, near the city wall. He began to build Saint Mary's church within the walls, but he left it unfinished. Ommatius occupied the see for four years and five months. When he died he was buried in Saint Martin's church.

Leo was consecrated as the thirteenth Bishop.[115] He had previously been a priest in Saint Martin's church. His hobby was wood-carving. He made a number of pyramidal font-covers, which he then gilded. We still have some of them today. He was talented in other handicrafts, too. Leo occupied the see for six months only and was buried in Saint Martin's church.

Francilio was consecrated as the fourteenth Bishop.[116] He was from Poitiers and came of a senatorial family. He had a wife called Clara, but no sons. They both possessed a great deal of land, most of which they left to Saint Martin's church. The rest they bequeathed to their relations. Francilio occupied the see for two years and six months. When he died he was buried in Saint Martin's church.

Injuriosus was fifteenth.[117] He was a citizen of Tours. He came from a poor family, but he was born free. Queen Clotild died during his episcopate.[118] He finished building Saint Mary's church within the walls of Tours. It was also in his time that the church of Saint Germanus was built, and that the villages of Neuilly and Luzillé were constructed. He instituted the saying of tierce and sext in the cathedral. This still continues today, in the name of God. Injuriosus occupied the see for sixteen years, eleven months and twenty-six days. When he died he was buried in Saint Martin's church.

115. Leo was Bishop of Tours in A.D. 526. He seems to have been an interesting person.
116. Francilio was Bishop of Tours from A.D. 527 to 529.
117. Injuriosus was Bishop of Tours from A.D. 529 to 546.
118. Queen Clotild, now Saint Clotild, died in Tours in A.D. 545.

Baudinus was consecrated as the sixteenth Bishop.[119] He had been one of King Lothar's Referendaries. He had sons of his own. He was much given to charity. He distributed among the poor the money which his predecessors had left, giving away more than twenty thousand pieces of gold. In his day the second village of Neuilly was constructed. It was he who instituted the *mensa* for the canons. Baudinus occupied the see for five years and ten months. When he died he was buried in Saint Martin's church.

Gunthar was consecrated as the seventeenth Bishop.[120] He had been Abbot of the monastery of Saint Venantius. He was formerly a man of great discretion, and during his tenure of office as Abbot he was often sent on diplomatic missions between the various Frankish kings. After his consecration as Bishop he took to drink. He became almost half-witted. This weakness so affected his reason that he was unable to recognize guests whom he knew very well, and he would assail them with insults and abuse. Gunthar occupied the see for two years, ten months and twenty-two days. When he died he was buried in Saint Martin's church. The bishopric then remained vacant for a whole year.

The priest Eufronius was consecrated as the eighteenth Bishop.[121] He came of one of the senatorial families which I have mentioned a number of times. He was a man of great piety and had been a cleric from his early years. In his day much of the city of Tours was burnt down and all the churches with it. He managed to restore two of them, but the third, which was the oldest, he left derelict. Later on Saint Martin's church was burnt by Willichar, when he took refuge there after Chramn's revolt. Eufronius roofed it in with tin, being helped financially in this by King Lothar. Saint Vincent's church was built in his time. Churches were also built in the villages of Thuré, Céré and

119. Baudinus was Bishop of Tours from A.D. 546 to 552.

120. Gunthar was Bishop of Tours from A.D. 552 to 554.

121. Saint Eufronius was Bishop of Tours from A.D. 555 to 573. He was Gregory's first cousin once removed, and the senatorial family which Gregory has mentioned a number of times is his own.

Orbigny. Eufronius occupied the see for seventeen years, died at the age of seventy, and was buried in Saint Martin's church. The bishopric then remained *sede vacante* for nineteen days.

All unworthy as I am, I, Gregory, have been the nineteenth Bishop.[122] When I took over Tours cathedral, in which Saint Martin and all these other priests of the Lord had been consecrated to the episcopal office, it had been destroyed by fire and was in a sorry state of ruin.[123] I rebuilt it, bigger and higher than before, and in the seventeenth year of my episcopate I re-dedicated it.

I was told by certain very elderly priests that the relics of the Agaune martyrs[124] had been deposited there by the men of long ago. In the treasury of Saint Martin's church I came upon the reliquary. It had been taken there because of the miraculous power of the martyrs. The relics themselves were in a terrible state of putrefaction. While vigils were being celebrated in their honour, I took it into my head to pay them another visit, carrying a lighted taper. As I was examining the relics with great care, the church sacristan said to me: 'There is a stone here with a lid on it. I don't know what it contains. I found that those who were sacristans here before me did not know either. I will bring it, and you can examine it carefully and see what is inside.' He fetched the stone and I, of course, opened it. Inside I found a

122. Gregory was consecrated on 24 August 573.

123. The cathedral of Tours, built by Bishop Litorius, 337–71, was destroyed by fire during the episcopate of Gregory's predecessor, Bishop Eufronius. It was left to Gregory to rebuild it. He presumably completed the new building in A.D. 580. Venantius Fortunatus sent him a poem of congratulation, 'Ad ecclesiam Toronicam quae per Episcopum Gregorium renovata est', *Carmina*, 10, 6.

124. The Emperor Diocletian sent the Theban legion to Gaul in A.D. 287 to quell a revolt. These troops, under their commander Mauritius, were Christians. They refused to take part in official pagan sacrifices and they were martyred. The monastery built on the spot in the fourth century was called Saint-Maurice-d'Agaune. Its present building dates from 1707–13. Saint-Maurice is on the River Rhône, near to where it runs into the eastern end of the Lake of Geneva. It was the Celtic Acaunum. Sigismund, King of Burgundy, restored the monastery and took refuge there in A.D. 523, cp. *HF*, III, 5–6.

silver reliquary, which contained not only the relics of those who had actually seen the Holy Legion but also the remains of many saints, martyrs and holy men. I took charge of it, and at the same time I also took a number of other hollowed-out stones in which had been preserved the relics of other holy apostles and martyrs. I was delighted with this gift sent by God. In my gratitude to Him I kept a number of vigils and said Masses. Then I placed in the cathedral all that I had found, except that I put the relics of the martyrs Saint Cosmas and Saint Damian[125] in Saint Martin's cell, which adjoins the cathedral.

I found the walls of Saint Martin's church damaged by fire.[126] I ordered my workmen to use all their skill to paint and decorate them, until they were as bright as they had previously been. I had a baptistery built adjacent to the church, and there I placed the relics of Saint John and Saint Sergius[127] the martyr. In the old baptistery I put the relics of Saint Benignus the martyr.[128] In many other places in Tours and its immediate neighbourhood I dedicated churches and oratories, and these I enriched with relics of the saints. It would be too long to give you a complete list.

I, Gregory, have written the ten books of this *History*,[129] seven books of *Miracles*[130] and one on the *Lives of the*

125. Saint Cosmas and Saint Damian were martyred in Cilicia in the third century. For their church in Rome see *HF*, X, 1.

126. *Basilicae sanctae parietes*, the walls of Saint Martin's church, as distinct from *ecclesiam urbis Turonicae*, Tours cathedral, p. 601, note 123. The cathedral had been burnt at some time during the episcopate of Saint Eufronius, A.D. 555–73. The church was burnt by Willichar *c.* 560 and King Lothar restored the roof, *HF*, IV, 20. Maybe the walls still lacked frescoes. On the other hand, in his poem on the restoration of the cathedral, Venantius Fortunatus expressly mentions the murals commissioned by Gregory. There may be confusion here; but the walls of both buildings would have frescoes.

127. Saint Sergius was martyred in Syria in the third century; cp. *HF*, VII, 31.

128. Saint Benignus was martyred in Dijon *c.* 179.

129. The *Historiae* or *Historia Francorum*.

130. The *Liber in gloria Martyrum Beatorum*, the *Liber de passione et*

Fathers.[131] I have composed a book of *Commentaries on the Psalms.*[132] I also wrote a book on the *Offices of the Church.*[133] I know very well that my style in these books is lacking in polish. Nevertheless I conjure you all, you Bishops of the Lord who will have charge of Tours cathedral after my unworthy self, I conjure you all, I say, by the coming of our Lord Jesus Christ and by the Judgement Day feared by all sinners, that you never permit these books to be destroyed, or to be rewritten, or to be reproduced in part only with sections omitted, for otherwise when you emerge in confusion from this Judgement Day you will be condemned with the Devil. Keep them in your possession, intact, with no amendments and just as I have left them to you.

Whoever you are, you Bishop of God, even if our own Martianus (Capella) himself has given you instruction in the Seven Arts,[134] if he has taught you grammar so that you may read, if he has shown you by his dialectic how to follow the parts of a disputation, by his rhetoric how to recognize the different metres, by his geometry how to reckon the measurements of surfaces and lines, by his astronomy how to observe the stars in their courses, by his arithmetic how to add and subtract numbers in their relationships, by his book on harmony how to set together in your songs the modulation of mellifluous sounds, even if you are an acknowledged master in all these skills, and if, as a result, what I have written seems uncouth to you, despite all this, do not, I beg you, do violence to my Books. You may rewrite them in verse if you wish to, supposing that they find favour in your sight; but KEEP THEM INTACT.

---

virtutibus Sancti Juliani martyris, the *De virtutibus beati Martini episcopi* in four Books, and the *Liber in gloria Confessorum* make up the 'seven books of *Miracles*'.

131. The *Liber vitae Patruum*.

132. *In Psalterii tractatum commentarius*. This is lost, apart from the *incipit* and the chapter-headings.

133. The *De Cursu Stellarum ratio*.

134. This paragraph refers to the *Satiricon* of Martianus Capella, *fl.* in the fifth century: see the Introduction, p. 49. The book is also known as the *Liber de nuptiis Mercurii et Philologiae* ('The marriage of Philology and Mercury'), the *Disciplinae* and *De septem disciplinis*.

I finished writing this History in the twenty-first year after my consecration. In the section above I have listed the Bishops of Tours and set out their years of service. I have not recorded the years in order as in a chronicle, for I have not been able to discover the exact intervals between the consecrations.

The total sum of years since the world began is, then, as follows:

From the Beginning until the Deluge, 2242 years.

From the Deluge until the Passage of the Red Sea by the Children of Israel, 1404 years.

From the Passage of the Red Sea until the Resurrection of our Lord, 1808 years.

From the Resurrection of our Lord until the death of Saint Martin, 412 years.

From the death of Saint Martin until the year mentioned above, that is the twenty-first after my own consecration, which is the fifth year of Gregory, Pope of Rome, the thirty-third of King Guntram and the nineteenth of Childebert II, 197 years.

This makes a grand total of 5792 years.[135]

IN THE NAME OF CHRIST HERE ENDS BOOK X
OF MY HISTORY

135. As the figures stand the total is, of course, 6063. All the figures are given in roman numerals, which are often miscopied by scribes.

INDEX

What follows is at once an index and an *index raisonné* of my translation of Gregory's *Historiae*. Every proper name and place-name mentioned in the text is listed in this index; and all the major events and most of the minor ones which occur are given in succinct form under the names of the persons concerned in them.

A

Aaron, 161, 310

Abel, 65; he is killed by his brother Cain, 70

Abijah, son of Rehoboam, 78; second King of Judah, 78

Abiud, son of Zerubbabel, 79

Abraham, 65; son of Terah, 72; born in the reign of Ninus, King of Nineveh, 72; received the promise of the birth of Christ, 72; he offered the sacrifice of Isaac on Mount Calvary, 72; received circumcision, 72; originally called Abram, 73; father of Isaac, 73; contemporary with Ninus, King of Nineveh, 73; 80, 161, 248, 249, 310, 564

Abraham, Abbot of the monastery of Saint-Cyr in Clermont-Ferrand, 134

Achim, son of Sadoc, 79

Adam, 65; Gregory begins his *History of the Franks* with Adam, 69; created by God in His own image, 69; before he had committed sin, similar to our Lord and Saviour, 69; expelled from Paradise, 70; from Adam to Noah there are ten generations, 71; buried in the land of the Anakim, 71; 452

Aegidius, Roman general, Master of Both Services, (=Afranius Syagrius Aegidius), 101, 128; chosen as King of the Franks during the deposition of Childeric and reigns for eight years, 128; his death, 132; he leaves a son called Syagrius, 132; once lived in Soissons, 139

Aelia, name for Jerusalem, as restored by Hadrian, 85

Aeneid quoted: I, 46–7, 141; I, 100–101, 118, 224; III, 56–7, 242; III, 56–7, 454; VIII, 148–9, 486

Aetherius, Bishop of Lisieux, 326; is greatly maligned and nearly killed by an evil priest from Le Mans, 366–70; escapes to King Guntram, 369; is reinstated and returns in triumph to Lisieux, 369–70; signs the letter to Bishop Gundegisel about the revolt in Saint Radegund's nunnery, 533

Aetherius, Bishop of Lyons, 587; is present at the baptism of Lothar II, 587

Aetius, Archdeacon of Paris, 276; speaks up for Saint Praetextatus, 276

Aetius, Roman general, 101; defeats Attila, King of the Huns, outside

605

Orleans, 116–17; the wife of Aetius prays to the Apostles Peter and Paul to save her husband, 117; defeats Attila in a second battle, 118; mentioned by the historian Renatus Profuturus Frigeridus in Book XII of his *Historia*, 118–19; as Governor of the Palace sent as an envoy to the Huns by John the tyrant, 119; his father was Gaudentius, 119; his mother was a wealthy Italian noblewoman, 119; like his father, a member of the Praetorian Guard, 119; sent to Alaric II, King of the Visigoths, as hostage, 119; and to the Huns, 119; marries the daughter of Carpilio, 119; his personal qualities, 119; murdered by the Emperor Valentinianus III, 119; his trumpeter Occila kills Valentinianus III, 119

Africa, the Vandals cross over to, 108; the Catholics there persecuted by the Arian Vandals, 108; Ingund thought to be there, 453

Agastus, second King of the Athenians, 80

Agatadis, sixteenth King of the Assyrians, 80

Agathais, the, rob King Chilperic's ambassadors when they are wrecked, 327–8

Agaune, 601; see also Saint-Maurice d'Agaune

Agde, in Septimania, Visigothic territory, 327; Chilperic's ambassadors wrecked there, 327; Pronimius had been Bishop there, but expelled, 512

Agen, attacked by Duke Desiderius, 344; 384; Saint Vincent martyred there, 418; his church, 418; Antidius is Bishop, 435; 517

Ageric, Saint, Bishop of Verdun, 191; exorcises a false prophetess, 426–7; 479; intercedes with Childebert II for Duke Guntram Boso, whom he had baptized, 488; produces Guntram Boso at court, 488–9; put in charge of Guntram Boso by Childebert II, 489; grieved by the killing of Duke Berthefried in his church-house, 495; dies, 511

Agila, King of the Visigoths in Spain after Theudegisel, 187; the Emperor Justinian sends an army against him, 202; assassinated, 202

Agilan, an Arian, sent as envoy by Leuvigild to King Chilperic, 307; Gregory of Tours disputes with him on the Holy Trinity, 307–10

Agin, represents Tetradia, when sued by her ex-husband, Count Eulalius, 556

Aginus, Count, 502; supports Chramnesind in his troubles, 502

Agiulf, deacon of Tours, 543; in Rome to seek relics, 543; sees floods and resulting plague there, 543; describes to Gregory of Tours the election of Gregory the Great as Pope, 543–7

Agnes, first Mother Superior of the nunnery of the Holy Cross in Poitiers, 530, 535, 536, 537, 538; for details of her role in the revolt, see Holy Cross, the nunnery of the, in Poitiers

Agricius, Bishop of Troyes, 464; sent by King Guntram to the court of Lothar II to investigate the murder of Saint Praetextatus, 464–5

Agricola, Bishop of Nevers, signs the letter to Bishop Gundegisel about the revolt in Saint Radegund's nunnery, 533

Agricola, Saint, 131; his relics brought from Bologna to Clermont-Ferrand by Bishop Namatius, 131

Index

Agricola, Saint, Bishop of Chalon-sur-Saône, 252; his worthy life, 312; dies, 312; seen in a vision by King Guntram, 438

Agricola, the patrician, 218; dismissed by King Guntram, 218

Agroetius, Head of Chancery to Jovinus, killed by the army commanders of the Emperor Honorius, 124

Ahaz, son of Jotham, 78; King of Judah, 78

Aire, 414; Rusticus is Bishop, 414; added to the territory over which Ennodius is Duke, 487; 504

Aisne, River, 370; with the help of an eagle, the head and body of Abbot Lupentius are fished out of it in two sacks, 370

Aix-en-Provence, 240; Pientius is Bishop, 343

Alais, small bishopric under the jurisdiction of Saint Dalmatius, Bishop of Rodez, 260; Munderic is Bishop, 260

Alamanni, the, ruled over by King Chroc, 88; they invade Gaul, 88–9; they kill Saint Privatus, Bishop of Javols, 89–90; they are also called the Suebi, 106; they occupy Galicia, 106; they quarrel with the Vandals, 106; they cross to Tangiers, 108; they make a treaty with the tyrant Eugenius, 123; 124; beaten by Childeric and Odovocar, 132; King Clovis beats the Alamanni and is baptized as a result, 143; 153

Alani, the, defeated in battle by Thorismund the Goth, 118; their King Respendial, 123; 124

Alaric II, King of the Visigoths, 102; Aetius is sent to him as a hostage, 119; Syagrius flees to him in Toulouse, but Alaric hands him back to Clovis, 139; 148; makes a treaty with Clovis at Amboise, 150; beaten and killed by Clovis at the battle of Vouillé, 153–4; 161

Albi, 113; Saint Eugenius, Bishop of Carthage, is exiled there by King Hunderic, 113; Diogenianus is Bishop, 129; 154; Saint Salvius is Bishop, 311; 356; plague, 364; 388; 389; Desiderius is Bishop, 455; given back to Childebert II by King Guntram, 476; Duke Desiderius withdraws to Toulouse as a result, 476; 504

Albigeois, the, 389, 455

Albinus made Governor of Provence by King Sigibert, 238; assaults and fines the Archdeacon Vigilius in Marseilles, 239; Sigibert makes him pay back four times the sum, 239; 337; becomes Bishop of Uzès, 337; dies, 337

Albinus, Saint, 347

Albofled, sister of King Clovis, 144; baptized, 144; immediately dies, 144; consoling letter from Saint Remigius to Clovis, 145

Alboin, King of the Longobards, 196; marries Chlothsind, daughter of King Lothar I, 198; 235; invades Italy, 235; marries Rosamund, 236; she poisons him, 236; 272; 273

Alchima, wife of Apollinaris, 162; aunt of Arcadius, 171; arrested and sent into exile, 171

Alithius, Bishop of Cahors, 129

Allier, River, in spate, 295

Amalaric, son of Alaric II, 154; fought at Vouillé, 154; escaped to Spain,

154; marries Clotild, daughter of King Clovis, 162; maltreats her because of her Catholic faith, 170; Childebert I visits his sister Clotild in Spain, 170; Amalaric is killed in Barcelona, 170; 187

Amalasuntha, daughter of Theodoric, King of Italy, and Audofleda, 160; according to Gregory, has a slave Traguilla as her lover, 187–8; poisons her mother, 188; killed by Theudat, King of Tuscany, 188

Amalo, Duke, 479; attempts to rape a young woman, but she kills him, 513–14

Amandus, Bishop of Bordeaux, 129

Amalaberg, wife of Hermanfrid, King of the Thuringians, 164; her evil influence over her husband, 164

Amatus the patrician, 236; replaces Celsus, 236; beaten in battle by the Longobards, 236

Amboise, an island in the River Loire, 150; King Clovis and Alaric II make a treaty there, 150; Saint Martin built the church there, 595

Ambrosius, citizen of Tours, 325; killed by his wife's lover, 345; the name of the murderer was Vedast, 390

Amelius, Bishop of Bigorra, 457; apparently in a plot to murder Childebert II and Brunhild, 457; an impostor in Paris turns out to be one of his servants, 486

Amminadab, son of Ram, 77

Amo, leader of the Longobards, 239; with Rodan and Zaban invades Gaul, 239; marches through Embrun, 240; camps at Saint-Saturnin, 240; captures Arles, 240; ravages La Crau, 240; retreats into Italy, 241

Amon, son of Manasseh, 78; King of Judah, 78; 80

Amsivarii, the, a tribe of Franks, 122

Anakim, the land of the, where Adam was buried, 71; another name for Hebron, 71

Ananias, 309, 349, 535

Anastasius, Abbot of the monastery of Saint Victor in Marseilles, 343; revolts against Bishop Theodore, 343

Anastasius, the Emperor, 154; confers the consulate on King Clovis, 154

Anastasius the priest, 195; lived in Clermont-Ferrand, 205; given some land by Queen Clotild, 205; Bishop Cautinus tries to steal it, 205; buried alive in the crypt of the church of Saint Cassius the martyr, 205; escapes, 205–6

Anatolius, the boy-martyr of Bordeaux, 468–9; becomes insane, 468–9; lives in Tours for a while and helped by Saint Martin, 469

Andarchius, 196; slave and *lector* of Felix, who lived in Marseilles, 241; literary pretensions, 241; leaves Marseilles with Duke Lupus, 241; given employment by King Sigibert, 241; goes to Clermont-Ferrand, 241; tries to marry the daughter of a citizen called Ursus, 241–3; appears before Sigibert in Berny-Rivière, 242; follows Ursus to Le Velay, 243; burnt to death there, 243

Andelot, 503

Index

Andelot, Treaty of, made between King Guntram and King Childebert II, 493–4; Guntram has the whole Treaty read aloud in Chalon-sur-Saône to Gregory of Tours and Bishop Felix, 503–7

Andica, 376; marries the sister of Euric, King of Galicia, 376; forces Euric to become a priest, 376; replaces Euric as King of Galicia, 376; marries Sisegunth, widow of King Mir, Euric's father, 376

Angers, 132; Odovocar, King of the Saxons, reaches Angers, 132; he takes hostages from there, 132; occupied by Childeric, 132; 243; Eunius, Bishop of Vannes, banished there, 292; 305; man from Angers cured of deafness and dumbness by Saint Hospicius, 334–6; earthquake, 350; 359; earthquake, 395; Theodulf is Count, 450; he is expelled by Domigisel, 450; reinstated by Duke Sigulf, 451; Angers harassed by Duke Beppolen, 473; Antestius comes to punish Bobolen for the murder of Domnola, 474; Duke Ebrachar's army there on its retreat from Brittany, 558; Audioveus is Bishop, 566; the deacon Theudulf moves there from Paris, falls over the city wall when drunk and kills himself, 566–7; famine, 584; Saint Licinius was born there and founded a monastery there, 598

Angoulême, 154; Theudebert buried there, 247; Nantinus is Count, 299; his uncle Marachar had been Count before him, 299; Marachar becomes Bishop of Angoulême, 299; Frontinus is Bishop, 299; Heraclius is Bishop, 299; Eparchius a recluse there, 325; 338; Gundovald the Pretender was there, 407; Nicasius is Bishop, 435; 459

Anianus, Saint, Bishop of Orleans, 116; he prays when the Huns advance on the city, 116; goes to Arles to seek help from Aetius, 116; his prayers help Aetius to beat the Huns twice, 116–17

Anille, monastery near Le Mans, 267; Merovech sent there by his father, 267

Animodius, helps Chuppa to escape, 552; is allowed to go free by Flavianus, 553

Anjou, 267, 290

Ansovald, Duke, 258; when Siggo deserts to Childebert II, King Chilperic gives his property to Ansovald, 258; sent to Tours to depose Count Leudast, 313; sent to Spain concerning Rigunth's dowry, 348; comes back, 348; discusses with Gregory of Tours the ways in which Leuvigild, the Arian King of the Visigoths, persecutes the Catholics in Spain, 349; sets out with Rigunth, 379; rallies to Lothar, four-month-old son of the assassinated Chilperic, 392; leaves King Guntram, 441; with Fredegund, 463

Antestius, 432; takes Duke Desiderius to King Guntram, 456; sent to Angers to punish those involved in the death of Domnola, 474; confiscates the goods of Bobolen, 474; moves to Nantes and harasses Bishop Nonnichius for his son's implication in the same murder, 474; moves to Saintes, 474; sent by Guntram to attack Septimania, 517

Anthony, the monk, dies, 64; he was one hundred and five years old, 91

Antichrist, the, 68; he proclaims himself Christ, 68

Antidius, Bishop of Agen, 435; King Guntram is sarcastic to him, 435

Antioch, 85; Saint Ignatius is Bishop. 85; Saint Babylas is Bishop, 86;
   according to Gregory, it is in Egypt, 235; captured by the Persians, 235;
   church of Saint Julian there burnt down, 235; Saint Simeon the Stylite
   lived there, 447; 541; in Armenia, according to Gregory, 582; how the
   city fell to the Persians, 582; the story of the man who, like Lot near
   Sodom, witnessed the destruction of Antioch, 583–4

Antolianus, Saint, martyred at Clermont-Ferrand, 89

Antoninus, the Emperor, 85

Apamea in Syria, 235; captured by the Persians, 235

Apocalypse, the, 562

Apollinaris, son of Saint Sidonius Apollinaris, 154; fought at Vouillé, 154;
   159; his wife Alchima, 162; his sister Placidana, 162; seeks the bishopric
   of Clermont-Ferrand, 162–3; visits Theuderic, 163; is made Bishop of
   Clermont-Ferrand, 163; dies, 163

Apostles, the Passion of the, 64; persecuted by Herod, 83

Aprunculus, Saint, brother of Saint Sidonius Apollinaris, 136; Bishop of
   Langres, 137; expelled by the Burgundes, 137; escapes by being lowered
   from the walls of Dijon, 137; becomes Bishop of Clermont-Ferrand, 137;
   151; death, 162

Aptachar (or Authari). King of the Longobards, 550; takes refuge in
   Pavia, 550; sends peace envoys to King Guntram and Childebert II, 551;
   dies, 551

Aquileia, destroyed by the Huns, 118; the tyrant Maximus went to live
   there, 120

Aquitaines, the two, *Aquitania Prima* and *Aquitania Secunda*, invaded by
   Euric, King of the Visigoths, 138

Aravatius, Bishop of Tongres, 101; foresees the coming of the Huns, 114;
   goes to Rome to pray to Saint Peter, 114; says goodbye to his flock, 115;
   dies in Maestricht, 115; his life is recounted in the *Liber in gloria
   Confessorum*, 115

Arbogast, Frankish leader in the Roman service, 121; winters in Trier, 122;
   comes to Cologne, 122

Arcadius, Senator of Clermont-Ferrand, 169–70; on hearing false rumour
   that Theuderic has been killed, he invites Childebert I to Clermont-
   Ferrand, 170; flees from Theuderic to Bourges, 171; his mother Placidina
   and his aunt Alchima are arrested, 171; sent by Lothar I and Childebert
   to threaten the young sons of Chlodomer, 180

Arcadius, the Emperor, 97, 595

Ardennes, the, 453

Aredius, Saint (=Saint Yrieix), Abbot of Limoges, 445; Saint Vulfolaic
   was his disciple, 445; takes Duke Desiderius to see King Guntram, 456;
   542; dies, 589; came from Limoges, 589; in the household of King Theudebert, 589; a dove alights upon him and accompanies him everywhere,
   589; when his father dies, he goes home to console his mother, Pelagia,
   590; founds a monastery, 590; his miracles, 590–91; a water-diviner,

590–91; cures Wistrimund of toothache, 591; goes to Tours to die and stays with Gregory of Tours, 591; the Saints are present at his passing, 591–2

Aregisel, military commander of Theuderic, 174; besieges and kills the Pretender Munderic in Vitry-le-Brûlé, 174–5

Aregund, third wife of King Lothar I, 197; sister of his wife Ingund, 197; mother of King Chilperic, 197

Argaeus, King of the Macedonians, 80; contemporary of Amon, 80

Argentoratum, old name of Strasbourg, 579

Argives, the, reigned over by Trophas in the time of Moses, 80

Arian heresy, 107; established in Spain by Trasamund, King of the Vandals, 107; the Arians persecute the Catholics in Spain, 107; Cyrola the Arian disputes with Saint Eugenius, Catholic Bishop of Carthage, 110; King Clovis hates the Arians, 151; an evil sect, 161; 302; Goiswinth, second wife of Leuvigild, King of the Visigoths, is an Arian, 302; Arianism is supposed to have been condemned on his deathbed by Leuvigild, 477

Aridius, retainer of King Gundobad, 146; makes peace between Gundobad and King Clovis, 146–7

Arius, 135; how he died in the lavatory, 135; 137; 161; 309; 498

Ark, the, 70; Noah, his wife, his three sons and their wives were all saved in the Ark, 70; represents the Mother Church, 70–71

Arles, receives Saint Trophimus as its Bishop, 87; Chroc, King of the invading Alamanni, is captured and killed there, 90; Saint Anianus, Bishop of Poitiers, visits Aetius there, 116; 184; attacked by King Sigibert, 196; plague in Arles, 199; Theudechild put in a nunnery in Arles, 221; Sigibert sends the men of Clermont-Ferrand under Count Firminus to attack Arles, 223; Celsus attacks Arles, 223; captured by Amo the Longobard, 240; 462; Leudegisel put in charge of the whole area, in order to withhold Recared, 462; Sabaudus is Bishop, 471; Licerius is Bishop, 471; attacked by the Visigoths, 488; Virgil, Abbot of Autun, becomes Bishop, 511; Saint Caesarius had been Bishop, 528; 530; 584

Armenia, 582; a Bishop called Simon arrives in Tours from there, 582; tells how his country was invaded by the Persians, 582–3

Armentarius the Jew, comes to Tours to collect payment, 405; murdered, 406; Injuriosus, the Vice-Count, and Eunomius, the Count, are suspected, with Medard, but the case is not proven, 405–6

Armentius replaces Justinian, who had replaced Saint Bricius as Bishop of Tours, 106; he dies, 106; 595

Arnegisel, 455; in ill favour with Childebert II, who suspected him of having stolen King Sigibert's treasure, 455; his property sequestered, 456; Gregory of Tours saves him from being beheaded, 456

Arphaxad, son of Shem, 72

Arthemius, Saint, Bishop of Clermont-Ferrand, 64, 94; while still a young man, chosen as an envoy to go from Trier to Spain, 94; falls ill and is cured by Saint Nepotianus, 94–5; replaces Saint Nepotianus as Bishop on the latter's death, 95; he himself dies, 129

Arthemius, Saint, Bishop of Sens, 464; sent by King Guntram to the court of Lothar II to investigate the murder of Saint Praetextatus, 464–5

Asa, third King of Judah, 78

Ascension Day, 596

Ascension, the, of Christ, 66, 83, 149, 332

Asclepius, Duke, kills King Chilperic's guards, 349; King Guntram makes amends, 350

Ascovindus, a well-intentioned retainer of Chramn, 211

Ascyla, mother of Theudemer, 125

Asher, son of Jacob, 73

Assyrians, the, ruled over by Ninus, 80; their sixteenth King was Agatadis, 80; their King Eutropes, 80

Asteriolus, servant of Theudebert, 160; he quarrels with Secundinus, 189–90

Asterius, a patrician, 124

Athaloc, an Arian bishop in Spain, 498; refuses to be converted to Catholicism with King Recared, 498–9; dies of depression, 498

Athanagild, King of the Visigoths in Spain, 202; his daughter Brunhild marries King Sigibert, 221; his daughter Galswinth marries King Chilperic, 222; dies, 233; his wife was Goiswinth, 301; 512

Athanaric, King of the Goths, 101; he persecutes the Christians, 113–14; is banished, 114; his relation Gundioc, 141

Athenians, the, ruled over by Agastus, 80

Attalus, 159; his enslavement, 159; nephew of Saint Gregory, Bishop of Langres, and a relative of Saint Gregory of Tours, 175; sent as a hostage and then a slave to Trier, 175; with the help of Leo, the cook of Saint Gregory, he escapes, 175–9

Attica, ruled over by Cecrops, 80

Atticus, Consul, 97

Attila, King of the Huns, 116; he invades Gaul, 116; he advances from Metz to Orleans, 116; defeated there by Aetius, he retires to the plain of Moirey, 116; there he is defeated a second time by Aetius, 118; he retreats, 118

Auch, 454; Faustus is Bishop, 454; Saius is Bishop, 454; Childeric the Saxon flees there, 581

Audinus, citizen of Tours, 429, 517

Audo, accomplice of Fredegund in her malpractices, 399; exacted taxes from free Franks, 399; stripped of all his possessions, 399; seeks sanctuary with Fredegund, 399

Audofleda, sister of King Clovis, 187; marries Theodoric, King of Italy, 187; has a daughter Amalasuntha, 187; she is poisoned by her daughter, 188

Audovald, Duke, one of Childebert II's military commanders, 549; leads an army against the Longobards in Italy, 549; ravages Metz on the way, 549; attacks Milan, 549; returns home after very small success, 550–51

Audovarius, military leader of King Sigibert, 224; beaten by Celsus at Arles, 224

Audovera, first wife of King Chilperic, 223; she bears him three sons, Theudebert, Merovech and Clovis, 223; in Rouen, 255; visited by Merovech there, 255; murdered by Chilperic, 304; the nun Basina was her daughter, 365

Augustus, the second Emperor of Rome, according to Gregory of Tours, 81; originally called Octavian, 81; the month of August is named after him, 81; Jesus Christ was born in the forty-fourth year of his reign, 81

Aunacharius, Bishop of Auxerre, signs the letter to Bishop Gundegisel about the revolt in Saint Radegund's nunnery, 533

Auno, citizen of Tours, 429; killed by Sichar, 429

Aunulf, the man who found Theudebert's body on the battlefield, 247

Aurelius, Bishop of Le Puy, 585; he is assailed by the bogus Christ of Bourges, 585; Aurelius has the impostor killed, 585

Ausanius, friend of Parthenius, the tax-collector, 192; Parthenius murders him, 192

Austadius, Bishop of Nice. 336–7; buries Saint Hospicius, 337

Austrapius, Duke, Governor of Touraine and Poitou, 195; fears Chramn, 214; takes refuge in Saint Martin's church in Tours, 214; favoured by King Lothar I, 214; takes orders and becomes Bishop of Champtoceaux, 214; tries to become Bishop of Poitiers, 214; killed by the Theifali, 214–15

Austrechild, wife of King Guntram, 219; known to her friends as Bobilla, 219; she bears Guntram two sons, Lothar and Chlodomer, 219; 252; maligned by the sons of Magnachar, 274; maligned by Bishop Sagittarius, 286; she had been one of Magnachar's servants, 286; dies of dysentery, 298; expresses a wish that the two doctors who tried to save her should be executed for their pains, 298–9

Austregesil, citizen of Tours, 428–9

Austrinus, Bishop of Orleans, 501; his father's name was Pastor, 501

Austrovald, Count, 476; attacks Carcassonne with Duke Desiderius, 476–7; withdraws from the siege, 477; made Duke when Desiderius is killed, 477; organizes expeditions against the Gascons, 488; sent by King Guntram to attack Carcassonne, 517; insulted by Boso, 517

Authari, see Aptachar

Autun, 131; Saint Eufronius builds the church of Saint Symphorian there, 131; besieged by Childebert I and Lothar I, 171; Saint Syagrius is Bishop, 261; 262; Virgil is Abbot, 511; 531; 586; 587

Auvergne, has a swarm of locusts, 215–16; miraculous portents seen there, 255–6; floods, 295; kept in order by Duke Nicetius, 450

Auxerre, 236; Peonius is Count, 236; Mummolus, his son, replaces him, 236; 272; Aunacharius is Bishop, 533

Avignon, 146; Gundobad takes refuge there, 146; captured by Celsus for

King Guntram, 223; restored by Guntram to King Sigibert, 224; 238; 240; Count Mummolus takes refuge there, 327; the bishopric is offered to Domnolus, who refuses it, 339–40; Gundovald the Pretender joins Mummolus there, 352; Duke Guntram Boso visits Mummolus there, 354; Gundovald, Mummolus and Desiderius all there together, 394; 420; 422; 425; 436; bubonic plague, 582

Avitus, Saint, Abbot of the monastery of Saint-Mesmin-de-Micy, 166; pleads with Chlodomer for Sigismund, 166; 277; 434

Avitus, Saint, Bishop of Clermont-Ferrand, 196; his election, despite the opposition of Count Firminus, 229–30; consecrated in Metz, 230; 251; converts the Jews in Clermont-Ferrand, 265–7; pleads for the gaolbirds of Clermont-Ferrand when by a miracle their chains are twice broken, 553

Avitus, Saint, Bishop of Vienne, 148; tries in vain to convert the Arian Gundobad, 148–9; his polemics against the heresies of Eutychus and Sabellius, 149; his *Homilies* and *Letters*, 149

Avitus, the Emperor, 101; as Senator, 128; came from Clermont-Ferrand, 128; how he became Emperor, 128; his libidinous life, 128; later became Bishop of Piacenza, 128; his death, 128; buried in Brioude, 128; he was succeeded as Emperor by Maiorianus, 128; his daughter married Saint Sidonius Apollinaris, 134

Avius, see Vedast

Avranches, 504

Azor, son of Eliakim, 79

B

Baal-zephon, place near the Red Sea, 76

Babel, 65; the Tower of Babel was built in the plain of Senachar, 71; the confusion of tongues, 71; according to Gregory, another name for Babylon, 71; described by Orosius, 72

Babylas, Saint, Bishop of Antioch, martyred, 86

Babylon, another name for Babel, 71; built by Hebron, son of Chus, 72; Orosius describes the town, 72; different from Babylon in Egypt, 74; Nebuchadnezzar was King, 78; the Babylonian captivity, 78; 249

Babylon in Egypt, 74; granaries built by Joseph there (=the pyramids), 74

Babylonian Captivity, The, 65, 78; Zerubbabel frees the Israelites from, 79; symbolic of the enslavement of the soul of a sinner, 79; lasted seventy-six years, 79; 80; 249

Baddo, 479; tried in Paris by King Guntram for high treason, 496; eventually released, 496

Badegisil, Mayor of the Palace, 340; becomes Bishop of Le Mans, 340; Fredegund accuses his brother Nectarius of having stolen part of King Chilperic's treasure, 399; Badegisil speaks up for his brother, 399; dies, 470; evil behaviour, 470–71; evil behaviour of his wife, 471; Chuppa tries to abduct his daughter, 553; his widow, Magnatrude, drives Chuppa away, 553

Baderic, King of the Thuringians, 164; his brother Hermanfrid conspires with Theuderic against him, 164; they kill him, 164

Balesmes, where the church was built by Saint Perpetuus, 597

Ballomer, a Frankish word meaning Pretender, applied to Gundovald, 397, 419, 423, 514

Baptism, Catholic, 31

Barrou, ravaged by Count Berulf, 344; the church there was built by Saint Perpetuus, 597

Basil, Saint, The Rule of, 590

Basilius, mob-leader in Poitiers, 241; put down by Count Mummolus, 241

Basilus, Bishop, correspondent of Saint Sidonius Apollinaris, 138–9

Basina, daughter of King Chilperic and Audovera, 305; shut up by her father in Saint Radegund's nunnery in Poitiers, 305; when Theuderic dies, Chilperic thinks of marrying her to Recared in place of Rigunth, 364–5; Basina is unwilling and Saint Radegund scotches the idea, 365; 480; see Holy Cross, the nunnery of the, in Poitiers, for details of her role in the revolt, 541; 568; quarrels with Clotild, 568; repents, 569; rejoins the dissidents, 569; 571; is found guilty on all counts by the commission of bishops set up by Childebert II to try her, and is suspended from communion, 575; appeals to Childebert II against the verdict, but the appeal is dismissed, 575; begs for forgiveness and is allowed to return to Saint Radegund's nunnery, 580

Basina, wife of Bisinus, King of Thuringia, 128; she runs away from her husband and goes to live with Childeric, 129; Childeric marries her, 129; she is the mother of King Clovis, 129

Bathsheba, wife of King David, 77; mother of Solomon, 77; with the help of Nathan the prophet, she raises Solomon to the throne, 77

Baudegil, a deacon, 271; places King Chilperic's letter on Saint Martin's tomb, 271

Baudinus, Bishop of Tours, sixteenth in order, 198; dies, 199; had been a Referendary of King Lothar I, 600; had sons of his own, 600; constructed the second village of Neuilly, 600; started the canons' *mensa* in Tours, 600; was Bishop for five years, 600; buried in Saint Martin's church, 600

Bavaria, 203; Garivald is Duke, 203

Bayeux, 496; Leudovald is Bishop, 496; Saxons settle near there in the Bessin, 556

Bazas, 347; burnt down, 350; Orestes is Bishop, 414; he is present at the consecration of Faustianus as Bishop of Dax, 414

Beaucaire, attacked by Recared, 462; attacked by the Visigoths, 488

Belial, 264

Belisarius, beaten repeatedly in battle by Buccelin, 189; replaced as military commander in Lower Italy by Narses, 189; made Count of the Stables, 189

Belley, Felix is Bishop, 533

Bellinzona, where Duke Olo, one of Childebert II's army commanders, is killed, 549

Index

Belphegor, the worship of, 126

Benignus, Saint and martyr, 602; Gregory of Tours placed his relics in the old baptistery by Saint Martin's church in Tours, 602

Benjamin, son of Jacob, 73; his mother was Rachel, 73; sent for by his brothers in Egypt, 74

Beppolen, Duke, 292; fights against the Bretons, 292; 432; with Fredegund in Rouen, 463; badly treated by Fredegund, 473; goes over to King Guntram, 473; made Duke of the cities belonging to Lothar II, 473; Rennes refuses to accept him as Duke, 473; harasses Angers, 473; his son dies in Rennes, 473; quarrels with Domigisel, 473; his son had married the wife of Wiliulf, 496; with Duke Ebrachar in joint command of King Guntram's army against the Bretons, 556; they quarrel incessantly, 556; taken by a priest to where all Waroch's men are assembled, 556; beaten and killed by Waroch, 557

Beregisil, relative of the priest Eufrasius, 229

Beretrude, leaves her wealth to her daughter, 522; Count Waddo invades one of her estates, 522–3; he is killed ignobly by the bailiff's son, 523

Berny-Rivière, royal villa, 217; King Chilperic seizes the treasure of his dead father, Lothar I, there, 217; Andarchius arraigned before King Sigibert there, 242; Chilperic there, 289; Dagobert, young son of Chilperic and Fredegund, died there, 298; Chilperic and Fredegund send Clovis there, in the hope that he will catch dysentery, 303; Gregory of Tours is tried there for treason and calumny, 319–21

Berthar, King of the Thuringians, 164; killed by his brother Hermanfrid, 164; leaves a daughter Radegund, 164

Berthefled, daughter of King Charibert, 518; a nun in Ingitrude's convent in Tours, 518; flees to Le Mans, 518

Berthefried, one of the rebellious Dukes, harasses Duke Lupus, 329; 479; conspires with Duke Rauching against Childebert II, 489; marches with Duke Ursio as part of the Rauching conspiracy, 491; they reach Ursio's estate on the River Woëvre, 491; Brunhild tries to persuade him to detach himself from Ursio, 491; escapes from the battle on the Woëvre to the church-house in Verdun, 495; killed there, 495; 511; 576

Berthegund, daughter of Ingitrude 518; her quarrels and lawsuits with her mother, 518–21; persuaded by Ingitrude to leave her husband and become Abbess of Ingitrude's convent in Tours, 519; returns to her husband, 519; returns to the convent, stealing most of her husband's goods, 519; is the sister of Bertram, Bishop of Bordeaux, 519; goes to stay with him, 519–20; returns to Poitiers, 520; the priest Theuthar is sent to settle her affairs, 521; 541; on her deathbed her mother forbids her to enter the convent or ever to pray at her tomb, 560; authorized by King Childebert II to inherit all her mother's and father's possessions, 560; she strips the convent bare, 560

Bertram, Bishop of Bordeaux, 277; 281; Count Leudast alleges that he is the lover of Queen Fredegund, 314; when challenged, Leudast says that it is Gregory of Tours who started the rumour, 316; speaks against Gregory at his trial, 319; conspires with the Pretender Gundovald and Count Mummolus in Bordeaux, 413; tries to force the merchant Eufronius to enter the Church, so that he can steal his possessions, 413–14; the ridiculous affair of Gundovald, Mummolus, Bertram and the finger-bone of Saint Sergius, 413–14; 420; in ill odour with King Guntram for having received Gundovald, 434–5; he is Guntram's kinsman on his mother's side, 435; quarrels openly with Palladius, Bishop of Saintes, 439; must pay an indemnity to the deposed Faustianus, Bishop of Dax, 450; Bertram dies immediately after the Council of Mâcon, 454; harbours his sister, Berthegund. against the will of her husband, 519–20; is the son of Ingitrude, 519

Bertram, Bishop of Le Mans, 471; was earlier Archdeacon of Paris, 471; has trouble with his predecessor's wife over church property, 471; one of King Guntram's envoys to the Bretons, 471; signs the letter to Bishop Gundegisel about the revolt in Saint Radegund's nunnery, 533

Bertram, see Waldo the deacon

Berulf, Duke, 318; alleges that Gregory of Tours is planning to invite King Guntram to take over his city, 318; after the trial and the exoneration of Gregory of Tours, tries to catch Leudast, 322; ravages Yzeures, 344; ravages Barrou, 344; attacks Bourges, 359; 431; deposed from his one-time position as Duke of Tours and Poitiers, 455; captured by Duke Rauching, 455; his property sequestered, 455, Gregory of Tours saves him from being beheaded, 456

Bessin, the, 290

Bethlehem, city of David, 81; this was the scene of Christ's birth, 81

Béziers, attacked by Theudebert, 183

Bigorra, where Amelius is Bishop, 457; 486

Birth, the, of Christ, 65

Bisinus, King of Thuringia, 128; he welcomes Childeric, King of the Franks, 128; his wife Basina then runs away to Childeric, 128

Bladast, Duke, 344; beaten in Gascony, 344; attacks Bourges, 359–60; devastates Tours, 360–61; in Toulouse with the Pretender Gundovald, 409; accompanies Gundovald to Saint-Bertrand-de-Comminges, 417; he is there in the siege, but he escapes by a trick, 421: at the request of Gregory of Tours, is pardoned by King Guntram, 438; his mother was Leuba, 457

Blessed Virgin Mary's church in Rome, the, 546

Blois, the war of, and the men of Orleans against Châteaudun, 389; 402

Boantus, 431; executed by King Guntram, 441–2

Boaz, son of Salma, 77

Bobilla, nickname of Queen Austrechild, wife of King Guntram, 219

Bobo, Duke, retainer of King Chilperic, 304; plays a part in the murder of Clovis, 304; son of Mummolen, 379; sets out with Rigunth, 379

Bobolen, Referendary of Fredegund, 465; kills Domnola, whose vineyard he covets, 465; his goods are confiscated to the public treasury by Antestius, 474

Bodegisil, son of Mummolen, 547; came from Soissons, 547; sent by Childebert II on a mission with Grippo to the Emperor Maurice Tiberius, 547; murdered in Carthage, 548

Bodic, Breton chieftain, 273; makes a treaty with Macliaw, the Breton Count, 273; dies, 273; leaves a son called Theuderic, 273

Bodigisil, Count, dies, 454

Bologna, 131; Saint Namatius brings the relics of Saint Agricola and Saint Vitalis from Bologna to Clermont-Ferrand, 131

Bonghéat, 179; a villa there was given to Saint Julian's church in Clermont-Ferrand by Saint Tetradius, 179

Bordeaux, 129; Amandus is Bishop, 129; 154; 196; Saint Leontius is Bishop. 219; miracle of the corn saved from rain in a monastery there, 228–9; 243; Bertram is Bishop, 277; earthquake, 295; fireball, 296; 340; wolves roam the streets, 350; 366; the Pretender Gundovald is there with Bishop Bertram, 413–14; 417; 434; Garachar is Count, 438; Gundegisel is Bishop, 454; Anatolius, the boy-hermit, lived there, 468–9; portents, 483; 505; 517; 519; 532

Boso, military commander of King Guntram, 423; receives the surrender of the Pretender Gundovald, 423; sent to attack Septimania, 517; quarrels with Austrovald, 517

Bouges, near Bourges, 502; Chramnesind hides there, 502

Bourg-de-Déols, 132; many Bretons killed there by the Goths, 132

Bourges, the church at, 66; Saint Ursinus, Bishop of Bourges, seeks a church there, 87; the Senator Leocadius offers a house there to the Christians, 88; the relics of Saint Stephen the martyr in Bourges, 88; the Bretons expelled from Bourges by the Goths, 312; Arcadius flees there from Theuderic, 171; plague, 227; 251; 265; hailstorm, 296; 305; Leudast flees there, 320; 325; 344; attacked by Duke Berulf and Duke Bladast, 359–60; Remigius is Bishop, 371; Saint Sulpicius is Bishop, 371; 395; 396; 406; Ullo is Count, 423; 426; 459; 502; 578; the bogus Christ of Bourges, 584–6; Eustasius is Bishop, 586

Brachio, Abbot of the monastery of Ménat, 251; a Thuringian, 267; in his youth had been a huntsman in the service of Duke Sigivald, 267; dies, 267

Braye, where Saint Eustochius built the church, 595

Brèches, where Saint Bricius built the church, 595

Breslingen, 431; in the Ardennes, 453; Childebert II calls a meeting of his nobles there, 453; Brunhild appeals in vain for help for Ingund, 453; inquiry into the evil behaviour of Duke Guntram Boso in the church of Saint Remigius in Metz, 453–4

Bretons, the, expelled from Bourges by the Goths, 132; many killed at Bourg-de-Déols, 132; their counts, 195; their Count, Chanao, 198; their Count, Chonomor, 199; 252; 273; attack Rennes, 292; reach Corps-Nuds, 292; Duke Beppolen sent to fight them, 292; attack Nantes and Rennes,

294; 479; attack Nantes, 500; King Guntram sends envoys to them, 500; they promise to pay compensation, 500; attack Nantes and Rennes, 512; attack Rennes and Nantes, 556

Bricius, Saint, Bishop of Tours, fourth in order, 101; as a young man he used to tease Saint Martin, 104; succeeds Saint Martin as Bishop, 104; accused of being the father of his washerwoman's child, 104; the child, just thirty days old, denies that Bricius is his father, 105; Bricius walks to Saint Martin's tomb with burning coals in his cassock, 105; expelled and flees to Rome, 105; replaced by Justinian, 105; spends seven years in Rome, 106; when Justinian dies, Armentius is the second replacement for Saint Bricius as Bishop of Tours, 106; on his journey home, Saint Bricius arrives at Mont-Louis just in time to hear of the death of Armentius, 106; he is restored, 106; he dies, 106; the story of his life, 595; consecrated when Arcadius and Honorius were Emperors, 595; spent seven years in exile in Rome, 595; built the first small church over Saint Martin's tomb, 595; was buried there beside Saint Martin, 595; with his two periods added together, was Bishop for forty-seven years, 595; built churches in Clion, Brèches, Ruan, Brizay and Chinon, 595

Brioude, 128; church and tomb of Saint Julian there, 128; Cautinus, Bishop of Clermont-Ferrand, attacked by Chramn when he was processing there in Lent, 207–8; 591

Britanus, Count of Javols, 233; father of Count Palladius, 233; the wife of Britanus was Caesaria, 233

Brittany, 252, 273, 287; attacked by King Chilperic, 290; 541; attacked by King Guntram's army with Duke Beppolen in command, 556; Duke Beppolen is beaten and killed, 557; the remnants of the army cross back over the River Vilaine, 508; Count Waroch sends his son Canao to harass the stragglers, 558

Brives-la-Gaillarde, 394–5; Saint Martin's church there burnt down, 394–5; restored by Bishop Ferreolus of Limoges, 395

Brizay, where Saint Bricius built the church, 595

Bructeri, the, a tribe of the Franks, 122

Brunhild, daughter of King Athangild, 196; marries King Sigibert, 221; she was an Arian, but she becomes a Catholic, 221–2; her mother was Goiswinth, 233; 247; 251; her distress at her husband's assassination, 254; seized by King Chilperic, 254; banished to Rouen, 254; her daughters, Ingund and Chlodosind, are held in custody in Meaux, 254–5; Merovech comes to Rouen and marries her, 255; for a short time she takes sanctuary in Saint Martin's church in Tours, 255; 256; Merovech, who comes to seek sanctuary in Saint Martin's church, plans to visit Brunhild, who has left, 268; Merovech escapes to her, 272; 275; 279; 305; allegedly libelled by Lupentius, Abbot of the monastery of Saint Privatus in Javols, 370; 383; Fredegund attempts to have her assassinated, 401–2; 417; receives Duke Waddo after the siege of Saint-Bertrand-de-Comminges, 426; King Guntram jokes about Brunhild's having threatened to murder him,

437; appeals to Childebert II's nobles, assembled at Breslingen, for help
for Ingund, 453; Fredegund and Leuvigild apparently plan to assassinate
Brunhild, 456; Fredegund sends two priests to assassinate Brunhild and
Childebert II, 457–8; 480; 481; she is perpetually being insulted by Duke
Guntram Boso, 488; 489; she tries to persuade Duke Berthefried to
withdraw from the conspiracy against Childebert II and to abandon
Duke Ursio, 491; present in Trier at the conference between Childebert II
and Guntram, 492; Childebert gives Cahors back to Brunhild, 494; she
rages at Chramnesind for having murdered Sichar, 502; 503; 505; 507;
sends a golden salver to King Recared, 514–15; 518; the conspiracy
against Brunhild and Faileuba led by Septimima, Sunnegisil, Gallomagnus
and Droctulf, 524–6; 578

Buccelin captures Upper Italy for Theudebert, 189; fights against Belisarius
in Lower Italy, 189; beats him repeatedly, 189; beats Narses repeatedly,
189; occupies Sicily, according to Gregory of Tours, 189; killed by
Narses, 203

Buccovald, Abbot, puts in for the bishopric of Verdun, 511; he is known
facetiously as Buccus Validus, 511

Buchau, the forest of, 155; King Sigibert the Lame is murdered there by
his son Chloderic, 155

Burgolen, son of Severus and brother-in-law of Duke Guntram Boso, 290;
he was the first husband of Domnola, 465; his daughter Constantina in
Saint Radegund's nunnery in Poitiers, 531

Burgundes, 124; Arians, 125; they lived across the River Rhône, 125; they
expel Bishop Aprunculus from Langres, 137; their King, Gundioc, 140;
conquered by the Franks, 167

Burgundians, the, 459; see Burgundes

Burgundio, nephew of Saint Felix, Bishop of Nantes, 346; proposal that
he should succeed his uncle as Bishop, 346–7; Gregory of Tours, the
Metropolitan, refuses firmly, 347

Burgundy, famine in, 102; 137; attacked by Childebert I and Lothar I, 159;
attacked by Chlodomer and his brothers, 166; attacked by Lothar and
Childebert, 171; taken over by the Franks, 171; 267; 277; 598

Burial of Saint Martin, Feast of, 596

C

Cabaret, captured by Recared, 462

Cabrières, invested by Theudebert, 183

Caesarea, where Eusebius was Bishop, 18

Caesaria, Saint, Mother Superior of the nunnery of Saint Caesarius in
Arles, 530; her Rule was accepted by Saint Radegund for the nunnery
of the Holy Cross, 530; 535

Caesaria, sister-in-law of Count Firminus, 208; takes refuge with Firminus in the cathedral of Clermont-Ferrand, 208; seized by Scapthar, Chramn's emissary, 208; she escapes, 208; wife of Count Britanus of Javols, 233; mother of Count Palladius of Javols, 233

Caesarius, Consul, 97

Caesarius, Saint, Bishop of Arles, 528; his Rule, 528; his Rule accepted by Saint Radegund for the nunnery of the Holy Cross, 530; 535

Cahors, 129; Alithius is Bishop, 129; 171; attacked by Theudebert, 244; 252; Saint Maurilio is Bishop, 306; Saint Ursicinus petitions for the bishopric, 306; Ursicinus is Bishop, 371; Innocentius, Bishop of Rodez, tries to remove certain parishes from the diocese of Cahors, 371; the Abbot of the monastery of Cahors is discovered by King Guntram to be carrying secret messages for Gundovald the Pretender, 412–13; 452; Cahors is given back to Brunhild by Childebert II, 494; 505

Cain, 65; kills his brother Abel, 70; 561

Calumniosus, surnamed Egilan, King Guntram's military commander, 462; deposed after Recared's successful invasion, 462

Caluppa the recluse, 251; lived in the monastery of Méallet, 265; dies, 265

Calvary, Mount, 72; according to Sulpicius Severus, Abraham offered the sacrifice of Isaac there, 72; Christ crucified there, 72; in Jerusalem, 72; there stood the Holy Cross, 72

Cambrai, 125; Clodio, King of the Franks, sent spies there, 125; he captured the town from the Romans, 125; he lived there, 125; Ragnachar lived there, 156; 326; King Chilperic sought refuge there, 374

Campus Martius, the, in Rome, 119; the Emperor Valentinianus III was assassinated there, 119

Canaan, 74; Jacob was buried there, 74

Canao, son of Waroch, Count of the Bretons, 558; sent by his father to harass the remains of Duke Beppolen's army, 558

Candes, 97; Saint Martin of Tours died there, 97; his church there, 472; 594; it was he who built the church, 595

Canini lowlands, the, near Lake Maggiore, 549; Childebert II's troops engaged there with the Longobards, 549

Caprasius, Saint, of Agen, 344

Captivity, the, of the Israelites, 63; the Captivity in Babylon, 63, 79

Carcassonnais, the, 459, 476

Carcassonne, in Septimania, entered by King Guntram's army, 459; attacked by Duke Desiderius and Count Austrovald, 476–7; attacked by Count Austrovald, 517; attacked by Boso, 517

Carietto, Roman general, 121

Carignan, 445; Gregory of Tours meets Saint Vulfolaic there and is told the story of his life, 445–7; Gregory sees portents in the sky there, 449

Carpilio, father-in-law of Aetius, 119; he is Head of the Imperial Household and Governor of the Palace, 119

Carpitania, the district round Toledo, 363; plague of locusts there, 363

Index

Carthage, Saint Eugenius is Catholic Bishop, 109; Grippo, Bodegisil and Evantius, Childebert II's envoys, reach there safely, 547; Bodegisil and Evantius are then murdered, 548

Carthaginians, the, 254; what Orosius had to say about them, 254

Cassian, Saint, the Rule of, 590

Cassius, Saint, martyred at Clermont-Ferrand, 89; his church there, 205; the priest Anastasius buried alive in the crypt there by Bishop Cautinus, 205

Castinus, Master of the Imperial Household under Honorius, 124; fights against the Franks, 124

Catholic faith, the, split by heresies, 23; Gregory of Tours' credo as a Catholic, 67–9; disputation between Gregory of Tours and Agilan the Arian, 307–10; disputation between Gregory of Tours and King Chilperic, 310–11; disputation between Gregory of Tours, King Chilperic and Priscus the Jew, 330–33; disputation between Gregory of Tours and Oppila the Arian, 371–4; Leuvigild, Arian King of the Visigoths, is supposed to have become a Catholic on his deathbed, 477; Recared, Arian King of the Visigoths, debates the Catholic credo with his bishops, 497–8; he becomes a Catholic, 498

Cato the priest, 195; tries to become Bishop of Clermont-Ferrand, 200–201; elected as Bishop, 201; threatens the Archdeacon Cautinus, 201; his feud with Cautinus, 201–2; on the death of Gunthar, he is proposed for the bishopric of Tours, possibly by Bishop Cautinus, 203; refuses the bishopric of Tours, 204; promised the bishopric of Clermont-Ferrand by Chramn, 204; calumniates Cautinus, 204; tries to depose Cautinus, 210; in the end is ready to accept the bishopric of Tours, but it is too late, 210; behaves valiantly in the plague in Clermont-Ferrand, but dies, 226

Cautinus, the Archdeacon of Clermont-Ferrand, 195; threatened by Cato, 201; his feud with Cato, 201–2; made Bishop of Clermont-Ferrand, 202; it is possibly he who proposes Cato for the bishopric of Tours, 203; calumniated by Cato, 204; takes to drink, 204; seizes other people's land, 205; tries to seize the land of the priest Anastasius, 205; has him buried alive, 205–6; rebuked by King Lothar I, 207; always buying things from the Jews, 207; attacked by Chramn when processing to Brioude, 207–8; Chramn's evil behaviour towards him, 211; behaves ignobly in the plague in Clermont-Ferrand and dies, 226–7; 229; permits Count Eulalius to take communion, 554

Cavaillon, Saint Veranus is Bishop, 464; 483

Cecrops, King of Attica in the time of Moses, 80

Cedinus, Duke, one of Childebert II's army commanders in Italy, 550

Celsus the patrician, 195; appointed by King Guntram to replace Agricola, 218; seizes church property, 218; repents, 218; sent by Guntram to capture Avignon and attack Arles, 223; beats King Sigibert's troops, 224; replaced by Amatus, 236

Cenchris, twelfth King of the Egyptians, drowned in the Red Sea, 80

Index

Céré, where the church was built by Eufronius, Bishop of Tours, 600

Chalon-sur-Saône, 212; captured by Chramn, 212; plague, 227; Bishops Sagittarius and Salonius are tried and deposed at a council there, 291; Saint Agricola is Bishop, 312; Saint Flavius is Bishop, 312; King Guntram there, 433; attempt to assassinate Guntram there, 482; Baddo imprisoned there, 496; Gregory of Tours summoned there urgently by King Guntram, 502; 514; Guntram's Chamberlain, Chundo, is locked up there, 559; 587; 589

Châlons-sur-Marne, 305; Saint Elafius was Bishop, 305; Felix is Bishop, 533

Chamavi, the, a tribe of the Franks, 122

Champagne, 178; Lupus is Duke, 241; 255; 272; 329; 443; Wintrio is Duke, 450; 489; 549

Champenois, the, 587

Champtoceaux, sub-bishopric of Poitiers, 214; Austrapius becomes Bishop, 214; its parishes are restored to the diocese of Poitiers after the death of Austrapius, 215

Chanao, Count of the Bretons, 198; he kills three of his brothers, 198; he imprisons the fourth brother, Macliaw, 198; tries to kill Macliaw, 199; his death, 199; Chramn seeks refuge with him, 215; killed by King Lothar I while fighting with Chramn, 216

Chararic, King of the Salian Franks, 102; his death, 102; neutral in the war between Syagrius and King Clovis, 156; captured by Clovis, 156; he and his son murdered by Clovis, 156

Charbonnière, the forest of, 120; Nanninus and Quintinus beat the Franks there, 120

Charegisel, King Sigibert's Chamberlain, 248; murdered with him at Vitry, 248

Charibert, King of the Franks, son of Lothar I, 196; his wives, 196; his mother was Ingund, 197; sent to the Limousin by Lothar with Guntram to deal with Chramn, 212; Chramn escapes, 212; on the death of King Lothar I, Charibert, Guntram, Chilperic and Sigibert divide between them the lands of the Franks, 217; Charibert takes the kingdom of Childebert I, with Paris as his capital, 217; marries Ingoberg, 219; dismisses Ingoberg and marries Merofled instead, 219; has a mistress, Theudechild, 219; restores the deposed Emerius to the bishopric of Saintes, 220; marries Marcovefa and is excommunicated as a result, 220; dies, 220; 241; 269; 270; 314; takes up the Pretender Gundovald, 352; 383; 392; 395; 504; 513; 516; his daughter Berthefled, 518; 536

Charimer, Bishop of Verdun, 511; had been a Referendary, 511

Chariulf, supporter of the Pretender Gundovald in the siege of Saint-Bertrand-de-Comminges, 421; escapes after the siege, 424; seeks sanctuary in Saint Martin's church in Tours, 426

Charivald, one of three Franks of Tournai, 586-7; killed by Fredegund, 587

Charterius, Saint, Bishop of Périgueux, 325; treasonable letters signed by him are intercepted by Nonnichius, Count of Limoges, 351; they were

623

written by his enemy, the deacon Frontinus, 351; exonerated, 351; harassed by the Pretender Gundovald, 408

Chartres, 246; blood in the Communion bread, 296; 383; 389; Pappolus is Bishop, 400; 441; portents, 483; 504

Chaste Lovers, the, 66; the husband was Injuriosus of Clermont-Ferrand, 95–7; the story is told again in Gregory's *Liber in gloria Confessorum*, 97

Chastel-Marlhac, the siege of, 159; description of the place, 172–3; forced to pay a ransom to Theuderic, 173

Châteaudun, 247; attacked by the men of Orleans and Blois, 389–90; Promotus is Bishop, 400; deposed, 400; 409; 504

Châteaumeillant, 578

Chatti, the, a tribe of Franks, 122

Chelles, royal estate near Paris, 303; King Chilperic and Fredegund stay there, 303; they summon Clovis to stay with them there, 303; Chilperic is assassinated there, 379; 390; 578

Cher, River, in spate, 306

Childebert I, King of the Franks, son of King Clovis, 159; shares the kingdom of Clovis with Theuderic, Chlodomer and Lothar, 162; invited to Clermont-Ferrand on false rumour that Theuderic is dead. 170; he visits Spain because of the maltreatment of his sister Clotild by her husband Amalaric, 170; he brings her home, but she dies on the journey, 170; he and Lothar attack Burgundy, 171; Childebert and Theuderic make a treaty, exchange hostages, but immediately quarrel, 175; after his death, Childebert and Lothar threaten the sons of Chlodomer, 180; they kill Theudovald and Gunthar, but Chlodovald escapes, 180–82; Childebert and Lothar share between them the lands of Chlodomer, 182; on the death of his father they attack Theudebert, 184; Childebert makes peace with Theudebert, 184; Childebert and Theudebert attack Lothar, 185; they make peace, 186; Childebert and Lothar besiege Saragossa, 186–7; Childebert, Lothar and Theudebert threaten Theudat for having killed Amalasuntha. 188; he gives them *wergeld*, most of which is seized by Childebert, 188–9; 195; at the funeral of his mother, Queen Clotild, 197; conspires with Chramn against Lothar, 211; allies with Chramn, 213; attacks Rheims, 213; dies in Paris, 215; buried in the church of Saint Vincent (=Saint-Germain-des-Prés), 215; his kingdom seized by Lothar, 215; on Lothar's death Childebert's kingdom inherited by Charibert, 217; 247; 299; 339; had received Gundovald the Pretender when the latter was a boy, 352; 399

Childebert II, King of the Franks, son of King Sigibert and Brunhild, 248; succeeds to his murdered father, 248; 251; his life was saved by Duke Gundovald, 254; proclaimed King, 254; Siggo the Referendary joins him, 257–8; 263; 268; makes treaty with King Guntram at the Stone Bridge, 274–5; made Guntram's adopted son, 275; 280; Duke Guntram Boso goes over to him, 289; 291; 295; 313; 325; 326; breaks the peace which he had made with Guntram and allies with Chilperic, 327; sends

Index

Egidius, Bishop of Rheims, on an embassy to Chilperic, 328; they ally against Guntram, 328; 341; asks for half of Marseilles from Guntram, 341–2; quarrels with Guntram, 344; 345; ambassadors from Spain visit him, 349; 354; makes a new alliance with Chilperic, 359; his troops rebel against the diplomacy of Egidius, Bishop of Rheims, 361; Guntram gives him the second half of Marseilles, 363; 371; 374; attacks the Longobards in Italy, 375; plans to invade Spain, 375; had been paid by the Emperor Maurice Tiberius to put down the Longobards, 375; visits Chilperic in Paris, 377–8; 383; 384; after the assassination of Chilperic takes over Fredegund's treasure, 390; argument with Guntram about the right to enter Paris, 391–2; demands the surrender of Fredegund, 392; 395; 396; sends Bishop Egidius, Duke Guntram Boso and Sigivald to confer with Guntram, 397; 407; 415; summoned urgently by Guntram to confer about Gundovald the Pretender, 415–7; Guntram makes him his heir, 416; hands over to him everything that Sigibert had held, 417; 420; he receives a half-share of the treasure of Mummolus from Guntram, 425; 431; 432; 436; 442; receives messengers from Guntram about a proposed church council in Troyes, 443–4; pressed for the return of the money which the Emperor Maurice Tiberius had given to him, 449; sends an army into Italy, 449–50; Childeric the Saxon joins him, 450; at the Council of Mâcon, 453; calls a meeting of his nobles at Breslingen, 453; Leuvigild and Fredegund are apparently planning to assassinate Childebert and his mother Brunhild, 456; Fredegund sends two priests to assassinate them, 457–8; has Magnovald executed while watching a wild-beast show in Metz, 469; has a son called Theudebert, 470; envoys come from Leuvigild, 470; receives Albi back from Guntram, 476; 479; 480; 481; receives envoys from Recared, 481; has a second son, Theuderic, 482; 487; decides to deal with the case of Duke Guntram Boso, 488–9; conspiracy of Duke Rauching to assassinate him, 489; alerted by Guntram, 489; has Rauching killed, 489–90; 491; called to confer with Guntram in Trier, 491–2; makes the Treaty of Andelot with King Guntram, 493–4; gives Cahors back to Brunhild, 494; sends an army to kill Dukes Ursio and Berthefried, 494–5; pardons Egidius, Bishop of Rheims, 497; receives envoys from Recared, become a Catholic, 499; Recared asks for the hand in marriage of Chlodosind, Childebert's sister, 499; Chramnesind comes to ask pardon for having murdered Sichar, 502; Gregory of Tours assures Guntram that Childebert is observing the conditions of the Treaty of Andelot, 502–3; Guntram has the Treaty of Andelot read in full to Gregory of Tours and Bishop Felix, in case they have forgotten it, 503–7; 509; 510; had previously promised his sister Chlodosind in marriage to Authari, King of the Longobards, 512; since then had promised her to Recared, now King of the Visigoths, 512; had promised the Emperor Maurice Tiberius that he would drive the Longobards out of Italy, 512; sends an army against the Longobards, but it is cut to pieces, 512–13; 515; celebrates Easter Day in Mainz with Bishop

Index

Sigimund, 515; sends an army against the Longobards, 515; revises the tax-lists of Poitiers, 515; attempts to tax Tours, but Gregory of Tours stops him, 515–17; goes to stay in Strasbourg, 523; is invited to send Theudebert to go to live in Soissons, 523–4; his Queen, Faileuba, has another child, who dies immediately, 524; conspiracy against Faileuba and Brunhild, led by Septimima, Sunnegisil, Gallomagnus and Droctulf, 524–6; 531; sends Count Macco to put down the revolt of Clotild and the nuns of Saint Radegund's nunnery, by main force if necessary, 523; sends the priest Theuthar to negotiate with the nuns, 538–9; they refuse to listen to him, 539; most of the nuns go home, but Clotild and Basina remain in the nunnery, 539; 541; 543; sends Grippo, Bodegisil and Evantius on a peace mission to the Emperor Maurice Tiberius, but the two last get themselves murdered in Carthage, 547–9; sends an army under Duke Audovald, Duke Wintrio and Duke Olo to attack the Longobards in Italy, 549–51; Maurice Tiberius sends the murderers of Bodegisil and Evantius to Childebert who refuses to molest them, as he is sure that they are the wrong men, 551–2; 552; remits arrears of taxes owed by the clergy of Clermont-Ferrand, 553; 558; allows Berthegund to inherit all the property of her mother Ingitrude, 560; sets up a commission of Bishops to settle affairs in Saint Radegund's nunnery, 569; turns down an appeal against the verdict of the commission by the nuns Clotild and Basina, 575; Fredegund sends twelve assassins to murder him, but they are caught, 576; tries Bishop Egidius for high treason, 577–80; 582; 587; offended by Guntram's having baptized Lothar II, 588; 604

Childeric, King of the Franks, son of Merovech, 125; his debauched life, 128; he flees to Thuringia, 128; recalled by the Franks after eight years, 128; marries Basina, Queen of Thuringia, and she becomes mother of Clovis, 129; fights a battle at Orleans, 132; occupies Angers, 132; Odovacar joins him to beat the Alamanni, 132; his death, 139

Childeric, King of the Vandals, 101; fights a battle at Orleans, 101; his death, 113

Childeric, second son of Lothar I and Ingund, 197, 198

Childeric the Saxon, 390; one of his men kills Vedast, 390; loses favour with King Guntram, 450; takes sanctuary in Saint Martin's church in Tours, 450; Gregory of Tours gains permission for his wife to join him there, 450; they escape, cross the Loire and join King Childebert II, who makes him Duke of the cities beyond the Garonne, 450; 541; commits many crimes, 581; flees to Auch, 581; dies in his bed, 581; thought to have been with the nun Clotild in Saint Hilary's church in Poitiers when the bishops were knocked about, 581

Children of Israel, the, 604; see Israelites

Chilperic, King of the Franks, son of Lothar I and Aregund, 195; his mother was Aregund, 197; after the death of Lothar I, Chilperic takes possession of his treasury, 217; enters Paris and takes possession of Childebert I's kingdom, 217; on Lothar's death, Charibert, Guntram,

Index

Chilperic and Sigibert divide between them the lands of the Franks, 217; Chilperic inherits Lothar's kingdom, with Soissons as his capital, 217; attacks Rheims and other towns belonging to Sigibert, 217–18; beaten by Sigibert, 218; marries Galswinth, the elder sister of Brunhild, 222; is already married to Fredegund, 222; has Galswinth garrotted, 222; his brothers drive him out of his kingdom, 223; his earlier wife, Audovera, by whom he had three sons, 223; attacks Tours and Poitiers, 241; 243; quarrels with Sigibert, 244; sends Theudebert to invade Tours and Poitiers, 244; attacked by Sigibert, 245; retreats to Havelu, near Chartres, 246; makes peace, 246; allies with Guntram against Sigibert, 246; attacks Rheims, 247; takes refuge in Tournai, 247; he is besieged there by Sigibert, 247; emerges when he learns that Sigibert has been assassinated, 248; buries Sigibert in Lambres, 248; 251; 252; goes to Paris and seizes Sigibert's treasure, 254; seizes Brunhild and banishes her to Rouen, 254; sends Merovech to attack Poitiers, 255; is furious when his son Merovech marries Brunhild, widow of the murdered Sigibert, 255; takes Merovech to Soissons, 255; beats the Champenois and relieves Soissons, 255–6; suspects Merovech of plotting, 256; locks him up, 256; his relations with Godin, 256; 257; his relations with Siggo, 257–8; 258; quarrels with Munderic, 260; 261; sends Clovis to Tours, 267; has Merovech tonsured, ordained a priest and sent to the monastery of Anille, 267; learns that Merovech has escaped and sought sanctuary in Saint Martin's church in Tours, 268; 270; Gregory of Tours sees in a vision the death of Chilperic and all his sons, 270; writes a letter to the tomb of Saint Martin to ask if the Saint will please expel Duke Guntram Boso from sanctuary, 271; after the escape of Merovech and Guntram Boso from Saint Martin's church, ravages Tours, 272; busy building amphitheatres in Soissons and Paris, 275; has Saint Praetextatus, Bishop of Rouen, tried by a council of bishops in Paris for conspiring against him, 275–82; 288; attacks Poitiers, 289; deposes Count Ennodius, 289; attacks Waroch, son of Macliaw, in Brittany, 290–91; tries to impose new taxes, 292; riot in Limoges put down with great brutality, 292; loses his young sons Chlodobert and Dagobert through dysentery, 297; in remorse destroys the tax demands, 297; in mourning in the forest of Cuise, 303; tries to infect his son Clovis with the dysentery which is raging in Berny-Rivière, 303; summons Clovis to Chelles, 303; has him murdered for alleged conspiracy, 304; has his first wife Audovera murdered, 304; puts his daughter Basina in the nunnery of Saint Radegund in Poitiers, 305; locks up the ambassadors sent by Mir, King of Galicia, to Guntram, 306; after a year he sends them home, 306; 307; publishes a decree denying the distinction of Persons, 310; Gregory of Tours disputes with him about this, 310–11; his poetry, which was a poor imitation of Sedulius, 312; adds four Greek letters to the Roman alphabet, 312; 313; tries Gregory of Tours at Berny-Rivière for alleged treason and calumny, 319–21; 325; 326; makes an alliance with Childebert II, 327; after three years his ambassadors return from the Emperor Tiberius II, 327; at war with Guntram, 327; the ambassadors wrecked at Agde, 327–8; robbed by the Agathais, 328; visited at Nogent-sur-Marne by Gregory of Tours, 328; shows him a gold salver and medallions which he has received from the Emperor Tiberius II, 328; receives Egidius, Bishop of Rheims, on an embassy from Childebert II, 328; they ally against Guntram, 328; disputes with a Jew called Priscus, 329–30; Gregory of Tours joins in the disputation, 330–33; asks Gregory of Tours for his blessing, 333; 341; sends Duke Desiderius to attack Guntram, 344; 345; has a number of Jews baptized, 347–8; ambassadors from Spain visit him, 349; posts guards on the bridge over the River Orge near Paris against Guntram's men, 349; Asclepius kills them, 349; Guntram makes amends, 350; appoints counts to the cities which he has captured from Guntram and exacts taxes, 350; has a son Theuderic, 351; has him baptized in Paris, 355; makes a new alliance with Childebert II, 359; attacks Guntram, but they make peace, 360; has Leudast tortured to death, 363; his ambassadors arrive home from Leuvigild in Spain, 363; envoys arrive from Leuvigild concerning the betrothal of Rigunth to Recared, 364; loses his son Theuderic, 364; tortures Mummolus the Prefect for alleged implication in Theuderic's death, 366; Oppila arrives as envoy from Leuvigild, 371–4; retires to Cambrai, 374; has a son, Lothar, 375; more Visigothic envoys come to Paris, 377; assassinated at Chelles, 379; compared with Nero and Herod, 379; his evil character and behaviour analysed, 380; buried by Mallulf, Bishop of Senlis, in Saint Vincent's church in Paris (=Saint-Germain-des-Prés) 381; 383; 389; 391; 392; 394; 396; 399; 401; 407; 415; 420; 431; 433; seen in visions by both King Guntram and Gregory of Tours, 437–8; 440; 464; 474; 485; 489; 505; 536; 552; 577; 578; 579

Chilperic, son of Gundioc, King of the Burgundes, 141; killed, with his wife, by his brother Gundobad, 141; Gundobad drives into exile Chilperic's two daughters, the younger of whom is Clotild, 141

Chinon, 251; earth-tremor there during Mass, 274; 345; Saint Bricius built the church there, 595

Chlochilaich, King of the Danes (=Hygelac), 163; invades Gaul, 163; killed by Theudebert, 164

Chloderic, son of King Sigibert the Lame, 153; fought at Vouillé, 153; persuaded by King Clovis to kill his own father, 155–6; killed in turn by Clovis, 155

Chlodobert, young son of King Chilperic and Fredegund, dies of dysentery, 297; expires in the church of Saint Medard in Soissons, 298; 323

Chlodomer, King of the Franks, second son of King Clovis and Clotild, 142; he is baptized, 142; 159; divides the kingdom of Clovis with Theuderic, Childebert I and Lothar I, 162; encouraged by his mother Clotild, he attacks the Burgundian Kings, Godomar and Sigismund, 166; he captures Sigismund, 166; murders Sigismund and his wife,

166–7; summons Theuderic to help him against Godomar, 167; killed by Godomar's troops through advancing too fast, 167; his widow was Guntheuc, 167; his three sons were Theudovald, Gunthar and Chlodovald, 167; Queen Clotild cares for them, 167; Lothar and Childebert threaten the sons of Chlodomer, 180; Lothar murders Theudovald and Gunthar, but Chlodovald escapes, 180–82; Chlodomer's treasure is seized by Lothar, 189; on Lothar's death, Guntram inherits Chlodomer's kingdom, 217; 277

Chlodomer, son of King Guntram and Austrechild, 219

Chlodosind, daughter of King Sigibert and Brunhild, 254–5; when her father is assassinated, she is banished to Meaux, 254–5; present at the conference in Trier between Childebert II and Guntram, 492; King Recared asks Childebert II and Brunhild for Chlodosind's hand in marriage; 499; 505; 507; 512; 515

Chlodovald, third son of Chlodomer (=Saint Cloud), 167; Queen Clotild brings him up, 167; escapes being murdered with his brothers by Lothar, 180–82; becomes a priest, 182

Chlothsind, daughter of Lothar I and Ingund, 197; marries Alboin, King of the Longobards, 198; 235; she dies, 236

Chonomor, Count of the Bretons, 199; hides Macliaw, 199

Chramn, son of King Lothar I, 195; his mother was Chunsina, 197; 198; sent to Clermont-Ferrand, 203; his evil behaviour there, 207; insults Count Firminus, 207; replaces him by Salustius, 207; attacks Firminus and his sister-in-law Caesaria, 208; his other crimes in Clermont-Ferrand, 211; hostility towards Bishop Cautinus, 211; leaves Clermont-Ferrand for Poitiers, 211; conspires with Childebert against his father Lothar, 211; moves to the Limousin, 211; attacked by Charibert and Guntram at Nigremont, 212; escapes to Chalon-sur-Saône, 212; enters Dijon, 212; consults the *Sortes Biblicae* with Saint Tetricus, Bishop of Langres, 212–13; marries Chalda, daughter of Wilichar, 213; comes to Paris, 213; allies with Childebert, 213; flees to Brittany, 215; seeks refuge with Count Chanao, 215; fights against his father Lothar in Brittany, 216; is captured and burnt alive by his father, 216; Lothar dies on the first anniversary of his death, 217

Chramnesind, citizen of Tours, son of Audo, 429–30; develops a great friendship with Sichar, 501; murders Sichar and hangs his naked body on the garden-fence, 502; goes to Childebert II to seek pardon, 502; is raged at by Brunhild, 502; hides in Bouges, 502; goes to Childebert II a second time to crave pardon, 502; his property is handed to Flavinius, who gives it back again, 502

Christ, see Jesus Christ

Christians, i.e. Catholics, persecuted by the Arian Vandals, 31; their happiness, believing as they do in the Holy Trinity, 161; 252; persecuted in Spain by Queen Goiswinth, 301; persecuted in Spain by King Leuvigild, 349

Christmas, 428, 437, 440, 474, 596

Christopher the merchant, 384; he is murdered, 427

Chroc, King of the Alamanni, 66; he invades Gaul, 88; he burns down a shrine near Clermont-Ferrand called Vasso Galatae, 89; he and his men murder Saint Privatus, Bishop of Javols, 90; captured in Arles and killed, 90

Chrodin, Duke, dies, 325; his charitable deeds, 350

Chroma, elder daughter of Chilperic, son of Gundioc, King of the Burgundes, and thus sister of Clotild, 141; becomes a religious, 141

Chundo, King Guntram's Chamberlain, 541; is accused of having killed an aurochs in the royal forests in the Vosges, 559; locked up in Chalon-sur-Saône, 559; tries to seek sanctuary in the church of Saint Marcellus, 559; Guntram has him stoned to death, 559

Chunsina, fourth wife of King Lothar I, 197; mother of Chramn, 197

Chuppa, Master of the Stables to King Chilperic, 305; brings the treasure of King Clovis from Bourges, 305; tortured by Fredegund for his pains, 305; freed at the request of Gregory of Tours, 305; sent by Fredegund to bring home Rigund, 425; 541; ravages the district round Tours, 552; helped to escape by Animodius, 552; bribes Flavianus and is allowed to go free, 553; tries to abduct the daughter of Badegisel, late Bishop of Le Mans, 553; breaks into her house at Mareil, 553; is driven away by the girl's mother, Magnatrude, 553

Chus, 65; eldest son of Ham, 71; magician and inventor of idolatry, 71; worshipper of fire and of the stars, 71; goes to live among the Persians, 71; father of the giant Hebron, 72

Cieutat, 505

Ciran-la-Latte, where Saint Martin built the church, 595

Ciuciolo, Count of the Palace to King Sigibert, 283; supports Merovech, 283; executed, 283

Clain, River, 533; the deacon Desiderius swims his horse across, 533

Claudius, sent by King Guntram to drag Eberulf out of Saint Martin's church in Tours and kill him, 409–12; visits Fredegund on the way, 409; kills Eberulf, 411; is killed by Eberulf's men, 412

Claudius, the Emperor, 84; the Apostle Peter came to Rome in his reign, 84

Clement, Saint, the third Pope, martyred by Trajan, 85; his church in Rome, 546

Cleophas, father of Saint Simeon, 85

Clermont-Ferrand and the shrine there, 66; receives Saint Stremonius as its Bishop, 87; the shrine called Vasso Galatae destroyed there by Chroc, 89; Saints Liminius and Antolianus martyred there, 89; Saints Cassius and Victorinus martyred there, 89; Saints Urbicus, Legonus, Illidius, Nepotianus and Arthemius were Bishops there, 94; Injuriosus, the husband in the story of the Chaste Lovers, lived there, 95; Saints Venerandus and Rusticus were Bishops there, 101; Saint Namatius is Bishop, 101; the church of Saint Stephen *extra muros*, 101; the Senator

Avitus, who became Emperor, came from there, 128; Saint Julian martyred there, 128; Saint Venerandus is Bishop, 129; Saint Rusticus is Bishop, 130; Saint Namatius is Bishop, 131; he builds the great church there, 131; the church of Saint Stephen outside Clermont-Ferrand is built and decorated by the wife of Bishop Namatius, 131–2; Duke Victorius goes there, 132; builds churches there, 132; Saint Eparchius is Bishop, 133; Saint Sidonius Apollinaris is Bishop, 134; Abraham is Abbot of Saint-Cyr there, 134; Saint Aprunculus is Bishop, 137; Saint Quintianus takes refuge there, 151; Saint Eufrasius is Bishop, 151; 154; visited by Childebert I, 159; attacked by Theuderic, 159; the destruction there, 159; 162; 169; Childebert invited there by the Senator Arcadius, 170; Theuderic sends his troops to ravage the neighbourhood, 171; damaged by Theuderic, 171; garrisoned by Theuderic, with Sigivald in charge, 173; 184; Theudebert, become King, remits the taxes to the churches in Clermont-Ferrand, 185; 196; Saint Gall is Bishop, 199; spared the plague thanks to Saint Gall, 199–200; Cautinus is Bishop, 202; 203; bishopric promised to Cato by Chramn, 204; Anastasius lived there, 205; Chramn comes there, 207; his evil behaviour there, 207; 211; he leaves, 211; plague in the city, 212; the men of Clermont-Ferrand attack Arles, 223; a crested lark puts out all the lamps in the sacristy of one of the churches, 226; a bird puts out the lamps in Saint Andrew's church, 226; plague, 226; 227; Saint Avitus is Bishop, 229–30; 233; 235; 238; Andarchius comes there and tries to marry the daughter of a citizen called Ursus, 241–3; 265; 267; 289; 318; Duke Guntram Boso retires there with the treasure of Gundovald the Pretender, 353; 354; council of bishops held there to settle the dispute between Innocentius, Bishop of Rodez, and Saint Ursicinus, Bishop of Cahors, 371; Nicetius is Count, 450; Eulalius is Count, 450; Nicetius is Duke, 450; 454; 460; 462; 474; 476; 541; the gaolbirds of Clermont-Ferrand are freed by a miracle, despite the efforts of Count Eulalius, 553; Childebert II remits arrears of taxes owed by the clergy, 553; 554; 599

Clion, where Saint Bricius built the church, 595

Clodio, an early King of the Franks, 125; lived in Duisburg, in Thuringia, 125; sent spies to Cambrai, 125; he captured the town from the Romans, 125; he lived there, 125; he occupied territory up to the River Somme, 125; King Merovech was descended from him, 125

Clotild, daughter of King Charibert, 480; a nun in Saint Radegund's nunnery in Poitiers, 526; see Holy Cross, the nunnery of the, in Poitiers, for details of her role in the revolt, 541; 567; 571; found guilty on all counts by the commission of bishops set up by Childebert II, and suspended from communion, 575; appeals to Childebert II against the verdict, but the appeal is dismissed, 575; is pardoned, refuses to return to Saint Radegund's nunnery, and is given the estates of Count Waddo to live on, 580; 581

Clotild, daughter of King Clovis, 162; marries Amalaric, 162; maltreated by her husband, 170; her brother Childebert visits her in Barcelona, and Amalaric is killed, 170; she is brought home with her treasure, 170; dies on the journey, 170; buried in Paris, 170

Clotild, daughter of King Guntram, 504

Clotild, Saint and Queen, marries Clovis, King of the Franks, 102; the younger daughter of Chilperic, son of Gundioc, King of the Burgundes, 141; death of her son Ingomer after baptism, 142; Chlodomer, her second son, is baptized, 142; she persuades Clovis to be baptized, 143; on his death she comes to live in Tours and becomes a religious there, 158; encourages her sons to avenge the death of her father and mother on the Burgundes, 166; cares for the three sons of Chlodomer after his death, 167; living then in Paris, 180; sadly she buries Theudovald and Gunthar, the two older sons of Chlodomer, murdered by King Lothar I, 181; her blameless life, 182; she prays to Saint Martin for peace between Theudebert, Childebert and Lothar, 185–6; she dies in Tours, 197; buried in Paris, 197; had given land to the priest Anastasius, 205; 206; 598; 599

Clovis, King of the Franks, 102; his early victories, 125; his father was Childeric and his mother Basina, ex-Queen of Thuringia, 129; on the death of his father Childeric, he becomes King of the Franks, 139; with Ragnachar, Clovis attacks Syagrius, 139; he kills Syagrius, 139; he was a pagan, 139; how his men sacked Christian churches, 139–40; in Soissons he killed one of his men who disagreed over booty, 140; he conquers the Thuringians, 140; marries Clotild, the Burgundian princess, 141; their first son, Ingomer, dies immediately after baptism, 142; their second son, Chlodomer, is baptized, 142; Clovis is baptized, following his victory over the Alamanni, 143; Saint Remigius explains the Catholic faith to Clovis and baptizes him and his men, 143–4; beats Gundobad on the River Ouche, 145; pursues Gundobad to Avignon, 146; accepts tribute from Gundobad, 147; makes a treaty with Alaric II at Amboise, 150; marches on Poitiers, 151; kills a soldier who forages on land belonging to Saint Martin's church, 152; seeks a message from Saint Martin's church, 152; crosses the River Vienne, 152; beats Alaric II at Vouillé, near Poitiers, 153–4; receives the consulate in Saint Martin's church in Tours, 154; establishes his government in Paris, 154; persuades Chloderic to kill his father, King Sigibert the Lame, 155–6; kills Chloderic, 155–6; the Ripuarian Franks accept his rule, 156; kills Chararic, King of the Salian Franks, 156; they accept his rule, 156; he bribes the *leudes* of Ragnachar, 157; he kills Ragnachar and his brother Ricchar, 157; he kills their brother Rignomer, 157; gradually extends his dominion over Gaul, 158; kills one after another of his blood-relations, 158; dies in Paris and buried there, 158; he had reigned for thirty years, 158; his four sons, 162; 193; 197; 199; 249; 253; 597; 598

Clovis, son of King Chilperic and Audovera, 223; expelled from Tours by Count Mummolus, 241; escapes to Bordeaux, 243; attacked by Sigulf,

243; escapes via Angers, 243; 252; expelled from Soissons by the Champenois, 255; sent to Tours by Chilperic, 267; occupies Saintes, 267; his father Chilperic tries to infect him with dysentery, 303; ordered to go to join his father at Chelles, 303; murdered at Noisy-le-Grand for alleged conspiracy, 304; his treasure is seized by Chilperic, 305; 321; 431; his earthly remains discovered, 440–41; King Guntram has them buried in Saint Vincent's church in Paris (=Saint-Germain-des-Prés), 441

Clysma, harbour in the Gulf of Suez (=Tell Kolzum), 75

Coblenz, confluence of the River Moselle and Rhine, 443; Gregory of Tours there when messengers to Childebert II arrive from King Guntram, 444

Cologne, attacked by the Franks, 120; Arbogast comes there in winter, 122; King Sigibert the Lame lives there, 155; full name is Colonia Claudia Agrippinensis, 352; Gundovald the Pretender at one time exiled there, 352

Comminges, see Saint-Bertrand-de-Comminges

Compiègne, King Lothar I dies there, 217

Constans, son of the tyrant Constantine, 123; comes from Spain to meet his father, 123; leaves his wife in Saragossa, 123; leaves his affairs in the hands of Gerontius, 123; frightened by Gerontius, who had proclaimed Maximus as Emperor, 123–4

Constans, the Emperor, 91, 593

Constantina, daughter of Burgolen, 531; one of the rebellious nuns of Saint Radegund's nunnery in Poitiers, 531; drops out of the revolt and joins a nunnery in Autun, 531

Constantine, the Emperor, 90; Saint Martin was born in the eleventh year of his rule, 91; poisoned his son Crispus, 91; drowned his wife Fausta in a hot bath, 91; the wood of the True Cross was discovered by his mother Helena, 91; 144

Constantine II, the Emperor, 91

Constantine, the tyrant, 123; summons his son Constans from Spain, 123; besieged in Arles, 124; beheaded on the River Mincio, 124

Constantinople, entered by Theodosius as a conqueror, 25; Justinian dies there, 234; Tiberius II is Emperor there, 235; Tiberius II crowned there, with the Patriarch of Constantinople present, 293; Gundovald the Pretender lives there, 352; 354; 415; 419; rumour that Ingund has been sent there, 449–50; 571

Constantius, the Emperor, 91; pardons Saint Hilary and recalls him from exile, 91

Corinthians, the, ruled over by Oxion, 80

Cornelius, Saint, martyred in Rome, 88

Corps-Nuds, village in Brittany, 292; attacked by the Bretons, 292

Cosmas, Saint and martyr, 546; Gregory of Tours found his relics in Tours cathedral when he was tidying up, and placed them in Saint Martin's cell nearby, 602

Cournon, the monastery of, 234; Palladius was buried in unconsecrated ground there, 234

Couserans, 504

Coutances, 282; Saint Romachar is Bishop, 463

Creation, the, 69; God makes heaven and earth, 69; He makes man in His own image, 69; 248; 331; 452; 604

Crescens, goes to see Saint Hospicius as he is dying, 336–7

Crispian, Saint, martyr, 490

Crispin, Saint, martyr, 298; church of Saint Crispin and Saint Crispinian in Soissons, 298; Chlodobert, young son of Chilperic and Fredegund, buried there, 298; 490

Crispinian, Saint, martyr, 298; church of Saint Crispin and Saint Crispinian in Soissons, 298; Chlodobert, young son of Chilperic and Fredegund, buried there, 298

Crispus, son of the Emperor Constantine, 91; poisoned by his father, 91

Cuise, the forest of, 217; King Lothar I falls ill there, 217; King Chilperic and Fredegund go there to mourn the death of their sons Chlodobert and Dagobert, 303

Cymulus, secular name for Emerius, Bishop of Saintes, 220

Cyprian, Saint, Bishop of Carthage, 88; martyred there, 88

Cyrola, so-called Arian bishop, 101, 108; seizes Saint Eugenius, Catholic Bishop of Carthage, 109; they dispute, 110; Cyrola's false miracle, 110–11; he is punished by God, 111; 498

D

Dacolen, Duke, son of Dagaric, 252; in the service of King Chilperic, 289; captured by Duke Dragolen, 289; murdered, 289

Dagaric, father of Duke Dacolen, 289

Dagobert, young son of King Chilperic and Fredegund, dies of dysentery, 297; died at Berny-Rivière, 298; buried in Saint Denis, 298; 323

Dagulf, Abbot, 431; fornicator, 451; killed by an outraged husband, 451

Dalmatius, Saint, Bishop of Rodez, 252; administers the small bishopric of Alais, 260; dies, 312

Damian, Saint and martyr, 546; Gregory of Tours found his relics in Tours cathedral when he was tidying up, and placed them in Saint Martin's cell, 602

Dan, son of Jacob, 73

Danes, the, attack Gaul, 159; 163

Daniel, the prophet, 78; in the lions' den, 78

David, the generations of the Israelites down to, 65; second King of Israel, 77; son of Jesse, 77; father of Solomon, 77; his death, 77; 78; 81; 103; 126; 161; Psalms of David, 287; 308; 310; slays Goliath, 330; 331; 561

Day of Judgement, the, see Judgement Day

Dax, 414; Nicetius, brother of Rusticus, Bishop of Aire, is Count, 414;

King Chilperic had agreed to the nomination of Nicetius as Bishop of
Dax, 414; instead Faustianus is made Bishop by Gundovald the Pretender
and Count Mummolus, 414; Faustianus deposed by the Council of
Mâcon, 452; Nicetius is Bishop, 452

Decimus Rusticus, Master of the Offices to the tyrant Constans, 124;
Prefect to Constans, 124; killed by the military leaders of the Emperor
Honorius, 124

Decius, the Emperor, 86; persecutes the Christians, 86; as Consul, 87; 593

De Cursu Stellarum ratio, the, 603

Deluge, the, see the Flood

Denis, Saint, Bishop of Paris, 591–2; see also Dionysius

Desert, the Israelites in the, 65; for forty years they dwelt there, 77

Desideratus, Bishop of Verdun, 190; maltreated by Theuderic, 190; is given
a loan for his city by Theudebert, 191–2; dies, 191; his son is Syagrius, 191

Desiderius, Bishop of Albi, 455

Desiderius, Bishop of Eauze, 454

Desiderius, deacon of Autun, 533; terrified by the rebellious nuns of Saint
Radegund's nunnery in Poitiers he runs away and swims his horse
across the River Clain, 533

Desiderius, Duke, Chilperic's military commander, 267; beaten by Count
Mummolus, 267; plays a part in the murder of Clovis, 304; sent by
Chilperic to attack Guntram's territory, 344; beats Duke Ragnovald, 344;
occupies Périgueux, 344; attacks Agen, 344; attacks Bourges, 359–60;
devastates Tours, 360–61; 383; 384; when he hears of her father's
assassination, he locks up Rigunth's treasure in Toulouse, 394; joins
Count Mummolus and Gundovald the Pretender in Avignon, 394;
sponsors Gundovald, 408; in Toulouse with Gundovald, Mummolus and
Duke Waddo, 408; knocks Bishop Magnulf about, 408–9; deserts
Gundovald, 417; 426; 432; received by King Guntram, 456; living with
the wife of Duke Eulalius, 456; her name is Tetradia, 476; he has moved
all his goods to Albi, 476; when Guntram gives Albi back to Childebert
II, Desiderius withdraws to Toulouse, 476; leads an army against the
Visigoths, 476; attacks Carcassonne, 476–7; killed at the siege of
Carcassonne, 477; 554

Desiderius the impostor, 483; in Tours, 483–4

Deuteria, 159; a woman of Cabrières, 183; she becomes the mistress of
Theudebert, 183; she bears him a daughter, 184; marries him, 184;
murders her daughter in Verdun, 185; she has a son, Theudebald, by
Theudebert, 185; Theudebert abandons her, 185

Deutherius, Bishop of Vence, dies, 511

Deutz, attacked by the Saxons, 213

Devil, the, 161; encourages Palladius to commit suicide, 234; 266; 270;
330; 331; 357; 368; 528; 529; one of the ringleaders in the rebellion of
the nuns of Saint Radegund's nunnery in Poitiers, 533; inspires the
bogus Christ of Bourges, 584–5; 603

Index

De virtutibus beati Martini episcopi, the, 97, 246, 258, 263

Diana, 446; Saint Vulfolaic destroys a statue to her in Trier, 446

Die, 240

Dijon, 137; Saint Aprunculus is lowered over the walls, 137; 145; 151; 159; description of Dijon, 182–3; should be a bishopric, 183; excellent wine, 183; built by the Emperor Aurelian, 183; 191; 195; entered by Chramn, 212–13; plague, 227; 261

Dinifius, Bishop of Tours, eleventh in order, 159, 162; dies, 179; was Bishop for ten months only, 598; buried in Saint Martin's church, 598

Dio, fortress sacked by Theudebert, 183

Diocletian, the Emperor, 90; persecutes the Christians, 90; slaughters many Christians at Easter, 90; 91; 244

Diogenianus, Bishop of Albi, 129

Dionysius, Saint, Bishop of Paris, 87; one of the Seven Bishops, 87; martyred, 87; 252; see Saint Denis

Disciola, nun in Saint Radegund's nunnery of the Holy Cross in Poitiers, 356; niece of Saint Salvius, Bishop of Albi, 356; she dies and the Archangel Michael comes to collect her soul, 357

Division, the, of the Kingdom of Israel, 65

Documents quoted at length, or in full: the *Historia* of Renatus Profuturus Frigeridus on Aetius, 118–19; the *Historia* of Sulpicius Alexander on the early rulers of the Franks, 120–23; the *Historia* of Renatus Profuturus Frigeridus on the tyrant Constantine and his son Constans, 123–4; the terms of the Treaty of Andelot, 503–7; the letter of the seven Bishops, Eufronius, Praetextatus, Germanus, Felix, Domitianus, Victorius and Domnolus, to Saint Radegund, when she proposes the foundation of the nunnery of the Holy Cross in Poitiers, 527–9; the reply of ten bishops to the letter in which Bishop Gundegisel says that he has excommunicated the rebellious nuns of Saint Radegund's nunnery in Poitiers, 533–4; Saint Radegund's letter of foundation for the nunnery of the Holy Cross, 535–8; the address of Pope Gregory the Great to the people of Rome during the plague, 544–6; the *procès-verbal* of the trial of the rebellious nuns of Saint Radegund's nunnery in Poitiers, 571–5

Dolo, son of Severus and brother-in-law of Duke Guntram Boso, 290; killed, 290

Dolus, where Saint Eustochius built the church, 595

Domigisel, 348; sent to Spain concerning Rigunth's dowry, 348; returns, 348; sets out with Rigunth, 379; expels Duke Theodulf from Angers, 450; quarrels with Duke Beppolen, 473

Dominicus, man cured of blindness by Saint Hospicius, 336

Domitian, the Emperor, 85; persecutes the Christians, 85; exiles the Apostle John to Patmos, 85

Domitianus, Saint, Bishop of Maestricht, 527; signs the letter to Saint Radegund, 527

Domnola, wife of Nectarius, 432; widow of Burgolen, 465; daughter of

Index

Victorius, Bishop of Rennes, 465; killed by Bobolen, Fredegund's Referendary, because he covets her vineyard, 465; the murderers are punished, 474

Domnolus, Bishop of Le Mans, 325; had been head of a religious community in Saint Lawrence's church in Paris, 339; faithful supporter of King Lothar I, 339; offered the bishopric of Avignon by Lothar, 339; refuses it, 339–40; becomes Bishop of Le Mans, 340; signs the letter to Saint Radegund, 527

Dordogne, River, 409, 415

Dragolen, Duke, 252; in the service of King Chilperic, 289; captures Duke Dacolen, who is murdered, 289; ambushes Duke Guntram Boso, who kills him, 289–90

Droctigisel, Bishop of Soissons, 480; dipsomaniac, 524; by the council of Sorcy allowed to remain Bishop, 524

Droctulf, 524; conspires with Septimima, Sunnegisil and Gallomagnus against Faileuba and Brunhild, 524–6; he is the lover of Septimima, 525; disfigured and sent to labour in the vineyards, 525

Duisburg, residence of King Clodio in Thuringia, 125

Dunois, the, see Châteaudun

Dynamius, Governor of Provence, 325; harasses Saint Theodore, Bishop of Marseilles, 341; blocks Duke Gundulf, sent to Marseilles by King Guntram, 342; captures Bishop Theodore, 343; joins Childebert II, 494; his son Evantius is killed in Carthage, 548

E

Easter, 251; dispute about the date, 274; 18 April in Gaul, 274; 21 March in Spain, 274; the springs at Osser always begin to run on 18 April, 274; 371; 436; 440; 515; 539; 541; 568; dispute about the date, 581–2; opinion of Victorius of Aquitaine, 581; view of Gregory of Tours, 582; Gregory's view is substantiated by the date of the flowing of the spring at Osser, 582; 596

Eauze, 454; Laban is Bishop, 454; Desiderius is Bishop, 454

Eber, son of Shelah, 72

Ebero, Treasurer of King Childebert II, 396; left in charge of Poitiers, 396

Eberulf, 384; Treasurer of King Chilperic, 402; Fredegund wanted him to be her lover, 402; she accuses him of having killed Chilperic, 402; in Touraine, 402; seeks sanctuary in Saint Martin's church in Tours, 402; the men of Orleans and Blois who are set to see that he does not come out rob the church instead, 402; his property is removed, 402–3; his evil behaviour, 403; Gregory of Tours had baptized his son, 403; desecrates Saint Martin's church, 403–5; Guntram sends Claudius to drag Eberulf out of Saint Martin's church and kill him, 409–12; Eberulf is killed by Claudius, 412; his wife is reduced to penury, 412

Eberulf, citizen of Tours, 429

Index

Ebrachar, Duke, sent by King Guntram to capture Ebregisel on his mission
to King Recared in Spain, 514; with Duke Beppolen in joint command
of King Guntram's army against the Bretons, 556; they quarrel incessantly,
556; Ebrachar stands on one side while the Bretons beat and kill Beppolen, 557; withdraws to Vannes, where welcomed by Bishop Regalis, 557;
withdraws across the River Mayenne at Angers, 558; his troops maltreated by the Angevins, 558; his troops ravage Tours, 558; thought to
have been bribed by Waroch the Breton, 558; bitterly reproached by
King Guntram, 558

Ebregisel, Bishop of Cologne, 569; appointed by Childebert II as one of
the commission to settle the revolt in Saint Radegund's nunnery, 569

Ebregisel, retainer of Queen Brunhild, 514; she sends him to King Recared,
who hopes to be her son-in-law, 514; King Guntram sends Duke Ebrachar
to seize Ebregisel, as he is under the impression that Brunhild is communicating with the sons of Gundovald the Pretender, 514–15; he is
freed, 515

Ecdicius, 102; how he relieves a famine in Burgundy from his own resources,
137–8; how he repelled a band of Goths almost single-handed, 138

Edobech, supporter of Constans the tyrant, 124

Edom, the 'earthly one', another name for Esau, 73

Egidius, Bishop of Rheims, 283; possibly responsible for the capture of
Merovech, 283; comes to King Chilperic in Nogent-sur-Marne on an
embassy from Childebert II, 328; leads a new embassy from Childebert II
to Chilperic, 359; the troops of Childebert II rebel against the diplomacy
of Egidius, 361; with some difficulty he escapes on his horse to Rheims,
361; sent by Childebert II to negotiate with King Guntram, 397; Guntram
is very rude to him, 397; Guntram warns Childebert II against him, 416;
479; makes his peace with Childebert II, 497; makes peace with Duke
Lupus, 497; 541; under torture, Sunnegisil implicates him in the plot
against Childebert II of Dukes Rauching, Ursio and Berthefried, 576;
imprisoned in Metz, 576; his trial in Metz for high treason, 577–80;
Duke Ennodius is prosecutor, 577; he breaks down and pleads guilty,
579; taken to Strasbourg, 579; deposed and exiled, 580

Egypt, 65; the Ishmaelites take Jacob to Egypt, 74; famine in Egypt, 74;
Jacob's brothers visit him there, 74; Benjamin is summoned to Egypt,
74; the Israelites are in bondage there, 74; the plagues of Egypt, 74;
irrigated by the River Nile, 74; ships from the Indies come to Clysma in
Egypt, 75; 126; 235; 249; the plagues of Egypt, 332; 377

Egyptians, the, pursue the Israelites, 75; they are drowned in the Red Sea,
75; the sixteenth dynasty of Pharaohs, 80; their Pharaoh Thephei, 80;
their Pharaoh Vafres, 80

Elafius, Saint, Bishop of Châlons-sur-Marne, 252; dies in Spain while on
a mission for Brunhild, 305; buried in his own cathedral, 305

Eleazar, son of Eliud, 79

Eliakim, son of Abiud, 79

Index

Elisha the prophet, 103, 373, 561

Eliud, son of Achim, 79

Embrun, 236, 238, 240; Count Mummolus beats the Longobards Rodan and Zaban there, 240

Emerius, Bishop of Saintes, 219; expelled by his Metropolitan, Saint Leontius, Bishop of Bordeaux, 219; his secular name was Cymulus, 220; restored to his bishopric by King Charibert, 220

Emerius, cousin of a nun abducted by Count Eulalius, 555; Eulalius murders him, 555

Emperius, Bishop of Toulouse, 129

Ennodius, Count of Tours and Poitiers, 289; deposed by King Chilperic, 289; Duke of Tours and Poitiers, 455; 479; Aire and Lescar are added to his responsibility, 487; Tours and Poitiers reject him, 487; prosecutor in the trial of Egidius, Bishop of Rheims, 577

Enoch the Righteous, 65; he walks with God, 70; son of Jered, 71

Enosh, son of Seth, 71

Eparchius, Saint, Bishop of Clermont-Ferrand, 101; succeeds Namatius, 133; his experience with Satan, 133; builds the monastery of Mont Chantoin, 133–4; goes into retreat there during Lent, 134; dies, 134

Eparchius, the recluse of Angoulême, 325; sanctity and miracles, 338; came from Périgueux, 338; dies, 338; how he saved a robber from the gibbet, 338–9

Epiphanius, Abbot of the monastery of Saint Remigius in Rheims, gives evidence against Bishop Egidius at his trial, 578–9; deposed, 580

Epiphanius, Bishop of Fréjus, 353; implicated in the Gundovald affair and locked up by King Guntram, 353; dies in custody, 353

Epiphany, 258, 596

Episcopate of Saint Peter, Feast of, 596

Epolon, boy martyr, 86

Esau, 65; son of Isaac and Rebecca, 73; also called Edom, the 'earthly one', 73; sold his birthright, 73; ancestor of the Idumaeans, 73; Jobab or Job descended from him, 73; God hated him, 73

Estoublon, near Riez, 237; the invading Saxons encamp there, 237

Esvres, where the church was built by Saint Perpetuus, 597

Etampes, 504, 578

Eucherius, Senator of Clermont-Ferrand, 133; killed by Duke Victorius, 133

Eufrasius, Saint, Bishop of Clermont-Ferrand, 151, 162

Eufrasius the priest, 229; son of Evodius, 229; asks for the bishopric of Clermont-Ferrand, 229

Eufronius, merchant of Bordeaux, 413–14; hated by Bishop Bertram, who had tried to force him into the Church in order to steal his possessions, 413–14; apparently a Syrian, 413; the ridiculous affair of the Pretender Gundovald, Count Mummolus, Bertram and the finger-bone of Saint Sergius, 413–14

Eufronius, Saint, Bishop of Autun, 131; he builds the church of Saint

Symphorian there, 131; he sends a marble top for the tomb of Saint Martin in Tours, 131

Eufronius, Saint, Bishop of Tours, eighteenth in order, 195; the people of Tours ask Lothar for Eufronius as Bishop, 210; he is the nephew of Saint Gregory, Bishop of Langres, and thus a relative of Gregory of Tours, 210–11; made Bishop of Tours, 210; he refuses to support the priest Heraclius in his attempt to replace Emerius, Bishop of Saintes, 220; 321; refuses to allow the Tourangeaux to be taxed, 516; signs the letter to Saint Radegund, 527; leads the service of installation of the fragment of the True Cross in Saint Radegund's nunnery, 530; much of Tours burnt down in his day, 600; in his time, too, Willichar the priest burned down Saint Martin's church while he was taking sanctuary there, 600; Eufronius has a tin roof put on it, being helped financially by King Lothar I, 600; built Saint Vincent's church in Tours, 600; built churches in the villages of Thuré, Céré and Orbigny, 600–601; was Bishop for seventeen years, 601; buried in Saint Martin's church, 601

Eugenius, a tyrant, 123; he advances to the Rhine and makes a treaty with the Alamanni and the Franks, 123

Eugenius, Saint, Bishop of Carthage, 108; seized by Cyrola the Arian, 108; his letter to his flock quoted in full, 109–10; disputes with Cyrola, 110; 112; under sentence of death, 112; he is exiled to Albi by King Hunderic, 113

Eulalius, Count of Clermont-Ferrand, 450; his wife leaves him for Duke Desiderius, 456; her name is Tetradia, 476; Desiderius marries her, 476; Desiderius is killed, 477; 541; tries to prevent the escape of the gaolbirds of Clermont-Ferrand when they are freed by a miracle, 553; he brings a lawsuit against his ex-wife, Tetradia, for restitution of property, 554; his evil life as a young man, 554; suspected of having garrotted his own mother, 554; permitted to take communion by Cautinus, Bishop of Clermont-Ferrand, 554; had seriously maltreated Tetradia, 554–5; his nephew Virus fell in love with her, 555; Virus sent her to Duke Desiderius for protection, 555; Eulalius murdered Virus, 555; Tetradia married Desiderius, 555; Eulalius abducted a nun, 555; murdered the nun's cousin Emerius, 555; murdered a brother of his own half-sister, called Socratius, 555; gave his son John to Innocentius, Bishop of Rodez, to be a priest, 555–6; sues the widowed Tetradia for restitution of property, 556

Eunius, Bishop of Vannes, 252; sent by Waroch as an emissary to King Chilperic, 291; Chilperic banishes him from his diocese, 291; recalled, 292; banished by the Bretons to Angers, 292; becomes a heavy drinker, 305; has a stroke, 305

Eunius, other name of Count Mummolus, 236; see Mummolus, Count

Eunomius, Count of Tours, 252, 313; alleges that Gregory of Tours is planning to invite King Guntram to take over the city, 318; suspected of the murder of Armentarius the Jew, 405–6

Index

Euphemia, Saint and martyr, her church in Rome, 546

Euric, King of Galicia, 376; son of Mir, 376; allies with Leuvigild, 376; deposed by Andica, 376

Euric, King of the Visigoths, 102, 132; puts Duke Victorius in charge of the Seven Cities, 132; his death, 133; how he crossed the Spanish frontier and harassed Gaul, 138; his death, 139

Europs, King of Sicyon, 80

Eusebius, Bishop of Caesarea, 69; his *Chronicles*, 69; he continues his *Chronicles* down to the twenty-first year of Constantine, 91; 103; 498

Eusebius, Bishop of Paris, 586; a Syrian, 586; had been a merchant, 586; fills his household with Syrians, 586

Eusebius, Saint, Bishop of Vercelli, 311

Eustasius, Bishop of Bourges, 586; had been deacon of Autun, 586

Eustochius, Saint, Bishop of Tours, fifth in order, 101; replaces Saint Bricius as Bishop, 106; his death, 130; 154; his life, 595; was Bishop for seventeen years, 595; built a church inside Tours, 595; also built churches in Braye, Yzeures, Loches and Dolus, 595; buried in Saint Martin's church, 595

Eutropes, King of the Assyrians, 80

Eutyches, the heresy of, 149

Evantius, Saint, Bishop of Vienne, 471; dies, 471

Evantius, son of Dynamius, 547; came from Arles, 547; sent by Childebert II on a mission with Grippo to the Emperor Maurice Tiberius, 547; killed in Carthage, 548

Eve, 65; created by God from one of Adam's ribs, 69; expelled from Paradise, 70; she conceives and bears two sons, 70; 452; 528

Evodius, father of Salustius, Count of Clermont-Ferrand, 207; also father of the priest Eufrasius, 229

Ezekiel, the prophet, 78, 561

Ezra, the prophet, 78

F

Faileuba, wife of King Childebert II, 492; present at the conference in Trier between Childebert II and King Guntram, 492; 505; has a second child, who dies immediately, 524; conspiracy against Faileuba and Brunhild led by Septimima, Sunnegisil, Gallomagnus and Droctulf, 524–6

Faramod, priest, brother of Bishop Ragnemod, 586; when Ragnemod dies, Faramod puts his name forward for the bishopric of Paris, 586

Faraulf, alleged to be planning to assassinate King Guntram, 400–401; dies, 401

Farro, adviser to Ragnachar, 156–7

Fausta, wife of the Emperor Constantine, 91; he drowns her in a hot bath, 91

Faustianus the priest, 414; made Bishop of Dax by the Pretender Gundovald and Count Mummolus, 414; Bertram, Bishop of Bordeaux, avoids consecrating him, 414; Palladius, Bishop of Saintes, performs the consecration, 414; Orestes, Bishop of Bazas, is present, 414; 434; deposed by the Council of Mâcon, but is paid an indemnity, 452

Faustus, Bishop of Auch, 454

Feast of Saint Peter and Saint Paul, the, 597

Felix, Bishop of Belley, signs the letter to Bishop Gundegisel about the revolt in Saint Radegund's nunnery, 533

Felix, Bishop of Châlons-sur-Marne, goes to Chalon-sur-Saône with Gregory of Tours to assure King Guntram that Childebert II is observing the terms of the Treaty of Andelot, 507; Guntram jokes with Felix about the enmity between Brunhild and Fredegund, 507; tells Guntram that Recared is asking Childebert II for the hand of Chlodosind, 507–8; and that Childebert II wants him to help in attacking the Longobards, 508; Felix, Gregory and Guntram dine amicably together, 509; signs the letter to Bishop Gundegisel about the revolt in Saint Radegund's nunnery, 533

Felix, head of a mission from Guntram to Childebert II, 443–4

Felix, member of a senatorial family (in Marseilles?), 241

Felix, Saint and martyr, 484

Felix, Saint, Bishop of Nantes, 198; saves the life of Macliaw the Breton, 198; visits Saint Friard the hermit as he lies dying, 233; writes an abusive letter to Gregory of Tours, alleging that his brother Peter had killed his own Bishop, Silvester of Langres, 259; sends a deputation to the rebellious Bretons, 294; 321; 325; catches plague, 346; dies, 347; had refused the hand of his niece to Pappolen, 347; Pappolen abducts the girl and marries her, 347; Felix signs the letter to Saint Radegund, 527

Ferreolus, Saint, Bishop of Limoges, 292; saves the life of Mark the tax-collector, 292; restores Saint Martin's church in Brives-la-Gaillarde, 395

Ferreolus, Saint, Bishop of Uzès, 325; dies, 325; 337; his volumes of letters, 337

Festus, King of the Lacedaemonians, 80

Firminus, Count of Clermont-Ferrand, 195; deposed by Chramn, 207; takes refuge in the cathedral in Clermont-Ferrand, 207; his sister-in-law Caesaria with him, 207–8; Imnachar, one of Chramn's men, drags him out of sanctuary, 208; he escapes, 208; attacks Arles with the men of Clermont-Ferrand, 223; beaten by King Guntram's troops under Celsus, 224; opposes the election of Saint Avitus to the bishopric of Clermont-Ferrand, 229–30; brother-in-law, says Gregory (really uncle) of Palladius, 234; sent by King Sigibert as an envoy to the Emperor Tiberius II, 235

Flavianus, court official of King Childebert II, 553; Animodius appears before him, but is allowed to go free, 553; is bribed by Chuppa to allow him to go free, 553; frees Leubovera, Mother Superior of Saint Radegund's nunnery, when the nun Clotild locks her up, 568

Index

Flavinius, retainer of Queen Brunhild, 502; she gives him Chramnesind's property, but he hands it back to Chramnesind, 502

Flavius, Saint, Bishop of Chalon-sur-Saône, 312; had been King Guntram's Referendary, 312; is present at the baptism of Lothar II, 587

Fleury-sur-Ouche, near Dijon, 191; Syagrius murders Syrivald in a villa there, 191

Flood, the, 65; sent by God, 70; 248; 331; 604

Florentianus, Mayor of the Household, sent by Childebert II to revise the tax-lists of Poitiers, 515

Forty-eight Martyrs, the church of the, in Antioch, 582; the Persians attempt in vain to burn it down, 582

Francilio, Bishop of Tours, fourteenth in order, 179; had been a Senator, 179; poisoned, 180; came from Poitiers, 599; had a wife called Clara, 599; was Bishop for two years only, 599; buried in Saint Martin's church, 599

Franks, the, 101, 118; in his *Historia*, Sulpicius Alexander discusses their early leaders, 120; they invade the Roman province of Germania, 120; their early leaders were Genobaud, Marcomer and Sunno, 120; attack Cologne, 120; threaten Trier, 120; beaten by Nanninus and Quintinus in the forest of Charbonnière, 120; destroy the army of Quintinus in their forests, 120–21; ravage Germania, 121; their 'regales' or petty kings, 122; their tribes, the Bructeri, the Chamavi, the Amsivarii, the Chatti, 122; they make a treaty with the tyrant Eugenius, 123; long description of their early wars by Renatus Profuturus Frigeridus in his *Historia*, 123–4; annihilate the Vandals under their King Godigisel, 123; 124; they sack Trier, 124; their early kings are never named, 125; came from Pannonia, 125; colonized the banks of the Rhine, 125; marched through Thuringia, 125; their early long-haired kings, 125; Theudemer an early king, 125; Clodio an early king, 125; the early Franks were idol-worshippers, 125–7; they expel Childeric because of his debauched life, 128; Aegidius, the Roman general, reigns over them for eight years during the deposing of Childeric, 128; they recall Childeric, 129; on the death of Childeric, Clovis becomes King, 139; the Franks are baptized with Clovis, 144; the kingdom of Clovis divided after his death between Theuderic, Chlodomer, Childebert and Lothar, 162; they conquer the Burgundes, 167; attack and conquer the Thuringians, 168; they conquer Burgundy, 171; beaten under Lothar I by the Saxons, 209–10; on the death of King Lothar I, the lands of the Franks are divided between Charibert, Guntram, Chilperic and Sigibert, 217; their never-ending civil wars, 253; a Frankish army under Duke Beppolen is cut to pieces by the Bretons, 557

Fredegund, the wife of King Chilperic, 222; sends two emissaries to assassinate King Sigibert at Vitry, 248; expelled from Soissons by the Champenois, 255; is furious when she learns that Merovech has escaped from Anille, 268; 269; persuades Duke Guntram Boso to lead Merovech into an ambush, but it fails, 270–71; tries to bribe Gregory of Tours to speak against Saint Praetextatus, 279; 283; rejects her son Samson, 288;

he dies, 288; loses her young sons Chlodobert and Dagobert through dysentery, 297; ascribes this to Chilperic's new taxation, 297; in mourning in the forest of Cuise, 303; tries to infect her stepson Clovis with dysentery, 303; tortures Clovis's girl-friend and the girl's mother, 304; has Clovis murdered for alleged conspiracy, 304; the allegation by Count Leudast that Gregory of Tours is putting it about that Bertram, Bishop of Bordeaux, is her lover, 316; 319; 322; stops a fight between Duke Berthefried and Duke Ursio on the one hand and Duke Lupus on the other, 329; Leudast, whom she has had deprived of communion, throws himself at her feet, 362; she and Chilperic have Leudast tortured to death, 363; grief at the death of her son Theuderic, 365; tortures and kills a number of Parisian housewives for allegedly causing Theuderic's death, 365; destroys all Theuderic's possessions, 366; tortures Mummolus the Prefect for alleged implication in Theuderic's death, 366; has a son, Lothar, 375; contributes vast sums and quantities of goods to the dowry of her daughter Rigunth, 378; takes refuge in the cathedral in Paris when her husband Chilperic is assassinated, 381; 383; seeks sanctuary with Bishop Ragnemod, 390; her treasure is taken to Childebert II in Meaux, 390; seeks help from King Guntram, 390–91; her surrender is demanded by Childebert II, 392; her crimes listed, 392; she is pregnant again, 392; Guntram refuses to surrender her to Childebert II, 397; still in Paris, 399; rages when she hears how badly Rigunth is being treated, 399; speaks against the restoration of Praetextatus to the bishopric of Rouen, 400; sent to Rueil, near Rouen, under guard of ex-Bishop Melanius, 401; sends a cleric to assassinate Brunhild, 401; murders him when he fails, 402; wanted Eberulf, King Chilperic's Treasurer, to be her lover, 402; accuses him of having killed Chilperic, 402; encourages Claudius to kill Eberulf, 409; 417; sends Chuppa to bring home Rigunth, 425; 432; Guntram intercepts a secret letter from Leuvigild to Fredegund, 456; sends two priests to assassinate Childebert II and Brunhild, 457–8; they are intercepted by Duke Rauching and executed, 458; still in Rouen, 462; exchanges bitter remarks with Praetextatus, 462; Praetextatus is murdered in his own cathedral, apparently at the instigation of Fredegund, 463; she goes to watch him die, 463; poisons one of the Rouennais who says that it is a bad thing to murder bishops, 463–4; tries to murder Leudovald, Bishop of Bayeux, 464; Bobolen, her Referendary, kills Domnola, 465; to protect herself, alleges that one of her servants killed Praetextatus, 472–3; treats Duke Beppolen badly, 473; sends messages to Spain, 474; sends envoys to Guntram, 475; one of them is thought to be an assassin, 475–6; 480; sends no one to speak up for Baddo at his trial, 496; 507; her endless quarrels with her daughter Rigunth lead to her trying to choke the girl with the lid of Chilperic's treasure-chest, 521–2; 542; orders the Saxons of the Bessin to dress up as Bretons and fight against Duke Beppolen, 556–7; gives a large donation to Saint Martin's church when she learns that her son Lothar is seriously ill, 559; has Waroch release the prisoners from Duke Beppolen's army. 559; 575; sends twelve assassins to murder King Childebert II, but they are all caught, 576; has three Franks killed in Tournai, Charivald, Leudovald and Waldin, 586–7; asks Guntram to baptize her son Lothar, 587

Fréjus, 353; Epiphanius is Bishop, 353

Friard, Saint, the hermit, 196; his holy life, 232–3; visited by Saint Felix, Bishop of Nantes, as he lies dying, 233

Frontinus, 299; poisons Marachar, Bishop of Angoulême, with a fish's head, 299; becomes Bishop of Angoulême himself, 299; dies, 299

Frontinus, deacon of Périgueux, 351; apparently wrote treasonable letters which he signed in the name of his enemy, Bishop Charterius, 351; pardoned, 351

G

Gad, son of Jacob, 73

Gailen, Merovech's servant, 267; kills his master at his own request, 282; is foully done to death, 282–3

Gaiso, Count of Tours, 516; tries to tax the Tourangeaux, 516

Galicia, occupied by the Vandals, 106; occupied by the Suebi, 106; 252; Saint Martin is Bishop, 301; Mir is King, 306; 326; 375; Euric is King, 376; Andica becomes King, 376; 469

Galienus, friend of Gregory of Tours, 316–17; arrested, 317

Galilaeans, the, 83

Gall, Saint, Bishop of Clermont-Ferrand, 195, 199; his vision during the plague, 199–200; he institutes Rogations, 200; dies, 200; 207

Gallienus, the Emperor, 88; persecutes the Christians, 88

Gallomagnus, Referendary to Childebert II, 524; conspires with Septimima, Sunnegisil and Droctulf against Faileuba and Brunhild, 524–6; sent into exile, 525–6; recalled after a plea by King Guntram, 526

Gallo-Roman speech, 433

Galswinth, daughter of Athanagild, King of the Visigoths, 222; elder sister of Brunhild, 222; she was an Arian, but becomes a Catholic on her marriage to Chilperic, 222; jealous of Fredegund, Chilperic's other wife, 222; Chilperic has her garrotted, 222; the miracle at her tomb, 223; 505

Garachar, Count of Bordeaux, pardoned by King Guntram at the request of Gregory of Tours, 438

Gararic, Duke, supporter of Childebert II, 396; comes to Limoges, 396; moves to Poitiers, 396; advises the Tourangeaux to retain their allegiance to Childebert II, 396; leaves Ebero in charge of Poitiers, 396; robs Marileif, one-time physician to Chilperic, 407

Garivald, Duke of Bavaria, 203; receives Vuldetrada, widow of King Theudebald, 203

Garonne, River, 138, 417, 418, 450

Gascons, the, 479, 487; probably = the Basques

Index

Gascony, 344

Gatianus, Saint, Bishop of Tours, first in order, 87; one of the Seven Bishops, 87; 99; his life, 593; came when Decius was Emperor, 593; was Bishop for some fifty-odd years, 593; buried in the town, 593; his body was translated to Saint Litorius' church by Saint Mar.in, 594

Gaudentius, the father of Aetius, 119; born in Scythia, 119; member of the Praetorian Guard, 119; rose to be Master of the Horse, 119

Gaul, the decline of literature in, 63; the Seven Bishops sent to Gaul, 87; invaded by the Alamanni, 88; by the Vandals, 106; by the Huns, 114; by Euric, King of the Visigoths, 138; keen to submit to the rule of the Franks, 150; Clovis gradually extends his dominion over Gaul, 158; attacked by the Danes, 159; 163; plague in Gaul, 199; attacked by the Huns after the death of King Lothar I, 217; 235; attacked by the Longobards, 236; the Saxons accompany the Longobards in their attack on Gaul, 237; 292; terrible outbreak of dysentery, 296; invaded by the Longobards, 333–4; portents and epidemics, 377; 415; 420; 422; famine, 427; 432; 435; 436; 456; 459; 469; 512; 527; 541; plague, 584; religious impostors in, 586

Gauls, the, preached to by the Seven Bishops, 66; 87

Gaza, the wine of, 411

Geilamir, King of the Vandals, 113; defeated and killed by the Romans, 113

Genesis, the Book of, 561

Geneva, flooded by a blockage in the River Rhône at Tauredunum (=Les Evouettes), 225

Geneviève, Saint, 197

Genebaud, early leader of the Franks, 120

Gentiles, the different kingdoms of the, 65; their idolatrous behaviour, 101; 310

Germania, Roman province on the left bank of the Rhine, 120; invaded by the Franks, 120; 124

Germanus, Prefect of the City of Rome, intercepts a letter from Gregory the Great to the Emperor Maurice Tiberius, 544

Germanus, Saint, 133; his church in Saint-Germain-Lanbron built by Duke Victorius, 133; his spirit frees the prisoners in the gaol in the great fire of Paris, 466; his tomb is in the church of Saint Vincent in Paris (now Saint-Germain-des-Prés), 466

Germanus, Saint, Bishop of Auxerre, 272; Merovech seeks sanctuary in his church, 272

Germanus, Saint, Bishop of Paris, 220; he excommunicates King Charibert for marrying two sisters, Merofled and Marcovefa, 220; tries to make peace between Sigibert and Chilperic, 247–8; 251; dies, 264; his miracles 264; these are described by Venantius Fortunatus in his *Vita Sancti Germani*, 264; 268; signs the letter to Saint Radegund, 527; consecrates Agnes as the first Mother Superior of Saint Radegund's nunnery in Poitiers, 536

Gerontius, supporter of the tyrant Constans in Spain, 123; proclaims Maximus as Emperor, 123

646

Index

Gervasius, Saint and martyr, 546, 595

Gévaudan, the, 554

Goar, King of the Alani, 123

God the Father Almighty, 67; makes heaven and earth, 69; creates Adam and Eve, 69; takes Enoch the Righteous, 70; sends the Flood, 70; the wrath of God, 70; He causes the confusion of tongues, 71; offers Solomon any gift, 77; punishes Herod, 81; 162; His position in the Trinity debated between Gregory of Tours and Agilan the Arian, 307–10; similar disputation between Gregory of Tours and King Chilperic, 310–11; Chilperic and Gregory of Tours debate the Godhead with a Jew called Priscus, 330–33; 349; Gregory of Tours and Oppila debate the Godhead; 371–4; 385; 446; 448; 483; 491; 494; 498; 503; 507; 527; 528; 534; 535; 537; 545

Godigisel, Duke, 494; leads the army of Childebert II against Duke Berthefried and Duke Ursio, 494; had married the daughter of Duke Lupus, 494; 495; fights the battle on the River Woëvre against Duke Berthefried and Duke Ursio, 494–5

Godigisel, Duke, Sigibert's military commander, 247; with Duke Guntram Boso fights and kills Theudebert, 247

Godigisel, King of the Vandals, 102; his death, 102; 123

Godigisel, son of Gundioc, King of the Burgundes, 141; with his brother Gundobad rules over the province of Marseilles and the territory round the Rivers Rhône and Saône, 145; an Arian, 145; conspires with Clovis against Gundobad, 145; Clovis and Godigisel beat Gundobad near the River Ouche, 145–6; returns home to Vienne, 146; besieged by Gundobad there, 147–8; 162

Godin, supporter of King Sigibert, 256; transfers to Chilperic, who rewards him, 256; beaten in battle, 256; loses Chilperic's favour, 256; dies, 256; Duke Rauching marries his widow, 256

Godomar, King of the Burgundes, 162; brother of Sigismund, 166; with Sigismund is attacked by Chlodomer, 166; beaten by Chlodomer and Theuderic at the battle of Vézeronce, 167; although beaten three times, wins back his kingdom, 167; beaten by Childebert and Lothar and forced to flee, 171

Gogo, the governor and nutritor of the young King Childebert II, 313; dies, 327

Goiswinth, wife of Athanagild, King of the Visigoths, 233; later second wife of Leuvigild, King of the Visigoths, 233; by Athanagild, mother of Brunhild, 233; widow of Athanagild, 301; later married Leuvigild, 301; persecutes the Catholics in Spain, 301; punished by a cataract, 301; maltreats her daughter-in-law Ingund because she will not become an Arian, 302; Goiswinth herself is an Arian, 302; 481

Goliath, the Philistine, 103; slain by David, 330

Goths (often meaning the Visigoths), beat the Romans in Thrace, 92; they kill the Emperor Valens, 92; Athanaric is their King, 113; how they

647

captured and destroyed Rome, 123; expel the Bretons from Bourges, 132; Count Paul attacks the Goths, 132; attacked by Theudebert and Gunthar, the sons of Theuderic and Lother I, 183; 260

Gracina, an island off Poitou, 314; Leudast was born there, 314

Gratianus, the Emperor, 92; makes Theodosius his colleague, 92; captured and killed by Maximus, 93

Gratus, Consul, 87

Greeks, the, 302; troops of the Emperor Tiberius II in Spain, 302; they fail to support Hermangild in his war against his father Leuvigild, 302–3; Ingund is in their hands, 371

Gregory, Saint, Bishop of Langres, 159; Attalus was his nephew, 175; how he loved Dijon, 182; buried in Dijon, 261; great-grandfather of Gregory of Tours, 261

Gregory, Saint, Bishop of Tours, nineteenth in order, and why he wrote *The History of the Franks*, 63; his literary style, 63; his Catholic faith, 67; pretends to have little knowledge of Latin grammar, 67; his credo as a Catholic, 67–9; has questioned men who have actually visited the Red Sea, 75; his ancestor, the Senator Leocadius, gives a house to the church in Bourges, 88; his ancestor Vettius Epagatus martyred in Lyons, 86; 88; the hostage Attalus was a relative of his, 175; witnesses miracles in the church of Saint Medard in Soissons, 215; sees the monk Julian perform a miracle in Saint Julian's church in Clermont-Ferrand, 227; his first-person evidence first becomes important with the arrival of Roccolen in Tours, 258; refuses to drive Duke Guntram Boso out of sanctuary, 258; receives an abusive letter from Saint Felix, Bishop of Nantes, 259; his sarcastic reply, 259; the murder of his brother, Peter the deacon, 260–62; Saint Gregory, Bishop of Langres, was his great-grandfather, 261; laments the fact that his Latin is so provincial, 263; compelled to give communion to the fugitive Merovech, 268; Nicetius, the husband of his niece, 268; refuses King Chilperic's order to expel Merovech, 268; helps Marileif, Chilperic's physician, when he is attacked by Merovech, 269; has a meal with Merovech, 269; reads some biblical passages to him, 269; in a vision foresees the death of Chilperic and all his sons, 270; has no choice but to receive a never-ending flood of evildoers in sanctuary in Saint Martin's church, 270; speaks up firmly for Saint Praetextatus, Bishop of Rouen, at his trial, 276–7; his speech reported verbatim, 276–7; Chilperic tries to bully him, 277–9; Fredegund tries to bribe him, 279; ordains Winnoch as a priest, 288; sees portents in the sky over Tours while celebrating Mass, 288–9; has Chuppa, Chilperic's Master of the Stables, freed, 305; disputes with Agilan the Arian over the Holy Trinity, 307–10; disputes with King Chilperic over the distinction of Persons, 310–11; is seriously calumniated by Count Leudast, who alleges that it is he who started the scandal that Bertram, Bishop of Bordeaux, is the lover of Queen Fredegund, 316; it is then alleged by Count Berulf and Eunomius, Count of Tours, that Gregory is planning to invite King Guntram to take over Tours, which is treason, 318; Gregory is advised to flee to Clermont-Ferrand, but he refuses, 318; the trial of Gregory of Tours at Berny-Rivière for treason and calumny, 319–21; Bertram, Bishop of Bordeaux, like himself a Metropolitan, speaks against him, 319; Rigunth fasts and prays for Gregory, 319–20; he is exonerated on all counts, 319; returns in triumph to Tours, 321; finds a sorry mess, 321; before leaving Berny-Rivière, chats with Saint Salvius, Bishop of Albi, outside the court-house, 322–3; Salvius points out the sword of the wrath of God which is hanging in the sky over the house where Chilperic is staying, but, although he screws up his eyes, Gregory cannot see it, 323; visits King Chilperic at Nogent-sur-Marne and is shown a gold salver and some medallions which the Emperor Tiberius II has sent, 328; joins in a religious disputation between the Jew Priscus and King Chilperic, 330–33; gives communion to King Chilperic, 333; himself questions a deaf and dumb man cured by Saint Hospicius, 337; also questions an official concerned with a miracle performed by Eparchius the recluse, 339; saves the lives of the men who broke into Saint Martin's church, 341; puts up Duke Gundulf, who is a relation of his, 342; discusses with Duke Ansovald, newly returned from Spain, the latest arguments used by King Leuvigild in his persecution of the Catholics, 349; writes to Fredegund about Leudast, 362; debates the Catholic and Arian faiths with Oppila, the envoy from Leuvigild, 371–4; his account of the life of Saint Salvius had been given to him by Salvius himself, 388; had baptized Eberulf's son, 403; intervenes in a dispute between six citizens of Tours, 429; dines with King Guntram in Orleans, 434; Guntram visits Gregory's lodging and they have a drink together, 434; Guntram asks Gregory's deacon to sing, 436; he shows Gregory some of Count Mummolus' plate, 436; Guntram and he admit that they have both seen the dead Chilperic in a vision and that he is not too happy, 437–8; intercedes with Guntram on behalf of Duke Bladast and Garachar, Count of Bordeaux, 438–9; is told a sad story about Saint Theodore, Bishop of Marseilles, by Saint Magneric, Bishop of Trier, 442–3; present in Coblenz when messengers from Guntram come to Childebert II, 444; nearly drowned there when crossing the river late at night after dining with Childebert II, 444; meets Saint Vulfolaic at Carignan and is told the story of his life, 445–7; Vulfolaic tells Gregory of miracles performed by Saint Martin, 448–9; sees a striking portent in the sky over Carignan, 449; intercedes for Childeric the Saxon, 450; saves Berulf and Arnegisel from being beheaded, 456; 479; goes to the funeral of Saint Radegund in the nunnery of the Holy Cross in Poitiers, 481; how he came next after the impostor in Saint Julian's church in Paris, 486; meets Wiliulf and his son dying of dysentery on the road near Rheims, 496; is on his way to Metz to see Childebert II, when summoned urgently to Chalon-sur-Saône by Guntram, 502; assures Guntram that Childebert II is observing the conditions of the Treaty of Andelot, 502–3; has to listen while Guntram has the entire Treaty read aloud, 503–7; jokes with

Index

Guntram about the bitter enmity between Brunhild and Fredegund, 507; tells Guntram that Childebert II does not want to hold a council of bishops, 508–9; Gregory, Felix, Bishop of Châlons-sur-Marne, and Guntram dine amicably together, 509; helps Ingoberg, one-time wife of King Charibert, to make her will, 513; prevents Childebert II from taxing Tours, 515–17; advises the rebellious nun Clotild to return to Poitiers, 526; he reads to her the letter of the seven Bishops to Saint Radegund, 527–9; he insists that at least she and her forty sister-nuns spend the rest of the winter in Tours, 531; his deacon Agiulf gives Gregory an eye-witness account of the plague in Rome and the election of Gregory the Great as Pope, 543–7; has to intervene with the nuns of Ingitrude's convent in Tours, when they object to her niece being appointed as Mother Superior, 560; disputes with one of his own priests, who denies the resurrection of the body, 560–66; appointed by Childebert II as one of the commission to settle the revolt in Saint Radegund's nunnery, 569; refuses to sit until the civil authorities put down the rioting, 569; quotes in full the *procès-verbal* of the trial and the verdict, 571–5; his views on the date of Easter, 581–2; Simon, a Bishop from Armenia, arrives in Tours and tells Gregory about the sack of Antioch and the invasion of Armenia by Adarmaanes, Chosroes' general, 582–3; Saint Aredius, albeit unwillingly, tells Gregory about his miracles, 591; Aredius stays with Gregory in Tours and dies there, 591–2; how Gregory had to rebuild Tours cathedral, which had been burnt down when Saint Eufronius was Bishop, 601; he re-dedicated it in the seventeenth year of his episcopate, 601; he discovered the relics of the Agaune martyrs, and placed them in Tours cathedral, 601–2; he placed the relics of Saint Cosmas and Saint Damian in Saint Martin's cell by the cathedral, 602; he repainted the walls of Saint Martin's church, 602; he built a new baptistery by Saint Martin's church, 602; he placed the relics of Saint John and Saint Sergius there, 602; he placed the relics of Saint Benignus in the old baptistery, 602; dedicated many churches and oratories, 602; his writings consist of the ten books of the *Historiae Francorum*; the seven books of the *Liber in gloria Martyrum Beatorum*, the *Liber de passione et virtutibus Sancti Juliani martyris*, the *De virtutibus beati Martini episcopi* and the *Liber in gloria Confessorum*; the *Liber vitae Patruum*; the *In Psalterii tractatum commentarius*; and the *De Cursu Stellarum ratio*, 603–4; his style lacks polish, 603; he exhorts any future bishop of Tours who is responsible to keep these books intact and unchanged, 603; if he wants something to do, he can put them into verse, 603; Gregory finished writing his *Historiae* in the twenty-first year after his consecration, 604; for convenience he has added a list of the bishops of Tours, 604; adds up the years since the Creation of the World, 604

Gregory the Great, Saint and Pope, 541; was a deacon in Rome, 543; of a very noble family, 543; founded six monasteries in Sicily and a seventh in Rome, 543–4; his abstinence, 544; sends a letter to the Emperor Maurice

Tiberius to say that he does not wish to be Pope, 544; it is intercepted by Germanus, Prefect of the City of Rome, 544; Gregory is made Pope, 544; his address to the people of Rome quoted in full, 544–6; he organizes prayers and processions against the plague in Rome, 546–7; consecrated as Pope in Saint Peter's, 547; 604

Grenoble, 240; Rodan the Longobard encamps there, 240; Hesychius is Bishop, 533

Grèzes, 90; the people of Javols shut up in a castle there when the Alamanni come, 90

Grindio, Merovech's retainer, 283; foully done to death, 283

Grippo, envoy of Childebert II to the Emperor Maurice Tiberius, 541; arrives back from his mission, 547; had landed with two companions and their servants in North Africa, 547; travelled to Carthage, 547; as the result of a theft committed by their servant, the three were involved in a fracas in Carthage and all but Grippo killed, 547–8; Grippo had seen the Emperor, 549; 552

Gundegisel, Count of Saintes, surnamed Dodo, 454; becomes Bishop of Bordeaux, 454; as Metropolitan, visits the rebellious nuns of Saint Radegund's nunnery and their male confederates in Saint Hilary's church, 532; they knock him over, 532; he excommunicates Clotild and the rebellious nuns, 533; he writes to a council of Bishops called by King Guntram to say what he has done, 533; their reply quoted in full, 533–4; appointed by King Guntram as one of the commission to settle the revolt in Saint Radegund's nunnery, 569; 573

Gunderic, King of the Vandals, 106; he invades Gaul and then Spain, 106; dies, 107

Gundioc, King of the Burgundes, 140–41; a relation of Athanaric, 141; his four sons, Gundobad, Godigisel, Chilperic and Gundomar, 141

Gundobad, King of Burgundy, 102; son of King Gundioc, 141; kills his brother Chilperic and Chilperic's wife, 141; drives Chilperic's two daughters into exile, the younger being Clotild, 141; allows Clovis to marry his niece Clotild, 141; with his brother Godigisel rules over the province of Marseilles and the territory round the Rivers Rhône and Saône, 145; an Arian, 145; beaten by Clovis and Godigisel near the River Ouche, 145–6; takes refuge in Avignon, 146; Aridius makes peace between Gundobad and Clovis, 146–7; besieges Godigisel in Vienne, 147–8; rules over all Burgundy, 148; considers the possibility of becoming a Catholic, but remains an Arian, 148–9; 162; dies, 165

Gundobad, son of King Guntram and his mistress Veneranda, 218; packed off to Orleans by his stepmother, Marcatrude, 218; she murders him, 218–19

Gundovald, Count of Meaux, 451; killed by Werpin, 451

Gundovald, Duke, military commander of King Sigibert, 244; beaten by Theudebert at Poitiers, 244; on the murder of Sigibert, saves the child Childebert, 254; proclaims him King, 254

Gundovald the Pretender, 325; maintains that he is the son of King Lothar

I and a woman not named, 352; in Constantinople, 352; lands in Marseilles, 352; his career, 352; seen by Childebert I, rejected by Lothar I, taken up by Charibert, rejected by Sigibert and exiled to Cologne, 352; escapes to Narses in Italy, 352; goes to Constantinople and marries, 352; invited (by Duke Guntram Boso?) to return to Gaul, 352; lands in Marseilles, 352; joins Count Mummolus in Avignon, 352; escapes to an island in the Mediterranean, 353; Guntram Boso steals his treasure, 353; 383; 384; again with Mummolus in Avignon, 394; after the assassination of Chilperic joined there by Duke Desiderius, 394; raised on the shield, 394; portents of his coming death, 395; 397–8; moves to Poitiers and then Angoulême, demanding oaths of allegiance, 407–8; goes to Périgueux, where he harasses Bishop Charterius, 408; in Toulouse, where he causes trouble to Bishop Magnulf, 408–9; Guntram's army sets out after him, 409; sends the Abbot of Cahors to his supporters with a message, but it is discovered, 412–13; in Bordeaux with Bishop Bertram, 413–14; the ridiculous affair of Gundovald, Mummolus, Bertram and the finger-bone of Saint Sergius, 413–4; sends two messengers to King Guntram, who has them flogged, tortured and thrown into prison, 415; 417; is pursued by Guntram's army, 417; crosses the Garonne, 417; deserted by Duke Desiderius, 417; retires to Saint-Bertrand-de-Comminges, 417; accompanied by Count Mummolus, Duke Bladast and Count Waddo, 417; is besieged there, 417–23; taunted by Guntram's troops, 419; tells the story of his life, 419–20; emerges from the besieged fortress, 423; is slaughtered, 423; 425; 434; 438; his sons in Spain, 514; 518; 581

Gundulf, Duke, 342; sent to Marseilles by King Guntram, 342; a relative of Gregory of Tours, who puts him up, 342; blocked by Dynamius, 342; enters Marseilles with Bishop Theodore, 342; sent to the siege of Avignon by Childebert II, 355

Gunthar, Bishop of Tours, seventeenth in order, 199; had been Abbot of the monastery of Saint Venantius in Tours, 199; dies, 203; had gone on many diplomatic missions for the Frankish Kings, 600; became an alcoholic, 600; was Bishop for two years only, 600; buried in Saint Martin's church, 600

Gunthar, eldest son of Lothar I, 183; attacks Rodez, 183; his mother was Ingund, 197; 198

Gunthar, second son of King Chlodomer, 167; his grandmother, Queen Clotild, brings him up, 167; murdered by King Lothar I, 180–82

Guntheuc, wife of King Chlodomer, 167; after Chlodomer's death, she marries his brother, King Lothar I, 167

Guntram, King of the Franks, fourth son of King Lothar I, 195; his mother was Ingund, 197; sent to the Limousin by Lothar I with Charibert to deal with Chramn, 212; Chramn escapes, 212; on Lothar's death, Charibert, Guntram, Chilperic and Sigibert divide between them the lands of the Franks, 217; Guntram takes Chlodomer's kingdom, with Orleans as his capital, 217; dismisses the patrician Agricola and appoints Celsus in his place, 218; makes Veneranda his mistress, 218; marries Marcatrude, 218; he dismisses Marcatrude, who dies, 219; marries Austrechild, 219; on Charibert's death, Theudechild offers her hand to Guntram, 220–21; he takes her treasure and puts her in a nunnery in Arles, 221; quarrels with Sigibert, 244; calls a council of bishops in Paris, 244; 245; allies with Chilperic against Sigibert, 246; 251; 261; 267; kills the sons of Magnachar, who had maligned Austrechild, 274; loses his own two sons, Lothar and Chlodomer, by dysentery, 274; makes treaty with Childebert II at the Stone Bridge, 274–5; makes Childebert II his adopted son, 275; 285; has the Bishops Sagittarius and Salonius tried, 285–6; shuts them up in two monasteries, 286; 289; appoints a council to try Sagittarius and Salonius at Chalon-sur-Saône, 291; they are imprisoned, 291; they escape, 291; loses his wife, Austrechild, 298; 305; Childebert II breaks the alliance with him, 327; Count Mummolus leaves him, 327; at war with Chilperic, 327; Chilperic and Childebert II ally against him, 328; Duke Lupus takes refuge with him, 329; 341; 343; quarrels with Childebert II, 344; 345; 359; attacked by Chilperic, but they make peace, 360; gives the second half of Marseilles to Childebert II, 363; 371; 374; 383; 384; goes to Paris, where Fredegund is, 391; argument with Childebert II about right to enter Paris, 391–2; asks his subjects not to assassinate him, 393; 394; invests Tours, Poitiers and Mareuil, 395; 396; with Lothar II and Childebert II as infants, really rules the whole of Gaul, 396; 397; Bishop Egidius, Duke Guntram Boso and Sigivald come to confer, as representatives of Childebert II, 397; Guntram refuses to give up any cities or to surrender the person of Fredegund, 397; he dismisses the envoys with insults, 398; allows Saint Praetextatus to be reinstated as Bishop of Rouen, 399–400; in Paris, 400; allegation that a man called Faraulf is planning to assassinate him, 400–401; hands back to its rightful owners property misappropriated during Chilperic's reign, 401; sends Fredegund to the manor of Rueil, near Rouen, under guard of ex-Bishop Melanius, 410; goes to Chalon-sur-Saône to investigate Chilperic's death, 402; his men invade Poitiers and Tours, 406–7; 407; 408; his army pursues the Pretender Gundovald, 409; sends Claudius to drag Eberulf out of Saint Martin's church and kill him, 409–12; 412; flogs, tortures and imprisons two messengers sent by Gundovald, 415; confers with Childebert II about Gundovald the Pretender, 415–17; makes Childebert II his heir, 416; warns him against Egidius, Bishop of Rheims, 416; restores to him everything that King Sigibert had held, 417; warns him against Fredegund, 417; sends his army against Gundovald, 417; besieges Gundovald in Saint-Bertrand-de-Comminges, 417–24; shares the treasure of Count Mummolus with Childebert II, 425; attempts to fine anyone who had not joined in the expedition against Saint-Bertrand-de-Comminges, 426; 431; 432; leaves Chalon-sur-Saône and travels through Nevers to Orleans, 433; is entertained by the townsfolk of Orleans, 433–4; is hostile to the Jews, 433–4; Gregory of Tours dines with him in Orleans, 434; he has a

Index

drink with Gregory, 434; asks Gregory's deacon to sing to them, 436; shows Gregory the plate of Count Mummolus, 436; alleges that Saint Theodore, Bishop of Marseilles, was responsible for Chilperic's murder, 437; he and Gregory confide in each other that they have both seen the dead Chilperic in a vision, 437–8; pardons Garachar, Count of Bordeaux, and Duke Bladast, at the request of Gregory of Tours, 438–9; goes to Paris, 440; questions if Lothar II really is Chilperic's son, 440; buries the remains of Merovech and Clovis in Saint Vincent's church in Paris (=Saint-Germain-des-Prés), 440–41; has Boantus executed, 441–2; locks up Saint Theodore, Bishop of Marseilles, 442; sends messengers to Childebert II about a proposed church council in Troyes, 443–4; plans to take over the territory of Lothar II, 450; makes Theodulf Count of Angers, 450; at the Council of Mâcon, 451; so ill at the Council that they thought he would die, 453; pardons Duke Desiderius at the instance of Antestius and Saint Aredius, 456; prepares to send an army into Spain, 456; intercepts a secret letter from Leuvigild to Fredegund, 456; sends an army to ravage Septimania, 459–60; sacks Nîmes, 459; enters Carcassonne, 459; the army retreats, instead of going on into Spain, as Guntram had planned, 459–60; Guntram meets the leaders in Autun and discusses the reason for the army's ineffectualness, 460–62; Recared counterattacks, 462; sends Saint Arthemius, Saint Veranus and Agricius, Bishop of Troyes, to the court of Lothar II to see how Saint Praetextatus came to be murdered, 464–5; gifts arrive for Guntram from Leuvigild, 469; sends gifts to Childebert II's newly-born son Theuderic, 470; sends Antestius to punish those who murdered Domnola, 474; receives envoys from Fredegund, one of whom is thought to be an assassin, 475–6; envoys come to Guntram from Spain, 476; gives Albi back to Childebert II, 476; 479; 480; refuses to receive Recared's envoys, 481; attempt to assassinate him in Chalon-sur-Saône, 482; 488; 489; hears of Duke Rauching's conspiracy and alerts Childebert II, 489; confers with Childebert II in Trier, 492; makes the Treaty of Andelot with Childebert II, 493–4; tries Baddo in Paris for high treason, but eventually lets him go, 496; angry because Childebert II receives Egidius, Bishop of Rheims, 497; refuses to receive the envoys of Recared, become a Catholic, 499; sends envoys to the Bretons, who have attacked Nantes, 500; summons Gregory of Tours urgently to Chalon-sur-Saône to explain why Childebert II is not observing the conditions of the Treaty of Andelot, 502; grumbles because Childebert II has not handed over half of Senlis, 503; has the Treaty of Andelot read in full to Gregory of Tours and Bishop Felix, 503–7; jokes with Gregory and Felix about the enmity between Brunhild and Fredegund, 507; told by Felix that Recared wants to marry Chlodosind, 507–8; refuses to send an army against the Longobards, 508; agrees with Gregory of Tours not to call a council of bishops, 508–9; gives Gregory and Felix a fine dinner, 509; his charity, 509; his pastoral behaviour during the plague, 509–10; a fragment cut from his cloak cures a quartan ague, 510; seizes Ebregisel on his mission to Spain for Brunhild, as he thinks that she is communicating with Gundovald's sons, 514–15; advises Childebert II to make peace with the Longobards, 515; sends an army to attack Septimania, but it is beaten, 517; puts the blame on Childebert II and his relations with Recared, 518; angered by Childebert II, who had sent his son Theudebert to Soissons, 518; tries to intervene in the lawsuits between Ingitrude and her daughter Berthegund, 519–21; pleads with Childebert II for Sunnegisil and Gallomagnus, 526; receives his niece Clotild, the rebellious nun from Saint Radegund's nunnery in Poitiers, but quickly sends her back to Tours, wise man, 531; 533; 536; 541; sends an army under Duke Beppolen and Duke Ebrachar against the Bretons, 556; the army crosses the River Vilaine and the River Oust, 556; Duke Beppolen's troops are beaten, 557; bitterly reproaches Duke Ebrachar on his return, 558; goes hunting in the Vosges, 558–9; has his Chamberlain Chundo stoned to death for allegedly killing an aurochs in the royal forests, 559; travels as far as Sens on his way to Paris when he hears a false rumour that Lothar II is dead, 559; 569; 578; 582; goes to Paris and baptizes Fredegund's son Lothar at Nanterre, 587–9; has gout, 587; 604

Guntram Boso, Duke, Sigibert's military commander, 247; with Duke Godigisel fights and kills Theudebert, 247; 252; takes sanctuary in Saint Martin's church in Tours, 258; Roccolen orders Gregory of Tours to expel him, 258; Gregory refuses, 258; advises Merovech to escape from the monastery at Anille and to join him in sanctuary, 267; 268; consults a soothsayer, 269–70; to please Fredegund, leads Merovech into an ambush, but it fails, 270–71; swears that he will never leave sanctuary without Chilperic's permission, 271; emerges from sanctuary with Merovech, 272; possibly responsible for the capture of Merovech, 283; collects his daughters from Tours and takes them to Poitiers, 289; joins King Childebert II, 289; ambushed by Dragolen, 289–90; kills Dragolen, 290; his father-in-law, Severus, is banished, 290; his brothers-in-law, Burgolen and Dolo, are murdered, 290; 326; probably the person who invited Gundovald the Pretender to return to Gaul, 352; arrests Saint Theodore, Bishop of Marseilles, for having received Gundovald, 352; steals Gundovald's treasure and takes it to Clermont-Ferrand, 353; locked up by King Guntram, 354; allowed to visit Count Mummolus in Avignon, 354; Mummolus nearly drowns him, 355; sent by Childebert II to confer with King Guntram, 397; Guntram accuses him of having brought the Pretender Gundovald into Gaul, 397–8; 415; 419–20; 422; he and his men despoil the church of Saint Remigius in Metz, 453–4; the case is looked into by Childebert II's nobles, but Guntram Boso escapes, 454; 479; begins to canvass bishops and nobles for support, 488; never ceases to heap abuse on Queen Brunhild, 488; Childebert II decides to put an end to him, 488; seeks sanctuary in Verdun cathedral, 388; Saint Ageric, Bishop of Verdun, pleads for him, 488; Guntram Boso is put in Saint

Index

Ageric's charge, 488–9; condemned to death at the conference of Trier, 492; killed, 493; his evil life, 493; his children go to live with Bishop Ageric in Verdun, 511

Gyges, King of the Lydians, 80; contemporary of Amon, 80

H

Habakkuk, the prophet, 126, 592

Hadrian, the Emperor, 64; full name Aelius Hadrianus, 85; restored Jerusalem, 85; Jerusalem therefore called Aelia, 85

Ham, second son of Noah, 71

Havelu, near Chartres, 246; King Chilperic retreats there before King Sigibert, 246

Hebron, name for the land of the Anakim, 71

Hebron, the giant who built Babel, 72; son of Chus (in mistake for Nimrod), 72

Hebrews, the, pursued in Egypt by the Pharaoh, 75; they enter the Red Sea, 75; see the Israelites

Helena, mother of the Emperor Constantine, 91; she discovers the wood of the True Cross, 91

Heraclius, priest in Bordeaux, 219; abortive attempts to make him Bishop of Saintes, 219–20; 252; made Bishop of Angoulême, 299; had been a priest in Bordeaux and one of Childebert II's ambassadors, 299; harassed by Count Nantinus, 299–300

Heraclius, tribune of the Jovinian Legion, killed by the Franks, 121

Hermanfrid, King of the Thuringians, 159; his death, 164; kills his brother Berthar, 164; his wife Amalaberg, 164; conspires with Theuderic against Baderic, 164; quarrels with Theuderic, 164–5; attacked by Theuderic and Lothar, 167–8; beaten in battle, 168; summoned to Zülpich by Theuderic, 169; killed there, 169

Hermangild, elder son of Leuvigild, King of the Visigoths, 233; marries Ingund, daughter of King Sigibert, 233; on his marriage given a city by Leuvigild, 302; is persuaded to become a Catholic by his wife Ingund, 302; is baptized as John, 302; makes overtures to the military commanders of the Emperor Tiberius II, 302; his father Leuvigild decides to kill him, 302; they fight, 302–3; the Greeks let Hermangild down, 302; Leuvigild and Recared deceive Hermangild, 303; he is seized and sent into exile, 303; attacked by his father Leuvigild, 348; his attempted alliance with the generals of Tiberius II, 348; imprisoned by Leuvigild, 371; 375; fights his father Leuvigild, 375–6; imprisoned in Toledo, 376; exiled, 376; 432; killed by his father, 456

Herod, the death of, 64; fears for his kingdom, 81; the Massacre of the Innocents, 81; his death, 81; 83–4; 207; 298; compared with King Chilperic, 379

Herpo, military leader of King Guntram, 272; captures Merovech, but lets

656

him escape, 272; fined by Guntram and dismissed for his incompetence, 272

Hesychius, Bishop of Grenoble, signs the letter to Bishop Gundegisel about the revolt in Saint Radegund's nunnery, 533

Hezekiah, King of Judah, 78, 103

Hezron, son of Pharez, 77

Hilary, Saint, Bishop of Poitiers, 91; sent into exile, 91; his books, 91; pardoned by the Emperor Constantius, 91; dies in Poitiers, 92; his church there, 152; 161; 252; Guntram Boso leaves his daughters in Saint Hilary's church in Poitiers, 289; 311; Leudast takes sanctuary there, 322; 391; 537; 591

Hippolytus, Saint, martyred, 86

Historiae Francorum, the, 63, 602, 604

Holofernes, 513

Holy Cross, the nunnery of the, in Poitiers, founded by Saint Radegund, 168; King Chilperic shuts his daughter Basina up there, 305; the soul of the nun Disciola is fetched by the Archangel Michael, 356–7; the nameless nun who has a vision of the Well of Living Water, 357–8; 480; the great scandal begins, 526; the nun Clotild, daughter of King Charibert, begins a revolt against the Mother Superior, Leubovera, 526; she walks out with the nun Basina King Chilperic's daughter, and forty others, 526; she comes to Tours and is advised by Gregory of Tours to go back, 526; he reads to Clotild the letter of the seven Bishops to Saint Radegund, 527–9; she takes no notice, 529; how Saint Radegund had founded the nunnery, 530; how she had brought a fragment of the True Cross from the East and Saint Eufronius, Bishop of Tours, had led the service of installation, 530; Maroveus, Bishop of Poitiers, had taken no interest down the years, 530; Agnes appointed as the first Mother Superior, 530; took its Rule from Saint Caesarius and Saint Caesaria in Arles, 530; when Saint Radegund died, Maroveus was virtually forced to become Visitor, 531; Clotild at least agrees to spend the winter in Tours, on Gregory's advice, 531; in the spring she leaves Basina in charge of the forty nuns in Tours, and herself sets off for the court of King Guntram, her uncle, 531; he treats her kindly and immediately sends her back to Tours, 531; there she and the other rebellious nuns wait for Bishop Maroveus to do something, which he avoids sedulously, 531; many of the nuns get tired of waiting, and get married instead, 531–2; the rest return to Poitiers and become the partners in crime of a gang of cut-throats based on Saint Hilary's church there, 532; joined by a half-crazy woman recluse, 532; they are visited there by Gundegisel, Bishop of Bordeaux, their Metropolitan, and three other supporting Bishops, Nicasius of Angoulême, Safarius of Périgueux and Maroveus of Poitiers, 532; they knock the four Bishops over, 532; Desiderius the deacon is so astonished by this that he runs away and swims his horse across the River Clain, 533; Clotild takes over the nunnery property and appoints her own bailiffs, 533; she threatens to toss Leubovera, the Mother Superior, over the nunnery wall, 533; Bishop Gundegisel excommunicates Clotild and the rebellious nuns, 533; he writes to a council of bishops called by King Guntram to say what he has done, 533; their reply quoted in full, 533–4; Leubovera, the Mother Superior, reads out Saint Radegund's letter of foundation to the rebellious nuns and sends a copy to all local bishops, 534–5; letter quoted in full, 535–8; Bishop Maroveus asks if he may give communion to the nuns, 538; refused, 538; King Childebert II sends the priest Theuthar to negotiate, 539; the nuns refuse to listen to him, 539; most of the nuns go home, 539; Clotild and Basina remain in the nunnery and continue the revolt, 539; 541; Clotild tries to drag the Mother Superior, Leubovera, out of the nunnery, 567; in error she seizes the Prioress Justina instead and assaults her, 567; drags Justina to Saint Hilary's church, 567; realizes her mistake, 567; seizes Leubovera and locks her up, 568; she and her associates loot the nunnery, 568; Bishop Maroveus tries to free Leubovera, 568; Flavianus succeeds in freeing her, 568; Leubovera seeks refuge in Saint Hilary's church, 568; Clotild quarrels with Basina, 568; Childebert II sets up a commission of bishops to settle the revolt: Ebregisel of Cologne, Maroveus of Poitiers, Gregory of Tours, Gundegisel of Bordeaux. 569; Count Macco puts an end to the rioting by main force, 569–70; Clotild seizes the fragment of the Holy Cross and brandishes it, 570; the trial of the rebellious nuns by the commission of of bishops, 570–71; *procès-verbal* of the trial quoted in full, 571–5; the Mother Superior, Leubovera, is completely exonerated, but given some avuncular advice, 573; Clotild and Basina are found guilty on all counts and suspended from communion, 575; the verdict is made public. 575; Clotild and Basina appeal to King Childebert II, but the appeal is turned down, 575

Holy Cross, the shrine of the, in Saint Radegund's nunnery in Poitiers, 567; the Mother Superior, Leubovera, takes refuge there during the revolt, 567; the nun Clotild picks up the reliquary and brandishes it, 570; 574

Holy Ghost, the, 68, 76; and the Birth of Jesus Christ, 79; 107; 111; 161; 162; 267; 297; His position in the Trinity debated between Gregory of Tours and Agilan the Arian, 307–10; His position in the Trinity debated between Gregory of Tours and King Chilperic, 310–11; reveals the coming of the Longobards to Saint Hospicius, 333; 349; Gregory of Tours and Oppila debate the position of the Holy Ghost in the Trinity, 371–4; 385; Recared, Arian King of the Visigoths, debates the concept of the Trinity with his bishops, 497–8; 536; 571; 589

Holy Legion, the. see Saint-Maurice d'Agaune

Holy Scriptures, the, 265, 287, 306, 498, 560, 565, 566

Holy Trinity, the, 68, 107, 109, 110, 161, 222, 302; debated between Gregory of Tours and Agilan the Arian, 307–10; debated between Gregory of Tours and King Chilperic, 310–11; 349; Gregory of Tours and the

Arian Oppila debate the Holy Trinity, 371–4; Recared, Arian King of the Visigoths, debates the Catholic doctrine of the Holy Trinity with his bishops, 497–8; 507; 527; 594

Honorius, the Emperor, 97; his death, 118; his army commanders kill Decimus Rusticus and Agroetius, 124; 595

Hortensius, 229

Hospicius, Saint, the recluse, 325; lives near Nice, 333; his abstinence, 333; prophesies the coming of the Longobards, 333–4; his miracles when they come, 334; cures a man from Angers of deafness and dumbness, 334–6; cures a man called Dominicus of blindness, 336; his other miracles, 337; announces his approaching death, 336; visited by a man called Crescens, 336–7; dies, 337; buried by Bishop Austadius, 337

Huneric, King of the Vandals, 108; in Africa, 108; annoyed by the failure of the Arian Cyrola to perform a miracle, 112; persecutes the Catholics, 112; kills himself, 113

Huns, the, 101; they prepare to invade Gaul, 114; come from Pannonia, 115; burn Metz, 115; under King Attila they advance on Orleans, 116; defeated by Aetius outside Orleans, 116–17; defeated a second time by Aetius on Moirey plain, 118; they retreat, destroy Aquileia and ravage Italy, 118; attacked by Sigibert, 195–6; invade Gaul after the death of Lothar I, 217; Sigibert puts them to flight, 217; he fights against them once more, 223; skilled in necromancy, 223; their king is always called the Khan, 223

I

Idumaeans, the, descended from Esau, also called Edom, 73

Ignatius, Saint, Bishop of Antioch, 85; martyred by Trajan, 85

Illidius, Saint, Bishop of Clermont-Ferrand, 66; his sanctity, 94; summoned to Trier to cure the Emperor's daughter, 94; his life recounted in Gregory's *Liber vitae Patruum*, 94; buried in Clermont-Ferrand, 94; the miracles at his tomb, 94

Immanuel, 331; see Jesus Christ

Imnachar, one of Chramn's gang, 208; drags Firminus from the cathedral in Clermont-Ferrand, 208

Indies, ships from the, come to Egypt, 75

Ingitrude, the religious of Tours, 288; the miracle of the water and the wine at Saint Martin's tomb, 288; 420; 480; founds a convent in the forecourt of Saint Martin's church, 518; complains to Childebert II about her daughter Berthegund, 518; Berthefled, daughter of King Charibert, is one of Ingitrude's nuns, 518; her quarrels and lawsuits with her daughter, 518–21; the priest Theuthar is sent to settle affairs, 521; she falls ill, 560; appoints her niece as Mother Superior of her convent, 560; the nuns object and Gregory of Tours has to intervene, 560; refuses to allow her daughter Berthegund to enter her convent or pray at her tomb, 560; she dies, 560; Berthegund inherits everything and strips the convent bare, 560

Ingoberg, wife of King Charibert, 219; has a daughter Adelberg, 219; tries to stop Charibert's relations with her two servants, Marcovefa and Merofled, 219; is dismissed as a result, 219; 479; woman of great wisdom and saintly life, 513; Gregory of Tours helps her to make her will, 513; she dies, 513; her daughter Adelberg married Ethelbert, King of Kent, 513

Ingomer, first child of King Clovis and Clotild, 141; he is baptized and immediately dies, 141–2

Ingund, daughter of King Sigibert and Brunhild, 254–5; when her father is assassinated, she is banished to Meaux, 254–5; sets off to Spain to marry Hermangild, elder son of King Leuvigild, 301; is maltreated by Goiswinth, second wife of Leuvigild, because she will not become an Arian, 302; persuades her husband to become a Catholic, 302; 371; left by Leuvigild in the hands of the Greek troops of the Emperor Tiberius II, 371; 432; rumour that she has been sent to Constantinople, 449–50; at the meeting of Childebert II's nobles at Breslingen, Brunhild calls for help for her daughter, now thought to be in Africa, 453; dies in Africa, 456; had been warned by Pronimius, Bishop of Agde, not to become an Arian, 512

Ingund, second wife of Lothar I, 197; her sons were Gunthar, Childeric, Guntram and Sigibert, and her daughter Chlothsind, 197; 198

Injuriosus, Bishop of Tours, fifteenth in order, 180, 197; refuses to pay tax to Lothar I, 197; dies, 198; born in Tours, 599; came of a poor family, 599; finished building Saint Martin's church, 599; built the church of Saint Germanus in Tours, 599; constructed the villages of Neuilly and Luzillé, 599; instituted the saying of tierce and sept, 599; was Bishop for sixteen years, 599; buried in Saint Martin's church, 599

Injuriosus, husband in the story of the Chaste Lovers, 95; lived in Clermont-Ferrand, 95

Injuriosus, Vice-Count of Tours, suspected of the murder of Armentarius the Jew, 405–6

Innocentius, Bishop of Le Mans, 340; dies, 340

Innocentius, Count of Javols, 370; accuses Lupentius, Abbot of the monastery of Saint Privatus, of having libelled Brunhild, 370; Lupentius is found not guilty, but he is first assaulted and then murdered by Innocentius, 370; becomes Bishop of Rodez, thanks to the support of Brunhild, 370; harasses Ursicinus, Bishop of Cahors, over certain parishes, 371; takes John, the young son of Count Eulalius and Tetradia, to make a priest of him, 555–6

Innocents, the Massacre of the, 65

In Psalterii tractatum commentarius, the, 603

Irenaeus, Saint, the martyrdom of, 66, 86; Bishop of Lyons, 86

Isaac, 65; Rebecca bore him twin sons, Esau and Jacob, 73; his tomb in Canaan, 74; the son of Abraham, 73; 77; 210; 331

Isaiah, the prophet, 127; 561

Index

Isère, River, 240

Ishmaelites, the, buy Joseph. 74; take him to Egypt, 74

Israel, name taken by Jacob, 73

Israel, the division of the kingdom under Rehoboam and Jeroboam, 63; 78; the ten northern tribes under Jeroboam keep the name of Israel, 78

Israelites, the, 65; took their name from Israel, i.e. Jacob, 73; travel to Egypt, 74; bondage in Egypt, 74; Moses frees them, 74; their departure from Egypt, 76; dwelt in the desert for forty years. 77; they assimilate the Law, 77; cross the Jordan, 77; enter the Promised Land, 77; forced to submit to the domination of foreign peoples, 77; through Samuel they ask for a king, 77; their departure from Egypt, 77–8; divided under Rehoboam and Jeroboam, 78; worship idols under Jeroboam, 78; taken captive to Babylon by Nebuchadnezzar, 78; freed by Zerubbabel, 79; subsequent idolatry, 79; in the power of the Gentiles, 79; redeemed by the Birth of Christ, 79; other kingdoms contemporary with them, 80; brought out of the land of Egypt, 136; follow the cloud, 161; 249; 604

Issachar, son of Jacob, 73

Italy, ravaged by the Huns, 118; 184; invaded by Theudebert, 189; Buccelin captures Upper Italy for Theudebert, 189; Buccelin invades Lower Italy, 189; invaded by Alboin, King of the Longobards, 196; under Imperial rule, 203; invaded again by Alboin, 235–6; 272; 284; 326; Childebert II attacks the Longobards there, 375; 419; 431; 479; Childebert II sends an army against the Longobards, but it is cut to pieces, 512–13; 541; the Longobards in Italy attacked by an army sent by Childebert II, 549–51; 594

J

Jacob, 65; twin son of Isaac and Rebecca, born immediately after Esau, 73; God loved him, 73; took the name Israel, 73; father of twelve patriarchs, 73; dies in Egypt. 74; buried by Joseph in Canaan, 74; son of Isaac, 77; 161; 310; 331; 332; 333

Jacob, son of Count Macliaw, the Breton, 273–4; killed by Theuderic, son of Bodin, 273–4

Jacob, son of Matthan, 79

James, Saint, Bishop of Nisibis, 66; lived when Constans was Emperor, 91

James the Apostle, brother of Jesus, 65, 66; swears never to eat bread until he sees the risen Christ, 82; surnamed the Just, 83; his martyrdom, 84; 443

Japheth, third son of Noah, 71

Javols, 89; Saint Privatus is Bishop, 89; people of Javols shut up in a castle at Grèzes when the Alamanni come, 90; Britanus is Count, 233; his son Palladius becomes Count, 233; Parthenius is Bishop, 233; 326; Lupentius is Abbot of the monastery of Saint Privatus, 370; the bogus Christ of Bourges comes there 585

Index

Jechonias, son of Josiah, 79

Jehoram, son of Jehoshaphat, 78; King of Judah, 78

Jehoshaphat, son of Asa, 78; fourth King of Judah, 78

Jered, son of Mahalaleel, 71

Jeremiah, the prophet, 127

Jeroboam under whom ten of the twelve tribes revolt against King Rehoboam, 78; becomes King of Israel, 78

Jerome, Saint, 69; writes his *Chronicle* from the twenty-first year of the Emperor Constantine, 91; the end of his *Chronicle*, 91; 92; 103

Jerusalem, 68; on Mount Calvary there Abraham offered the sacrifice of Isaac, 72; Christ crucified there, 72; rebuilt by Zerubbabel after the Babylonian captivity, 79; Saint Simeon is Bishop, 85; restored by Hadrian, 85; therefore called Aelia, 85; visited by the matron Melania, 92; disasters during the reign of Hezekiah, 103; visited by Licinius, later Bishop of Tours, 154–5; 267; 287

Jesse, son of Obed, 77

Jesus Christ, 65; the faith of, 67; born of the Father, 67; His Godhead and His Manhood, 67; faints in His Passion, 69; produces water and blood from His side, 69; stretched on the Cross, 70; the promise of His Birth received by Abraham, 72; crucified on Mount Calvary in Jerusalem, 72; redeems the Israelites by His Birth, 79; Son of Mary, 79; the fourteen generations leading to Jesus Christ, 79; born in Bethlehem in the forty-fourth year of the reign of Augustus, 81; the Three Wise Men worship Him, 81; Herod's attempt to kill Him, 81; His preaching and miracles, 81; persecuted by the Jews and crucified, 81–2; buried by Joseph of Arimathaea, 82; His tomb guarded by soldiers, 82; His Resurrection, 82; shows Himself to James His brother, 82; for forty days He appears to His disciples, 82; the Ascension, 82; His Passion, 249; 254; 266; His position in the Trinity debated between Gregory of Tours and Agilan the Arian, 307–10; then between Gregory of Tours and King Chilperic, 310–11; His divinity denied by Priscus the Jew, 330; 335; 336; 349; Gregory of Tours and Oppila debate the position of Jesus Christ in the Trinity, 371–4; 452; 486; 498; 535; 536; 537; 543; 561–6; 603

Jews, the, 207; sell objects to Bishop Cautinus of Clermont-Ferrand, 207; 251; converted in great numbers by Saint Avitus, Bishop of Clermont-Ferrand, 265–7; 325; a number baptized on the orders of King Chilperic, 347–8; Jews in Orleans welcome King Guntram in their own language, 433; his hostility to them, 433

Job, 63; also called Jobab, 73; son of Zerah, 73; his illness and his recovery, 73; 561

Job, the Book of, 306

Jobab, see Job

Joel the prophet, 379

John, name taken by Hermangild, son of Leuvigild, King of the Visigoths, when he becomes a Catholic, 302

662

John III, Pope, 285; Bishops Sagittarius and Salonius appeal to him, 285

John, Saint, the Apostle and Evangelist. 64; exiled to Patmos by Domitian, 85; returns after Domitian's death, 85; climbs into the tomb while still alive, 85; 109; 308; 372; 538; his church in Rome, 546; 562; Gregory of Tours placed certain relics to do with him in the new baptistery which he had added to Saint Martin's church in Tours, 602

John the tyrant, in Rome, 118; sends envoys to the Emperor Valentinianus III, 118; sends Aetius as a hostage to the Huns, 119

Jonah, the prophet, 72; describes Nineveh, 72

Jonzac, village near Tours, 271; Merovech and Duke Guntram Boso go riding there, 271

Jordan, River, 77; the Israelites cross it, 77

Joseph, in Egypt, 65; the son of Jacob, 73; his mother was Rachel, 73; Jacob loved him, 73; his visions, 74; the vision of how his brothers' sheaves of corn worshipped him, 74; the vision of how the sun, the moon and eleven stars fell prostrate, 74; his brothers hate him, 74; sold by his brothers to the Ishmaelites, 74; taken by them to Egypt, 74; famine in Egypt, 74; Joseph's brothers arrive, 74; he recognizes them, 74; Joseph forces them to send for Benjamin, 74; he reveals himself to them, 74; buries his father Jacob in Canaan, 74; he dies, 74; built granaries in Egypt (=the pyramids), 74

Joseph (of Arimathaea) buries Christ, 63; 82; imprisoned and guarded by the high priests, 82; freed by an angel, 82

Joseph, the husband of Mary, son of Jacob, 79; also the father of the Apostle James, 83

Joshua, 63; leads the Israelites across the Jordan, 77; dies, 77

Joshua, the Book of, 71

Josiah, son of Amon, 78; King of Judah, 78

Jotham, son of Uzziah, 78; King of Judah, 78

Jovinian Legion, the, beaten by the Franks, 121

Jovinius, Governor of Provence, 238; deposed by King Sigibert, 238; gives evidence against his successor Albinus, 239; Governor of Provence, 337; nominated as Bishop of Usèz, but never installed, 337; harasses Bishop Marcellus, 337; 341

Jovinus the tyrant, 124; assumes the rank of Emperor, 124

Judah, son of Jacob, 73, 77, 332

Judah, the southern kingdom, the two tribes who accepted the rule of Rehoboam, 78; list of the kings of Judah, 78; Amon is King, 80

Judas, a Hebrew, locates the wood of the True Cross, 91; baptized and called Quiriacus, 91

Judas Iscariot, 281

Judgement Day, 23, 31, 507, 536, 563, 565, 603

Judgement of Solomon, the, 77

Judith, 513

Julian, monk of Randan, 196; his miracles, 227; dies, 227

Julian, Saint, of Antioch, 235; his church is burnt down, 235

Julian, Saint, of Vienne, 128; martyred at Clermont-Ferrand, 128; his church and tomb at Brioude, 128; Avitus died en route for Brioude, 128; Avitus buried there, 128; Saint Julian's church in Clermont-Ferrand added to by Duke Victorius, 133; damaged by Theuderic's troops, 172; a villa at Bonghéat belonged to the church, 179; Sigivald seizes it, but he is stricken by Saint Julian and repents, 179; processions to his church during the plague, 200; 486; his church in Paris, 486; 554; his church in Brioude, 590; 591

Julius Caesar, first Emperor of Rome, according to Gregory of Tours, 22

Jupiter, 141

Justin, Saint, the martyrdom of, 66; 85

Justin II, the Emperor, 196; 234; avaritious, 234; a Pelagian, 234; becomes insane, 234; co-opts Tiberius, 234; mad, 283; dies, 292–3

Justina, Prioress of Saint Radegund's nunnery in Poitiers, 567 (she is the daughter of the sister of Gregory of Tours); for details of her role in the revolt, see Holy Cross, the nunnery of the, in Poitiers

Justinian, nephew of the Emperor Justin II, 293; plots against the Emperor Tiberius II, 293; pardoned, 293; Tiberius II offers his daughter in marriage to Justinian's son, but nothing happens, 294

Justinian, replaces Saint Bricius as Bishop of Tours, 105; he dies in Vercelli, 106; 595

Justinian, the Emperor, 202; sends an army against Agila, King of the Visigoths in Spain, 202; dies in Constantinople, 234

Justus, Saint, Archdeacon of Clermont-Ferrand, 94; buried with his Bishop, Saint Illidius, 94

Juvencus, a Spanish priest (=Caius Vettius Aquilinus), rewrites the Gospels in verse, 91

K

Kenan, son of Enosh, 71

Khan, the name of the kings of the Huns, 223

Kingdom of Heaven, the, 519

Kings, the Book of, 78

Kyrie eleison, the, 546

L

Laban, Bishop of Eauze, 454

Labourd, 504

Lacedaemonians, the, ruled over by Festus, 80

La Crau, 240; ravaged by Amo the Longobard, 240

Lambres, 248; King Sigibert buried there by Chilperic, 248

Lamech, son of Methuselah, 71

Index

Lampadius, deacon in Langres, 260; dismissed by his Bishop, Saint Tetricus, 260; accuses Peter the deacon, brother of Gregory of Tours, of having murdered Silvester, *episcopus electus* of Langres, 261; murders Peter, 261; is deposed, 262

Langeais, where Saint Martin built the church, 595

Langres, 137; Saint Aprunculus is Bishop, 137; expelled by the Burgundes, 137; Saint Tetricus is Bishop, 212; 251; 260–61; Pappolus is Bishop, 262; Mummolus is Bishop, 262

Lanthechild, sister of King Clovis, 145; she was an Arian, 145; baptized as a Catholic, 145

Laon, Duke Lupus leaves his wife there, 329

Last Trump, the, 484

Latium, the fifth King of which was Silvius, 80; the wine of Latium, 411

Latte, the monastery of, 196; attacked by Theudebert's troops, 244–5; relics of Saint Martin there, 245

Laurentius, Saint, Archdeacon, martyred, 86; his church in Clermont-Ferrand built by Duke Victorius, 133

Law, the, assimilated by the Israelites in the desert, 77

Lawrence, Saint, 335

Lazarus, 308, 563, 564

Legonus, Saint, Bishop of Clermont-Ferrand, 94

Le Mans, 157; Rignomer killed there by King Clovis, 157; 267; 325; Innocentius is Bishop, 340; Domnolus becomes Bishop, 340; Badegisil is made Bishop, 340; 366; 470; Bertram is Bishop, 471; 513; famine, 584

Lent, 259, 333, 417

Leo of Poitiers, evil companion of Chramn, 211; maligns Saint Martin and Saint Martialis, 211; they strike him deaf and dumb, 211

Leo, one of the cooks of Saint Gregory, Bishop of Langres, 176; he manages to free Saint Gregory's nephew, Attalus, from slavery, 176–9; rewarded, 179

Leo, Bishop of Tours, thirteenth in order, 179; a carpenter, 179; dies, 179; had been a priest in Saint Martin's church, 599; some of the font-covers which he carved still there, 599; Bishop for six months only, 599; buried in Saint Martin's church, 599

Leocadius, Senator of Bourges, offers a house as a Christian church, 88

Leontius, Saint, Bishop of Bordeaux, 219; expels Emerius, Bishop of Saintes, 219; fined by King Charibert for having done so, 220

Le Puy, 585; Aurelius is Bishop, 585

Lescar, added to the territory over which Ennodius is Duke, 487; 505

Leuba, the mother of Duke Bladast, 457; apparently involved in a plot by Leuvigild and Fredegund to assassinate Childebert II and Brunhild, 457

Leubast, Abbot, keeper of martyrs' relics in the diocese of Tours, 203; sets out to summon Cato of Clermont-Ferrand to the bishopric, 203–4

Leubovera, Mother Superior of the nunnery of the Holy Cross in Poitiers, 526; see Holy Cross, the nunnery of the, in Poitiers, for details of her role in the revolt; 567; 568; accusations levelled against her, 570–73; after the trial she is completely exonerated, but given some avuncular advice, 573

Leucadius, a slave, 314; father of Count Leudast, 314

Leudast, Count of Tours, 252; tries to catch Merovech as he emerges from sanctuary, 269; his crimes, 313; deposed, 313; calumniates Gregory of Tours, 313; calumniates Queen Fredegund, 314; thrown into prison, 314; was born in Gracina, the son of a slave called Leucadius, 314; humble beginnings, 314; becomes Master of the Stables to Queen Marcovefa, 314; made Count of Tours, 314; his evil behaviour, 315; becomes the avowed enemy of Gregory of Tours, 315; alleges that Gregory of Tours is putting about a rumour that Queen Fredegund is the mistress of Bertram, Bishop of Bordeaux, 316; banned from all churches for his scurrilous behaviour, 320; takes refuge in Paris, 320; flees to Bourges, 320; 322; takes sanctuary in Saint Hilary's church in Poitiers, 322; 326; reappears in Tours, 361; goes to see King Chilperic in Melun, 362; throws himself at Fredegund's feet, 362; tortured to death, 363

Leudegisel, King Guntram's Master of the Stables, 420; in charge of the siege of Saint-Bertrand-de Comminges, 420–24; kills Count Mummolus after the siege, 424; hands the treasure of Mummolus over to Guntram, 425; at the Council of Mâcon, his servants quarrel with those of Priscus, Bishop of Lyons, 452–3; put in charge of the Arles district to hold Recared, 462

Leudes, or personal bodyguard, 157; the *leudes* of Ragnachar are bribed by King Clovis, 157; the *leudes* of Theudebert help him to establish himself on the throne, 184; the *leudes* of Guntram, 440; the *leudes* of Lothar I, Sigibert and Guntram, 506

Leudovald, Bishop of Bayeux, 328; sent on an embassy by Chilperic to Childebert II, 328–9; closes all the churches in Rouen after the murder of Bishop Praetextatus, 464; Fredegund tries to murder him, 464; obtains the liberation of Baddo after his trial, 496

Leudovald, one of three Franks of Tournai, 586–7; killed by Fredegund, 587

Leunard, Fredegund's servant, 399; she maltreats him when he reports the plight of Rigunth, 399

Leunast, Archdeacon of Bourges, 251; loses his sight, 263; cured by Saint Martin, 263; consults a Jew and goes blind again, 263

Leuva, King of the Visigoths, 233; dies 233; 512

Leuvigild, King of the Visigoths, 233; brother of Athanagild, 233; married Goiswinth, widow of Athanagild and mother of Brunhild, 233; his two sons Hermangild and Recared, 233; his marriage to Goiswinth, 310; his elder son, by his first wife, married Ingund, daughter of King Sigibert, 310; his younger son, Recared, by his first wife, was engaged to Rigunth, daughter of King Chilperic, 301; gives a city to Hermangild and Ingund on their marriage, 302; decides to kill Hermangild because he has become a Catholic, 302; fights him, 303–4; with the help of Recared, deceives Hermangild, seizes him and sends him into exile, 303; his capital is Toledo, 303; sends Agilan, an Arian, as envoy to King Chilperic, 307; attacks Hermangild, 348; captures Merida, 348; still fighting Hermangild, 356; again sends envoys to King Chilperic concerning the betrothal of Recared to Rigunth, 364; sends Oppila as envoy to Chilperic, 371–4; fights his son Hermangild, 375–6; 432; kills Hermangild, 456; his secret letter to Fredegund intercepted by King Guntram, 456; 462; sends Recared to attack some of Guntram's cities, 462; loots ships sailing from Gaul to Galicia, 469; sends gifts to Guntram, 469; sends envoys to Childebert II, 470; dies, 477; supposed to have banned Arianism and become a Catholic on his deathbed, 477; 481; 512

Le Velay, 354; the bogus Christ of Bourges is there, 585

Levi, son of Jacob, 73

Lex Gundobada, the, 148

Liber de passione et virtutibus Sancti Juliani martyris, 172, 179, 602

Liber in gloria Confessorum, 97, 115, 434, 482, 498, 602

Liber in gloria Martyrum Beatorum, 131, 582, 602

Liber vitae Patruum, 94, 134, 151, 163, 212, 230, 233, 264, 265, 602–3

Licerius, Bishop of Arles, 471; had been Referendary to King Guntram, 471; dies, 511

Licinius, Bishop of Tours, ninth in order, 102; had been to the East and in Jerusalem, 154–5; 158; 162; came from Angers, 598; on his return from the East, founded a monastery in Angers, 598; became Abbot of the monastery of Saint Venantius in Tours, 598; lived in the days of King Clovis, 598; was Bishop for twelve years, 598; buried in Saint Martin's church, 598

Limagne, the plain of, 170; Childebert wants to see, 170; under water, 295

Liminius, Saint, martyred at Clermont-Ferrand, 89

Limoges, receives Saint Martialis as its Bishop, 24; 251; invaded by Count Mummolus, 267; riot against King Chilperic's new taxes put down with great brutality, 292; Saint Ferreolus is Bishop, 292; Nonnichius is Count, 350–51; held by Duke Gararic for Childebert II, 396; Terentiolus had been Count, 459; 505; 542; Saint Aredius came from there, 589; consuming fire from Heaven, 592

Limousin, the, 211; Chramn moves there, 211; swarm of locusts, 215; invaded by Theudebert, 244

Lisieux, 366; Aetherius is Bishop, 366; 367

Litorius, Saint, Bishop of Tours, second in order, 99; his life, 593–4; consecrated when Constans was Emperor, 593–4; was born in Tours, 594; was Bishop for thirty-three years, 594; was buried in the church named after him, 594

Loches, where Saint Eustochius built the church, 595

Loire, River, 98; the body of Saint Martin carried along the river on a boat, 98; the Romans occupied territory up to the Loire, 125; 150; 258; 270; in spate, 295; 306; 450

Longinus, Saint, Catholic Bishop in Africa, 110; his miracles, 110; 112
Longobards, the, 196; Alboin is their King, 196, invade Italy, 196; attacked
by Count Mummolus, 196; 198; 235; invade Gaul, 236; beat Amatus,
236; invade Gaul again, 236; beaten by Mummolus at Plan de Fazi, 236–7;
invade Gaul under their leaders Amo, Rodan and Zaban, 239; their
invasion of Gaul prophesied by Saint Hospicius, 333–4; attacked by
King Childebert II, 375; 480; King Guntram refused to help Childebert II
attack them, 508; Childebert II had once promised his sister Chlodosind
in marriage to Authari, King of the Longobards, 512; he had promised
Emperor Maurice Tiberius that he would drive the Longobards out of
Italy, 512; sends an army against the Longobards, but it is cut to pieces,
512–13; Childebert II attacks the Longobards, 515; attacked by an army
sent by Childebert II, 549–51; Aptachar (=Authari) is their King, 551;
according to Gregory of Tours, Paul is their King, 551
Lot, 583, 584
Lothar I, son of King Clovis and King of the Franks, 159; divides
the kingdom of Clovis with Theuderic, Chlodomer and Childebert 162;
marries Guntheuc, widow of Chlodomer, 167; with his half-brother
Theuderic attacks Hermanfrid, 167; brings home Radegund, daughter of
King Berthar, as booty, 168; marries her, 168; Theuderic prepares a trap
for him, 169; he and Childebert attack Burgundy, 171; Lothar and
Childebert threaten the sons of Chlodomer, 180; Lothar murders
Theudovald and Gunthar, but Chlodovald escapes, 180–82; Lothar and
Childebert share the lands of Chlodomer, 182; sends his son Gunthar to
attack the Goths, 183; Lothar and Childebert attack Theudebert on the
death of his father, 184; Childebert and Theudebert attack Lothar, 185;
he takes refuge in the Forêt de Brotonne, 185; they make peace, 186;
Lothar and Childebert besiege Saragossa, 186–7; Lothar, Childebert and
Theudebert threaten Theudat for having killed Amalasuntha, 188; he
gives them *wergeld*, 188; Lothar is cheated out of this, 189; he seizes
Chlodomer's treasure, 189; at the funeral of his mother, Queen Clotild,
197; tries to tax the churches, 197; his four wives, Radegund, Ingund,
Aregund and Chunsina, 197; his seven sons, Gunthar, Childeric, Chari-
bert, Guntram, Sigibert, Chilperic. and Chramn, 197; his daughter,
Chlothsind, 197; how he married Aregund, Ingund's sister, 198; takes over
Theudebald's kingdom on his death, 203; seduces Theudebald's widow,
Vuldetrade, 203; attacks the Saxons and the Thuringians, 203; 204;
confirms the priest Anastasius in the possession of his land, 207; seizes
the land of the Ripuarian Franks, 209; attacks the Saxons, who beat him,
209–10; asks why Cato never became Bishop of Tours, 210; makes Saint
Eufronius Bishop of Tours, 210–11; his son Chramn conspires with
Childebert against him, 211; the Saxons again revolt against him, 213;
when Childebert I dies, Lothar seizes his kingdom, 215; builds a new roof
for Saint Martin's church in Tours, 215; fights his son Chramn in Brittany
216; captures him and burns him alive, 216; goes on a pilgrimage to

Saint Martin's church in Tours, 216; falls ill in the forest of Cuise, 217; dies at Compiègne, 217; his kingdom inherited by King Chilperic, 217; 220; 235; 247; 272; 297; 339; Gundovald the Pretender maintains that he is Lothar's son, 352; Lothar rejects him, 352; 396; 415; 419; 420; 490; 506; 516; Saint Radegund founded her nunnery in his day, 530; 535; 536; 600; gave Bishop Eufronius financial help to build a tin roof on Saint Martin's church in Tours, 600

Lothar II, son of King Chilperic and Fredegund, 375; born, 375; brought up in the manor of Vitry, 375; only four months old when his father was assassinated, 392; called Lothar, 392; Ansovald and the other nobles true to Chilperic rally to him, 392; King Guntram questions his legitimacy 440; Guntram plans to seize his territory, 450; Guntram sends three bishops to the court of Lothar II to investigate the murder of Saint Praetextatus, 464–5; Guntram puts Duke Beppolen in charge of his cities, 473; 474; 489; 500; 541; 542; very seriously ill, 559; recovers thanks to a large donation by Fredegund to Saint Martin's church, 559; baptized by Guntram at Nanterre, 588

Lothar, son of King Guntram and Austrechild, 219

Lugano, Lake, 549; Childebert II's troops engaged with the Longobards near there, 549–50

Lupentius, Abbot of the monastery of Javols, 326; accused by Innocentius, Count of Javols, of having libelled Brunhild, 370; exonerated, 370; maltreated and then murdered by Innocentius, 370; his head and body are fished out of the River Aisne in two sacks, 370; miracles at his tomb, 370

Lupus, citizen of Tours, 325; widower, 345; wants to enter the church, 345; murdered, 345; his murderer was called Vedast, 390

Lupus, Duke of Champagne, 241; visits Marseilles, 241; the slave and *lector* Andarchius joins him, 241; Lupus recommends Andarchius to King Sigibert, 241; 325; harassed by Duke Ursio and Duke Berthefried, 329; protected by Fredegund, 329; leaves his wife in Laon, 329; takes refuge with King Guntram, 329; 479; joins Childebert II, 494; his daughter had married Godigisel, 494; makes peace with Egidius, Bishop of Rheims, 497; his son Romulf becomes Bishop of Rheims, 580

Luzillé, village built by Bishop Injuriosus of Tours, 599

Lydians, the, ruled over by Gyges, 80

Lyons, the founding of, 65; Saint Photinus and Saint Irenaeus martyred there, 66; founded during the reign of Augustus, 81; the martyrdoms there, 81; 86; Gregory's ancestor Vettius Epagatus martyred there, 86; 88; the River Rhône flows through Lyons, 125; 151; Sigismund flees there, 166; plague, 227; Sacerdos is Bishop, 230; Saint Nicetius is Bishop, 230–31; Saint Priscus is Bishop, 231–2; 260–61; trial of Bishops Sagittarius and Salonius there, 285; council of bishops there, 327; 509; Aetherius is Bishop, 587

Lytigius, local official in Clermont-Ferrand, 173; harasses Bishop Quintianus, 173; arrested and then disappears, 173

Index

M

Macco, Count of Poitiers, deputed by Childebert II to put down the revolt of Clotild and the nuns of Saint Radegund's nunnery, 533; he stops the rioting by main force, 569–70; tries in vain to capture the two sons of Count Waddo, 580

Macedonians, the, ruled over by Argaeus, 80

Macliaw, brother of Chanao, Count of the Bretons, 198; imprisoned by Chanao, 198; hidden by Chonomor, 199; flees to Vannes, 199; becomes Bishop of Vannes, 199; excommunicated, 199; 251; makes a treaty with Bodic, another Breton chieftain, 273; dispossesses Bodic's son, Theuderic, 273; Theuderic kills Macliaw and his son Jacob, 273–4; Macliaw's son Waroch inherits part of his land, 274; 290

Mâcon, the wine of, 183; the Council of, 431; the Council assembles, 451–3; King Guntram is there, 451; dispute as to whether 'man' in the Bible includes 'woman', 452; King Childebert II is there, 453; Recared's envoys halted there, 481

Maestricht, Aravatius, Bishop of Tongres, dies there, 115

Magnachar, father of Marcatrude, wife of King Guntram, 218; 251; dies, 274; Guntram kills his two sons, Guntio and Wiolich, who had maligned Austrechild, 274; 286

Magnatrude, wife of Badegisil, Bishop of Le Mans, 471; her evil behaviour, 471; prevents Chuppa from abducting her daughter, 553

Magneric, Saint, Bishop of Trier, 442; tells Gregory of Tours of how he succoured Saint Theodore, Bishop of Marseilles, when he was in the custody of Childebert's men, 442–3; baptizes Childebert II's son Theuderic, 470; present at the conference of Trier between Childebert II and Guntram, 492; tries to protect Duke Guntram Boso, 492–3

Magnovald, 432; executed by Childebert II in Metz, 469

Magnovald, Duke, replaces Duke Rauching, 491

Magnulf, Bishop of Toulouse, 384; unwillingly receives Gundovald the Pretender, 408; forced to dine with Gundovald, Count Mummolus and Duke Desiderius, who knock him about, 408–9; put in charge of Rigunth, 415

Mahalaleel, the son of Kenan, 71

Maine, 255; under Roccolen the men of Maine steal the very nails from one of Gregory's church-houses near Tours 258; 290

Maine, River, 304

Mainz, 120; Nanninus retreats there from the Franks, 120; Sigimund is Bishop, 515

Maiorianus, the Emperor, 128; succeeds Avitus, 128

Mallulf, Bishop of Senlis, 381; buries King Chilperic in Saint Vincent's church in Paris (=Saint-Germain-des-Prés), 381

Mamertus, Saint, Bishop of Vienne, 149–50; he institutes Rogations there in a time of disaster, 150

Manasseh, son of Hezekiah, 78; King of Judah, 78

Manichaeans, the, 83; some say that Pilate was one, 83

Manthelan, village near Tours, 428; built by Saint Volusianus, seventh Bishop of Tours, 597

Marachar, Count of Angoulême, 299; his nephew, Nantinus, becomes Count of Angoulême in his turn, 299; joins the church, 299; becomes Bishop of Angoulême, 299; murdered by Frontinus, 299; Nantinus claims his property, 299

Maratis, King of the Sicyonians, 80

Marcatrude, daughter of Magnachar, 218; King Guntram marries her, 218; murders her stepson Gundobad, 218–19; dismissed by Guntram, 218; she dies, 218

Marcellinus, Saint, his church in Rome, 546

Marcellus, deacon of Uzès, 337; son of Felix, 337; becomes Bishop of Uzès, 337; harassed by Jovinus, 337

Marcellus, Saint, church, in Chalon-sur-Saône, 291; Bishops Sagittarius and Salonius are locked up there, 291; 482; Chundo the Chamberlain tries to take refuge there, 559

Marcion, the heresy of, 85

Marcomer, early leader of the Franks, 120, 122

Marcovefa, servant of Queen Ingoberg, 219; Charibert falls in love with her, and with her sister Merofled, 219; Charibert marries her while he is still married to her sister Merofled, 220; she dies, 220; had made Leudast her Master of the Stables, 314

Mareil, where Magnatrude lived with her daughter, 553

Mareuil, church burnt down by Guntram's troops, 395; miracle there, 395–6

Marileif, court physician to King Chilperic, 269; waylaid and robbed by Merovech, 269; Gregory of Tours helps him, 269; lives in Poitiers, 269; 384; robbed by Duke Gararic, 407; robbed again and reduced to penury, 407

Mark, Saint, the Apostle and Evangelist, 66; his martyrdom, 84

Mark the Referendary, 326; dies 355–6

Mark the tax-collector, nearly killed in a riot in Limoges, 292; saved by Bishop Ferreolus, 292; 297

Marlenheim, royal villa, 525; Septimima disfigured and sent to grind corn there, 525; Fredegund sends twelve assassins to murder Childebert II there, but they are caught, 576

Marmoutier, 594; church of Saint Peter and Saint Paul built there by Saint Martin of Tours, 593–4; Saint John's church there built by Saint Volusianus, 597

Marne, River, in spate, 353; remains of Clovis fished out of the river, 441

Maroveus, Bishop of Poitiers, 406; resists King Guntram's troops, 406–7; in the end buys them off, 407; asks Childebert II for a revision of the tax-lists of Poitiers, 515; 526; criticized by the nun Clotild, 529; 530; refused to be present at the installation of the fragment of the True Cross in Saint Radegund's nunnery, 530; he had steadfastly refused to help the nunnery, 530; when Saint Radegund died, he was virtually forced to become Visitor, 531; obliged to accompany his Metropolitan, Gundegisil, Bishop of Bordeaux, on a visit to the rebellious nuns and their male confederates in Saint Hilary's church, 532; they knock him over, 532; asks if he may give communion to the nuns, 538; tries to free Leubovera, Mother Superior of Saint Radegund's nunnery, when the nun Clotild locks her up, 568; appointed by Childebert II as one of the commission to settle the revolt in the nunnery, 569

Mars, 141

Marseilles, 145; the province ruled by the Burgundian Kings, Gundobad and Godigisel, 145; 196; Vigilius is Archdeacon, 239; 240; 241; 259; 267; Saint Theodore is Bishop, 325; 327; 341; 342; Gundovald the Pretender lands there, 352; 359; second half given to Childebert II by Guntram, 363; 442; Nicetius becomes governor, 474; 479; plague there, 509–10

Martha, the sister of Lazarus, 563

Martialis, Saint, Bishop of Limoges, 87; one of the Seven Bishops, 87; 211; 591

Martianus Capella, author of the *Satiricon* and an authority on the Seven Arts, 603

Martin, Saint, Bishop of Galicia, 252; dies, 301: born in Pannonia, 301; travelled in the East, 301; composed the verses over the southern portal of Saint Martin's church in Tours, 301

Martin, Saint, Bishop of Tours, third in order, 64; born in Sabaria, in Pannonia, 91; begins to preach in Gaul, 91; restores three dead men to life, 92; visits the Emperor Maximus, 93; his death in Candes, 97; the men of Poitiers and Tours are rivals for his body, 97–8; his first monastery was in Milan, 98; succeeded as Bishop of Tours by Saint Bricius, 104; how Saint Bricius used to tease him, 104; Bishop Perpetuus builds an immense church outside Tours over Saint Martin's tomb, 130; Saint Eufronius, Bishop of Autun, sends a marble top for Saint Martin's tomb, 131; King Clovis seeks a message from Saint Martin's church, 152; 158; 197; 198; 199; Duke Austrapius takes refuge in Saint Martin's church, 214; the priest Willichar burns the church down, 215; Lothar I pays for the building of a new roof, 215; Lothar goes on a pilgrimage there, 216–17; his relics at Ciran-la-Latte, 245; 249; 251; destroys Roccolen by his miraculous power, 255; Duke Guntram Boso finds sanctuary in Saint Martin's church, 258; miracles at his tomb, 263; Merovech takes sanctuary there, 267–8; miracle of the water and the wine at Saint Martin's tomb, 288; the verses over the southern portal of his church in Tours were composed by Saint Martin of Galicia, 301; 310; 318; his church in Tours is broken into, 325; 340–41; 383; 384; 391; 426; 431; his feast-day is 4 July, 433; 434; his relics save Gregory of Tours from drowning in

Index

Coblenz, 444; he is the inspiration behind Saint Vulfolaic, 445; oil from his church cures Saint Vulfolaic of a skin disease, 447; Saint Vulfolaic tells Gregory of Tours of other miracles performed by Saint Martin, 448–9; during the great fire of Paris his oratory saved by a miracle, 466–7; helps Anatolius, the boy-hermit of Bordeaux, 469; 472; 484; 494; 513; 516; 527; 537; instrumental in curing Lothar II when he is seriously ill, 559; 591; his life reviewed, 594–5; consecrated when Valens and Valentinian were Emperors, 594; came from Sabaria in Hungary, 594; founded a monastery in Milan, 594; his miracles, 594; translated the body of Saint Gatianus to Saint Litorius' church, 584; died in Candes, 594; buried in Tours, 594; built a church in Marmoutier, 594; built churches in the villages of Langeais, Sonnay, Amboise, Ciran-la-Latte, Tournon and Candes, 595; was Bishop for twenty-six years, 595; 604

Martin the priest, 232; supporter of Saint Priscus, Bishop of Lyons, 232; visited in a vision by Saint Nicetius, 232; dies, 232

Mary, companion of the bogus Christ of Bourges, 585; captured and tortured, 585–6

Massacre of the Innocents, the, 65, 81

Matthan, son of Eleazar, 79

Mauretania, the Vandals cross over to, 108

Maurice Tiberius, the Emperor, succeeds to Tiberius II, whose daughter he marries, 358–9; pays King Childebert II to put down the Longobards, 375; presses for the return of the money, 449; 512; 541; Gregory the Great writes to him to say that he will never be Pope, 544; his joy when Gregory is elected, 544; Childebert II sends Grippo, Bodegisil and Evantius on a mission to the Emperor, but the two last are murdered in Carthage, 547–9; Maurice Tiberius sends the murderers to Childebert II, who refuses to punish them, as he is quite sure that they are the wrong men, 551–2

Maurilio, Saint, Bishop of Cahors, 252; suffers from gout, 306; dies, 306; protector of the poor, 306; knew all the genealogies of the Old Testament by heart, 306

Maxentius, Abbot of a monastery in Poitiers, 152–3; performs a miracle when his monastery is attacked by the troops of King Clovis, 153

Maximinus, Saint, Bishop of Trier, 91

Maximus, the tyrant, 66; victorious over the Britons, 93; made Emperor by his soldiers, 93; makes Trier his capital, 93; captures and kills Gratianus, 93; Saint Martin visits him, 93; put to death by Theodosius, 93; went to live in Aquileia, 120; his son Victor murdered, 121; proclaimed Emperor by Gerontius, 123; 277; 594

Mayenne, River, 558; Duke Ebrachar's army crosses at Angers, on its retreat from Brittany, 558

Méallet, monastery near Clermont-Ferrand, 265; Caluppa the recluse lived there, 265

Index

Meaux, 255; when King Sigibert is assassinated, his daughters Ingund and Chlodosind are banished to Meaux by King Chilperic, 255; 390; 409; Werpin is Count, 451; Gundovald is Count, 451; 504; 523

Medard, assistant to Injuriosus, Vice-Count of Tours, suspected of murder of Armentarius the Jew, 406

Medard, Saint, Bishop of Vermand, Noyon and Tournai, 195; dies, 215; buried by King Lothar in Soissons, 215; Lothar begins to build the church of Saint Medard in Soissons, 215; this was later finished by Sigibert, 215; Lothar I buried there, 217; Sigibert buried there, 248; 256; Chlodobert, young son of Chilperic and Fredegund, died there, 298; 319; 490

Melania, the matron, 66; lives in Rome, 92; goes on a pilgrimage to Jerusalem, 92; canonized as Saint Thecla, 92; her son Urbanus, 92

Melanius, Bishop of Rouen during the exile of Saint Praetextatus, 401; deposed when Praetextatus restored, 401; made guardian of Fredegund in the manor of Rueil, 401; supposed to have bribed the murderer of Praetextatus, 473; after the death of Praetextatus, made Bishop of Rouen, 473

Melun, attacked by Chilperic, 360; battle of Melun, 360; 362

Ménat, the monastery of, 267; Brachio is Abbot, 267

Mende, 90; Saint Privatus, Bishop of Javols, prays in a cavern near Mende when the Alamanni come, 90; 591

Mercury, 141

Merida, captured by King Leuvigild, 348

Merofled, servant of Queen Ingoberg, 219; Charibert falls in love with her, and at the same time with her sister Marcovefa, 219; he dismisses Ingoberg and marries Merofled, 219

Merovech, King of the Franks, 125; descended from Clodio, 125; father of Childeric, 125

Merovech, son of King Chilperic and Audovera, 223; sent by Chilperic to attack Poitiers, 255; attacks Tours, 255; goes to Rouen and marries the widowed Queen Brunhild, 255; takes sanctuary in Saint Martin's church in Tours, 255; taken to Soissons by Chilperic, 255; suspected of plotting by his father, 256; Chilperic locks him up, 256; tonsured, ordained a priest and put into the monastery of Anille, 267; advised by Duke Guntram Boso to join him in sanctuary in Saint Martin's church in Tours, 267; escapes from Anille, 267; finds sanctuary in Saint Martin's church, 268; Gregory of Tours, who is saying Mass, is forced to give him communion, 268; Gregory refuses Chilperic's order to expel him, 268; plans to visit Brunhild, 268; Leudast, Count of Tours, tries to catch him, 269; Gregory of Tours has a meal with him, 269; reads some Biblical passages to him, 269; 270; led into an ambush by Duke Guntram Boso, but it fails, 270–71; tries the *Sortes Biblicae*, 271–2; escapes from sanctuary in Tours with Guntram Boso, 272; captured by Duke Herpo near Auxerre, but escapes, 272; seeks sanctuary in the church of Saint Germanus in Auxerre, 272; escapes to Queen Brunhild, 272; 275; 280; 281; rumoured to be planning to seek sanctuary again in Saint Martin's church in Tours, 282; portents of his death, 282; hides near Rheims, 282; surrounded, 282; his servant Gailen kills him at his own request, 282; 315; 431; King Guntram buries his remains in Saint Vincent's church in Paris (=Saint-Germain-des-Prés), 441

Methuselah, son of Enoch, 71

Metz, 101; the Huns ravage the city, 115; the oratory of Saint Stephen there is saved from the Huns, 115–16; Attila, King of the Huns, advances from Metz to Orleans, 116; 230; 451; Magnovald is executed there, 469; dysentery there, 496; 502; ravaged by Duke Audovald and Duke Wintrio on their way to Italy, 549; Egidius, Bishop of Rheims, imprisoned there by Childebert II, 576–7

Michael the Archangel, collects the soul of the nun Disciola from Saint Radegund's nunnery, 356–7

Migdol, place near the Red Sea, 76

Milan, 98; Saint Martin of Tours was a monk there, 98; attacked by Duke Audovald, Childebert's army commander, 549; 594

Mincio, River, 124; the tyrant Constantine is beheaded there, 124

Mir, King of Galicia, sends ambassadors to King Guntram, 305; they are locked up by Chilperic, 306; after a year, he sends them home, 306; 375; beaten by Leuvigild, 376; dies, 376; his son and successor is Euric, 376

Moab, the women of, 126

Modestus, a carpenter, 318; thrown into gaol for supporting Gregory of Tours at his trial, 318–19; released by a miracle, 319

Moirey, the plain of, to which Attila, King of the Huns retreats after the battle of Orleans, 117; he is beaten there by Aetius, 117

Mont Chantoin, 133; Saint Eparchius builds the monastery there, 133–4

Mont-Louis, village where Saint Bricius learns that Armentius, his replacement, has died, 106; Saint Perpetuus builds Saint Lawrence's church there, 597

Morgengabe, the, 505

Moselle, River, 177, 443

Mosaic Law, the, 265

Moses, frees the Israelites in Egypt, 74; he divides the Red Sea, 75; the passage of the Red Sea occurred in his eightieth year, 76; contemporary with Trophas, King of the Argives, and Cecrops, King of Attica, 80; Moses and the second Commandment, 125–6; the burning bush, 161; 265; 310; 330; 373

Mougon, where the church was built by Saint Perpetuus, 597

Mount Calvary, see Calvary, Mount

Mount Sinai, the Israelites come to, 75

Mummolen, father of Duke Bobo, 379; his son Bodegisil killed in Carthage, 548

Mummolus, Count of Auxerre, 196; also known as Eunius, 236; made a patrician by King Guntram, 236; son of Peonius, 236; Guntram sends him to combat the Longobards, 236; he beats them at Plan de Fazi, 236; he beats the Saxons near Estoublon, 237; owned the villa of Saint-Saturnin, 240; beats the Longobard Rodan, 240; beats the Longobards Rodan and Zaban at Embrun, 240; appointed by Guntram and Sigibert to rescue Tours and Poitiers from Chilperic, 241; expels Clovis, son of Chilperic, from Tours, 241; 251; attacks Duke Desiderius, Chilperic's commander, and soundly beats him, 267; 286; 325; 326; flees from King Guntram and takes refuge in Avignon, 327; joined in Avignon by Gundovald the Pretender, 352; visited there by Duke Guntram Boso, 354; nearly drowns him, 355; 384; 389; still with Gundovald in Avignon, 394; joined by Desiderius after Chilperic's assassination, 394; in Toulouse with Gundovald, Desiderius and Waddo, 408–9; knocks Bishop Magnulf about, 408–9; the affair of the finger-bone of Saint Sergius, 413–14; encourages Gundovald to make Faustianus Bishop of Dax, 414; accompanies Gundovald to Saint-Bertrand-de-Comminges, 417; is there during the siege, 417–24; betrays Gundovald, 422–3; is killed by Leudegisel after the siege, 424; his wife is left destitute, 425; one of his servants was a giant, 425; 431; 436

Mummolus the Good, Abbot, 262; becomes Bishop of Langres, 262

Mummolus the Prefect, 326; tortured by Fredegund and Chilperic for alleged implication in the death of Theuderic, 365–6; packed off to Bordeaux, 366; dies of the torture, 366

Munderic the Pretender, 159; his death, 159; leads a revolt against Theuderic, pretending to be of royal blood, 173–5; besieged in Vitry-le-Brûlé, 174–5

Munderic, *episcopus electus* of Langres, 260; remains as arch-priest of Tonnerre, 260; incurs the displeasure of King Chilperic, 260; escapes to King Sigibert, 260; becomes Bishop of Alais, 260

N

Nahshon, son of Amminadab, 77

Namatius, Bishop of Orleans, 479; one of Guntram's envoys to the Bretons, 500; dies in Angers, 501; buried in Saint Anianus' church in Orleans, 501

Namatius, Saint, Bishop of Clermont-Ferrand, 101; his wife, 101; his election, 131; builds the great church there, 131; sends to Bologna for the relics of Saint Agricola and Saint Vitalis, 131; his wife builds the church of Saint Stephen outside Clermont-Ferrand, 131–2; dies, 133

Nanninus, Roman general, protects Trier from the Franks, 120; beats the Franks in the forest of Charbonnière, 120; retreats to Mainz, 120

Nantais, the, 501

Nanterre, King Guntram baptizes Lothar II there, 588

Nantes, 198; Saint Felix is Bishop, 198; 259; attacked by the Bretons, 294; 346–7; Nonnichius is Bishop, 347; 359; Atestius there, 474; attacked by the Bretons, 500; ravaged by the Bretons, 512; attacked by the Bretons, 556; famine, 584; epidemic, 592

Nantinus, Count of Angoulême, 252; dies of dysentery, 299; his uncle was Marachar, also Count of Angoulême, 299; Marachar becomes Bishop of Angoulême and when he dies Nantinus claims his property, 299; harasses Heraclius, Bishop of Angoulême, 299; murders a priest, 300; dies in torment, 300–301

Naphtali, son of Jacob, 73

Narbonne, receives Saint Paulus as its Bishop, 87; plague, 346; plague, 364; attacked by Recared, 470; Recared, Arian King of the Visigoths, sends to Narbonne the news of his conversion to Catholicism, 498

Narses, made military commander in Lower Italy in place of Belisarius, 189; repeatedly beaten by Buccelin, 189; kills Buccelin, 203; dies, 284; his treasure, 284–5; Gundovald the Pretender joins him in Italy, 352; 419

Nathan the prophet, helps raise Solomon to the throne of Israel, 77

Nativity of Saint John, Feast of, 596

Nativity of Saint Hilary, Feast of, 596

Nebuchadnezzar, King of Babylon, 78; takes the Israelites captive to Babylon, 78; 80

Nectarius, brother of Badegisil, Bishop of Le Mans, 399; Fredegund accuses him of having stolen part of Chilperic's treasure, 399; Badegisil speaks up for him, 399

Nectarius, husband of Domnola, 432, 465, 474

Nepotianus, Saint, Bishop of Clermont-Ferrand, 66, 94; cures Arthemius, later to become Bishop in his place, 94–5

Nero, the Emperor, 66; persecutes the Christians, 84; his debauched life, 84; executes the Apostles Peter and Paul, 84; commits suicide, 84; 207; King Chilperic is compared with him, 379

Neuilly, village built by Bishop Injuriosus of Tours, 599; a second village of the same name was added by Bishop Baudinus, 600

Neuss, Quintinus crosses the Rhine there against the Franks, 120

Nevers, 433; King Guntram there, 433; Agricola is Bishop, 533

Nicaea, the first Council of, 68; the points of doctrine which it established, 68

Nicasius, Bishop of Angoulême, 435; King Guntram is sarcastic to him, 435; with his Metropolitan, visits the rebellious nuns of Saint Radegund's nunnery and their male confederates in Saint Hilary's church in Poitiers, 532; they knock him over, 532; 533

Nice, 238; Saint Hospicius the recluse lived near there, 333; Austadius is Bishop, 336–7

Nicene Creed, the, 519

Nicetius, 432; Count of Clermont-Ferrand, 450; deposed, 450; made Duke of Clermont-Ferrand, Rodez and Uzès, 450; ineffectual role in Guntram's invasion of Septimania, 460; put in charge of the frontiers to hold Recared, 462; becomes Governor of Marseilles, 474; 510

Nicetius, Count of Dax, 414; brother of Rusticus, Bishop of Aire, 414; nominated by King Chilperic as Bishop of Dax, 414; becomes Bishop of Dax, 452

Nicetius, husband of Eustenia, the niece of Gregory of Tours, 268; when he reports to Chilperic the arrival in sanctuary of Merovech, Fredegund says that he must be a spy, 268

Nicetius, Saint, Bishop of Lyons, 196; 230; his virtues, 230–31; dies, 231; his miracles, 231; after his death denigrated by his successor, Saint Priscus, 231–2; visits Saint Priscus and his wife in a vision, 232; punishes the priest Martin, 232; receives Munderic the Pretender, 260; tries Peter the deacon for murder, 261; brought up Bishops Sagittarius and Salonius, 285; present at their trial in Lyons, 285; seen in a vision by King Guntram, 438

Nicetius, Saint, Bishop of Trier, 589; Saint Aredius becomes his disciple, 589

Nigremont, place in the Limousin where Charibert and Guntram try in vain to capture Chramn, 212

Nile, River, flows through Egypt, 74; the monasteries on its banks, 20

Nîmes, in Septimania, sacked by King Guntram's army, 459; Recared the Visigoth withdraws there, after his successful counter-attack on Guntram's territory, 462

Nineveh, built by Ninus, 72; also called Ninus, 72; Ninus was King, 72; 545

Ninus, 65; King of Ninus or Nineveh, 72; contemporary with Abraham, 72; 80

Ninus, another name for Nineveh, 72

Nisibis, Bishop James of, 66, 91

Noah, saved in the Ark, 70; his wife, his three sons and their wives are saved, too, 70; son of Lamech, 71; his three sons were Shem, Ham and Japheth, 71; his first son Shem, 72

Nogent-sur-Marne, manor of King Chilperic, 328; Gregory of Tours visits him there, 328; 329

Noisy-le-Grand, royal estate, 304; Clovis is murdered there, 304

Nonnichius, Bishop of Nantes, 347; threatened judicially by Antestius for the part which his son had played in the murder of Domnola, 474; brought before King Guntram, but sent home again as the case is not proven, 475

Nonnichius, Count of Limoges, 350–51; intercepts treasonable letters apparently from Saint Charterius, Bishop of Périgueux, 351; dies of a stroke, 351

North Africa, Grippo, Bodegisil and Evantius land there, 547

Novatianus, Antipope, persecutes the Christians, 86

O

Obed, son of Boaz, 77

Occila (=Optila), the trumpeter of Aetius, 119; assassinates the Emperor Valentinianus III, for having killed his master, 119

Octavian, the original name of the Emperor Augustus, 81

Octavianus, Saint, Archdeacon of Carthage, martyred by King Hunderic, 113

Odovacar, King of the Saxons, reaches Angers, 101, 132; he takes hostages from Angers, 132; joins Childeric against the Alamanni, 132

Old Testament, the, 306, 452

Olo, Duke, one of Childebert II's army commanders, 549; killed in Bellinzona, 549

Ommatius, Bishop of Tours, twelfth in order, 179; protégé of Chlodomer, 179; dies, 179; came from Clermont-Ferrand, 599; restored the church of Saint Gervasius and Saint Protasius in Tours, 599; began to build Saint Mary's church in Tours, 599; buried in Saint Martin's church, 599

Oppila, envoy from Leuvigild to Chilperic, 371; comes to Tours, 371; Gregory of Tours debates the Catholic and Arian beliefs with him, 371–4

Orbigny, where the church was built by Saint Eufronius, Bishop of Tours, 601

Orestes, Bishop of Bazas, 414; at the illegal consecration of Faustianus, Bishop of Dax, 414; must pay an indemnity to Faustianus when the latter is deposed, 452

Orge, River, 325; Chilperic posts guards on the bridge over the River Orge against Guntram's men, 349; Asclepius kills them, 349; Guntram makes amends, 350

Orleans, 101; attacked by Attila, King of the Huns, 116; he is defeated there by Aetius, 116–17; Saint Anianus was Bishop at the time, 116; Childeric, King of the Franks, fought a battle there, 132; Guntram makes Orleans his capital, 217; 218; conflagration, 296; 383; war of Orleans and Blois against Châteaudun, 389–90; 402; 406; 427; 431; King Guntram is entertained by the townsfolk, 433–4; portents, 483; Namatius is Bishop, 500; Astrinus is Bishop, 501; 519

Orosius, 69; his *Chronicles*, 69; his description of Babylon or Babel, 72; in his *Chronicles* he takes over from Jerome, 92; describes the campaigns in Gaul of Stilicho, 124; on the Carthaginians, 254

Osser, near Seville, 274; the springs of water run there on Easter Day, 18 April, 274; fortress, 376; burnt down by King Leuvigild, 376; how the springs there mark Easter by their running, 582

Otto, one-time Referendary of King Childebert II, 577; a document allegedly signed by him was produced at the trial of Egidius, Bishop of Rheims, 577–8

Ouche, River, 145; King Clovis and Godigisel beat Gundobad near the river, 145–6; river on which Dijon stands, 182

Oust, River, 556; King Guntram's army crosses the river to attack the Bretons, 556

Oxion, second King of the Corinthians, 80

P

Palladius, Bishop of Saintes, 414; consecrates Faustianus as Bishop of Dax, 414; 431; in ill odour with Duke Guntram for having received Gundovald the Pretender, 434–5; Guntram offended by his saying Mass, 439; quarrels openly with Bertram, Bishop of Bordeaux, 439; must pay an indemnity to the deposed Faustianus, 452; castigates his clergy for having attacked him, 454; alleged to be an intermediary for letters passed to Spain by Fredegund, 474; brought before King Guntram, but the case is not proven, 475

Palladius, Count of Javols, 196; son of Count Britanus, 233; quarrels with Parthenius, Bishop of Javols, 233; deposed by King Sigibert, 233; quarrels with Romanus, 234; although watched by his mother, Caesaria, and his uncle, Firminus, commits suicide, 234; buried in unconsecrated ground near the monastery of Cournon, 234

Pannonia, country bounded by the River Danube to the north and east and by Italy and Dalmatia to the south (=Austria, Western Hungary and Northern Yugoslavia), 91; Saint Martin of Tours was born in Sabaria in Pannonia, 91; the Huns came from Pannonia, 115; the Franks came from Pannonia, 125; Saint Martin of Galicia came from there, 594

Papianilla, wife of Parthenius the tax-collector, 192; he murders her, 192

Pappolen, 325; abducts the niece of Saint Felix, Bishop of Nantes, 347; marries the girl, 347

Pappolus, Archdeacon of Autun, 262; becomes Bishop of Langres, 261; sees Saint Tetricus in a vision, 262; dies, 262

Pappolus, Bishop of Chartres, has Promotus demoted from the Bishopric of Châteaudun, on the argument that his small diocese is only really part of Chartres, 400; fetches Merovech's body for King Guntram, 441

Paradise, 70; Adam and Eve are happy there, 70; expelled for misconduct, 70; 528

Parian marble, 205

Paris, receives Saint Dionysius as its Bishop, 87; King Clovis establishes his capital there, 154; Clovis dies there and is buried, 158; the younger Clotild buried there beside her father Clovis, 170; Queen Clotild lives there, 180; King Sigibert there, 196; Chramn there, 213; King Chilperic enters Paris, 217; King Charibert makes Paris his capital, 217; 220; 244; villages round Paris sacked by Sigibert's troops, 246; 247; 251; Brunhild there when Sigibert was assassinated in Vitry, 254; Saint Germanus is Bishop, 268; dies, 268; Ragnemod is Bishop, 268; 275; Saint Praetextatus, Bishop of Rouen, tried in Saint Peter's church there, 275–82; two Parisian families quarrel over a woman who committed adultery, 294–5; 305; 306; 326; 333; rains blood, 346; Chilperic's son Theuderic baptized there, 355; 360; Leudast throws himself at Fredegund's feet there, 362; Parisian housewives tortured to death for alleged implication in the death of Theuderic, 365; 377; Chilperic is buried in Saint Vincent's church (=Saint-Germain-des-Prés), 381; 383; Fredegund in sanctuary there, 390; argument between Guntram and Childebert II about the right to enter Paris, 391–2; Fredegund still there, 398–9; 400; 409; 432; 433; the great fire of Paris, 465–7; the spirit of Saint Germanus frees the prisoners in the gaol, 466; Saint Martin's oratory saved by a miracle, 466–7; an impostor comes from Tours to Paris, 485–6; Bishop Ragnemod expels him, 485; Baddo tried there by King Guntram, 496; 504; 514; Eusebius, a Syrian, is Bishop, 586

Parthenius, Bishop of Javols, 233; quarrels with Count Palladius, 233

Parthenius, the tax-collector, 160; seeks refuge in Trier, 192; had murdered his wife Papianilla and his friend Ausanius, 192; he is murdered in a church in Trier, 192

Pascentius, Bishop of Poitiers, 214

Passion of Saint John, Feast of the, 597

Pastor, father of Austrinus, Bishop of Orleans, 501

Patiens, Saint, Bishop of Lyons, 138; relieves a famine there, 138; letter of Saint Sidonius Apollinaris about this, 138

Patmos, scene of the exile of the Apostle John by Domitian, 85

Patriarch of Constantinople, the, 293; at the coronation of the Emperor Tiberius II, 293

Patroclus the recluse, 251; lived near Bourges, 265; his piety and way of life, 265; his miracles, 265; dies, 265

Paul, Count, attacks the Goths, 132; killed, 132

Paul, King of the Longobards, according to Gregory of Tours, 551

Paul, Saint, the Apostle, executed by Nero, 84; he intervenes to save the oratory of Saint Stephen in Metz from the Huns, 115–16; 309; 332; 335; 349; 372–4; 483; 534; his church in Rome, 546; 564; 565; 566

Paulellus, priest in Rheims, 178; helps Attalus, the nephew of Saint Gregory, Bishop of Langres, to escape from slavery, 178–9; an old acquaintance of Saint Gregory, 179

Paulinus of Périgueux, quoted, 129

Paulus, Saint, Bishop of Narbonne, 87; one of the Seven Bishops, 87

Pavia, reached by Theudebert in his invasion of Italy, 189; 550

Pegasus, Bishop of Périgueux, 129

Pelagia, mother of Saint Aredius, 590

Pelagian heresy, the, 234; the Emperor Justin was a Pelagian, 234

Pelagius, citizen of Tours, 432; his evil behaviour, 471–2; dies, 472

Pelagius III, Pope, dies of the plague in Rome, 543

Peleg, son of Eber, 72

Pentecost, 266

Peonius, Count of Auxerre, 236; replaced by his son, Count Mummolus, 236

Périgueux, 129; Pegasus is Bishop there, 129; Eparchius the recluse came from there, 338; occupied by Duke Desiderius, 334; 459; 517; Safarius is Bishop, 532

Perpetuus, Saint, Bishop of Tours, sixth in order, 101; his death, 102; replaces Saint Eustochius, 130; he builds an immense church over Saint Martin's tomb outside Tours, 130; he builds the church of Saint Peter and Saint Paul, 131; built a new church over Saint Martin's tomb, 596;

instituted the fasts and vigils observed in the cathedral and Saint Martin's church in Tours, 596–7; built Saint Peter's church in Tours, 597; built Saint Lawrence's church in Mont-Louis, 597; built churches in Esvres, Mougon, Barrou, Balesmes, Vernou, 597; occupied the see for thirty years, 597; buried in Saint Martin's church, 597

Persarmenians, the, 235

Persians, the, 71; they welcome Chus, son of Ham, the fire-worshipper, 71; they call him Zoroaster, 71; they themselves worship fire, 71; 235; they capture Antioch and Apamea, 235; beaten in a battle by the Emperor Tiberius II, 294; they invade and ravage Armenia, 582–3

Peter, deacon of Langres, 259; brother of Gregory of Tours, 259; Saint Felix, Bishop of Nantes, writes an abusive letter to Gregory in which he alleges that Peter had killed Silvester, Bishop of Langres, 259; accused by Lampadius the deacon and by the son of Silvester, *episcopus electus* of Langres, of having murdered Silvester, 261; exonerated after a trial in Lyons, 261; murdered by Lampadius, 261; buried in Dijon, 261

Peter, Saint, the Apostle, comes to Rome to preach when Claudius is Emperor, 84; executed by Nero, 84; he intervenes to save the oratory of Saint Stephen in Metz from the Huns, 115–16; 309; 335; 349; 483; his church in Rome, 546

Pharaoh, the, receives the Israelites in Egypt, 74; death of the Pharaoh, 74; drowned in the Red Sea, 74; pursues the Hebrews, 75

Pharez, son of Judah, 77

Phatyr, a Jew converted by King Chilperic, 348; murders Priscus, a Jew who had refused baptism, 348; murdered by the relations of Priscus, 348

Phineas, son of Eleazar, 126

Phineas, son of the high priest Eli, 103

Photinus, Saint, the martyrdom of, 66; 86; Bishop of Lyons, 86

Piacenza, 128; how the Emperor Avitus became Bishop, 128

Pientius, Bishop of Aix, 343; helps Saint Theodore, Bishop of Marseilles, 343

Pientius, Saint, Bishop of Poitiers, 214; dies, 214

Pi-hahiroth, place near the Red Sea, where the Israelites camped, 76

Pilate, the death of, 66; sends accounts of Christ's death and the imprisonment of Joseph of Arimathaea to the Emperor Tiberius, 82; tells Tiberius of the miracles, crucifixion and Resurrection of Christ, 83; his report still exists, 83; the Roman Senate refuses to accept the report, 83; Pilate killed himself with his own hands, 83; some say that he was a Manichaean, 83

Placidana, sister of Apollinaris, 162; mother of Arcadius, 171; arrested and sent into exile, 171

Plan de Fazi, near Embrun, 236; Count Mummolus beats the Longobards there, 236–7

Plato, Archdeacon of Tours, Gregory's friend, 316–7; arrested, 317

Poitevins, the, 491; plan to implicate them in Duke Rauching's attempted assassination of Childebert II, 491

Index

Poitiers, 91; Saint Hilary was Bishop there, 91; dies there, 92; 98; the men of Poitiers and Tours are rivals for the body of Saint Martin, 98; King Clovis marches on Poitiers, 151–2; Saint Hilary's church there, 152; Clovis beats Alaric II at Vouillé near Poitiers, 153–4; Saint Radegund builds her nunnery there, 168; Chramn moves there, 211; Saint Pientius is Bishop, 214; Pascentius is Bishop, 214; attacked by Chilperic, 241; saved by Count Mummolus, 241; attacked by Theudebert, 244; 251; 255; 259; 269; Duke Guntram Boso leaves his daughters in Saint Hilary's church, 289; 306; 326; 359; 379; 383; 384; invested by Guntram, 395; occupied by Duke Gararic for Childebert II, 396; goes over to Guntram, 396–7; attacked by Guntram, 406; Maroveus is Bishop, 406; he resists Guntram's troops, 407; Gundovald the Pretender is there, 407; 409; 420; Ennodius is Duke, 455; 480; 487; 496; 502; 504; tax-lists revised by Childebert II, 515; for the revolt of the nuns Clotild and Basina, see Holy Cross, the nunnery of the, in Poitiers, 529; the trial there of the rebellious nuns and the full *procès-verbal*, 571–5

Poitiers, Saint Radegund's nunnery in, see Holy Cross, the nunnery of the, in Poitiers

Poitou, 314

Polycarp, Saint, martyrdom of, 66; 86; disciple of Saint John the Apostle, 86

Polyeuctes the martyr, 391

Pompierre (=the Stone Bridge), 274; Guntram and Childebert II make a treaty there, 274–5

Ponthion, 218; Theudebert imprisoned for a year in a villa there by King Sigibert, 218; Lupentius, Abbot of the monastery of Saint Privatus in Javols, maltreated there by Innocentius, 370

Porcarius, Abbot of Saint Hilary's monastery in Poitiers, 538; sent by Bishop Maroveus to ask if he may give communion to the rebellious nuns of Saint Radegund's nunnery, 538

Portus, port of Rome, 547

Praetextatus, Saint, Bishop of Rouen, 251; tried by a council of bishops in Paris for conspiring against King Chilperic, 275–82; found guilty, 282; exiled to an island off Coutances (=Jersey), 282; 383; restored to his bishopric after the death of Chilperic, 399–400; 432; at the Council of Mâcon recites the prayers which he has composed, but they are received coldly, 452; exchanges bitter remarks with Fredegund, 462; he is murdered in his own cathedral, no doubt at her instigation, 463; she goes to watch him die, 463; 472; 508–9; signs the letter to Saint Radegund, 527

Prefect of Africa, the, official of the Emperors of Constantinople, 547; based on Carthage, 547; 548; 552

Prilidanus, boy-martyr, 86

Prince of Darkness, the, 467

Priscus, Saint, Bishop of Lyons, 231–2; his wife Susanna, 231–2; their denigration of Saint Nicetius, 231–2; their evil behaviour, 231–2; visited in a vision by Saint Nicetius, 232; at the Council of Mâcon his servants quarrel with those of Leudegisel, 452–3

683

Priscus the Jew, 330; supplies King Chilperic with goods, 330; disputes with the King, 330; denies the Divinity of Christ, 330; disputes with Gregory of Tours, 330–33; refuses baptism, as he wants to marry a Jewess in Marseilles, 348; murdered by Phatyr, a converted Jew, 348

Privatus, Saint, Bishop of Javols, 66; prays in a cavern near Mende when the Alamanni come, 89–90; killed by the Alamanni, 90; monastery named after him in Javols, 370; 591

Proculus, joint-Bishop of Tours, tenth in order, with Theodorus, 179; came from Burgundy, 179; appointed by Clotild, 179; dies, 179; buried in Saint Martin's church, 598; had been joint-Bishop for two years only, 598

Proculus, priest in Marseilles, 343; revolts against Bishop Theodore, 343

Proculus, priest in Vollore, 172

Promised Land, the, 77; the Israelites enter it, 77

Promotus, Bishop of Châteaudun, 383; installed at the command of King Sigibert, 400; deposed on the plea by Pappolus, Bishop of Chartres, that his see was part of that of Chartres, 400

Pronimius, Bishop of Vence, 479; had lived in Bourges, 511; moved to Septimania, 511; became Bishop of Agde, 512; warns Ingund not to become an Arian, 512; expelled from his diocese as a result and flees to Childebert II, 512

Protasius, Saint and martyr, 546, 595

Provence, 238; Jovinus is Governor, 238; Albinus is Governor, 238; 334; 432; 460; epidemic, 471

Psalms of David, the, 287, 317

Pyrenees, the, reached by the army commander Stilicho, 124; crossed by Euric, King of the Visigoths, 138; landslides, 296

Q

Quintianus, Saint, Bishop of Rodez, 102; driven out of Rodez by the Goths because of his sympathy with the Franks, 151; flees to Clermont-Ferrand, 151; 159; becomes Bishop of Clermont-Ferrand, 162–3; 172; harassed by a local official called Lytigius, 173; dies, 199; 229

Quintinus, Roman general, protects Trier against the Franks, 120; beats the Franks in the forest of Charbonnière, 120; crosses the Rhine near Neuss, 120; his army is cut to pieces by the Franks, 121

Quiriacus, baptismal name of a Jew called Judas, who located the wood of the True Cross, 91

Quirinus, Saint, Bishop of Siscia (=Sissek), 66, 90; martyred by being thrown into a river with a millstone tied to his neck, 90

R

Rachel, wife of Jacob, 73; mother of Joseph and Benjamin, 73

Radegund, Saint, Thuringian princess, 164; daughter of Berthar, King of

Index

Thuringia, 168; captured in the wars between the Franks and the Thuringians, 168; brought home as booty by King Lothar I, 168; he marries her, 168; becomes a religious, 168; builds a nunnery in Poitiers, 168; Chilperic shuts up his daughter Basina there, 305; the soul of the nun Disciola is fetched by the Archangel Michael, 356–7; the nameless nun who had a vision of the Well of Living Water in Saint Radegund's nunnery, 357–8; scotches the idea of Basina's marrying Recared in place of Rigunth, 365; 420; 479; 480; dies; and Gregory of Tours goes to her funeral in her nunnery, 481; 526; the letter written to her by the seven Bishops, Eufronius, Praetextatus, Germanus, Felix, Domitianus, Victorius and Domnolus, when she founded the nunnery, quoted in full, 527–9; she founded it in the days of Lothar I, 530; sends to the East for a piece of the True Cross, 530; Saint Eufronius, Bishop of Tours, had led the service of installation for this relic, 530; down the years Maroveus, Bishop of Poitiers, had shown no interest, 530; appointed Agnes as the first Mother Superior, 530; accepted the Rule of Saint Caesarius and Saint Caesaria in Arles, 530; when Saint Radegund died, Maroveus was virtually forced to become Visitor, 531; 533; her letter of foundation for the nunnery of the Holy Cross, 535–8; 571; 572

Ragnachar, petty King of the Franks, 102; helps Clovis in his attack on Syagrius, 139; lived in Cambrai, 156; his debauchery, 156; his adviser Farro, 156–7; captured and killed by King Clovis, 157

Ragnemod, Bishop of Paris, 268; 277; 295; baptizes Chilperic's son Theuderic, 355; gives Fredegund sanctuary after her husband's assassination, 390; speaks in favour of the restoration of Saint Praetextatus to the bishopric of Rouen, 400; expels an impostor, 485–6; 542; excommunicates the deacon Theudulf for absenteeism, 566; dies, 586

Ragnovald, Duke, 344; King Guntram's military commander, 344; beaten by Duke Desiderius, 344; his wife seeks sanctuary from Desiderius, 344; he returns from Spain and collects his wife, 394

Ram, son of Hezron, 77

Randan, monastery near Clermont-Ferrand, 196, 227

Rathar, Duke, 431; in the service of King Childebert II, 442; sent by King Guntram to arrest Saint Theodore, Bishop of Marseilles, 442; pillages the church there, 442; as a result his son dies and he is very ill, 442

Rauching, Duke, 251; marries the widow of Godin, 256; infamous character, 256; how he tortured his slaves, 256; buries a girl and a man alive, 256–7; captures Duke Berulf, 455; captures two priests sent by Fredegund to assassinate Brunhild and Childebert II, 457–8; 479; conspires against Childebert II, 489; killed, 489–90; news sent to his wife in Soissons, 490; he had given it out that he was a son of King Lothar I, 490; 576

Rebecca, wife of Isaac, 73; mother of Esau and Jacob, 73

Recared, second son of Leuvigild, King of the Visigoths, 233; engaged to Rigunth, daughter of King Chilperic, 233; envoys arrive from Leuvigild to Chilperic about this betrothal, 364; counter-attacks Guntram's

685

territory, 462; captures Cabaret, 462; ravages the land round Toulouse, 462; attacks Beaucaire, 462; takes shelter in Nîmes, 462; attacks Narbonne, 470; on the death of Leuvigild becomes King of the Visigoths in Spain, 477; 479; comes to terms with Goiswinth, his father's widow, 481; sends envoys to Guntram and Childebert II, 481; debates the Catholic credo with his bishops, 497–8; becomes a Catholic, 498; sends to Narbonne the news that he has been converted, 498; sends envoys to Guntram and Childebert II, 499; asks for the hand in marriage of Chlodosind, sister of Childebert II, 499; Bishop Felix tells Guntram about this, 507–8; Brunhild sends him a golden salver, 514–15

Red Sea, the crossing of the, 65, 74, 76; Pharaoh drowned there, 74; Moses parts it, 75; the ruts of chariot-wheels are still visible there, 76; it is a symbol of our earthly existence, 76; the Pharaoh drowned was Cenchris, 80; 604

Regalis, Bishop of Vannes, 557; welcomes Duke Ebrachar and his army, 557; swears loyalty to King Guntram, 557

Rehoboam, son of Solomon, 78; under him the kingdom of Israel was divided, 78; two tribes accept his rule and are called Judah, 78

Remigius, Bishop of Bourges, 326; dies, 371

Remigius, Saint, Bishop of Rheims, 143; he explains the Catholic faith to King Clovis, 143–4; he baptizes Clovis and his men, 144; his learning and his miracles, 144; his consoling letter to Clovis on the death of Albofled, 145

Renatus Profuturus Frigeridus, the historian, 118; passage on Aetius quoted from his *Historia*, 118–19; series of passages quoted on the Franks and their early opponents, 123–4

Rennais, the, 473

Rennes, attacked by the Bretons, 292; again attacked by the Bretons, 294; Victorius is Bishop, 465; refuses to accept Beppolen as Duke, 473; ravaged by the Bretons, 512; attacked by the Bretons, 556

Reovalis, doctor of medicine, who gives evidence in the trial of the rebellious nuns of Saint Radegund's nunnery, 570–71

Respendial, King of the Alani, 123

Ressons, 505

Resurrection of Christ, the, 65, 82; took place on a Sunday, 83; 155, 274, 509, 592, 604

Resurrection of Jesus Christ our Lord, Feast of, 596

Reu, son of Peleg, 72

Reuben, son of Jacob, 73

Reuel, son of Esau, 73

Revocatus, Saint, Bishop in Africa, 113; abjures the Catholic faith, 113

Rheims, 143; Saint Remigius is Bishop, 143; 178; King Sigibert makes Rheims his capital, 217; attacked by Chilperic, 217; again attacked by Chilperic, 247; 282; Egidius is Bishop, 328; Bishop Egidius escapes there on his horse, 361; Gregory of Tours travelling there, 496; 497; 541;

Bishop Egidius is found guilty of high treason, deposed and exiled, 579–80; Romulf is Bishop, 580

Rhine, River, 120; Quintinus crosses the Rhine against the Franks at Neuss, 120; Arbogast crosses the Rhine against the Franks, 122; Eugenius comes to the Rhine, 123; Stilicho crosses the Rhine into Gaul, 124; the banks of the Rhine were early colonized by the Franks, 125; 155, 245; 246; 247; meets the Moselle at Coblenz, 443

Rhône, River, 125; the Burgundes lived across the river, 125; it flows through Lyons, 125; 145; 146; 224; blocked by the collapse of its bank at Tauredunum (= Les Evouettes), which causes floods up to Geneva, 224–5; 238; 260; in spate, 295; 354; 459

Ruthénois, the, 151

Ricchar, brother of Ragnachar, 157; killed by King Clovis, 157

Richemer, father of Theudemer, an early King of the Franks, 125

Riculf the priest, of Tours, 316; conspires with Count Leudast against Gregory of Tours, 316–17; had the conspiracy succeeded, was to have been made Bishop of Tours, 321; after the trial and exoneration of Gregory of Tours, takes refuge with Saint Felix, Bishop of Nantes, 321–2

Riculf, the sub-deacon of Tours, emissary between Duke Guntram Boso and Merovech, 267; conspires with Count Leudast against Gregory of Tours, 316–17; tortured, but Gregory saves his life, 320; had the conspiracy succeeded, was to have been made Archdeacon of Tours, 321

Riez, 237; Urbicus is Bishop, 533

Rignomer, brother of Ragnachar, 157; killed by King Clovis, 157

Rigunth, daughter of King Chilperic and Fredegund, 319–20; she fasts during the trial of Gregory of Tours at Berny-Rivière, 319–20; 326; problems concerning her dowry and betrothal to Recared, son of Leuvigild, 348; envoys come from Leuvigild to Chilperic about this betrothal, 364; still more envoys, 377; preparations for her journey to Spain, 377–8; sets out for Spain with an immense dowry, 378; is pillaged on the way, 379; 383; reaches Toulouse, 393; the news of her father's assassination reaches her there, 394; Duke Desiderius locks up what has not been stolen of her dowry, 394; she takes refuge in Saint Mary's church in Toulouse, 394; Fredegund rages when she hears how badly Rigunth is being treated, 399; 409; put in the charge of Magnulf, Bishop of Toulouse, 415; her treasure now seized by Gundovald, 415; 418; on Fredegund's orders, brought home by Chuppa, 425; endless quarrels between Fredegund and Rigunth, 521–2; in the end Fredegund tries to choke her daughter with the lid of one of Chilperic's treasure-chests, 521–2

Ripuarian Franks, the, 102; Sigibert the Lame is their King, 102; they submit to King Clovis, 156; after the death of Theudebald, their land seized by Lothar I, 209; attacked by the Saxons, 213

Roccolen, 251; harasses Tours, 255; killed by Saint Martin, 255; attacks Tours, 258; dies of jaundice, 258–9

Rodan, leader of the Longobards, 239; with Amo and Zaban invades Gaul,

239; besieges Grenoble, 240; attacked by Count Mummolus and beaten, 240; rejoins Zaban, 240; he and Zaban beaten at Embrun by Mummolus, 240; retreats to Susa, 240

Rodez, 102; Saint Quintianus is Bishop, 102; the Ruthénois expel him, 151; 154; 162; attacked by Gunthar, 183; Saint Dalmatius is Bishop, 312; Theodosius is Bishop, 313; 370; Innocentius, Count of Javols, becomes Bishop, 370; Nicetius is Duke, 450; 555

Rogations, instituted by Saint Mamertus, Bishop of Vienne, 149; then by Saint Gall, Bishop of Clermont-Ferrand, 200; 207; 485; 510; 592

Romachar, Saint, Bishop of Coutances, 463; buries Bishop Praetextatus, 463

Romagnat, the plain of, 216; swarm of locusts there, 216

Romans, the, ruled over by Servius Tullius, 80; Julius Caesar their first Emperor, according to Gregory of Tours, 80; their second Emperor was Augustus, according to Gregory of Tours, 81; beaten in Thrace by the Goths, 92; their wars with the Saxons, 101; 132

Romanus, 234; quarrels with Palladius about the countship of Javols, 234

Rome, Saint Peter comes there, 84; Saint Cornelius martyred there, 88; Saint Bricius spends seven years there in exile, 105–6; captured and destroyed by the Goths, 123; 253; 335; great floods there, followed by plague, 543; Pope Pelagius III dies of this plague, 543; Gregory the Great becomes Pope, 544; his address to the people of Rome quoted in full, 544–6; he organizes prayers and processions against the plague, 546–7

Romulf, Bishop of Rheims, 580; son of Duke Lupus, 580

Romulf, Count of the Palace, sent by Childebert II to revise the tax-lists of Poitiers, 515

Rouen, King Sigibert advances as far as, 247; Saint Praetextatus is Bishop, 251; after the assassination of Sigibert, Brunhild is banished there by Chilperic, 254; Audovera there, 255; Praetextatus is deposed, 275–82; the Count of Rouen executed by Chilperic, 360; Praetextatus is restored as Bishop, 399–400; Melanius had been Bishop during the exile of Praetextatus, 401; Fredegund is sent to Rueil, near Rouen, and put in the charge of Melanius, 401; Fredegund in Rouen itself, 462; 472; Melanius is Bishop, 473

Rouergue, the, 554

Ruan, where Saint Bricius built the church, 595

Rueil, royal villa near Rouen, 401; Guntram sends Fredegund there under the guard of ex-Bishop Melanius, 401; Wiliulf and his son die there, 496; King Guntram stays there, 588

Rufinus, Bishop of Saint-Bertrand-de-Comminges, 418

Rusticus, Saint, Bishop of Clermont-Ferrand, 101; his election, 130; dies, 131

Index

S

Sabaria (=Szombathely), now in Hungary, town in Pannonia, 91; Saint Martin born there, 91; 594

Sabaudus, Bishop of Arles, 223–4; exhorts Sigibert's troops to issue from Arles and attack Guntram's army, 224; dies, 471

Sabellius, the heresy of, 149

Sacerdos, Saint, Bishop of Lyons, 230; dies in Paris, 230

Sadoc, son of Azor, 79

Sadducees, the, 560

Safarius, Bishop of Périgueux, 532; with his Metropolitan, visits the rebellious nuns of Saint Radegund's nunnery and their male confederates in Saint Hilary's church in Poitiers, 532; they knock him over, 532; 533

Saffarac, Bishop of Paris, 230; deposed, 230

Sagittarius, Bishop of Gap, 237; fought at the battle of Plan de Fazi against the Longobards, 237; brother of Salonius, 237; 251; 252; brought up by Saint Nicetius, Bishop of Lyons, 285; tried by a council of Bishops in Lyons for unseemly behaviour, 285; assaults Victor, Bishop of Saint-Paul-Trois-Châteaux, 285; deposed, 285; Pope John III reinstates him, 285; continues to behave badly, 285–6; had fought with Count Mummolus against the Longobards, 285; denigrates King Guntram and Austrechild, 286; shut up in a monastery by Guntram, 286; freed and reinstated, 287; continued evil behaviour, 287; tried at Chalon-sur-Saône and deposed, 291; locked up in the church of Saint Marcellus, 291; escapes, 291; 384; supports Gundovald the Pretender, 409; with Gundovald at the siege of Saint-Bertrand-de-Comminges, 421–4; betrays Gundovald, 422–3; is killed after the siege, 424–5

Saint Albinus' church in Nantes, 347; Pappolen takes sanctuary there with the niece of Saint Felix, Bishop of Nantes, 347

Saint Andrew's church in Clermont-Ferrand, 226; a bird puts all the lamps out, 226

Saint Anianus' church in Orleans, 501; Bishop Namatius buried there, 501

Saint Avitus' church in Orleans, 434

Saint-Bertrand-de-Comminges, 384; description of the town and fortress, 417; Gundovald the Pretender retreats there with Count Mummolus, Duke Bladast and Duke Waddo, 417; the siege, 417–24; all the inhabitants are destroyed after the siege, 424

Saint Bricius' Day, 597

Saint Caprasius' church in Agen, 344

Saint Clement's church in Rome, 546

Saint Cosmas' and Saint Damian's church in Rome, 546

Saint Crispin's and Saint Crispian's church in Soissons, 490; Duke Rauching's wife on her way to Mass there when she hears of his death, 490

Saint Cyr, monastery in Clermont-Ferrand, 134; Abraham is Abbot, 134

Index

Saint Denis, church of, in Paris, 298; Dagobert, young son of King Chilperic and Fredegund, buried there, 298

Saint Denis, tomb of, 294

Saint Euphemia's church in Rome, 546

Saint-Germain-Lanbron, church of Saint Germanus there built by Duke Victorius, 133

Saint Germanus' church in Tours built by Bishop Injuriosus, 599

Saint Gervasius' and Saint Protasius' church in Tours, 599; restored by Bishop Ommatius, 599

Saint Hilary's church in Poitiers, 480; the rebellious nuns from Saint Radegund's nunnery take up residence there as the partners of a band of cut-throats, 532; they are visited there by their Metropolitan, Gunde-gisel, Bishop of Bordeaux, and three other Bishops, 532; they knock them over, 532–3; Clotild has Justina, the Prioress of the nunnery, dragged there in mistake for Leubovera, the Mother Superior, 567–8; Leubovera seeks refuge there, 568; Basina seeks temporary refuge there, 569; 573; Childeric the Saxon implicated in the rioting there, 581

Saint Hilary's Day, 597

Saint John's and Saint Paul's church in Rome, 546

Saint John's church in Marmoutier built by Saint Volusianus, 597

Saint John's Day, 440

Saint Julian's church in Brioude, 590; Saint Aredius and his mother Pelagia go there on a pilgrimage, 590

Saint Julian's church in Paris, 348; Phatyr, the converted Jew, takes sanctuary there, 348; Gregory of Tours staying in the church-house when an impostor arrives, 486

Saint Lawrence's church in Mont-Louis built by Saint Perpetuus, 597

Saint Lawrence's church in Paris, 339, 353

Saint Litorius' church in Tours, 594; he is buried there, 594; the body of Saint Gatianus translated there by Saint Martin, 594

Saint Litorius' Day, 597

Saint Marcellinus' and Saint Peter's church in Rome, 546

Saint Marcellinus' church in Chalon-sur-Saône, 291; Bishops Sagittarius and Salonius locked up there, 291; attempt to assassinate King Guntram there, 482; 514; Chundo the Chamberlain tries to seek sanctuary there, 559

Saint Martin's church in Brives-la-Gaillarde burnt down, 394–5; restored by Ferreolus, Bishop of Limoges, 395

Saint Martin's church in Candes, 472; the evil-doer Pelagius had a tomb there, 472

Saint Martin's tomb in Tours, see Tours

Saint Martin's church on the Woëvre, 494; Duke Berthefried and Duke Ursio take refuge there, 494

Saint Martin's Day, 597

Index

Saint Martin's oratory in Paris saved by a miracle during the great fire of Paris, 466–7

Saint Mary's church in Toulouse, 394; Ragnovald's wife in sanctuary there, 394; Rigunth takes refuge there, 394

Saint Mary's church in Tours, 599; begun by Bishop Ommatius, 599; finished by Bishop Injuriosus, 599

Saint-Maurice d'Agaune, 165; monastery there built by Saint Sigismund, King of Burgundy, 165; Gregory of Tours found the relics of the Theban Legion, or the Holy Legion, which was martyred at Saint-Maurice d'Agaune, in the treasury of Saint Martin's church in Tours, and placed them in his cathedral, 601–2

Saint Maximinus' church in Trier, 443

Saint Medard's church in Soissons, 490; Duke Rauching's wife seeks sanctuary there, 490

Saint-Mesmin de Micy, monastery, 166; Saint Avitus is Abbot, 166

Saint-Paul-Trois-Châteaux, 285; Victor is Bishop, 285

Saint-Péravy-la-Colombe, 166–7; Sigismund and his wife were murdered there, 166–7

Saint Peter and Saint Paul, Feast of, 597

Saint Peter's and Saint Paul's church in Marmoutier, built by Saint Martin of Tours, 594–5

Saint Peter's and Saint Paul's church in Tours, 597

Saint Peter's church in Clermont-Ferrand, 226

Saint Peter's church in Paris (=Sainte Geneviève), 197; Queen Clotild is buried there, 197; Leudast seeks sanctuary there, 320

Saint Peter's church in Rome, 117

Saint Peter's church in Tours built by Saint Perpetuus, 597

Saint Protasius' and Saint Gervasius' church in Rome, 546

Saint Radegund's nunnery in Poitiers, see Holy Cross, the nunnery of the, in Poitiers

Saint.Remigius' church in Rheims, 579; Epiphanius is Abbot, 579

Saint Remigius' church outside Metz, despoiled by Duke Guntram Boso, 453–4

Saint-Saturnin, villa near Avignon, 240; given to Count Mummolus by King Guntram, 240; occupied by Amo the Longobard, 240

Saint Saturninus' church in Toulouse, 344

Saint Stephen's church in Rome, 546

Saint Symphorian's church in Autun, 101, 131, 460

Saint Symphorian's Day, 597

Saint-Symphorien-d'Ozon, near Lyons, 509; plague there, 509

Saint Victor's church in Marseilles, 511

Saint Vincent's church in Agen, 384, 418; sacked by King Guntram's troops, 418

Saint Vincent's church in Paris (=Saint-Germain-des-Prés), 381; Mallulf, Bishop of Senlis, buries King Chilperic there, 381; King Guntram buries the remains of Merovech and Clovis there, 441; just before the great fire of Paris a woman sees in a vision a pyromaniac coming out of this church, 466; the tomb of Saint Germanus is there, 466

Saint Vincent's church in Tours, built by Bishop Eufronius, 600

Saintes, 219; Emerius is Bishop, 219; occupied by Clovis, 267; 300; Waddo is Count, 379; Palladius is Bishop, 414; 434; Gundegisel is Count, 454; 459; Antestius there, 474; 517

Saius, Bishop of Auch, 454

Salathiel, son of Jechonias, 79

Salian Franks, the, 156; Chararic is their King, 156; they submit to King Clovis, 156

Salma, son of Nahshon, 77

Sallust, 208; *Catilina* quoted, 208–9, 388

Salonius, Bishop of Embrun, 237; fought at the battle of Plan de Fazi against the Longobards, 237; brother of Sagittarius, 237; 251; brought up by Saint Nicetius, Bishop of Lyons, 285; tried for unseemly behaviour by a council of bishops in Lyons, 285; assaults Victor, Bishop of Saint-Paul-Trois-Châteaux, 285; deposed, 285; Pope John III reinstates him, 285; continues to behave badly, 285–6; had fought with Count Mummolus against the Longobards, 286; shut up in a monastery by King Guntram, 286; freed and reinstated, 287; continued evil behaviour, 287; tried at Chalon-sur-Saône and deposed, 291; locked up in the church of Saint Marcellus there, 291; escapes, 291

Salustius, son of Evodius, 207; made Count of Clermont-Ferrand by Chramn, 207

Salvius, Saint, Bishop of Albi, 252; joins in argument about the Holy Trinity and the distinction of Persons between Gregory of Tours and King Chilperic, 311–12; chats with Gregory after his trial at Berny-Rivière, 322–3; sees the sword of the wrath of God hanging in the sky over the house where King Chilperic is staying, 322–3; the nun Disciola was his niece, 356–8; 383; dies, 385; his early life, 385; as Abbot, 385–8; his apparent death and vision of Heaven, 386–8; elected Bishop of Albi, 388; his good deeds, 389; dies, 455

Samson, son of King Chilperic and Fredegund, 251; born during the siege of Tournai, 288; rejected by his mother, 288; baptized, 288; dies, 288

Samuel, through whom the Israelites ask God for a king, 77; 103

Saône, River, 145; in spate, 295; 459

Sapphira, 535

Saragossa, the tyrant Constans leaves his wife there, 123; besieged by Childebert I and Lothar, 186–7

Satan, tempts Saint Eparchius, Bishop of Clermont-Ferrand, in his own cathedral, 133; 349

Saturn, 141

Saturnius, Saint, Bishop of Toulouse, 87; martyred, 87; one of the Seven bishops, 87; his church in Toulouse, 344; 591

Saul, first King of Israel, 77

Saxons, the, fight the Romans, 101; 132; they revolt against Lothar I, 195; attacked by Lothar, 203; attacked again by Lothar, but, in desperation, they beat him, 209–10; stirred up by Childebert, they again revolt against Lothar, 213; invade Italy with the Longobards, 237; turn back against Gaul, 237; encamp at Estoublon, near Riez, 237; beaten by Count Mummolus, 237; two invading forces of Saxons meet at Avignon, 238; they destroy the harvest, 238; they are settled by King Sigibert, 238; 251; attack the Swabians, who have settled in their territory, 272–3; they are badly beaten, 273; the Saxons of the Bessin are ordered by Fredegund to dress up as Bretons and fight against Duke Beppolen, 556–7

Scapthar, one of Chramn's gang, 208; drags Caesaria from the cathedral in Clermont-Ferrand, 208

Scheldt, River, 155

Scythia, birthplace of Gaudentius, father of Aetius, 119

Secundinus, servant of Theudebert, 160; his quarrels with Asteriolus, 190; commits suicide, 190

Sedulius, 312; King Chilperic imitates his poetry, 312

Seine, River, 245; in spate, 353; 459

Senachar, the plain of, 71; site of the Tower of Babel, 71

Senlis, 346; prodigyt here, 346; Mallulf is Bishop, 381; 503; 504; 505; 506

Senoch the recluse, 251; lived in Tours, 264; one of the Theifali, 264; his cell, 264; dies, 264

Sens, Saint Arthemius is Bishop, 464; King Guntram is there, 559

Septimania, ruled by the Visigoths, 432; King Guntram prepares to attack, 456; attacked and ravaged by Guntram's army, 459–60; 469; 480; 481; attacked by Guntram, but his army is beaten, 517–18

Septimima, nurse to the royal children for Childebert II and Queen Faileuba, 524; conspires with Sunnegisil, Gallomagnus and Droctulf against Faileuba and Brunhild, 524–6; mistress of Droctulf, 524; disfigured and sent to grind the corn in Marlenheim, 525

Sergius, Saint, the martyr, 384; Gundovald the Pretender seeks relics of Saint Sergius in Bordeaux, 413–14; Gregory of Tours placed certain of his relics in the new baptistery which he had added to Saint Martin's church in Tours, 602

Serpent, the, 70

Serug, son of Reu, 72

Servius Tullius, sixth King of Rome, 80

Seth, third son of Adam and Eve, 71

Seven Arts, the, 603

Seven Bishops, the, sent to preach among the Gauls, 66, 87

Seven Cities, the: Clermont-Ferrand, Bourges, Rodez, Cahors, Limoges, Le Gévaudan, Le Velay, 132

Severus, father-in-law of Duke Guntram Boso, 290; banished, 290; his two sons, Burgolen and Dolo, killed, 290

Shelah, son of Arphaxad, 72

Shem, eldest son of Noah, 71; ancestor of Abraham, 72; the line of descent from Shem, 72

Sicamber (from Sicambri), title of the Frankish kings, 144

Sichar, attacks Poitiers, 396

Sichar, citizen of Tours, 428–30; kills Audo, 429; 479; develops a great friendship with Chramnesind, 501; Chramnesind murders him, 502; his widow Tranquilla goes to Pont-sur-Seine and marries again, 502; only twenty, 502; loose-living young man, 502

Sicily, occupied by Buccelin, according to Gregory of Tours, 189; Gregory the Great founded six monasteries there, 543–4

Sicyon, ruled over by Europs, 80

Sicyonians, ruled over by Maratis, 80

Sidonius Apollinaris, Saint, Bishop of Clermont-Ferrand, 101; had married the daughter of the Emperor Avitus, 134; his eloquence, 134; his gifts to the poor, 134; two of his priests rebel against him, 135; his fatal illness, 135–6; the vision seen by one of the rebellious priests, 136–7; his letter about Saint Patiens, 138; his letter to Bishop Basilus about the attack on Aquitaine by Euric, King of the Visigoths, 138; quoted on Bishop Cautinus, of Clermont-Ferrand, 205; 337

Sigeric, son of King Sigismund and Ariagna, 165; throttled to death, 165

Siggo the Referendary, 257; served King Sigibert, 257; transferred to Chilperic, 257; deserted Chilperic for Childebert, 258; deprived of his property in Soissons, 258; his wife dies, 258; he marries again, 258

Sighar, mob-leader in Poitiers, 241; put down by Count Mummolus, 241

Sigibert, King of the Franks, fifth son of King Lothar I, 195; his mother was Ingund, 197; completes the church of Saint Medard in Soissons, 215; on the death of Lothar, Charibert, Guntram, Chilperic and Sigibert divide between them the lands of the Franks, 217; Sigibert takes Theuderic's kingdom, with Rheims as his capital, 217; beats the Huns, 217; attacks Soissons and captures Theudebert, 217; beats Chilperic, 218; marries Brunhild, daughter of Athanagild, King of the Visigoths, 221; fights against the Huns, 223; sends the men of Clermont-Ferrand under Count Firminus to attack Arles, 223; sends envoys to the Emperor Tiberius II, 235; 237; settles a horde of Saxons in his territory, 238; 241; quarrels with Guntram, 244; marches against Chilperic, 245; they make peace, 246; Chilperic and Guntram ally against him, 246; advances to Rouen, 247; besieges Chilperic in Tournai, 247; assembles his troops at the royal villa of Vitry, 248; is murdered by the emissaries of Fredegund, 248; buried temporarily at Lambres by Chilperic, 248; buried in the church of Saint Medard in Soissons beside his father, King Lothar I, 248; 249; 254; 256; 257; 263; 272; 283; his daughter Ingund marries Hermangild, son of Leuvigild, 301; 315; 328; rejects the Pretender Gundovald, 352; 359, 391, 395, 396, 407, 417, 436–7, 455–6, 476, 504, 505, 506, 516, 530, 536

Sigibert the Lame, King of the Ripuarian Franks, 102; his death, 102; his son Chloderic fought at Vouillé, 153; wounded in the battle of Zülpich against the Alamanni, 153; he is murdered by his son, 155

Sigila the Goth, 248; one of King Sigibert's close associates, 248; wounded when Sigibert was assassinated in Vitry, 248; foully done to death by Chilperic, 248

Sigimund, Bishop of Mainz, 515

Sigismund, Saint, King of Burgundy, 159; son of Gundobad, 165; builds the monastery of Saint-Maurice d'Agaune, 165; loses his first wife, Ariagna, daughter of Theodoric, King of Italy, 165; marries again, 165; at the instigation of his second wife, throttles his son Sigeric, 165; remorse, 165–6; flees to Lyons, 166; his daughter Suavegotha marries Theuderic, 166; with his brother Godomar is attacked by Chlodomer, 166; captured by Chlodomer, 166; he and his wife are murdered at Saint-Péravy-la-Colombe by Chlodomer, 166–7; 277

Sigivald, Duke, 159; left in charge of the garrison of Clermont-Ferrand by Theuderic, 173; his evil behaviour there, 179; he seizes the villa of Bonghéat, belonging to the church of Saint Julian, 179; stricken by Saint Julian, he repents, 179; killed by Theuderic, 183; his son, the younger Sigivald, saved by Theudebert, 183–4; Brachio, Abbot of Ménat, had once been his huntsman, 267

Sigivald the younger, saved by Theudebert, 183–4; flees to Arles and then to Italy, 184; returns to Theudebert on Theuderic's death, 184–5

Sigivald, sent by Childebert II to confer with Guntram, 397

Sigulf, a pretender, 408; had caused trouble to Magnulf, Bishop of Toulouse, 408

Sigulf, Duke, 451; restores Count Theodulf to his position in Angers, 451

Sigulf, retainer of King Sigibert, 243; attacks Clovis, son of Chilperic, in Bordeaux, 243

Silvester, *episcopus electus* of Langres, 260–61; dies of an epileptic fit, 261; his son and the deacon Lampadius accuse Peter the deacon of having murdered him, 261

Silvester, Saint, and Pope, 144; his miracles, 144

Silvius, fifth King of Latium, 80; contemporary of Solomon, 80

Simeon, Saint, Bishop of Jerusalem, son of Cleophas, 85; martyred by Trajan, 85

Simeon, Saint, the Stylite, of Antioch, 447; Saint Vulfolaic emulates him, 447; 583

Simeon, son of Jacob, 73

Simois, River, 224

Simon, a Bishop from Armenia, arrives in Tours, 582; tells Gregory of Tours how Adarmaanes, Chosroes's general, had captured Antioch and sacked Armenia, 582; the invaders attempted to burn down the church of the Forty-eight Martyrs, 582; he himself had been led off into captivity, 582–3

Simon Magus, the necromancer, 84; helps Nero in persecuting the Christians, 84; 137, 317, 371

Simplicius, Bishop of Vienne, 129

Sirus, Roman general, 121

Siscia (=Sissek), 90; Saint Quirinus is Bishop, 90

Sisinnius, Master of the Troops of the Emperor, 240; lived in Susa, 240

Sixtus, Saint and Pope, martyred, 86

Socratius, brother of the half-sister of Count Eulalius, 555; Eulalius murders him, 555

Sodom, 332, 584

Soissons, 139; Aegidius lived there and after him his son Syagrius, 139; King Clovis kills one of his own men there in a disagreement about booty, 140; Saint Medard buried there by Lothar I, 215; Lothar begins to build the church of Saint Medard, 215; finished by King Sigibert, 215; Lothar buried there, 217; becomes the capital of King Chilperic, 217; attacked by Sigibert, 217; Sigibert buried there in the church of Saint Medard, 248; 255; Chilperic wins a battle there against the Champenois, 255; 256; 258; 275; 298; prodigies, 346; walls collapse, 350; 364; 458; 480; Duke Rauching's wife there, 490; 518; the inhabitants ask Childebert II to send his son Theudebert to live among them, 523–4; Droctigisel is Bishop, 523; 576

Solomon and the building of the Temple, 65; third King of Israel, 77; son of David and Bathsheba, 77; raised to the throne by the efforts of Bathsheba and Nathan the prophet, 77; chooses wisdom when God asks him to choose any gift, 77; Judgement of, 77; built the Temple, 77; death, 78; 80, 247, 249, 269, 309, 310

Somme, River, 125; Clodio, King of the Franks, occupied territory up to the River Somme, 125

Sonnay, where Saint Martin built the church, 595

Sophia, the Empress, 283; wife of Justin II, 283; widowed, 292–3; plots against Tiberius II, 293; punished, 293; when Tiberius II is dying, she proposes Maurice, later the Emperor Maurice Tiberius, as his successor, under the impression that she can marry him, 358

Sorcy, 524; a council of bishops held there allows Droctigisel to remain Bishop of Soissons, despite his heavy drinking, 524

Sortes Biblicae, the, 212; Chramn tries them, 212–13; Merovech tries them, 271–2

Spain, invaded by the Vandals, 106; the Christians in Spain, i.e. the Catholics, are persecuted by Trasamund, the Arian King of the Vandals, 107; Constantine, the tyrant, summons his son Constans from Spain, 123; attacked by Childebert and Lothar, 160; the Kings of Spain, 160; visited by Childebert, 170; the Kings of Spain, 195–6; 233; 252; 274; earthquake, 295; persecution of the Catholics by Goiswinth, 301; 325; ambassadors come and go between Chilperic and Leuvigild, 349; Chilperic's ambassadors again return from Leuvigild, 363; Childebert II plans to invade, 375; 394; 432; King Guntram prepares to attack, 456; 462, 470, 476, 481, 497; a ship from Spain brings plague to Marseilles, 510–11; 514, 594

Stephen, Saint, the Levite and protomartyr, 84; his martyrdom, 84; his relics kept in Bourges, 88; his oratory in Metz, 101; his church outside Clermont-Ferrand, 101; the oratory in Metz saved from being burnt by the Huns by the intervention of Saint Peter and Saint Paul the Apostles, 115–16; his church outside Clermont-Ferrand built and decorated by the wife of Bishop Namatius, 131–2; his church in Rome, 546

Stilicho, an army commander, 124; crosses the Rhine into Gaul, 124; comes to the Pyrenees, 124

Stone Bridge, the, (=Pompierre), 274; King Guntram and King Childebert II make a treaty there, 274–5

Strasbourg, 523; King Childebert II stays there, taking Brunhild and Chlodosind, 523; old name was Argentoratum, 579; after his trial, Egidius, Bishop of Rheims, was taken there and condemned to exile for life for high treason, 579–80

Stremonius, Saint, Bishop of Clermont-Ferrand, 87; one of the Seven Bishops, 87; succeeded by Saint Urbicus, 93

Suebi, the, another name for the Alamanni, 106; they occupy Galicia, 106; they quarrel with the Vandals, 106; see Swabians

Sulpicius Alexander, the historian, 120; in his *Historia* he discusses the early leaders of the Franks, 120; passage quoted from Book III, 120–21; passages quoted from Book IV, 121–3

Sulpicius, Saint, Bishop of Bourges, 371; a poet, 371; 542; dies, 586

Sulpicius Severus, 72; tells us in his *Chronicle* that Abraham offered the sacrifice of Isaac on Mount Calvary, 72; 103; Gregory of Tours has read his *Life of Saint Martin*, 594

Sunday, day of the Resurrection, 83

Sunnegisil, Count of the Stables to Childebert II, 524; conspires with Septimima, Gallomagnus and Droctulf against Faileuba and Brunhild, 524–6; sent into exile, 525–6; recalled after a plea by King Guntram, 526; under torture implicates Egidius, Bishop of Rheims, in the revolt of Dukes Rauching, Ursio and Berthefried against Childebert II, 576

Sunniulf, Abbot of Randan, 196; dies, 227; his vision, 227–8

Sunno, early leader of the Franks, 120, 122

Susa, 240; the Longobards Rodan and Zaban retreat there, 240; Sisinnius, the Emperor's Master of the Troops, lived there, 240

Susanna, evil wife of Saint Priscus, Bishop of Lyons, 231–2

Suzon, River, 182; stream on which Dijon stands, 182

Swabians, the, 251; settled in Saxon territory by Lothar and Sigibert, 272; they are attacked by the Saxons, but beat them, 272–3; Mir is their King, 305; Chilperic locks up their ambassadors for a year and then lets them go, 305–6; see Suebi

Syagrius, Saint, Bishop of Autun, 261; tries Peter the deacon, brother of

Gregory of Tours, for murder, 261; backs Virgil, Abbot of Autun, for the bishopric of Arles, 511; Desiderius is his deacon, 533; signs the letter to Bishop Gundegisel about the revolt in Saint Radegund's nunnery, 533; is present at the baptism of Lothar II, 587

Syagrius, son of Aegidius, 132; lived in Soissons, 139; attacked by Clovis and Ragnachar, 139; beaten, he flees to King Alaric II in Toulouse, 139; handed over to Clovis and murdered, 139; 156

Syagrius, son of Desideratus, Bishop of Verdun, murders Syrivald, who had denounced his father to Theuderic, 191

Symphorian, Saint, 101; his church at Autun. 101; built by Saint Eufronius, 131; 460

Syria, 235

Syrians, welcome King Guntram in Orleans, 433; Eusebius, Bishop of Paris, is a Syrian, 586; he fills his household with Syrians, 586

Syrivald, 160; it was he who denounced Desideratus, Bishop of Verdun, to Theuderic, 191; murdered by Syagrius, son of Desideratus, 191

T

Tangiers, the Alamanni cross over to, 108

Tatto, see Wistrimund

Tauredunum (=Les Evouettes), 196; part of the bank of the River Rhône collapses there, blocks the river and causes immense floods, 225

Temple, the building of the, and Solomon, 65; how the Antichrist will place his image there, 68; built by Solomon, 77-8; the Temple adornments taken to Babylon by Nebuchadnezzar, 78; the destruction of the Temple, 78; rebuilt by Zerubbabel, 79; 83; burnt down in Vespasian's reign, 84; 249

Terah, son of Serug and father of Abraham, 72

Terentiolus, Count of Limoges, 459; killed at Carcassonne, 459

Tetradia, wife of Count Eulalius, 456; she leaves her husband and goes to live with Duke Desiderius, 476; Desiderius marries her, 476; he is killed, 477; Eulalius brings a case against her for restitution of property, 554; he had seriously maltreated her when she was his wife, 555; his nephew Virus had fallen in love with her, 555; Virus sent her to Duke Desiderius for safety, 555; she took most of her property, 555; Eulalius murdered Virus, 555; Tetradia married Desiderius, 555; now the widowed Tetradia is sued by her one-time husband for restitution of property, 556; she is represented by Agin, 556; the decision is that Tetradia should repay fourfold all that she has taken, but retain all her own property, 556

Tetradius, Saint, Bishop of Bourges, 179; dies, 227

Tetricus, Saint, Bishop of Langres, 212; Chramn consults the *Sortes Biblicae* with him, 212-13; dismisses the deacon Lampadius, 260; dies, 260-61; appears in a vision to Bishop Pappolus, 262; seen in a vision by King Guntram, 438

Theifali, the, revolt against Austrapius, Bishop of Champtoceaux, and kill him, 214–15; the recluse Senoch was one of them, 264

Theodore, Saint, Bishop of Marseilles, 325; harassed by Dynamius, Governor of Provence, 341; re-enters his city with Duke Gundulf, 342; captured by Dynamius, 343; helped by Pientius, Bishop of Aix, 343; again enters his city, 343–4; in fresh trouble over Gundovald the Pretender, 352; receives Gundovald when he lands in Marseilles, 352; arrested by Duke Guntram Boso for having done so, 352; locked up by King Guntram, 353; 431; Guntram alleges that he was responsible for Chilperic's murder, 437; locked up by Guntram, 442; a man of great sanctity, 442; Bishop Magneric's story to Gregory of Tours of how he helped Theodore when he was in the custody of Childebert's men, 442–3; restored to his bishopric by the Council of Mâcon, 453; 510–11

Theodoric, King of Italy, 160; his daughter Ariagna marries Sigismund, King of Burgundy, 165; he himself had married Audofleda, sister of King Clovis, 187; dies, leaving a daughter Amalasuntha, 187

Theodoric, King of the Visigoths, 116; with Aetius at the battle of Orleans against Attila, 117; killed in the battle against Attila on Moirey plain, 118

Theodorus, joint-Bishop of Tours, tenth in order, with Proculus, 179; came from Burgundy, 179; appointed by Clotild, 179; dies, 179; 598; buried in Saint Martin's church, 598; had been joint-Bishop for two years only, 598

Theodosian code of laws, the, 241

Theodosius, Archdeacon of Rodez, 313; becomes Bishop, 313; 326; dies, 370

Theodosius, the Emperor, 66; given a share of the Imperial power by Gratianus, 92; his trust in God, 92; enters Constantinople as a conqueror, 92; captures and kills Maximus, 93; makes Valentinianus III Emperor, 118

Theodulf, Abbot of the monastery of Le Mans, 340; proposed as Bishop by Domnolus, 340

Theodulf, made Count of Angers by King Guntram, 450; expelled from Angers by Domigisel, 450; restored by Duke Sigulf, 451

Thephei, King of the Egyptians, 80

Thérouanne, 282; the people of Thérouanne betray Merovech, 282

Thessalonians, Saint Paul's first Epistle to the, 564–5

Theuda, King of the Visigoths in Spain after Amalaric, 187; assassinated, 187

Theudat, King of Tuscany, 188; kills Amalasuntha, 188; threatened by Childebert, Lothar and Theudebert, 188; he buys them off, 188

Theudebald, King of the Franks, son of Theudebert and Deuteria, 185; he succeeds to his father, 193; dies, 195; 200; 201; marries Vuldetrada, 202; an evil man, 202–3; his death and the portents which foretold it, 203

Theudebert, son of Childebert II and a concubine, 470; baptized by Saint Magneric, Bishop of Trier, 470; 480; 489; 505; has a tumour in his throat, 515; 518; takes up residence in Soissons at the invitation of the inhabitants, 523–4

Theudebert, son of Chilperic, 196; captured by Sigibert, 218; imprisoned for a year in a villa in Ponthion, 218; swears never to fight against Sigibert again, 218; son of Audovera, 223; attacks Tours and Poitiers, despite his promise to Sigibert, 244; beats Duke Gundobald at Poitiers, 244; invades the Limousin, 244; attacks Cahors, 244; 246; killed in battle by Duke Godigisel and Duke Guntram Boso, 247; body found by a man called Aunulf, 247; buried in Angoulême, 247; 248, 270, 283, 315

Theudebert, son of Theuderic, 159; his ability, 162; repels a Danish invasion, 163–4; with his father Theuderic and his uncle Lothar, attacks the Thuringians, 168; betrothed to Wisigard, 183; sent by his father Theuderic to attack the Goths, 183; reaches Béziers, 183; sacks Dio, 183; enters Cabrières, 183; makes Deuteria his mistress, 183; saves the younger Sigivald, 183–4; his father dies, and Childebert and Lothar attack him, 184; he establishes himself on the throne, 184; he marries Deuteria, 184; makes peace with Childebert, 184; a good king, 185; remits taxes to the churches in Clermont-Ferrand, 185; he abandons Deuteria and marries Wisigard, but she dies, 185; Theudebert and Childebert attack Lothar, 185; they make peace, 186; Theudebert, Childebert and Lothar threaten Theudat for having killed Amalasuntha, 188; he gives them *wergeld*, 188; invades Italy, 189; advances as far as Pavia, 189; loans money to Bishop Desideratus for the city of Verdun, 190–91; refuses repayment, 191; dies 191; 193, 249, 589

Theudechild, mistress of King Charibert, 219; she was a shepherd's daughter, 219; on Charibert's death, she offers her hand to King Guntram, 220–21; he takes her treasure and puts her in a nunnery in Arles, 221; she tries to escape with a Goth, 221; dies in the nunnery, 221

Theudegisel, King of the Visigoths in Spain after Theuda, 187; assassinated, 187

Theudemer, King of the Franks, 125; son of Richemer and Ascyla, 125

Theuderic, King of the Franks, son of King Clovis by his mistress, 141; after Vouillé, sent to Albi, Rodez and Clermont-Ferrand, 154; joins his father in Paris, 154; divides the kingdom of Clovis with Chlodomer, Childebert and Lothar, 162; 163; conspires with Hermanfrid against Baderic, 164; quarrels with Hermanfrid, 164–5; marries Suavegotha, daughter of Sigismund, 166; joins Chlodomer against Godomar, 166; with his half-brother Lothar, attacks Hermanfrid, 167; prepares a trap for Lothar, 169; summons Hermanfrid to Zülpich and kills him, 169; false rumour that he has been killed in Thuringia, 169; he refuses to join Lothar and Childebert in their attack on Burgundy, 171; sends his troops to ravage Clermont-Ferrand, 171; they damage the church of Saint Julian, 172; Munderic, a pretender, leads a revolt against him, 173–5; Theuderic and Childebert make a treaty, exchange hostages and immediately quarrel, 175; 183; sends Theudebert to attack the Goths,

183; kills Sigivald, 183; dies, 184; his maltreatment of Desideratus, Bishop of Verdun, 190; 191; on the death of Lothar, Sigibert inherits Theuderic's kingdom, with Rheims as his capital, 217

Theuderic, son of Bodin, the Breton chieftain, 273; dispossessed by Count Macliaw, 273; kills Macliaw and his son Jacob, 273–4

Theuderic, son of King Childebert II and Faileuba, 482; baptized by Saint Veranus, Bishop of Cavaillon, 482; 489, 505

Theuderic, son of King Chilperic and Fredegund, 326; 351; baptized in Paris, 355; dies of dysentery, 364; buried in Paris, 364

Theudovald, eldest son of Chlodomer, 167; Queen Clotild brings him up, 167; murdered by King Lothar I, 180–82

Theudulf the deacon of Paris, 541; moves to Angers, 566; attaches himself to Bishop Audioveus, whom he had known years before, 566; excommunicated by Bishop Ragnemod for absenteeism, 566; falls over the city wall when drunk and kills himself, 566–7

Theuthar the priest, 480; had been one of King Sigibert's Referendaries, 521; sent to settle the affairs of Ingitrude and Berthegund in Tours, 521; sent by Childebert II to negotiate with the rebellious nuns of Saint Radegund's nunnery, 538–9; they refuse to listen to him, 539; 574

Thorismund, son of Theodoric, King of the Goths, 117; helps Aetius in his two victories over Attila, King of the Huns, outside Orleans and on Moirey plain, 117–18; defeats the Alani, 118; garrotted by his brothers, 118

Thrace, 92; the Romans are beaten there by the Goths, 92; 122

Three Persons, the distinction of the, 68; King Chilperic publishes a decree denying it, 310; Gregory of Tours disputes with him, 310–11; disputed between Gregory of Tours and Oppila the Arian, 371–4; Recared, Arian King of the Visigoths, debates the distinction of the Three Persons with his bishops, 498

Three Wise Men, the gifts of the, 65; they see Christ's star, 81; their gifts and worship, 81

Thuré, where the church was built by Saint Eufronius, Bishop of Tours, 600

Thuringia, through which the Franks marched, 125; King Clodio lived in Duisburg in Thuringia, 125; when driven into exile, Childeric, King of the Franks, takes refuge there, 128; Bisinus is King and Basina Queen, 128; attacked by Theuderic, Lothar and Theudebert, 167; submitted to Frankish rule, 168; 169; attacked by Lothar, 203

Thuringians, the, 140; attacked and conquered by King Clovis, 140; their Kings, Baderic, Hermanfrid and Berthar, 164; their alleged outrages against the Franks, 167–8; invaded by the Franks under Theuderic, Lothar and Theudebert, 168; massacred and submitted to Frankish rule, 168; attacked by Lothar, 203; Brachio, Abbot of Ménat, was a Thuringian, 267

Tiber, River, floods Rome, 543; a dragon and water-snakes swim down the river, 543

Tiberius, the Emperor, 82; sent the news of Christ's crucifixion and the imprisonment of Joseph of Arimathaea by Pilate, 82; he is told by Pilate of the miracles, Passion and Resurrection of Christ, 83

Tiberius II, the Emperor, 234; co-opted as Caesar by the Emperor Justin II, 234; his virtues, 234–5; above all a true Christian, 235; King Sigibert sends envoys to him, 234; 251; 252; his immense charity, 283; finds a treasure under a flagstone, 283–4; finds the treasure of Narses, 284–5; co-opted Caesar until the death of the Emperor Justin II, he then becomes full Emperor, 293; his coronation, 293; Justinian, the nephew of the Emperor Justin II, plots against him, 293; pardoned, 293; the Empress Sophia, widow of Justin II, plots against him, 293; offers his daughter in marriage to Justinian's son, but nothing happens, 294; beats the Persians in battle, 294; captures twenty elephants, 294; his troops in Spain, 302; Hermangild makes overtures to them, 302; they fail Hermangild in his war with his father Leuvigild, 302–3; 326; King Chilperic had sent envoys to him, 327; sends gold medallions to Chilperic, 328; dies, 358; before his death discusses the succession with the Empress Sophia, 358; she proposes Maurice (=the Emperor Maurice Tiberius), whom she hopes to marry, 358; Tiberius marries his daughter to Maurice, 358–9; 375

Toledo, Visigothic capital in Spain, 363; plague of locusts, 363; Hermangild is imprisoned there, 376; the locusts spread, 376

Tongres, 114; Aravatius is Bishop, 114; 115

Tonnerre, 260; Munderic, *episcopus electus* of Langres, is arch-priest there, 260

Toulouse, receives Saint Saturninus as its first Bishop, 87; Emperius is Bishop, 129; Alaric II, King of the Visigoths, resident there, 139; 148; 154; Rigunth reaches the city on her bridal journey, 393–4; Gundovald the Pretender is there, 408; Magnulf is Bishop, 408; 415; 426; 459; lands ravaged by Recared, 462; Duke Desiderius moves his wife and his goods there, 476; 517; 591; Saint Volusianus was exiled and died there, 597

Touraine, 267, 274, 290; portents, 295; 322, 541

Tourangeaux, the, 491; plot to implicate them in Duke Rauching's attempt to assassinate Childebert II, 491; 595

Tournai, King Chilperic takes refuge there, 247; Sigibert besieges him there, 247; 288; Leudast's wife exiled there, 320; Fredegund has three Franks killed there, 586–7

Tournon, where Saint Martin built the church, 595

Tours, receives Saint Gatianus as its first Bishop, 87; the men of Tours and Poitiers are rivals for the body of Saint Martin, 98; Saint Bricius is Bishop after Saint Martin, 104; the Tourangeaux expel Saint Bricius, 105; Justinian and Armentius act in turn as Bishops, 106; Saint Bricius is restored, 106; Saint Eustochius replaces Saint Bricius, 106; Saint Perpetuus replaces Saint Eustochius, 130; he builds an immense church over the tomb of Saint Martin outside the city, 130; 150; Licinius is

Bishop, 154–5; after the death of King Clovis, Clotild takes up residence there and becomes a religious in Saint Martin's church, 158; Licinius is Bishop, 162; Dinifius is Bishop, 162; Ommatius and Leo are Bishops in turn, 179; Theodorus and Proculus are joint-Bishops, 179; Francilio is Bishop 180; Injuriosus is Bishop, 180; 196; Queen Clotild dies there, 197; Baudinus is Bishop. 198; Gunthar is Bishop, 199; on Gunthar's death, the bishopric is offered to Cato, 203–4; he refuses, 204; Saint Eufronius is Bishop, 210–11; Willichar the priest burns down Saint Martin's church, 215; King Lothar pays for the building of a new roof, 215; 219; attacked by Chilperic, 241; saved by Count Mummolus, 241; attacked by Theudebert, 244; 247; 251; harassed by Roccolen, 255; attacked by Merovech, 255; 258–9; 264; 267; Tours is ravaged because Gregory of Tours refuses to expel Merovech from sanctuary, 268; 278; Winnoch comes there, 287; portents in the sky, 288; 289; 291; 301; Gregory of Tours returns there after his trial, 321; finds a sorry mess, 321; 325; 344–5; portents, 350; ball of fire, 353; 359; devastated by Duke Bladast and Duke Desiderius, 360–61, 361; 383; 384; invested by King Guntram, 395; advised by Duke Gararic to remain faithful to Childebert II, 396; Willachar is Count, 396; Eberulf seeks sanctuary in Saint Martin's church, 402; men set to guard him rob the church, 402; Eberulf desecrates Saint Martin's church, 403–5; murder there of Armentarius the Jew, 405–6; Count Eunomius and Injuriosus the Vice-Count suspected 405–6; attacked by Guntram, 406; 409; Eberulf and Claudius kill each other there, 409–12; 420; Chariulf seeks sanctuary in Saint Martin's church after the siege of Saint-Bertrand-de-Comminges, 426; 428; feud between six citizens of Tours, Audinus, Auno, Austregesil, Chramnesind, Eberulf and Sichar, 428–30; Gregory of Tours intervenes, 429; Garachar. Count of Bordeaux, and Duke Bladast in sanctuary in Saint Martin's church, 438; Childeric the Saxon seeks sanctuary there, 450; Ennodius is Duke, 455; 471; 480; Desiderius the impostor appears there, 483; the story of a second impostor, 484–6; 487; the feuds begin again between the citizens, 501–2; 504; 513; Childebert II attempts to tax the Tourangeaux, but Gregory of Tours stops him, 515–17; troubles in Ingitrude's convent in Tours, 518–21; Clotild the nun arrives there and is advised by Gregory of Tours to return to Poitiers, 526; 542; neighbourhood ravaged by Chuppa, 552; ravaged again by Duke Ebrachar's retreating army, 558; Simon, a Bishop from Armenia, comes to Tours, 582; 591; epidemic, 592; complete list of the nineteen Bishops of Tours, 593–602; list of the fasts and vigils instituted by Saint Perpetuus and observed in the cathedral and in Saint Martin's church in Tours, 596–7; much of Tours burnt down in the time of Saint Eufronius, 600; in his time, too, Willichar the priest, who was in sanctuary there, burned the roof off Saint Martin's church, 600; Eufronius, helped financially by King Lothar I, put a tin roof on it, 600; it was Gregory of Tours who rebuilt Tours cathedral, burnt down when Eufronius was Bishop, 601; he located the relics of the Holy Legion, martyred at Saint-Maurice d'Agaune, in Tours cathedral, 601–2; he located the relics of Saint Cosmas and Saint Damian and placed them in Saint Martin's cell, 602; he had the walls of Saint Martin's church newly frescoed after the fire, 602; he added a new baptistery to Saint Martin's church, 602; there he placed the relics of Saint John and Saint Sergius, 602; he placed the relics of Saint Benignus in the old baptistery, 602; he conjures future bishops of Tours to take every care of his books, 603

Traguilla, a slave, the lover of Amalasuntha, 188; killed, 188

Trajan, the Emperor, 66; persecutes the Christians, 66; responsible for the martyrdom of Saint Clement, Saint Simeon and Saint Ignatius, 85

Tranquilla, wife of Sichar, 502; came from Pont-sur-Seine, 502; marries again when Sichar is murdered, 502

Transobadus the priest, 312–13; aspires to become Bishop of Rodez, 312–13; dies of a stroke, 313; 370

Trasamund, King of the Vandals, 107; persecutes the Christians, 107; establishes the Arian heresy in Spain, 107; he tortures a young Catholic girl to death, 107; dies, 108

Treaty of Andelot, the, see Andelot

Trier, 91; Saint Maximinus is Bishop, 91; the capital of Maximus, 93; Saint Arthemius lived there as a young man, 93; protected by Nanninus and Quintinus against the Franks, 120; Arbogast winters there, 122; sacked and burnt by the Franks, 124; Parthenius, the tax-collector, seeks refuge there, 191; Saint Magneric is Bishop, 442; pagan inhabitants converted by Saint Vulfolaic, 446; 470; Childebert II and Guntram hold a conference there, 491–3; Saint Nicetius is Bishop, 589

Trojans, the, 224

Trophas, King of the Argives, 80; contemporary of Moses, 80

Trophimus, Saint, Bishop of Arles, 87; one of the Seven Bishops, 87

Troyes, suggested by Guntram to Childebert II as suitable place for a church council, 443; Saint Agricius is Bishop, 464

Trudulf, Count of the Royal Palace to Childebert II, 495; killed at the battle on the Woëvre, 495

True Cross, 66; the wood of the True Cross discovered by Helena, mother of the Emperor Constantine, 91; a Hebrew called Judas actually located it, 91; 283, 331

True Cross, the, fragment in the nunnery of the Holy Cross in Poitiers, 357; Saint Radegund sent for it, 530; Maroveus, Bishop of Poitiers, refused to have anything to do with it, 530; Saint Eufronius, Bishop of Tours, led the ceremony of installation, 530

U

Ullo, Count of Bourges, receives Gundovald the Pretender as he emerges from Saint-Bertrand-de-Comminges, 423; kills him with a rock, 423

Ultrogotha, wife of Childebert I, 215; sent into exile with her two daughters by Lothar, on Childebert's death, 215; Saint Ursicinus was her Referendary, 306

Unstrut, River, 168; the Thuringians massacred there by the Franks, 168

Urbanus, boy-martyr, 86

Urbanus, son of the matron Melania, who became Saint Thecla, 92

Urbicus, Bishop of Riez, signs the letter to Bishop Gundegisel about the revolt in Saint Radegund's nunnery, 533

Urbicus, Saint, Bishop of Clermont-Ferrand, 66; married man, 93; relations with his wife, 93–4; buried at Chantoin, 94

Ursicinus, Saint, 306; was Queen Ultrogotha's Referendary, 306; asks for the bishopric of Cahors, 306; Bishop of Cahors, 371; harassed by Innocentius, Bishop of Rodez, over certain of his parishes, 371; excommunicated for three years for having received the Pretender Gundovald, 452

Ursinus, Saint, Bishop of Bourges, 24; seeks a building as a church, 24

Ursio, Duke, harasses Duke Lupus, 329; 479; conspires with Duke Rauching against Childebert II, 489; marches with Duke Berthefried as part of the Rauching conspiracy, 491; they reach Ursio's estate on the River Woëvre, 491; killed there by Childebert II's troops, 495; 576

Ursus, citizen of Clermont-Ferrand, 241; Andarchius tries to marry his daughter by a series of tricks, 242–3; flees to Le Velay, 243

Uzès, 337; Saint Ferreolus is Bishop, 337; Albinus is Bishop, 337; Marcellus is Bishop, 337; Nicetius is Duke, 450

Uzziah, King of Judah, 78

V

Vafres, Pharaoh of the Egyptians, 80

Valence, 240; the Longobard Zaban encamps there, 240

Valens, the Emperor, 66; succeeds to the whole Empire on the death of Valentinianus I, 92; his violent death, 92; 594

Valentinianus I, the Emperor, persecutes the Christians, 86; 92; his death, 92; 594

Valentinianus III, the Emperor, 118; made Emperor by his cousin Theodosius, 118; receives the envoys of John the tyrant with contempt, 118–19; has Aetius murdered, 119; assassinated in the Campus Martius by Occila, the trumpeter of Aetius, 119; shut up in Vienne, 122

Valentinus, historian, 120

Valentinus, the heresy of, 85

Valerianus, the Emperor, 88; persecutes the Christians, 88

Vandals, the, invade Gaul, 101; Gunderic is their King, 106; they invade Spain, 106; occupy Galicia, 106; quarrel with the Alamanni or Suebi, 106; Trasamund becomes their King, 107; they cross over to Mauretania and Africa, 108; persecute the Christians, 108; their King Huneric, 108; their King Childeric, 113; their King Geilamir, 113; the Vandals are defeated and destroyed by the Romans, 113; their King Godigisel is killed by the Franks, 123

Vannes, 199; Macliaw flees there, 199; Waroch promises to restore it, 291; 292, 455, 501; Duke Ebrachar and his army withdraw there, 557; Regalis is Bishop, 557

Vasso Galatae, a shrine near Clermont-Ferrand, burnt by Chroc, King of the Alamanni, 89

Vedast, surnamed Avius, 383; he was the man who had murdered Ambrosius and Lupus in Tours, 390; killed by one of the men of Childeric the Saxon, 390

Venantius Fortunatus, 264; his *Vita Sancti Germani*, 264

Venantius, Saint, Abbot of the monastery named after him in Tours, 598; Licinius was later Abbot of the monastery, before becoming Bishop of Tours, 598; Saint Venantius buried there, 598; Gunthar was Abbot before becoming Bishop of Tours, 600

Vence, 511; Deutherius is Bishop, 511; Pronimius is Bishop, 511

Veneranda, mistress of King Guntram, 218; she bears a son, Gundobad, 218

Venerandus, Saint, Bishop of Clermont-Ferrand, 101; succeeds Saint Arthemius, 129; passage quoted from Paulinus of Périgueux about him, 129; dies, 129

Veranus, Saint, Bishop of Cavaillon, 464; sent by Guntram to the court of Lothar II to investigate the murder of Praetextatus, 464-5; baptizes Theuderic, son of Childebert II and Queen Faileuba, 482; his miracles, 482-3; signs the letter to Bishop Gundegisel about the revolt in Saint Radegund's nunnery, 533

Vendôme, 504

Vercelli, 106; Justinian, the replacement of Saint Bricius as Bishop of Tours, dies there, 106; 595

Verdun, 160; Theudebert makes a loan to the Verdunois, 160; Deuteria murders her daughter there, 185; Desideratus is Bishop, 190; Saint Ageric is Bishop, 191; 427; Duke Guntram Boso seeks sanctuary in the cathedral, 488; Berthefried escapes from the battle on the Woëvre to the church-house in Verdun, 495; is killed there, 495; 511; Charimer is Bishop, 511; 577

Vernou, where the church was built by Saint Perpetuus, 597

Verus, Bishop of Tours, eighth in order, 102; died in exile, 598; was Bishop for eleven years, 598

Vespasian, the Emperor, 84; the Temple was burnt down in his reign, 84; he persecutes the Christians, 84

Vettius Epagatus, martyred in Lyons, 86, 88

Vézeronce, in the Viennois, 167; the armies of Chlodomer and Theuderic join there, 167

Victor, Bishop of Saint-Paul-Trois-Châteaux, 285; assaulted by Bishops Sagittarius and Salonius, 285; punished for forgiving them, 286

Victor, Saint and martyr, 511

Victor, son of Maximus, killed, 121

Victorinus, Saint, martyred at Clermont-Ferrand, 89; he was converted and baptized by Saint Cassius, 89

Victorius, Bishop of Rennes, 465; Domnola was his daughter, 465; signs the letter to Saint Radegund, 527

Victorius, Duke of Auvergne, 101; put in charge of the Seven Cities by Euric, King of the Visigoths, 132; goes to Clermont-Ferrand, 132; erects columns in Saint Julian's church, 133; builds Saint Lawrence's church, 133, builds the church of Saint Germanus in Saint-Germain-Lanbron, 133; nine years in Clermont-Ferrand, 133; quarrel with the Senator Eucherius, 133; he kills Eucherius, 133; flees to Rome, 133; killed there, 133; 134

Victorius of Aquitaine, 69; his enquiries into the dating of Easter, 69; his views on the subject, 581

Vidimael, leader of the Bretons who had attacked Nantes, 500; promises better behaviour and compensation to Guntram's envoys, 500

Vienne, 35; the Emperor Valentinianus III shut up there, 35; Simplicius is Bishop, 129; Godigisel lived there, 146; Gundobad besieges Godigisel there, 147–8; Saint Avitus is Bishop, 149; Saint Mamertus is Bishop, 149; Saint Evantius is Bishop, 471; Virus is Bishop, 471

Vienne, River, 98; the body of Saint Martin of Tours is carried down the river, 98; Clovis crosses the river, 152

Viennois, the, 167

Vigilius, Archdeacon of Marseilles, 196, 239; his men steal wine from a ship in harbour, 239; Albinus, Governor of Provence, assaults him and fines him, 239; Albinus is forced to pay back four times the fine, 239

Vilaine, River, 290; King Guntram's army crosses the river, 556; the remains of Duke Beppolen's troops cross back in retreat, 558

Vincent, Saint, the martyr of Agen, 186; his tunic, 186; his church in Paris (=Saint-Germain-des-Prés), 215; Childebert II buried there, 215; 484

Vindimialis, Saint, Catholic Bishop in Africa, 110; his miracles, 110; 112; martyred by King Hunderic, 113

Virgil quoted. *Aeneid* I, 46–7, 141; I, 100–101, 118, 224, 241; III, 56–7, 242; III, 56–7, 454; VIII, 148–9, 486

Virgil, Bishop of Arles, 511; had been Abbot of Autun, 511

Virgin Mary, the Blessed, 68; and the Birth of Christ, 79; mother of Christ, 79; 81, 331, 452, 537, 538; Her church in Rome, 546

Virus, Bishop of Vienne, 471

Virus, nephew of Eulalius, falls in love with Tetradia, wife of Eulalius, who is lovely in distress, 555; he sends her to Duke Desiderius for protection, 555; Virus is murdered by Eulalius as a result, 555

Visigoths, the, in Spain, 187; their habit of assassinating their kings, 187; the Emperor Justinian sends an army against them, 202; Agila is King,

202; Athanagild is King, 202; Leuvigild is King, 233; rule over Agde, which is in Septimania, 327; 459; on the death of Leuvigild, Recared becomes King, 477; attack Arles and Beaucaire, 488; Recared, their King, becomes a Catholic, 497–8; they beat the army sent by King Guntram to attack Septimania, 517–18

Vitalis, Saint, 131; his relics brought from Bologna to Clermont-Ferrand by Bishop Namatius, 131

Vitry, royal villa, 248; King Sigibert assembles his troops there, 248; he is assassinated there, 248; 254; Lothar, son of Chilperic and Fredegund, to become King Lothar II, brought up there, 375

Vitry-le-Brûlé, 174; the Pretender Munderic besieged there by Theuderic, and then killed, 174–5

Viviers, bubonic plague, 582

Vollore, besieged by Theuderic, 159; his troops destroy the fortress, 172

Volusianus, Saint, Bishop of Tours, seventh in order, 102, 139; relation of Saint Perpetuus, his predecessor, 597; lived in the days of King Clovis, 597; exiled to Toulouse and died there, 597; built the village of Manthelan, 597; built Saint John's church in Marmoutier, 597; was Bishop for seven years, 597

Vosges, the, 558; King Guntram goes hunting there, 558–9

Vouillé, the battle of, in which King Clovis beats and kills Alaric II, 153–4, 158

Vuldetrada, daughter of Wacho, King of the Longobards, 202; marries King Theudebald, 202; after Theudebald's death, she is seduced by Lothar I, 203; handed over to Garivald, Duke of Bavaria, 203

Vulfoliac, Saint, the deacon (=Saint Walfroy), 431; a Longobard, 445; meets Gregory of Tours in Carignan and tells him the story of his life, 445–7; inspired by Saint Martin of Tours, 445; disciple of Saint Aredius, Abbot of Limoges, 445; moved to Trier, 445; converted the pagan inhabitants of Trier to Christianity, and destroyed their statues, including one of Diana, 446; cures himself of a skin disease with some oil from Saint Martin's church in Tours, 447; imitates Saint Simeon the Stylite, but the weather in Trier is not suitable, 447; tells Gregory of Tours of miracles performed by Saint Martin, 448–9

W

Waddo, Count of Saintes, 379; major-domo of Rigunth's household, 379; sets out for Spain with her, 379; 384; in Toulouse with Gundovald the Pretender, Duke Desiderius and Count Mummolus, 409; accompanies Gundovald to Saint-Bertrand-de-Comminges, 417; is there during the siege, 417–24; betrays Gundovald, 422–3; escapes after the siege, 424; received by Brunhild, 426; 480; invades a villa belonging to a woman called Beretrude, 522–3; is killed ignobly by the bailiff's son, 523; 541; his estates are made over to Clotild, the ex-nun of Saint Radegund's nunnery, 580; his two sons commit various crimes in the Poitiers region, 580; Count Macco tries to put them down, 580; they are captured and tried, 580–81; one is exiled and one executed, 581

Waldin, one of the three Franks of Tournai, 586–7; killed by Fredegund, 587

Waldo the deacon, baptized in the name of Bertram, 454; hopes for the Bishopric of Bordeaux, but does not get it, 454

Wandalen becomes governor or nutritor of King Childebert II, 327; 431; dies, 454; Brunhild, the Queen Mother, does not replace him, 454

Warinar the Frank, sent by King Sigibert as an envoy to the Emperor Tiberius II, 235

Waroch, son of Macliaw, Count of the Bretons, 274; inherits part of his father's territory, 274; attacked by Chilperic's troops, 290–91; gives in and promises to restore Vannes, 291; attacks Nantes, 500; promises better behaviour and compensation to Guntram's envoys, 500; fails on both counts, 501; assembles his army to fight Duke Beppolen, 556; beats Beppolen and kills him, 557; loses his treasure at sea, 557; makes peace with Duke Ebrachar and his army, 557; swears that he will never again cause trouble to King Guntram, 557–8; thereupon sends his son Canao to harass Ebrachar's retreating troops, 558; Fredegund, frightened by her son Lothar's serious illness, makes Waroch release the prisoners from Beppolen's army, 559

Werpin, Count of Meaux, 451; replaced by Gundovald, 451; kills Gundovald, 451; Gundovald's relations kill Werpin, 451

Whitsun, 596

Whit Sunday, 437, 597

Wilichar, father, of Chramn's wife, Chalda, 213; same as Willichar the priest?

Wiliulf, citizen of Poitiers, 486; dying of dysentery, 496; Gregory of Tours meets him on the road near Rheims, 496; he and his son die in the villa of Rueil, 496; evil life, 496; his widow married Duke Beppolen's son as her third husband, 496; buried in Poitiers, 496

Willachar, Count of Orleans, 396; becomes Count of Tours, 396; attacks Poitiers, 396; with Duke Ebrachar in Brittany, 558; thought to have been bribed by Waroch, Count of the Bretons, 558

Willichar the priest, 215; seeks sanctuary in Saint Martin's church in Tours, 215; burns the church down, 215; Lothar pays for a new tin roof, 215; 600; same as Wilichar?

Winnoch the Breton, 251; abstinence, 287; comes to Tours, 287; ordained a priest by Gregory of Tours, 288; miracle of the water and the wine at Saint Martin's tomb, 288; becomes an alcoholic, 467–8; dies insane, 468

Wintrio, Duke of Champagne, 450; expelled, 450; reinstated, 450; accompanies an army sent by Childebert II against the Longobards in Italy, 549

Wisigard, daughter of Wacho, King of the Longobards, 159; becomes engaged to Theudebert, 159; he marries her after some hesitation, 159; 185; dies, 185; 190

Index

Wistrimund, known to his friends as Tatto, citizen of Tours, 591; cured of toothache by Saint Aredius, 591

Woëvre, River, 491; Duke Ursio has an estate there, 491; 494

Y

Yzeures, ravaged by Count Berulf, 344; Saint Eustochius built the church there, 595

Z

Zaban, leader of the Longobards, 239; with Amo and Rodan invades Gaul, 239; passes through Die, 240; camps at Valence, 240; he and Rodan beaten by Count Mummolus at Embrun, 240; retreats to Susa, 240

Zebulun, son of Jacob, 73

Zerah, son of Reuel, 73

Zerubbabel, frees the Israelites from the Babylonian captivity, 79; rebuilds the Temple and the city of Jerusalem, 79; son of Salathiel, 79

Zoroaster, the Living Star, as Persian name for Chus, son of Ham, 71

Zülpich, the siege of, 153; Hermanfrid is killed there by being pushed over the city wall, 169

READ MORE IN PENGUIN

In every corner of the world, on every subject under the sun, Penguin represents quality and variety – the very best in publishing today.

For complete information about books available from Penguin – including Puffins, Penguin Classics and Arkana – and how to order them, write to us at the appropriate address below. Please note that for copyright reasons the selection of books varies from country to country.

In the United Kingdom: Please write to *Dept. EP, Penguin Books Ltd, Bath Road, Harmondsworth, West Drayton, Middlesex UB7 ODA*

In the United States: Please write to *Consumer Sales, Penguin USA, P.O. Box 999, Dept. 17109, Bergenfield, New Jersey 07621-0120*. VISA and MasterCard holders call 1-800-253-6476 to order Penguin titles

In Canada: Please write to *Penguin Books Canada Ltd, 10 Alcorn Avenue, Suite 300, Toronto, Ontario M4V 3B2*

In Australia: Please write to *Penguin Books Australia Ltd, P.O. Box 257, Ringwood, Victoria 3134*

In New Zealand: Please write to *Penguin Books (NZ) Ltd, Private Bag 102902, North Shore Mail Centre, Auckland 10*

In India: Please write to *Penguin Books India Pvt Ltd, 706 Eros Apartments, 56 Nehru Place, New Delhi 110 019*

In the Netherlands: Please write to *Penguin Books Netherlands bv, Postbus 3507, NL-1001 AH Amsterdam*

In Germany: Please write to *Penguin Books Deutschland GmbH, Metzlerstrasse 26, 60594 Frankfurt am Main*

In Spain: Please write to *Penguin Books S. A., Bravo Murillo 19, 1° B, 28015 Madrid*

In Italy: Please write to *Penguin Italia s.r.l., Via Felice Casati 20, I–20124 Milano*

In France: Please write to *Penguin France S. A., 17 rue Lejeune, F–31000 Toulouse*

In Japan: Please write to *Penguin Books Japan, Ishikiribashi Building, 2–5–4, Suido, Bunkyo-ku, Tokyo 112*

In Greece: Please write to *Penguin Hellas Ltd, Dimocritou 3, GR–106 71 Athens*

In South Africa: Please write to *Longman Penguin Southern Africa (Pty) Ltd, Private Bag X08, Bertsham 2013*

A CHOICE OF CLASSICS

Aeschylus	**The Oresteian Trilogy**
	Prometheus Bound/The Suppliants/Seven Against Thebes/The Persians
Aesop	**Fables**
Ammianus Marcellinus	**The Later Roman Empire (AD 354–378)**
Apollonius of Rhodes	**The Voyage of Argo**
Apuleius	**The Golden Ass**
Aristophanes	**The Knights/Peace/The Birds/The Assemblywomen/Wealth**
	Lysistrata/The Acharnians/The Clouds
	The Wasps/The Poet and the Women/The Frogs
Aristotle	**The Art of Rhetoric**
	The Athenian Constitution
	Ethics
	The Politics
	De Anima
Arrian	**The Campaigns of Alexander**
St Augustine	**City of God**
	Confessions
Marcus Aurelius	**Meditations**
Boethius	**The Consolation of Philosophy**
Caesar	**The Civil War**
	The Conquest of Gaul
Catullus	**Poems**
Cicero	**Murder Trials**
	The Nature of the Gods
	On the Good Life
	Selected Letters
	Selected Political Speeches
	Selected Works
Euripides	**Alcestis/Iphigenia in Tauris/Hippolytus**
	The Bacchae/Ion/The Women of Troy/Helen
	Medea/Hecabe/Electra/Heracles

READ MORE IN PENGUIN

A CHOICE OF CLASSICS

Hesiod/Theognis	**Theogony/Works and Days/Elegies**
Hippocrates	**Hippocratic Writings**
Homer	**The Iliad**
	The Odyssey
Horace	**Complete Odes and Epodes**
Horace/Persius	**Satires and Epistles**
Juvenal	**The Sixteen Satires**
Livy	**The Early History of Rome**
	Rome and Italy
	Rome and the Mediterranean
	The War with Hannibal
Lucretius	**On the Nature of the Universe**
Martial	**Epigrams**
Ovid	**The Erotic Poems**
	Heroides
	Metamorphoses
	The Poems of Exile
Pausanias	**Guide to Greece** (in two volumes)
Petronius/Seneca	**The Satyricon/The Apocolocyntosis**
Pindar	**The Odes**
Plato	**Early Socratic Dialogues**
	Gorgias
	The Last Days of Socrates (Euthyphro/
	The Apology/Crito/Phaedo)
	The Laws
	Phaedrus and Letters VII and VIII
	Philebus
	Protagoras/Meno
	The Republic
	The Symposium
	Theaetetus
	Timaeus/Critias

A CHOICE OF CLASSICS

Plautus	**The Pot of Gold and Other Plays**
	The Rope and Other Plays
Pliny	**The Letters of the Younger Pliny**
Pliny the Elder	**Natural History**
Plotinus	**The Enneads**
Plutarch	**The Age of Alexander** (Nine Greek Lives)
	The Fall of the Roman Republic (Six Lives)
	The Makers of Rome (Nine Lives)
	The Rise and Fall of Athens (Nine Greek Lives)
	Plutarch on Sparta
Polybius	**The Rise of the Roman Empire**
Procopius	**The Secret History**
Propertius	**The Poems**
Quintus Curtius Rufus	**The History of Alexander**
Sallust	**The Jugurthine War/The Conspiracy of Cataline**
Seneca	**Four Tragedies/Octavia**
	Letters from a Stoic
Sophocles	**Electra/Women of Trachis/Philoctetes/Ajax**
	The Theban Plays
Suetonius	**The Twelve Caesars**
Tacitus	**The Agricola/The Germania**
.	**The Annals of Imperial Rome**
	The Histories
Terence	**The Comedies (The Girl from Andros/The Self-Tormentor/The Eunuch/Phormio/The Mother-in-Law/The Brothers)**
Thucydides	**History of the Peloponnesian War**
Virgil	**The Aeneid**
	The Eclogues
	The Georgics
Xenophon	**Conversations of Socrates**
	A History of My Times
	The Persian Expedition

READ MORE IN PENGUIN

A CHOICE OF CLASSICS

ANTHOLOGIES AND ANONYMOUS WORKS

The Age of Bede
Alfred the Great
Beowulf
A Celtic Miscellany
The Cloud of Unknowing and Other Works
The Death of King Arthur
The Earliest English Poems
Early Irish Myths and Sagas
Egil's Saga
English Mystery Plays
Eyrbyggja Saga
Hrafnkel's Saga
The Letters of Abelard and Heloise
Medieval English Verse
Njal's Saga
Roman Poets of the Early Empire
Seven Viking Romances
Sir Gawain and the Green Knight

READ MORE IN PENGUIN

A CHOICE OF CLASSICS

Honoré de Balzac	**The Black Sheep**
	César Birotteau
	The Chouans
	Cousin Bette
	Eugénie Grandet
	A Harlot High and Low
	Lost Illusions
	A Murky Business
	Old Goriot
	Selected Short Stories
	Ursule Mirouet
	The Wild Ass's Skin
J. A. Brillat-Savarin	**The Physiology of Taste**
Marquis de Custine	**Letters from Russia**
Pierre Corneille	**The Cid/Cinna/The Theatrical Illusion**
Alphonse Daudet	**Letters from My Windmill**
René Descartes	**Discourse on Method and Other**
Denis Diderot	**Writings**
	Jacques the Fatalist
	The Nun
	Rameau's Nephew/D'Alembert's
	Dream
Gustave Flaubert	**Selected Writings on Art and Literature**
	Bouvard and Pecuchet
	Madame Bovary
	Sentimental Education
	The Temptation of St Anthony
Victor Hugo	**Three Tales**
	Les Misérables
Laclos	**Notre-Dame of Paris**
La Fontaine	**Les Liaisons Dangereuses**
Madame de Lafayette	**Selected Fables**
Lautréamont	**The Princesse de Clèves**
	Maldoror and Poems

READ MORE IN PENGUIN

A CHOICE OF CLASSICS

Molière	**The Misanthrope/The Sicilian/Tartuffe/A Doctor in Spite of Himself/The Imaginary Invalid**
	The Miser/The Would-be Gentleman/That Scoundrel Scapin/Love's the Best Doctor/ Don Juan
Michel de Montaigne	**Essays**
Marguerite de Navarre	**The Heptameron**
Blaise Pascal	**Pensées**
	The Provincial Letters
Abbé Prevost	**Manon Lescaut**
Rabelais	**The Histories of Gargantua and Pantagruel**
Racine	**Andromache/Britannicus/Berenice**
	Iphigenia/Phaedra/Athaliah
Arthur Rimbaud	**Collected Poems**
Jean-Jacques Rousseau	**The Confessions**
	A Discourse on Inequality
	Emile
Jacques Saint-Pierre	**Paul and Virginia**
Madame de Sevigné	**Selected Letters**
Stendhal	**Lucien Leuwen**
	Scarlet and Black
	The Charterhouse of Parma
Voltaire	**Candide**
	Letters on England
	Philosophical Dictionary
Emile Zola	**L'Assomoir**
	La Bête Humaine
	The Debacle
	The Earth
	Germinal
	Nana
	Thérèse Raquin

READ MORE IN PENGUIN

A CHOICE OF CLASSICS

St Anselm	**The Prayers and Meditations**
St Augustine	**Confessions**
Bede	**Ecclesiastical History of the English People**
Geoffrey Chaucer	**The Canterbury Tales**
	Love Visions
	Troilus and Criseyde
Marie de France	**The Lais of Marie de France**
Jean Froissart	**The Chronicles**
Geoffrey of Monmouth	**The History of the Kings of Britain**
Gerald of Wales	**History and Topography of Ireland**
	The Journey through Wales and **The Description of Wales**
Gregory of Tours	**The History of the Franks**
Robert Henryson	**The Testament of Cresseid and Other Poems**
Walter Hilton	**The Ladder of Perfection**
Julian of Norwich	**Revelations of Divine Love**
Thomas à Kempis	**The Imitation of Christ**
William Langland	**Piers the Ploughman**
Sir John Mandeville	**The Travels of Sir John Mandeville**
Marguerite de Navarre	**The Heptameron**
Christine de Pisan	**The Treasure of the City of Ladies**
Chrétien de Troyes	**Arthurian Romances**
Marco Polo	**The Travels**
Richard Rolle	**The Fire of Love**
François Villon	**Selected Poems**